OXFORD HISTORY OF MODERN EUROPE

OXFORD HISTORY OF MODERN EUROPE

The Struggle for Mastery in Europe 1848–1918
Available in paperback
A.J.P. Taylor

The Russian Empire 1801–1917
Available in paperback
Hugh Seton-Watson

A History of French Passions
Available in paperback in two volumes
Ambition, Love, and Politics
Intellect, Taste, and Anxiety
Theodore Zeldin

Germany 1866–1945
Available in paperback
Gordon A. Craig

The Low Countries 1780–1940
E. H. Kossman

Spain 1808–1975
Available in paperback
Raymond Carr

German History 1770–1866
Available in paperback
James J. Sheehan

A People Apart: A Political History of the Jews in
Europe 1789–1939
Available in paperback
David Vital

The Transformation of European Politics 1763–1848
Available in paperback
Paul W. Schroeder

The Lights that Failed
European International History
1919–1933
Available in paperback
Zara Steiner

Bulgaria
R. J. Crampton

Ireland

The Politics of Enmity 1789–2006

PAUL BEW

OXFORD

UNIVERSITY PRESS

OXFORD

UNIVERSITY PRESS

Great Clarendon Street, Oxford OX2 6DP

Oxford University Press is a department of the University of Oxford.
It furthers the University's objective of excellence in research, scholarship,
and education by publishing worldwide in

Oxford New York

Auckland Cape Town Dar es Salaam Hong Kong Karachi
Kuala Lumpur Madrid Melbourne Mexico City Nairobi
New Delhi Shanghai Taipei Toronto

With offices in

Argentina Austria Brazil Chile Czech Republic France Greece
Guatemala Hungary Italy Japan Poland Portugal Singapore
South Korea Switzerland Thailand Turkey Ukraine Vietnam

Oxford is a registered trade mark of Oxford University Press
in the UK and in certain other countries

Published in the United States
by Oxford University Press Inc., New York

British Library Cataloguing in Publication Data

Data available

Library of Congress Cataloging in Publication Data

Data available

Typeset by Laserwords Private Limited, Chennai, India
Printed in Great Britain
on acid-free paper by
Biddles Ltd., King's Lynn, Norfolk

ISBN 978-0-19-820555-5

1 3 5 7 9 10 8 6 4 2

For Mary, Greta, and John

Preface

> The King shall drink to Hamlet's better breath,
> And in the cup an union shall he throw.
>
> (*Hamlet*, V. ii. 268–9)

> It is the wittiest partition that ever I heard discourse, my lord.
>
> (*A Midsummer Night's Dream*, V. i. 1179)

At the end of October 1904, D. P. Moran's *The Leader*—strongly Catholic nationalist in tone—published a clever pastiche of William Shakespeare's *A Midsummer Night's Dream*. In this version, 'The Bigots of the Wood', which takes place near Castle Saunderson, the 'home' of Colonel Saunderson, the landlordist Ulster Unionist leader of the day, Puck, the Fairy, amuses himself by playing tricks on the enemies of the Irish cause:

> An Orangeman drunk I diverted from home,
> And now he is sunk in a bog cursing Rome.
> With signs and guiles a Freemason I led
> For fully six miles from his home and his bed.

Puck then encounters a 'caste of bigots'—Bottom, Billy, Boyne, Howler, and Scorcher—all rehearsing a play, 'The Triumph of the Saved?' The Protestant and unionist 'Bigots of the Wood' roar out their lines—'Now is the Summer of our discontent | Made roaring winter by the Winds of Rome'—and celebrate their triumphs over everything, Catholic and nationalist. The author of the pastiche ('J. M. W.', the pen-name of John Swift) makes it clear that this is also a triumph over the values of toleration:

> For our mighty Bottom an ambush soon got 'em
> And proudly o'er them the victor's flag waved.
> Sound the loud timbrel o'er famed Sandy Row, etc.,
> Now where's toleration and Ireland a nation?
> Vanished and melted like last winter's snow.

Exasperated, Puck places asses' heads on the whole unsavoury crew: 'perceiving each other', the bigots set up 'a horrible screaming', and with cries of Popery and witchcraft 'rush madly off in various directions'. As the dawn breaks, Puck reluctantly removes their beastly heads: for 'bigots always should wear asses' heads'. *The Leader's* pastiche perfectly expresses the mutual contempt which characterized the relationship between the two main traditions—Protestant, 'British', and unionist on the one hand, Catholic and nationalist on the other—on the island of Ireland at the beginning of the last century, and is not so much diluted at the beginning of this century, as the violence which met the Ulster Unionists in the 'Love Ulster' march in Dublin in February 2006 demonstrated.

Such animosity is the theme of this book. The book is about the conflict between the Protestant British—both on the British 'mainland' and in Ireland itself—and the Catholic Irish. It is perhaps more particularly about the ideas and attitudes which underpin that conflict: it is about rationalization and self-justification. During the nineteenth century mainland Britain became both less ardently Protestant and less emotionally engaged in this Irish battle of communal wills: in 1852 Benjamin Disraeli described 'hatred of the Pope' as one of the defining features of English public opinion; his biographer, J. A. Froude, however, noted the 'decay' of such protestant feeling by the late 1860s. In the 1880s British liberalism detached itself from the cause of Irish Protestantism: the Tory leadership stuck with it for much longer, but was visibly losing enthusiasm by the late 1930s. Irish neutrality in the Second World War re-created a new type of London unionism. Nevertheless, by the end of the twentieth century Britain was perceived to have formally declared itself neutral, save perhaps for a vestigial element of concern for the protestant community in Northern Ireland, expressed in support for the principle of 'consent', the idea that Northern Ireland could only leave the United Kingdom when a majority within Northern Ireland so desired it.

This is the conflict which, for many, defines the modern Irish question. Norrey Jephson O'Conor, in his *Changing Ireland*, published by Harvard University Press in 1924, wrote that 'many laymen outside of Ireland' had come to accept a particular view of that history as a history of 'tyranny supposedly unexampled in modern times—a great and supposedly liberal nation taking unfair unadvantage of a smaller'. At the heart of this relationship is the problem of the management of enmity. The union of Great Britain and Ireland in 1801 was, above all, presented as a sophisticated attempt to manage that enmity: a new benign framework for Irish development. Not everyone accepted British professions of good faith. At the time, anti-union writers seized on the reference to 'an union' in *Hamlet* as a suitably ambiguous and threatening image: after all, the King wishes to place 'an union' (a jewel) in Hamlet's goblet at a moment when he wants to see Hamlet destroyed. Did not Britain, despite all the deceitful Claudius-like professions of good-will, not really wish to destroy Ireland? All the other great experiments since—Home Rule, partition and independence, the Anglo-Irish Agreement of 1985, and the Belfast Good Friday Agreement of 1998—have been conceived as attempts to divert the full flood of rage into a place of relative calmness. Partition based on the principle of consent remains the order of the day in Ireland: but it is also the case that the recently revised constitution of the Irish Republic declares it to be the 'firm will' of the Irish people to achieve political unity on the island of Ireland, admittedly only with the support of a democratic majority in Northern Ireland.

These issues—and this great unresolved and ambiguous project—provide the context for this book. To treat the problems raised with any degree of seriousness, it is necessary to re-create the worlds of the political class in London, Dublin, and Belfast and to study their interaction. But it is also important to convey the mood of popular politics. In this work, as in others, I have laid particular emphasis on the press, including the vibrant Irish provincial press: inevitably, such sources tend to reflect the passions of particular localities, sometimes in a very unmediated, even crude, way. One rather intellectual Irish viceroy in the 1860s, Lord Kimberley, referred to a 'despicable' Irish press, in which there were only two 'tolerably able papers', the *Northern Whig* of Belfast and the *Cork Examiner.* There is a fair amount here from the *Whig* and the *Examiner*, but I have employed many of the more 'despicable' organs as well.

In his Wiles Lectures, given in Belfast in 1985, Eric Hobsbawm declared: 'To be Irish and proudly attached to Ireland—even to be proudly catholic Irish or Ulster protestant Irish—is not in itself incompatible with the study of Irish history.' He adds: 'To be a Fenian or an Orangeman, I would judge, is not so compatible ... unless the historian leaves his or her conviction behind when entering the study.' These are interesting remarks. The issue of objectivity in the writing of Irish history is a fraught one. The fact remains that very many people in Ireland, Fenians and Orangemen in particular, regard their history as almost a personal possession and resent what is often seen as a subversive and impious challenge by scholars in ivory towers. Given the scale of the emotional investment that has traditionally been made, it is difficult to contemplate the possibility that, for all its sound and fury, the tale might not entirely have the comforting significance attributed to it. Even when this doubt surfaces, there is always, as 'The Bigots in the Woods' shows, the absurdity of the opposing 'collectivity' to reassure and keep one warm at night. Ernest Renan, the friend of the great nineteenth-century Irish historian W. E. H. Lecky, pointed out, in a famous lecture on nationalism, that, in the formation of national consciousness, sacrifice is more important than success and historical error more important than historical truth. Such a context creates an almost insoluble problem for historians.

As William Cooke Taylor, one of the most interesting of the Irish historical writers to be discussed in the following pages, honestly noted in the 1847 preface to his own study of Daniel O'Connell: 'Professions of impartiality from Irishmen are not unjustly received with suspicion.' In his memoir published in 1895, William O'Connor Morris wrote: 'To this hour Ireland has produced no genius who has been able to bridge over the chasm existing between her divided people, to do justice to the sons of English and Scottish colonists, and to portray the habits and life of the Catholic Irishry.' William Cooke Taylor therefore made a reduced claim for his work. 'This writer, therefore, limits himself to claiming perfect accuracy in his statement of facts—many of them little known; the soundness in his opinions is a very different question, which he leaves to be solved by his readers.' The author of this work makes a still more reduced claim: he has attempted to achieve accuracy in the statement of facts, little known or otherwise.

Acknowledgments

In the writing of this book I have incurred four major debts to institutions—to Magdalene College, Cambridge, for a Parnell Fellowship, 1996–7; to the British Academy for the support of a research assistant—the excellent Gorden Gillespie—in the same year; to the Burns Library, Boston College, for the visiting Burns Professorship in 1999–2000; and to the Institute of Governance at Queens University, Belfast, for a visiting fellowship 2001–2. Without the knidness and support of all these institutions this work could not have been completed. I owe a particular debt to the librarians who work in the Henry Collection at Queens, but also to Robert O'Neill and John Attebury at the beautiful Burns Library, with its outstanding collection of Irish material. I owe a debt also to the Centre for Contemporary British History and in particular, to Sir John Chilcot who chairs the committee with such skill.

My friend Henry Patterson has always been a major influence. I owe much to the encouragement of others in my department—Richard English, Graham Walker, Brian Walker, and Margaret O'Callaghan; also gratitude is due to my former colleague Alvin Jackson, now in Edinburgh. Much is also owed to the encouragement and friendship of Dean Godson and the late Arthur Green. It is a matter of deep regret to me that I was unable to show the finished work to Peter Jupp and Frank Johnson, who both died late in 2006. Eamon Duffy, Richard Luckett, and Ronald Hyam were very kind to me at Magdalene, as were Kevin O'Neill and Bob Savage in Boston—blessed be the memory of Adele Dalsimer.

Two have helped me above all. Patrick Maume is the outstanding Irish scholar of his generation—as Professor Gearóid Ó Tuathaigh has written, his research is outstanding 'by any standards'. I have drawn on Dr Maume's many articles and books; but I have also benefited time and again from his conversation. Colin Armstrong has been a source of advice and other assistance. Colin's grasp of detail is an inspiration.

A. J. L. 'Tony' Morris initiated the project at OUP at a time when Lord Bullock and Sir William Deakin were the general editors of the series; Rupert Cousens, Zoe Washford, and Jeff New completed the task. Professor Geoffrey Warner of Brasenose made helpful comments on the 'Troubles' chapter. Richard Bourke also provided significant help.

The greatest support came from my immediate family. In a country where there is a perception that the past matters more than the future, a controversial Irish historian may be a mixed blessing. My maternal grandfather attended the same school as Eamon de Valera in Co. Cork; my paternal grandfather is described in a recent book as believing that the accident of his birth—English—was in itself an 'accolade'. These are two different angles of vision on the material presented here. Nevertheless, my family has responded to my historical labours with consistent sympathy and good humour.

Paul Bew
Belfast
January 2007

Contents

1. Impact of the French Revolution: 'The Battle of Burke'—Tone or Castlereagh?   1

2. The Union Between Britain and Ireland: One People?   49

3. Daniel O'Connell and the Road to Emancipation 1810–1829   87

4. The Repealer Repulsed: O'Connell 1830–1845   125

5. The Politics of Hunger, 1845–1850   175

6. The Fenian Impulse   231

7. Parnellism: 'Fierce ebullience linked to constitutional machinery'   302

8. Squelching, 'by way of a *hors d'oeuvre*': Conflict in Ireland, 1891–1918   361

9. The Politics of the Gun or a 'Saving Formula', 1919–1923   393

10. 'Melancholy Sanctity' in the South, 'Perfect Democracy in the North': Ireland 1923–1966   444

11. 'Unbearably Oldfashioned and Pointless': The Era of the Troubles, 1968–2005   486

12. Conclusion   556

Index   583

1

Impact of the French Revolution: 'The Battle of Burke'—Tone or Castlereagh?

I forgot a phrase which O'Connell made use of when the conversation hinted at a connection between France and Ireland. He said that Britain would then be between the *blades* of the *scissors*, and she knew well that her own existence would be in such jeopardy as not to resist such a connection to the last drop of her blood.

(William Drennan to Sam McTier, 8 Apr. 1795, in Jean Agnew (ed.), *The Drennan–McTier Letters,* vol. 2 (1999), 147. Daniel, Count O'Connell (1745–1833), *ancién régime* French general, uncle of Daniel O'Connell, the Liberator)

Is Mr Burke to be always the authority for despotic acts, and of no weight on the side of freedom?

(George Barnes, *The Right of the Imperial Crown of Ireland Attested and Maintained against Edward Cooke* (1799), 67)

'My dear Sir—Tone died this morning of his wound.'[1] With this laconic note on 19 November 1798, Lord Castlereagh, in a striking contemporary judgement considered to be 'the effective Prime Minister of Ireland',[2] or simply 'the Minister for Ireland', informed the senior British spymaster, William Wickham,[3] that Wolfe Tone—the greatest of those Irish republican separatist revolutionaries who had, with French support, pitted their will

---

[1] *Memoirs and Correspondence of Lord Castlereagh, Second Marquis of Londonderry, edited by his Brother, Charles Vane, Marquis of Londonderry,* vol. II, *Arrangements for a Union* (London, 1843), 7.

[2] *Sketches of Irish Political Characters of the Present Day* (London, 1799), 247. *The Star* called him 'the Minister for Ireland', quoted in the *Belfast News Letter,* 13 Feb. 1801.

[3] Michael Durey, 'William Wickham, the Christ Church Connection and the Rise and Fall of the Security Service in Britain, 1798–1801', *English Historical Review,* 121: 4 (2006), 714–45.

against the British state in Ireland in the 1790s—had committed suicide following capture. As the United Irish revolt crumbled, Castlereagh's mind was already turned to the project of a legislative union. So stark was the opposition between the position of the two men, Tone and Castlereagh (originally Robert Stewart)—one at the apex of political power, and the other, captured, imprisoned, and suicidal—that it requires an effort of will to cast the mind back to the spring of 1790 when these two young, talented, progressive, and ambitious Irish protestants seemed, for a moment, to stand on very much the same liberal, reform-minded political ground. Both men sympathized with the French revolution of 1789.

Both men were highly ambitious and sought out membership of political elites.[4] Castlereagh's access to such circles was, by virtue of his birth (in September 1789 his father was created Baron Londonderry), wealth, and later marriage to Lady Emily Hobart in 1794, vastly more assured than that of Tone. Tone, born to the 'middle race of men', was dependent on the more contingent factors of his very considerable ability and charm. The most brilliant of the Irish Protestant 'patriots' of the 1840s, Thomas Davis, brilliantly captured the ambiguities, social, financial, and political, which lay at the heart of Wolfe Tone's career. 'The son of a man half farmer, half coachmaker, a poor and briefless lawyer with a wife and a parcel of children, he resolved to redress the wrongs of the Catholics, restore representation in the Commons, and with these, or failing in them to make his country an independent republic.'[5] There was from the start clear evidence that both Tone and Stewart might find the lure of the political establishment hard to resist. This evidence was, in fact, if anything more clear-cut in the case of Tone. Tone entered the legal profession at a moment when Ireland was achieving that overproduction of barristers which was to be a marked feature of the nineteenth century. 'The tardiness, with which his profession furnished him with the *res pecuniae*, afforded but a barren prospect for the future support of his growing family',[6] noted a hostile observer. Tone certainly was not untypical of the Dublin lawyer class in leaning towards radicalism.[7] But his first impulses lay elsewhere. Noting that Tone considered a career in the East India Company, James

---

[4] For this milieu see Neil Herman, 'The Irish Whigs and Popular Politics, 1789–92', in R. Gillespie (ed.), *The Remaking of Modern Ireland 1788–1950* (Dublin, 2003), 49–72.

[5] 'A Barrister' (Thomas Davis), *Speeches of the Rt. Hon. John Philip N. Curran* (Dublin, 1843), p. xii.

[6] *Biographies and Anecdotes of Founders of the Late Irish Rebellion* (London, 7 Aug. 1799), 2.

[7] R. B. McDowell, 'The Dublin Society of United Irishmen', in *Historical Essays, 1938–2001* (Dublin, 2003), 119.

Anthony Froude noted cynically: 'He could have become a faithful subject of King George if Pitt had offered him a writership of India.'[8] Even more remarkably, in August 1788 Tone had submitted a proposal to Prime Minister William Pitt in support of the establishment of a British military colony in the Sandwich or Hawaiian Islands in the North Pacific.[9] In the period from September to December 1790, Tone renewed the proposal in communications to the Duke of Richmond and Lord Grenville. Tone, however, had more than one iron in the fire in 1790. His plan rejected again, he used his skills as a pamphleteer to pursue an alternative path for patronage within the Whig reformist interest which was so strong in Dublin legal circles. In April 1790 Tone, borrowing the pen-name 'The Independent Irish Whig', published his first pamphlet, *A Review of the Conduct of Administration during the Seventh Session of Parliament* (Dublin, 1790). The pamphlet—its language full of hostility towards the arbitrary power of the Irish executive and the patronage resources which sustained it—appeared in the same month as the manifesto offered by a young parliamentary candidate in Co. Down, Robert Stewart. Tone's opinions quickly radicalized thereafter. By July 1791 he had become a separatist Irish republican.[10] On 22 August 1791 Tone published *An Argument on Behalf of the Catholics of Ireland*, insisting on the common political interests uniting Catholics and Protestants—at the time, William Sampson, a key political ally, tells us, Tone was scarcely acquainted with a single Catholic; Tone's mother came from a Catholic business family, but she had formally adopted Protestantism in 1771.[11]

This pamphlet did not, however, display the privately held separatist beliefs of the author. It was, instead, a brilliant attempt to persuade Irish Protestants to support the Catholic cause. Tone found it easy to dismiss the 'violent' and 'ignorant' anti-Catholic' prejudices of many Irish Protestants, not because he had a close knowledge of Irish Catholicism, but because he believed traditional Irish Catholicism was in a process of disintegration anyway. In his private letter to his friend Thomas Russell on 9 July 1791, which announced his view that separatism 'would be the regeneration' of Ireland, Tone had written: 'Look at France and America;

[8] *The Times*, 4 Apr. 1874.

[9] T. W. Moody, R. B. McDowell, and C. J. Woods (eds.), *The Writings of Theobald Wolfe Tone*, vol. 1, *Tone's Career in Ireland to June 1795* (Oxford, 1998), 10–16.

[10] Ibid. 104–6, T. Thomas Russell, 9 July 1791; J. Quinn, 'Theobald Wolfe Tone and the Historians', *Irish Historical Studies*, 125 (May 2000).

[11] Marianne Elliott, *Wolfe Tone* (London, 1989), 11; William Sampson, *Memoirs of William Sampson: An Irish Exile* (London, 1832), 341. Sampson wrote: 'It is remarkable that at the time he was scarcely acquainted with any one Catholic, so great was the separation which barbarous institutions had created between men of the same nation, formed by nature to befriend and love each other.' *Memoirs*, 344.

the Pope burnt in effigy in Paris, the English Catholics at this moment seceding from the church.'[12] Tone assumed that Irish Catholicism was equally vulnerable to the broad international trend whereby the progress of enlightenment eroded the intensity of traditional religious feeling. Tone was always removed—intellectually and morally—from mainstream Catholic opinion: he considered that 'Irish priests' had 'all along acted execrably in Ireland, and they hated the very name of the French revolution'.[13] Stephen Gwynn has offered an acute summary of Tone's political thought:

The country of which he thought was not a Gaelic Ireland: he was little more concerned with its past than the Americans with that of America. His natural affinity was with the republican dissenters. But history taught him to believe that the Catholic Irish must be at the bottom of their hearts inveterately hostile to England. He probably agreed with Fitzgibbon, the opponent of their claims, that admitting them to full political rights must mean separation, and that was to him a reason for desiring emancipation. Yet he was always a practical politician, and put forward no aim beyond reform within the 'constitution'.[14]

Wolfe Tone's pamphlet enjoyed a great success and was reprinted by the Northern Whig Club, who elected its author as a member.[15] In this remarkable text Tone insisted that the emancipation of Catholic Ireland could be achieved safely, because 'the wealthy and moderate party of their own persuasion, with the whole Protestant interest, would form a barrier against invasion of property strong enough and solid enough'. In a later, fifth edition he added the words 'joined to the "trifling power of England"',[16] and in a significant footnote cited 'Burke' in favour of this argument.[17] Intriguingly, Tone saw Edmund Burke, the greatest Irishman of his era, as a supporter of Irish reform; or at any rate as a name to be employed to encourage those who were fearful of a reformist strategy. With the publication of his pamphlet, Tone established himself as a coming man in Irish politics.

Robert Stewart had achieved such status a year earlier. The Stewart family had emerged out of the dissenting Ulster bourgeoisie of the eighteenth century: a group distinguished by their commitment to constitutional reform. Local intellectual and professional families, such as the Halidays, the Drennans, the Bruces, and the Joys, naturally saw young Robert Stewart as the man to put their case before the world.

---

[12] *Writings of Wolfe Tone*, i. 105.
[13] T. W. Moody, R. B. McDowell, and C. J. Woods (eds.), *The Writings of Theobald Wolfe Tone*, vol. 2 (Oxford, 2001), diary, 23–7 Mar. 1796, p. 128.
[14] Stephen Gwynn, *The History of Ireland* (Dublin and London, 1923), 393–4.
[15] John Savage, *'98 and '48: The Modern Revolutionary History and Literature of Ireland* (New York, 1856), 40.
[16] *Writings of Wolfe Tone*, i. 119.   [17] Ibid.

Like many other leading Presbyterian families, the Stewarts had been educated at the Glasgow University—much influenced, long after his death, by the humane liberal thinking of the brilliant scholar Francis Hutcheson (1694–1746), the leading Ulster Presbyterian thinker of his generation.[18] Robert Stewart, born in Dublin on 15 August 1769, was subsequently baptized by the Revd Dr John Moody, a typical Glasgow University product. During the general election of 1783 Robert Stewart senior stood unsuccessfully as a reform candidate; he was defeated by Lord Kilwarlin, the son of the Earl of Hillsborough, thus inaugurating decades of intensive competition between the Stewart and the more conservative Downshire interests, the two being the most powerful families in Co. Down. The young Robert Stewart was caught up in the excitement of the contest, delighted that radical Presbyterianism clergy like the Revd Steel Dickson backed his father's cause.[19] By 1789, however, the Stewarts had succumbed somewhat to the lure of the political and religious establishment: Robert's father had been created Baron Londonderry, and the family were now members of the Church of Ireland. The Revd Henry Cooke probably had the Stewarts in mind when he told the Lords Select Committee in Ireland in 1825: 'There is one class of persons who inevitably joined the Establishment from the Dissenters; that is the people who grow rich.'[20] The young Robert Stewart was educated at St John's College, Cambridge, not Glasgow: a significant moment in his intellectual formation. Maria Edgeworth, in her classic novel *The Absentee* (1812), discusses the sensibility of the young Lord Colambre; in particular, Edgeworth notes the impact of a set of 'clever young men with whom he was at Cambridge'. The consequence for the young Irish peer is stated clearly: 'English and Irish had not been invidiously contrasted in his mind. He had lived with men who were too well informed and liberal to misjudge or depreciate a fellow country.'[21] In Edgeworth's novel, when reproached with 'Curse your English education!', Colambre replies, describing himself as 'as warm a friend to Ireland as your heart could wish and as someone who hopes that his English education will enable him

---

[18] Michael Brown, *Francis Hutcheson in Dublin: The Crucible of His Thought* (Dublin, 2002); Ian Hazlett, 'The Students at Glasgow University from 1747 to 1768 Connected with Ireland: An Analytical Probe', in W. Donald Patton (ed.), *Essays in Church History in Honour of R. Finlay G. Holmes* (Belfast, 2002), 220–89; Mark G. Spencer, ' "Stupid Irish Teagues" and the Encouragement of Enlightenment: Ulster Presbyterian Students of Moral Philosophy in Glasgow University, 1730–1795', in David A. Wilson and Mark G. Spencer (eds.), *Ulster Presbyterians in the Atlantic World: Religion, Politics and Identity* (Dublin, 2006), 50–61.

[19] W. T. Latimer, *Ulster Biographies Chiefly Relating to the Rebellion of 1798* (Belfast, 1897), 79.

[20] *Sessional Papers, 1825*, 18 Mar. 1825, p. 217.

[21] Maria Edgeworth, *The Absentee* (London and New York, 1895), 94.

to become all that a British nobleman ought to be'.[22] This imagined voice of a young Irish nobleman is very much the actual voice of Robert Stewart. The progressive Presbyterian intelligentsia looked with enthusiasm on the young man in 1790—and were surprisingly slow to abandon their faith in him over the next few years.

April 1790 was an ideal moment for a progressive candidature. Co. Down was enjoying a period of unparalleled prosperity—a relatively even balance existed between agriculture and linen manufacturing: with 11,000 freeholders, Co. Down topped the list of Irish electorates.[23] With a large Presbyterian community living alongside a relatively small Catholic community, there was relatively little Catholic–Protestant sectarian animosity. Robert Stewart's most important group of supporters was the Northern Whig Club, which declared it was 'not satisfied with the [Irish] House of Commons, in which the voice of the nation is with difficulty to be heard, with the majority of the House by rotten boroughs filled through ministerial profligacy, with 104 pensioned hirelings'. Not only was the Irish Parliament still dependent, it was highly unrepresentative: of 150 constituencies represented in the Irish House of Commons, 107 were under the control of an individual or a small group of parties.[24] The Whig Club enunciated a series of questions, which, it argued, voters should put to candidates. The Club wanted to know, for example:

Will you ... with all your ability, promote the success of a Bill for mending the representation of the people?

... A Bill for limiting the number of placements and pensioners and the amount of pensions?

A Bill for preventing revenue officers from voting or interfering in elections?

A Bill for rendering the servants of the Crown of Ireland responsible for the expenditure of public money?

A Bill to protect the personal safety of the subject against arbitrary and executive bias and against the stretching of the power of attachment beyond the limits of the constitution, and will you, so far as in you lies, prevent any renewal of the Police Act?

In later years Castlereagh was to claim that his support for the franchise reform embodied in the Catholic Relief Act of 1793 met his electoral commitments. In fact, it is clear that he was elected on a much broader

---

[22] Valerie Kennedy, 'Ireland in 1812: Colony or Part of the Imperial Main? The "Imperial Community" in Maria Edgeworth's *The Absentee*', in Terrence McDonough (ed.), *Was Ireland a Colony? Economics, Politics and Culture in Nineteenth-Century Ireland* (Dublin, 2003), 273.

[23] Nancy Curtin, 'Rebels and Radicals: The United Irishmen in County Down', in Lindsay Proudfoot, *Down: History and Society* (Dublin, 1997), 267.

[24] Alvin Jackson, *Ireland 1798–1898* (Oxford, 1999), 7.

programme, and that the emotions that he deliberately aroused were far more intense. The declaration of the first United Irish Society of Dublin, 9 November 1791, had declared: 'We are ruled by Englishmen and the servants of Englishmen, whose object is the interest of another country ... and these men have the whole of the power and patronage of the country.' It is clear that the Whig Club and the United Irishmen—at this early point in the 1790s—stood on similar terrain. Castlereagh and an electoral ally described their project thus in April 1790: 'We are now embarked on a much more interesting and glorious cause than our success as candidates—we are called forth as instruments and young hands to emancipate the country.'[25] Naturally, Castlereagh's opponents drew attention to the ambiguity of his social-religious position.[26] In July 1790, after a close-fought campaign, Robert Stewart squeaked home for a narrow victory. Enthusiastically, he told his supporters at the count that his 'young heart would never be separated from the cause of the people'.[27] But how long would such a mood last? In the autumn of 1790 Edmund Burke, the most celebrated Irish politician of his day, published his notable attack on the French revolution, immediately inspiring a debate, not only in England but in his own country too.[28] For Wolfe Tone this was a moment of quite decisive importance. 'At length, Mr Burke's invective [*Reflections on the Revolution in France*, 1790] appeared; and this in due season produced Paine's reply, which he called *The Rights of Man*. This controversy, and the gigantic event which gave rise to it, changed, in an instant, the politics of Ireland.'[29] Burke's *Reflections* were published on 1 November 1790, Thomas Paine's reply, *The Rights of Man*, on 13 March. These words of Wolfe Tone—simultaneously striking, profound, and incomplete—constitute an excellent if ambiguous introduction to Irish politics in the 1790s. The force of Tone's observation is undeniable. Burke immediately provoked a number of Irish replies and commentaries. *The Rights of Man* sold well over 40,000 copies. The spy Leonard MacNally reported that

several thousand copies of his various writings were printed in Belfast and Cork and distributed *gratis* by those who contributed to the first expense, many of whom were

[25] *Belfast News Letter*, 30 Apr. 1790; Patrick Geoghegan, *Lord Castlereagh* (Dublin, 2002), 9.
[26] Public Records Office of Northern Island, Belfast (PRONI) T3367/3/11. Questions put by an independent freeholder from Newry ' ... to the Rt. Hon. the Lord Baron Londonderry, the Master Robert Stewart ... 5 May 1790'.
[27] *Belfast News Letter*, 20 Apr. 1790; 23 Aug. 1822.
[28] Hugh Fenning, 'Imprints of Catholic Interest', *Collectanea Hibernica*, 46 and 47 (2004–5), 95.
[29] Thomas Bartlett (ed.), *Life of Theobald Wolfe Tone: Compiled and Arranged by William Theobald Wolfe Tone* (Dublin, 1998), 39.

men of wealth. I am assured and I believe it to be true that in the county of Cork, Paine's works are read by the boys at almost every school and that in most places they now supply the places of the psalter and prayer book.[30]

One pamphleteer insisted that Paine had a lock on 'the mind of the Irish peasant and lower tradesman'.[31]

The French revolution challenged the principles of aristocracy and monarchy in Ireland. Burke was for many the classic analyst of the inevitably disastrous consequences of the revolution, Paine its classic defender. Castlereagh was certainly impressed by some of Burke's arguments from the start: he was quick to read and absorb his copy of the *Reflections*. He told his fellow Irish Whigs that they were much too enthusiastic about the events in Paris. His uncle Charles Pratt, first Earl of Camden, wrote to him: 'I am glad you fought Burke's [battle] so strongly with the Whig Club—because I am afraid that your kingdom has caught the spirit of the National Assembly.'[32] Throughout most of 1791 Castlereagh's political behaviour continued to be satisfactory to his traditional Presbyterian supporters, but late in that year he visited France and was shocked by the chaos created by the revolution.

It is important to note that Castlereagh was influenced only in part by Burke. His two powerful analyses of the state of affairs in France—almost sixty pages of handwritten script between them—employ characteristic Burkean notions; he is happy to condemn the abstract doctrine of the rights of man ('delirium ... this metaphysical mode') and the revolution's treatment of the Catholic Church and its fiscal policies. So far, so explicitly Burkean; but Castlereagh's tone was altogether more cool than that of Burke. He stressed the 'inexhaustible complexity' of the revolution. He was contemptuous of the French émigré aristocracy, and was capable of feeling some sympathy for the popular cause. 'I feel as strongly as any man that an effectual change was necessary for the happiness and dignity of a great people, living in a state of degradation.' Castlereagh insisted that foreign armies should not be used to effect regime-change in France. But he was convinced that the revolution's political arrangements were doomed; 'essential alterations' were in the wind. The French revolution's visible failure would assist the cause of stability elsewhere. It would now be

---

[30] Thomas Bartlett, *Revolutionary Dublin 1795–1801: The Letters of Francis Higgins to Dublin Castle* (Dublin, 2004), 79; David Dickson, 'Paine and Ireland', in David Dickson, Daire Keogh, and Kevin Whelan (eds.), *The United Irishmen: Republicanism, Radicalism and Rebellion* (Dublin, 1993), ch. 11.

[31] Anon, *Some Observations on a Late Address titled Thoughts on the Present Crisis ... to which is added, Remarks on Sarsfield's Letter which appeared in the Dublin Evening Post* (Dublin and London, 1797), 9.

[32] PRONI D3030/F/7, 23 Jan. 1791.

possible 'to check the romantic projects of the people by their failure, their failure in recent history'. Castlereagh concluded:

> If Ireland should be convulsed, I trust with the assistance of Great Britain, she may escape many of the distresses France is doomed to suffer, and that, as an affectionate attachment to each other is decidedly the predominant feature of both, that it will even by an instinctive impulse perpetuate their connection.[33]

Throughout 1792, Castlereagh maintained this position, and a certain estrangement from the radical elements of his Ulster support-base began to appear: his first cold meeting with William Drennan took place at the beginning of 1793, three days after the execution of Louis XVI.[34] The French declaration of war on Britain and Holland on 1 February intensified Castlereagh's hostility to the revolution and its Irish supporters. He was infuriated also by what he saw as the unpatriotic, disloyal tone of the Ulster Volunteer Convention of February 1793. But he remained a strong supporter of measures of Catholic relief, such as that passed on 9 April 1793.

Tone, in this respect, got it right: the Burke–Paine debate was important in Ireland. But it is worth noting that Irish radicals—men like Drennan and Russell—rejected Paine's anti-Christianity, whilst important 'moderates' (William Bruce and Henry Joy) rejected Burke's militant reactionary tone. The 'lethargy' of Irish political life in the late 1780s was, however, shaken up by the impact of the French revolution; more than that, before the end of the decade the entire life of the island was to be convulsed by it. In Tone's own words, 'oppressed, plundered, insulted' Ireland was transformed politically. The French revolution had a striking impact upon the debate about the status of Catholics in Ireland. *Ancien régime* peculiarities, for so long tolerated in both Ireland and France, were being destroyed in France. When the French revolutionaries gave Protestants civil and political equality, it both highlighted the injustice of Catholic inequality in Ireland and demonstrated that Catholics in power need not be 'natural oppressors'.[35] This was an argument Irish radicals sought to

---

[33] Royal Irish Academy (RIA), Ms 12 R22, two letters of the Honourable Robert Stewart to Earl Camden 'on the prospect of France', dated 1 Sept. and 11 Nov. 1791.

[34] William Drennan to Mrs Ann Drennan, 24 Jan. 1793, in Jean Agnew (ed.), *The Drennan–McTier Letters*, vol. 1 (Dublin, 1998), 469.

[35] William Doyle, 'The Union in a European Context', *Transaction of the Royal Historical Society*, 6th ser., 10 (2003), 178; James Livesy (ed.), *Arthur O'Connor: The State of Ireland 1799* (Dublin, 1998), 101. In the section devoted to 'Effects of the French Revolution on the Irish Mind', Arthur O'Connor wrote: 'When this great Catholic nation [France] established her liberties on the ruin of religious and political tradition, the Protestants of Ireland were convinced that no particular religion, in this enlightened state of the European world, was incompatible with political freedom.'

exploit, whilst others of a different (Burkean) disposition argued that as the French regime fought bitterly with the Catholic Church, it became realistic to argue with a renewed urgency that Catholicism in Ireland might be turned into a conservative rather than a subversive constituency.

The years 1791 and 1798 became a kind of contest between the British government and the militant elements of the Society of United Irishmen (founded in 1791) to influence the Catholics of Ireland. The United Irishmen were middle class and Presbyterian in Belfast. In Dublin they were also middle class, but there was a sprinkling of gentry and aristocracy, with a roughly equal Catholic–Protestant split. The United Irishmen needed active Catholic support. For the government the task was rather different: whilst outright Catholic alienation was to be avoided, it was enough to ensure a certain political ambivalence. The United Irish operated initially as a club of radical reformers, but developed clandestine insurrectionary structures by 1795, partly as a result of an inherent radicalizing momentum, and partly as a reaction to government repression.[36] Especially after May 1797, the Irish Parliament was less and less relevant: a clear harbinger of its destruction in 1800. But there were powerful figures in Dublin political life who favoured neither the radical project of the United Irish nor the British government project of absorbing the Catholics within the system, or at any rate, reducing their alienation from that system. This was the historical moment when the term 'Ascendancy', actually invented by highly partisan Protestants, entered the public discourse for the first time. Like the term *ancien régime* in France, it soon came to imply a description of a social order which was on the verge of disintegration,[37] as both pro-Catholic and radical thinkers derided it contemptuously.

In early 1794 Tone prepared his own, empirically rather rough-and-ready, analysis of the disposition of forces in Irish society. First, he noted the Protestant members of the Established Church in Ireland, 450,000 strong, comprising the 'great body of the aristocracy, which supports and is supported' by England. This was the reactionary, oppressive, elitist segment of society. Secondly, he talked of the Dissenters, 900,000 of them, who formed a large and respectable portion of the middle ranks of the community—all, 'to a man, sincere Republicans, devoted with enthusiasm to the cause of liberty and France'. Thirdly, he noted 'The Catholics who were 3,150,000 strong. These are the Irish, properly so called, trained

[36] McDowell, 'The Dublin Society of United Irishmen', 118–19; Nancy Curtin, 'The Transformation of the Society of United Irishmen into a Mass-Based Revolutionary Organisation, 1794–6', *Irish Historical Studies*, 24: 96 (Nov. 1985), 463–93.

[37] Thomas Bartlett, *The Fall and Rise of the Irish Nation: The Catholic Question, 1690–1830* (Dublin, 1992), 151.

from their infancy in a hereditary hatred and abhorrence of the English name, which conveys to them no ideas but those of blood, pillage and persecution.'[38] A decade later, a wide-ranging survey by Robert Bell made the same point concerning the disposition of the Irish peasant masses:

> The political character of the Irish peasants ... was distinguished by their hatred of the English name and of the laws under which they lived. Whenever they spoke to the English, and of their descendants who settled in Ireland, it was in terms of derision and detestation. The usual expression was *na Sassanich broddagh*, the execrable Saxons.[39]

Bitter memories of dispossession, both as to land and political rights, had a central place within Catholic culture. Popular discontent found its direct and sharpest expression through agrarian secret societies such as the Whiteboys, an economically driven movement that tapped into traditional notions of communal revenge, custom, and justice within Irish society.[40]

For Tone, the recent change in the disposition of the Dissenters was of decisive importance. The Dissenters, in Tone's assessment, had always been inclined to oppose the 'usurpations' of England and the Anglican aristocracy. They felt that they had created the wealth of a thriving Belfast, and regarded their achievement with enormous pride. In their 'Preface' to the reformist *Belfast Politics: Thoughts on the British Constitution*, published in 1794, William Bruce and Henry Joy claimed proudly:

> Belfast, by its consequence on the Scale of Commerce, Manufacturers and Revenue, contributes eminently to the prosperity of the kingdom ... When credit was tottering to its base in almost every corner of Europe, here it held its ground. Its merchants blended prudence with enterprise, and reaped the reward for unsullied integrity.[41]

Bruce and Joy had to accept that Belfast remained the sole political property of the Marquess of Donegall. Nevertheless, much as they despised the elite above them, the Presbyterians had also despised the Catholic natives as 'slaves'. But in the years after 1790 the impact of the French revolution—according to Tone—decisively transformed their mentality. They saw that, while they had thought that they were the 'masters' of

---

[38] Bartlett (ed.), *Life of Theobald Wolfe Tone*, 605–7; *Writings of Wolfe Tone*, i. p. xxxviii.

[39] R. Bell, *A Description of the Condition and Manners as well as of the Moral and Political Character, Education of the Peasantry of Ireland such as they were between the Years 1780 and 1790, when Ireland was supposed to have arrived at its Highest Degree of Prosperity and Happiness* (London, 1804).

[40] Maureen Wall, 'The Whiteboys', in T. D. Williams (ed.), *Secret Societies in Ireland* (Dublin, 1973), 13–25; but see also Vincent Morley, *Irish Opinion and the American Revolution 1760–83* (Cambridge, 2002), 48–9.

[41] J. P. A. Bew (ed.), *William Bruce and Henry Joy: Belfast Politics: Thoughts on the British Constitution (1794)* (Dublin, 2005), 39.

the Catholics, they were, in fact, but their 'jailers'; the establishment of unbounded liberty of conscience in France had mitigated their horror of Popery; 110 years of peace had worn away very much of the old animosity which former wars had raised and fomented. Inspired by the example of France, they understood that the only 'guide' to 'liberty' was 'justice'; they saw that they neither deserved nor could obtain independence while their Catholic brethren, as they then for the first time called them, remained in slavery and oppression. Reflecting this analysis, the United Irishmen stressed the common cause of Catholic, Anglican, and Dissenter, and utilized the radical press to produce ground-breaking propaganda.

The elements of truth in Tone's analysis help to explain why the insurrection of the United Irishmen in 1798 was, in principle, so formidable and why the French revolutionaries were willing to give it material help. Nevertheless, it had obvious flaws. Tone never really faced up to the growing scepticism about French intentions which affected many Irish Presbyterian reformers by the mid-1790s,[42] in particular after the eruption of continental war in 1792, with Britain and Ireland joining against France in 1793. Furthermore, was the Dissenter change of attitude quite so complete and irreversible? For example, Tone elsewhere speaks only of the 'best men' among them. Tone certainly did not give an adequate account of the 'rootedness' of the British state—the so-called Dublin Castle 'junta' which governed Ireland—within Irish society. Irish loyalism, Protestant and even Catholic in some cases, turned out to be a rather more profound popular obstacle to the success of an insurrection than any follower of Tone's analysis of the disposition of forces would have expected. After all, in 1788 Tone himself had been sufficiently seduced by the British Empire to attempt to sell a scheme of colonial expansion to William Pitt. How was it reasonable to expect others to be suddenly immune to such a resonant and powerful appeal?[43] Above all, however, problems existed concerning Tone's analysis of the Catholic Irish, the Irish 'properly so called'. Tone insisted that Irish Catholicism was evolving along a 'French' path; a cultural inheritance, no doubt, but not any longer a driving force, capable of expressing anti-Protestant bigotry on a large scale. Tone, in short, ascribed a consciousness to the Catholics of Ireland more definitely secularized, more 'enlightened', than they themselves may have felt.

Tone's solution to the 'Irish crisis' was disputed by Edmund Burke, the greatest Irishman in British public life and the greatest intellectual opponent of the French revolution. But the stark opposition one might

---

[42] See J. P. A. Bew (ed.), *Belfast Politics* (Dublin, 2004), introduction.
[43] Thomas Bartlett, 'Theobald Wolfe Tone: An Eighteen-Century Republican and Separatist', *The Republic*, 2 (Spring–Summer 2001).

expect—emblematic revolutionary (Tone) versus emblematic counter-revolutionary (Burke)—is only partially present. In some important respects, it was Tone rather than Castlereagh who fought the 'Battle of Burke'. For if Castlereagh shared Burke's analysis of the significance of events in France, Wolfe Tone was arguably closer to Burke's analysis of the politics of Ireland. For what appears first to be a stark polarity (the Tone–Burke relationship) is, in fact, more complex: a messy world of overlapping personal connections and of conflicting political allegiances, which, while ultimately incompatible, nonetheless included a significant amount of common ground. At first glance, this may be difficult to grasp.

One of the first replies to Burke came from the pen of 'An Irishman', entitled *An Answer to the Rt Hon Edmund Burke: Reflections on the Revolution in France with some Remarks on the Present State of the Irish Constitution Generally.*[44] 'An Irishman' accused Burke in general terms of an absurd 'violent' ancestor worship, but he also asked:

What are the consequences of the stationary policy if adopted in this country? … Shall we ever sit above 'our neighbours' [or] admit them to their rights? Shall no continuance of submission, of allegiance, of patience, of common sufferings and fears, of common wishes, exertions and triumphs induce us to afford to our Roman Catholic brethren a power of promoting the common prosperity?

In short, 'An Irishman' feared that Burke's critique of the French revolution could be utilized against the demands for reform in Ireland. 'An Irishman' was not alone in expressing such a view. In 1791 J. Towers argued that Burke's allies—the Portland faction in British politics—were staunch opponents of Catholic emancipation in Ireland.[45] Although explicitly disagreeing on this point, Bernard Bousfield of Cork also published in Dublin a refutation of Burke, *Observations on the Rt Hon Edmund Burke's Pamphlet 'The Subject of the French Revolution'*, which pleased elements in the United Irish leadership,[46] perhaps because it raised the question of how Mr Burke, a 'great advocate of the Church of England', could 'express such a veneration' for the French Catholic Church. But, in truth, neither 'An Irishman', Towers, Bousfield, or United Irish satires like Thomas Russell's and William Sampson's anti-Burkeian 'A Review of the Lion of Old England' (1794) are a complete guide to Burke's message for Ireland in the 1790s.

---

[44] Published and printed by J. Moore in Dublin (1791), 31. See also William Sampson and Thomas Russell's United Irish satire, directed explicitly against Burke. Mary Helen Thuente, 'The Belfast Laugh: The Context and Significance of United Irish Satire', in J. Smyth (ed.), *Revolution, Counter-Revolution and the Union* (Cambridge, 2001), 73–5.

[45] J. Towers, *Thoughts on the Commencement of a New Parliament* (Dublin, 1791), 4.

[46] Agnew (ed.), *The Drennan–McTier Letters*, Drennan to Sam McTier, 18 Aug. 1792, p. 412.

EDMUND BURKE: 'INCONSISTENTLY ENOUGH' A 'TRUE NATIVE'?

An important hint of the real complexity of Burke's role in Irish politics is caught by the celebrated Presbyterian Francophile radical William Drennan, who noted that Irish Catholics 'idolised' Burke who, 'inconsistently enough, is a true native'.[47] For if Burke was guilty of 'ancestor worship', as 'An Irishman' claimed, who were *his* ancestors? Edmund Burke's father may have been the Catholic Richard Burke who conformed to the Established Church in 1722. His mother followed her Catholic faith and Burke's sister Julianne was brought up as a Catholic. A sickly child, Burke spent a considerable amount of time with his Nagle Catholic relatives in Munster. Lord Acton lays particular stress on Burke's affection for a Catholic uncle and Catholic nurse.[48] The *Dublin University Magazine* later noted that it was also 'well for Burke ... that he was not sent to an English public school, and that the strong affection he felt for his Roman Catholic relatives were not exposed to any distracting influences'.[49] Burke was the greatest single opponent of the French revolution. There was a paradox at the heart of his thought: Edmund Burke, solid defender of the *ancien régime* in France, was well known to be a critic of the *ancien régime* in Ireland.[50]

There is no doubt as to Burke's strong empathy with the plight of Catholic Ireland. In fact, Edmund Burke was related by marriage to Father Sheehy,[51] who was executed for alleged Whiteboy activities in 1766. Burke was personally alarmed by the whole affair, and it left the deepest impression. Some forty substantial local Catholics had been arrested, as powerful Protestant forces insisted that Whiteboyism was a form of political subversion. David Nagle, the wealthiest Cork Catholic landowner, felt it wise to slip out of the country. Burke was a private secretary to the Chief

[47] William Drennan to Sam McTier, 8 Apr. 1795, in Jean Agnew (ed.), *TheDrennan-McTier Letters*, vol. 2, *1794–1811* (Dublin, 1998), 146.

[48] Acton explicitly derived this argument from Thomas McKnight's study of Burke, *Essays on the History of Liberty*, ed. J Rufus Fears (Indianapolis, 1985), 139.

[49] 'The Life and Times of Edmund Burke', *Dublin University Magazine*, 55:325 (Jan. 1860), 156.

[50] T. McLoughlin and J. T. Boulton, *The Writings and Speeches of Edmund Burke*, introduction, vol. 1, (Oxford, 1997), but see also F. P. Lock, *Edmund Burke, 1730–84*, vol. 1 (Oxford, 1998), 1–29; J. C. Beckett, 'Burke, Ireland and the Empire', in O. McDonagh, W. P. Mandle and Padraig Travers (eds.), *Irish Culture and Nationalism* (London, 1983), 81–174.

[51] Father Nicholas Sheehy's sister was married to Richard Burke's first cousin. R. B. McDowell (ed.), *The Writings and Speeches of Edmund Burke, vol. 9* (Oxford, 1991), 414.

Secretary William Hamilton in Dublin Castle from 1761 to 1764, and in a position to see much and be horrified by the crude bias of the system.[52]

Burke constructed a new career outside Ireland. Elected to the British Parliament in 1765, he emerged as a leading orator and theorist of the new reformist Whig Party.[53] Some in Ireland claimed that Burke had forgotten his Irish roots.[54] But in 1783 he published 'A Letter from a Distinguished English Commoner' (*Rt. Hon. E. B. to a Peer of Ireland on the Penal Laws against Irish Catholics, Previous to the Late Repeal of a Part Thereof of the Session of the Irish Parliament, held AD 1782*), where he cautiously accepted that it might be necessary to keep the 'leading parts' of the military and political system in the hands of those who were judged most trustworthy. But it did not follow that any group should be 'subjected to a total exclusion from the Commonwealth'. From this point onwards, Burke's latent Catholic sympathies became the subject of debate.[55] In March 1808 the *Irish Magazine* went so far as to claim that Burke formally adopted the Catholic faith before his death: 'Perhaps it is not generally known that the ornament of Ireland who, during his lifetime, was often reproached for his attachment to the Roman Church, died a Catholic.'[56] There is no definite proof on such a point. The Victorian historian James Anthony Froude offered a more nuanced account, which does, however, fit the public record:

Burke was not himself a Catholic, but as little was he a Protestant. His sympathies were with the old faith. His most intimate friends were Catholics to the end, and at the end even more than at the beginning. His advice to Pitt, his advice to the world,

[52] Luke Gibbons, *Edmund Burke and Ireland* (Cambridge, 2003), 22; David Dickson, 'Jacobitism in Eighteenth-Century Ireland: A Munster Perspective', *Eire–Ireland*, 3: 3–4 (Fall–Winter 2004), 97; and id., *Old World Colony: Cork and South Munster 1630–1830* (Cork, 2005), 279.

[53] Gibbons, *Edmund Burke and Ireland*, 23.

[54] See Anon., *Edmund Burke, by Birth an Irishman, by Adoption an Englishman* (Dublin, 1780).

[55] Ibid. 7; Duke of Argyll, *Irish Nationalism: An Appeal to History* (London, 1893), 264.

[56] See, above all, on this point Conor Cruise O'Brien, introduction, to Edmund Burke, *Reflections on the Revolution in France* (Harmondsworth, 1968). This thesis is extended in the same author's *The Great Melody: A Thematic Biography of Edmund Burke* (London, 1992). The most impressive recent statement is L. M. Cullen, 'Burke's Irish Views and Writings', in Ian Crowe (ed.), *Edmund Burke: His Life and Legacy* (Dublin, 1997), 62–75; Seamus Deane, 'Factions and Fictions: Burke, Colonialism and Revolution', *Bullan: An Irish Studies Journal*, 4 (Winter 1999–Spring 2000), 5–27; T. McLoughlin, *Contesting Ireland: Irish Voices against England in the Eighteenth Century*, vol. 12 (1997), 7–28; Kevin Whelan, 'An Underground Gentry? Catholic Middlemen in Eighteenth-Century Ireland', in J. S. Donnelly Jr. and Kerby Miller (eds.), *Irish Popular Culture 1650–1850* (Dublin and Portland, Oreg., 1999), 161–4; Katherine O'Donnell, 'To Love the Little Platoon': *Edmund Burke's Jacobite Heritage* (Dublin, 2007), 16–28 in Sean Patrick Dolan (ed.), *Edmund Burke's Irish Identities* (Dublin, 2006).

was to save his countrymen from the revolutionary temper by restoring to them the privileges of citizenship.[57]

In 1791 Thomas McDonnell, the United Irish printer, reprinted Burke's 1783 advocacy of a policy of conciliation of Catholics; by this time Burke was in a more outspoken mood. The French revolution had changed everything. Sir Hercules Langrishe, who had discussed the matter extensively with Burke, told the 'Ascendancy' Irish Parliament: 'The old dangers of Popery which used to alarm you, are now extinct to all intents and purposes; and new dangers have arisen in the world, against which the Catholics are your best and natural allies.'[58] This was precisely the message which Burke wished to drive home. W. E. H. Lecky was an early sharp critic of Froude's historical work on Ireland, but on this point he agreed with him:

Burke, who had just seceded from the Whig party through his hostility to revolution, and who had lately published his *Reflections* on that revolution, the most profound and eloquent of all defences of the Constitution, was the steady friend of the Catholics, and at a time when he was preaching with unrivalled power the danger of tampering with the framework of the existing British Constitution, he argued that the Constitution of Ireland could not but be better strengthened by introducing gradually and carefully a Catholic element of property and education into political life.[59]

Burke insisted that the Irish Constitution was a bastard form; not a simple aristocratic *ancien régime*—which, for Burke, might logically have been more acceptable—but a Protestant *ancien régime* integrally linked to a 'plebeian' Protestant element which also had rights not allowed to the entire Catholic community. A plebeian Protestant might consider himself superior to a Catholic nobleman. Not everyone accepted this argument: 'Does not entirely the same distance exist between Lord Fingal and his footman, whether that footman be a Protestant or not, as between as any other nobleman or footman?'[60] Edmund Burke was convinced that there was nothing in the coronation oath which committed the King to deny a 'Roman Catholic to the use of any franchise whatsoever', an argument

---

[57] J. A. Froude, *The English in Ireland* (London, 1895), iii. 27.

[58] *A Full and Accurate Report of the Debates in the Parliament of Ireland in the Session 1793: On the Bill for the Relief of his Majesty's Catholic Subjects* (Dublin, 1793), 4 Feb. 1793, p. 71; see also *Some Objections on a Later Address of Dublin and the Present Crisis* (Dublin and London, 1797), 40.

[59] W. E. H. Lecky, *Leaders of Public Opinion in Ireland* (London, 1903), 135.

[60] Anon., *Review of a Celebrated Speech on the Catholic Claims, Delivered in the Imperial House of Commons on the Session of 1813 in a Letter Addressed to the Hon. W. C. Plunket* (London, 1813), 31.

sharply and effectively disputed by the Irish Anglican hierarchy.[61] Burke claimed that Ireland was profoundly unstable because of the denial of Catholic rights and the radical humiliation of that community. With a keen personal eye, in a pamphlet first published in February 1792 and frequently reprinted in the 1790s, he argued that there were 'thousands in Ireland who have never conversed with a Roman Catholic in their whole lives, unless they happened to talk to their gardener's workmen ... I remember a great, and in many respects a good, man, who advertised for a blacksmith, but at the same time added he must have a Protestant blacksmith'.[62]

This passage showed Burke's perception of the blinkered outlook of the Protestant ascendancy. But the brilliance of his analysis goes beyond such a conventional observation. He had also a profound insight into the angle of vision of Catholic Ireland living cheek by jowl with an entire community that considered itself superior; a claim of superiority made all the more irritating by the obvious fact that many of the dominant community were such ordinary, unimpressive, and worse than unimpressive people. 'Our grievance is that many men beneath us in birth, education, morals and fortune are allowed to trample us', wrote John Keogh, a wealthy Catholic merchant and ally of Burke.[63] Burke's dramatic and insightful passage on this point goes right to the heart of much of Irish history in the nineteenth and even the twentieth centuries:

We know that the Government of Ireland (the same as the British) is not in its constitution wholly Aristocratical, and as it is not such in its form, so neither is it in its spirit. If it had been inveterately aristocratical, exclusions might be more patiently submitted to. The lot of one plebeian would be the lot of all; and a habitual reverence and admiration of certain families might make the people content to see government wholly in hands to whom it naturally seemed to belong. But our constitution has a plebeian member, which forms an essentially integral part of it. A plebeian oligarchy is a monster in itself: and no people, not absolutely domestic or predial slaves will long endure it ... I hold it to be absolutely impossible for two millions of plebeians, composing certainly a very clear and decided majority in that class, to become so far in love with six or seven hundred thousand of their fellow citizens (to all outward appearances plebeians like themselves, and many of

---

[61] A. P. W. Malcolmson, *Archbishop Charles Agar: Churchmanship and Politics in Ireland, 1760–1810* (Dublin, 2002), 516–19.

[62] 'Letter from Rt. Hon. Edmund Burke in the Kingdom of Great Britain to Sir Hercules Langrishe', 3 Jan. 1792, in McDowell (ed.), *Writings and Speeches of Edmund Burke*, vol. 9. Sir Hercules Langrishe was a supporter, at times hesitantly, of pro-Catholic reform in the Irish House of Commons.

[63] E. Hay (ed.), *A Sketch of a Speech by John Keogh Esq at a Meeting of the Catholics of Dublin* (Dublin, 1807), 14.

them tradesmen, servants, and otherwise inferior to some of them) as to see with satisfaction, or even patience, an exclusive power vested in them.[64]

On Irish affairs, Burke now spoke 'like a revolutionary':[65] evoking a loyalty to an 'interior history of Ireland, the genuine voice',[66] rather than histories which justified Protestant ascendancy. Burke appeared to believe that 'the system that excluded Catholics from political office and from many common rights, if it could not be reformed at once, deserved to be overthrown'.[67] Burke's principal message, however, was that England would be stronger if it responded to Catholic grievances;[68] by 1791 fear of a revolution throughout Europe had dominated his thinking on Ireland.

Burke's reasoning, combined with his enormous personal prestige, attracted the attention of the leadership, both clerical and secular, of the increasingly important Irish Catholic middle class. On 13 August 1790 Thomas Hussey (1746–1803), former chaplain to the Spanish ambassador in London, and from 1793 to 1803 Catholic bishop of Waterford, wrote to Burke, including a letter to his son, Richard Burke, as a professional gentleman,[69] and asking for his help on behalf of the Irish Catholics. From this point on Burke and his son formally engaged themselves in the affairs of the Irish Catholics. In 1791 Burke introduced the wealthy Dublin Catholic merchant John Keogh to prominent figures in London political life. The objective was to argue the case for a measure of Catholic relief. Burke's relationship with Keogh was characterized by a definite unease: in 1795 John Keogh had visible pro-Jacobin leanings which disturbed Burke. Replying to Keogh's praise of Burke on 20 July 1796—Keogh had described him as an Irishman living an English political life but remaining true to Ireland—Burke, in his letter of 17 November 1796, accepted the praise but reversed the proposition with strong ulterior purpose: 'I can not conceive that a man can be a genuine Englishman without being a true Irishman ... I think the same sentiments ought to be reciprocal on the part of Ireland, and, if possible, with much stronger reason.'[70] Elsewhere, Burke stated that 'the closest connection between Great Britain and Ireland is essential to the well-being, I had almost said to the very

---

[64] 'Letter to Sir Hercules Langrishe, 1792', in McDowell (ed.), *Writings and Speeches of Edmund Burke*, ix. 600.

[65] David Bromwich, *On Empire, Liberty and Reform: Speeches and Letters of Edmund Burke* (New Haven and London, 2000), 416.

[66] Thomas McLoughlin, *Contesting Ireland: Irish Voices against England in the Eighteenth Century* (Dublin, 1999), 166.

[67] Bromwich, *On Empire*, 416.

[68] McLoughlin, *Contesting Ireland*, 74; F. P. Locke, 'Unpublished Burke letters (iii) 1793–6', *English Historical Review*, 118: 478 (Sept. 2003), 973–4.

[69] Cruise O'Brien, *The Great Melody*, 468.   [70] Ibid. 579.

being of the two kingdoms'. Burke added: 'By separation Ireland would be the most completely undone country in the world, the most wretched, the most distracted and the most desolate part of the inhabitable globe.'[71] 'Ireland,' said Burke in his most vivid phrase on the subject, could not be 'separated from England, she could not exist without her; she must ever remain under the protection of England, her guardian angel.'[72] But Irish opinion was escaping Burke's clutches. On 10 May 1795 the United Irishmen reformed in a new guise—as a secret, oath-bound, revolutionary organization. In mid-May 1795 Burke denounced the separatist language at a Dublin meeting which had been called to attack the idea of a union between the two kingdoms. He insisted: 'Ireland, therefore as Ireland, taken civilly, constitutionally or commercially, suffers no grievance. The Catholics as Catholics do.'[73] There was, he insisted, a fundamental identity of interest between the two countries—it was only the denial of Catholic emancipation which threatened that fundamental identity of interest.

In 1791, however, such dangers lay in the future. In order to assist the Catholic cause, Richard Burke became Secretary to the Catholic Committee in Dublin in September of that year, and threw himself into the battle of ideas on the Catholic side in a pamphlet, published significantly enough by Patrick Byrne, the United Irish printer.[74] Richard Burke's reputation has suffered on all sides; the conventional scholarly wisdom is that he served with 'little ability and less tact'.[75] He was a habitual sender of explosive epistles to powerful men in the British ruling class, who did not expect to be addressed in such a tone. Richard Burke's capacity to irritate and exasperate was undoubted. Within days of the young Burke's appointment to his post as Secretary, Henry Dundas, Home Secretary, was protesting to him: 'I had a visit from your father this evening. I took the occasion to state to him my surprise at the contents of your last letter.'[76] The Earl of Charlemont

---

[71] Edmund Burke, in Mathew Arnold (ed.), *Irish Affairs*, with an introduction by Conor Cruise O'Brien (London, 1988), 379–80.

[72] Burke, quoted in Viscount Wellesley, *The Irish Question Considered in its Integrity* (Dublin, 1844), 25.

[73] *Memoirs and Correspondence of Lord Castlereagh*, iii. 122.

[74] Richard Burke, *A Letter from Richard Burke Esq*, pp. xxv–xxxx; Esq. of Cork, *In which the Legality and Propriety of the Meeting then Commended by Mr Byrne's Circular Letter, are Discussed: Together with Some Observations on a Measure Proposed by a Friend, to be Substituted in the Place of the Catholic Committee*, (Dublin: 'printed by P. Byrne', 1792); for Patrick Byrne, bookseller and lottery-office keeper, see R. B. McDowell, *Historical Essays* (Dublin, 2003), 228.

[75] Sean Patrick Donlan, 'Edmund Burke: Scorned Loyalty and Allegiance', *History Ireland*, 12:2 (Summer, 2004), 21. But see Danny Mansergh, *Grattan's Failure: Parliamentary Opposition and the People in Ireland 1779–1800* (Dublin, 2005), 137.

[76] National Library of Ireland, Dublin (NLI) Ms54, Dundas to Richard Burke, 20 Sept. 1791.

wrote to Dr Haliday on 21 January 1792, with heavy sarcasm, of Burke's 'modesty scarcely to be paralleled ... This Catholic plenipotentiary, this truly consistent French aristocrat and Irish demagogue'.[77] Wolfe Tone, who eased Richard Burke out of his position as secretary to the Catholic Committee and took the post for himself in the summer of 1792, described Richard Burke as talented but woefully deficient in judgement, in temper, and especially the art of managing.[78] Certainly Tone found it easy enough to persuade Keogh that he was the right man to step into Burke's job on 25 July 1792.

Conor Cruise O'Brien has suggested that Richard's often extravagant and turbulent behaviour may reflect the impact of the tuberculosis which killed him in 1794.[79] Richard Burke himself admitted to Dundas that his Irish friends considered him lacking in 'temperance' and 'practicality'.[80] But there is another side to this story. Richard Burke flailed mercilessly and bravely against a government which remained inert in the face of a major and pressing political problem. He identified Major Hobart, the Chief Secretary in Dublin, and politicians such as Sir John Parnell as the supporters of oppressive Protestantism. He assailed Hobart to his face, in private letters, behind his back, in communication with other Cabinet ministers, and, in public, in an angry pamphlet. 'Great Britain has always governed Ireland by the Protestants ... instead of being governed by His Majesty's opinions in consideration of his Catholic citizens', he told Henry Dundas, Viscount Melville. Richard Burke added in the same letter, with some vigour: 'Whether the Catholics are right or not in their understanding of things is not the question. But they are right. However respectable and plausible the words *English government* may sound ... they signify the destruction of Ireland in the times past and in the present time.'[81]

Some of this was undoubtedly counter-productive, but there is no evidence of that venality which Tone claimed to observe: Tone described Richard Burke's salary requests as 'sublime' and 'ridiculous'. There is also evidence of a surprising degree of effectiveness. Dundas, after all, remained a loyal friend to pro-Catholic reform in Ireland, and even thought of appointing Burke's ally, Henry Grattan, as Chief Secretary in Dublin.[82] Catholic opinion in Ireland could easily fall into a mood of morose pessimism. A writer styling himself 'An Irish Helot', for example, believed

[77] Royal Irish Academy, Ms 12 R22.
[78] O'Brien, *Great Melody*, 473. [79] Ibid. 474.
[80] NLI MS54, Burke to Dundas, 6 Apr. 1792.
[81] NLI MS 54, Richard Burke to Dundas, 6 Apr. 1792.
[82] Michael Fry, *The Dundas Despotism* (Edinburgh, 1992), 178.

there was no inevitability about any pro-Catholic reform; rather, he feared, 'the misfortunes of the Roman Catholics are likely to increase, as the country shall improve in prosperity and freedom'.[83] It was this defeatist mentality which Richard Burke challenged by his aggressive effrontery. Significantly, Hobart, Richard Burke's arch-enemy, confessed on 4 October 1792: 'The Catholics appear to have acquired fresh vigour since the arrival of Mr Richard Burke who continues to encourage them with the expectation of British neutrality.'[84]

On 3 January 1792 Edmund Burke told Sir Hercules Langrishe that the refusal to allow Catholics to enjoy 'the ancient, fundamental and tried advantages of a British constitution,' had a tendency, 'deeply to ulcerate their minds'. 'What the consequence of such feelings must be, it is for you to look to ... To warn is not to menace.'[85] Another active supporter of pro-Catholic reform makes a very precise reference to this passage in an unpublished reply to a pamphlet published that year. In a deliberate echo of Burke, Wolfe Tone wrote: 'I am far from wishing to bully the legislature, yet I can not help thinking that perhaps three million of people now in Ireland are discontented, and with reason, with many of our laws. To warn, says Burke, is not to threaten.'[86]

Tone's use of Burke's language should not be cause for surprise. Tone knew both the Burkes, having met the son in 1791 and the father in 1795. Tone was an important part of the world of pro-Catholic political activism. More than this, Burke's language always seems to rattle around Tone's mind. When he arrived in Paris in 1795, he was relieved, for example, to find that (to his own satisfaction) the 'age of chivalry' had not been destroyed by the French revolution, as Burke had proclaimed. Tone was well aware that Burke's advocacy of the Catholic cause plagued Dublin Castle. Hobart opined: 'In proportion as Popery declines in France, Mr Burke is determined to make it flourish in Ireland.'[87] In 1793 Lord Clare

---

[83] *Vindiciae Catholicae: A True Defence of the Declaration of Catholic Society of Dublin* (Dublin, 1792), 40.

[84] NLI MS54.

[85] 'Letter to Sir Hercules Langrishe, 3 January 1792', in McDowell (ed.), *Writings and Speeches of Edmund Burke*, ix. 630.

[86] Wolfe Tone, unpublished reply to a pamphlet entitled 'The Protestant Interest in Ireland Ascertained', January 1792, in *Writings of Wolfe Tone*, i. 178.

[87] Chief Secretary Major Hobart to Evan Nepean, 1 Nov. 1792, A. Froude, *The English in Ireland* (London, 1895), iii. 73. For other evidence of the Castle's concern about Burke's stand, see A. Marsden to W. Wickham, 9 Mar. 1803, PRONI T 2627/5/IC/66. Richard Burke picked up on Hobart's hostility to his father's Irish cause, and was blunt both in his direct communications with Hobart, and also in talking about Hobart to the members of the government, PRONI, Hobart Papers, T 2627/1/3, 28 Oct. 1793, Burke to Hobart, T 2627/1/12, accusing Hobart of betraying the government.

claimed that Edmund Burke had betrayed Pitt in the name of 'Popish democracy'.[88] Symptomatically, in late 1793 Burke met the United Irish radical Arthur O'Connor, who recorded that Burke seemed to imagine that 'I, like himself, had a hankering after Popery'.[89] Ian McCalman has argued that, for Burke, 'Irish Jacobinism, as distinct from its wanton English strain, stemmed from terrible hunger, distress and injustice. If such sympathy did not push Burke into becoming a republican revolutionary like Irish Whig counterparts Arthur O'Connor and Wolfe Tone, he verged on complicity.'[90]

As part of the project of Catholic emancipation, the Burkes developed an interesting range of contacts. They did not confine themselves to the small landed, business, and clerical elite in the Catholic community. Edmund Burke maintained friendly relations with Henry Grattan, the leading Protestant Liberal patriot reformer. In 1792–3 William Cusack Smith was brought within the Burke circle. Educated at Eton and Christ Church, Oxford, elected to the Royal Irish Academy in 1790, he was one of the cleverest young men in the Dublin of the 1790s. It is not difficult to see the purely academic side of Smith's appeal to Burke: Smith had read Montesquieu, spoke excellent French, and was capable of publishing, in 1791, an elegant rebuttal of Paine, dedicated to Burke. *The Rights of Citizens* was sent to Burke for his approval, and the great man responded with a warm letter.[91] There was also a more personal dimension. Like Burke,[92] Smith had been brought up as a Protestant, but his mother and several close relatives were Catholics.[93] Smith's background seems to mirror, in a rather precise way, that of Burke: Smith was influenced both by his Catholic connections and his superior educational experiences. As F. Elrington Ball observed of Cusack Smith: 'In his opinions, he was affected by the fact that his mother belonged to a Roman Catholic family and professed that religion and by a sense of superiority at having been a

[88] Clare to Auckland, 8 June 1798, in A. P. W. Malcolmson and D. A. Fleming (eds.), *A Volley of Execrations: The Letters and Papers of John Fitzgibbon, Earl of Clare* (Dublin, 2005), 342.

[89] Jane B. Hames, *Arthur O'Connor, United Irishman* (Cork, 2001), 83.

[90] Ian McCalman, 'Popular Constitutionalism and Revolution in England and Ireland', in Isser Woloch (ed.), *Revolution and the Meanings of Freedom in the Nineteenth Century* (Stanford, 1996), 140.

[91] Burke to William Cusack Smith, 1 July 1791, in A. Cobban and R. A. Smith (eds.), *The Correspondence of Edmund Burke* (Chicago, 1967).

[92] James Prior, *Memoirs of the Life and Character of the Rt. Hon. Edmund Burke* (London, 1826), 321; T. H. D. Mahoney, *Edmund Burke and Ireland* (Cambridge, Mass., 1960), 243.

[93] W. Cusack Smith, *Letter on the Catholic Claims Written to the Rt. Hon. Edmund Burke* (London, 1808), 7.

gentleman commoner in the House at Oxford and a frequent visitor to the Continent.'[94] William Cusack Smith visited Edmund Burke at Beaconsfield and became friendly with Richard. In 1793 Cusack Smith published *The Patriot*, a political pamphlet, also dedicated to Burke. The most important essay, actually written on 28 May 1792, was devoted to the Catholic question. Cusack Smith made a critically important reference to Cicero: 'That great [*sic*] conceived that the possession of privileges was calculated to produce allegiance to the system under which they were enjoyed, and that we might promote the loyalty of the subject by giving him an interest in the defence of the Constitution.' In conventionally Burkean style, he insisted that Cicero built no conclusions on 'Imaginary Rights of Man'. These belonged to 'the obscurity consigned to Tom Paine'.[95] By October of 1793 Dublin reviewers knew of the Burke–Cusack Smith relationship[96] and, indeed, in November of that year Cusack Smith published Burke's letter of July 1791, which had praised his rejection of abstract, over-theoretical reasoning, and the introduction to his revised version of *The Rights of Citizens*.[97]

But if William Cusack Smith was an obvious intellectual soulmate and ally for the Burkes, it can not be said that Protestant, pro-French radicals like Wolfe Tone and William Drennan were. Yet Richard Burke had extensive dealings with such figures. There was always an underlying tension: the intellectualist and internationalist republicans like Drennan supported Catholic emancipation, but as part of a wider separatist and radical project.[98] For the Burkes, on the other hand, Catholic emancipation was an end in itself, and they had no sympathy with the wider project. Indeed, Catholic emancipation in Ireland was seen as a means of blocking that wider project. Edmund Burke instinctively did not find it easy to be accommodating to the northern Dissenters, whose radicalism he detested—indeed, the second edition of the 'Letter to Hercules Langrishe' contained an apology for offence unintentionally caused, in the first edition, to that community.[99] Burke had criticized the northerners for their intense

[94] F. Elrington Ball, *The Judges in Ireland 1221–1921*, vol. 2 (London, 1926), 239–40.

[95] *The Flapper: Miscellanies in Prose*, vol. 1, *Including The Patriot: A Collection of Political Essays* (Dublin, 1793), 107.

[96] *Anthologica Hibernica, or Monthly Collection of Science, Belles-Lettres and History*, 2 (Oct. 1793), 367.

[97] Ibid. 3 (Nov. 1793), 367.

[98] David Wilson, *United Irishmen, United States: Immigrant Radicals in the Early Republic* (Ithaca and London, 1998), 12–13.

[99] The Catholic Committee insisted on an advertisement appended to the 2nd edn., claiming that it was 'never Mr Burke's intention to throw any imputation whatever on that great and respectable body'. These allegations had created a furore within the

radicalism. One nineteenth-century Burke scholar, Thomas McKnight, recalls: 'In a direct reply to Burke, certain members of the Northern Whig Club ... passed a resolution ... declaring that they were what he said they were.'[100] Drennan and his friends believed that Richard Burke was quite happy to employ the threat of a northern Presbyterian–Irish Catholic alliance in order to stir the British state into reform. But they also believed that the Burkes would have no difficulty in ultimately siding with the British state against such an alliance if actually cemented on United Irish principles. The Presbyterian radicals also believed that the Burkes would support any British policy of *divide et impera*: uncomfortably aware of this sort of thinking, Drennan declared that the Catholic cause 'is selfish compared to ours'.[101] In an attempt to revitalize a more genuine reformism, Drennan penned a Dublin Society of United Irishmen declaration: 'Citizen soldiers to arms!', favouring revival of volunteering in preference to establishment of government-controlled militia, and advocating the holding of another Volunteer convention.

The outbreak of war between Britain and France in February 1793 heavily implied that Irish affairs could not be allowed to drift. There appeared to be a polarizing momentum at work. Joseph Pollock, once a passionate radical and friend of Tone, urged the largely Presbyterian Dungannon Convention later that month—which had been called to maximize pressure for equality of political representation—that they should not reject the government's pleas for military support against the French,[102] but felt himself isolated.[103] It became essential for the government to detach middle-class Catholics from the United Irish movement, which was growing in confidence. Britain persuaded the Irish Parliament that it was desirable to pass a Catholic Relief Bill that April. Two of the brightest young stars of the Irish Parliament supported the legislation. On 9 February 1793 Robert Stewart argued that

---

United Irish Society, which expressed itself in hostility towards the printer Patrick Byrne. See M. Durey, 'The Dublin Society of United Irishmen and the Politics of the Cary–Drennan dispute, *Historical Journal*, 33:1 (1994), 89–161.

   [100] *Ulster As It Is*, vol. 2 (London, 1896), 373.

   [101] William Drennan to Martha McTier, 25 Nov. 1792, in Agnew (ed.), *Drennan–McTier Letters*, i. 429. For other important references on this point see ibid. 385, 391, 560.

   [102] A. T. Q. Stewart, *A Deeper Silence: The Hidden Roots of the United Irish Movement* (London, 1995), 183; *Belfast News Letter*, 15–19 Feb. 1793; Fleming and Malcolmson (eds.), *A Volley of Execrations*, 240.

   [103] Joseph Pollock, *Letter to the Inhabitants of the Town and Lordship of Newry* (Dublin, 1793) 49, 73–4; S. Small, *Political Thought in Ireland 1776–1798* (Oxford, 2002), 222–3. Pollock had, in 1779, chosen as a pen-name Owen Roe O'Nial, the commander of the invasion which would liberate Ireland. Morley, *American Opinion and the Irish Question*, 217.

it was time to put an end to the 'great evils of representation' in Ireland
and allow the 'public vote' to operate fully in the representative assembly'.
On 25 February Arthur Wellesley argued that Catholics—like everyone
else—were swayed by various 'passions' and 'interests' and would not
accept dictation by their priests.[104] The strategy of the Burkes—essentially
to frighten the British ruling class into an awareness of its true interests
in Ireland—had thus an early success. The Catholic Relief Act of 1793
removed almost all the remaining Catholic disabilities from the penal law
era. The franchise was now extended to Catholics. They were enabled to
hold high civil and military offices. The statutory ban on holding university
degrees was removed. Catholics were now admitted to the franchise, but
they were, it is important to note, still excluded from Parliament. Burke
declared that this measure had his hearty approval: but it must, he said, be
made 'subservient to the tranquillity of the country and the strength of the
Empire'.[105] John Fitzgibbon, the Irish Lord Chancellor, took a much more
pessimistic view: at this moment, he told the Prime Minister, Burke and
Dundas had 'betrayed' Pitt by opening up a revolution of rising expectations
in Ireland. The only possible remedy was a new union between the two
islands.[106]

John Fitzgibbon was not alone in seeing the importance of Burke's role.
William Drennan wrote to Sam McTier on 1 September 1793:

I do believe that Mr Burke was called into the closet of the King who acknowledged
his numerous obligations for benefits to himself, his family and his government, and
asked Burke what return *he* could make for his abuse against France and his good
service to the monarchy. I do believe that Mr Burke answered to this effect: nothing
for himself, 'but much for three millions of my loyal and suffering countrymen, the
friends and victims of their attachment to monarchy. Sir, I warn you to do this
immediately, an alliance which a little time will make more natural than it now
appears, is about to take place between three million Catholics and half a million
disaffected Presbyterian republicans, deeply intoxicated with French notions and
French practices. The Constitution will be changed even here, and monarchy itself
will be endangered'. I do believe our King said: 'Burke, Burke, let it be done, let
the Catholics be emancipated immediately, and let me get the credit before it is
too late'.

Drennan argued that 'all was accomplished without any communication
with the Irish cabinet, and that the grand juries and the Chancellor
and the Council here were well instructed what was going on in the

[104] *Parliamentary Register of Ireland*, 313.

[105] J. C. Beckett, 'Burke, Ireland and the Empire', in McDonagh, Mandle, and
Travers (eds.), *Irish Culture and Nationalism 1750–1950*, 2.

[106] Fleming and Malcolmson, *A Volley of Execrations*, Clare to Auckland, 8 June
1798, p. 342.

backstairs conference'.[107] William Drennan's analysis may have lacked literal truth, but in a more broad sense Drennan, who, after all, had several meetings with Richard Burke under his belt, was describing the reality which underpinned the government's new strategy. In the same letter Drennan noted that 'Siberia' was more 'fitted' to be a republic than Ireland—his underlying reasoning is clear: Drennan believed that the British state was containing the threat of Protestant radicalism by winning over Catholicism, ironically, along the line suggested by Tone's revised fifth Dublin edition of *Arguments on Behalf of the Catholics of Ireland.*

Full Catholic emancipation was, however, now realistically placed on the political agenda for the first time. 'The sitting in Parliament seems almost to proceed from the privilege of voting for MPs, which was conceded by the Act of 1793', wrote Lord Hardwicke to Lord Redesdale; a striking admission to find in the correspondence ten years later of two senior Protestant leaders of the British political establishment.[108] It is important to note that the electoral emancipation of the poorer section of the Catholic electorate—whilst at the same time denying a parliamentary presence to the Catholic elites—in some respect sharpened the alienation of those elites, while at the same time increasing their sense of political ethnic power. Certainly, the prospect of revolution had not passed. In June 1793 Colonel Eleazer Oswald, an agent of the revolutionary government, secretly visited Ireland. Fears grew of a link-up between Irish and French revolutionaries. On 16 August 1793 the increasingly authoritarian government responded with the Convention Act, which prohibited assemblies purporting to represent the people under pretence of preparing petitions to the King or Parliament: it was the definitive, if heavy-handed, riposte to the Dungannon Convention and the Catholic conventions which had been held in Dublin in 1792–3.[109]

It is clear that Burke's powers of persuasion had influenced the thinking of key British political leaders. On 3 January 1794 Pitt held a briefing conversation with the Burkean Sylvester Douglas (later Lord Glenbervie), recently appointed as Irish Secretary. His remarks were fascinating; they indicate an underlying drift of policy which was pro-Catholic, but also a remarkable vagueness on how to implement such a policy; almost a belief that there were, in fact, no means of implementation, because Ireland, that 'subject', as Pitt called it, was characterized by a certain

[107] Agnew, *Drennan–McTier Letters*, i. 360.

[108] PRONI T 3030/3/13, Redesdale Papers, Hardwicke to Redesdale, 9 May 1803.

[109] C. J. Woods, 'The Personnel of the Catholic Convention, 1792–3', in *Archivium Hibernicum*, 150: 7 (2003), 26–76.

'debilitating distaste'.[110] Burke felt no such inhibition: he gave Douglas his blessing. Burke advised also that Douglas keep his distance from the old ruling clique (Foster, Fitzgibbon, and Beresford) and draw Grattan into his confidence.[111] In Ireland itself the 'government of expedients'—to use Pitt's description—continued. On 29 January 1794 one of the most intellectually brilliant United Irishmen, Archibald Hamilton Rowan, was arrested on the charge of distributing a seditious paper and sentenced to a fine of £500 and imprisonment for two years. On 28 April 1794 the Irish-born Revd William Jackson, agent of the French revolutionary government, was arrested on a charge of high treason. His conversations with Irish radicals provided enough evidence to endanger Wolfe Tone and help justify the suppression of the Dublin United Irishmen. Hamilton Rowan fled to America; Tone eventually negotiated a deal with the authorities, which allowed him to leave for the United States, though interestingly, before leaving he met Edmund Burke as part of a Catholic delegation. On 23 May the Dublin Society of United Irishmen was suppressed by a police raid on a meeting. On 25 June William Drennan was tried for seditious libel: John Philpot Curran, in a brilliant defence of liberty of conscience, managed to secure his acquittal.[112]

THE FITZWILLIAM EPISODE: 'REFORM FROM ABOVE?'

In July 1794 a powerful section of the Whig Party under the Duke of Portland, anxious to support Pitt in the war against France, seceded and joined the Pitt government. Burke played, in Lecky's view, a 'very considerable part' in the formation of this new coalition.[113] In December 1794 Burke's ally Lord Fitzwilliam was appointed as Viceroy in Ireland. It became clear that Fitzwilliam's agenda was a dramatic one—total Catholic emancipation. Within a mere six weeks the old guard in Dublin Castle was changed, new liberal appointments were made, and the promise of a positive response to Catholic grievances hung in the air. The displaced guardians of Irish Protestant ascendancy fought back and put pressure on Pitt to recall Fitzwilliam. In the midst of this crisis, at the beginning

---

[110] John Ehrman, *The Younger Pitt: The Reluctant Transition* (London, 1983), 436–7.
[111] Mansergh, *Grattan's Failure*, 162.
[112] John Larkin (ed.), *The Trial of William Drennan* (Dublin, 1991), 27.
[113] Lecky, *Leaders of Public Opinion*, 169; but, as David Wilkinson points out, Portland was quite capable of forming an independent judgement against the French Revolution and regarded Burke as over-ideological: nor did Portland support Burke's pro-Irish Catholic strategies.

of 1795, William Cusack Smith sent Burke a rather uncertain letter. He remained 'disposed to give the Catholics what they asked', but he admitted that his personal knowledge of the ambitions of the Catholics gleaned from his mother's people was not altogether reassuring. Indeed, he wondered if Burke was not slightly too enthusiastic in his advocacy of the Catholic cause.[114] Clearly feeling it necessary to stiffen his young friend's resolve, Burke replied magisterially on 29 January 1795. He hailed the 'present excellent Lord Lieutenant' and his 'perfectly pure intentions with regard to Ireland'. He then offered his classic prescription for Ireland: without reform, the 'half citizen' would become the 'whole Jacobin'. 'You have now your choice for full four-fifths of your people, the Catholic religion or Jacobinism ... They [the Catholics] are considered as no better than half citizens. If they are kept such for any length of time, they will be made whole Jacobins'.[115]

For a few brief weeks Henry Grattan, leader of the Irish Whigs, enjoyed an unprecedented degree of influence. But on 21 February 1795 Fitzwilliam was suddenly recalled to London. The ostensible reason for his recall was that he had removed senior figures from office—thus breaking a clear agreement that his appointment was not to lead to a general remodelling of the Irish administration. But ministers in London were also profoundly worried by Fitzwilliam's requests for permission to support a Catholic Relief Bill that Henry Grattan had introduced on 21 February.

On 28 February 1795 William Cusack Smith responded to rumours of Fitzwilliam's recall by writing—under a pseudonym—a pamphlet defending a strategy of Catholic emancipation. Cusack Smith had reflected on Burke's half citizen/whole Jacobin formulation and found a way of giving it more dramatic effect: 'Let an individual reflect whether he could be zealous in the interest of one who admitted him as a half-acquaintance. He will be the better judge, whether *half-citizenship* can purchase zeal among the Catholics.'[116] In fact, Cusack Smith argued, it might well be that post-emancipation very few Catholics could be returned to the

---

[114] Cusack Smith, *A Letter on the Catholic Claims* (London, 1808); R. B. McDowell (ed.), *The Correspondence of Edmund Burke*, vol. 8, *1794–96* (Cambridge, 1969), letter to Burke, 20 Jan. 1795, pp. 118–21; letter to William Smith, 29 Jan. 1795, in McDowell (ed.), *The Writings and Speeches of Edmund Burke*, ix. 658–85. For the considerable impact of these remarks, which were quickly published, see the discussion by C. J. Fox's Irish adviser, J. B. Trotter, *Five Letters to Sir William Smith* (Dublin, 1813), 7. Also, see Sir James Mackintosh's comments in Parliament in April 1821, in *Freeman's Journal*, 13 Apr. 1821.

[115] *Correspondence of Edmund Burke*, vol. 8, Burke to Smith, *c*.15 May 1795, p. 243.

[116] *Letter to His Excellency Earl Fitzwilliam, on the Rumour of His Excellency's Intention of Quitting the Government of this Kingdom*, by a Member of Parliament (Dublin, 1795), 15.

House of Commons, but the principle of granting a sense of ownership of the constitution for Irish Catholics was the decisive one. It had been Fitzwilliam's intention to 'put our excellent constitution into the hands of its rightful owners, the Irish nation'.[117] It was time to forget the religious bigotry of the past. 'Will any man deny that the French principles ... are what constitutes the danger in our times?'[118] But all these arguments fell on deaf ears. Nonetheless, Cusack Smith made a vital point when he noted that: 'expectation had been raised to the highest; and what well wisher to this country would seek to dash it to the ground?'[119] Confirmation of Fitzwilliam's removal depressed the hopes of Catholic and Protestant reformers alike. His removal revealed also the dangerous ambiguity which lay at the heart of Pitt's Irish policy. At one level Pitt fully shared some of Burke's most important ideas. Like Burke, he did not regard the Ascendancy as sincere in its protestations of danger to the Protestant faith—indeed, like Burke, he felt that the Christian religion was in mortal danger from Jacobins—and this posed a larger issue than the overthrow of Protestantism by Popery. Like Burke, Pitt believed that the Catholics, being the great majority of the inhabitants of Ireland, must be admitted by degrees to a full participation in all the advantages previously held exclusively by Protestants. But unlike Burke, Pitt also believed this had to be done on a gradualist basis, 'as it were insensibly to the Protestants', particularly when the Dublin Castle machinery was dominated by many strong partisan defenders of the Protestant interest.[120] Fitzwilliam was right to insist that Pitt approved 'in principle'[121] of his policy, but wrong to believe that Pitt had ever felt it was possible to break with previously loyal supporters in Ireland and radically shake up the Dublin administration. Of course, the obvious implication here was a complete policy paralysis: unless, that is, the whole political relationship of Ireland and England could be recast in a way which simultaneously defended the Protestant interest and opened up a path towards Catholic emancipation. In 1795 Pitt, when dining with Irish friends and associates, became increasingly explicit in his advocacy of the union as the only logical way forward in Irish affairs.[122]

For the immediate future, however, the policy was more brutally 'pragmatic'. Fitzwilliam's replacement, Camden, reassured the Protestant old guard immediately on his arrival. In short, the Catholic Relief Bill was to be dropped. The new Chief Secretary, Pelham, was a Portland Whig,

---

[117] Ibid. 26.   [118] Ibid. 19.   [119] Ibid. 24.

[120] *Glenbervie Journals*, 11 Jan. 1794, p. 36; David Wilkinson, *The Duke of Portland and Party in the Age of George III* (Basingstoke, 2003), 142.

[121] *A Letter from a Venerated Nobleman Recently Returned from this Country to the Earl of Carlisle, Explaining the Cause of that Event* (Dublin, 1795), 14.

[122] *Personal Recollections of Lord Cloncurry* (Dublin, 1849), 38.

and although Fitzwilliam's opponents like Beresford and Cooke returned to office, Pelham relied for assistance also on Camden's young step-nephew Robert Stewart, who had been returned to Parliament as an opposition Whig. There was, perhaps, not a complete reversal of policy.[123] It was stated that Downing Street, not Dublin Castle, would direct Irish policy. Catholic emancipation was now no longer on the immediate agenda, but some concerns were addressed. In particular, the idea of establishing Catholic colleges had solid support. The fact remains that the Fitzwilliam episode, concluding in his removal, was a classic example of government generating the frustration of a revolution of rising expectations in Ireland. When the system of governance, apparently so close to Catholic emancipation, suddenly changed tack, it significantly increased the chance of open rebellion. Burke, who feared precisely such an outcome, bitterly resented Fitzwilliam's departure from Dublin.

On 4 May 1795 there was, however, to be a little personal comfort for Burke. William Cusack Smith, despite Fitzwilliam's removal and the certainty of defeat, threw his weight in the Irish Parliament behind Catholic emancipation: 'Are not Catholics possessed of rights? Consider this mainly, they are the great body of your people; it is not very extravagant hyperbole to call them *Ireland*.'[124] Cusack Smith added: 'Jacobinism is abroad; the lower class of society are his prey; these are Catholics. Shall we shut the gate of our constitution,' and push them towards 'this monster?' A truly Burkean crescendo was now within reach:

Half-citizens and whole Jacobins might become synonymous in these days ... Protestantism is the established religion of the state; but I will go a step further and say that Christianity is ... our religion. In the permanent bonds of this sublime religion, whose very name suggests good will to all men, we are connected with our fellow subjects.[125]

In the same debate, however, Patrick Duigenan denounced Burke's pro-Catholic leanings vigorously: Burke, according to Duigenan, had defended the American revolution only because it was then supported by Catholic France; only the French revolution's destruction of Catholicism had led to Burke's 'recantation of republicanism'.[126] Duigenan's militant Protestant

---

[123] McDowell, *Grattan: A Life*, 137; Gillian O'Brien, 'Camden and the Move Towards Union 1798–85', ch. 6, in D. Keogh and K. Whelan (eds.), *Acts of Union: The Causes, Contexts and Consequences of the Act of Union* (Dublin, 2003), 106–25.

[124] *Report of the House of Commons on the Bill Presented by Henry Grattan for the Further Relief of his Majesty's Popish and Roman Catholic Subjects* (Dublin, 1795), 37; *Parliamentary Register of Ireland, History of the Proceedings and Debates of the House of Commons of Ireland*, vol. 15 (Bristol, 1999), 247.

[125] *Report*, 38.   [126] *Parliamentary Register*, 345.

assault created some uneasiness even within the Ascendancy elements. The powerful Protestant Beresford interest disliked the way that this debate degenerated into 'abuse of Catholicism'; Robert Stewart's speech was one of the few efforts on 'our side' to be considered worthy of positive comment.[127] John Philpot Curran, the leading Dublin advocate and eloquent parliamentarian, felt it necessary to protest[128] against Duigenan's personal abuse of Burke; indeed, Curran went further and published an open letter to Edmund Burke, which lamented the passing of the promise of reform associated with the Fitzwilliam viceroyalty. Supporters of Fitzwilliam plainly saw that the crisis had arrived in which by 'delay' all would be 'hazarded' and by 'refusal irretrievably lost'.[129] Duigenan had, however, no monopoly on criticism of Burke: others attacked Burke from an entirely different angle. 'Bolingbroke', a Dublin pamphleteer and friend of William Drennan, denounced him for his naive faith in Pitt's reformist agenda.[130]

POLARIZATION AND FRUSTRATION: THE ROAD TO REVOLUTION, 1796–1798

At the end of May 1796 Tone visited Belfast for the last time. With Russell, Simms, McCracken, and other United Irishmen, he took a solemn obligation on Cave Hill 'never to desist in our efforts until we had subverted the authority of England over our country'.[131] The United Irishmen were moving to a new secret revolutionary organizational structure—they also sought to link up with the Catholic Defenders, an organization which, anyway, they were perceived to have influenced. The *Westmeath Journal* opined that 'a great part of the peasantry, through the wicked industry of the democrats and United Irishmen, on scattering their doctrines throughout the land, are becoming defenders'.[132] The Defenders were a popular

---

[127] *The Correspondence of the Rt. Hon. John Beresford, Illustrations of the Last Thirty Years of the Irish Parliament, Selected from his Original Papers and Edited with Notes, by his Grandson, the Rt. Hon. William Beresford* (London, 1854), ii. 108–9.

[128] Ibid. 128.

[129] *A Letter to Edmund Burke on the Present State of Ireland* (Dublin, 1795), 40.

[130] 'Bolingbroke', *A Letter Addressed to a Noble Lord, by Way of a Reply to the Rt. Hon. Edmund Burke* (Dublin, 1796); J Agnew, *Drennan–McTier letters*, ii. 226, Drennan to Martha McTier, 18 Apr. 1796, from Dublin, that a 'young fellow left my room this moment, who bellowed out an answer to Burke under the forced signature of Bolingbroke'. The author in question was a young lawyer who felt it necessary for career reasons to keep his identity secret. The point had been made earlier by J. Towers, *Thoughts on Commencement of a New Parliament* (Dublin, 1791).

[131] *Writings of Wolfe Tone*, ii. 333.

[132] William Kidd, *Westmeath Journal*, 15 Aug. 1795; see also Thomas Bartlett (ed.), 'Defenders and Defenderism in 1795', *Irish Historical Studies*, 24 (May 1985), 373–95.

underground conspiracy. They had a wholly independent existence and a crude but relatively coherent political world-view: in the 1790s new ideas absorbed from America, from France, and from middle-class Irish radicalism blended confusingly with more traditional themes: 'resentment of Protestant dominance, some broad ideal of an Ireland independent of English rule and cloudy aspirations to the recovery of lost rights and possessions.'[133]

Something at least—from Burke's point of view—was rescued from the wreckage of Fitzwilliam's viceroyalty. On 7 March Portland had sent a reassuring letter to Thomas Hussey; he should remain in Ireland, a concession to Catholic interests was on the way.[134] By the summer of 1795 it was clear that Pitt had decided to deliver one boon to Catholic Ireland, and, perhaps, to Burke: St Patrick's College, Maynooth, which became the principal seminary for the training of Irish Catholic priests. Pitt's decision to endow a Catholic educational foundation and then concede it de facto autonomy was a major development in Britain's Irish policy. Above all, it clearly reflected the force of the continuing hope that Catholic Ireland might still be a reliable ally against French Jacobinism.[135]

If, as has been cogently argued, 'the radicalisation of Catholics was [neither] immediate or universal in the wake of the Fitzwilliam episode', other factors, nonetheless, now conspired to intensify that radicalization.[136] In Co. Armagh, Protestants and Catholics shared an increasingly contested territory. Here, unlike in Co. Down, Catholics and Protestants coexisted in roughly equal numbers; it was experiencing also a massive growth in linen manufacture. Clashes in and around Armagh in the summer and autumn of 1795 escalated into a localized civil war. George Ensor, a liberal Protestant gentleman in Co. Armagh, commented bitterly on 'Protestant *banditti*' who had launched 'a private war'.[137] These clashes appeared to have been characterized by a certain loss of social control exercised by the

---

This newspaper cutting is to be found in the Acton collection in the Cambridge University Library. In his celebrated essay, published in 1862, on nationalism, Lord Acton, then a Liberal MP for the Irish constituency of Carlow, laid great emphasis on the way in which the French Revolution taught the people to regard their own wishes and wants as the 'supreme criterion' of night.

[133] S. J. Connolly, 'Eighteenth-Century Ireland', in D. George Boyce and Alan O'Day (eds.), *The Making of Modern Irish History* (London and New York, 1996), 28.

[134] PRONI T2905/22/40/PW/109.

[135] Cruise O'Brien, *The Great Melody*, 516, 544.

[136] Deirdre Lindsay, 'The Fitzwilliam Episode Revisited', in David Dickson, Daire Keogh and Kevin Whelan (eds.), *The United Irishmen: Republicanism, Radicalism and Rebellion* (Dublin, 1893), 207.

[137] George Ensor, *A Defence of the Irish and the Means of their Redemption* (Dublin, 1825).

local gentry. Lord Gosford, Governor of Armagh, denounced these 'terrible proceedings' as 'contrary' to 'humanity' and 'policy'.[138] It appeared that the impact of rural industrialization may have been linked to a less deferential attitude amongst the Protestant lower orders towards their social superiors and amongst Catholics in their attitudes to Protestants. In September 1795 the Orange Order—Burke called them 'zealots in Armagh'[139]—was set up—following the victory of the Orange Boys, an offshoot of the 'Peep Of Day Boys', over the Catholic Defenders at the Battle of the Diamond, when dozens of Catholics lost their lives.

The Protestant victors—largely Episcopalian by notional affiliation, though including some Presbyterians—returned to the village of Loughgall, where, in the inn of James Sloan, they formally established the Orange Order. The Order dedicated itself to sustaining the 'glorious and immortal memory' of King William III and his victory at the Boyne. More concretely, they drove some 700 Catholic families out of north Armagh. The Orange Order rapidly became the site of a struggle, as the local gentlemen attempted again to reassert leadership over the Protestant community.[140] On 14 February 1797 Dr William Richardson, a Tyrone-based Church of Ireland clergyman, reported to the Duke of Abercorn:

The Orangemen had no moderation after their victory. They continued harassing the Catholics with great cruelty for many months, with little interruption from the magistrates. They followed them, too, into Tyrone, and endeavoured to incite the same persecutions among us, but the police of the two counties being very different, the activity and unanimity of our magistrates instantly repressed them.[141]

Many Catholics had been driven out of their homes in Armagh and scattered throughout the island. These Defenders carried with them bitter tales of

[138] William Wenman Seward, *Collectanea Politica or the Political Transactions of Ireland*, 3 vols. (Dublin, 1801–4), iii. 159.

[139] Daire Keogh, 'Burke's Political Testament: Thomas Hussey and the Irish Directory', in Richard English and Joe Skelly (eds.), *Ideas Matter: Essays in Honour of Conor Cruise O'Brien* (Dublin, 1998), 217. For a suggestive analysis, see Peter Gibbon, 'The Origins of the Orange Order and the United Irishmen', *Economy and Society*, 1, pp. 134–64. But see David W. Miller, 'The Origins of the Orange Order in County Armagh', in A. J. Hughes and William Nolan (eds.), *Armagh: History and Society* (Dublin, 2001), 583–615; James Wilson, 'Orangeism in 1798', in T. Bartlett, D. Dickson, D. Keogh, and K. Whelan (eds.), *1798: A Bicentenary Perspective* (Dublin, 2003), 295–462; W. H. Crawford, 'The Linen Triangle in the 1790s', *Ulster Local Studies*, 18: 2 (Spring 1997), 43–53.

[140] D. W. Miller, *Peep O'Day Boys and Defenders: Selected Documents on the Disturbances in County Armagh, 1784–1796* (Belfast, 1990); Allan Blackstock, 'The Invincible Mass: Loyal Crowds in Mid Ulster, 1795–96', in P. Jupp and E. Magennis (eds.), *Crowds in Ireland c. 1720–1920* (London, 2000).

[141] Miller, *Peep O'Day Boys*, 136.

Protestant violence and state partisanship: this was the context in which the United Irishmen attempted to seal their alliance with the Defenders. Tone arrived in France on 1 February 1796 from the United States and began to move comfortably in official circles—forming, in particular, a good relationship with General Hoche and Lazare Carnot of the Directory,[142] as he made the case that France should grant assistance to radical Irish separatism. Tone found it easy enough to make the case that Ireland was a deeply disturbed country. On 22 February 1796 William Cusack Smith protested in the Irish House of Commons against a partial administration of the law: how could it be right to call for special measures of repression against Defenders but not against Orangemen?[143]

These developments distressed Burke enormously. After he met with Tone as part of a Catholic Committee grouping in 1794, he had rebuked the Catholics for having such republican connections, but Burke found that he had other, more personal, problems to face. Throughout 1796 the government was well aware that the United Irishmen and the Catholic Defenders were amalgamating for rebellion and that a French invasion was imminent. This placed Burke in a very exposed position. In early 1796 William Augustus Miles, spy, journalistic hack, and an occasional adviser to William Pitt on French matters, published a disobliging commentary on Burke's alleged crypto-Catholicism. Miles was a friend of Edward Newenham, a strong Ascendancy politician, who probably supplied him with the details of Burke's youth. Miles was sidelined by Pitt after 1794, and resented Burke's continuing influence on Anglo-French affairs—even obsessively claiming, probably wrongly, that Burke was allowed into a Cabinet meeting to urge intervention against France.[144] Miles insisted on the importance of Burke's early life and family connections:[145] 'His confessions in early life can not altogether be effaced from memory.'[146] Miles launched a campaign against Burke, alleging that his advice to Pitt was tainted by a hidden 'papist' agenda. A later commentator noted correctly that Miles had attacked Burke with 'peculiar severity for his attachment to Popery and his endeavours to give it legal sanction in the British Empire'.[147]

---

[142] Moody, McDowell, and Woods, *Writings of Wolfe Tone*, ii. 232–7.

[143] *Parliamentary Register*, xvi. 15.

[144] Ian Hampsher-Monk, 'Edmund Burke's Changing Justification for Intervention', *Historical Journal*, 48:1 (Mar. 2005), 85.

[145] Howard Evans, 'William Pitt, William Miles and the French Revolution', *Bulletin of the Institute of Historical Research*, 42: 108 (Nov. 1970), 190–213.

[146] *A Letter to Henry Duncombe Esq on Mr Burke's Reply to a Noble Lord* (Dublin, 1796), 2.

[147] *Considerations on the Late and Present State of Ireland in Refutation of Observations and Reflections thereon by Robert Stearns Tighe Esq and a Letter to the Earl of Wycombe from Mr Miles on the Present State of Ireland* (Dublin, 1804), 50.

Burke was sufficiently stung to write to Joseph Moser on 5 April 1796 that Miles was an 'illiterate, stupid and impudent railer'.[148]

Thomas Townsend MP (*c.* 1768–1856) drew Burke's attention to this attack by Miles in March 1796.[149] Townsend's defence—completed on 13 March—cites Burke's specific support for the Established Church. 'He [Miles] considers him [Burke]' as a 'zealot and bigot of the Romish form of Christian worship'; Townsend considered Burke to be an exemplary Protestant.[150] Burke, however, offered no such defence, and preferred to treat Miles' arguments with lofty disdain. But this did not mean he was unconcerned by the activity of Miles—indeed, he was exasperated when Townsend made public Burke's private approval of his defence.[151] Burke's exasperation is not surprising, he confessed to a Catholic friend: 'I am in mortal fear lest the suspicion of Popery should attach upon me.'[152] He need not have worried quite so much; in 1797 Pitt dispensed with Miles, partly because of the attacks on Burke. Five years later Townsend merely added that, if Burke had been a Catholic or crypto-Catholic, as his enemies alleged, neither his 'genius' nor his 'fame' would be impaired.[153] Burke could only plough on his chosen path: his first 'Letters on a Regicide Peace', published in October 1796, laid stress again on the potential value of a contented Ireland for Britain's war effort against France.[154]

At the beginning of December 1796 Henry Grattan wrote to French Laurence that the system of government in Ireland was 'radically bad ... our friend, Mr Burke, understands this better than anyone'.[155] How 'radically bad' Burke felt it was emerges in a most striking text of that month. On 9 December 1796 Burke produced his last and most defiantly pro-Catholic political testament, a lengthy letter to the Revd Thomas Hussey.[156] The letter is dominated by the devilish choice facing Irish Catholics, 'grievous oppression' or 'refuge in Jacobinism'.[157] 'You and I hate Jacobinism as we hate the Gates of Hell—Why? Because it is a system of oppression. What can make us in love with oppression because the Syllables Jacobin are not put before the *ism*, when the very same things are done under

[148] McDowell (ed.), *Burke Correspondence*, viii. 547.

[149] Burke to Thomas Townsend, 29 Mar. 1796, in ibid. 452–3.

[150] *A Summary Defence of the Rt. Hon. Edmund Burke in Two Letters ... Including Strictures upon a Pamphlet written by William Miles* (London, 1796), 81.

[151] *Sketches of Irish Political Characters of the Present Day* (London, 1799), 244.

[152] Burke to the Revd Thomas Hussey (*post* 9 Dec. 1796), quoted in Daire Keogh, 'Burke's Political Testament', 222.

[153] T. Townsend, *Part of a Letter to a Noble Earl Containing a Very Short Vindication of the Yeomanry and Catholics of the City of Cork* (Dublin, 1801), 39.

[154] McDowell, *Burke Correspondence*, ix. 230.

[155] McPeake Papers, PRONI T 3048/A/10, Mr Grattan to Mr Laurence, 1 Dec. 1796.

[156] Daire Keogh, 'Burke's Political Testament'.   [157] Ibid. 215.

the *ism* preceded by any other Name in the Directory of Ireland.'[158]
Burke here labels the Dublin Castle regime—'the little narrow Faction that
domineers'—as being morally on a par with the leaders of the French revolutionary government, the Directory. Indeed, the whole letter is evidence
of Burke's willingness to equate the spirit of Irish Protestant ascendancy
with Jacobinism, even to the extent of using the terms interchangeably,
so that a French revolutionary general became a 'Protestant'. 'I suppose
General Hoche is eagerly expected in Ireland,' wrote Burke in a bitterly
hostile tone, which showed how intense was his opposition to the idea
that Hoche was an ally of Ireland's Catholics: for 'he, too, is a most
zealous Protestant',[159] as Hoche had shown by his cruelty towards French
Catholicism. It is easy to see why Burke felt this way: Hoche had been in
charge of suppressing the Royalist uprising in the Vendée, which Burke
had openly supported. In fact, Carnot's instructions for the invasion of
1796 instructed Hoche to accept the leadership of Catholic forces and
guard against the pro-British religions of Anglicanism and Presbyterianism.
In the longer term, though, a 'national religion with a deistic basis' was
considered to be most suitable for French purposes. 'It seems that Ireland
is not yet ripe for a religious revolution which the benefits of a free press
will inevitably bring in time.'[160] In that respect Burke's worst fears were
justified.

To have put their faith in men like Hoche was not the only error which
Burke attributed to the United Irishmen:

You feel the thing very rightly—all the evils of Ireland originate within itself. That
unwise body, the United Irishmen, have had the folly to represent those Evils as
owing to this Country, when in Truth its chief neglect is in its total neglect, its
utter oblivion, its shameful indifference and its entire ignorance, of Ireland and
of everything that relates to it, and not in any oppressive disposition towards that
unknown region.[161]

Burke's letter circled uneasily around the political options open to the
leaders of Irish Catholicism. He implies heavily that any advantages Ireland
derived from having its own parliament were fast eroding; it was a 'breach
of order' to discuss Ireland in the Westminster Parliament. 'If the people
of Ireland were to be flayed alive by the predominant faction, it would be
the most criminal of all attempts so much as to discuss the subject in any
public Assembly upon this side of the Water.'[162] It is arguable that here
is an implicit pro-union message, combined, as it is, with an injunction

[158] Daire Keogh, 'Burke's Political Testament' 228.   [159] Ibid. 222.
[160] Copy of extracts from the Executive Directory, Thermidor 4, 20 July 1796,
McPeake Papers, PRONI T3048/D/12.
[161] Keogh, 'Burke's Political Testament', 223.   [162] Ibid.

to be patient.[163] Not surprisingly, Burke's missive was regarded by the senior Castle official, Alexander Marsden, as 'a most curious letter'.[164] The intensity of Burke's invective against the Dublin Castle establishment conveys the intensity of the excruciating dilemma in which he found himself. As revolutionary France became increasingly plausible as an ally of Irish Catholicism, Burke, in the last year of his life, was being forced to choose between two unpalatable extremes: Protestant ascendancy in Ireland or the radical Jacobin alternative. In fact, the possibility of a revolution in Ireland seems to have convinced Edmund Burke, formerly an opponent of union, that even the 'bold experimental remedy' might be 'justified, perhaps called for, in some nearly desperate crisis of the whole Empire'.[165] He continued to the end (his death came in May 1797) to reject both these alternatives, but he no longer retained the ability to influence the course of events, which he had held in the mid-1790s.

Burke's death did not, however, end the argument. Indeed, the significance of Burke's legacy was to be one of the most crucial themes in Irish political debate over the next fifteen years. The key figure here was Patrick Duigenan:[166] a militant Orange Protestant, whose first wife, however, was a Catholic, Miss Cusack, a relative of William Cusack Smith, who was allowed Catholic servants and a Catholic chaplain. From 1795 onwards Duigenan launched a full-scale assault on Burke's status as a political thinker. Duigenan, through his association with John Fitzgibbon—whose Catholic family had been close to the Burke family—was well aware of Burke's 'papist' family history. He insisted that Burke had not really been an opponent of the French revolution at all. Burke's support for the American revolution was proof enough for Duigenan that Burke had no inherent difficulty with popular uprisings. Burke, in Duigenan's view, had only opposed the French revolution because he saw it as creating the opportunity to make the case for Irish Catholics.

[163] Ibid. 229.

[164] PRONI T 2627/5/K/66, cf also PRONI T 2627/5/D/53, Wickham to Addington, 1 Apr. 1803.

[165] Manuela Ceretta, 'Like a Phoenix from the Ashes: United Irish Propaganda and the Act of Union', in Brown, Geoghegan, and Kelly (eds.), *The Irish Act of Union*, 86; McDowell, 'Burke and Ireland', in Dickson, Keogh, and Whelan, *The United Irishmen*, 113–14.

[166] This most bitter of Protestant partisans finally brought his public and private life into some harmony when he married Miss Heppenstall, sister of Lt. Heppenstall, a violent anti-Catholic. Barrington spoke suggestively of Duigenan's 'hot, rough, intrepid mind ... his intolerance was too outrageous, too unreasonable to be sincere'. Sir Jonah Barrington, *Historic Memoirs of Ireland* (London, 1835), 92–3. For Duigenan, see Peter Jupp, 'Dr Duigenan Reconsidered', in Sabine Wichert (ed.), *From the United Irishmen to Twentieth-Century Unionism* (Dublin, 2004), 79–96.

Robert Bellew, a member of an important Catholic gentry family with commercial interests on the continent, replied to Duigenan by pointing out that the objective differences between the American and French revolutions were quite sufficient in themselves to explain Burke's differing response.[167] Sir John Hippisley pointed out that if Burke really was an 'active agent of Rome', as Duigenan suggested, why did the University of Oxford praise his eminent service, both to the civil and religious constitutions?[168] But Duigenan never relented:

Mr Burke himself sprang from parents who were Irish Romanists; he received his early education in the College of Dublin; but having quitted Ireland at a very early stage of his period of life, with all his relations by blood or alliance being Irish Romanists, he became thoroughly tinged, or rather dyed, in the grain with the political sentiments of that class of people.[169]

His line of argument became commonplace; Sir Richard Musgrave, the partisan anti-Catholic polemicist, reiterated it.[170] 'Huri', in the *Dublin Journal*, claimed to be a great admirer of Burke: 'His speech dropped like dew drops from the honey-scented thorn.' 'But,' Huri felt compelled to add, 'he was a Papist though ... for political reasons he professed conformity to the Protestant Church, his very soul was riveted to the superstitions of his ancestry.'[171] Duigenan insisted that Burke convinced several 'very powerful and popular English noblemen' that the 'only method of retaining Ireland in obedience to the British Crown, and maintaining the connexion between the two countries, was the complete establishment of Popery in Ireland'.[172] Duigenan spoke of the 'spirit of Burkism', and set himself the task of overthrowing the 'Burkean system with respect to Ireland'.

[167] Robert Bellew, *Hibernia Trinoda Necessitas* (London, 1803), 87–8. For the Bellew family, see Karen J Harvey, *The Bellews of Mount Bellew* (Dublin, 1998).

[168] Sir John Hippisley, *The Substance of Additional Observations intended to have been delivered in the House of Commons on the Debate of the Petitions of the Roman Catholics of Ireland on the 13th and 14th May 1805* (London, 1806), 96.

[169] Patrick Duigenan LL D, *Answer to the Address of the Rt. Hon. Henry Grattan, Representative of the City of Dublin, to his Fellow Citizens of Dublin*, 4th edn., with additions (Dublin, 1799), 19.

[170] Cruise O'Brien, *The Great Melody*, 37–8.

[171] *Dublin Journal*, 26 Mar. 1813, also 20 May 1813. Duigenan's ally, John Gifford, was then at the zenith of his influence with the moving spirit behind the *Dublin Journal*; for Gifford, see B. Inglis, *The Freedom of the Press in Ireland 1784–1841* (London, 1954), 113–14, and Jacqueline Hill, 'Dublin After the Union', in Brown, Geoghegan, and Kelly (eds.), *The Irish Act of Union*, 144–56.

[172] *A Fair Representation on the Present Political Situation in Ireland* (Dublin, 1799), 20. But by 1810 Duigenan openly admitted that he had not succeeded in this self-appointed task, see his *The Nature and Extent of the Demands of the Irish Roman Catholics Fully Explained: in Observations and Structures in a Pamphlet entitled A History of the Penal Laws Against the Irish Roman Catholics* (London, 1810), 130.

For Duigenan the answer lay elsewhere. The British state should continue to gamble on loyal Protestant Ireland, which was strong enough—if supported properly by London—to hold the country. With such a bitter tone dominating public debate, it is hardly surprising that in 1796 and 1797 Ireland moved inexorably towards explosion: Protestant loyalists watched in horror as United Irish and Catholic Defenders militarily attempted to ally with revolutionary France; an alliance that, if achieved, would destroy the Irish Protestant landed class and its supporters. In September 1796 Thomas Russell, Samuel Neilson, and several others with French sympathies were arrested in Belfast on charges of high treason.

Neilson's arrest, significantly enough, was supported by Lord Castlereagh, even though Neilson had been one of his supporters in the Co. Down election in 1790. There is one even more dramatic and even more personal example of a Castlereagh 'betrayal'. Luke Teeling, a wealthy linen bleacher and wine merchant, as a Catholic, could not vote for Robert Stewart in 1790—but he did help finance the campaign of his friend: 'The penal laws at the time operated against my father's personal exercise of the elective franchise, but neither his fortune nor his best exertions were unemployed in the service of his friend.'[173] On 16 September 1796 Luke's son Charles was arrested on a charge of high treason by Castlereagh himself. There seems to have been a element of protective regard in Castlereagh's behaviour. He dined over wine with Luke Teeling—'The prisoner of state seemed, for a moment, to have forgotten the kinder feelings of the earlier friend'—and he seemed to be moved by recollections which, under present circumstances, he would perhaps rather have 'suppressed'.[174] Charles Teeling was released the following summer upon showing signs of ill-health—generally regarded as an act of clemency.[175]

Castlereagh was not the only erstwhile reformer who was moving to the right. On 10 November 1796 Joseph Pollock, who had been reading Burke's letters on the 'Regicide' peace, wrote to Lord Downshire concerning the need to put

some arguments to the people of this country, as to the dangers they must incur, if they join any party but England in the probably approaching invasion—England who will fight here rather than at home, and must desolate this country rather than give it up (for to give it up to France is to give it up herself).

---

[173] C. H. Teeling, *History of the Irish Rebellion* (Glasgow and London, 1876), 13; see also the National Library of Ireland, Report on Private Collections, The Teeling Papers, no. 262.

[174] Teeling, *History*, 19.

[175] Bartlett (ed.), *Revolutionary Dublin 1795–1801*, Higgins to Edward Cooke, 29 Aug. 1798, p. 177; H. Montgomery Hyde, *The Rise of Castlereagh* (London, 1993), 80–1, notes that Castlereagh took care to deliver clothes to the young Teeling in jail.

But Pollock noted in the same letter that it was probably already too late to advance such a case.[176] On 26 November 1796 the senior Castle official Edward Cooke reported: 'The north very bad.' He added: 'The United Irishmen boast they have 150,000 sworn, including Defenders, and I really believe they have two thirds of the numbers.'[177] In Belfast, at a dramatic public meeting at the turn of the year, the radicals, led by William Sampson, were strong enough to defy the government over the issue of arming the town in the event of a French invasion.[178] It is worth noting, however, that the Belfast radicals feared the continued existence of a significant moderate body within the ranks of erstwhile reformers.[179]

At the same time, a fleet of French ships, carrying a large army led by General Hoche, with Wolfe Tone on board, approached the south-west coast. On this occasion a ferocious wind—soon to be known as the Protestant wind—prevented the French from landing. But it was, after all, the weather and not the Royal Navy which had saved Ireland from invasion. The reality of the French threat, and the prospect of internal rebellion, appeared still very real to radicals and conservatives alike. On 29 January 1797 Francis Higgins, the spy, reported to Edward Cooke in grim mood, expressing his less-than-comforting assessment: 'What if Hoche made good a landing, and only maintained his ground for a few days? Government would have soon found the difference of the boasted attachment of the people. The people have long felt their oppressions, and they care not who shall be their taskmasters, if oppression shall be continued.'[180] The Prince of Wales, in his Cabinet memorandum of February 1797, showed that he had grasped the crucial psychological importance of the fact that the French now knew that their general inferiority to the Royal Navy did not necessarily prevent an invasion of Ireland.[181] In Ulster, the centre of disaffection and the likely destination of any future invasion attempt, membership of the United Irishmen doubled within three months of the scare at Bantry Bay. In the spring of 1797 the Carrickfergus local historian Samuel McSkimmin, however, reported that new recruits continued to flood into the United Irishmen in the north: 'Not a few through fear or a

[176] Brendan Clifford (ed.), *Lord Downshire and the United Irishmen: A Selection from the Downshire Papers, 1793–1799* (Belfast, 1998), 26.

[177] PRONI T 3229/2/10.

[178] *Belfast News Letter*, 9 Mar. 1798; in an angry speech in the Irish House of Commons, Castlereagh recalls this event with evident anger, claiming that the radicals claimed to know nothing of Bantry Bay, when, in fact, it was their obsessive topic of private discussion.

[179] Higgins to Cooke, 8 Jan. 1796, in Bartlett (ed.), *Revolutionary Dublin*, 125.

[180] Francis Higgins to Edward Cooke, 29 Jan. 1797, ibid. 129.

[181] PRONI T33/9/9.

belief that the union cause was the strongest.'[182] At the same time, liberal reformers—among them some United Irishmen—debated whether to side with the government or the revolutionary movement; the very real prospect of French armies on their soil complicated the situation further.

On 12 March the government hit back. General Lake ordered the handing-in of all weapons in Ulster. The government arranged for the formation of a secret committee of the Irish House of Commons to examine a rebel Irish turncoat, Edward Newell, and the papers of two Belfast United Irish cells seized on his information. The bulk of the fifteen members of the committee were staunch supporters of the government, but there was a certain leavening of the committee with the inclusion of a Whiggish and even pro-Catholic element. The report was presented on 10 May 1797, and had a decisive impact. It purported to prove the existence of a mass revolutionary organization: reform and emancipation, it was claimed, were mere screens for this deeper purpose: the establishment of an Irish Republic under French protection.[183] William Cusack Smith resisted the increasingly repressive course of the government, insisting that he could not support repression without a commitment to the 'corrections of abuse'. Cusack Smith also invoked Burke's name again in the Irish House of Commons. He reminded the House that the policy of conciliation had been rejected in the debate of May 1795. Jacobinism had made great progress in Ireland. The disastrous policy which had been followed was one of 'shedding the patient's blood' and 'keeping him in hot water'.[184]

On 19 May, in a decisive moment, the presses of the radical *Northern Star* were broken up by the Monaghan Militia. Cusack Smith voted with the heavily defeated minority—which also included Henry Grattan and Lord Edward Fitzgerald, the most aristocratic of the United Irish revolutionaries—against such one-sided repression in the Irish Parliament on 24 May 1797.[185] But this was the last stand of parliamentary Whigs and radicals alike.[186]

1798: RISING AND REPRESSION

In 1798 Ireland was to experience not one but three quite distinct risings. The arrest of Arthur O'Connor and Father Coigley at Margate in February 1798 represented an early triumph for the authorities.[187] The seizure of

[182] RIA, 12F36; Samuel McSkimmin, 'Union Cause', *Recollections 1795–1799*, 8.
[183] Mansergh, *Grattan's Failure*, 222.   [184] *Parliamentary Register*, xvii. 550.
[185] *Belfast News Letter*, 24 May 1797.   [186] Mansergh, *Grattan's Failure*, 224.
[187] *Belfast News Letter*, 5 Mar. 1798.

O'Connor's papers compromised many of the United Irish leaders, and possibly even contained embarrassment for Grattan.[188] On 5 March 1798 the Orange Order leadership (William Blacker and Wolsey Atkinson) moved with surprising shrewdness. In a public statement, they praised some indications of Catholic loyalism ('contriteness') and declared that they held no hostility to anyone 'on account of their religion', but would co-operate with all loyalists.[189] Virtually the entire Dublin executive of the United Irishmen was captured on 12 March—one of those who escaped, Lord Edward Fitzgerald, was arrested by Major Sirr on 19 May.[190] As early as 22 May Pitt wrote to Camden: 'Can not crushing the rebellion be followed by an act appointing commissions to treat for an union?'[191] Fitzgerald died of the wounds sustained on his capture on 4 June 1798, thus removing the one aristocrat-Protestant leader with serious military experience.

There was, however, a volatile mood in the countryside. Word of the brutal behaviour of Crown forces reached Kildare and Wicklow very quickly. On 23 May rebels successfully attacked and wiped out the garrison in Prosperous, Co. Kildare. The military then moved to attack the rebels in Kildare, but their action served only to provoke fierce rebellion in Wexford. Stories of daily flogging and house-burning provoked a Catholic peasant revolt, led by some priests. On 28 May Enniscorthy was taken; the entire county, with the exception of New Ross, was soon in the hands of rebels. The United Irish leadership, supposedly in charge, found itself frequently overwhelmed by the impassioned force of an angry Catholic peasantry. The Wexford rebellion took on all the appearance of a naked sectarian confrontation.[192] One Wexford representative of a heavily involved family wrote shortly afterwards: 'Though I can hardly think it was the original intention of the United Men to murder all the Protestants, for many of the heads of them were of that persuasion, yet when the mob rose, they murdered almost all of them.'[193] This testimony is particularly valuable because John Colclough, who was a friend of the pro-Catholic reformer Hercules Langrishe, also protested bitterly against the machinations of

---

[188] Before his death, Arthur O'Connor was working on a memoir said to contain 'strange revelations with respect to the movement and to men prominent in public life not suspected of identification with the revolutionary party', *Freeman's Journal*, 11 May 1852.
[189] For Coigley's trial, see *Belfast News Letter*, 1 June 1798.
[190] Ibid., 25 May 1798.   [191] PRONI T2627/4/222/6.
[192] J. S. Donnelly, 'Sectarianism in 1798 and in Catholic Nationalist Memory', in L. Geary (ed.), *Rebellion and Remembrance in Modern Ireland* (Dublin, 2001), 15–37; Tom Dunne, *Rebellions Memoir, Memory and 1798* (Dublin, 2004), ch. 7, a work of major importance.
[193] PRONI T30248/C/118, John Colclough, Fishguard, to Caesar Colclough, Ulm, 30 July 1798.

the Protestant ascendancy faction.[194] Nonetheless, at the end of the year his revulsion against the insurgents had not diminished: 'You can not, nor did I, conceive it possible that man could be so ferocious, and I am convinced that, had the country remained another week under them, a single protestant, in particular a gentleman of any kind, could not have been left alive.'[195] From 30 May to 21 June Wexford town was occupied by insurgents. On 5 June over 100 Protestants were burned to death in a barn at Scullabogue.[196] On 20 June rebels in Wexford town systematically executed seventy Protestants on the long bridge which spanned the Slaney. On 26 June 1798 Jeffrey Paul reported to his wife Jane: 'I saw the bridge like a slaughter house thick with the blood of those 70 Protestants.'[197] The reporting of these events in Belfast from 7 July to 11 June the following year laid great stress on the brutal, annihilating anti-Protestantism of the Catholic masses: 'if the gates of hell were opened there could not come a worse enemy than our neighbours were.' [198] These Belfast reports left out the wave of brutal military repression which preceded the worst crimes of the rebels.

For two weeks rebellion was confined to the south. The Presbyterian north, for so long the cradle of the United Irish movement, appeared to have been cowed by the government wave of repression in 1797. But on 7 July the Antrim United Irish, just before news of Scullabogue reached the north, seized Ballymena and gave vent to their enthusiasm with shouts of 'Ballymena's our own—Hurrah for the United Irishmen!' 'Up with the green and down with King Geordie!'[199] On the same day they took Antrim, but were ultimately defeated by the arrival of loyal

---

[194] Same to same, 27 Aug. 1798.   [195] Same to same, 20 Dec. 1798.

[196] 'The Killing at Scullabogue', in Dunne, *Rebellion*, ch. 13, for an important treatment.

[197] *Memoirs of Chief Justice Lefroy*, by his son Thomas Lefroy (Dublin, 1877), 70.

[198] *Belfast News Letter*, 7 July 1798, which places the Protestant dead at Scullabogue at 'near 200'. It is worth contrasting the recent accounts of two major actors in Anglo-Irish relations and the peace process of the 1990s. Sir David Goodall, a direct descendant of Thomas Monck Goodall, who witnessed the events on the bridge at Wexford, has published a version which emphasizes conflicting loyalties—his ancestor was a Protestant married to a Catholic—confusion, and fear: 'Conflicts of Loyalty: The Dixons and the Hunte's Cavalry in 1798', *Journal of the Wexford Historical Society*, 17 (1998–9), 83. Contrast this with the remarks of Dr Martin Mansergh, who apologized to the descendants of three local peasant families who had brutally murdered his ancestor, Col. Richard Mansergh St George, in 1798. Mansergh spoke as a representative of a family who once had the 'undeserved privilege' of being local landlords, *Ireland on Sunday*, 15 Feb. 1998. See M. Mansergh, 'The Assassination of St George and Uniacke', in id., *The Legacy of History* (Cork, 2003), 163–6.

[199] *Old Ballymena: A History of Ballymena during the 1798 Rebellion*, published in the *Ballymena Observer* in 1857 under the title of 'Walks About Ballymena'.

reinforcements from Belfast and Lisburn. Antrim was followed a few days later by Down. Northern Catholics, however, held back, it was later said, repelled by the Presbyterian United Irishmen singing psalms which contained expressions offensive to them. The *Belfast News Letter* took great pleasure in noting the difference between the northern and the southern Catholics.[200] Munroe's reported, though unlikely, call—for he was himself Church of Ireland—for a Presbyterian government was also said to have given offence.[201] A young Presbyterian witness, James Thomson, later to be a distinguished mathematician and father of Lord Kelvin, has left us a picture of the northern United Irish army on the eve of battle:

They wore no uniform; yet they presented a tolerably decent appearance, being dressed, no doubt, in their Sunday clothes—some better and some worse; but none in the ragged costume that is often to be seen in other parts of Ireland. The only thing in which they all concurred was the wearing of green.[202]

Munroe's forces went down to heavy defeat, and sixty out of the 110 houses in Ballynahinch were destroyed by the military. On 15 June 1798 the *Belfast News Letter* reported: 'This rebellion in the part of the country may now be considered completely suppressed.' In every town and village the people, 'heartfelt sorry for their late conduct', delivered up their arms, leaders, and even latent supporters as the last resort. 'There is every reason to conclude that the insurgents of the county of Down, vexed with disappointment and terrified by the consequences of their late conduct, will not again be able to collect in considerable numbers.'

Significantly, the Orange Order had played a strategic role. When General Nugent took the field at Ballynahinch, Belfast was 'secured for the King' by a 'few gentlemen' who brought up over a thousand Orangemen to hold the town.[203] On 30 June the Orange leadership announced its decision to call off the Twelfth of July celebrations; it had more important work to do in the localities, and it now had the arms—distributed by the grateful authorities—to help it in its task.[204] In a telling letter that expressed the ambiguity of the government's attitude to such 'debts', Camden wrote to Castlereagh on 4 November 1798: 'That the violence of the partisans of the Protestant interest should be repressed, I believe you know, I sincerely think, but that a condemnation of them should take place will infinitely

200 *Belfast News Letter*, 7 July 1798.
201 See Gavan Duffy, *My Life in Two Hemispheres*, vol. 1 (London, 1903), 118–19.
202 A recollection of the Battle of Ballynahinch by an eyewitness, Iota, *Belfast Magazine* (Feb.–July 1825), 58.
203 PRONI T2627/1/7/96, 2 Mar. 1811, John Pollock to the fourth Earl of Buckinghamshire.
204 *Belfast News Letter*, 10 July 1798.

hurt the English interest in Ireland.'[205] The Presbyterians paid a high price for their radicalism; not least, the shock of seeing some of their number, erstwhile radicals, flood into the loyalist ranks.[206] The principal leaders, including Presbyterian clergy, were executed, and some key leaders seized the opportunity to avoid a similar fate by fleeing to the United States.[207]

The 'third rising' was a western affair. General Jean Humbert, a typically able soldier of the French Republic, landed at Killala in Mayo on 22 August 1798, with a force of only 1,000 men. They distributed arms among those Irish peasants who were prepared to support them. At Castlebar Humbert's troops inflicted a humiliating defeat on the troops of the Crown, but eventually a vastly superior British force, under the command of General Cornwallis, of 20,000 men compelled the French to surrender on 8 September. The French were honourably treated as prisoners of war; 2,000 of their Irish allies, including 500 Longford militiamen being found with arms, were slaughtered. On 24 August 1798 a senior British officer, William Wellesley-Pole, reported to the Earl of Mornington: 'In this horrible rebellion, the King's troops never gave quarter to the rebels; hundreds and thousands of wretches were butchered while unarmed on their knees, begging mercy.'[208] As late as 2 October 1798 the *Sligo Journal* claimed: 'The scourge ... has fallen with tenfold vengeance on the recreant tribe, nor is the sword yet sated.'[209]

In mid-September Tone sailed in an expedition from Brest, in a valiant but, as he himself acknowledged, self-evidently hopeless attempt to reinforce General Humbert's now destroyed expedition. The ship, the *Hoche*, was easily captured by the British, and Tone was just as easily recognized.[210] Rightly fearing the worst, Tone wrote to Castlereagh on 9 November 1798, asking to be treated as a captured French officer.[211] At his trial on 10 November Tone conducted himself with bravery: 'The British connection, in his opinion, was the bane of his country's prosperity, and it was his objective to destroy this connection, and in the event of his exertions he succeeded in raising three millions of his countrymen to a sense of their national debasement.'[212] With a fluent eloquence—which did not convince everyone—he dissociated himself from the 'sanguinary' horrors

[205] Charles Vane (ed.), *Memoirs and Correspondence of Viscount Castlereagh*, vol. 1 (London, 1848), 425.

[206] John A. Crozier, *The Life of the Rev Henry Montgomery*, vol. 1 (London, 1837), 12.

[207] Wilson, *United Irishmen, United States*, 33.

[208] L. S. Benjamin (ed.), *The Wellesley Papers*, vol. 1 (London, 1914), 75.

[209] PRONI D2707/A/3/126, Earl of Shannon to Henry, Viscount of Boyle, 26 Sept. 1798.

[210] Oliver Knox, *Rebels and Informers* (London, 1997), 225.

[211] PRONI T3048/J3.   [212] *Dublin Journal*, 13 Nov. 1798.

of the rebellion. The author of the profile of Tone in the *Dublin Journal* shuddered: 'He attempted to identify the interests of the Roman Catholics with his conduct and even affected to be thought ... as acting under their direction.'[213] On 11 November Tone was told of his sentence: to be hanged until dead and then to have his head cut off and displayed in a conspicuous public place. The next day Tone was discovered, convulsed with agony, grasping a bloody razor with which he had attempted unsuccessfully to cut his own throat. For days Tone lingered, apparently expressing repentance of his unsuccessful attempt to end his own life, but on 19 November he died in the Provo Prison in Dublin.[214]

Two days later, on 21 November 1798, Lord Castlereagh wrote to a close political ally, Maurice Fitzgerald, the Knight of Kerry: 'I take the earliest opportunity of intimating to you in the strictest confidence that the incorporation of the two countries by legislative union is seriously looked to.'[215] Within a month of Tone's death the *Dublin Journal* noted the change in the political atmosphere: 'The question of a union ... seems to have settled into a subject of "serious" and temperate discussion.'[216] The union concept was, indeed, now being discussed with renewed seriousness at the highest level. But while it did not lack 'serious' and 'temperate' supporters, in particular several of Cornwallis's commanders, who took pains to rein in the post-rising repression, the union also had some very aggressive partisan loyalist support.

But what of the reputation of Lord Castlereagh? The young reformer of 1790 was now apparently at the very heart of government repression. Father James Coigley, the United Irishman from Armagh, on the eve of his hanging for high treason in June 1798, was the first to lay stress on the alleged informer role of Castlereagh.[217] The Catholic priest was then supported by a Presbyterian clergyman on his way to exile, Thomas Ledlie Birch. Ledlie Birch's *A Letter from an Irish Emigrant* (1799) accused Castlereagh of having 'arrested his former supporters in the Whig Club and at the Down election'.[218] Charles Grey (1764–1845), later to be Earl Grey and Prime Minister from 1830 to 1834, took a similar view and accused Castlereagh

---

[213] *Dublin Journal*, 20 Nov. 1798, biographical sketch no. 1, Theobald Wolfe Tone.
[214] *Belfast News Letter*, 23 Nov. 1798.
[215] NLI Ms 2007, Lord Castlereagh to the Knight of Kerry, 21 Nov. 1798.
[216] *Dublin Journal*, 8 Dec. 1798.
[217] Daire Keogh (ed.), *A Patriot Priest: The Life of James Coigley 1761–1798* (Cork, 1998), 39.
[218] Kenneth Robinson (ed.), *Thomas Ledlie Birch: A Letter from an Irish Emigrant to his Friend in the United States, Giving an Account of the Rise and Progress of the Commotions in Ireland of the United Irishmen and Orange Societies and of Several Battles and Military Executions* (Philadelphia, 1799; repr. Belfast, 2005), 56.

of betraying those he had misled in his own radical 'Jacobin' phase.[219] The Prime Minister, William Pitt, came to Castlereagh's defence, pointing out that there was clear enough difference between a parliamentary reformer and a Jacobin. It was a reasonable and solid defence, but it does not disguise the fact that there had been realignment, and a remarkable one at that.

William Sampson, an unrepentant United Irish radical, writing in 1807, compared the 'tests' of the young Robert Stewart's electoral programme of 1790 with the 'tests' of the United Irishmen, and he argued that 'there is not so much difference that the taker of one should be exalted on a gallows and the other to a peerage. The only difference is this: he that was true to his test was hanged; and he that was foresworn, hanged him.'[220] Sampson had a point: the United Irish oath—promoted by William Drennan rather than Tone—had two basic principles: an attainment of an impartial adequate representation of the Irish nation in Parliament, and union of power among Irishmen of all religious persuasions.[221] Castlereagh's reply would, however, have been a simple one: the United Irishmen of 1790–1 and the Whigs were reformers. By 1795 the United Irishmen had become revolutionaries in alliance with Jacobinism. He was certain that such an alliance would destroy his own country. The fact remains that allegations of disloyalty to old friends and allies would always be associated with Castlereagh's career.

'Who fears to speak of '98?' This line of the poem by John Kells Ingram, written in 1843, is well known. But the harsh fact remains that Irish people did fear to speak of '98 until sufficient time had elapsed and its terrors had faded into the past. Then the sentimentality which could be found, for example, in the 1898 commemoration could emerge.[222] It was a sentimentality which infuriated Lecky, who saw the 1798 rising as the most divisive and poisonous event in Irish history, even as he acknowledged it had been provoked by bad government: 'It had planted in Ireland the hatred which has been the chief obstacle to all rational self-government.'[223] The bloodshed and murder confirmed two awful

[219] *Dublin Evening Post*, 19 Mar. 1801. Report of the debate in the House of Commons, 12 Mar.

[220] *Memoirs of William Sampson: Including Particulars of the Adventures in Other Parts of Europe* (New York, 1807), App. V, pp. 383–4.

[221] J. F. Larkin, *The Trial of William Drennan* (Dublin, 1994), 8.

[222] Peter Collins, *Who Fears To Speak of '98?: Commemoration and the Continuing Impact of the United Irishmen* (Belfast, 2004), 37.

[223] Lecky, *A Memoir of W. E. H. Lecky*, 321. Not surprisingly, the main nationalist press dismissed Lecky's view as 'pedestrian'. See Marc Mulholland, 'Not Historical but Prospective Application? The 1798 Rising, as Recalled in the Irish Popular Press of 1898', in D. G. Boyce and Alan O'Day, *The Ulster Crisis 1885–1921* (London, 2005), 165–81.

lessons. For Catholics and (radical Presbyterians), that the state and its allies (especially perhaps its Orange allies) would, if provoked, impose a bloody terror on the countryside. For Protestants, on the other hand, it became easy to claim that Catholics could not be trusted: given a chance, they would use their power, as at Scullabogue, to destroy the other community. Both sides now believed the worst of each other, and not without justification.

2

The Union Between Britain and Ireland: One People?

Pitt intended to pay the priests. This was the complement of the Union policy which took away the Irish parliament. The bigotry of George the Third prevented the success of a great scheme of settlement when the settlement was possible. We shall pay for this.

(T. A. Jenkins (ed.), *The Parliamentary Diaries of Sir John Trelawny, 1858–65*, entry for 27 Feb. 1865)

The 1798 rebellion and its bloody aftermath had as its most significant impact an increase in sectarianism—'the evil divisions of race and faith in the Irish community were deepened and widened'.[1] Tone's sincere desire to promote the 'common name of Irishman' in place of the existing political and religious divisions was cruelly mocked. Loyalist ideologues derived great satisfaction from the fact that the rebellion was crushed by Irish forces before substantial English reinforcement arrived.[2] 'Be it remembered that the yeomanry and militia of Ireland, with a very few regulars, had put down the rebellion in Ireland before Lord Cornwallis and his forces arrived; for the last affair of any importance was the defeat of the rebels at Vinegar Hill, the day before his Lordship arrived in Dublin.'[3] The interpretation of the 1798 rebellion became a key battleground; for hardline Protestants it became a matter of necessity to insist that the rebellion was inspired essentially by visceral Catholic sectarianism. Patrick Duigenan, who was closely allied with the ultra-Protestant polemicist Sir Richard Musgrave in this debate, claimed that 1798 was a 'Romish rebellion', and Catholic emancipation could only be conceived of thereafter as a reward for 'the cruel murders of Irish Protestants'.[4] Both authors were consciously working

---

[1] W. O'Connor Morris, *Ireland from 1798 to 1898* (London, 1989), 47.

[2] Thomas Bartlett, 'Defence, Counter-Insurgency and Rebellion: Ireland 1793–1803', in T. Bartlett and K. Jeffrey, *A Military History of Ireland* (Cambridge, 1906), 287–8.

[3] *Dublin Journal*, 12 Jan. 1811.   [4] Ibid., 23 July 1805.

with Sir William Temple's account of the 1641 massacre in mind. In this carefully constructed history, 1798 was a 'revolution of Irish Romanists', which was 'suppressed by the Protestants of Ireland'.[5] Viridicus (Sir Richard Musgrave), in his *A Concise Account of the Material Events and Atrocities which Occurred in the Late Rebellion and the Causes which Produced them* (1799), felt that no defence could be offered against changes of mass, bloody-minded sectarianism. It was an interpretation that allowed no room for nuance. For example, Viridicus analysed the evidence of the Wexford yeoman William Goodhall, that 'no person' at Wexford could have prevented the 'effusion of blood'[6] but the priests, as, in effect, a suggestion of priestly responsibility for the effusion of blood that did occur. Dublin Castle tended to argue that both Musgrave and his United Irish critics like Edward Hay were equally 'extreme', and fell short of endorsing Duigenan's analysis. Instead, it was assumed that Duigenan's objective was to frighten the Castle.[7]

Duigenan's analysis was, moreover, unequivocally supported by the powerful figure of John Fitzgibbon (1749–1802) Irish Lord Chancellor, created Earl of Clare in 1795, son of a self-made Catholic lawyer who had converted to Protestantism in 1731. Dr Clare O'Halloran has argued that Fitzgibbon represented 'the extreme mainstream Protestant reaction against the liberal pluralism of the previous decades'.[8] Ann C. Kavanaugh, Fitzgibbon's biographer, has surmised that his attitude towards his own people and culture 'originated in a contempt born of self-hatred'.[9] Fitzgibbon believed in the futility of any attempt to conciliate Catholic interests in Ireland; Catholic Ireland could only be satisfied by the complete overthrow of the existing order.[10]

This was no mere public posture: it represented personal conviction drawn from private experience. On hearing Sir Laurence Parsons make a pro-Catholic speech in the Irish Parliament at this time, attacking the policy

---

[5] *A Fair Representation on the Present Political Situation in Ireland* (Dublin, 1999), 84–90.

[6] *A Concise Account of the Material Events and Atrocities which Occurred in the Late Rebellion and the Causes which Produced them: And an Answer to Veritatis's Vindication of the Roman Catholic Clergy of the Town of Wexford* (Dublin and London, 1799), 25. See also Stuart Andrews, *Irish Rebellion: Protestant Polemic* (London, 2006), 24–5.

[7] PRONI T 2627/8/K/88, Marsden to Wickham, 26 Mar. 1803.

[8] *Golden Ages and Barbarous Nations: Antiquarian Debate and Cultural Politics in Ireland c. 1750–1800* (Cork, 2004), 69.

[9] *John Fitzgibbon: Earl of Clare* (Dublin, 1997), 364–5.

[10] *The Speech of the Rt. Hon John, Lord Baron Fitzgibbon (now Earl of Clare), Lord High Chancellor of Ireland, in the House of Lords on the second reading of the Bill for the relief of Her Majesty's Roman Catholic subjects, 13 March* (London, 1798), 37; see also one of his last key statements, *Dublin Evening Post*, 17 Feb. 1801.

of repression, Fitzgibbon drew him aside to make the same point: 'My father was a Papist recusant. He became a Protestant ... but he continued to have terms of familiarity with his Roman Catholic relations and friends ... if they had the chance, they would overthrow the government and church and remove the Protestants.'[11] Duigenan, whose own father, some alleged, had converted under the persuasion of Fitzgibbon's father, performed the same function for Hercules Langrishe, telling him first in 1793 and then in 1798 that the Catholics had recently produced maps asserting their claims to land forfeited 'as long ago as Charles I'.[12]

This compelling testimony—the story of the 'real' intentions of the Catholics—was the stock-in-trade of Duigenan and Fitzgibbon: 'real intentions' concerning which they alone had the personal authority and experience that allowed them to offer an authentic interpretation. Against this, Protestant liberals asserted the complexity of the motivations involved in 1798. Henry Grattan insisted that 1798 could not be classed simply as a Catholic rebellion. He spoke of 90,000 mobilized in the Protestant north, while the south remained loyal. His final verdict was more qualified: 'He admitted that the Catholics had been drawn into the vortex of the rebellion, but the rebellion had not therefore been Catholic.'[13] Much of this argument is actually also an argument about the posthumous influence of Edmund Burke. Both Sir Richard Musgrave and Patrick Duigenan in 1798 denounced the legacy of Burkeism, and Duigenan continued with his self-appointed task of overthrowing 'the Burkean system respecting Ireland'[14] In this respect Duigenan had only limited success. Prime Minister William Pitt consistently maintained a Burkean position. Pitt insisted that Jacobinism, not Catholicism, was the driving force of the rebellion: 'Jacobin principles were the foundation of the rebellion, yet I do not mean to deny the influence of the priests, themselves tainted with Jacobin principles.'[15] In the aftermath of the rebellion, Pitt's intentions follow logically from this analysis. He wished to bring in a further act of Catholic relief as part of the new proposed union; Lord Cornwallis, Lord-Lieutenant of Ireland, canvassed support for the Act of Union from Catholics on this basis. The government, however, considered it necessary to attach two conditions to any new measure of Catholic relief. They wished to establish a royal veto on the appointment of Catholic bishops by the Pope, and they also wished to implement some form of state financial

[11] *Belfast News Letter*, 9 Mar. 1798; Ann C. Kavanaugh, 'John Fitzgibbon, Earl of Clare', in David Dickson, Daire Keogh, and Kevin Whelan, *The United Irishmen: Republicanism, Radicalism and Rebellion*, Dublin (1993), 119.
[12] *Belfast News Letter*, 2 Feb. 1798.   [13] *Dublin Journal*, 16 May 1805.
[14] *A Fair Representation on the Present Political State in Ireland* (Dublin, 1799), 25.
[15] *Dublin Journal*, 23 May 1805.

provision for the Catholic clergy. When Castlereagh and Cornwallis raised these issues with the Catholic bishops in 1799, they received a friendly response. The Catholic bishops, meeting in Dublin on 17–19 January, secretly adopted resolutions in favour of state remuneration of clergy and government veto on appointments of bishops. 'There was no settlement with Lord Castlereagh about salaries for the bishops and clergy; although he made no explicit or formal promise of emancipation, he distinctly said the union would facilitate it', the conservative Archbishop Troy of Dublin was to tell Denys Scully some thirteen years later.[16] Both sides to this dialogue presumed that the Papacy would be sympathetic. But in the end nothing came of it. Pope Pius VI died in French captivity at Valence on 29 August 1799, but the cardinals assembled in Venice and elected a new pope, Pius VII, on 4 March 1800. The failure to reach an agreement on state provision for the clergy is highly significant. Writing fifty years later, a shrewd observer, William Cooke Taylor, saw it as a decisive moment of failure: a bad omen, indeed, for the whole union project.[17]

Britain's Irish policy from 1778 onwards was influenced by the increasing demands of war. The objective of British policy was to create an armed nation with loyal Catholic support. This implied Catholic recruitment, and it implied, logically, conciliation of Catholic grievances; one-third of the regulars in the British army at this time were Irish. In 1799 and 1800 Pitt and his ministers persistently advocated a particular interpretation of Anglo-Irish relations. Ireland's grievances were acknowledged in a sombre historical overview: England had, over some centuries, persistently mistreated Ireland by means of conquest and oppression. This was followed, after 1782, by the very narrow policy of devolving power to the Protestant elite. English mismanagement, therefore, had a great responsibility for that foundation of 'Catholic exclusion' which explained the emergence of the French disease in Ireland.[18] In Pitt's mind, historical considerations of this sort were allied to pressing contemporary considerations of national security. Catholic emancipation represented the answer to the historical problem, while a union of the two countries represented the solution for the problem of national security.

The Prime Minister William Pitt was always explicit about the strategic considerations involved in the Anglo-Irish relationship. In one of his key

[16] J. T. Troy to Denys Scully, 8 June 1813, in Brian MacDermott (ed.), *The Catholic Question in Ireland and England* (Dublin, 1988), 463.

[17] *Athenaeum* (1849), 110–11.

[18] Peter Jupp, *Britain and the Union 1797–1801: Transactions of the Royal Historical Society*, 6th ser., 10 (Cambridge, 2000), 209.

statements, Pitt recalled the activity of our 'natural and implacable enemy' (France), which was using 'every means, secret clandestine machination' as well as 'open force'.[19] Castlereagh never lost sight of this dimension; during the peace negotiations at the Congress of Vienna he extracted from Louis XVIII a commitment that the French army would never again engage an Irish brigade.[20] Powerful though it appeared to the British ruling elite, there were many in Ireland who could not see the force of the strategic argument. In January 1799 Castlereagh attempted to defend the principle of union before a hostile Irish House of Commons. This was to be a bruising experience: by the end of the week the Chief Secretary was forced to acknowledge that 'the measure could not be proceeded with until the mood of the country changed'.[21] Essentially, Irish opponents of union argued that the danger was passed; that a repeat of 1798 was an impossibility; that British politicians, like old generals, were fighting the last battle rather than thinking about the future. 'Good God, is it because a few ambitious young men place themselves at the head of a ridiculous mob in the interior parts of Ireland that the genius, the spirit and the loyalty of Dublin are to be sacrificed?'[22] wrote Isaac Burke Bethel. An 'Irish Logician' dismissed the 1798 crisis as 'recent, partial and temporary'.[23] Anyway, as Pemberton Rudd pointed out, the danger had passed: 'The seas are clear, France humbled and rebellion crushed.'[24] The anonymous author of *Observations For and Against an Union between Great Britain and Ireland* asked the rhetorical question: 'Can it be supposed now rebellion has tried its utmost strength, that it will again risk peril?'[25]

Pitt, however, remained unimpressed by such arguments. He continued to push ahead with a unionist strategy in which Burkean considerations of pro-Catholic reform were inextricably linked to considerations of national security.[26] The joint address of both Houses of Parliament on the union resolutions conveys perfectly this combination of underlying principles:

[19] *Belfast News Letter*, 29 Apr. 1800, Pitt in Parliament on 21 April.
[20] Ibid., 3 January 1815.
[21] Patrick Geoghegan, *Lord Castlereagh* (Dundalk, 2002), 28.
[22] Isaac Burke Bethel, *A Reply to the Gentleman who has Published a Pamphlet, Entitled Arguments For and Against a Union* (Dublin, 1799), 12.
[23] An Irish Logician, *A Union to be Subjection* (Dublin, 1799), 11.
[24] Pemberton Rudd, *An Answer to the Pamphlet Entitled For and Against a Union, Letter Addressed to Edward Cooke Esq* (Dublin, 1799), 21.
[25] (Dublin, 1799), 11, printed by J Stockdale & Co., 62 Abbey St., Dublin.
[26] W. J. McCormack, 'Between Burke and the Union', in J. Whale (ed.), *Edmund Burke's Reflections on the Revolution* (Manchester, 2000), 68, argues that no writer in favour of the union or opposed to it made extensive use of Burke. But, as Clare Connolly has more recently shown, Burkean language was significant during the union debate: see Connolly's 'Writing the Union', in D. Keogh and K. Whelan (eds.), *Acts of Union* (London, 2001), 176–8. A classic example is the explicitly Burkean advocacy of

We entertain a persuasion that a completed and entire union between Great Britain and Ireland, founded on equal and liberal principles, on the similarity of laws, constitution and government by providing the security, wealth and commerce of the respective kingdoms, and by allaying the distinctions which have unhappily prevailed in Ireland, must afford fresh means of opposing at all times an effectual resistance to the destructive projects of our foreign and domestic enemies and must tend to confirm and augment the stability, power and resources of the Empire.[27]

Publicly, at least, deference was paid to Irish sensibilities. William Pitt expressed a hope, in 'stately Virgilian' numbers, that 'two unconquered nations' would come together in 'perpetual concord'.[28] In Pitt's most remarkable flight of rhetoric he insisted—following Burke—that he wished to see a convergence of the interests of the two countries so that 'a man can not speak as a true Englishman, unless he speaks as a true Irishman; nor can he speak as a true Irishman, unless he speaks as a true Englishman'.[29] Significantly, Burke's young friend William Cusack Smith was to be excited and moved by these Burkean words at the end of April, and, after initial

---

Anglo-Irish conciliation to be found in Joseph Cawthorne, *The Means of Restoring the Tranquillity of Ireland* (London, 1798), 17, or George Cooper, *Letters on the Irish Nation written on a Visit to that Kingdom in the Autumn of the Year 1799*, 2nd edn. (London, 1801), 72. But Professor McCormack is quite correct on the more substantive point: Burke's legacy was a tricky one for all in the union debate. The debate continues to this day. Conor Cruise O'Brien sees Pitt's project of the union, combined with Catholic emancipation, as essentially Burkean in concept; as does R. B. McDowell, 'Burke and Ireland', in Dickson, Keogh, and Whelan, *The United Irishmen*, 114. On the other hand, Kevin Whelan insists that in 1800 Pitt embarked on an 'experiment of forced' union, turning Burkean (pro-Catholic) principles entirely on their head: Keogh and Whelan (eds.), *Acts of Union*, 31. Whelan is determined to defend Burke's reputation as an opponent of injustice in an Irish context. From an entirely different perspective, Tom Nairn, *Pariah: Misfortunes of the British Kingdom* (London, 2002), 113–14, appears to presume that Burke's reactionary stance would in itself damn the union project by contamination. The union, combined with Catholic emancipation, was advocated as specifically Burkean rhetorical principles by Pitt, Castlereagh, and William Cusack Smith—a point well understood by anti-Catholics like Miles and Duigenan—but without Catholic emancipation in place, it did not work on Burkean principles. There is no doubt that many writers, notably George Barnes and also Henry Grattan (*An Answer to a Pamphlet Entitled The Speech of the Earl of Clare* (Dublin, 1800), 7), employed Burke's name in arguments *against* the union. Professor Tom Bartlett has, however, concluded: 'As an Irish-born English statesman of Catholic descent, Burke was uniquely placed to contemplate the blighted promise of the Old Empire, and surely he would have applauded the fresh start the union offered': 'Ireland: Empire and Union 1690–1801', in Kevin Kenny (ed.), *Ireland and the British Empire* (Oxford, 2004), 82.

[27] Sir Henry Parnell, *A Speech Delivered in the House of Commons, 24 June 1823, on the Disturbances in Ireland* (London, 1823), 54.

[28] O'Connor Morris, *Ireland 1798–1998*, 61.

[29] *The Speech of the Rt. Hon. William Pitt in the British House of Commons on Thursday, 31 January 1799* (Dublin, 1799), 127.

doubt, confirmed in his pro-union sentiment.[30] 'By a union we shall become one people',[31] said Robert Peel, father of the future Prime Minister, on 14 February 1799. This speech from a prominent English manufacturer promised English willingness to make material sacrifices for the economic development of Ireland.

Some of Pitt's most interesting language on this theme came in his speech of 22 January which has been overshadowed by a second major effort which came a week later. In the speech of 22 January the Prime Minister defined the Irish problem as 'the hereditary feud existing between two nations on the same land'.[32] He insisted that the Irish legislature, not from any 'defect' of 'intention', but from its 'own nature', was incapable of sustaining the progressive development of Irish society.[33] In short, the 1798 rebellion had destroyed the credibility of the Dublin Parliament once and for all. The Irish Parliament reflected the Protestant–Catholic antagonism in pure form; only when that parliament was absorbed in a larger entity was there any chance of providing a political context which might reduce, rather than intensify, Irish divisions. The union, William Cusack Smith explained in an open letter to Grattan, would work to improve the condition of Catholics; 'by making them one in four, instead of being three to one', concessions to Catholic claims became a feasible and realistic project.[34] Cusack Smith's friend Charles Kendal Bushe took a more cynical, subversive line: 'For instance, it is obvious that the Catholics can never hereafter complain of not participating in the Constitution, but because there will be no constitution for them to participate in.'[35] Charles Hall argued that the union was the best means, not of ending the sectarian struggle, 'but to provide for its unceasing continuance'.[36]

The advocates of union remained unperturbed; they continued to say that only in such a context was Catholic emancipation a safe project; Catholic emancipation would overwhelm Protestant interests in an Irish parliament, but in a United Kingdom parliament its effects could, in principle, be contained: 'That influx of Cathoic power, which, under the constitution of 1782, would be subversive to the Protestant interest, will be, by an union, attended with no danger of that sort.'[37] Pitt also laid great emphasis on the

[30] *Review of a Publication Entitled The Speech of the Rt. Hon. John Foster in the House of Commons by William Cusack Smith* (Dublin, 1799), 41.
[31] *Belfast News Letter*, 18 Feb. 1799.
[32] *A Fair Representation on the Present Political State in Ireland* (Dublin, 1799), 215.
[33] *Belfast News Letter*, 25 Jan. 1799.
[34] *A Letter to Henry Grattan Esq* (Dublin, 1800), 34–5.
[35] *Cease Your Funning* (Dublin, 1798).
[36] *A Union Neither Necessary Nor Expedient for Ireland* (Dublin, 1798), 25.
[37] George Cooper, *Letters on the Irish Nation* (London, 1800), 317.

alleged economic advantages: a closer political union was a precondition for the influx of English capital. The Prime Minister concluded:

The situation of the country is indeed deplorable. Rent by party distraction, torn by the division of sects, subject to the revival of inflamed hostility, a prey to the hereditary animosity of the old Irish and English settlers, the scene of constant prejudices proceeding from superstition and ignorance. Add, Sir, to this true colouring the infusion of that deadly poison, Jacobinism.[38]

Pitt went on to offer the union, or more precisely, the Parliament of the new union, as a way out:

The deplorable situation of the country can only be cured by gradual, sober dispassionate improvement and civilisation: if much of it that is justly complained of can only be remedied by the circulation of capital, by the social intercourse naturally followed from improved trade and commerce, by the infusion of social habits, by the discrimination of liberal sentiment, by removing party distractions, by suppressing factious associations, and by allaying hereditary feuds subsisting between two nations living on the same land, we must look to the provisions of an independent legislature removed from the immediate seat of these evils, which shall not be partial to either party but the fair arbiter and kind parent of both.[39]

Pitt gave a particularly significant response to a speech by Richard Brinsley Sheridan against the union. On 23 January 1799 Pitt responded to Sheridan's strictures on British policy towards Ireland:

that he did not admit that England had oppressed Ireland for 300 years, but he would say that for 100 years the country had followed a very narrow policy with regard to that kingdom. When this country exercised a supremacy over Ireland, the policy tainted and perverted by selfish notions treated Ireland with illiberality and neglect [and] did not look upon her prosperity as that of the Empire at large.[40]

The decisive test for the new arrangement is unambiguously declared: that they avoid 'illiberality' and 'neglect', that Britain internalize Ireland's needs. Unsurprisingly, Pitt's acknowledgement of British historical failures in Ireland did not win any unreserved Irish applause. He was refused 'closure' in the matter. Irish writers pointed out that his condemnation of the bad side of Britain's record had not gone far enough. Patrick Lattin noted sardonically:

May I be allowed to follow, to follow this great man and finish the picture? Lamentable as this situation is, it is not all. There was yet another, a deeper curse in reserve for Ireland. In every other country domestic union would have been

---

[38] *Belfast News Letter*, 25 Feb. 1799.   [39] Ibid.
[40] Anon., published by Edward Moxon, *Past and Present Policy of England towards Ireland* (London, 1848), 102; quoted by R. Barrett, *Cork Examiner*, Jan. 1847.

a consequence of such external oppression; it is the precious jewel in the head of adversity.[41]

The point was that Ireland had to suffer not only the effects of foreign oppression, but the complicating effects of sectarian communal division. (The *Cork Examiner*, almost five decades later, picked up Pitt's language only to mock British government strategy.)[42] Pitt's most celebrated speech on the union—given on the last day of January 1799—hinted that the objections to Catholic emancipation could be removed if the Protestant legislature was 'no longer separate and closed, but general and opened and the Catholics themselves would at once feel a mitigation of the most goading and irritating of their present causes of complaint'.[43] Dr Patrick Geoghegan notes: 'That Pitt was prepared to make this assertion, despite all the opposition to Catholic relief in both countries, demonstrated a remarkable degree of confidence.'[44] Precisely in the use of the words 'goading' and 'oppressive', Patrick Duigenan detected Burke's influence in what he admitted otherwise to be an impressive speech. Burke was the 'active and able Romish agent' who had transformed the opinion of the English ruling elite on Ireland: Pitt would never have got so far in his efforts to placate Catholics but for 'the uncontrolled influence, respecting Irish affairs which Mr Edmund Burke had obtained'.[45] Duigenan's attacks on Burke became more and more extravagant:

His parents were Irish Romanists; he was endowed with very showy talents; his style was elegant; he was well read on all parts of polite literature; he was laborious and indefatigable; but his vanity, attendant on a weak judgement, was unbounded, and his zeal for promoting all the political views of Popery was enthusiastic. This zeal will account for the extraordinary anomalies of his political conduct.[46]

Those who worked to seduce Pitt away from the path of concession to Catholic interests knew that they had to take on the legacy of Burke: Hobart told Pitt that the Catholics exaggerated their own strength, but the government had itself encouraged them in this delusion, acting, as it had, 'under the influence of Mr Burke'.[47]

But important parts of the British political elite refused to accept Duigenan's analysis. Indeed, a belief persisted in the basically good intentions

[41] *Observations on Dr Duigenan's Fair Representation in the Present State of Ireland: Particularly with Reference to the Strictures on a Pamphlet Entitled the Case of Ireland Reconsidered* (Dublin, 1800), 48.

[42] *Cork Examiner*, 14 Jan. 1847.

[43] Patrick Geoghegan, *The Irish Act of Union* (Dublin, 1999), 70.   [44] Ibid.

[45] Patrick Duigenan, *The Nature and Extent of the Demands of the Irish Roman Catholics fully Explained* (London, 1800), 162.

[46] *A Fair Representation on the Present Political State of Ireland* (Dublin, 1799), 82.

[47] PRONI 3318/72, Hobart to Pitt, 2 Nov. 1799.

of Catholics. Duigenan, therefore, had every reason to be exercised by the Burkean legacy. It is important here to look at the speech in the Irish Parliament which most attracted the attention of Castlereagh, who drew Pitt's attention to it and subsequently introduced the young parliamentarian to the Prime Minister. It was by William Cusack Smith, Edmund Burke's young interlocutor, and coincidentally a relative by marriage to Patrick Duigenan. Cusack Smith's speech began with a lament for the condition of Ireland in the late 1790s: he regretted that Catholics had responded to early glimmerings of reform by associating with separatists; he repeated that Protestant ascendancy had degenerated into bigotry and faction, but these brutal realities made the case for the union. Cusack Smith then recalled his celebrated exchange with Burke:

In a letter, which the late Mr Burke did the honour of writing to me four years ago of what was termed Catholic emancipation, the necessity for interesting as many classes of people as may be, in the conservation of the present political establishment, and thus administering an antidote to Jacobinical poison—this, I say, forms the hinge on which all his arguments on behalf of the Catholic demands turn. Would to God these principles had been acted upon! If not in granting the Catholic requests (for the expediency of the great measure I feel to be questionable though I supported it), yet doing graciously what we felt compelled to do.[48]

The British Constitution was secure, free, and respected—the Irish Constitution could never be. That constitution, Cusack Smith argued, was a light, ambiguous affair, with little historical legitimacy. Irish 'distinctiveness' in this sense was anything but an advantage. This was easily the most effective speech in favour of the union to be given in the Irish House of Commons: the reprinted text rapidly ran through six editions.[49] Lord Auckland asked John Beresford, who was Cusack Smith? Beresford's reply was hardly flattering to the young lawyer. Cusack Smith, it said, had almost always been in opposition since he entered Parliament, and was vain, eccentric, ill-tempered, and whimsical, refusing to accept direction from anyone, even his own father. 'He is certainly very able on this occasion and is a very ingenious young man, but would be, I believe, very impracticable and hard to work with.'[50] There was some truth in this—by the summer of

---

[48] *The Substance of William Cusack Smith's Speech on the Subject of a Legislative Union Between this Country and Great Britain, Delivered in the House of Commons, on Thursday 24 January 1799, and now Reduced to the Form of an Address to the People of Ireland*, 4th ed. (London, 1800), 69.

[49] William Cusack Smith, *Introduction to the 1831 Edition* ... .

[50] The Rt. Hon. William Beresford (ed.), *The Correspondence of the Rt. Hon. John Beresford, Illustrative of the last Thirty Years of the Irish Parliament* (London, 1954), Beresford to Lord Auckland, 16 Feb. 1799, p. 214.

1799 Cusack Smith rejected as insufficient the government's first offer of patronage.[51]

Castlereagh,[52] in Dublin widely seen as the effective Prime Minister of Ireland, remained at the centre of the process, cynically manipulating all the local forces, leaving many ambiguous traces. It is easy to see why in later life he was so keen to find a historian who would give his version of these events.[53] Castlereagh's own public advocacy of the union avoided controversy. He stressed, above all, the defective nature of the 'present mode of connexion'[54] with England, and proposed the union as a remedy: Ireland, therefore, did not have the proper benefits of the British Constitution. But what did this mean? It is necessary to turn to this private correspondence to gain a fuller picture of Castlereagh's real agenda. It is perfectly true that the union was sold both to ultra-Protestants and pro-Catholic reformers as being in their particular interests. At first sight this was a blatant political deceit, but it is clear that Castlereagh genuinely believed that a stable accommodation for Irish Catholics and Protestants could be found within the union.

In early 1799 Castlereagh nonetheless laid most stress on winning over Orange support: in February to March 1799 many Orange Lodges had passed resolutions against the union. Castlereagh decided to appeal to senior politicians of an Orange hue. He unsuccessfully recommended the union to George Ogle MP, for example, by telling him that he knew 'no member of the legislature who more anxiously endeavoured to strengthen the constitution in church and state'.[55] The message here was that the Protestant Church in Ireland would be strengthened by the union. In the same month he corresponded with Patrick Duigenan on the same agenda.[56] Castlereagh probably knew he was pushing at an open door: during the 1793 debate on Catholic relief Duigenan had expressed pro-union sentiment.[57] Rather than endure the impact of Catholic political power in Ireland, Duigenan had said as early as 1793 that 'he would be the man to propose an union'.[58] Castlereagh worked also with Lewis O'Beirne, the Bishop of Meath—another aggressively anti-Catholic convert and opponent of Burke's influence in Irish affairs.[59]

[51] PRONI D3030/851.

[52] *Sketches of Irish Political Characters of the Present Day* (London, 1799), 247.

[53] Vane (ed.), *Memoirs and Correspondences of Castlereagh*, i. 81.

[54] *The Speech of the Rt. Hon. Lord Viscount Castlereagh upon Delivering to the House of Commons of Ireland His Excellency the Lord-Lieutenant's Message on the Subject of an Incorporating Union with Great Britain, with the Resolutions: Containing the Terms on which it is Proposed to Carry that Measure in Effect*, 5 Feb. 1800 (Dublin, 1800), 11.

[55] NLI Ms, Castlereagh to the Rt. Hon. G Ogle, 4 Dec. 1798.

[56] Duigenan to Castlereagh, 20 Jan. 1798, in Vane, *Castlereagh*, i. 52.

[57] *Report of the Debates in the Parliament of Ireland.*

[58] *Belfast News Letter*, 1 Jan. 1799.   [59] Vane, *Castlereagh*, iii. 37.

Yet, there is another side to Castlereagh's project. His key officials—Edward Cooke and the solidly Burkean Walter Elliott—presumed
Castlereagh to be strongly anti-Duigenan and in favour of Catholic emancipation.[60] There is no doubt that they correctly read his mind: in November
1799 he urged the Cabinet in London that Catholic emancipation was necessary. Castlereagh was capable of praising Duigenan's anti-Burkean attacks
on anti-unionists like Grattan, writing to his wife: 'I have been very amused
by Duigenan's answer to Grattan. It has very great merits as a piece of brutal
controversy.'[61] But this was hardly an endorsement of Duigenan's overall
world-view. When Maurice Fitzgerald, the Knight of Kerry (1772–1849),
an ardent Catholic emancipationist, complained about Duigenan's anti-
Catholic polemics, Castlereagh responded sympathetically, making it clear
that Cusack Smith's approach was the one closest to his own heart: 'I shall
see Dr Duigenan without delay. If Government had complained of being
censured by the learned author, it would have been the truth, but Cerberus
must be appeased. Smith is too valuable with all his impracticalities ever to
be neglected by me, and I hope we shall not only keep him but make him
happy.'[62] William Percy's pamphlet *Irish Salvation* (1800), dated 'Comber,
4 May 1800', by one of Castlereagh's northern neighbours, presented itself
as an 'insider's account'—'If you knew as much of the internal policy as
I do'—and, citing Castlereagh's words, presented Castlereagh as a strong
backer of the liberal version of the union.[63] Government policy in Ireland,
it said, could no longer be based on any one partisan or religious group.[64]
It is not difficult to see why, however, when the penny dropped on 15
January 1801 with Clare—'for the first time, Lord Castlereagh opened the
whole of his project to me'—Clare denounced him angrily for an 'act of
treachery to the gentlemen of Ireland'.[65]

The security of the state provided the justification for the extensive use
of bribery that was employed to buy off the surprisingly stern resistance
to the union within the Irish Parliament. The defence against this charge
of excessive bribery has been to admit that the government did, indeed,
employ large-scale patronage, but to insist that unionists were acting

[60] Vane, *Castlereagh*, ii. 29, iv. 27, Cooke to Castlereagh, 6 Feb. 1802. For Cooke's
vigorous defence of Catholic emancipation in a letter to Clare (10 Feb. 1801) see *A
Volley of Execrations*, 421–2.
[61] PRONI D 3030T/MC3/291, late June/mid-July 1798, Castlereagh to his wife.
[62] PRONI MIC 639/7/30, Castlereagh to Maurice Fitzgerald, June 1800.
[63] *Irish Salvation*, 23. Ian McBride points out that *Irish Salvation* was the only
pamphlet published in Belfast on the union issue, 'Ulster Presbyterians and the Passing
of the Act of Union', Brown, Geoghegan, and Kelly, *The Irish Act of Union*, 106.
[64] Ibid. 17.
[65] PRONI D2707/A/2/156, 13 Feb. 1801, Fitzgibbon to Richard Boyle, Earl of
Shannon.

according to the conventions of the time. Thus, given the reality that the control of parliamentary boroughs was regarded as a form of property, it was inevitable that government would have to compensate borough-owners for the loss occasioned by the abolition of the Irish Parliament. But the fact remains that the government only acknowledged that it would compensate the borough-owners *after* its defeats in the Irish Parliament of January 1799 and February 1799. In short, the necessity of manipulating opinion was the driving impulse behind the government's recognition of property right of the borough-owners. The creation of peerages—and advances within the peerage—caused much satirical comment at the time. Cornwallis and Castlereagh were told that they could make such promises; though in the end—once the Act was passed—Pitt did not always want to remember them.

There is no doubt that the government broke its own law in applying secret-service funding to the cause of the union. While the government could not legally spend more than £5,000 a year out of the secret-service budget in the country, it doled out some £32,336 in 1799–1800 to aid the purchase of votes and seats.[66] The government undeniably felt it was justified in breaking its own rules, as the union was a matter of such vital national security. In the end, between January and June 1800 the Irish Parliament's resistance was worn down, by force of argument no doubt, but also force of bribery: at a more populist level, Cornwallis was also careful to allow government rice to be sold at low prices, in order to save 'many from starvation'[67] in the poorer parts of Dublin. But such threat of starvation was a sharp reminder of a crucial fact: the union, if it was to work, had to achieve a substantial modernization of the Irish economy and social life. The union received the royal assent; it was destined to come into effect on 1 January 1801. On 2 January 1801 the *Belfast News Letter* hailed the union between the two countries: 'Yesterday morning the union flag was hoisted at the Market House, and at one o'clock a Royal salute was fired by the Royal Artillery in garrison, in consequence of the legislative union between the kingdoms of Great Britain and Ireland taking place.' The editorial eloquently continued:

It may not be impertinent on the occasion to observe that, however inimical some of the people of Ireland may have heretofore been to the adoption of that certainly *awful*, and most important, measure, a legislative union, it is now become an *interest*

---

[66] David Wilkinson, 'How Did They Pass the Union? Secret Service Expenditure', *History*, 82: 266 (Apr. 1997); Geoghegan, *Lord Castlereagh*, 31–3.

[67] Thomas Bartlett, *Revolutionary Dublin 1795–1801: The Letters of Francis Higgins to Dublin Castle* (Dublin, 2004), Higgins to Alexander Marsden, 28 Sept. 1800 and 29 Sept. 1800, pp. 293–5.

as well as the *duty* of the whole to bury, if possible, all political differences—all religious animosities—all local prejudices; to consider the Empire, not as composed of distinct political bodies, each having views incompatible with the happiness and prosperity of the rest—but as containing only one people, united in interest as in dominion—whose services ought to be reciprocal—the whole objects are undoubtedly the same viz tranquillity, prosperity and security.

The implications of the union reinforced the subdued mood of Presbyterian radicalism. Eliza MacCrone wrote to the Revd John Tennent, father of William Tennent, a United Irish activist, arrested in 1798 and still imprisoned at Fort George:

Yesterday we became united with the mother country. The union flag was hoisted in the Market House, and a royal salute was fired by the artillery and answered by the garrison. It was feared that there could have been some averse to it, and that perhaps some dispute would be to the consequence, but thank goodness, all is quiet as if nothing had happened. Long may it continue so. I will never again be an advocate for an opinion that persevering with it will be attended with bad consequences to any of my fellow creatures.[68]

This new quietism expected, of course, a return from government: that the remaining prisoners in Fort George would be released. Castlereagh continued to worry about the loyalty of the Presbyterian community; this explains his keen support for *regium donum* arrangements to pay their clergy. As late as 1813 he declared: 'The principles of Presbyterianism were very much republican, whereas, on the contrary, the fundamental principles of the Roman Catholic religion are purely monarchical.'[69] But the truth lay elsewhere—the Irish republican phase of the Presbyterian community's history was effectively over by 1800.

Professor Oliver MacDonagh has argued that the Act of Union was 'the most important single factor in shaping Ireland as a nation in the modern world'. The subordination of Ireland to Great Britain had preceded the union for several centuries before 1800, but the union transformed the relationship. 'The experience of being assimilated by, and resisting assimilation into, a powerful and alien empire—perhaps the master culture of the nineteenth century—was truly traumatic.'[70] At the level of trade there was already a full measure of 'union'. About 85 per cent of Irish exports were going to Britain by 1800, and 75 per cent of Irish imports were produced in Britain: the economies of the two islands were substantially integrated and interdependent.[71] But at the level of religion matters stood

---

[68] PRONI D1748/A/1/2/1, 3 Jan. 1801.   [69] *Dublin Journal*, 20 May 1813.
[70] MacDonagh, *Ireland: The Union and its Aftermath* (1997 edn.), 10.
[71] Gearóid Ó Tuathaigh, 'Ireland under the Union: Historiographical Reflections', *Australian Journal of Irish Studies*, 2: 2 (2002), 8.

differently. Ireland was not only a majority Catholic country, but it had its own language. At the time of the union Ireland probably held a population of 2 million Irish-speakers, one-and-a-half million Irish–English bilinguals, and one-and-a-half million English-speakers.

The conception of a union of Britain and Ireland which might lead to the creation of 'one people' was, indeed, a powerful one: and even its opponents paid some formal obeisance to it.[72] But clearly it was dependent on the reduction of political 'differences', 'religious animosities', and 'local prejudices'. Powerful forces were, however, opposed to any rapid move. Pitt's plans to link Catholic emancipation to the union ran into serious difficulties; faced by an unusually determined King—backed by the Church of England and a majority of peers—Pitt and his allies were forced to abandon the linkage and resign from government on 3 February 1801. On 7 February the *Star* reported 'doubts in the highest place'; His Majesty felt that the terms of the coronation oath to 'defend' and 'maintain' the Protestant religion conflicted with support for Catholic emancipation. On 9 February 1801 the *News Letter* reported: 'The rumours which for some days [have been] in circulation, and have so much agitated the public mind, appear to have been well founded.'[73] There were severe differences in Cabinet on the Catholic question—Pitt, Dundas, Grenville, Earl Spencer, and Windham all resigned; it was clear, too, that Pitt was supported by Lord Castlereagh. One strong supporter, both of the union and Catholic emancipation, the Knight of Kerry, was impressed by Pitt's action. On 13 February 1801 he wrote to Castlereagh: 'Mr Pitt retires in a manner which will cover him with honour, and I should suppose must attract to him the hearts of all honest Irishmen.'[74] Castlereagh replied that, while 'the hopes of seeing the foundation' of tranquillity in Ireland laid upon a 'solid basis' were for 'the moment disappointed', he hoped that the logic of the union, 'the wisdom of the system', would assert itself in a benign way.[75] W. E. H. Lecky, however, refused any praise for Pitt's conduct: 'There has seldom been a resignation which deserves less credit', he wrote, insisting that Pitt could have done more to face down the King.[76]

---

[72] Robert Sterne Tighe, *Observations and Reflections on the State of Ireland Respectfully Submitted to the British Nation* (London, 1804), Addington's speech dated 11 Feb. 1799, pp. 37–9. Addington quoted Duigenan: 'If we were one people within the Empire, it would not be necessary ... to curb Romanists by any exclusive law whatsoever', *Substance of the Speech of the Rt. Hon. Henry Addington in the House of Commons on the 12th February 1799* (London, 1799), 30. In fact, however, as Duigenan made clear, he did not include full political emancipation.
[73] *Belfast News Letter*, 9 Feb. 1801.   [74] NLI Ms 2007.   [75] Ibid.
[76] Lecky, *Leaders of Public Opinion*, 259.

The *News Letter* explained that all the members of this group were

strenuously of opinion, all restrictions with respect to religious opinion should be
done away with, and it was known that many of the persons who supported the
union, supported it under [the impression] that such a measure would be among
the first ... granted by the imperial parliament.[77]

Pitt moved quickly to calm frustrations in Ireland; on 28 February he sent
a message to the Lord-Lieutenant, Lord Cornwallis, pointing out that he
and his friends had sacrificed office in the Catholic cause; in return, he
needed steady, moderate behaviour from Irish Catholics; in particular, they
should refuse all alliances with 'Jacobinism'.[78] In the end, it was implied, the
cause of Catholic emancipation would triumph: Cornwallis, on his personal
initiative, went a step further and told Catholic leaders that Pitt and his
friends were pledged not to return to office until their cause was won.
The perception among those who supported the concept of a 'Protestant'
union—who were disgusted by the tone of this communication—was that
Mr Pitt had not actually written this communication but had certainly
known of it before it went.[79] John Foster endorsed a sneering *Morning
Chronicle* (12 March 1801) article, which pointed out that the whole
tone of this epistle implicitly isolated the King and the leadership of the
Established Church.[80] John Wilson Croker, almost forty years later, asked
Lord Sidmouth (then aged 82), who, as Henry Addington, had succeeded
Pitt as Prime Minister, whether the Catholic question was not rather the
'colour' than the 'cause' of Pitt's resignation, and whether his real object
was not to have peace made. Lord Sidmouth said no, that the Catholic
question was the real and, he believed, the sole cause of Pitt's retirement. 'In
fact, I can not call it retirement, for the King *positively dismissed* him, when
Pitt, in the closet, disclosed that he could not accede from his proposition
for emancipation.'[81] But despite Pitt's efforts to assuage Catholic fears, his
ally Cornwallis was withdrawn as Lord-Lieutenant in May and replaced by
Philip Yorke, Earl of Hardwicke (1757–1834), who held the position until
May 1806. Hardwicke was a former Foxite, who had drifted to the right in
Irish issues, though he later became a supporter of Catholic emancipation.

---

[77] PRONI D 2707/A/2/2/156, 13 Feb. 1801, Lord Chancellor Clare to the Earl of
Shannon, Dublin, 13 Feb. 1801. Clare, on 2 October 1801, censored the 'perfidy, folly
and presumption of Castlereagh', PRONI T 2827/7/6/1.

[78] *Dublin Evening Post*, 26 Feb. 1801.

[79] *Diary and Correspondence of Charles Abbott, Lord Colchester, edited by his Son,
Charles, Lord Colchester, in Three Vols*, vol. 1 (London, 1861), 250.

[80] PRONI D205/7/65.

[81] Louis F. Jennings (ed.), *Correspondence and Diaries of the Rt. Hon. John Wilson
Croker* (London, 1884), ii. 340.

The structure of government thus established for Ireland within the United Kingdom was implicitly authoritarian. The construction of the Irish government under a Lord-Lieutenant remained unchanged. The implication was stark; the Lord-Lieutenant in Dublin Castle was granted almost all the powers of colonial government without any significant restraint flowing from local representative structures of government; though, of course, the 'colonialist' aspect was mitigated by the responsibility of the Irish administration to the new Union Parliament at Westminster. The Irish Parliament of 200 members having been abolished, Irishmen at Westminster could take part in imperial legislation. They could expect to hold the highest offices of state—provided, of course, that they were not Catholic. Ireland, in accordance with its population share of the new United Kingdom, was to be represented at Westminster by 100 MPs, sixty-four sitting for counties, one for Dublin University, and the remaining thirty-five for thirty-three boroughs. The Irish were to be represented in the House of Lords at Westminster by four (Protestant) bishops and twenty-eight temporal peers or noblemen elected for life by the whole body of Irish peers from among themselves. An important side-effect of these changes was to abolish the Irish 'rotten' or 'pocket' boroughs, one of the great abuses of the old system. Irish Members of Parliament could not, however, expect, even if entirely united, to prevail against a determined and opposed English majority on an Irish question, or, indeed, any other. Irish MPs could join the existing English parties or they could form their own parties—but Catholics could not become Irish MPs, even though Irish MPs were elected in significant measure by Catholic votes. The Irish Protestant Church was to remain the state church and was to be called the Established Church of England and Ireland. From the perspective of those opposed to the union, or even its more liberal supporters, these were harsh realities. They hardly suggested an auspicious future for this new political project. The Union Flag of the United Kingdom was altered by the addition of a red saltire cross on a white background: the so-called Flag of St Patrick.

The most thoughtful and searching critique of the union came from Henry Grattan. Attempting to exploit Burkeism *against* Pitt, he argued that Pitt was displaying a Jacobin contempt for Ireland's ruling elite and traditional institutions. Grattan argued that the union as proposed was not an 'identification' of two nations, it was merely the 'merger' of the parliament of one nation in that of another. 'There is no identity in anything save in legislation, in which there is complete and utter absorption.'[82] Others

---

[82] W. O'Connor Morris, *Present Irish Questions* (London, 1901), 258; R. B. McDowell, *Grattan: A Life* (Dublin, 2001), 168.

were less subtle but equally powerful in their denunciation of bribery and military coercion. O'Neill Daunt was even more blunt in his riposte to Pitt: 'Thus if French bayonets overawed the English people, and if French gold bribed the English House of Commons into a legislative union with France, the English people according to Mr Pitt ... would be just as free, independent, happy as they are at present.'[83]

A young Catholic leader, Daniel O'Connell (1775–1847), joined his voice to those who criticized the union. The informer Francis Higgins believed that O'Connell had been a United Irishman, and he certainly appears to have operated within the ambience of the movement: on the eve of the rebellion, however, O'Connell had removed himself to untroubled Kerry.[84] A later unionist critic sneered that, at a time when so many others had taken great risks for Ireland, O'Connell had passed through the 'ordeal of 1798, unhurt, unnoticed, unsuspected'. But on 18 June 1800 O'Connell did speak out in even more remarkable terms against the union. O'Connell argued that the continuation of an Irish parliament, even if accompanied by continued Catholic inferiority, was superior to the union, even if the existing Catholic relief measures were repealed and the penal laws reinstated in full. This was pure rhetoric on O'Connell's part, as there was no danger of a return to the penal laws.[85] But it was an early indication of an ability to use the most striking language. In later years O'Connell painted an angry picture of violent, uncontrolled repression at this moment; certainly, his tone at the time was careful indeed: 'It was an effort which caution rendered admirable. Not one allusion to the whippings, and the incarcerations which had goaded Irish patriots into madness.'[86] Discretion at this moment was undoubtedly the better part of valour. But the harsh truth was that O'Connell and his allies in the aspirant Catholic bourgeoisie had had to endure a double rebuff: no Irish parliament, but no Catholic emancipation either. But as a class they remained in place, determined not to accept the moderation of a conservative Catholic hierarchy: the ideological beneficiaries of those in the Protestant elite who had thwarted the Burkean conception of the union.[87]

[83] *Freeman's Journal*, 21 Jan. 1834.   [84] Bartlett, *Revolutionary Dublin*, 227.

[85] W. J. Battersby, *The Repealers' Manual or Absenteeism: The Union Reconsidered* (Dublin, 1833), 317–20, makes it clear that O'Connell, in 1800, did not think any local Irish parliament would reinstate the penal laws.

[86] *Dublin University Magazine*, 10: 57 (Sept. 1837); 'A Provisional Character of Daniel O'Connell', *The Nation*, 20 May 1843.

[87] Gearóid Ó Tuathaigh, 'Political History', in Laurence M. Geary and Margaret Kelleher (eds.), *Nineteenth-Century Ireland: A Guide to Recent Research* (Dublin, 2005), 8–9.

UNION WITHOUT CATHOLIC EMANCIPATION

In the aftermath of Pitt's resignation the conduct of Britain's Irish policy was to be shaped by other, decidedly less liberal forces. There is no dispute as to the anti-Catholic views of the Prime Minister, Addington, and those who moved into the key positions in the governance of Ireland: Earl Hardwicke was appointed Lord-Lieutenant in March 1801, whilst Charles Abbott became Chief Secretary at the same time. Hardwicke and Abbott had been shocked to the core by 1798. They had little doubt that lower-class Catholics and their priests had revealed themselves to be determined on the bloody destruction of the Protestant community in Ireland. They were quite prepared to discuss privately the need to employ 'Cromwellian' methods of repression. They wished to see not only a union without Catholic emancipation, but a more general project of gradually 'Protestantising the country',[88] and took great comfort from the visible revival of anti-Catholic suspicions within the north's Presbyterian community in the early 1800s. The Prime Minister, Addington, wrote to Lord Redesdale on 7 January 1803: 'Let me assure you in the meantime that no impression can be more deeply rooted in my mind than the importance of rendering Ireland a Protestant country, nor more remote than that of an estate for the Catholic religion.'[89] One senior Dublin Castle official noted: 'A separation has taken place between Catholics and Protestants which, however to be lamented in respect of the general welfare of the country, will work materially for us in case of Ireland becoming the seat of war.'[90] Thomas Newenham was quite correct when he wrote in the following month: 'Perhaps some, on Machiavellian principles, may think it expedient to keep up divisions and political jealousy in Ireland a little longer.'[91] These remarks should not, however, be taken as representing the existence of *divide et impera* policy, accepted by all levels of the British political establishment. On 30 September 1803 Edward Cooke, who had resigned from Dublin when Catholic emancipation did not accompany the union, but who was still a British state insider, wrote to John Beresford:

I am very happy that you feel so strong in the north, though I fear the religious feeling which makes you so strong there, makes you proportionately weak in the

---

[88] *Colchester Diary and Correspondence*, i. 356, 410; cf also Addington to Redesdale, PRONI T 3030/3/10, 7 Jan. 1803.

[89] PRONI T3030/3/10/X15.

[90] Marsden to Wickham, 15 Mar. 1803, PRONI T 2627/5/K/77.

[91] Thomas Newenham, *An Obstacle to the Ambition of France; or Thoughts on the Expediency of Improving the Political Conditions of His Majesty's Irish Roman Catholics* (Oswestry, 1803), 31, dated 14 Apr. 1803.

south. There seems to be no confidence between the sects in each other, and until that can be produced in Ireland, Ireland must be in a state of weakness and insecurity.[92]

There was a little softness at the edges of the new policy. It was made clear that Irishmen were eligible for the key offices in the United Kingdom state and Cabinet. The Catholic hierarchy was, at least, to be treated with some decorum by Dublin Castle.[93] Both Clare and Duigenan detected a dangerous liberalism. There was also some desire to avoid exclusive reliance on the emergency powers granted to the Irish authorities under the terms of the Rebellion Act of 1799, which remained in force until 1802.[94] The government, in particular the Lord Chief Justice Kilwarden, was anxious to rely on the ordinary law rather than the repressive anti-rebellion measures which had led to the execution of twenty-four men as late as the period between November 1800 and February 1801.[95] 'Rebellion cases' in Wicklow and Kildare were to be tried by normal jury system as early as November 1801. No sentimentality was to be allowed to stand in the way of efficient and effective government.

ROBERT EMMET: THE MAKING OF A LEGEND

The government's strategy of 'normalization', combined with amnesia, was, however, to be challenged by Robert Emmet (1778–1803), the younger brother of Thomas Addis Emmet, a prominent United Irishman, and son of a prosperous Dublin physician. Expelled from Trinity College in 1798, following the Clare/Duigenan visitation of 1798, the young Emmet visited the continent, where he discussed plans to liberate Ireland with Napoleon and Talleyrand. On his return to Ireland in 1802 Emmet became involved in a conspiracy designed to achieve a new rebellion, focused, above all, on the capture of Dublin. At the core of his projected plan, Emmet and his co-conspirators attempted to overwhelm Dublin Castle, the seat of the Irish administration.[96]

---

[92] *Beresford Correspondence*, ii. 168.

[93] *Colchester Diary and Correspondence*, i. 250.

[94] Lord Kilwarden in particular was in favour of repeal of the Insurrection Act, 15 Jan. 1802, PRONI T 2627/5/W/6, remarks by Lord Kilwarden, 5 Jan. 1802, in conversation with Abbot.

[95] Marianne Elliott, *Robert Emmet: The Making of a Legend* (London, 2003), 56; PRONI T G27/5/W/6, Lord Kilwarden Document, dated 15 Jan. 1802; *Dublin Evening Post*, 19 Mar. 1801.

[96] R. O'Donnell, *Aftermath: Post-Rebellion Insurgency: Wicklow 1793–1803* (Dublin and Portland, Oreg., 2000), 127.

Emmet was a man of considerable idealism and drive, but the human material he had to work with was unimpressive. His plan relied heavily on the use of explosives, but these were not properly prepared. He relied much on support from Michael Dwyer's men in Wicklow—nonetheless, his communications with his Wicklow supporters were hopelessly mishandled. Michael Dwyer later told the Castle authorities: 'If Emmet had had a brain to his education, he would have been a fine man.'[97] Although Emmet placed great emphasis on secrecy, the authorities had a significant awareness of his plans. 'Great praise is due to Marsden for the accuracy of the information he had obtained ... Be assured that the government was not surprised', wrote Wickham on 16 August 1803.[98] 'It is utterly untrue that the government was surprised on the 23 July', wrote Redesdale in similar vein to Spencer Perceval on the same day.[99] But the army commander-in-chief, Lieutenant-General Henry Fox, brother of Charles, and the Earl of Hardwicke, the Viceroy—who were in the midst of a personal power struggle—responded sluggishly. J. W. Croker concluded savagely: 'The peril of Ireland was forgotten in a squabble between the governor and the general.'[100] As a result, a confused, violent mêlée took place in the streets of Dublin; the insurrectionists stopped a carriage containing Henry Robert Cole, a young British officer, and his wife. They offered him a pike and asked him to join the rising. Upon giving an unsatisfactory answer, Cole was then stabbed in seventeen places, though his wife was not harmed; then, leaving Cole for dead, the crowd turned on a following carriage. This contained the Lord Chief Justice of Ireland, Lord Kilwarden. Less fortunate than Cole, he was piked to death.[101]

Soon after, the insurrectionists were easily dispersed by the army. Nevertheless, it had been a shock: the pro-government *Dublin Journal* shuddered that the Emmet conspiracy 'was in extent nearly equal and in ferocity

[97] PRONI T 303/12/1, Redesdale, 11 Jan. 1804; Redesdale's cool analysis, dated 10 Dec. 1803, of the government's handling of the rebellion is to be found at T 303/10/9.
[98] PRONI T303/6/7/1. For the role of Marsden see J. W. Croker, *The Opinion of an Impartial Observer Concerning the Late Transactions in Ireland* (Dublin, 1803), 17; Patrick Geoghegan, *Emmet*, 166–7. On 14 November 1803 Marsden blamed Fox for the system's poor performance. PRONI D3030/1840. See Thomas Bartlett, 'Three Failures and a Success: Dublin Castle's Intelligence, 1796–1803', in Ennan O'Halpin, Robert Armstrong, and Jane Ohlmeyer (eds.), *Intelligence, Statecraft and International Power* (Dublin, 2006), 79–93.
[99] PRONI T303/6/7/1.
[100] *Sketch of the State of Ireland: Past and Present* (London, 1808), 20; Allen Blackstock, 'The Union and the Military, 1801 to c. 1830', in *Britain and the Union 1797–1801*, 338; Ruan O'Donnell, *Robert Emmet and the Rising of 1803* (Dublin, 2003), 61, 174–5.
[101] Elizabeth Bonython and Anthony Burton, *The Great Exhibitor: The Life and Work of Henry Cole* (London, 2003), 14. This young soldier was to be the father of the celebrated Victorian Henry Cole, the 'great exhibitor'.

much superior'[102] to the United Irishmen's effort of May 1798. Rumours circulated that the Castle had been under siege; that Kilwarden had been deliberately assassinated; that nineteen counties were in a state of revolt and the authorities were completely caught by surprise. It soon appeared that Kilwarden had 'been taken by accident' and much of the rest of the most frightening stories were without real foundation.[103] Dubliners were invited to survey the extent of the captured military equipment assembled by the rebels. Following Emmet's arrest and execution in September however, confidence, rapidly returned: the self-made Mr Luke White, the representative of the 'monied interest' in Ireland, called the Castle to offer a half-a-million-pound loan on the easiest of terms, and the *Dublin Journal* now described the Emmet affair as 'one of those efforts of riot and licentiousness to which mad enthusiasm can almost at any time, with the aid of a little money, rouse the desperate profligacy of a great capital'.[104] It was a 'contemptible ebullition' of 'confused treason', and there was no reason for 'well grounded apprehension in the public mind'.

Professor Marianne Elliott has offered a shrewd explanation of Emmet's persistence in a clearly futile rebellion: Professor Elliott sees Emmet and his colleagues as behaving like classic impoverished 'middle class revolutionaries': 'Only the truly rich and the truly poor know how to cut their losses. Having expended nearly all their resources on preparations, and struggling to find more, fear of losing them all at this stage became the prime reason for the decision to rise prematurely.'[105] Emmet's speech had a profound impact on Irish history,[106] but he cannot have imagined his full impact as a nationalist martyr. The fact remains that Dublin Castle authorities had the chance to make a deal with Emmet; he was prepared to forgo his celebrated speech in favour of a Dublin Castle offer of protection for his sweetheart, Sarah Curran, the daughter of John Philpot Curran, the 1790s lawyer and reformer. In fact, Dublin Castle paid no attention to Emmet's offer—even though they had no intention of arresting Sarah Curran. The Castle instead took comfort from the lack of realism at the least of Emmet's project. The Castle's laid-back attitude had a profound unintended effect: Emmet's oratory took pride of place in Irish patriotic consciousness, the speech cast a retrospective glow of nobility over the squalor of the actual revolt.

But this long-term impact, stretching across the generations, contrasted with the nullity of short-term effect. Dr Daire Keogh has recently argued

---

[102] *Dublin Journal*, 28 July 1803.

[103] J. W. Croker, *The Opinion of an Impartial Observer Considering the Late Transactions in Ireland* (Dublin, 1803), 4–5.

[104] *Dublin Journal*, 29 Sept. 1803.   [105] *Robert Emmet*, 56.

[106] See Donald Akenson's review essay of recent Emmet literature, 'Remember Emmet', *Irish Studies Review*, 12: 2 (2004), 339–43.

that within the Castle there was a chilling awareness and universal relief that the rebels' ill-judged timing had saved the day, rather than any efforts of their own.[107] Dublin Castle was well aware that their internal personality conflicts had shown the administration in an undignified light; but the fact remains that the more the authorities looked into Emmet's project, the less substantial it appeared to be. Wickham told John Foster, 'they were not yet all agreed'[108] on the basis of strategy. Hardwicke wrote: 'It is, at least so far, satisfactory to learn, from the testimony of the principal conspirator, that the difficulty of inciting the country is so considerable, not only from the scarcity of supply of money, but from the unwillingness of the people to rise.'[109] When citing Emmet's fate as a warning for the Young Irelanders, W. Cooke Taylor argued that:

Emmet had an imperfect conception of the end to which he aimed, as he had of the adequacy of the means by which it was to be effected. He speaks [in his final speech] of a thousand pounds as a sufficient supply of money, and of a thousand men as an adequate army. He trusted to the chance of success, for the means by which the success was to be achieved.[110]

Redesdale privately explained that the 'history of rebellions' showed that the calculation of 'probable success' plays little part; the 'vaulting ambition' of Emmet led him to attempt he 'did not know what'.[111] The execution of Thomas Russell, Emmet's co-conspirator, soon followed in Downpatrick in the north: Russell's failure to mobilize even the 'lowest dregs of Presbyterians ... a fact established beyond doubt',[112] in sharp contrast with the events of 1798, was noted with great satisfaction.[113] If, as Russell believed, six of the jurors who condemned him, whom he had known personally, had taken the oath of the United Irishmen, the effect was all the more marked.[114] Even more remarkable, perhaps, was the willingness of local Catholics to give evidence against Russell. Standish O'Grady, the

[107] *History Ireland: Special Issue, Robert Emmet Bicentenary*, 2: 3 (Autumn 2003), 56.

[108] PRONI T 2627/5/1/26, 6 Sept. 1803.

[109] PRONI T 2627/5/X/25, Hardwicke to Charles Yorke, 26 Sept. 1803.

[110] W. Cooke Taylor ('A Munster Farmer'), *Reminiscences of Daniel O'Connell MP* (London, 1847), 16.

[111] PRONI T 303/10/9, dated 10 Dec. 1803; Geoghegan, *Robert Emmet*, argues, however, that Emmet's plans were ingenious and complex; Ruan O'Donnell, *Robert Emmet and the Rising of 1803*, 218, speaks of the 'underrated rising of 1803'; see also *History Ireland*, 2: 3 (Autumn 2003), special issue.

[112] *Belfast News Letter*, repr. in *Dublin Journal*, 27 Oct. 1803.

[113] I. McBride, *Scripture Politics: Ulster Presbyterianism and Irish Radicalism in the Late Eighteenth Century* (Oxford, 1995), 208.

[114] M. MacDonagh (ed.), *The Viceroy's Post Bag: Correspondence Hitherto Unpublished by the Earl of Hardwicke, First Lord-Lieutenant of Ireland After the Union* (London, 1904), 426.

Downpatrick magistrate, reported to Wickham on 22 October 1803 that those who supported the case against Russell were of all religions, but 'principally Popish'.[115] But it is a remarkable fact that even government propagandists conceded the idealism of Emmet and Russell, if not their followers. Emmet was described as a man of whom, in other circumstances, 'his country might justly have been proud',[116] and of being capable of eloquence in the Grattan style. Robert Emmet's famous final declaration certainly had its own force: 'I have but one request to ask at my departure from this world—it is the *charity* of its silence. Let no man write my epitaph ... when my country takes her place among the nations of the earth, then, and only then, may my epitaph be written.'

Robert Emmet's trial speech was also reported at the time to include an attack on France:

It never was the intention of the provisional government of Ireland to form a permanent alliance with France ... On the contrary, it is evident from the introductory paragraphs of the address of the provisional government of Ireland that every hazard affecting an independent effort was deemed to be preferable to the fatal risk of introducing a French army into the country. How could we speak of freedom to anyone ... see how she [France] has behaved to Switzerland, to Holland and to Italy. Could we expect better treatment towards us? No![117]

Despite these words, much publicized by the government, not everyone could accept Emmet's anti-French credentials. 'Is there a man in either country that believes, or can believe, that Mr Emmet could ever have entertained a hope of ultimate success independent of French assistance?'[118] One well-placed senior legal figure, however, did not doubt the sincerity of Emmet's dislike of Napoleon; and it is important to note that William Cusack Smith fully accepted the validity of Emmet's anti-French remarks.[119]

---

[115] PRONI T2627/5/Y/38.   [116] *Dublin Journal*, 22 Sept. 1803.

[117] William Ridgeway, *A Report of the Proceedings in Cases of High Treason at a Court of Oyer and Terminer held at the New Sessions House with a Special Commission in the Months of August and September 1803* (Dublin, 1803), 97. There is some doubt as to whether Emmet actually did criticize the French; see Helen Landreth, *The Pursuit of Robert Emmet* (London, 1948), 332 n.; but Patrick Geoghegan, *Robert Emmet*, 249–54, is confident that Emmet did, indeed, make these criticisms. 'A Munster Farmer' (William Cooke Taylor), in his *Reminiscences of Daniel O'Connell MP*, in an account of Emmet's rebellion, claims to have had access to 'peculiar sources of information', which 'enables us to give the real history of an event which hitherto has been most grossly misrepresented' (p. 12), arguing that Emmet's meeting with Napoleon had been profoundly disillusioning.

[118] R. S. Tighe, *A Letter to Mr Fox, on that Part of his Speech in Parliament on the First Day of the Present Session which related to Ireland* (Dublin, 1803), 6.

[119] F. Danier (ed.), *Letters from Literary Characters to E. Barton, with a Prefatory Notice by EB of Captain Rock* (Dublin, 1824), p. ix.

Thomas Russell's trial speech contained no criticism of France; indeed, his captors believed he still had serious hope of French assistance which would rescue him. When Russell spoke of the need to improve 'the condition of the lower classes', one commentator interjected with exasperation: 'Infatuated and inconsistent man! Who could ever for a moment concede that the state of either the beggar or the gentleman would be ameliorated by the introduction of French armies?'[120] Nevertheless, even Russell received his measure of praise: his display of religious fervour, 'with which, it appears, his mind had long been tinctured', was contrasted favourably with the infidelity of Thomas Paine. In fact, Russell's last projected book was 'a collection of notes' on a publication by the celebrated visionary Mr Dobbs, 'tending to enforce that writer's interpretation of certain prophecies [which], according to him and his disciples, indicated the near approach of the millennium'.[121] There was a certain logic here. Francis Dobbs was an MP who opposed the union on millenarian principles. His 1800 work, *A Concise View from History and Prophecy of the Great Predictions in the Sacred Writing*, predicted that the Messiah would first appear in Ireland. Russell's message was a disturbing one to the authorities: 'The saviour of the world will show his sign on to mankind, and the boundaries of the nations will be pointed out.' Russell was, indeed, obsessed with finishing a 'religious work'; his last political statement (dated 'Downpatrick', 17 October 1803) argued that the institution of landed property was in conflict with the divine will.[122] Even so, the *Belfast News Letter*, like the *Dublin Journal*, strongly pro-government at this point, concluded: 'The general tenor of his life was gentle and humane.'

A paper published by the *Belfast News Letter* in October exploited further Russell's alleged Francophilia; although, in fact, Russell probably shared Emmet's cool assessment of Bonapartist France. It claimed that 'every honest United Irishman' detested Russell's cause. But there was another Russell, who remained an icon. The United Irish had appealed to the British radical tradition, but 'what was the cause for which Russell, Hamden [*sic*] and Sydney contended? For the blessings of a British constitution.' Thomas Russell, on the other hand, stood for the abolition of the British state in favour of French tyranny and French slavery. Having failed to win over more than a handful of supporters from the 'lower dregs' of Presbyterians, he was forced to employ the Catholic Defenders as the desperate engine of his revolt,

120 *Belfast News Letter*, repr. in the *Dublin Journal*, 27 Oct. 1803.
121 *Memoirs and Correspondence of Viscount Castlereagh*, edited by his brother, vol. 4 London (1850), 272. For more complex, rich details on this point, see James Quinn, *Soul on Fire: A Life of Thomas Russell* (Dublin, 2002), 272–5, 290–5.
122 MacDonagh (ed.), *The Viceroy's Post Bag*, 426–7.

there being no alternative source of support. This inevitably unleashed the demon of sectarianism, hence the condemnation of every honest United Irishman.[123] This was a serious argument, but inevitably it involved an element of nervous special pleading; in fact, in 1784 William Drennan had specifically rejected even the Hampden/Sydney tradition as a form of historical false consciousness—'a fairytale of infancy'—inappropriate for a movement of the 'native Irish under an English pale'. Two decades later it is tempting to see a sign here of the rapid formation of a particularly British form of liberal unionism. In Dublin also the Emmet affair had the unintended consequence of weakening the broad anti-union position in political life. Most strikingly, Wolfe Tone's eloquent lawyer friend W. C. Plunket agreed to prosecute Emmet. Wickham described this decision by Plunket to come 'on our terms' as a 'clear blow to the anti-union root at the bar'.[124]

A POST-EMMET STABILIZATION?

In fact, while a significant section of the erstwhile opposition to the union melted away, within a segment of the elite who had brought it about, and who were generating it, there were, for the first time, serious doubts. William Wickham, now the Chief Secretary in Dublin Castle, whose intelligence skills had done so much to undermine the Emmet rebellion, nonetheless retained Emmet's brave and courteous last note to him in his private papers. Wickham noted that he could never again, 'by my official duty ... prosecute to death men capable of thinking and acting as Emmet has done in his last moments, for making an effort to liberate their country of grievances the existence of which none can deny'.[125] He told Redesdale he wanted to leave Dublin Castle for financial and health reasons, he complained to others of confused lines of command; but the real reason seems to have been very much more profound: Wickham felt morally compromised by his role in the destruction of Emmet.[126] Perhaps even more revealingly, Castlereagh appears to have been disturbed and personally upset by the Emmet revolt. Redesdale reported in August 1803 to a future Prime Minister, Spencer Perceval, that 'Lord Castlereagh can not see the

[123] *Belfast News Letter*, 25 Oct. 1803; for a careful reconstruction of Russell's views, see James Quinn, *Soul on Fire*. Quinn (p. 232) argues that Russell had no illusions about what he termed the 'corruption' and 'tyranny' of the French government.

[124] PRONI T 2627/5/G/53, Wickham to Castlereagh, 21 Sept. 1803.

[125] PRONI T 2627/5/7/26; see M. Elliott, *Partners in Revolution: The United Irishmen and France* (New Haven, 1982), 282–322.

[126] Elizabeth Sparrow, *Secret Service: British Agents in France 1792–1815* (Woodbridge, 1999), 307–8; Geoghegan, *Robert Emmet*, 271.

change which his own great measure of the union has effected in Ireland'.[127] Emmet's proclamation had quoted out of context a passage of a Castlereagh speech, which appeared to assert that Britain oppressed Ireland; in fact, in 1799 Castlereagh regularly argued against the illusion of constitutional equality under an Irish parliament in favour of a more genuinely beneficial connexion with the British Constitution under the union. Nonetheless, Castlereagh may well have been shaken to see his words used in this context, especially as the union lacked Catholic emancipation. But such doubts could not be expressed in public; rather, the failure of the Emmet rebellion opened the way for a reactionary offensive.

For Lord Redesdale, Fitzgibbon's successor as Irish Lord Chancellor, the failure of Emmet's rising opened up the opportunity to go onto the ideological attack. Perhaps influenced by a warning from Lord Eldon that political Protestantism was on the wane in the British political class, he decided to inject some militancy into the debate.[128] In the immediate aftermath of Emmet, a sharp-tongued and lengthy private correspondence between Lord Redesdale, the Lord Chancellor, and Lord Fingall, the leading figure in Irish Catholic society, was somehow leaked to the press: Redesdale laid great emphasis on the 'disloyal' or anti-Protestant traits in the behaviour of the Irish Catholic Church in recent years. In fact, Archbishop Troy and O'Reilly of Armagh, accompanied by Lord Fingall, had done everything possible to register their disapproval of Robert Emmet's rebellion.[129] Fingall's efforts to stress the moderate and conciliatory character of Irish Catholicism fell—humiliatingly— on deaf ears.[130] In the autumn of 1804 Napoleon had decided that an invasion of Ireland had a distinct place in his second great project of invading England. He told Vice-Admiral Decrès that he wished to employ 30,000 or 40,000 men, and considered that 'le nord de la baie Lough Swilly est, á mon sens, le point le plus advantageaux'.[131] It was a dangerous moment. Lord Henry Petty told Thomas Creevey that Henry Parnell, a liberal, unlike his father Sir John, had convinced him that the Catholic movement in Dublin had assumed a 'very formidable aspect',[132]

---

[127] PRONI D 3030/17/8, Redesdale to Perceval, 29 Aug. 1803. As early as 9 October 1801 Castlereagh spoke with contempt of the 'cabal' in Dublin Castle, in a letter to Camden, PRONI T2627/4/127.

[128] Eldon to Redesdale, 5 Oct. 1803, PRONI T303/6/7: 'I think the time will come … when ours will not be the prevailing opinion.'

[129] Ambrose Macaulay, 'Catholicism and Nationalism: A Historical Reflection', Dennis Kennedy (ed.), *Nothing but Trouble? Religion and the Irish Problem* (Belfast, 2004), 26.

[130] *Dublin Journal*, 11 Feb. 1804.

[131] *Correspondance de Napoleon* (Paris, 1858–69), ix. 556–7, 29 Sept. 1804.

[132] Lord Henry Petty (afterwards first Marquess of Lansdowne) to Creevey, 23 Nov. 1804, in J. Gore (ed.), *Thomas Creevey's Papers 1793–1838* (London, 1985), 20.

but Redesdale continued to treat it with disdain; even as he reappointed Fingall to the magistracy, he reduced the benefit of that gesture.

Lord Redesdale, a man of exceptional legal ability as well as with a sharp eye for lucrative opportunity, had similarly unflinching views on the broad aspect of Irish issues. He denounced the 'bigotry of Burke', who had 'stimulated' the Catholics to make unreasonable demands. These were Redesdale's genuinely held principles. He had not intended these private communications to reach the public domain, but he was not dismayed when they did so. Redesdale felt that the tide was going his way. Pitt seemed to confirm this impression later in 1804, however, when he took office again as Prime Minister. Pitt fettered himself by a promise not to disturb the prejudices of the royal conscience. He even refused to present the petition which had been entrusted to his charge by the Catholic body. Many in Catholic Ireland came to believe that he had acted in deliberate bad faith all along, and duped them. 'They can not be surprised',[133] wrote one pamphleteer; but they were—both surprised and angered. The liberal 'small u' unionist historians of nineteenth-century Ireland were particularly unforgiving towards Pitt. W. O'Connor Morris insisted: 'The subsequent conduct of Pitt can not be justified in the mature judgement of history.'[134] George Lewis Smith strongly agreed,[135] and W. Cooke Taylor claimed:

His Late majesty, William IV, when speaking as Duke of Clarence, on the Catholic question, in 1829 more than insinuated that Pitt could have redeemed his pledge to the Irish nation, had he not been distracted by jealousy of Fox, whom he was unwilling to admit into his cabinet with a substantive share of power.[136]

The doyen of this school, W. E. H. Lecky, simply opined: 'Pitt's conduct on this occasion is, and probably always will be, differently judged.' But there can be no doubt, he added, as to the 'calamitous' effect of his actions upon 'Irish history'.[137] It is more than possible that Pitt, who was already a seriously ill man, simply could not bring himself to reopen such a traumatic issue with the King.

On 12 March 1805 a visibly ailing Pitt met privately with a group of Irish Catholic noblemen, including Lord Fingall and the Earl of Shrewsbury, and

[133] James Mason, *Considerations Upon the Necessity of Discussing the State of the Irish Catholics* (London, 1804), 16.
[134] *Ireland from 1798 to 1898* (London, 1898), 60.
[135] George Lewis Smith, *Ireland: Historical and Statistical*, 3 vols. (London, 1844, 1847, 1849), ii. 258.
[136] *Reminiscences of Daniel O'Connell MP*, 17.
[137] W. E. H. Lecky, 'Ireland in the Light of History', in *Historical and Political Essays* (London, 1910), 78.

other leading Irish Catholics to discuss the issue. A watery-eyed Pitt was sympathetic and courteous, but made it clear that he considered Catholic emancipation, whilst desirable, not such a question of basic justice that it should be implemented regardless of considerations of timing and political circumstances. At present political circumstances were highly unfavourable. The delegation left, permeated with a sense of bitterness which was immediately conveyed to one of the rising stars of Catholic politics, Daniel O'Connell.[138]

But if Pitt had pragmatically and opportunistically diluted his Burkean pro-Catholic principles, others had not. In 1805, under the aegis of Lord Fitzwilliam's patronage, Grattan, explicitly presented as a 'favoured friend of Edmund Burke', was returned to Parliament for Malton, Burke's old seat. Grattan immediately raised the issue of Catholic emancipation in Parliament. His petition was debated in May 1805; but the outcome was an exceptionally heavy defeat—178 to 49 in the Lords and 336 to 124 in the Commons. Pitt voted against Grattan on the issue, and defended himself against the idea that he had given any pledge—whatever Cornwallis might have said. He insisted to Parliament, in his words:

I must also remind the House that I considered the period of the union as the period favourable for the adoption of such a measure—not because any pledge had been given, but because there was a likelihood that the measure might be adopted after the union ... [rather] than before it.

These vague formulations—obviously highly elastic as to timing—left a bitter taste in the mouth of Catholic Ireland; for Catholic Ireland Pitt had revealed himself as the 'Machiavel of modern times',[139] incapable of generosity or justice.

IRELAND AND THE MINISTRY OF ALL THE TALENTS

Following Pitt's death on 25 January 1806, none of his ministers felt able to form a ministry. The King sent for Lord Grenville; Grenville insisted that Charles James Fox, a noted sympathizer with Catholic Ireland, should be included in the new Cabinet: 'It was Grenville's support for emancipation

---

[138] B. McDermott (ed.), *The Diary of Denys Scully*, 12 Mar. 1805, p. 81; John Ehrman, *The Younger Pitt: The Consuming Struggle* (Stanford, 1996), 774–5; Maurice O'Connell (ed.), *Correspondence of Daniel O'Connell*, vol. 1, *1792–1814* (New York, 1972), 133, O'Connell to Scully, 19 Mar. 1805.

[139] Father John Regan, *Reflections on an Important Subject Respectfully Addressed to the Roman Catholics of Ireland* (Dublin, 1809), 8–13.

which made possible this alliance with Fox.'[140] The Irish journalist Eaton Stannard Barrett dubbed the new administration 'the Ministry of All the Talents'. Hardwicke and the Protestant hardliner Redesdale were removed from Dublin Castle. The Duke of Bedford, whom Burke had mocked, was appointed Lord-Lieutenant, and the Burkean William Elliott became the new Irish Secretary. Sir John Newport was brought in alongside them to work as Chancellor of the Irish Exchequer.[141] George Ponsonby, one of the most important Irish Whigs, became Lord Chancellor. The Duke of Bedford was the first Lord-Lieutenant not to take part in the annual Orange parade around the statue of King William. Henry Brooke Parnell was made a Treasury Commissioner;[142] his brother William Parnell was well known as the author of several vigorously pro-Catholic tracts.[143] Most suggestively of all, Fox's secretary, the Irishman J. B. Trotter, an old associate of the United Irish intelligentsia, moved into Downing Street and opened up a friendly correspondence from there with his old friends.[144] Fox accepted the impossibility of changing the King's mind over the admission of Catholics to Parliament or to high office. He nevertheless felt that something could be achieved within the existing legal framework. He hoped to remove magistrates who had been notoriously partisan in their judgements. He wished to make Catholic entry into the army or the corporations of towns easier. Fox also wished to make the tithe system less oppressive.[145] One hopeful observer, William Drennan, was quick, however, to perceive Fox's potential weakness, seizing on the significance of a hesitant phrase used by Fox: 'If proper means be adopted to conciliate the feelings and interests of Ireland.' Drennan noted shrewdly: 'A predominant minister would not put an "if" into that sentence.'[146] Fox died in the summer of 1806, but not before his reputation, and that of Grenville, had suffered with radicals because of the failure to institute an inquiry into serious allegations made against the conduct of the Wellesley family in India. For all its trimming, the mild reformism of Fox's sympathies with 'Ireland' was always balanced

---

[140] J. C. D. Clark, *English Society 1600–1832: Religion, Ideologies and Politics During the Ancient Regime* (Cambridge, 2000), 507; Martin Powell, 'Charles James Fox and Ireland', *Irish Historical Studies*, 33 (2002), 169–90.

[141] Peter Jupp, *Lord Grenville 1759–1834* (Oxford, 1985), 363.

[142] Henry Parnell, *A History of the Penal Laws Against the Irish Catholics* (London, 1808), 22, 181.

[143] Notably *A Historical Apology for the Irish Catholics*, 3rd edn. (London, 1808), 180.

[144] Trotter to William Drennan, 31 Mar. 1806, in Jean Agnew (ed.), *The Drennan–McTier Letters*, vol. 3 (Dublin, 1999), 447.

[145] D. Keenan, *Ireland 1800–50* (Philadelphia, 2000), 56.

[146] William and Sarah Drennan to Martha McTier, 10 Apr. 1806, in Agnew (ed.), *Drennan–McTier Letter*, iii. 463.

by a respect for existing structures of power.[147] Nonetheless, the 'Talents' set the King's nerves on edge: in March 1807 George III took alarm at the government's evident intention of further concessions to Catholic claims, and demanded a written declaration from them that they would propose no more. The Foxite Whigs refused, were then dismissed, and were excluded from office until 1830.[148] It was an important moment in the radicalization of Daniel O'Connell. Indeed, the enlightened language of the Ministry of all the Talents had merely, in the end, infuriated Irish Catholic opinion. As John Keogh declared: 'They indeed volunteer to defend the liberties of Germany or the Blacks of Africa, but they are silent to our suffering millions.'[149]

In March 1807 the Duke of Portland was appointed Prime Minister. In May/June 1807 a general election, very much fought on 'No Popery' principles, confirmed Portland's position. The new Prime Minister had been for several years a hero to Irish Protestants, as, indeed, was his Lord-Lieutenant, the Duke of Richmond.[150] The Burkean Canning succeeded Fox at the Foreign Office. The penniless Trotter asked Canning, whose parents were both Irish, for help, even as he admitted that his position with Fox had been 'so confidential' that he could not expect to stay on. Canning wrote to the Duke of Richmond in Dublin Castle to ask if any role could be found for a capable Irish intellectual, but nothing happened—that position was reserved for J. W. Croker, who acted as aide to Arthur Wellesley, the new Chief Secretary.[151] Sir John Newport, who broke the news of Wellesley's appointment to William Elliott, was appalled by the tough-minded ingratitude of the Wellesley family, who had enjoyed such protection from the outgoing administration: 'You will no doubt be surprised when you learn the name of your intended successor, Sir Arthur Wellesley,' Newport noted grimly; 'human nature is very bad.'[152]

AN ERA OF ILL-FEELING: 1807–1810

At any rate, the new man in Dublin Castle did not intend to rely on Irish human nature. On 7 May 1807 Arthur Wellesley drew up a plan

---

[147] Martin Powell, 'Charles James Fox and Ireland', *Irish Historical Studies*, 2: 33 (2002), 169–90.

[148] Clark, *English Society*, 508.

[149] John Keogh, *A Sketch of a Speech Delivered by John Keogh* (Dublin, 1807), 12.

[150] *Dublin Journal*, 12 July 1798.

[151] NLI, Ms 59, George Canning to the Duke of Richmond, 12 Oct. 1807.

[152] Newport to Elliott, 28 Mar. 1807, Queen's University Belfast, The Henry Collection, MS 37/17/18; Peter Spence, *The Birth of Romantic Radicalism: War, Popular Politics and English Radical Reformism, 1800–1815* (Aldershot, 1996), 128.

for the military defence of Ireland. Its striking feature was its dark tone. While he wanted a naval station in Bantry Bay, he preferred to construct a defensive line, based on inland stations. He insisted that the people were 'disaffected', and that 'we have no strength here but our army'.[153] William Saurin, a strong-willed Protestant of Huguenot extraction, was appointed Attorney-General. Patrick Duigenan, Secretary of the Grand Orange Lodge of Ireland, became a privy councillor. The effect can easily be imagined: for most Irish Catholics, Orangeism was simply another name for anti-Catholic violence. The parliamentary grant to Maynooth, which the previous administration had intended to increase significantly, was kept at a fixed lower sum. These provocations, which greatly soured the atmosphere, made life difficult for Henry Grattan. Nevertheless, Grattan made a serious attempt to address the Catholic issue in 1808, but this time under different terms. A series of contacts had convinced him that the Catholic hierarchy was willing to accept a royal veto on the appointment of Irish Catholic bishops by the Pope: British sensitivities on this matter had been exacerbated by the Papacy's visible subordination to Napoleon. Armed with 'acceptance' of the veto, Grattan felt that he had a serious chance of winning the argument for Catholic emancipation. It seemed that the obvious solution was at hand. But although there is little doubt that Grattan had reason to believe that he had been authorized to make his proposal on behalf of Catholic Ireland, 'sentiment changed and the authorisation was withdrawn'.[154] Grattan had proved to be vulnerable to the classic weakness of the liberal Protestant reformer: a presumption that Irish Catholics held the views hypothetically ascribed to them by Irish liberal Protestants.[155]

The issue of Pitt's good faith played a significant part in this debate. Watty Cox's *Irish Magazine*, a new and powerful voice, poured scorn on all those who believed in British good faith, its graphic illustrations reminding its readers of the dreadful repression of 1798. Dublin Castle was well aware of 'Cox's role in inflaming opposition to the British connection'.[156] A few of the most self-confident and privileged Irish Catholic intellectuals, for example, the Revd Charles O'Conor and the poet Thomas Moore, took a radically different view. They urged Irish Catholics to take a more independent line, less deferential towards the Papacy. But O'Conor came

---

[153] Sir Herbert Maxwell, *The Life of Wellington* (London, 1900), i. 83–4.

[154] For an excellent explanation of the confusion, see McDowell, *Grattan*, 206–7.

[155] Ibid.; Revd Thomas Elrington Ball, *Remarks Occasioned by the Supplement and Postscript to the Second Edition, Revised and Augmented by Dr Milner's Tour of Ireland* (Dublin, 1812), 155. Milner was the 'ambassador' of the Irish Catholic clergy in 1808 who had raised Grattan's expectations. Milner's defence was to say that he had never advocated the veto 'as generally understood'.

[156] Jennings (ed.), *Croker Correspondence and Diaries*, i. 90.

from a distinguished and long-established Catholic family. Moore, a child of the Dublin Catholic middle class, was one of the first Catholics to attend Trinity College, Dublin, after it opened its doors to Catholics in 1793. Charles O'Conor noted sadly that 'our national hatred of England' has driven 'our writers into an odious system of ultramontanism, unworthy of a generous war-like and independent nation'.[157] Moore, in 1810, passionately declaimed:

And, therefore, I appeal to that love of liberty, which is natural to you as Irishmen, and avowed by you as Catholics, and I ask whether you can think, without shame and indignation, that, for a long period, you have been the only people in Europe (with the exception of a few petty states, in the neighbourhood of the Pope) who have sunk so low.[158]

But privileged self-confident intellectuals like O'Conor and Moore—who in different ways had escaped the sense of humiliation which inspired so many others—were unable to influence mainstream opinion. One bitter drawing in Cox's *Irish Magazine* of ascendancy cruelty outweighed a dozen such elegant arguments.

Nevertheless, important as it was, the polemics of the *Irish Magazine* were not the only source of the union's ideological weakness. Many asked the obvious question: where was the much-promised inflow of English capital? The *Dublin Journal* felt compelled to point out that those who advocated 'repeal of the union' used precisely that 'violent language' which frightened the English capitalists.[159] Ten years on, defenders of the union were reduced to arguing that there had, at least, been substantial technocratic improvement in the working of the government apparatus; the union had led to 'highly improved and judicial regulation in such areas of government activity as the revenue, the ordnance and the post office'.[160] But useful though such improvements were, neither Catholic nor Protestant argued that the union lived up to Pitt's promises and advance billing. Few could assert convincingly that Grattan's critique had been refuted.

Thomas Newenham was one who, as MP for Clonmel, had voted against the union in the Irish Parliament. He remained sceptical:

Ireland has not as yet become a principal theatre for the exertions of enterprising Britons; nor does a perfect knowledge of its circumstances appear to be requisite either to celebrity or advancement in the political world. With regard to commerce, the Irish people have no reason whatsoever to congratulate themselves upon the

---

[157] B. Clifford, *The Veto Controversy* (Belfast, 1985), 169.

[158] Thomas Moore, *Political and Historical Writings on Irish and British Affairs* (Belfast, 1993), 13.

[159] *Dublin Journal*, 6 June 1811.   [160] Ibid., 4 June 1811.

union. The commercial prosperity of Ireland has vastly declined since that measure was carried into effect.[161]

George Barnes had opposed the union in a vigorous pamphlet of 1799: he saw nothing in the first decade of the union's operations to change his mind. In 1811 he noted: 'Behold the reciprocity which Pitt has bequeathed to you by the union—to eat the crumbs which have fallen from the rich man's table.'[162]

On the other side of the Irish Sea there developed a growing sense of impatience with the complaints of the Irish. After all, as the distinguished Scottish Enlightenment statistician, Sir John Sinclair, put it: 'The Scots have now got the better of all absurd, local or provincial prejudices. They are awfully aware that if the Empire flourishes, they will share in its prosperity.' As for the claim that the 'dignity' of Ireland had been diminished, there was a ready reply: 'But if a native of Ireland can not be satisfied with the dignity and importance attached to the character of a British subject, it would be difficult to discover where he could obtain a more honourable distinction.'[163] James Gordon argued that, since the union, 'Ireland was not subject to Great Britain but as much part of the same kingdom as Northumberland and any other county'.[164] Yet, noted one angry English commentator, the Irish showed little sign of improvement: 'Who can tell me that the common Papist Boys of Ireland, at the present day are one jot more civilised or improved than the Cingalese, the Candyans, the Malabars of Ceylon were in their primitive state ... like these, they are naturally driven to sloth and laziness.'[165]

Resentful of such language, many Irish felt that there was no honourable distinction attached to their condition. Patrick Duigenan, of course, had no doubt where the blame for this unsatisfactory state of affairs lay: the pernicious, long-term impact of Edmund Burke's thought:

The present unsettled state of Ireland, so justly attributed to the influence this gentleman acquired with the English ministry. While Mr Pitt was at the helm, that

---

[161] Thomas Newenham, *A View of the Natural Political and Commercial Circumstances of Ireland* (London, 1809), 289. For Newenham's critics, who included T. R. Malthus, see H. D. Gribbon, 'Thomas Newenham 1762–1831', in J. M. Goldstrom and L. A. Clarkson (eds.), *Irish Population, Economy and Society: Essays in Honour of the Late K. H. Connell* (Oxford, 1981), 23.

[162] *A Statistical Account of Ireland Formed on Historical Facts* (London, 1811), 16.

[163] *A Letter from the Hon Sir John Sinclair, Bart MP to the Chancellor of the Exchequer in Ireland on the Proceedings which have Lately taken Place for Dissolving the Union Between the Two Kingdoms* (Edinburgh, 1810), 20–1.

[164] James Gordon, *An Address to the People of Dublin* (Dublin, 1803), 207.

[165] John Jervis White Jervis, *A Brief View of the Present State of Ireland* (Bath, 1813), 40–1.

great, honest and able minister, being utterly unacquainted with the conduct of some demagogues in the Irish Parliament, unluckily delivered himself up as to the management of Ireland, to Mr Edmund Burke: the children yet unborn have cause to rue it.[166]

But by far the most revealing commentary on the working of the union is to be found in a private correspondence between two self-conscious Burkeans, J. W. Croker, MP for Downpatrick, and William Cusack Smith. In 1806–7 the two gentlemen had struck up an intellectual friendship. The anti-union writer W. J. O'Neill Daunt was later to offer a rather cynical account of Croker and Cusack Smith's friendship and advocacy of the union and Catholic emancipation.[167] For O'Neill Daunt, the union was such an inherently bad idea that any advocacy of it—no matter how ostensibly generous—must contain an irreducible element of bad faith. O'Neill Daunt was keen to exploit Burke's judgement against the Protestant ascendancy as a judgement against the union. Croker, nonetheless, treasured a family connection with Burke, whilst Cusack Smith had participated in a widely admired public exchange with the same man. In 1807, Croker sent Cusack Smith an advance text of his book *A Sketch of the State of Ireland, Past and Present*. The book denounced the oppressive nature of the Irish land system. *A Sketch of the State of Ireland* was to enjoy an underground reputation over the next three decades; it was even said to be so subversive a text that it had had to be withdrawn. The *Dublin Review*, in 1842, notes 'a literary friend once declared ... [it] was the best, most vigorous and scathing exposure of the iniquities of the Irish landlords' that he had ever read.[168] In a phrase which was to have a precise echo in the language of Thomas Drummond in 1838, Croker spoke of property as having its duty to perform as well as its rights: 'The combinations of the peasantry' were, it was said, 'natural'.[169] Baron Cusack Smith, by now an experienced judge, hardly needed the lesson. The 'Threshers' overran much of Connaught and, indeed, Cavan and Longford in 1806: judges, for example, could not move safely around without a troop of dragoons to protect them.[170] The Threshers, in the state's view 'a description of persons not possessed of any rank—of any property—of any

---

[166] Patrick Duigenan, *The Nature and Extent of the Demands of the Irish Roman Catholics Fully Explained: In Observations and Structures in a Pamphlet Entitled A History of the Penal Laws Against the Roman Catholics* (London, 1810), 136.

[167] W. J. O'Neill Daunt, *Eighty-Five Years of Irish History 1800–1885* (London, 1888), 70–6.

[168] *Dublin Review*, 13 (Aug.–Nov. 1842), 'Fixity of Tenure', p. 556.

[169] Ibid. 73.

[170] *A Report of the Trials of the Caravats and the Shanavests at the Special Commissions for the Several Counties of Tipperary, Waterford and Kilkenny*, taken in shorthand by Randall Heron (Dublin, 1811), 11. For a 'class' interpretation of the Caravats–Shanavest rivalry, see Paul Roberts, 'Caravats and Shanavests: Whiteboyism and Faction Fighting in East

talent—of any education', took it upon themselves to redefine the law of the state both as to agrarian, but also religious, issues, opposing apparently payments both to Catholic and Protestant clergy.[171] Denis Browne, one of the largest landlords in Ireland and a locally sensitive magistrate in Mayo, offered an analysis of the variable aims and actions of the Threshers.

The first object of the association was the reduction of tithes and priests' dues—when it travelled into this part, it assumed that, and another shape, that of attacking the wages of weavers and other artificers—and latterly farmers. In different stages of its progress, it professed different objects—all kinds of payment, whether of tithes, industry, labour or farming—assemblies of people collected in disguise and wearing badges and armed, appeared in different parts of the country.[172]

In 1807 Grattan surprised British radicals like Francis Horner by his willingness to support the Insurrection Act of that year.[173] In 1810 the government reacted to a lull in agrarian disturbance by repealing coercive legislation; by the end of the year serious disaffection had surfaced in fifteen counties, and more troops had to be called in.[174] One pamphleteer railed against this 'military despotism': 'Are not persons and property in many districts, at the moment, at the entire will of military commanders?'[175]

The authorities perceived these agrarian conspiracies as having a principal objective—'the regulation of landed property'—but this was not the end of the matter. There was a broader political concern: there was the lingering fear, even after the victory of Trafalgar in 1805, that the French threat might resurface in Ireland. At the beginning of 1808 the distinguished French General Dumouriez—long since a defector to the British—prepared a memorandum for Castlereagh, *Mémoire militaire sur l'Irlande*, stressing British vulnerability.[176] John Pollock, in 1809, actually considered the

---

Munster 1802–1811', in Samuel Clarke and J. S. Donnelly (eds.), *Irish Peasants: Violence and Political Unrest, 1786–1904* (Manchester, 1983), 64–101. The Shanavests represent the stronger farming community and its allies, in this interpretation, while the Caravats represent the rural poor.

[171] *A Report of the Proceedings Under a Special Commission: Sligo, Mayo, Leitrim, Longford and Cavan*, M. Ridgeway (1806), held in Sligo, 2 Dec. 1806, p. 9.

[172] Brian Griffin, *Sources for the Study of Crime in Ireland 1801–1921* (Dublin, 2005), 82. See also Browne to Arthur Wellesley, 21 May 1808, T2627/3/2/274, a letter which stresses that his local effectiveness in enforcing the law depended on his reputation as being pro-Catholic emancipation.

[173] L. Horner (ed.), *Memoirs of Francis Horner* (Edinburgh, 1849), Horner to John Allen, 19 Aug. 1807, p. 195.

[174] B. Jenkins, 'The Chief Secretary', in D. G. Boyce and A. O'Day, *Defenders of the Union* (London, 2001), 52.

[175] Anon., *Dangers from the Policy of England in the Repression of Ireland: To the Rt. Hon. Spencer Perceval* (London, 1810), 64.

[176] PRONI D/3030/2586/1.

situation in Limerick and Tipperary to be one 'of actual rebellion' with French help.[177] In 1810 senior judicial opinion insisted:

If, at a future day, rebellion should ever again raise its head in the country, or the French should unfortunately effect an invasion, either the one or the other would find well prepared and willing auxiliaries in the armed peasantry of the Co Tipperary, habituated to crime and familiarised with blood.[178]

Steeped as he was in these brutal realities and paranoid fears, Cusack Smith broadly accepted Croker's analysis and wrestled with a deep inner turmoil: even Cusack Smith's contemporary critics, after all, accepted the sincerity of his pro-union views.[179] But he argued for a distinction between the 'theory and principle' of the union and the 'vile system' of its actual administration. Pitt would not have allowed it, Cusack Smith suggested, but for his illness. The fundamental difficulty was England's lack of interest in making a union work. In September 1810 Cusack Smith concluded:

How have the promises made by Unionists to Ireland been kept? Made by some—by myself, for example, honestly and *bona fide*? Has a single step been taken to mitigate the evils which that arrangement was destined to reduce? ... Has a step been taken to console the pride and soothe the exasperation of a country fallen from its high esteem? Can a Unionist avoid blushing when he contrasts the performance with the promise?[180]

Indeed, as he pointed out—how much more strongly would anti-unionists feel? Cusack Smith had convinced himself in 1799 that the union would not 'sink Ireland to a province'[181]—what about those who had never shared his confidence?

Thomas Newenham was one such figure. His writing became increasingly impassioned. Ireland he saw as a wasted resource for the British Empire. Newenham defended the natural ability of the 'lower Irish in many parts of the country', speaking two languages 'idiomatically and effectively different', and noting that the Irish, 'when in foreign countries', effected

---

[177] PRONI T26277/1/7/87, Pollock to the Earl of Buckinghamshire, 29 Jan. 1809.

[178] *A Report of the Trial of the Caravats and the Shanavests*, 9; Donal McCartney, *The Dawning of Democracy: Ireland 1800–1870* (Dublin, 1987), 75.

[179] E. Somerville and Martin Ross, *An Incorrigible Irishman: Being an Account of Chief Justice Charles Kendal Burke and of his Wife Nancy Crampton, and Their Times 1767–1843* (London, 1932), 60.

[180] For Croker and Ireland see William Thomas, *The Quarrel Between Macaulay and Croker* (Oxford, 2000), 32–59. The Smith–Croker correspondence is in the private possession of Peter Rowan.

[181] *Letter on the Budget Addressed to Messrs Saurin and Jebb in which Mr Jebb's Reply is Considered*, by a barrister (W. C. Smith) (Dublin, 1799), 19.

their 'business with great intelligence and success'.[182] He added, with a touch of desperation:

> Distant dependencies may even cease to be part of the British dominion; yet Great Britain and Ireland, firmly united, sagaciously and impartially governed, with all their various sources of wealth and strength fully disclosed and skilfully improved, may still constitute a flourishing and unvanquishable Empire. But if the prosperity of Ireland may be suffered to decline, Great Britain, whatever others may think, will hardly find an adequate compensation for the effects of that declension on her own prosperity.[183]

But who really believed him, among the British political elite? In Ireland, a sense of resentment began to intensify. English hypocrisy was all too visible. In the absence of a strategy, in Cusack Smith's phrase, to 'console the pride and soothe the exasperation of a country fallen from its high esteem', it was this sense of British indifference, and perhaps even contempt, which threatened to undermine the union. Another 'Burkeist' supporter of the union, George Moore, had insisted that under the union, whatever its other defects, 'at least we shall be delivered from the empire of prejudice or resentment'[184] ; but ten years later this claim was open to serious criticism.

---

[182] Thomas Newenham, *A View of the Natural, Political and Commercial Circumstances of Ireland* (London, 1899), p. xix. J. Gault agreed: 'There is an air of vivacity, restlessness, of intelligence and perhaps of mischief' in the Irish lower classes 'totally unlike the fat contented ignorance' of the English lower classes: *Sketches of History, Politics, Manners, taken in Dublin and the North of Ireland in the Autumn of 1810* (London, 1811), 43.

[183] Newenham, *A View*, p. iv.

[184] George Moore, *Observations on the Union, Orange Associations and Other Subjects of Domestic Policy with Reflections on the Late Events on the Continent* (Dublin, 1800), 41.

3

Daniel O'Connell and the Road to Emancipation 1810–1829

We ask the sober and rational opponents of Catholic claims, is it wise
to expose the nation to continual dangers for the sake of prejudices
which their children will laugh at?

(*Northern Whig*, 23 August 1827)

The debate about the import of the impact of the union on Ireland
became a debate in part about good faith. Parliament decisively rejected
Catholic political emancipation again in 1805 and 1808; nevertheless, it
was clear that some of the most able and thoughtful members of the British
political elite continued to support emancipation, much to the dismay of
the unreconstructed supporters of the 'Protestant union'. In 1811 the issue
of Pitt's intent and purpose on this matter was raised yet again. Despite
his private view that Pitt had been too pro-Catholic, Lord Redesdale rather
brazenly argued that Pitt's commitment to Catholic emancipation had not
been wholehearted.[1]

Earl Spencer disputed Redesdale's version: Spencer insisted that as a
close colleague of Pitt's he must have known his mind on this matter.
He was supported by Lord Grenville: 'The great opportunity was lost by
the misjudged councils and by the wicked misconceptions imposed on
the mind of the sovereign.' With a notable air of resignation, Grenville
added: 'An opportunity was lost that would never be restored.'[2] Castlereagh
agreed—insisting that Pitt never doubted the fundamental wisdom of
Catholic emancipation. In 1812 mainstream opinion moved away from
Redesdale at least to the extent that the Liverpool Cabinet decided to leave
Catholic emancipation as an open question which ministers were allowed
to differ upon.

---

[1] *Dublin Journal*, 25 June 1811.
[2] Ibid. reports these exchanges in the House of Commons, 18 June 1811.

Nevertheless, and hardly surprisingly, there was continued anger within Catholic circles. The Dublin Catholic Committee had a legal status, but when in 1811 it proceeded to organize elections for a Catholic parliament on the basis of ten delegates from each county and five each from each Dublin parish, it ran foul of the Convention Act of 1793, designed to prevent the election of unlawful assemblies. The very isolation of the Castle government predisposed it to be highly nervous when it appeared that an alternative source of legitimate authority might conceivably be in the process of construction. The Castle acted even though their spy in the Catholic Committee told them that the young Daniel O'Connell was simply itching to be arrested.[3] This 1793 legislation had been originally the government's response to the Ulster Protestant convention of volunteers in Dungannon as well as the Catholic Convention in Dublin, but now it was turned solely against the Catholics. Dr Edward Sheridan and successful merchant Thomas Kirwan were prosecuted: Sheridan was acquitted, but on 3 February Kirwan was found guilty by a carefully packed jury, and three days later fined a nominal sum.[4] On 18 June 1812 O'Connell, in confused circumstances, at the Catholic Committee read out a resolution (later known as the 'witchery' resolution) fiercely critical of the Prince Regent, speaking of the 'fatal witchery of an unworthy secret influence. To this impure source we trace but too distinctly our baffled hopes.' It was an entirely understandable but tactless outburst: the Prince Regent, when Prince of Wales, had offered support to the Catholic cause, which he now opposed. But this attack on his mistress, Lady Hertford, was never forgiven. William Parnell wrote to Denys Scully on 26 June 1812: 'You know how much public events depend on personal feelings, and I quite tremble for the catholic cause when I see how unnecessarily the Prince is attacked.'[5] The next day Castlereagh sent a long, private memorandum on emancipation to the Prince—but to little avail.[6] To make matters worse, Lord Liverpool decided to send Robert Peel, a young and passionate defender of the Protestant constitution, to Ireland as Chief Secretary and driving force of the administration there. The youthful

[3] PRONI T3228/5/27/f. 28, William Wellesley Pole to Richard Ryder, 12 Feb. 1811; see f. 31 for intelligence report dated 17 Feb. 1811.

[4] William Ridgeway, *A Report of the Proceeding in the Cases of Thomas Kirwan, Merchant, and Edward Sheridan MD for Misdemeanours Charged to be Committed in Violation of the Convention Act* (Dublin, 1811). For the police surveillance of the Committee, see in particular pp. 154–72. Ridgeway (p. 226) acknowledges the point that the Dungannon Convention inspired the original legislation and cites the discussion in Joseph Pollock, *Letters to the Inhabitants of the Town and Lordship of Newry* (Dublin, 1793), 11–49.

[5] Brian MacDermott, *The Catholic Question in Ireland and England 1798–1822* (Dublin, 1988), 357.

[6] PRONI T3076/2/55.

Peel was heavily influenced by three important senior figures,[7] Baron Manners, Lord Chancellor from 1807 to 1827, William Saurin, Attorney-General 1807 to 1822, and William Gregory, Under-Secretary from 1812 to 1831. Manners was a famously affable sportsman, Saurin a sharply intelligent product of French Huguenot stock, and Gregory had a profound grasp of detail. These three men opposed the appointment of Catholics to positions of influence and political power, but, just as strenuously, the appointment of any Protestant who favoured Catholic claims.[8] Peel, as long as he remained in Dublin Castle, remained a firm opponent, not only of Catholic emancipation, but of Protestants who supported their case.[9]

IRELAND AND 'ORANGE' PEEL, 1812–1821

The Dublin Castle agenda was thus firmly tilted against Catholic emancipation. One elder statesman, Henry Grattan, did not accept this anti-emancipation consensus. On 30 April 1813 Grattan's Relief Bill was introduced into Parliament, proposing that all disabilities should be removed from Catholics, provided only the British government should have the right to forbid the choice of any particular priest for a bishopric. Parliament rejected the proposal by 251 votes to 247 on 24 May. Parliament seemed to be edging towards some kind of acceptance of Catholic claims, but it was widely understood that the Catholic cause depended on a moderate advocacy, avoiding any hint of threat. At this very moment, however, the reverse was to happen: on 8 December 1813 Dr Thomas Dromgoole addressed the Catholic Committee in Dublin, Lord French in the chair. Dr Dromgoole's speech was directed against the idea that Irish Catholics might exchange their religious principles for civil rights. It attacked liberal Protestants like Grattan, who, under the cover of conciliation, connived at a dilution of Catholic principles. Worse, Dromgoole's language seemed to embody an offensive challenge to the Protestant Church in Ireland: 'If the Church of England trembles for its safety, it must seek it elsewhere, we have no security to give.'[10] Dromgoole argued that the Methodists, 'a

---

[7] W. E. H. Lecky, 'Sir Robert Peel', *Historical and Political Essays* (London, 1910), 171.

[8] Robert Shipkey, *Robert Peel's Irish Policy 1812–46* (London and New York, 1985), 4–5.

[9] PRONI T1638/10/2, Peel wrote on 11 July 1918: 'You will scarcely believe what I fear is too true, but Colonel Longfield has made the unworthy declaration of his intention to vote for the catholics.'

[10] *The Speech of Dr Dromgoole, a Physician at the Catholic Board in Dublin, on Wednesday, 8 December 1815, Lord French in the Chair* (Oxford, 1820), 21.

kind of Cossack infantry', and the 'Republican phalanx' of Presbyterianism also besieged the Established Church. In fact, Ulster Presbyterianism's republican phase was past;[11] whilst the growth of Methodism, though subject to surges of enthusiasm, was essentially stable.[12] The real perceived threat in Dromgoole's language lay in his reference to the 'columns of Catholicity ... collecting to challenge for the possession of the ark'; it was this force, above all, which threatened the Established Church with eclipse.

Such language inevitably provoked a reaction. Watty Cox's *Irish Magazine* naturally insisted that Dr Dromgoole was 'neither a fanatic nor a bigot',[13] but the problems created by his celebrated speech simply would not go away. Some leading Catholics quickly condemned it, and the Catholic Board disavowed it three days later. Daniel O'Connell's behaviour was uncharacteristically uncertain—according to Dromgoole, O'Connell at first praised the speech, but picking up on the Catholic Board's disapproval, he rapidly moved towards a more critical stance. In fact, O'Connell praised Dromgoole on 'policy'—the veto—but warned that 'mutual toleration' and 'respectful courtesy' should govern the speeches and publications of all sects of Christians.[14] O'Connell, for his part, wrote privately to his wife of his 'dislike' of Dromgoole.[15] Fifteen years later, with emancipation safely won, he recalled Dromgoole's speech as the one genuinely sectarian utterance which came from the Catholic ranks during the emancipation struggle.[16]

Inevitably, ultra-Protestant opinion—men like Patrick Duigenan and John Giffard, editor of *Faulkner's Dublin Journal*—felt vindicated by Dromgoole's rhetoric. The *Dublin Journal* declared: 'Protestant parents now had a clear duty in educating their children. Guard them against spurious liberality, and should you see them swerve from their duty or wax cold in their zeal a single jot, please enter in their ears the names of Dr Dromgoole and the Roman Catholic Board.'[17] Speaking to the House of Lords in 1825, Henry Cooke was still stressing Dromgoole's impact:

---

[11] Finlay Holmes, 'From Rebels to Unionists: The Political Transformation of Ulster's Presbyterianism', in R. Hanna (ed.), *The Union: Essays on Ireland and the British Connection* (Newtownards, 2001).

[12] David Hempton, 'Methodism in Irish Society', *Transactions of the Royal Historical Society*, 5th ser., 36 (1986), 125.

[13] *The Irish Magazine* (Jan. 1814), 8.

[14] *The Veto Controversy: Including Thomas Moore's Letter to the Roman Catholics of Dublin*, compiled by Brendan Clifford (Belfast and Cork, 1985), 132–9.

[15] M. R. O'Connell (ed.), *The Correspondence of Daniel O'Connell, vol. 1, 1792–1814* (Shannon, 1972), 21 Mar. 1814, p. 465.

[16] *Northern Whig*, 28 Apr. 1829, speech at Downpatrick.

[17] *Dublin Journal*, 11 Dec. 1813. See Jacqueline Hill, 'Dublin After the Union: The Age of the Ultra-Protestants 1801–1822', in M. Brown, P. Geoghegan, and James

in Cooke's controversial view, Dromgoole had been decisive in weakening the Presbyterian community's support for Catholic emancipation.[18] The *Freeman's Journal* wondered where Irish Catholics were to find allies for their cause if they threw over people like Grattan,[19] then at the peak of his parliamentary influence, in favour of a policy which ignored completely the balance of forces. There is no doubt that the legacy of the speech was poisonous — regularly reprinted as it was by Protestant sources keen to draw attention to the frightening messages it contained.

Dromgoole's speech was, however, firmly repudiated by Richard Lalor Shiel, who created a considerable stir by the strength of his opposition. Like Moore, Shiel was one of the first Catholics to go through Trinity College, Dublin; in his case, after Stonyhurst. Like O'Connell, he came from an established (if recently established) Catholic family. His father was a merchant turned landowner.[20] Shiel now emerged as O'Connell's main rival for the leadership of Catholic Ireland, but for all his ability, Shiel lacked the bravado and impulsiveness that were such an important part of O'Connell's drive and success. He also lacked O'Connell's passionate resentment of Protestant privilege. The *Dublin Evening Mail* observed: 'Nature has done much for his good disposition; but, as he himself often admitted, the society of his young friends in the Protestant University of Ireland had done much more.'[21] Shiel may have lacked the necessary pugilistic qualities, but O'Connell did not. It was all too easy for opponents to see him as a bully and braggart. O'Connell's fatal duel with John D'Esterre in 1815, followed by an aborted one with Peel, may have been messy and discreditable affairs (O'Connell was much shaken by D'Esterre's death), but they contributed to O'Connell's 'heroic' image.[22] (The legacy of the D'Esterre affair was more complex: opponents were infuriated by O'Connell's verbal abuse and subsequent refusal to duel on the grounds of guilt-feelings over D'Esterre.)

The novelist John Banim portrayed Shiel as a 'low, slight, little gentleman, with eyes so dark, fine and expressive', able to outmanoeuvre O'Connell by a superior grasp of fact, which O'Connell simply overran by appealing much

Kelly, *The Irish Act of Union: Bicentennial Essays* (Dublin, 2003), for the influential Giffard–Duigenan faction of ultra-Protestant Orange loyalism.

[18] *Sessional Papers, vol. ix, House of Lords, Reports (brought to the Lords) with Minutes of Evidence, 3 February–6 May 1825*, 220. Cooke's evidence was given on 18 Mar. 1825.

[19] *Freeman's Journal*, 8 Dec. 1813; R. B. McDowell, *Grattan: A Life* (Dublin, 2001), 208.

[20] 'Shiel', *Irish Quarterly Review*, 1 (Sept. 1851), 37–48.

[21] *Dublin Evening Mail*, 4 June 1851.

[22] James Kelly, *That Damn'd Thing called Honour: Duelling in Ireland 1750–1850* (Cork, 1995), 244.

more effectively to the sentiment of a Catholic Association audience.[23] One of O'Connell's most formidable opponents, Lord Stanley, provided an objective judgement of the competing styles of the two men:

Except Grattan, Shiel has no superiority among the speakers of his country. But the perfection of the orator was the weakness of the debater. He could not reply readily, except where the attack was foreseen, and the retort previously prepared ... Hence his inferiority to O'Connell, who cared not one farthing for the judgement of critics and would rather make a bad speech than none.[24]

O'Connell actually boasted of his capacity to be repetitive as opposed to the more fastidious style of Shiel.[25] It should not be thought that O'Connell's followers were blind to his defects. In his diary, a young Catholic supporter, James Keegan, expressed considerable unease about O'Connell's cold treatment of 'excellent men', such as Protestant reformers like Sharman Crawford. Ultimately, however, Keegan felt that O'Connell's services to the Catholic cause outweighed his visible defects.[26] Stanley's judgement is a widely shared one. O'Connell defined himself as the force of movement, compulsion even, within Irish popular politics. His notoriously violent language in denunciation of political enemies was not a weakness but a strength; his words expressed the real anger of the Catholic population. 'People used to say to me,' he once said, ' "O'Connell, you will never get anything so long as you are so violent". What did I do? I became more violent and I succeeded.'[27]

Robert Peel regarded such demagogy with revulsion. He was determined to bring more efficiency into the life of the Irish government, but he was not simply a narrowly focused technocrat. Peel believed that in the past British policy had disrupted Ireland and hindered its industrial development. The surplus labour force of Ireland was forced to stay on the land working smaller and smaller units. All this was only possible because of the widespread reliance on potatoes, which allowed the poor to support their families—the Irish population rose dramatically from 5 million in 1800 to 7 million in 1821. One-third, at least, of the population were so-called 'potato

    [23] John Banim, *The Anglo-Irish of the Nineteenth Century* (London, 1828), ii. 154–72. The Woodstock text (Poole, Washington, DC) of the 1973 edition has a fine introduction by John Kelly.
    [24] J. R. Vincent (ed.), *Disraeli, Derby and the Conservative Party: Journals and Memoirs of Edward Henry, Lord Stanley 1849–1869* (Hassocks, 1978), entry for 2 June 1854, p. 68.
    [25] W. Thomas McCullagh, *Shiel's Memoirs*, vol. 1 (1855), 150, for the comparison, see also vol. 2, p. 86, for evidence of Shiel's 'startling reserve'.
    [26] W. Clare (ed.), *A Young Irishman's Diary 1836–47: Being Extracts from the Early Journal of James Keegan* (March, 1928), 24 Dec. 1841, p. 50.
    [27] Lecky, *Leaders of Public Opinion*, ii. 736.

people', dependent on the crop.[28] It would appear, too, that, while Ireland experienced a rise in average income in the decades leading up to the famine of 1846–50, the rise coexisted with a deterioration in the socio-economic circumstances of the Irish poor, especially cottiers and labourers.[29] In the decades from the 1780s to the 1820s Irish population grew at a faster rate than any other country in western or northern Europe. This produced deepening poverty and distress, and competition for access (on favourable or, indeed, on any terms) to the vital resource of land, producing acute social tension, and 'erupting at regular intervals' into 'episodes of agrarian protest, disorder and violence'.[30] There was also the complication of sectarian disturbance associated with the role of the Orange Order.

Within the establishment, however, Orangeism was an issue which could hardly be ignored. The *Dublin Journal*, on 25 June 1813, lamented the continuing influence of 'Burke and the other nominal Protestants'. The lament was not without objective basis. Sir William Cusack Smith was asked in September 1813 to provide a report for the Irish executive on the state of party feeling in the North. Cusack Smith produced a careful analysis, which was, in fact, an extension of Edmund Burke's analysis in his *Hercules Langrishe* pamphlet of 1792. Like Burke, Cusack Smith focused in on the loyalty of the 'vulgar classes' on the Protestant side, so different, he claimed, from the 'loyalty of gentlemen'. This was the problem of the Ascendancy's democratic tail, so shrewdly noted by Burke; Cusack Smith extended the analysis, implying that violent anti-Catholicism within the Protestant lower classes was a displacement of a subversive emotion, 'a rebellious and insurrectionary propensity gone astray ... turbulent, bigoted, riotous and affronting, very saucy, and overbearing, almost proud of transgression'.[31] Cusack Smith was speaking with deep personal knowledge of rural violence and sectarianism.[32]

[28] Cormac Ó Grada, *Ireland: A New Economic History 1780–1939* (Oxford, 1994), 701; L. Clarkson and M. Crawford, *A History of Food and Nutrition in Ireland, 1500–2002* (Oxford, 2002), 87.

[29] Joel Mokyr and Cormac Ó Grada, 'Poor and Getting Poorer? Living Standards in Ireland Before the Famine', *Economic History Review*, 2 (1988), 211; Clarkson and Crawford, *A History of Food and Nutrition*, 87. But see also Frank Geary and Tom Stark, 'Trends in Real Wages During the Industrial Revolution: A View from Across the Irish Sea', *Economic History Review*, 2: 21 (May 2004), 388.

[30] Gearóid Ó Tuathaigh, 'Amhlaoibh Ó Súilleabháin as Historical Witness: An Historiographical Perspective', in Liam P. Ó Murchú, *Cinnlae Amaloibh uí Shúileabháin*, Irish Texts Society, Cumann na Scríbheann nGaedhilge, subsidiary series 14 (Dublin, 2004), 2.

[31] 'On the State of Catholics and Protestants in the North of Ireland, 4 September 1813', in Lady Augusta Gregory (ed.), *Mr Gregory's Letter-Box 1813–1835* (Gerrard's Cross, 1981), 32–3.

[32] Brian Griffin, *Sources for the Study of Crime in Ireland 1801–1911* (Dublin, 2005), 83.

Life at the bottom of Irish rural society was often grim indeed: solace came in part from an oath-bound agrarian conspiracy (Ribbonism), fuelled with millennarian hopes of delivery, perhaps at the hand of the French. Gregory rehearsed a government intelligence agent's report to Peel on 20 April 1815:

The Ribbon system, which has now become so general, has, he says, two objects: the first Extirpation of Heretics, which arises from religious hatred, but the second and more powerful is the possession of Protestant property when the present owners are disposed of. The thirst for the property of others has excited the fear of even the middling class of Catholics, and prevented them associating with Ribbonmen, so long as they apprehend that when the poor get possession of Protestant lands, if they are not sufficient to satisfy them, they will help themselves without any religious system, under the circumstances, he does not think any alarming Insurrection can break out.[33]

The same agent did report in June that there were links between Napoleon and prominent Irish Catholic leaders.[34] But on 18 June one of the Irish Parliament alumni, Arthur Wellesley, the old Dublin friend of the Parnell and Castlereagh families, defeated Napoleon at Waterloo.[35] In the same month a tiny vessel, driven by steam against tide and wind, crossed the Irish Sea.[36] At the very moment when the French threat was eclipsed, Ireland was drawn physically closer to England.

But even with the Napoleonic threat removed, Robert Peel's assessment of Ireland remained essentially pessimistic. The population growth of the country was perceived to be out of control: 'In England, marriage is powerfully operated against by want of victuals ... the advantages of making love on an empty stomach are incalculable and peculiar to Ireland.'[37] The willingness of the Catholic population to be tacitly complicit in agrarian outrage constituted a sharp condemnation of the moral inadequacies of the Catholic priesthood. Peel sent his Irish friend John Wilson Croker, Secretary to the Admiralty from 1809 to 1830, a copy of a letter of admonishment, written by a priest to a member of his flock whom he suspected of giving evidence of agrarian crime to the authorities. Peel sardonically described it as 'an admirable specimen of the purposes for which the priests of Ireland exert their spiritual authority'.[38]

---

[33] Mr Gregory's Letter-Box, 59.   [34] Ibid. 63.   [35] Ibid. 63.

[36] Desmond Keenan, The Grail of Catholic Emancipation, 1793–1829 (Philadelphia, 2002), 253.

[37] Edward Dubois, My Pocket Book ... To be Called the 'Stranger in Ireland' in 1805 (London, 1808), 70–1.

[38] Louis F. Jennings (ed.), Correspondence and Diaries of the Rt. Hon. John Wilson Croker (London, 1884), i. 90.

In 1814 W. S. Mason published in Dublin *A Statistical Account or Parochial Survey in Ireland*, and respectfully dedicated it to Robert Peel. The method of this work was to ask the local Protestant clergy to provide a detailed analysis of their loyalties. It was particularly suggestive in its account of the sectarian realities of Northern Irish society. The Revd Alexander Ross, rector of Dungiven, produced the analysis which attracted the most interesting comment. Ross described two distinct communities, the 'Scotch' and the 'Irish':

> Both are industrious ... but the industry of the Scotch is steady, patient and directed with great foresight ... that of the Irish is rash, adventurous and variable. The inferiority of the native inhabitants is not to be ascribed either to their religion or to the effect of restraining laws. It may, with more justice, be ascribed to remaining barbarous tastes and habits derived from their ancestors, which all the arts of civilisation have not been able entirely to remedy or overcome.[39]

The *Newry Magazine* commented, in a striking review: "Thus, in the parish of Dungiven, lines of distinction seem to be drawn between the portions of the people, so strong as they ever can be found among nations separated from one another by surrounding seas.'[40]

At the end of 1816 Peel was fully aware of the sectarian and brutal realities of Irish society, which led to much violence. But, he added, this agrarian crime seemed to be losing its political meaning. 'There is, however, as little disaffection towards the state as I have ever heard of, and less than I can remember'.[41] The best hope was loyal, hard-working Protestant Ulster, but even here there was a serious flaw. The loyalism of the Orange Order was desirable—but the Order had a distressingly marked tendency to involve itself in violent clashes with the Catholic community. Peel explained the problem in 1822: 'I wish to maintain in force those laws by which Roman Catholics are excluded from any material share in the direction of public affairs, but for this very reason I ought to feel, and do feel, anxious that the mortification inseparable from exclusion should not be increased by any irritating ceremonies.'[42] But 'irritating ceremonies' were a significant part of the North's political life: they were in large measure the *raison d'être* of Orangeism.

In the late summer–autumn of 1816 there occurred the burning alive of the entire family of Edward Lynch; these Co. Louth murders formed the basis for the chilling exposé in William Carleton's *Wildgoose Lodge*: the

---

[39] *A Statistical Account*, 307–8.   [40] *Newry Magazine* (1815), 52.
[41] Raymond Murray, *The Burning of Wild Goose Lodge: Ribbonism in Louth: Murder and the Gallows* (Armagh, 2005), 132.
[42] Brian Jenkins, *Henry Goulburn 1784–1856: A Political Biography* (Liverpool, 1996), 153.

most terrifying Irish short story of the nineteenth century, based, at least in part, on the personal experience of the author.[43] A story, above all, of horror, but also of how a Ribbon leader could impose his will on hesitant followers by slowly dragging them over a moral precipice, appealing all the while to group loyalty. Carleton himself had taken the Ribbon oath and was uniquely placed to convey such a sentiment at work.[44] Carleton ended his tale—'if tale it can be called', he said—with a graphic footnote.

This tale of terror is, unfortunately, too true. The scene of hellish murder detailed in it lies in Wildgoose Lodge, in the county of Louth, within about four miles of Carrickmacross and nine of Dundalk ... The language of the story is partly fictitious; but the facts are pretty closely such as were developed during the trial of the murder.

The local peasantry, seeing the hanging corpse of the ringleader, frequently proclaimed 'Poor Paddy'—Carleton concluded his story with the words: 'A gloomy fact which speaks volumes.'[45] Carleton even took it upon himself, ten years later, to write to Peel, showing that the Catholic clergy were condoning, or at least tolerating, Ribbon societies; but Peel—as his letter to Croker showed—needed no such instruction.[46]

To preserve the peace in such a difficult, conflict-ridden society, Peel, in 1814, convinced a reluctant Lord Liverpool of the need for two pieces of special legislation. Under the Peace Preservation Act the Lord-Lieutenant was permitted to proclaim a district as being in a state of disturbance. Another element of Peel's 1814 legislation had a more long-term significance. The Lord-Lieutenant was given the power of appointing a force of special constables, under the command of a paid magistrate, to assist in policing the proclaimed area. Each barony traditionally had had a force of twenty, often rather elderly, men; Peel now raised the salary for the police to allow the recruitment of more able and younger men, thus providing a new source of job opportunity mostly for Catholic ex-soldiers.[47] The first 'Peelers' were essentially 'flying squads', intended to put down outbreaks of civil disorder and prosecute crime.[48] By the beginning of 1825, and following some further refinement of the legislation by Goulburn[49]

[43] Benedict Kiely, *Poor Scholar: A Study of William Carleton* (Dublin, 1987), 38.

[44] Keenan, *The Grail of Catholic Emancipation*, 276; Julian Moynahan, *Anglo-Irish: The Literary Imagination in a Hyphenated Culture* (Princeton, 1995), 62.

[45] William Carleton, *Traits and Stories of the Irish Peasantry*, vol. 2 (London, 1844; repr. Gerrard's Cross, 1990), 362.

[46] Marjorie Howes, 'William "Carleton's Literary Religion"', in James H. Murphy (ed.), *Evangelicals and Catholics in Nineteenth-Century Ireland* (Dublin, 2005), 110.

[47] For vigorous defence of his policy, see Peel to Sir G. F. Hill, 8 Oct. 1816, PRONI MIC 593/D/642/31.

[48] Elizabeth Malcolm, *The Irish Policeman 1822–1922: A Life* (Dublin, 2006), 21.

[49] Jenkins, *Goulburn*, 146.

in 1822, Ireland had, in theory, a professional police, consisting of some 4,500 men distributed across the country:[50] ambiguously directed by local magistrates, yet also regulated by central government. Policing apart, 'Peelism' in office avoided dramatic initiatives. The administration of the country was more efficient—the worst excesses of jobbery and patronage were checked—but in the end the improvement of Ireland was considered to be a long-term task dependent on the development of more widespread prosperity and educational attainment. There was a place for compassion. In 1817 the potato crop failed again: Peel authorized an unusual amount of state action with the object of alleviating the suffering.[51]

Hunger was not, however, in a direct and immediate way, the trigger for agrarian revolt, which would typically take the form of threatening letters, arson attacks, and assassination attempts. Certainly, in 1821 local newspaper editors asked themselves the question why were the disturbances to be found 'in the richest parts of Ireland', while 'the poorest counties such as Mayo experienced peace and tranquillity'.[52] When famine reappeared in 1822, South Cork, which was hard hit, was relatively quiet, while North Cork, affected by a fall in agricultural prices but not actually starvation, became the centre of a new form of agrarian terrorism, the Rockite movement.[53] In fact, O'Connell himself believed that a revolution of rising expectations had hit a blockage, due in significant measure to a change of monetary policy:

The present disturbances in the country were indeed of a highly disturbing description. It was notorious, however, that the causes of these disturbances were local and such as no activity could control. The causes were attributable in a great measure to the drop in the value of land and the sudden change from a paper to a monied currency.[54]

Rockism became the new descriptive term for agrarian militancy. In March 1822 William Stawel of Doneraile, Co. Cork, received this notice: 'That in consequence of a new Code of Laws recently given out by General John Rock, Regulator Legislator General of Ireland, it is unlawful for any gentleman to hold any more lands than that which immediately adjoins his dwelling residence.' Failure to respect this threat, it was stated explicitly,

[50] G. Broecker, *Rural Disorder and Police Reform in Ireland 1812–36* (London, 1970), 60; D. Keenan, *Ireland 1800–50* (Philadelphia, 2001), 115.

[51] Brian Jenkins, 'The Chief Secretary', in D. G. Boyce and Alan O'Day (eds.), *Defenders of the Union* (London, 2001), 60.

[52] *Leinster Journal* and *Mayo Constitution*, quoted in *Freeman's Journal*, 5 Dec. 1821.

[53] Shinsuke Katsuka, 'The Rockite Movement in County Cork in the Early 1820s', *Irish Historical Studies*, 33: 131 (May 2003), 286; David Dickson, *Old World Colony: Cork and South Munster* (Cork, 2005), 489.

[54] *Freeman's Journal*, 12 Dec. 1821.

would lead to death.[55] Until his arrest in July 1823, this Rock, more usually known as Captain Rock, was David Nagle, a dashing member of an influential Catholic family—dressed in a blue coat with a sash and a sword, and wearing a military cap with a big white feather. The Rockite movement achieved a genuine intensity, to the extent that senior figures in government fearfully recalled 1798. It had an elaborated form of committee structure. Rockism tapped in not simply to agrarian grievance, but to broader sectarian and political themes, the Rockites taking the time, for example, to side with Daniel O'Connell on the veto controversy, rather than liberal Protestants—unlike Plunket, who was explicitly mentioned—who offered support for Catholic emancipation if accompanied by the veto.[56] This was, after all, no spasmodic eruption: Sir Henry Parnell pointed out in 1823 that, out of the preceding thirty-one years, no less than twenty-six had been years of actual insurrection or, at least, serious disturbance.[57]

O'Connell was clearly the focus of emotions which he could not himself hope to control. Personally, he despised the 'Pastorini' prophecies, which predicted the annihilation of Protestantism by the end of 1825. Yet he was undoubtedly considered by many to be the instrument of such an annihilation. In remote villages in many parts of Ireland, with strange but threatening symbolism, lighted turf was carried from cabin to cabin, greatly alarming local Protestants.[58] By 1823 an 'intensely political peasantry, volatile, disaffected, sectarianized, conscious of its strength in numbers, and thoroughly aware of its grievances, had developed in varying degrees from one end of Ireland to the other'.[59] William Carleton's short story 'The Poor Scholar' catches the mentality of popular Catholic consciousness: softened a little in this case by a sense of personalized humanity.

An doesn't Pastorhini say it? Sure whin Twenty-Five comes, we'll have our own agin: the right will overcome the might—the bottomless pit will be locked—ay, double boulted, if St Pether gets the keys, for he's the very boy that will accommodate the heretics wid a warm corner; and yet, father, there's many of them that myself ud put a good word for, afther all.[60]

Charlotte Elizabeth Tonna's *Irish Recollections*, first published as *Personal Recollections* in 1841, convey some of the impact of 'Pastorini' and Rockism

[55] S. R. Gibbons, *Captain Rock: Knight Errant: The Threatening Letters of Pre-Famine Ireland* (Dublin, 2004), 147.

[56] Katsuka, *The Rockite Movement*, 292.   [57] Lecky, *Leaders*, ii. 82.

[58] Gibbons, *Captain Rock*, 35. For Pastorini, see James S. Donnelly Jr., 'Pastorini and Captain Rock: Millennianism and Sectarianism in the Rockite Movement 1821–4', in Samuel Clark and J. S. Donnelly Jr. (eds.), *Irish Peasants: Violence and Political Unrest 1780–1914* (Manchester, 1983).

[59] Bartlett, *Fall and Rise*, 311.

[60] 'The Poor Scholar', in Carleton, *Traits and Stories of the Irish Peasantry*, ii. 258.

on a fearful Irish Protestantism. It is important to understand that this growing sense of threat was visible and striking. A guest at Vicarsfield, the Knocktopher parsonage of the Revd Dr Hamilton, Tonna was asked to look out of the drawing-room window at midday. She could see clearly 'a body of Rockites to the number of 40, well-mounted, formidably armed with cross-belts and cartridge-boxes, leisurely walking their horses within less than a quarter of a mile from the house, for the purpose of intimidation'.[61] To make matters worse, Irish landlords, already culturally separated from the bulk of tenantry by a difference of religion, spent little on improvement before the famine; in consequence, no legitimization of their role took place.

But it is important to note that within the peasantry there was also a pattern of violent conflict. At the top of the social structure there were approximately 50,000 rich to 100,000 'snug' farmers, the mean size of whose holdings was 80 and 50 acres respectively; together with the 10,000 or so landlords, they cultivated roughly half the land and controlled access to much of the rest. In the middle of the structure were 250,000 family farmers, the mean size of whose holdings was about 20 acres, and they usually did not employ labour from outside the family. But at the bottom there was a vast sea of humanity: 1.3 million poor peasants and labourers. Particularly in those regions where the social stratification was marked by sharp cleavages between the better-off farmers and the swollen ranks of the poor, conflict was often between farmers and labourers on the one side and farmers on the other. The more comfortable Catholic farmers were frequently the victims of agrarian violence, and the labourers, cottiers, and small occupiers of land, totalling some 590,000, were its main perpetrators.[62]

To problems of such depth and severity, O'Connell had no real answer. This is hardly surprising: there was no political answer available in the 1820s. Contemporaries feared that some awful calamity lay ahead. Population constantly pressed up to the 'limits of subsistence'. 'The next generation must either be supported by increased supplies', or suffer one of 'those awful visitations', which proportion the number of people according to 'their resources'.[63] Such agrarian conditions inevitably generated agrarian crime. There is no doubt that O'Connell hated agrarian crime and had a particular

---

[61] Patrick Maume (ed.), Charlotte Elizabeth Tonna, *Irish Recollections* (Dublin, 2004), 43.

[62] Sean Connolly, *Priests and People in Pre-Famine Ireland*, 2nd edn. (Dublin, 2001), 224; J. S. Donnelly, 'The Social Composition of Agrarian Nineteenth-Century Ireland: The Case of the Carders and Caravats 1813–1816', in P. J. Corish, *Radicals, Rebels and Establishment: Historical Studies*, 15 (Belfast, 1983), 151–70, for an excellent discussion.

[63] *A Letter to a British MP in the year 1825 by an Irish Magistrate* (London, 1825), 47.

distaste for those who organized it.[64] When approached by the 'Ribbon' leaders in December 1813 and asked for his advice, he replied publicly: 'It is the common lot of all secret societies to grow more evil every day.'[65] The surviving correspondence concerning the management of O'Connell's own estate in the early 1820s makes it clear that he and the peasants were ranged upon different sides in a land war.[66] O'Connell himself was to lose Catholic friends and political allies to the violence of the secret societies.[67]

Nevertheless, the fact remains that O'Connellism as a popular force—as opposed to O'Connell himself—inevitably had its radical dimension.[68] O'Connell, therefore, had to embrace to some degree the cause of land reform. He told the Catholic Association on 21 July 1824: 'Considering the degraded and neglected condition of the Irish peasant, perhaps a better atonement could not be made for the past suffering than by making him a proprietor of the soil to a certain extent—that is by giving him a right to be supported out of its produce.' He defended this vague prescription, which had, as he was aware, little hope of practical application. If they knew that the landlord had to support the peasantry in this way, they would not 'then have that incentive to lawless assemblies'.[69] But as Lecky shrewdly observed, O'Connell only really felt strongly religious disabilities rather than agrarian social injustices as such.[70] He felt this way, of course, because the religious disabilities applied to him personally, while the social injustices did not. But how best to deal with these religious disabilities? Who, in the British political class, could they rely upon?

At the beginning of 1815, at a meeting at Lord Fingall's home, Daniel O'Connell and Lord Fingall asserted that Pitt had not been a sincere friend of Catholic claims; Richard Lalor Shiel insisted, however, that Pitt had been, and Lord Castlereagh was still, a genuine supporter of emancipation.[71] O'Connell now began to define himself as leader of the section of Catholic opinion which would not tolerate any talk of a 'veto',

---

[64] Lecky, *Leaders*, ii. 49–54.   [65] *Freeman's Journal*, 10 Dec. 1813.

[66] Oliver MacDonagh, *States of Mind* (London, 1983), 43.

[67] Michael Beames, *Peasants and Power: The Whiteboy Movements and their Control in Pre-Famine Ireland* (Brighton, 1983), 194–7.

[68] K. Theodore Hoppen, 'Riding a Tiger: Daniel O'Connell: Reform and Popular Politics in Ireland 1800–47', in T. Blanning and P. Wende (eds.), *Reform in Great Britain and Germany 1780–1850* (Oxford, 1979), 120–3; Fintan Lane, *In Search of Thomas Sheehan: Radical Politics in Cork, 1824–36*, Maynooth Studies in Local History, 37 (Dublin, 2001), 47–60.

[69] *Proceedings of the Catholic Association in Dublin 1823–25* (London, 1828), 474.

[70] Lecky, *Leaders*, ii. 54. 'Nothing is more remarkable in the speeches of Grattan than the almost entire absence of those agrarian questions which have in modern days become so prominent … The early speeches of O'Connell were, in this respect, not very different from those of Grattan.'

[71] Keenan, *The Grail of Catholic Emancipation*, 246–7.

not exactly a Dromgoole man, but leaning to Dromgoole's side of the argument. In the absence of any real prospect of reform, O'Connell's became the winning position. A decided majority of Irish Catholics rejected any extension of state control over their Church. The issue was presented as the maintenance of the freedom of the Church for which so many Irish Catholics had suffered: to accept the notion of the veto was to show indifference to the trauma of the past. The fact that the Papacy might be said to support the veto, or that similar arrangements existed in other European countries, was irrelevant; Ireland had suffered too much at the hands of the British state to allow it any role in her religious affairs.

There was also a more local and pressing explanation for Catholic attitudes. In the aftermath of the victory over Napoleon in 1815 (an event easily presented by evangelicals as a providential sign of the divine favours enjoyed by the Protestant cause), a new impetus was given to Protestant conversion work in Catholic Ireland. Catholic leaders felt themselves to be under pressure and reacted against the claims of what came to be known as the 'New' or 'Second' Reformation. O'Connell made himself the focus of the defensive emotion thus generated, and his strategies became increasingly acceptable to the Catholic hierarchy and clergy: the consequence was, as Dr Irene Whelan has noted, 'the Catholic Irish were educated into citizenship in an atmosphere charged with the rhetoric of religious warfare'.[72]

The point was forcibly made in 1817, that it was certainly possible to enlist Burke on O'Connell's side on the veto controversy.[73] Never, in Burke's well-documented view, were the members of one religious sect fit to appoint pastors to another. Nevertheless, O'Connell's stand cost him the support of some moderate members of the Catholic gentry—a pro-veto minority, headed by Sir Edmund Bellew, Lord Trimleston, and Shiel, seceded from the Catholic Committee in 1815. Shiel insisted for several years that O'Connell's 'fiery vapours on the veto' did not speak the 'sentiments of the Roman Catholic body', but he could never prove his case. Encouraged, however, by Shiel and his speech, in May 1817 Grattan again brought the Catholic question before Parliament. He insisted: "The principle of our law is bad, it attaints the child for the crime of the father and makes discord and division of the foundation of your policy.'[74] Grattan

---

[72] Irene Whelan, *The Bible-War in Ireland: The 'Second Reformation' and the Polarisation of Protestant–Catholic Relations, 1800–40* (Dublin, 2005), 265–71.

[73] *Observations on the Laws and Ordinances which Exist in Foreign States Relative to the Religious Concerns of the Roman Catholic Subjects*, by a British Roman Catholic (London, 1817), 25; Sir John Hippisley, *The Substance of Additional Observations Intended to have been Delivered in the House of Commons in the Debate on the Petition of the Roman Catholics of Ireland on the 13th and 14th of May 1805* (London, 1806), 116.

[74] *Belfast News Letter*, 17 May 1817.

was supported by a glittering array of leading figures. Canning, a future Prime Minister, insisted that conciliation in Ireland was the right policy: to open the door of the House of Commons 'to Catholic representatives would nullify the mischief they had created'.[75]

Castlereagh, who, after his triumph at the Congress of Vienna in 1814–15, now adopted the mantle of an international statesman,[76] was the most expansive and interesting in his reasoning:[77] 'Whoever cast his eye over the actual state of Europe would see that Rome had no longer the power to convulse which she formerly abused. We are now living in very different days.'[78] Drawing on his experience as a highly skilled negotiator at the Congress of Vienna, he noted: 'In the late Treaty for the establishment of peace in Europe, religion never was the subject of discussion for a moment (hear, hear).' He supported Catholic emancipation because it would give Ireland 'mild temper' and 'internal repose', and allow Protestant and Catholic to 'learn to know each other' within the framework of the Constitution; in a strikingly effective passage he insisted: 'He was confident that the narrow system of law by which Ireland was governed could never be the basis of a permanent mode of government.'

The Prime Minister and the Irish Chief Secretary were not, however, to be moved. Lord Liverpool, the Irish Prime Minister, insisted: 'The Constitution was inseparably connected with the Protestant Church; it was a connexion which pervaded every part of our system ... If these concessions were made, Parliament would no longer be a Protestant Parliament.'[79] Robert Peel, the Irish Chief Secretary, resolutely supported this position—sincere Catholics, he argued, inevitably sought the overthrow of the established Protestant religion. He presumably had Dr Dromgoole in mind. This was Peel in 'Orange Peel' mode; embittered, perhaps, by sharp personal clashes with O'Connell which had almost led to a duel, he was now saying that he could *never* support Catholic emancipation.[80] This was a classic statement of 'Protestant' principles, based, above all, on the

---

[75] *Belfast News Letter*, 17 May 1817.

[76] Paul W. Schroeder, *The Transformation of European Politics 1763–1848* (Oxford, 1996); for a positive appraisal of the Congress of Vienna and Castlereagh's role, pp. 574–82.

[77] Sir Henry Parnell was a strong believer in the sincerity of Castlereagh's support for the Catholic cause. B. McDermott (ed.), *The Catholic Question in Ireland and England 1798–1822: The Papers of Denys Scully* (Dublin, 1998), Parnell to C. Mahon, 17 June 1815, p. 555.

[78] *Belfast News Letter*, 16 May 1817.   [79] Ibid.

[80] Robert Carl Shipkey, *Robert Peel's Irish Policy* (New York, 1985), 192; T. J. Jenkins, *Sir Robert Peel* (London, 1999), 14; J. C. D. Clark, *English Society 1660–1832: Religion, Ideology and Politics During the Ancien Regime* (Cambridge, 2000), 517–18.

assumption that the religion of the British people was intimately connected with the progress of the nation. One anonymous pamphleteer tackled Peel's reasoning. Peel's boast was quoted: 'That under the Constitution which we have derived from our ancestors, we have enjoyed more liberty, we have acquired more glory, we possess more character and power than has hitherto fallen to the lot of any other country on the globe.' But the writer of the pamphlet slipped in a challenge: 'If you have enjoyed more liberty than other nations, then share it with a sister country that pants for the same enjoyment.'[81]

Grattan died in London on 4 June 1820; in a most interesting deathbed comment, he told his son that the conflict with Castlereagh over the union was a thing of the past. Going further, he praised Castlereagh's loyalty to Ireland and declared that his continued political influence was vital, both to Ireland and the cause of Catholic emancipation.[82] Wolfe Tone's old friend and Emmet's prosecutor, William Conyngham Plunket, slipped easily into his place as the leading voice of Irish liberal patriotism.

Bringing the matter once again before Parliament in May 1821, Plunket's celebrated and impressive speech argued:

Do I mean to say that the established church is not in any danger? No. But I say that the danger, whatever it is, exists at this moment. It consists in the great disproportion between the population and the establishment — it lies in the narrowness of that basis — I defy the art of men to find any other remedy than that the interests of the population are connected with the state.[83]

Robert Peel's reply acknowledged the effectiveness of Plunket's speech; furthermore, Peel went out of his way to praise the exemplary liberal patriotism of Grattan.[84] But Peel did not accept that emancipation would bring in a new era of social harmony in Ireland; he also pointed out that the great Burke — when he opposed the repeal of the Test and Corporations Act of 1791 — had seen something in the temper of that constituency which rightly barred it from eligibility for office. On 17 April 1821, however,

---

[81] Anon., *A Letter to the Rt. Hon. Robert Peel: An Answer to his Speech on the Catholic Question delivered in the House of Commons, May 19 1817* (London, 1817), 67.

[82] Geoghegan, *Castlereagh*, 4.

[83] *Hansard*, 2nd ser., vol. 5, 20 Feb. 1821, col. 960. A Rockite catechism found near Shanagolden in 1821 denounced Plunket's 'hellish observation', Katsuka, 'The Rockite Movement', 292.

[84] *Hansard*, 20 Feb. 1821, col. 980. Even if he did not, as W. O'Connor Morris claims in *Ireland 1798–1898*, actually abandon his previous views or soften his personal dislike for Plunket. Was this, nonetheless, a neglected moment in the 'ripening' of Robert Peel? See Boyd Hilton, 'The Ripening of Robert Peel', in M. Bentley (ed.), *Public and Private Doctrine: Essays in British History Presented to Maurice Cowling* (Cambridge, 1993).

Plunket's Bill—subject to a government right of veto on appointment of bishops and deans—was defeated in the House of Lords by 159 votes to 20, having passed the Commons.

'A DIFFERENT HUE': A NEW TONE FOR THE IRISH ADMINISTRATION

The vote in the Commons nonetheless seemed to imply a significant shift in British political attitudes. In August 1821 the new King George IV visited Ireland. It was the first time that an English king had come to Ireland without an army. The Earl of Fingall presented the Catholic bishops to him; the Earl then presented Daniel O'Connell, who was graciously received. Lord Castlereagh reminded Archbishop Troy that he had not changed in twenty years and asked to be introduced to the other bishops. Something was clearly in the wind. At the end of December 1821 Richard, Marquess Wellesley (1760–1842), was sworn in as Lord-Lieutenant in Dublin Castle. Wellesley had in his own mind a definite agenda: 'Correct the notion, which has long unhappily prevailed in Ireland, that there was one law for the rich and another for the poor, one law for the Protestant and another for the Catholic.'[85] Castlereagh wrote to him, offering support in any pro-Catholic programme.[86] Richard Wellesley attempted to exploit his family's successes as imperial soldiers and statesmen: after all, for Irish Protestants the Wellesleys were the ultimate models of success. On 9 January 1822 the Lord-Lieutenant said of his brother Arthur at a Dublin banquet:

There does not exist on the face of the earth a man more warmly and firmly attached to, and fond of, this country than the Duke of Wellington. He knows—he feels that the greater part of his achievements have been accomplished by Irishmen—and he glows in the feeling. It is his peculiar pride to be an Irishman.[87]

Lord Redesdale, true to form, wrote to him, warning against reformist illusions.[88] Wellesley was not only the first Irishman to hold the post,

---

[85] British Library, Papers relating to Irish affairs 1782–1837, Ad MS 381603, sf131, Notes on State of Ireland upon Lord Wellesley's arrival in December 1821.

[86] L. S. Benjamin (ed.), *The Life and Correspondence of Richard Colley Wellesley, Marquess Wellesley*, 2 vols. (London, 1914), 144–4.

[87] R. R. Pearce, *Memoirs of the Most Noble Richard Marquess Wellesley* (London, 1846), iii. 327.

[88] PRONI T 3030/10/21, Redesdale to Wellesley, 8 Dec. 1821. Wellesley's celebrated brother, in 1821, had delivered a notable rebuff to the Orange Order when he refused an invitation to join that body. 'I confess that I do object to belong to a society preferring attachment to the Throne and Constitution of these realms [from] which ... a large

but he was also 'an open advocate of Catholic claims'. Wellesley made it clear that he came to 'administer and not to change the law'. Nevertheless, Wellesley's advent seemed to mark 'a considerable step to progress'.[89]

William Saurin, Irish Attorney-General for the past fifteen years, the symbol of inflexible anti-Catholicism, was dismissed, his post given to W. C. Plunket.[90] To give some reassurance to 'Protestant' opinion, Henry Goulburn, a committed anti-Catholic, was appointed Chief Secretary. Daniel O'Connell, despite his sharp dislike for Goulburn, attended Wellesley's first levee and was received with marked favour.[91] O'Connell was clearly pleased by these developments: 'A change of men is to a certain extent a change of measure; a new colour, a different hue, is given to that great chameleon "the administration" if not absolutely "green", [it] is "less glaringly Orange".'[92] O'Connell can only have been further pleased by Saurin's bitter response to his dismissal. Even Goulburn gained some credit for himself by his relatively humane response—following Peel in 1817—to the partial failure of the potato crop in 1822, when the government once again intervened to save lives and feed the suffering.[93] Parliament granted some £300,000, while subscriptions raised in Great Britain reached £350,000—local subscriptions reached £150,000.[94] Yet, there were those who were distinctly unimpressed. On 16 February 1822 Henry Stratford Persse reported to his sons: 'English generosity has interposed and sent relief, and what relief is it? Some of the food that, in our poverty early this season, we were obliged to send away, even though we knew we would want it in the spring.'[95] It was the beginning of an argument—that Ireland should not export food during a famine—which was to take more dramatic shape in the 1840s.

proportion of His Majesty's subjects must be excluded, many of them as loyal men as exist, and having as much attachment to the Constitution. The objection is natural from one who was born in the country in which a large proportion of people are Roman Catholic, and ... who has never found that abstracted from other circumstances, the religious persuasion of individuals ... affected their feelings of loyalty.' Gerard Morgan, 'The Duke of Wellington', *Irish Times*, 29 Aug. 2003.

[89] Lecky, *Leaders,*, ii. 2, 42.

[90] David Plunket, *The Life, Letters and Speeches of Lord Plunket*, edited by his grandson (London, 1867).

[91] Goulburn was to distinguish himself by turning down an application for citizenship from Charles Bianconi, an Italian Catholic transport entrepreneur. See Daniel O'Connell, *Observations on Corn Laws* (Dublin, 1840), 10.

[92] *Proceedings of the Catholic Association in Dublin 1823–25* (London, 1828), 31 July 1824, p. 474.

[93] Jenkins, 'The Chief Secretary', in Boyce and O'Day, *Defenders of the Union*, 60.

[94] Pearce, *Wellesley*, iii. 334 n.

[95] James L. Pethica and James C. Roy (eds.), 'To my Darling Boys', 10 July 1822, *'To the Land of the Free from the Land of Slaves': Henry Stratford Persse's Letters from Galway to America, 1821–32* (Cork, 1999), 95.

Saurin refused to depart the scene gracefully. He declined to take the peerage offered, and fulminated against the new order from the sidelines. A sense of personal repudiation led him to refuse also a lofty position on the bench. Instead, Saurin polemicized against his old masters, who had so churlishly thrown him over. In Saurin's analysis, 'two counties were now in open insurrection',[96] whilst O'Connell, he noted, who had done so much to 'loosen every bond of society',[97] was given 'marked and flattering treatment' at the first *levée* held by Wellesley, on a 'crowded' and 'brilliant' occasion.

Sir William Cusack Smith sensed the new mood and felt it safe to publish a pamphlet denouncing Saurin, an old enemy, who had been a leading opponent of the union. Cusack Smith now embodied the moderate reformist wing of the Irish establishment, which felt increasingly self-confident. Burke was cited as a 'high authority'[98] several times throughout the text. Saurin, it was said, was wrong to see the Whiteboys as a Catholic conspiracy; they were essentially a class-based phenomenon.[99] Anyway, Saurin had failed to suppress them when he had the power.[100] As to Saurin's complaints about Wellesley's undue warmth in greeting O'Connell, Cusack Smith noted savagely: 'An ill-bred person mistakes the ordinary courtesy of a polished nobleman for a peculiarly flattering reception.'[101] He acknowledged that O'Connell's language was sometimes extreme, but added: 'They [the Catholics] would not deserve to share our honours, if they were not stung by their exclusion.'[102] After all, Saurin had played a part in generating this alienation: 'The Catholic mind is sore, and after having contributed much to make it sore (aye even the 15 years of Mr Saurin's power) we are surprised and angry that what is sore is more available than what is sound.'[103]

Cusack Smith also reiterated his hostility to the Orange institution: 'What have I to say of that institution? Of several of its members, nothing ill; of itself nothing, less than nothing, good.'[104] Baron Smith's tone—whilst it reflected a long-standing animosity towards both Orangeism in general and Saurin in particular[105] —reflected also the mood of the new establishment. On 12 July 1822 the government repressed the Orange celebrations in Dublin. A response was not slow in coming. When Wellesley was visiting

[96] *First Year of Wellesley's Administration, One Year of the Administration of His Excellency, the Marquis of Wellesley, in Ireland,* by the Rt. Hon. William Saurin, 4th edn. (London, 1823), 30.
[97] Ibid. 36.
[98] *Recent Scenes and Occurrences in Ireland or Animadversions on a Pamphlet, entitled 'One Year of the Administration of the Marquis of Wellesley', in a Letter to a Friend in England,* by Baron Sir William Smith (Dublin, 1823), 30.
[99] Ibid. 3.   [100] Ibid. 4.   [101] Ibid. 34.   [102] Ibid. 69.
[103] Ibid. 71.   [104] Ibid. 181.   [105] Cusack Smith, *Animadversions.*

the theatre on 14 December 1822, a large quart bottle was thrown from the gallery at his head, in what came to be known as the 'bottle riot': populist revenge for the government's efforts to curb provocative public Orange manifestations. This was no trivial incident: R. R. Pearce regarded it as something akin to an assassination attempt: 'It [the bottle] providentially missed its mark, but glanced close to his face. It would very probably have killed him on the spot, had it struck his head, considering the weight of the bottle and the height from which it descended.'[106] Those opposed to Orangeism were delighted. Angered by such a crude challenge, the government increasingly suspected an Orange conspiracy. Plunket made great efforts to uncover it, and was assisted by Peel, now Home Secretary, in the House of Commons. In March 1823 Goulburn introduced the Unlawful Oaths Bill, making it 'an indictable offence to belong to any society bound together by an oath'. 'This, coming from a "no Popery man" as Mr Goulburn is, strikes deeply into [the] Orange', Daniel O'Connell observed with some pleasure.[107] The Orange Order felt it necessary to dissolve and reconstitute itself to keep within the law. In 1824 the annual Twelfth of July parades were cancelled by the Grand Orange Lodge of Dublin. On 29 October 1825 the Lord-Lieutenant married Marianne Peterson, the Catholic widow of a Baltimore merchant: the marriage was solemnized by *both* the Primate of Ireland and by the Roman Catholic Archbishop of Dublin.

These shifts in elite opinion inevitably acted as an encouragement to Catholic mobilization. In August 1823 O'Connell told Thomas Moore that he was aware (through the Catholic bishops) that the 'chiefs' of the 'system of organisation' in the Catholic countryside had intimated that they would turn out for the Lord-Lieutenant against the Orangemen if necessary.[108] The new regime had attracted the supportive interest not just of the Catholic aristocracy and middle classes, but also of the leaders of agrarian militancy. The establishment in 1823 of the Catholic Association slowly transformed the nature of an agitation which, though initially based on a small group of Dublin activists — 'how hard it was to procure the attendance of ten persons at its early meeting'[109]—evolved into a mass movement with organized support throughout the country. 'Since the year 1789 the Catholic population had nearly doubled in number, and it had increased twenty-fold in wealth and respectability,' said Thomas

---

[106] Pearce, *Wellesley*, iii. 369.   [107] Jenkins, *Goulburn*, 157.

[108] Lord John Russell, *Memoirs, Journals and Correspondence of Thomas Moore*, 8 vols. (London, 1853), iv. 117.

[109] The Rt. Hon. Thomas, Lord O'Hagan, *The O'Connell Centenary Address* (Dublin, 1875), 17.

Kirwan in the chair, 'yet the Catholic cause had not been advanced.' The new Association was intended to achieve a much greater unity of purpose.[110]

O'Connell insisted that the Catholic Association be resolutely opposed to Ribbonism: 'There are no greater enemies to Ireland than those who enter into such a system.' There was great concern lest 'any identification of Ribbonmen amongst the collectors of the Catholic rent be used to damage the Association'.[111] O'Connell's remarks here reflect the views of the Catholic hierarchy: Bishop James Warren Doyle of Kildare and Leighlin (JKL) had denounced the wicked 'conspiracy of the Ribbonmen in 1822'.[112] O'Connell had every reason to echo such concerns, because he was dependent on the active support of the Catholic clergy, especially after he decided to fund-raise by means of the Catholic rent.[113]

While O'Connell tapped into the aspirations of the very poor, he did not tap into their pockets, in large measure because there was nothing in them. It was the more prosperous elements in Irish Catholic society—strong farmers, but above all the business and professional elites of the towns—which gave him their financial support. Poorer regions—Connaught and much of Catholic Ulster—lagged well behind Leinster and Munster, provinces which were frequently dotted with nests of relatively prosperous Catholicity.[114] As one angry O'Connellite newspaper editor in Galway protested to his local readership: 'When the great question was questioned throughout the land, and every other county was pouring in those thundering broadsides of rent and eloquence, it is a melancholy fact that your great county sent not in the means of paying the expense of publishing her scanty resolutions.'[115] O'Connell used the money gathered to contest elections, subsidize and even create an O'Connellite press in areas where it was weak, to defend the peasantry in the law courts, and, of course, for electoral purposes. Agrarian terrorism went into decline, and even faction fighters turned away from their traditional antagonisms.[116]

O'Connell became the focus of a massive weight of historic expectation. He was the leader of a novel form of popular politics, but it gained its

[110] *Proceedings of the Catholic Association of Dublin from 13 May 1823 to 15 February 1825* (London, 1825), 24 Jan. 1824, pp. 164, 176.

[111] *Proceedings of the Catholic Association in Dublin 1823–25*, 14 June 1824, p. 392.

[112] Connolly, *Priests and People*, 212.

[113] W. O'Connor Morris, *Ireland 1798–1898*, 94.

[114] Fergus O'Ferrall, *Catholic Emancipation: Daniel O'Connell and the Birth of Irish Democracy, 1820–30* (Dublin, 1985), 165.

[115] *Western Argus* (Galway), 19 Mar. 1830.

[116] Garry Owens, 'A Moral Insurrection: Faction Fighters, Public Demonstrations and the O'Connellite Campaign 1828', *Irish Historical Studies*, 30: 20 (Nov. 1997), 513–41.

strength from the exploitation of a profoundly traditional resentment, quite uncomplicated by any notion of alliance with the liberal Protestant reformist forces in Irish society. O'Connell, who had never visited Down, Londonderry, or Antrim, nor indeed Fermanagh, Armagh, or Donegal,[117] was remarkably tactless in his attitude towards Presbyterian liberalism, now organized around the *Northern Whig* newspaper, founded in 1824 and strongly in favour of Catholic emancipation. He seems to have had little understanding of the size or importance of the northern Presbyterian community, and certainly no serious interest in its history or evolution. According to O'Connell's analysis of the events of 1798:

They [the northern Presbyterians] delivered some of the Catholics from the paths of duty, and when they made offenders of them, they were the first not only to abandon the dupes of their own actions, but to enter the ranks of the Orangemen[;] the identical Northern Liberals who first stimulated the rebellion were also, when the hope of success faded, foremost in the Orange ranks.[118]

The pro-emancipation activist Jack Lawless, the editor of the *Irishman*, was furious. In 1818 Lawless had published in Belfast a volume, *Belfast Politics; Being a Compendium of the Political History of Ireland in the Last Forty Years*, which was presented as an act of historical recovery, an insistence that Belfast's political history, particularly Belfast history in the 1790s, properly understood, revealed the possibility of Catholic and liberal Presbyterians co-operating together in a common cause. Yet here was O'Connell cutting the ground from underneath him by denigrating the legacy of the 1790s. Lawless wrote to the Catholic Association to protest at the terms in which the Liberator had spoken of the local liberal politicians. O'Connell, however, refused to express regret and repeated the offence.[119]

Nevertheless, the Catholic Association agitation undoubtedly moved the question forward. At the beginning of 1825 the government announced its intention to ban the Catholic Association, but significantly it also decided to ban the Orange Order. The principle of governmental impartiality—if not the practice—towards the Irish factions was now enshrined in legislation. O'Connell's personal star was in the ascendant. On 25 February 1825 he impressively answered questions from the Commons Committee on the state of Ireland. He was the soul of moderation in his advocacy

---

[117] O'Ferrall, *Catholic Emancipation and the Birth of Irish Democracy*, 98; *Sessional Papers, 1825 (8), Report from the Select Committee on the State of Ireland, Ordered by the House of Commons to be Printed 30 June 1825*, Daniel O'Connell evidence, 1 Mar. 1825, p. 76.

[118] *Northern Whig*, 16 Dec. 1824.

[119] Thomas MacKnight, *Ulster As It Is* (London, 1896), i. 211; Brendan Clifford, 'Daniel O'Connell and Republican Ireland', in *Spotlights in Irish History* (Mill Street, 1997), 87–102.

of Catholic claims.[120] 'The fact is, darling, that the Catholic cause has certainly advanced in spite of its enemies,' O'Connell wrote to his wife. 'It is probably vanity, but I thought they were struck with my evidence.'[121]

Signs of O'Connell's growing status were increasingly evident. On 27 February O'Connell dined at Brougham's London house, seated between the Dukes of Devonshire and Leinster, facing the Duke of Sussex sitting opposite.[122] On 28 February the radical Sir Francis Burdett, seconded by the Burkean Tory J. W. Croker, successfully sought leave to introduce a Catholic Emancipation Bill in Parliament. Croker made it clear that he thought the Bill would only pass if it included the so-called 'wings'. These 'wings' disenfranchised the 40 shilling freeholder and provided for a state payment to the Catholic clergy. What was O'Connell's attitude? Traditionally he had, of course, opposed any state interference with the Catholic clergy.

On 1 March O'Connell returned to the House of Commons Committee. Perhaps surprisingly, he succeeded in striking up a relationship with Peel's brother-in-law, Colonel Dawson, a resolute Irish Tory MP: 'Mr Dawson is a gentleman who we expect, one day or other, to be voting for the Catholics. I am not myself without hope of it.'[123] He spoke of the desirability of state payment of the Catholic clergy, creating 'a golden link' between the state and the priests.[124]   In private, on 4 March, O'Connell wrote excitedly to his wife that Dawson had admitted that O'Connell had alleviated his 'prejudices'.[125] O'Connell in return heavily implied his willingness to accept the 'wings'; indeed, according to some later reports his moderation became quite extravagant.

On 2 March Daniel O'Connell had a private meeting alone with Plunket. On 3 March he returned to meet Plunket again, this time accompanied by Lord Killeen and the Earl of Fingall. On the same day Shiel attended the Parliamentary Committee, drawing attention to the rarely used device of a patent 'of precedency'; in principle, this could give a Catholic barrister the same place 'of forwardness' at the bar as if 'he had always been a Protestant'. Plunket though had, in fact, gained twenty years earlier from such an offer, which moved him ahead in his profession.[126] On 7 March O'Connell formally announced that he was prepared to accept the 'wings';

[120] W. O'Connor Morris, *Present Irish Questions* (London and New York, 1901); *Sessional Papers (8)*, esp. 48–64.
[121] 'You will smile when you see my evidence', O'Connell (ed.), *The Correspondence of Daniel O'Connell*, iii. 122.
[122] Ibid., O'Connell to his wife, 28 Feb. 1825, p. 126.
[123] *Sessional Papers (8)*, 75, 1 Mar. 1825.   [124] Ibid. 81.
[125] O'Connell (ed.), *O'Connell Correspondence*, iii. 129.
[126] PRONI T 2627/3/2/159, Plunket to Wellington, 26 May 1807.

undoubtedly a compromise on a great matter of principle.[127] He was fully aware of the opposition he was likely to experience. He wrote to his wife that night, complaining about 'your friend Jack Lawless foaming about two things, just that there is nothing really to *complain* of about securities in point of religion, and secondly, that the forty shilling freeholders are likely to be extinct'.[128]

It seemed to some critics that O'Connell had been seduced into betraying his own convictions. An angry William Cobbett told O'Connell that people will think 'you have offered to sell your country for a silk gown'. On 10 March, at Cobbett's birthday party, Shiel told him—as evidence of the government's pro-Catholic good faith—that the promise of a device of a patent 'of precedency' had, indeed, been made to O'Connell.[129] Plunket later pointed out that the proposed patent of precedence would allow O'Connell precedence in the courts over barristers who had been promoted simply because they were Protestants. When cases were called in the courts, those involving King's Counsel were called first.[130] It confirmed Cobbett's worst fears; O'Connell's great weakness, he publicly observed, was not corruption but inordinate vanity.[131] O'Connell himself had told his wife at this time: 'I wish to God I could make my motives so pure and disinterested as to care little for gratitude and applause.'[132] On 11 March O'Connell addressed the Lords' Committee on Ireland. Once again he was the soul of moderation: 'I think it would be very desirable ... that the government should possess a legitimate influence over the Catholic clergy, so that in all the relations of the state with foreign powers, the government should be as secure of the Catholic clergy as they are of the Protestant clergy.'[133]

It was later claimed that, according to shorthand unrevised notes taken at the time, O'Connell argued that the Protestant establishment should

---

[127] O. MacDonagh, *O'Connell: The Life of Daniel O'Connell* (London, 1991), 223.

[128] O'Connell (ed.), *O'Connell Correspondence*, iii. 131.

[129] Shiel to O'Connell, ibid. 188. Shiel later explained to O'Connell: 'I do not exactly recall what passed between me and Cobbett. Whatever I said was uttered in the heedlessness of an after-dinner dialogue.' But he insisted that he had gained the impression, not least from O'Connell, that the 'liberal part' of the administration adhered to the patent of precedency.

[130] Keenan, *The Grail of Catholic Emancipation*, 357.

[131] For this episode see the version given in Jack Lawless, *The Irishman*, 18 Aug. 1825; Keenan, *The Grail of Catholic Emancipation*, 349–51. There is a marked symbolism, Daniel O'Connell had earlier defined himself in opposition to Shiel and Plunket. John Banin, *The Anglo-Irish of the Nineteenth Century* (London, 1828) ii. 154 ff. For O'Connell's vanity see Constantia Maxwell, *The Stranger in Ireland: From the Reign of Elizabeth to the Great Famine* (London, 1954), 272 and 278; R. Bentley, *An Angler in Ireland* (London, 1834), 123–7.

[132] O'Connell (ed.), *O'Connell Correspondence*, ii. 112.

[133] *Sessional Papers (8)*, 154.

be 'rendered inviolable' and that his own platform rhetoric in Ireland did not have the 'sanction' of his judgement.[134] Whatever about these precise accusations—bitterly disputed by the O'Connellite *Freeman's Journal*—O'Connell did use some remarkably conciliatory language.[135] There is no question that O'Connell went out of his way to reassure both committees and exude a tone of non-sectarian moderation: speculating, for example, that he had seriously considered sending his son to Trinity College, Dublin.

In his evidence to the Lords Committee, O'Connell formally expressed his opposition to the veto, but added: 'For myself, I think that it would be desirable that the government should see the names before they went to Rome.'[136] Tantalizingly, he held out the prospect of ultimate stability arising from the concession of Catholic emancipation: 'The moment that we become actual subjects, all partisan interest should be done away in the general one of supporting the state.'[137]

In a letter of 13 Mar. to the *Morning Herald*, Jack Lawless once again challenged O'Connell's authority. He described the proposal for a greater state role in the affairs of the Catholic Church as equivalent to 'a species of ecclesiastical inquisition into the political as well as moral conduct of every Catholic clergyman and a powerful instrument of corruption in the hands of an artful minister'. As for the proposed disenfranchisement of the 40 shilling freeholders, Lawless recalled Grattan's famous description of the right to vote as the '*magna carta* of the poor man'.

It was claimed, he noted, that the 40 shilling freeholders were herded to the polls by the landlords—even if this was true, he shrewdly noted, 'the necessity of so bringing them up [to the polls] is, in fact, a great privilege to the Irish Catholic'.[138] But, in fact, he noted the 40 shilling freeholders often showed considerable independent spirit. They had, for example, played a key role in the election of the pro-emancipation candidate Henry White (son of Luke) in the Co. Dublin by-election of February 1823. The willingness to disenfranchise the freeholders seemed both to bow to English racist prejudice[139] against allowing illiterate 'bogtrotters' to vote, and also to show that at this point O'Connell had no strategy of popular electoral

---

[134] *Dublin Evening Mail*, 13 June 1838.

[135] *Sessional Papers (8)*, 154. For a defence of O'Connell against the claim that the unrevised notes show him as duplicitous, see *Freeman's Journal*, 15, 16, and 19 June 1838.

[136] *Northern Whig*, 21 Jan. 1843.   [137] *Sessional Papers (9)*, 149.

[138] *The Irishman*, 25 Mar. 1825. Lawless was perfectly correct. As early as 29 May 1807 Sir John Bagnell had written to Sir Arthur Wellesley: 'In many instances the Popish tenantry have voted against the positive mandates of their protestant landlord', PRONI T2627/3/2/161.

[139] A. Atkinson, *Ireland Exhibited to England in a Political and Moral Survey of the Population* (Dublin, 1823), 6: 'Not a single vote would we give to the bogtrotters of

intervention. But the state payment of the clergy was in many ways a more profound personal issue; it seemed to indicate a relaxation of that hostility to any interference of the British state with the Catholic religion which had previously defined O'Connell's career. For Protestant liberals, after all, there was a clear objective. The implications were profound: the Catholic clergy would have been placed more than ever before on a level with those of the Protestant Church, and a great stimulus to polemical zeal would thus have been removed. Question-marks now stood against O'Connell's consistency in 1825; was he now willing to make concessions which he had bitterly opposed in 1817? William Cobbett, in the end, decided to be forgiving: O'Connell had made mistakes because he had been in a state of high 'anxiety' to see the measure passed. He had acted out of character, and he had been betrayed. But all this was due to the essential goodness of O'Connell's nature and the wicked nature of the forces arrayed against him. 'How is a man to be a match for the devil, unless he be at least half a devil himself?'[140]

The *Dublin University Magazine* offered a more cynical assessment:

The veto project was originally conceived without his advice. Had it been successful, Catholic emancipation would have been accomplished without his assistance ... Therefore O'Connell opposed the veto. By 1825 he had acquired the power and reputation—whatsoever he could obtain from the British Crown and legislation, would have been ascribed to him.[141]

Cynical though it is, no better explanation has ever been offered. Such caustic analysis of O'Connell's motivation can not detract, however, from the significance of his initiative and its eventual failure in 1825. There was a considerable majority in the House of Commons for Catholic emancipation on this basis; however, the Bill was rejected by a majority in the Lords. The Parliament of the United Kingdom thus deprived itself of the opportunity for gracious concession to constitutional petition and argument. The last opportunity for wise and voluntary concession was lost—the day of Ireland's 'greatest calamity', according to one shrewd judge.[142]

John Wilson Croker noted, in particular, that it was not just the narrowly political project of Catholic representation at Westminster which was lost in 1825; there was also the failure (never to be rectified) to establish a co-operative, mutually beneficial relationship between the Catholic clergy

---

Leitrim, Galway, Roscommon or any other bogtrotters whatsoever, until their governor had first [sent] them to school to read.'

[140] *Political Register*, 21 May 1825, vol. 4, no. 8, pp. 401–2.

[141] *A Provisional Character, Daniel O'Connell* (1837), 319.

[142] Gerald Fitzgibbon, *Ireland in 1868: The Battle for English Party Strife, its Grievances, Real and Fatuous, Remedies, Abortive or Mischievous* (London and Dublin, 1868), 18.

and the government, whereby the Catholic clergy was granted 'an interest in, and therefore an attachment towards, the state'.[143] In Croker's view, 'all the political and social evils' of Ireland 'may be traced to the condition and influence of the Roman Catholic clergy of that country'.[144] Failure, therefore, to deal with this issue was failure to deal with the Irish question itself.

Inevitably, the 'insulted' Catholics of Ireland responded with a new mood of militancy; when Catholic emancipation eventually came, every Irish Catholic believed it was, above all, a concession to agitation. The Catholic Association was relaunched, this time with political and electoral ambitions, a line of strategy inspired, above all, by Thomas Wyse. The power and prestige of the Catholic Association was put to the test at the general election of 1826. It was a test the Association triumphantly survived. The Catholic rent was put to good use in providing for a series of successful contests—most notably that against the Beresford interest in Waterford, but other great Ascendancy houses in Louth, Westmeath, and Monaghan lost their seats to liberal Protestant candidates. When confronted by a capacity for revolt on this scale, landlord threats of retribution against the tenantry were rendered relatively insignificant.

POPULAR POLITICS AND THE CATHOLIC CAUSE: EMANCIPATION OR SECTARIAN CIVIL WAR?

After such triumphs O'Connell became increasingly optimistic about the prospects for emancipation. In 1827, when the Burkean Canning succeeded Liverpool as Prime Minister, Lawless regarded the change as being of no significance from an Irish Catholic point of view. O'Connell, on the other hand, disagreed sharply and clearly felt that a new era was at hand.[145] But Canning was ill, and died after a very short period of office. At the beginning of 1828 Wellington took office as Prime Minister. Even moderate aristocratic Catholic opinion feared that his appointment was a 'fatal omen',[146] but, in fact, Wellington shared a presumption in favour of Catholic emancipation.[147] Symbolically, in February 1828 Burke's old ally Baron William Cusack Smith had ruled in favour of the barrister O'Connell in a profoundly sectarian case—that of Father Thomas Maguire, who had been

[143] 'Outlines of the History of Ireland', *Quarterly Review*, 83: 165 (Sept. 1848), 599.
[144] Ibid. 598.   [145] *Northern Whig*, 12 July 1827.
[146] O'Connell, *Observations on the Corn Laws*, 10.
[147] Peter Jupp, *British Politics on the Eve of Reform: The Duke of Wellington's Administration* (London, 1998), 55–6.

accused of the seduction of a Protestant woman in Drumkeen, Co. Leitrim—adding some controversial and characteristically outspoken language on the respect due to the Catholic clergy.[148] Cusack Smith's friend Croker was sure that Wellington had decided to act on emancipation. O'Connell's conduct at this juncture was initially, at least, curiously indecisive. On 1 May 1828, responding to Wellington's decision to repeal the Test and Corporation Acts, he proposed at the Catholic Association meeting that a January resolution to oppose every ministerial candidate should be rescinded. The motion was strongly opposed, and it is clear that O'Connell became alarmed at the strength of militant feeling in the Association. Ironically, O'Connell's defeat at this meeting was to pave the way for his greatest triumph. Vesey Fitzgerald, one of the sitting members for Co. Clare, having been appointed to the presidency of the Board of Trade, was compelled to seek re-election. The Association, still committed to opposing the government, could not find any candidate; suddenly, on 27 June, Daniel O'Connell announced his intention of contesting the by-election. He was, in fact, pushing an open door. On the same day in late June Holland had written to Anglesey in Ireland:

There is a strong persuasion that the Duke of Wellington will next yield the question or devise some method of carrying it and inducing those who have hitherto resisted it to submit to necessity ... His silence when such inference was drawn from his speech by Lord Lansdowne, his reported advice to the ultra-Tories not to press him for a distinct explanation and the active assurance of some of his most intimate adherents favours such an explanation.[149]

It was possible for a member of an excluded group—Quakers had actually done this—to stand for Parliament and win an election, even if he could not actually take his seat. O'Connell was now employing the same tactic. Vesey Fitzgerald's liberality had made him a popular figure, but, in the event, O'Connell's campaign touched the deepest popular emotions and carried all before it. A Clare election street ballad catches the mood: 'O lose not an hour in repose or complaint | till bursting the Sassenach's wrongful restraint.' The same ballad advised its Clare audience not to expect 'freedom from foreign aid', but rather to place faith in O'Connell's 'high worth' and popular organization.[150] O'Connell's appeal to the electorate contained

[148] Proinsíos Ó Duigneáin, *The Priest and the Protestant Woman*, Maynooth Studies in Local History, 11 (Dublin, 1997).
[149] PRONI D 619/27/A/22, Holland to Anglesey, 27 June 1828.
[150] NLI Ms 7658. This Gaelic ballad was preserved by the 19th-cent. Gaelic scholar, Professor Eugene O'Curry, and translated into English by George O'Donovan.

an interesting shift from the issue of general oppression to more personal matters:

Our Protestant friends really think we are beings of degraded minds—that because we are Catholics, we have neither reasoning nor understanding; they imagine we are creatures of an inferior grade to themselves. Standing here, I may be considered the representative of the suffering of my country. Lord Manners, the very week before he left Ireland, put thirteen brother barristers over my head.[151]

The priests played a highly visible role in mobilizing—some said coercing—support amongst the peasantry for O'Connell. Sir Edward O'Brien assembled his tenants in a body to march to the hustings and vote for Fitzgerald.[152] In the last major speech, given in Irish to Irish-speakers, which actually moved a large audience in favour of a decisive action, Father Murphy of Corofin, the local parish priest, dramatically called upon these tenants 'to vote O'Connell in the name of their country and their religion'.[153] O'Connell's overwhelming victory over Vesey Fitzgerald in the Co. Clare by-election on 5 July 1828 confirmed the collapse of proprietorial control over Catholic voters; both Wellington and Peel, now in power, were convinced that emancipation had to be conceded.

The *Northern Whig* admirably conveyed the full extent of O'Connell's victory:

Mr Vesey Fitzgerald—a member of the King's Cabinet and possessed of extensive patronage—has been driven from a constituency which he had represented in Parliament for 20 years, where his property was most ample, and where he saw himself supported by the aristocracy and gentry of the place, all of whom were attached to him by personal friendship and bound by the obligations of gratitude.[154]

The Duke of Wellington could not but take note and continue further down the path he had already elected to follow.

At the end of July O'Connell had a private meeting with the pro-emancipation Lord-Lieutenant Anglesey. Anglesey, a distinguished soldier, recorded: 'Mr O'Connell seemed extremely anxious to impress upon my mind his abhorrence of insurrection and his conviction that none was to be expected. I assured him that I had no apprehension … yet that I felt bound to be prepared.' Anglesey then opened up a dreadful vista for contemplation, when he conjured up

151 *Western Argus and Ballinasloe Independent*, 9 July 1828, Clare election.
152 'A Munster Farmer', *Reminiscences of Daniel O'Connell*, 71.
153 'Clare Election', in *The Speeches of the Rt. Hon. Richard Lalor Shiel: With Memoir by Thomas McNevin*, 2nd edn. (Dublin, 1853), Sept. 1828, p. 53.
154 *Northern Whig*, 10 July 1828.

the most appalling of all cases—that of my being compelled in aid of the King's troops, to arm the Orange population. What, said I, must be the dreadful consequence of such a measure—war to extermination and the total destruction of all hopes of the Catholics!—For how could any government which had called for the energy of Protestants to put down Catholic rebellion, ever propose to the former to be received into the constitution upon an equality of rights with those who had been called upon to assist in subduing open rebellion?'[155]

O'Connell responded by expressing his shock at such a disastrous prospect; he signalled an immediate private willingness to sacrifice the 40 shilling freeholders, who had just so greatly assisted his triumph at the polls as part of an emancipation settlement. O'Connell was determined to avoid his tactical mistakes of 1825; this time the popular pressure had to be maintained, but the means of doing so were complex and subtle.[156] Yet the summer of 1828 had not completed its run of startling events. By mid-August 1828 George Dawson MP, Peel's brother-in-law, announced his conversion to the cause of Catholic emancipation. With remarkable bluntness, Dawson chose a striking moment for his declaration of a change of heart. At the 12 August Apprentice Boys celebrations of the relief of Derry, he broke the news to a crowd which had first been treated to renditions of 'God Save the King', 'Boyne Water', and 'Rule Britannia'. It was a surprising statement; three years previously, at the same event, Dawson had told the crowd that English opinion was hardening against emancipation.[157] His audience was at first slow to comprehend his message. 'I firmly believe', he explained, 'that it is not the wish of the Roman Catholic leaders to drive the people into rebellion.' Matters had reached a point, Dawson explained, where either it must be decided to 'crush the Catholic Association'—at this point he was interrupted by cheers lasting several minutes—or 'to look at the question with an intention to settle it'. He called for his supporters to abstain from 'irritating harangues' and grasp the full seriousness of the crisis. 'I speak here as an MP, as a member of the government, and as a citizen of the world. Is it possible I can look with apathy upon the degraded state of my Catholic fellow countrymen? (loud hisses).' Dawson responded to the crowd's defiance with a public defiance of his own: 'I can not express too strongly the contempt I feel for the persons who thus attempt to put me down.'[158] In private he told his

---

[155] PRONI D 619/32/B/2, Richview, 29 July 1828, Anglesey's signed memorandum of a conversation with O'Connell.
[156] MacDonagh, *O'Connell*, 257–9. [157] *The Irishman*, 30 Dec. 1825.
[158] *Northern Whig*, 21 Aug. 1828; Brian Jenkins, *Era of Emancipation: British Government of Ireland 1812–30* (Kingston and Montreal, 1988), 269–70; A. Macintyre, *The Liberator: Daniel O'Connell and the Irish Party 1830–47* (New York, 1965), 87.

brother-in-law, Robert Peel, that his hecklers were persons of no substance. Holland wrote to Anglesey:

Dawson's speech is the topic of every conversation—I conclude, it was in great measure, at least, the result of personal levity and imprudence—but it must, in its effects, produce hopes and fears and persuasion of concert with his colleagues which, whether true or false, will impair their strength in resisting the measure—Even in England it has much heightened the expectations of Wellington's acquiescence entertained by many friends of the Catholics.[159]

Daniel O'Connell wrote happily to Pierce Mahony: 'Do you know that nothing ever pleased me more than the conduct of Mr Dawson! He has done a great deal of good. You have seen that I hailed him cheerily, and I think delicately ... '[160]

Dawson may not have been speaking for Peel at this point—Peel did not tell Croker of his formal conversion on the Catholic question until January 1829, though one close observer, George Bentinck, believed that Peel and Wellington had formed an 'emancipist' understanding in the summer of 1828.[161] But it hardly matters either way. Most observers believed that Dawson was speaking for Peel. The tide was now all one way. All it needed was for one final demonstration of the precariousness of the situation; the precariousness, and perhaps also the indefensible nature of it. 'Honest Jack Lawless' was to be the agent of such a demonstration, not so much as a consequence of a deliberate, well-worked-out strategy, but as a result of one of the most powerful laws in politics, the law of unintended consequences.

In September 1828 Jack Lawless, honestly believing that he understood the political culture of the North, undertook to take the campaign for Catholic emancipation into Ulster. He explained:

I went to canvas the Northern counties to the payment of the Catholic rent, to expound its objects, and to explain the principles it was calculated to support: to inculcate brotherly love among all denominations and to demonstrate that this feeling could never be realised in Ireland but by the establishment of equal and impartial justice—common privileges and a national constitution.[162]

O'Connell claimed that he expected Lawless to attract another £100,000 to the Catholic Association's coffers.[163] In the event, Lawless was to be more

---

[159] PRONI D 619/27/A/26, 11–29 Aug. 1828, Holland, Chancellor of the Duchy of Lancaster, to Anglesey.

[160] O'Connell to Mahony, 17 Sept. 1828, in O'Connell (ed.), *O'Connell Correspondence*, iii. 409.

[161] *Croker Papers*, ii. 2.

[162] Lawless to R. D. Finlay, 27 Oct. 1828, *Northern Whig*, 30 Oct. 1828.

[163] *Northern Whig*, 18 Sept. 1828.

successful in exposing the absence of 'brotherly love' in Ireland; the absence also of 'equal and impartial justice'. Having arrived in Monaghan, Lawless announced an intention of entering Ballybay on 23 September. It was a strange decision. Ballybay was strongly Protestant; in the immediate vicinity there were 8,000 homes, it was claimed, in which there was not a single Catholic residing, while there was an Orange Lodge in each townland.[164] Sectarian passions on both sides were ignited. Lawless found himself at the head of a crowd of 20,000 Catholics, inevitably including Ribbon activists. Between 6,000 to 8,000 well-armed Orangemen flooded into Ballybay. They were led by Sam Gray (1782–1848), a terrifying figure, businessman, gangster, and baronial High Constable for the Ballybay area. Gray strutted around with two pistols on his belt.[165] Thought locally to be responsible for several murders, mothers elsewhere in Ireland warned naughty children that 'Bony' would 'get' them—in Monaghan, however, they warned that 'Sam' would take the offending child.

The young Charles Gavan Duffy, son of a Monaghan Catholic tradesman who had been a United Irishman, recalled later that Gray's activities—and the state's relative tolerance of them—made him 'a nationalist of the school of Rory O'Moore', that is, as 'someone who identified Irishmen with the Celtic race and the Catholic Church'.[166] The scene was set for bloodshed on a large scale. The rapid action of General Thornton, bringing troops from the Armagh garrison, helped to prevent a serious collision of forces.[167] Jack Lawless, anyway, had no wish to be a party to such a confrontation; he agreed to the request from the authorities to stay out of Ballybay—visiting instead the Catholic chapel which was a mile-and-a-half outside the town. The attitude of the *Northern Whig* to these events is instructive: it regarded Lawless as behaving in a way that was 'childish' and 'absurd'—lacking in all 'common sense'. But despite these strong criticisms, the *Whig* insisted that 'we entertain sentiments of the highest admiration for the splendour of his talents, the purity of his patriotism and the zeal of his devotion to the cause of human liberty'.[168] In the *Whig* Lawless remained an attractive, if misguided, figure (Alexis de Toqueville

[164] Ibid., 20 Sept. 1828.
[165] W. J. O'Neill Daunt, *A Life Spent for Ireland. Being Selections from the Journals of the late W. J. O'Neill Daunt* (London, 1896), 42.
[166] Patrick Maume, 'Monaghan Re-Imagined: *The Orangeman* (1915) an Ulster-American Original Narrative', *New Hibernia Review*, 6: 1 (Spring 2002), 115.
[167] The Irish University Press series of British Parliamentary papers, third report from the Select Committee on Orange Lodges in Ireland with Minutes of Evidence, Appendix and Index, Evidence of Mr Patrick McConnell, Qs 6563, 6564, p. 237. This committee was chaired by John Wilson Patten.
[168] *Northern Whig*, 30 Oct. 1828.

felt much the same way about him),[169] whilst Gray was precisely the type of Orange thug who made life miserable not only for Catholics but for liberal Presbyterians too. Significantly, the *Whig* also accepted that Lawless had proven that the operation of the law in Ireland was not impartial between the competing sects. The *Whig* fully supported the elite's efforts to prevent a 'tumultuous assemblage of unarmed Catholics', but it noted the failure of the civil authorities to 'discountenance' a 'simultaneous assemblage of armed Orangemen'.[170] When he was arrested at his Dublin home on 16 October, the *Whig* made it clear that it fully supported Lawless, who had, after all, backed away from a confrontation.[171]

These dramatic events greatly alarmed the *Whig*. There were other worrying developments. In Armagh, armed Orangemen had flooded the town, intending to repulse a Lawless visit; here the leaders of the Armagh Catholics quickly told Lawless that they had already long contributed to the Catholic rent and his visit as such was unnecessary. Then, in the county of Tipperary, a police barracks was razed to the ground by an angry Catholic crowd—'the fiercest peasantry in Europe', said the *Whig*—the policemen's lives only being saved by the timely intervention of the local priest. The *Whig* was terrified by the drift towards disaster: 'We do not hesitate to assert that the only alternative to granting emancipation which is left to the government is rebellion and civil war, the most horrible by which any country was ever scourged.'[172]

In February 1829 Peel, in effect, accepted the force of the *Whig*'s analysis. He argued that since 1794 'there has been division in the government on account of the Catholic question'. Cabinets were divided between those who accepted the Burkean case for Catholic emancipation and those who rejected it; often, the Irish administration was divided along similar lines. He conceded also the point first advanced in striking fashion in the House of Commons by Henry Parnell: 'That for hardly one year during that period that has elapsed since the union' has Ireland 'been governed by the ordinary course of law.' Peel remarked forcefully: 'He would demand of them whether it was possible to secure tranquillity in Ireland, if they went on from year to year as they had done with the Catholic question.'[173] Peel referred to those who talked of 'putting down' the Catholic Association. 'They might as well be talking of putting down the winds of heaven, or of

[169] *Alexis de Toqueville's Journey in Ireland July–August 1835*, trans. and ed. Emmet Larkin (Dublin, 1990), 26 July 1835, pp. 79–80.

[170] *Northern Whig*, 2 Oct. 1828.   [171] Ibid., 30 Oct. 1828.

[172] Ibid., 2 Oct. 1828; see also Suzanne T Kingon, 'Ulster Opposition to Catholic Emancipation', *Irish Historical Studies*, 21: 134 (Nov. 2004), 137–55; Kyla Madden, *Forkhill Protestants and Forkhill Catholics 1787–1858* (Liverpool, 2005), 73.

[173] *Hansard*, 10 Feb. 1829, 2nd ser., vol. 20, col. 181.

chaining the ceaseless tides of the ocean ... The Catholic Association was the people of Ireland. Its spirit was caused by the grievance of the nation, and its seat was the bosom of seven millions of its population.'[174]

In March 1829 Peel made his new position even more clear in the House of Commons. Irish opinion, including much respectable Protestant opinion, was firmly in favour of emancipation. The 'internal government' of Ireland was now incompatible with any 'system of exclusion'. Peel explicitly addressed the issue of civil war.

We have also had the experience of that other and greater calamity—civil discord and bloodshed. Surely it is no womanly fear that shudders at its recurrence, no degenerate impulse that prompts one to exclaim with Lord Falkland—'Peace! Peace! Peace!'—that looks with anxiety for the alternative by which civil war may be honourably averted; which may secure the natives of the same land, and the fellow subjects of the King from the dire necessity.[175]

One Irish provincial newspaper laid particular weight on one of Peel's remarks concerning the impact on Ireland of a foreign war: 'An exclusive system of government may be established—the system of exclusion might be carried on in time of peace; but what would be the result in the event of war? The very first announcement of a war would be a declaration of the perils in which the country would be placed.'[176] But Peel was not only driven by a profound sense of fear, even desperation—his speech also contained a more positive appeal to a better future:

Grant that by the admission of the Roman Catholics to a full and equal participation in civil rights, and by the establishment of a free and cordial intercourse between all classes of Her Majesty's subjects, mutual jealousies may be removed, and that we may be taught, instead of looking at each other as adversaries and opponents, to respect and value each other, and to discover the existence of qualities on each side that were not attributed to either.[177]

The leading English Catholic Earl of Shrewsbury rightly observed of the 'new' Peel: 'Those who survive a long political struggle may come out of it very different from what they were when they went in.'[178] On 13 April the Roman Catholic Relief Act provided a new oath of allegiance, enabling Catholics to enter Parliament, belong to any corporation, and hold civil and military offices—'Catholic emancipation' was at last a reality. The *Whig*, relieved beyond measure, carried the following suggestive report:

A Northern Presbyterian, on a walking tour, overheard the bursts of laughter and applause coming from a paid reading room—Ballybay, Co. Monaghan; on

---

[174] Ibid.   [175] Ibid., 5 Mar. 1829, col. 750.
[176] *Western Argus*, 11 Mar. 1829.   [177] *Hansard*, 5 Mar. 1829, col. 778.
[178] *A Third Letter to Ambrose Lisle* (London, 1842), 23.

entering, he found the best local reader regaling his audience with excerpts from recent speeches and editorials: the rhetoric of O'Connell was effective indeed, but even more effective was the hostile tone of the anti-emancipation press: 'Nor was it alone the appeals of O'Connell to the "hereditary bondsmen" that made the life blood pulse beat quicker in many a rustic breast'. The threatening denunciations of those meek holy men who spoke with such Christian calmness of exterminating 7,000,000 of people, were read with an emphasis suited to the subject, and though in general contemptuous laughter was the only outward manifestation of feeling expressed on that occasion, yet sometimes the swarthy flush that kindled on many a sunburnt brow, fully explained why even the soldier of a 100 fights, who never shrunk from personal danger, would hesitate to coerce into desperation the fiercest peasantry in Europe.[179]

In short, emancipation was conceded above all to the strength of the popular mobilization rather than the abstract justice of the case. Ireland's celebrated 'culture of agitation' was now fully formed; a development which had profound implications for the future. The unchallenged exponent of the agitational culture, the 'uncrowned King of Ireland', was Daniel O'Connell. The Emancipation Act allowed Catholics—without any assault on conscience—to occupy all civil and military offices except those of Regent, Lord Chancellor, and Lord-Lieutenant. There was, of course, a price to be paid. The Catholic Association was suppressed, the 40 shilling freehold was abolished and a £10 franchise established in its place. There was little outcry; even the young John Stuart Mill, flower of progressive liberalism, supported the measure.[180] Such an 'attempted' balancing of interests deserves some comment. It can, as Professor Peter Jupp has pointed out,

be traced back to the thinking of the Younger Pitt at the time of the Union and to a dominant strand in the approach to governing Ireland that had developed since then. The basic proposition of such thinking was that a fresh balance had to be struck between Protestant and Catholic interests which preserved those of Protestants but accommodated the interests of Catholics in the professions and trade. The legislation giving Catholics almost equal rights with Protestants was therefore counterbalanced by that which took away most of the political power which had been used to achieve it.[181]

It is perhaps suggestive that O'Connell's self-confidence now became so great that he could even afford to change his mind on a major issue of public debate. He now turned against the widespread Irish Catholic view—so

---

[179] *Northern Whig*, 23 Ap. 1829.
[180] Bruce Kinzler, *England's Disgrace? John Stuart Mill and the Irish Question* (Toronto, 2001), 27.
[181] Peter Jupp, *British Politics on the Eve of Reform: The Duke of Wellington's Administration, 1828–30* (London, 1998), 157.

frequently echoed by O'Connell himself—that the Younger Pitt had been a fraudster, who had cruelly deceived Catholics at the time of the union in 1800–1. But O'Connell now reversed his position in dramatic style, and insisted that careful historical study revealed Pitt's good intentions towards the Catholics all along.[182] For O'Connell to reverse his earlier view of Pitt in this way is perhaps not as surprising as it appears. By 1829 O'Connell was only too well aware that consistency is an overrated virtue in Irish politics. Having made himself the leader of popular Catholicism by opposing any British state interference with the Catholic clergy, he had opportunistically compromised that principle in 1825—but had lived to tell the tale. Having attempted to persuade the Catholic Association not to oppose Wellington's ministry in parliamentary contests, O'Connell had then, in the most successful move of his political career, thrown himself into the Clare by-election and defeated the ministry. Why not then turn around and reverse the young O'Connellite view of Pitt, if by doing so it put opponents of emancipation on the defence? O'Connell's career had been based not on precision of strategy, but rather on providing movement and drama. By 1830 O'Connell was the 'Liberator', the Irish leader who, many said, had defeated Wellington and thus succeeded where Napoleon had failed. The *Spectator* insisted repeatedly throughout the 1830s that O'Connell had compelled the Iron Duke to yield to fear that which he had been too obstinate to yield to justice. If a British liberal journal could make such a judgement, what did this imply for O'Connell's standing amongst the Catholics of Ireland? Who would dispute O'Connell's own claim? 'He [Wellington] did emancipate the Catholics, but he emancipated them because (as he himself avowed) emancipation was no longer to be resisted.' O'Connell added: 'We had our own Waterloo ... and our victory was more useful, if not more glorious. We chained the valiant duke to the car of our triumph, and compelled him to set us free.'[183]

But what of Robert Peel's hope, expressed during the emancipation debate, for a new era of good feelings and mutual respect in Irish politics? In the event, these hopes were destined to be disappointed. There was even a spiteful and self-defeating blow at O'Connell personally: 'There could be no doubt as to the abominable injustice of this case.' Thomas Creevey noted in his diary the unease of several senior figures in British politics.[184]

---

[182] *A Letter to the Members of the House of Commons of the United Kingdom of Great Britain and Ireland on the Legal Right of Roman Catholics to sit in Parliament to which is added a Reply to Edward Burkenshaw Sugden* (London, 1829), 21.

[183] *Observations on Corn Laws, on Political Pravity and Ingratitude* (Dublin, 1842), 11.

[184] *Thomas Creevey's Papers 1793–1838*, selected and ed. John Gore (Harmondsworth, 1985), 309.

The House of Commons refused to accept O'Connell upon the credit of his election prior to the Relief Act, and the Liberator was compelled to seek re-election. It was said that the King was here having his revenge—coldly served after seventeen years—for the 'witchery resolutions' of 1812. One close observer, Lord Cloncurry, argued that but for this snub, O'Connell 'would have quietly taken his hat' and pursued 'more moderate courses'.[185] But of 'moderate courses' there was to be little sign in Ireland. A year later the Tory *Galway Independent* newspaper was still resenting the effort made to conciliate a 'cabal of bog priests and bawling lawyers';[186] meanwhile its local Galway rival, the O'Connellite, pro-repeal *Western Argus*, reminded its readers that they had been treated as 'aliens in your native soil'[187] by oppressors who were still 'insatiable'. The more cynical Peel of the mid-1820s, however, would not have been surprised. On 3 November 1826 he had written to J. L. Foster of the consequences of Catholic emancipation, which he considered to be inevitable:

A much more marked division than there is at present between Catholics and heretics, and a much closer union among all classes of the latter. The Catholics having nothing to lose, will speak out more plainly. Those of the Protestants who contended for equality ... will be against Catholic domination—and that bond of union which exists between a large class of Protestants and the Catholics—arising out of feelings of pity and injustice, will be at end.[188]

An optimistic young liberal, John Stuart Mill, hoped that 'one people'[189] was at last being created in the United Kingdom; in 1826 Peel was considerably less sanguine and considerately more realistic.

---

[185] *Lord Cloncurry's Recollections of his Life and Times* (Dublin, 1849), 400; MacDonagh, *O'Connell*, 278–300.

[186] *Galway Independent Paper*, 21 Apr. 1830.

[187] *Western Argus and Ballinasloe Independent*, 17 Aug. 1830.

[188] RIA, Ms23 G39.   [189] Kinzler, *England's Disgrace?*, 36.

4

The Repealer Repulsed: O'Connell 1830–1845

The paramount importance of Catholic emancipation has so absorbed the nation, as to leave it little room for exploring its other grievances. That great measure at length was passed—but coupled with a fatal admission that it was surrendered to force—not a concession to justice.

That produced its full deleterious effect in Ireland, when we came into office, it found her popular leaders, seeing very clearly how much more remained to be achieved but animated by a seditious confidence in the efficacy of clamorous demands and the threats of physical force for the attainment of ever justifiable objects.

(PRONI D619/28/C/274, Cabinet paper attached to note dated 9 Oct. 1832, by Lord Anglesey, Lord-Lieutenant of Ireland)

The constant glow of political agitation, carried to such perfection as that science now is by Mr O'Connell, has a bewitchment about it that seems to captivate the senses. Ambition is as blind as love; Napoleon won a hundred battles, and lived to lose as many.

(Earl of Shrewsbury, *A Third Letter to Ambrose de Lisle Philipps Esq* (1842), 157)

Long may King William reign on his people | He spoke on behalf of the Catholic freedom | Three cheers for O'Connell both morning and evening | That silver-tongued man will redeem his people. | ... Good people, I hope it is no treason.

(Cambridge University Library, Irish mss, 44 Ad6565, 21R)

Emancipation as an issue defined Daniel O'Connell before 1829; it was the obsessive cause which engaged his attention and brought him fame. But after 1829 he was faced with more diverse challenges. He became a major figure in the House of Commons and, indeed, became a force in British high politics, a politician whose decisions affected both the making and life-span of ministries. In Ireland O'Connell immediately grasped that the passing of Catholic emancipation presented him with a potential problem. Writing to Pierce Mahony on 28/9 March 1829, he declared: 'The people will be taken out of *our* hands by emancipation, as we took them from Captain Rock by *our* agitation.'[1] Another Daniel O'Connell emerged in these years—the Daniel O'Connell who played a major role as an international humanitarian; a steadfast, unflinching opponent of slavery (even when it annoyed Irish–American supporters) and also, and perhaps even more remarkably, anti-Semitism, even when practised by the Pope.[2] He became, as one admirer, T. Maguire, claimed, 'the universal advocate of public liberty to which the black African, the Red Indian, the plundered Pole or the groaning Russian should look'.[3] Northern Presbyterian liberalism strongly admired and supported O'Connell's stand on these issues,[4] marred only, as it was, by O'Connell's own anti-Semitic attacks on the young Disraeli.

In 1812 Daniel O'Connell had once declared: 'It has been said that a repeal of the union was the ultimate aim of those who petitioned for Catholic emancipation.' He would be glad to see the man who would be bold enough to endeavour to bring forward the smallest evidence of such a fact; they would no longer see Lord Fingall at their heel, were that their aim. These charges were unfounded, and he thought it his duty that 'they and all others who imprinted *treason* or *disaffection* to the Roman Catholic body should not remain a moment uncontradicted'.[5] But emancipation achieved, O'Connell did indeed move on to the theme of repeal. In his acceptance speech in Clare, immediately following his famous victory, O'Connell had declared that he did not accept the impossibility of repeal. 'It was done in 1782. I hope I shall show that it may be done again. (Cheers.)'[6]

O'Connell also simultaneously set himself the target of breaking the power of the 'Orange Tory' interest in Ireland: this meant the arrival of Catholics into places traditionally reserved exclusively for Protestants in the judiciary, the police, and the town corporations. There was always,

---

[1] Maurice O'Connell (ed.), *The Correspondence of Daniel O'Connell 1824–32*, vol. 4 (Dublin, 1979) 35.

[2] Ibid. 95–7, for O'Connell's letter to Isaac Goldsmid (11 Sept. 1829), giving powerful expressions of O'Connell's sympathy with the Jewish cause.

[3] *Dublin Evening Mail*, 11 Jan. 1841. Lord O'Hagan stressed also O'Connell's support for 'the liberation of the Dissenters and the Jew', *The O'Connell Centenary Address 1875* (Dublin, 1875), 31. O'Hagan's text initiated the interpretation of O'Connell as the universalist, reformist, moral-force liberal which is still so influential today on the works of Fergus O'Ferrall and Oliver MacDonagh.

[4] J. L. McCracken, *New Light at the Cape of Good Hope: William Porter, the Father of Cape Liberalism* (Belfast, 1993), 35.

[5] *Dublin Evening Mail*, 18 Jan. 1841.   [6] *Western Argus*, 16 July 1828.

therefore, a tension at the heart of O'Connell's advocacy of repeal. He was well aware that the existence of a repeal movement acted as an important pressure for reform of the union in the Catholic interest. This, in turn, carried a dangerous implication—would not a reformed union reduce the basis of support for repeal? Would it not also make it harder to gain Protestant support for repeal if such reforms visibly strengthened Catholics at their expense? O'Connell explicitly asked himself this question in 1823: 'But may not the repeal be dispensed with if we get beneficent measures without it?' He gave his own answer:

This is a serious question and one upon which good men may well differ; but it is my duty to make up my mind upon it, and I have made up my mind accordingly—that there can be no safety for, no permanent prosperity in, Ireland without a repeal of the union. This is my firm and unalterable conviction. Irish affairs must be managed by Irishmen.[7]

The big theoretical question thus resolved to his own satisfaction, it still left open the issue of the precise O'Connellite tactics to be employed in any particular conjuncture.

In January 1830 O'Connell's 'Letter to the People of Ireland' put forward a new, comprehensive political programme, which included repeal of the union, but also stressed parliamentary reform and abolition of tithes. The union, wrote O'Connell in October 1830, 'should now be agitated in every possible shape'.[8] In eight days, he wrote, he had attended four public dinners and four meetings for petitioning and the redress of grievances. 'Agitate! Agitate! Agitate!' The government responded by harassment and prohibition of meetings. O'Connell hit back with highly personalized invective on 18 October 1830, describing Sir Henry Hardinge, the then Chief Secretary, as a 'paltry, contemptible little English soldier'. Hardinge challenged him to a duel; O'Connell, citing D'Esterre, rather ingloriously declined.[9] In November 1830 Orangemen 'completely wrecked' the Catholic village of Maghery in Co. Armagh, in the passive presence of Colonel Verner (a magistrate) and some of the constabulary police.[10] In January 1831 O'Connell exceeded his previous efforts by calling for a run on the banks.

[7] W. E. H. Lecky, *Leaders of Public Opinion in Ireland*, vol. 2 (London, 1903 edn.), 141.

[8] Charles Chenevix Trench, *The Great Dan: A Biography of Daniel O'Connell* (London, 1984), 200.

[9] Bruce Dolphin, 'Daniel O'Connell: An Interview from the Archives: Colonel George D'Aguilar's Memorandum of his Interview with Daniel O'Connell, 23 October 1830', *Canadian Journal of Irish Studies*, 27: 2 (Spring 2001), 39–40.

[10] Irish University Press Series of British Parliamentary Papers (BPP), *Third Report from the Select Committee on Orange Lodges in Ireland ... 1835, Civil Disorder 6* (Shannon, 1970), William John Hancock to E. G. Stanley, 28 Nov. 1830, pp. 172–3.

O'Connell, nonetheless, often declared that the success of his project required Irish Protestant support. Dr Fergus O'Farrell has written: 'Fundamental to O'Connell's policy was the hope of reconciliation, in the interests of Ireland, between Protestants and Catholics.'[11] But was O'Connell the type of politician possessed of the skills necessary to bring about reconciliation? It is true that he made serious efforts to win over—ultimately unsuccessfully—potentially 'patriotic' elements within Dublin intellectual Protestant conservatism.[12] Contrast this with his sometime northern ally Sharman Crawford's verdict: 'He is extremely kind and civil towards me when we meet, but has never shown the slightest desire to have communication on our actual views of a public question.'[13] O'Connell's failure in the north of Ireland, particularly his inability to work with liberal Presbyterians, was less predictable and all the more striking on this account. O'Connell has given his own analysis: 'After the emancipation I tried for five long years, I endeavoured to gain their confidence or, at least, to lessen their hostility. I thought to amalgamate all parties. I did all that I could.'[14] But had he, in fact, done all that he could? Liberal Presbyterians, after all, had supported Catholic emancipation; they continued, in the 1830s, to support three other great O'Connellite themes—parliamentary reform, municipal reform, and abolition of tithes. They fully supported O'Connell's broader international themes, including, in particular, anti-slavery. Yet O'Connell and the liberal Presbyterians had an awful falling-out in 1831. It is necessary to set these events in context; the whole unpleasant affair is characterized by complexity, misrecognition, and a degree of bad faith on all sides.

By the late 1820s Ulster Presbyterianism had become deeply divided, both on political and theological grounds. 'Zealous religion judiciously blended with loyalty', was the slogan of the Revd Henry Cooke, who emerged in the 1820s as the spokesman for an embattled populist Presbyterianism. Cooke himself was not an outright opponent of Catholic emancipation: he said he supported it in principle, provided sufficient assurances were given. Suggestively, he told the Lords Select Committee in 1825 that 'lower class' Protestants opposed Catholic emancipation because 'they understand by it some undefinable accession of power to the Roman Catholics, likely to turn to their injury'. At the same time he acknowledged that there was 'less fear' among the 'more informed' class of Presbyterians.

His main opponent in the Synod of Ulster, the 'New Light' preacher Revd Henry Montgomery, came from an intellectual, prosperous Co.

---

[11] Fergus O'Farrell, *Daniel O'Connell* (Dublin, 1981), 82.   [12] Ibid. 84.
[13] PRONI D856/9/34, William Sharman Crawford to John S. Crawford, 14 May 1835.
[14] *Northern Whig*, 4 Apr. 1839.

Antrim farming family with strong United Irish associations. Montgomery's elder brothers were involved in that movement, and in 1798 the young Montgomery (then 11 years old) had been present when Orange yeomen under local Tory command looted and burned the family farmhouse.[15] The more Arian Montgomery defended the rights of private conscience against Cooke's insistence on Trinitarian orthodoxy. Montgomery claimed that Cooke's success lay in his skill in uniting 'Evangelicalism [*sic*] and Orangeism',[16] and it was a fact that the evangelical revival created a common ground shared by Cooke and Anglicans such as Lord Roden, who had Orange views.[17] Cooke's support tended to come from smaller tenant farmers, while Montgomery could rely more easily on the more prosperous bourgeois and substantial farmers of East Ulster.[18] The theological conflict, both men believed, had definite political overtones; but it is important not to reduce the theological controversy to the political. In 1830 Montgomery and his party—not all of whom were Arian, but all of whom were supporters of Catholic emancipation—withdrew from the Synod of Ulster to form the Remonstrant Synod, which united with the long-established 'New Light' Presbytery of Antrim and the non-subscribers of the Synod of Munster as the Association of Non-Subscribing Presbyterian Churches of Ireland. But at the moment of Cooke's theological victory he had visibly failed to win an equal political triumph. As Professor Finlay Holmes has pointed out: 'When Cooke tried to have a special meeting of the Synod, called in 1829 to respond to the imminent concession of emancipation, he was unsuccessful even in his own presbytery.'[19]

In any case, O'Connell's first great row with Ulster Presbyterians was not to be with Cooke but with Montgomery, who, in January 1829, had spoken in favour of emancipation at a Catholic meeting in St Patrick's Chapel, Donegall Street, Belfast, presided over by William Crolly, then Catholic Bishop of Down and Connor. At first there was no hint of any row, rather the reverse. In December 1829 and January 1830 the *Northern Whig* published three unsigned articles denouncing the Irish land system in general, and the management of the absentee Marquess of Hertford's estate in particular. The Marquess of Hertford was a legendarily unpleasant man; he expected and obtained political subservience from his tenantry, but he had previously been

[15] J. A. Crozier, *The Life of the Rev Henry Montgomery LL D* (Belfast, 1875), 13.

[16] Finlay Holmes, *The Presbyterian Church in Ireland* (Dublin, 2000), 90; Andrew Holmes, 'Nineteenth-Century Liberal Presbyterian Perspectives on the 1798 Rebellion', in J. Augusteijn, *Irish History: A Research Yearbook* (Dublin, 2003).

[17] J. Venedey, *Ireland and the Irish* (Dublin, 1844), 271.

[18] Nigel Yates, *The Religious Condition of Ireland 1770–1850* (Oxford, 2006), 129.

[19] Holmes, *The Presbyterian Church*, 94; Ambrose Macaulay, *William Crolly: Archbishop of Armagh* (Dublin, 1994), 84–8.

considered to be a good landlord and was, indeed, admired by Cooke.[20] The language of the *Whig*'s articles was angry; the anonymous author was Henry Montgomery. J. A. Crozier, Montgomery's biographer, claimed that the articles marked the first articulation of a doctrine of tenant right. Certainly, Montgomery insisted that there were natural rights 'antecedent' to any legal title which meant the landlord was a 'steward', not an absolute proprietor.[21]

Provoked by an extract from the *Court Journal* describing the extravagant 'princely habits' of the Marquess of Hertford's retinue on its progress to Italy, Montgomery, in his first article, drew attention to the 'half-naked' children of the mountain tenantry on his Irish estates. The Marquess was a 'spoiled child of fortune'. Montgomery argued that now the 40 shilling freeholder had lost his vote, and thus, utility to the landlord, he was being ruthlessly squeezed out. (The latter charge was sharply denied by the Marquess of Hertford's agent.) But what is perhaps even more remarkable is the 'national' tone of Montgomery's remarks. 'The Hertford family', he said, 'have always been aliens to Ireland in connexion, feelings and residence.'[22] In a later speech Montgomery went so far as to hail the spirit of 'Captain Rock': 'This Rock is very popular and liberal-minded. He can raise recruits out of Protestant Ulster as successfully as out of Catholic Munster.'[23] The Rockite movement, which swept through Munster in the early 1820s, was associated with the millenarian anti-Protestant fantasy of the Pastorini prophecy.[24] The Rockite theme, even when articulated by sophisticates like Thomas Moore, was 'a vindication of Irish Catholics and an indictment of British misrule in Ireland'.[25] Mainstream Irish Protestants naturally regarded the Rockite movement with horror; Montgomery's apparent embrace of it, therefore, was a remarkable development.

The Marquess threatened to sue the *Whig* for libel; the *Whig* turned to Daniel O'Connell for legal help. The Liberator immediately offered his services for free. The Marquess of Hertford then decided not to continue with his legal action. His closer friends, who included John Wilson

---

[20] A. Atkinson, *Ireland: Exhibited to England*, vol. 2 (Dublin and London, 1823), 30–1.

[21] Crozier, *Montgomery*, i. 419–22.

[22] They appeared in the *Northern Whig* on 7 Dec. 1829, 7 Jan. 1830, 13 Jan. 1830.

[23] Ibid., 28 Dec. 1830.

[24] James S. Donnelly, 'Pastorini and Captain Cook: Millenarianism and Sectarianism in the Rockite Movement 1821–24', in S. Clark and J. J. Donnelly (eds.), *Irish Peasants: Violence and Political Unrest* (Dublin, 1983); Luke Gibbons, 'Between Captain Rock and a Hard Place: Art and Agrarian Insurgency', in T. Foley and S. Ryder (eds.), *Ideology and Ireland in the Nineteenth Century* (Dublin, 1998), 23–44.

[25] J. H. Murphy, *Ireland: A Social, Cultural and Literary History, 1791–1891* (Dublin, 2003), 59; Emer Nolan, 'Irish Melodies and Discordant Politics: Thomas Moore's Memoirs of Captain Rock (1824)', *Field Day Review*, 2 (2006), 41–53.

Croker,[26] suggested that the possibility of exposure of the exceptional peculiarities of his private life—he was, for example, estranged from his wife and lived openly with Lady Strachan[27]—might have deterred him. The whole incident has a broader significance: it marked the high point of the O'Connellite–Presbyterian liberal understanding.

Within a year, the Belfast liberals and O'Connellites were exchanging insults. Perhaps suggestively, the *Whig* was particularly contemptuous of O'Connell's effort to reduce Orange hostility.[28] O'Connell's attempt to win over the Orangemen was derided as a 'piece of false mummery'. There was always an element of parody in O'Connell's 'pro-Orange' gestures: did it really make sense to propose that a pro-repeal crowd should circle the statue of King William on College Green three times, the bands playing 'God Save the King, the Boyne water and St Patrick's Day'?[29] His theatrical public devices—the kissing of an Orange ribband; toasting the Orangemen in a bumper of water filled from the Boyne; the 'mock prayers' of forgiveness for past sins against Orangemen—impressed some: admirers, perhaps tongue-in-cheek, sent him gifts of Orange regalia.[30] But it did not impress the *Northern Whig*, which, at the beginning of January 1831, dismissed O'Connell's activities as 'being mostly of a hare-brained mob agitator rather than a man of his power'.[31] A great O'Connellite versus liberal Presbyterian row was not long delayed. On 20 January 1831 Montgomery sent an address to the Whig Viceroy, Lord Anglesey, praising his early support for Catholic emancipation, but reasserting Montgomery's support for the union. On 26 January 1831 O'Connell, who was in the process of facing down an Anglesey-inspired prosecution of his General Association, proclaimed that he held the most 'sovereign contempt' for Henry Montgomery, a 'fawning hypocrite', and denouncing his Arianism. What had gone wrong? Montgomery replied with a celebrated stinging letter, pointing out that O'Connell had not disdained his support for emancipation because of his disbelief in the Trinity.[32] It is easy to see that a bitter split was looming: a split which had a definite political basis.

O'Connell had responded to the achievement of emancipation by switching emphasis to repeal of the union and the establishment of a Dublin parliament. The *Whig* constituency, on the other hand, saw Catholic emancipation as a harbinger of further reforms to come; reforms which

[26] Myron Brightfield, *John Wilson Croker* (Berkeley, 1940), 94.
[27] William Thomas, *The Quarrel of Macaulay and Croker: Politics and History in the Age of Reform* (Oxford, 2002), 161–7.
[28] Erin R. Bishop (ed), *'My Darling Danny': Letters from Mary O'Connell to her Son, 1830–31* (Cork, 1998), Mary O'Connell to Daniel O'Connell, Jan. 1831, p. 39.
[29] *Spectator*, 1 Jan. 1831.   [30] *The Nation*, 25 Oct. 1845.
[31] *Northern Whig*, 3 Jan. 1831.   [32] Crozier, *Montgomery*, App. A.

would give real meaning to the union concept. The Whig Belfast activist and banker Robert Grimshaw explained: 'I admit that there should not be such a union as we have had hitherto. But let the past be forgotten. Better prospects have opened to our view.'[33] For the *Whig* editorialists, Catholic emancipation was a great moment of hope for the Irish people:

> We are not, it is true, an outcast people ... We have no peculiar mark fixed upon us, by which we are to be recognised at the door of the British Constitution and excluded from a participation in the privileges provided for the most favoured portion of our fellow subjects. We are no longer called to toil for the support of the stately and beautiful fabric, the sanctuary of whose vestibule would be polluted by our unhallowed tread.[34]

There was still a great work of reform to be carried out, and until it was completed Ireland remained a 'foreign province' within the British Empire. The project was to remove all signs of Irish inferiority or isolation within the system; not to separate from it in any way.

The basis of the *Whig*'s disillusionment with O'Connell now becomes clearer. The liberal Presbyterian constituency had supported an enhancement of Catholic political power because they wished to see the strengthening of a progressive reformist alliance within the United Kingdom. They felt that O'Connell now had a unique opportunity to drive forward a reformist agenda to eliminate the remaining sources of religious inequality. O'Connell's attempt to woo Orange and Tory elements appeared to them to be both insincere and futile, yet dictated at some level by the 'repeal demand'. For the *Northern Whig*, the realistic alliance was the Catholic–liberal Protestant one which had brought about emancipation. There was actually no particular point in trying to win over the Orange–Tory interest; rather, one attempted to marginalize it within the progressive polity of the United Kingdom.

This was an alliance which had the capacity to determine the political tune; providing, of course, the futile project of repeal was sidelined. The negative, fearful side of northern liberalism—the fear that O'Connellism embodied a new spirit of Catholic ascendancy—was real enough; but it has to be placed alongside the existence of more positive political ambitions and a willingness to work alongside Catholics to achieve common objectives. A very suggestive example here was the campaign against the payment of tithes to the Established Church in Ireland, an area where both Presbyterians and Catholics perceived a common injustice. Montgomery would not have disagreed with Captain Rock's summary of the tithes issue: 'Thirteen fourteenths of the people are taxed for the instruction

[33] *Northern Whig*, 3 Dec. 1829.   [34] Ibid.

of the small remaining fraction.'[35] The Montgomery–O'Connell row of 1831 was not, therefore, the end of the matter; when, at any point in the 1830s and 1840s, Daniel O'Connell seemed prepared to push repeal into the background and concentrated on more immediate grievances, he could count on a significant measure of Presbyterian liberal support. The whole exchange had contained more layers of ambiguity than many realized. O'Connell, at the very moment when he denounced Montgomery as a 'fawning hypocrite', was discussing seriously with Lord Cloncurry the possibility of dropping repeal in favour of a more moderate strategy which would, in effect, have placed the Liberator in very much the same political place as Montgomery.[36] Since 1828 Cloncurry, after all, had been a close friend and adviser to Anglesey.[37] Anglesey, it was said, told the Prime Minister that Montgomery had inflicted a smashing blow on repeal,[38] but O'Connell himself was already deciding to soften his position. The government's harassment of O'Connell was popular with some—the King was 'in perfect ecstasy'[39]—but policy was about to change.

DANIEL O'CONNELL: PATRON OF REFORM

On 1 March 1831 the government announced its scheme for parliamentary reform. O'Connell declared that the proposal was better than he had expected. As late as 3 March 1831 Anglesey wrote to Melbourne in a moment of black humour, and talked of sending O'Connell to some northern prison: Carrickfergus, for instance, where he would be surrounded by a Protestant population, which would 'take good care of him'.[40] The government was soon to retreat from any such notion: a new implicit understanding was reached with O'Connell. He agreed to disband the current repeal movement in return for the effective quashing of his own conviction, and some ameliorative Irish measures.[41]

---

35 Thomas Moore, *Memoirs of Captain Rock, the Celebrated Irish Chieftain, with some Account of the Ancestors, written by Himself,* 4th edn. (London, 1824), 301.
36 PRONI D 619/218/C, Anglesey to Lord Grey, 22 Jan. 1831. Cloncurry was a close ally of Anglesey; see his *Personal Recollections,* 351.
37 Marquess of Anglesey, FSA (ed.), *One-Leg: The Life and Letters of Henry William Paget, First Marquess of Anglesey 1768–1854* (London, 1963), 210–12, 245–69.
38 Crozier, *Montgomery,* 430.
39 John Gore (ed.), *Thomas Creevey's Papers 1793–1838* (Harmondsworth, 1985), Creevey to Miss Ord, 31 Jan. 1831, p. 319.
40 PRONI D 615/29/70.
41 O. MacDonagh, *O'Connell and Parnell* (Cambridge, 1998), 13.

The offer was, in effect, accepted: the project of parliamentary reform trumped everything. As William Cooke Taylor noted, the aid 'which he gave the Government on the Reform Bill was too valuable to be unrewarded; the Act under which he had been convicted was allowed to expire, and he was never called up for judgement'.[42] G. Shaw Lefevre has commented equally cynically: 'Doubtless, the introduction of the Reform Bill, the difficulties which the government met with, and the political necessity of keeping on *good* terms with the Irish members, accounted for the sudden abandonment of the policy of prohibiting meetings in Ireland and enforcing the law against O'Connell.'[43]

The new politicians in Dublin Castle constituted an interesting group. Anglesey, a 'premature' public supporter of emancipation, was now back as Lord-Lieutenant. The distinguished old soldier was very much in the 'Foxite orbit'; he was working alongside the Chief Secretary Lord Stanley, not Foxite, but serious and energetic.[44] On 8 March 1831 O'Connell 'repaid' the government with a celebrated speech on the Reform Bill.[45] On 24 April Tom Moore told O'Connell that he thought the repeal agitation had been 'premature' and ill-managed, but O'Connell did not seem to mind the reproach[46] at all. In truth, he had already moved on: O'Connell and the Whig government had established a working alliance. In the general election of May 1831, which followed the House of Lords' rejection of the first Reform Bill, O'Connell worked in complete harmony with and for the ministry, parcelling out Irish candidatures and helping to secure the return of prominent Irish ministers.

It was not alone the electoral reform issue which allowed O'Connell to rehabilitate himself so artfully; the darker problems of British rule in Ireland began to reassert themselves. Anglesey, in August 1831, wrote privately about the 'impossibility' of governing Ireland 'from Downing Street', bitterly lamenting the frustration of reformist impulse, and holding: 'were it not that no parliament in Dublin would be free to do its duty ... I would be against the union.'[47] Anglesey told Grey, as the year drew to a close, that Ireland was 'frightfully oppressed and degraded. It suffers injury and insult and oppression and exaction that no other people upon

[42] Patrick Maume (ed.), William Cooke Taylor, *Reminiscences of Daniel O'Connell: During the Agitations of the Veto, Emancipation and Repeal (1847)* (Dublin, 2005), 78.

[43] G. Shaw Lefevre, *Peel and O'Connell: A Review of the Irish Policy of Parliament from the Act of Union to the Death of Sir Robert Peel* (London, 1887), 125.

[44] Peter Mandler, *Aristocratic Government in the Age of Reform: Whigs and Liberals 1830–52* (Oxford, 1990), 70, 128.

[45] Chevenix Trench, *The Great Dan*, 201.

[46] T. Moore, 'Political and Historical Writings on Irish and British Affairs', *Moore's Journal*, introduction by B. Clifford (Belfast, 1993), 234.

[47] PRONI D 619/27/B, pp. 38–9, Anglesey to Holland, 12 Aug. 1831.

Earth would stand, and my only astonishment is that Ireland is not in open rebellion.'[48] Agrarian crime was mounting dramatically—at least, O'Connell was being helpful on the matter.[49] It was in the space created by these concerns that O'Connell operated.

Anglesey veered sharply between moods of conciliation and more repressive attitudes, all the while being haunted by a lack of self-confidence about the basis of the union itself. Such a context inevitably allowed the possibility of further bouts of O'Connellite co-operation. Melbourne told Anglesey on 25 October 1831: 'I have, for a long time, thought that we either lose Ireland, or hold her by means of the Protestants, and I hardly know which alternative opens to us the more melancholy and appalling prospect.' Anglesey, who, only six months before, had joked to Melbourne about locking up O'Connell in Carrickfergus jail and placing him in the good care of the local Protestants, responded sharply three days later: 'The bare mention of governing Ireland by means of the Protestants horrifies and appals me. I declare, that I will not be the man to attempt it.'[50] Anglesey became much more sympathetic to O'Connell, reporting to the Prime Minister on 6 November 1831: 'I believe but will not swear that O'Connell is working fairly, notwithstanding his occasional *écarts*, which I believe to be necessary to preserve him from totally falling in the people's estimation.'[51]

Anglesey's new Chief Secretary, Lord Stanley, found it difficult to be quite so understanding of O'Connell's peculiarities. His relationship with O'Connell tended to be confrontational. Stanley—considered to be the cleverest eldest son produced by the English aristocracy in a century[52]—nonetheless seized the moment in autumn 1831 to issue his ambitious instructions for the establishment of a national school system.[53] Stanley, interestingly, hoped to fund a non-denominational system which would facilitate the social integration of Catholics and Protestants. James Doyle (JKL), the Catholic Bishop of Kildare and Leighlin, was a strong believer in integrated education, as was Archbishop Whateley, the able new Whig-appointed Church of Ireland Archbishop of Dublin.[54] The steady weakening of liberalism within the Catholic hierarchy, combined with the heavily Catholic or Protestant composition of many school localities, had

---

[48] Anglesey to Grey, 19 Dec. 1831; the Marquess of Anglesey (ed.), *One-Leg*, 259.
[49] Trench, *The Great Dan*, 202.   [50] Marquess of Anglesey (ed.), *One-Leg*, 63.
[51] PRONI D 619/28/C/198.
[52] John Charmley, 'The View from Knowsley', *History Today*, 54: 3 (March 2004), 50.
[53] *Dublin Gazette*, 8 Dec. 1831. For a careful discussion see D. A. Akenson, *The Irish National Education Experiment: The National System of Education in the Nineteenth Century* (London, 1970), 117–22.
[54] Hugh Kearney, 'Context and Ideas of Nationhood 1800–1895', *Irish Review*, 20 (Winter–Spring 1997).

the effect that the system never delivered its full reconciling potential,[55] but it did much to improve the educational level of the Irish population, bringing about a dramatic fall in national illiteracy in under a decade.[56]

While Stanley promoted his educational plans, O'Connell at last received his decree of precedency—six years after the first serious discussions in 1825. On 20 October Anglesey had sent the liberal Protestant lawyer Louis Perrin, 'the most safe and serious man', to O'Connell to inform him that the government wished to 'place him where he ought to be in his profession'.[57] On 4 November O'Connell accepted the silk gown of the inner bar. The matter finally resolved, Anglesey reported to Holland with great pleasure: 'I rejoice in having done for him what has been done. He won the favour, or rather the act of justice, by a tolerable consistent support for the government upon reform. We have proven that there is no angry feeling towards him, and we are ready to do for him all he enables us to do.'[58] Within days the era of good feelings was over. On 14 November Holland recorded in his diary that 'O'Connell was once again behaving badly: scurrilously abusing Stanley and disparaging Lord Anglesey without provocation. The King is reported to have said: "The gloss was not off his silk gown before he began flinging dirt and kicking up a dust to defile it".'[59] But Anglesey, by now, was both used to, and resigned to, this sort of thing.

Despite the O'Connell–Montgomery row, one area of tacit Catholic–Presbyterian agreement was the issue of tithes. There was to many a manifest injustice in Catholics and Presbyterians having to support an incumbent parson, who might well be ministering only to a small number of Anglican parishioners. One senior aristocratic Whig, describing such a case, opined: 'Can you be surprised … that these tithes have never been collected since I have been there, without riot and almost bloodshed?'[60] There had been opposition to the payment of tithes expressed by the rural secret

[55] See the *Eleventh Report of the Commissioners of National Education in Ireland for the Year 1844* (Dublin, 1845), 24 Apr. 1845, para. 33. Here the commissioners openly state that their objective was not a system of 'united education' in that sense, but rather 'the system of united education which it was really desired to establish, and which has, in fact, been established is a system which does not exclude children of any denomination which will admit, without doing violence to the conscience of those, of whatever religious creed, who may wish for education.'

[56] MacDonagh, *The Economy and Society*, 233–4; D. H. Akenson, 'Pre-University Education, 1782–1870', in W. E. Vaughan (ed.), *Ireland Under the Union 1802–70* (Oxford, 1989), 530–5.

[57] PRONI D 619/273/20, Anglesey to Holland, 20 Oct. 1831.

[58] PRONI D 619/27/B/65, same to same, 5 Dec. 1831.

[59] Abraham D Kriegel (ed.), *The Holland House Diaries 1831–1880: The Diary of Henry Richard Vassall Fox, with Extracts from the Diary of Dr John Allen* (London, 1977), 78.

[60] Dorothy Howell-Thomas, *Duncannon Reformer, Reconciler* (Norwich, 1992), 167.

societies of the late eighteenth and nineteenth centuries. But it is important to note that Parliament's attempt to reform the tithe system in 1823–4 had the effect of increasing the tithe burden for large farmers; in particular, the exemption of grassland was no longer permitted.[61] The payment of tithes now tended to fall more on the middling and large farmers as against the smallholders (so numerically strong in Connaught) or agricultural labourers. Perhaps not surprisingly, therefore, the stronger farmers of Leinster and late Munster took the initiative in the tithe war. The anti-tithe campaign brought about frequent bloody clashes between police, process-servers, soldiers, and the farming population. But in one particularly celebrated clash 'the people' came out decisively on top: at Carrickshock—(*carraigseabhac*, 'the hawk's rock') in December 1831 seventeen people were killed. Four of these were tithe-resisters, but thirteen were constables, stoned to death while packed together on a constricted boreen.[62] Lord Melbourne grimly told Anglesey that he was put in mind of the 'ferocity' of the Hurons or the Iroquois. The victory at Carrickshock was, however, not typical: in other encounters of this kind, the crowds usually bore the brunt of the violence. Hence the need to construct a more effective, peaceful strategy: the system of passive resistance invented by Richard Lalor, a repeal MP for Queens County and a prosperous gentleman farmer.[63]

On 28 November 1832 Anglesey reported to Lord Grey: 'In Connaught, it is true, tithe [was] paid with less difficulty than I expected. In Ulster (Protestant as it is) with a bad grace, while in Leinster and Munster the resistance is universal.'[64] The anti-tithe warriors hit on a method of struggle: they sought to deny tithe-collectors any effective means of collection, though tithes, after delays made as long as possible, were often then paid under duress, at the point of a bayonet[65] 'Even in the event of a seizure of goods,' Gearóid Ó Tuathaigh has written of the conflict, 'a conspiracy to boycott or "fix" the ensuing auction could render it a Pyrrhic victory for the tithe owner.'[66] Such a form of struggle was accompanied by other actions designed to show the respectability and solidarity of those opposed to tithes. After one major demonstration, the point was driven home: 'In the evening

---

[61] S. Clark, *Social Origins of the Irish Land War* (Princeton, 1974), 92; Patrick O'Donoghue, 'Causes of Opposition to Tithes', *Studia Hibernica*, 5 (1968), 7–8.

[62] Gary Owens, 'The Carrickshock Incident, 1831: Social Memory and an Irish *cause celebre*', *Cultural and Social History*, 1: 1 (1994), 37. A 'boreen' is a small country road.

[63] James Fintan Lalor to Sir Robert Peel, 12 July 1843, in T. P. O'Neill, *James Fintan Lalor* (Wexford, 2003), 36–9.

[64] PRONI D 619/28/C/285.

[65] Patrick Egan, *Freeman's Journal*, 11 Aug. 1880.

[66] Gearóid Ó Tuathaigh, *Ireland Before the Famine* (Dublin, 1973), 177.

a company consisting of 150 gentlemen, wealthy graziers and substantial farmers sat down to an excellent dinner at Eiffe's hotel.'[67]

But if the strong farmers took the lead, other classes in Catholic rural and small-town society were happy to join in. The success of the emancipation campaign had infected the populace with a taste for the pleasures of political mobilization in a good cause. In Midleton, Co. Cork, for example, the 'entire population' looked on as the trades of the small town—the bakers, butchers, carpenters, masons, bookmakers, and brogue-makers, each under its own broad silk banner—took up their positions for an anti-tithe demonstration. Every individual composing these bodies wore a green-and-orange sash and had on his hat a laurel leaf, an emblem of victory.

From this position they shortly removed, preceded by the band belonging to the town, with its own flags and streamers to make room for another immense body of horse and foot, which took up for a moment in its place. This body also was preceded by a band, and had colours flying, and exhibited ingenious and elegant devices as well as the others; but it had beside these a distinct, characteristic feature. This was a bier, decorated with all due form, and borne with all due solemnity [carrying] a large coffin—inscribed in broad and legible letters with the words 'Tithes: Died 21 June 1832'.[68]

This recalled the local rector's recent failure to sell tithe-distrained cattle. It was reported that over 50,000 people marched behind this coffin. The widespread popularity of the anti-tithe campaign is not in doubt: in Munster in particular, the excitement it generated, brilliantly articulated by Feargus O'Connor, the nephew of the United Irish leader Arthur O'Connor, fed into the pro-O'Connellite passions of the 1832 general election.[69]

The general election of December 1832 provided a great national triumph for the Whigs—in Great Britain they defeated the Conservatives by 408 seats to 145, but in Ireland the Repealers did better than the government expected. They became the largest party, with forty-two seats; the Liberals had thirty-three and the Conservatives thirty. The Prime Minister, Grey, wrote to Anglesey: 'I always feared that the elections in Ireland would not prove favourable to us, but I did not expect they would be so entirely under the control of O'Connell.'[70] In agreement, the Lord-Lieutenant replied to Grey: 'In Parliament, O'Connell, I fear, will have a tail of 30 Repealers. A few of these only are so by choice, but all desperately afraid. The subject of repeal is now raging with intense violence, and the time is arrived when it must be crushed by some determined act.'

[67] *Western Argus and Galway Commercial Chronicle*, 31 June 1832.
[68] *Cork Chronicle*, 30 June 1832.
[69] Daniel O. Madden, *Ireland and its Rulers Since 1829* (London, 1843), 217.
[70] PRONI D 619/28 A–B/132, 14 Dec. 1832.

In 1833 the Whigs decided to tackle the issue of church reform via the Irish route. Some radicals attempted to subvert the principle of establishment in England by exploiting the greater vulnerability of the Irish Church. It was, however, also the case that Peel and many Tories felt that reform—to protect the Church—was both necessary and desirable; obvious abuses had to be ended.

The Whig Bill had contained a clause (147) providing for appropriation to secular use of surplus revenues. This was lost due to the scale of opposition in Parliament to the notion of any appropriation of sacred property. O'Connell attacked the Bill when the appropriation clause was removed.[71] Nevertheless, the clipped and enfeebled wings of Irish Toryism cannot have escaped his notice. For even when passed on 14 August, the Church Temporalities Act was highly controversial. Church rate was abolished, to the great delight of English Dissenters, and ten Irish bishoprics were abolished. A young Tory politician, W. E. Gladstone, denounced the policy of the Whigs with reference to the Church of Ireland, and expressed his belief that 'if it should be removed, they would not long be able to resist the repeal of the union'.[72]

In 1833 also, O'Connell fought a long and brilliant parliamentary battle against Lord Stanley's tough Coercion Bill. This gave the authorities more powers of arbitrary arrest and imprisonment and control of public meetings. O'Connell did, however, remove those sections which would have weakened an anti-tithe agitation.[73] At the same moment O'Connell was privately worried by the level of agrarian crime in Ireland, and was quite happy to say that soldiers should be used to put it down.[74] But it is important to note that for O'Connellites the anti-tithe campaign, even when it spilled over into serious violence, was a distinct phenomenon from that of agrarian terrorism. When, in 1833, O'Connell sent his head pacificator, Tom Steele, to Kilkenny, the move was regarded with great suspicions by the authorities,[75] but 'banditti' activities had virtually ceased by the spring of 1833. Twelve years later Steele told his side of the story. The same 'Carrickshock men' who had been so active in the tithe war kept clear of the armed, oath-bound secret society of the Kilkenny Whitefeet, 'whom they despised'. 'Indeed,' declared Tom Steele, 'they actually enrolled themselves under me as an O'Connellite police force to put down the midnight

---

[71] E. R. Norman, *A History of Modern Ireland* (London, 1971), 89.

[72] *Hansard*, ser. 3, vol. 27, col. 533; Thomas Webb, *Ipse Dixit or the Gladstonian Settlement of Ireland* (Dublin and London, 1886), 46.

[73] Lecky, *Leaders*, ii. 136–7.

[74] James Donnelly, 'The Land Question in Nationalist Politics', in T. E. Hachey and L. J. McCaffrey (eds.), *Perspectives in Irish Nationalism* (Lexington, 1989), 82.

[75] PRONI D619/29/B/183, Anglesey to Holland, 25 Feb. 1833.

disturbances in their district of the County of Kilkenny.[76] British soldiers and police, in short, should be used against agrarian assassins; but anti-tithe warriors were a very different group, essentially responsive to O'Connell's leadership, and ought not to be subject to state repression.

The year 1834 saw a surprising setback for O'Connell's parliamentary strategy. As early as December 1832 shrewd English observers had noted his capacity for alienating a favourable House of Commons.[77] But in February 1834 O'Connell seemed to have hit upon a winning issue, even if the issue itself was a surprising one—the conduct of Judge William Cusack Smith, Burke's old friend and a lifelong emancipationist. Cusack Smith was a very serious insomniac, and had developed the habit of opening his court hearings later and later in the day.[78] In the 1830s, irritated by the emergence of the repeal agitation, he had also taken to making rather political comments, even at the end of purely criminal trials. Even his personal friend, Bishop Doyle, publicly satirized Cusack Smith's *obiter dicta* on tithes-resistance.[79] Cusack Smith became increasingly unpopular—a large reward had to be offered for information concerning attacks on his house and property.[80] As Baron Smith openly admitted in 1834: 'For the last two years I scarcely lost an opportunity for making some "observations from the bench" on "the audacity of factional leaders".'[81] Other judges were exasperated, as Thomas Moore noted, by his vanity and explosive bad temper, and perhaps also by his endless use of pseudonyms in his writing of political pamphlets.[82] Some repealers remembered Cusack Smith's traditional sympathy for the Catholic cause and urged restraint upon O'Connell, but O'Connell felt he could not pass up an easy target. The liberal papers openly described the judge as a 'dotard'.[83]

O'Connell moved in February that the House of Commons appoint a select committee to enquire into the conduct of Baron Smith, both on the grounds of inefficiency and inappropriate political activity. O'Connell started out with the support of Stanley, who agreed that in England a judge who held such late hearings would be questioned. Stanley added that

---

[76] *The Nation*, 10 Jan. 1846; Galen Broeker, *Rural Disorder and Police Reform in Ireland 1812–1836* (London, 1970), 237.

[77] E. A. Smith, *Reform or Revolution: A Diary of Reform in England 1830–2* (Stroud, 1992), 152–3.

[78] Edith Somerville and Martin Ross, *An Incorruptible Irishman* (London, 1932), 61; O'Neill Daunt, *Eighty Years of Irish History* (London, 1886), 76.

[79] W. J. Fitzpatrick, *The Life, Times and Correspondence of the Most Rev. Dr Doyle, Bishop of Kildare and Leighlin* (Dublin, 1890), 392–3.

[80] PRONI T3069/D/3.

[81] *Charge of the Honourable Baron Smith at his Dublin Commission*, 18 Feb. 1834 (Dublin, 1834), 1.

[82] F. Elrington Ball, *The Judges in Ireland, 1221–1921* (London, 1926), ii. 333–4.

[83] *Charge of the Honourable Baron Smith*, 6.

Cusack Smith's political comments were foolish: 'By talking too much like so many others, he got himself into a scrape.'[84] But William Cusack Smith had his supporters. Robert Peel took the lead in reminding the House of Cusack Smith's status as the worthy recipient of two important Burke letters.[85] Robert Spankie declared:

Had not the House had enough of indiscretion already? Would it bring this judge, the friend and correspondent of Burke—a circumstance which was in itself a high honour to any man—could it bring him over from Ireland to this country for the purpose of generosity? Where, indeed, was the justice of rendering miserable the dying years of a noble man, merely because he had made reflections disagreeable to certain parties in Ireland?[86]

At first O'Connell won the day—by a majority of ninety-seven, the House ordered an inquiry into the conduct of the judge. On 18 February Cusack Smith defended himself in Dublin: he had merely been insisting that Ireland did not contain 7 million legislators; each individual was not entitled to legislate for himself.[87]

Then O'Connell proceeded to destroy the advanced position he had so carefully constructed. On 21 February the House debated the subject of agricultural distress: O'Connell unwisely seized the opportunity to attack the British state's solemn attitude towards the national debt. He treated with disdain talk of the 'violation' of the 'national faith'. He concluded that the national faith so-called was national injustice.[88] Stanley denounced O'Connell's 'absurd' and profligate opinions,[89] while Peel claimed that O'Connell made a 'jest of national honour'.[90] When the House moved on shortly afterwards to Cusack Smith, O'Connell could not reclaim the lost ground. Frederick Shaw made a fine 'Irish conservative' speech, defending the independence of judiciary and, more prosaically, Baron Sir William Cusack Smith's level of efficiency.[91] The House then agreed to rescind the resolution to hold a Select Committee to review Baron Smith. O'Connell reacted blithely to his defeat: in a letter to P. V. Fitzgerald on 22 February 1834, he denounced 'the foolish good nature' of the liberal politicians who had been soft towards Cusack Smith, and noted that 'miscreant judges' now knew they were 'not altogether free' of 'the possibility of punishment'.[92] Cusack Smith heaved a sigh of relief, acknowledging in a letter to a loyal friend, Lord Cloncurry, that he regarded political statements as 'inconsistent

---

[84] *Hansard*, 3rd ser., vol. 21 col. 299.
[85] Ibid., col. 302.   [86] Ibid., col. 303.   [87] *Charge of … Smith*, 7.
[88] *Hansard*, 21 Feb., col. 685.   [89] Ibid., col. 688.   [90] Ibid., col. 689.
[91] Ibid., cols. 726–31.
[92] Maurice O'Connell (ed.), *The Correspondence of Daniel O'Connell, 1833–36*, 8 vols. (Dublin, 1972–80), v. 104.

with the duties and station I hold'.[93] Shiel watched it all in horror, and reported to his wife—quite accurately—that O'Connell's speech on the agricultural distress notion had been a disaster: 'O'Connell made a dreadful slip last night ... he lost himself ... thus his order relative to Baron Smith was discharged.'[94] Daniel O. Madden, in his brilliant account of the debate, saw it as a sign of Peel's growing effectiveness—a blow to the ministry.[95] W. Cooke Taylor, Peel's Irish biographer, in a more detailed account supported this view.[96]

O'Connell had certainly managed to uncover all the latent fears about his integrity and stability and bring them to the surface of political life. Peel pointed out that 'in a few days' O'Connell would put repeal before the House, yet, as a result of O'Connell's demagogy on the debt, the question of the repeal of the union had already been decided.[97] Peel gleefully observed: anyone 'who had anything to lose, could ... draw the inference that if such slender pretences could be brought ... to justify the violation of the national faith, there could be no security for property of any description'.[98] On 29 April 1834 the repeal motion was defeated by a predictably immense majority of 523 votes to 38. The debate was noted as much for the sustained eloquence of Emerson Tennent's rebuttal of Home Rule as any speech made by the repealers. Emerson Tennent made much of the economic success Belfast had enjoyed under the union. In the first three decades of the nineteenth century Belfast's population had increased from about 20,000 to 53,000, as men and women from rural Ulster migrated to the city or its hinterland, to work as hand-loom weavers or as spinners in cotton factories, and increasingly, after 1830, in linen mills.[99] But he also stressed an important political theme: a more positive political vision of the union.

The Irish MP sits [in Parliament] to legislate ... for the interests of the most opulent and powerful empire in the universe ... [he helps to extend] the blessings of freedom from the confines of India to the remotest shores of the Atlantic, to liberate the Hindus, and to strike off the fetters of the African ... these are honours which

---

[93] W. C. Smith to Lord Cloncurry, 27 Mar. 1834, in *Personal Recollections of the Life and Times with Extracts from the Correspondence of Valentine Lord Cloncurry* (Dublin, 1849), 308.

[94] NLI Ms 1138, 22 Feb. 1834.

[95] Daniel O. Madden, *Ireland and its Rulers Since 1829: Volume the Second* (London, 1844), 138.

[96] W. Cooke Taylor, *The Life and Times of Sir Robert Peel*, vol. 5 (London, 1848), 364–76.

[97] *Hansard*, 21 Feb. 1834, col. 689.   [98] Ibid., col 689.

[99] Kerby A. Miller, 'Forging the "Protestant Way of Life" in Early Nineteenth-Century Ulster', in David A. Wilson and Mark G. Spencer (eds.), *Ulster Presbyterians in the Atlantic World* (Dublin, 2006), 137.

enable us, whilst we pride ourselves upon a birthplace as Irishmen, to add to our distinctions the glory of being Britons.[100]

At least the formal debate and defeat allowed O'Connell to move on to other issues, such as tithes, which had a more immediate political edge.[101]

O'Connell fought the 1835 election not on the slogan of repeal but on the slogan of 'No Tories, No Tithes'. It was an effective tactic. The main features of the election of January 1835 are clear: a decline in the position of the Whigs, a resurgence of the Tories, and an advance in radical strength. If the Whigs wished to regain power, they had little choice but to work closely both with O'Connell and the radicals.[102]

For O'Connell, there were real advantages in such an arrangement. For five years he had occupied a remarkable but isolated position in the House of Commons.[103] O'Connell had more friends in Cabinet than he realized, yet was never able to fully exploit this fact.[104] But in this new context created by the general election he was now the leader of a less united but larger Irish Party potentially allied to a government dependent on his support.

O'CONNELL AND THE WHIG GOVERNMENT: THE LICHFIELD HOUSE COMPACT

O'Connell's understanding with the Whigs emerged from meetings at Lichfield House, the Earl of Lichfield's residence, in March and April 1835. The 'compact', as it became known, had a simple, easily intelligible basis: the Whigs were returned to power while O'Connell was promised an Irish government sensitive to his agenda. Lord John Russell was later to acknowledge that an alliance undoubtedly existed.[105] It was often a frustrating partnership for both sides. Lord Melbourne, the Prime Minister, played little or no part in the negotiations of the compact, and always felt that, in the final analysis, Irish Protestants—for all their bigotry—were

---

[100] J. P. A. Bew, 'The Dilemmas of Liberal Unionism', M.Phil. thesis, Cambridge University (2002); Jennifer Ridden, 'Britishness as Imperial and Diasporic Identity: Irish Elite Perspectives c. 1820–1870', in Peter Gray (ed.), *Victoria's Ireland? Irishness and Britishness 1837–1901* (Dublin, 2004), 93.

[101] MacDonagh, *O'Connell*, 382–7.

[102] A. H. Graham, 'Historical Revision: The Lichfield House Compact 1835', *Irish Historical Studies*, 121 (Mar. 1961), 212.

[103] Macintyre, *The Liberator*, 145.

[104] Vincent (ed.), *Disraeli, Derby and the Conservative Party: The Political Journals of Lord Stanley* (Hassocks, 1978), 21 Aug. 1834, p. 224.

[105] Graham, 'Lichfield House Compact', 209; L. G. Mitchell, *Lord Melbourne 1779–1848* (Oxford, 1997), 178–81.

the sine qua non of the union which he supported. The Tories could easily intensify the Melbourne government's difficulties by suggesting that it danced to the Irish demagogue's tune. On 19 May 1835 Russell told the House of Commons: 'The subject of repeal was open to amendment or question like any other act of our legislature.' The Tory *Quarterly Review* responded with sarcastic anger: 'as open to question as a turnpike bill.'[106] On this point at least, interestingly, Karl Marx agreed with the *Quarterly Review*: this union—if Russell was to be taken seriously, which, of course, Marx doubted—was now subject to legislative amendment or question, in Marx's phrase, 'neither more nor less than any Bill dealing with beer'.[107]

O'Connell was often frustrated by the progress of his legislative prospects in the House of Commons, but from 1835 to 1841 he did consistently benefit from the entirely novel character of the Irish administration in Ireland itself. The new men in Dublin—Lord Mulgrave as Lord-Lieutenant, Lord Morpeth as Chief Secretary, and the driven, highly professional Scottish Hibernophile Thomas Drummond as Under Secretary to the Lord-Lieutenant—were very much to O'Connell's liking. Mulgrave chose to send out an immediate signal: the Viceroy took up his viceregency by leading a torchlight procession dressed in a new militia uniform of bright green.[108]

Shaw Lefevre described Drummond as a man of 'exceptional ability' and 'force of character'. Born in Edinburgh in 1797, Drummond was a classic technocrat, who rose via Edinburgh High School to the point where he attracted Lord Brougham's attention and was asked to work on the project of parliamentary reform in 1832. Every experience of Drummond's life inclined him towards a distaste for the force of privilege in Ireland. Maria Edgeworth, the literary voice of the reformist Irish gentry, an old friend, was one of the first to welcome him enthusiastically to Ireland. Formerly employed on the great Survey of Ireland, he had visited every part of the country and become inevitably acquainted with the Irish people of all classes; above all, Drummond had a great fund of human sympathy (especially valuable in dealing with the Irish people); a stern meritocrat, he was also a rather prickly personality.[109] Serious, high-minded, this

---

[106] 'Outline of the History of Ireland', *Quarterly Review*, 83:166 (Sept. 1848), 584.
[107] Karl Marx and Frederick Engels, *On Ireland* (London, 1971), 81.
[108] Peter Mandler, *Aristocratic Government in the Age of Reform: Whigs and Liberals 1830–52* (Oxford, 1990), 162.
[109] *Peel and O'Connell: A Review of the Irish Policy of Parliament from the Act of Union to the Death of Sir Robert Peel* (London, 1887), 176; J. H. Andrews, *A Paper Landscape: The Ordnance Survey of Ireland of Nineteenth-Century Ireland* (Dublin, 2001), 45–57; *Pall Mall Gazette*, 2 Aug. 1867.

group nonetheless set about a practical reformist agenda which pleased O'Connell above all because it moved Catholics into places of influence previously reserved for Protestants and offered the prospect of equality before the law.

Ten years later the Whig Duke of Bedford recalled the moment in a letter to a fellow Whig, the Duke of Leinster: 'It was the feeling of the old Tory government in Ireland not to discourage the faction fights that used to be so common ... by fighting among themselves they abstained from political agitation and insurrections against the government.' Now, however, Mulgrave and his aides decided to chart a radically different cause, based, above all, on

a good and impartial administration of justice throughout the country ... By degrees [the Irishman] saw that his government meant nothing but equal justice and the appointment of Catholic magistrates, and liberal Protestants by a friendly government gave him confidence, and we behold the beginning of a better state of things in Ireland.[110]

The legal system was significantly affected. Louis Perrin, a Protestant with strong liberal convictions, became Attorney-General.[111] Even more important, Michael O'Loghlen, a 'friend of Dan', became Solicitor-General in 1834, the first Catholic to hold high office in Ireland since the reign of James II. Extremely partial Orange magistrates like Colonel Verner were sacked in 1837;[112] indeed, at one point in 1838 the administration was trying to remove about one-third of the existing magistracy. Most dramatically, following the urging of a young Catholic lawyer, Thomas O'Hagan, Drummond overturned the controversial appointment of the notoriously violent Sam Gray as sub-sheriff in Monaghan by the simple device of dismissing the sheriff who had made the appointment.[113] The government made significant moves in the direction of professionalizing the magistracy—with a new important element involving significant Catholic patronage; control of policing, too, was effectively centralized. The Orange Order had a dreadful time. In 1835 a Select Committee report on Orangeism uncovered evidences of lodges in the army and—more dramatically—the outline of a rather unlikely plot to exclude Victoria from the throne and to replace her with the Duke of Cumberland, the King's younger brother and

---

[110] PRONI D 3979/3/33/37, Bedford to Leinster, 28 Mar. 1846.
[111] The best analysis remains M. A. G. Ó Tuathaigh, *Thomas Drummond and the Government of Ireland 1835–41* (Dublin, 1978).
[112] R. B. O'Brien, *Thomas Drummond: Life and Letters* (London, 1889), 261–4; see Lord Morpeth's letter to Verner, 26–4.
[113] O'Brien, *Thomas Drummond*; the source is a letter written by Gavan Duffy in 1888.

the Orange Grand Master. King William IV announced that he intended to discourage anywhere in his dominions 'Orange Lodges and ... political societies, excluding persons of a different faith, using secret signs and symbols and acting by means of associated branches'.[114] Having cancelled all military warrants, both Grand Lodges dissolved themselves. Even though this did not prevent county and local lodges from continuing to exist, the Irish administration maintained the onslaught on Orange morale, and was quite prepared to use large-scale troop movements of Hussars and Lancers to curtail any displays of Orange triumphalism, especially in the North, where the lodges remained a significant underground force.

How did matters stand on the other side of the communal divide? The government's view of the Ribbon movement in 1836 stressed its complexity and organizational development—an analysis shared later by Michael Davitt, whose father had been a Ribbonman. The county masters regularly travelled on a quarterly basis to Belfast or Armagh for central consultations. They reported back to the leaders of parish delegations, who then reported to local leaders, who typically had twenty or thirty men under their command. Nor were Ribbon objectives purely agrarian: there was a decidedly nationalist tone to the Ribbon password: 'May the sons of the Shamrock in union remain, till Erin becomes a nation again.'[115] Not surprisingly, the Orangemen felt increasingly ill-used by government, expected to rally to the support of the authorities in the event of any serious challenge, but otherwise to be quiet and unregarded. O'Connell drove home his advantage by becoming ever more 'royalist' in his pronouncements.

On 21 June 1837 the new Queen Victoria's accession was proclaimed at St James's Palace in London. Daniel O'Connell made his enthusiasm visible—even though he was hissed by sections of the London crowd. Professor James H. Murphy has shrewdly observed that for O'Connell the accession of the pro-Whig Victoria was a 'golden opportunity' to try once more to shift the parameters of loyalty. If he could show that Repealers and Whigs were the new monarch's true friends and the Tories her enemies, then perhaps the agenda of reform for Ireland and repeal of the union might succeed.[116] Queen Victoria was hailed as a millennial deliverer in many Gaelic ballads of this period. Cooke Taylor argued that she now took her place in the tradition which had once embraced the Young Pretender and Napoleon, alongside the Virgin Mary, Daniel O'Connell, and St

---

[114] Ruth Dudley Edwards, *The Faithful Tribe: An Intimate Portrait of the Loyal Institutions* (London, 1999), 198.

[115] PRONI T3069/D/5.

[116] James Hugh Murphy, *Abject Loyalty: Nationalism and Monarchy in Ireland During the Reign of Queen Victoria* (Cork, 2001), 21.

Francis.[117] O'Connell's royalist enthusiasm did seem at times to go beyond the merely tactical:

It was impossible not to recollect that on her depended the happiness of the most intellectual and commercial nation on the face of the earth and she was, at her tender age, sovereign of a mighty empire, upon whose limitless dominion the sun never sets (cheers). But she will not be happy or glorious if the distinctions that have so long existed ... be not done away with forever; if the wall of separation be not broken down and her subjects become one people, as they are ruled by the sovereign (cheers).[118]

On 21 February 1838 O'Connell and his sons were introduced to Queen Victoria at a levee in St James's Palace. There is little doubt that the Liberator was both flattered and impressed. In a letter to Nicholas Maher of 23 October 1838 O'Connell said of the Queen: 'Not only is she free of any prejudices against Her Irish subjects, but is actually and sincerely friendly towards the rights of the Irish people ... We have never had a Sovereign before her present Majesty who was not an actual enemy to the Irish people.'[119]

Most important of all, the Mulgrave administration demonstrated a quite distinctive attitude towards conflict between the forces of property and those of 'the people'. The government was not so much neutral as instinctively inclined to take the popular side. During the period from 1835 to 1838 Drummond made every effort to discourage tithe-owners from availing themselves of their full legal rights for tithe-recovery. In April 1838, following two murders—that of Austin Cooper and Francis Wayland—thirty-two members of the Tipperary magistracy, led by Lord Glengall and Lord Lismore, sent a memorial to the Lord-Lieutenant stressing that life and property were no longer safe, and that, due to the intimidation of juries, no one was brought to justice. They called for a forceful display of power to enforce the laws of the land—intervention by the state against the agrarian criminals who had placed Tipperary—with 190 violent crimes, ahead of the second Irish county, Limerick, with a mere seventy-six—at the top of the Irish outrage table between 1836 and 1838.[120] On 22 May 1838 Drummond replied dismissively to the document, including J. W. Croker's admonitory phrase: 'Property has its duties as well as its rights.' Within weeks this phrase—in a supposedly private communication—had entered the public domain and was widely circulated in Tipperary,[121] much to the anger of Irish

---

[117] 'Illustrations of Whiteboyism in Ireland', *Westminster Review*, 34 (1839), 98.
[118] *Northern Whig*, 11 July 1837.   [119] *Dublin Evening Mail*, 28 Oct. 1838.
[120] *Sessional Papers, Reports from Committees, State of Ireland (from the Lords) c. 1889*, vol. 12, table presented by Drummond, 27 June 1839, p. 1303.
[121] Lord Powerscourt, *The Merits of the Whigs* (London, 1840), 54–5; for the full document see the handwritten copy of Drummond's lengthy and cutting reply to the

landlordism. Gustave de Beaumont, de Tocqueville's friend, concluded: 'In truth the Whig government of Ireland and the aristocracy are at open war.'[122]

Drummond denied that there was serious evidence to support the idea that the intimidation of juries was increasing in Tipperary, but in his reply to the Earl of Donoughmore he then went much further, in a vigorous attempt to turn the tables on his opponents. Imagine the shock of the Tipperary magistracy: they had complained about the state of the country in the aftermath of two brutal murders. They might well have expected to be ignored in their request for further government support; it is most unlikely that they expected quite such a brutal rebuttal. But not only were they told that their concerns about an increased level of jury intimidation were baseless, they were told that, insofar as there were problems in the countryside, the fault lay at the door of the Tipperary landlord class.

The Tipperary landlords were accused of irresponsibly allowing small-holders to multiply on their lands for political reasons—until O'Connell smashed the ties of deference in the 1828 Clare by-election, it was presumed that these smallholders would vote for their landlord. In the changed political circumstances of the 1830s—with tenants neither so deferential, nor in many cases, following the abolition of the franchise for the 40 shilling freeholders, possessing a vote—the landlords reversed their policy. In line also with prevailing economic wisdom, they were perceived to be pushing for a different type of agricultural system, involving the consolidation of farms. The eviction rate in Tipperary had doubled in recent years, and this was clearly the core of the problem. The landlords, having been complicit for many years in a corrupt bargain with their tenantry, were now attempting to dissolve it at all-too-rapid a pace, inevitably invoking profound feelings of anger in the countryside. Such, at any rate, were Thomas Drummond's views about the Irish rural scene. Lord Glengall exploded: he did not accept the government view of agrarian outrage. 'The murders in consequence of landletting arose not from quarrels between landlord and tenant, but between tenant and tenant fighting for land.'[123] The anti-Whig press claimed there was a new Ribbon song: 'May Francis Henry Earl Musgrave sit on the Throne | For surely my friend he is one of our own.'[124]

Earl of Donoughmore, in NLI, Ms 7521, Larcom Papers, *Letters and Papers: Drummond,* 631–45; see also O'Brien, *Thomas Drummond,* 278–87; O'Flanagan suggests that the Catholic Attorney-General Stephen J. R. Woulfe invented the phrase: *The Irish Bar* (London, 1879), 262.

[122] *Ireland: Social, Political and Religious* (London, 1839; repr. Cambridge, Mass., 2006), 356. De Beaumont's translator was W. Cooke Taylor.

[123] PRONI T3069/D/22, Earl of Glengall to Lord Charlemont, 1838–9.

[124] *Dublin Evening Mail,* 4 Oct. 1839.

Drummond's views, however, were fully supported by William Cooke Taylor; in his analysis of Whiteboy ballads, he treated them as a cry from the distressed human heart. Taylor noted that even the killers of Austin Cooper—who was shot by mistake because he happened to be in the company of an 'obnoxious' person at the time—became the subject of a sympathetic song as they approached the gallows, the 'sorrowful lamentation' of Walsh and Hickey:

> Farewell unto Tipperary and all the country round
> To our friends and comrades our hearts were true and sound;
> We hope we'll be a warning to male and female kind
> To live and love in unity and your clergy for to mind.

For Taylor, the message was obvious—'their cause is that of their country'.[125] In similar tone, Thomas Drummond described the communal resentment of the Irish rural populace as 'enlisting feelings not just of self-preservation' but of 'guilt'; in other words, most farmers who were not being evicted felt guilty about the fate of their less fortunate brothers. Those were the emotions—understandable, in a sense even laudable—which explained the outbreak of agrarian crime.

It was only when he had completed the demolition of the case of landlordism that Drummond actually penned the passage which was to become so famous: 'Property has its duties as well as its rights.' It was 'neglect of these duties' in the past which had created the current problems of Irish society; and it was not repression, but a 'more faithful performance of these duties', which was the clue to a better condition of Irish society. How far was this a diatribe? Writing in 1867, O'Connor Morris, in the *Edinburgh Review*, praised Drummond without reserve.[126] But returning to the subject in 1898, he qualified a still largely positive judgement: Morris noted that Drummond:

showed undeserved dislike to the Irish landed gentry and was inclined to lay to their charge what was really the effects of a long term of misrule in the past. When he told them, in dictatorial language, that property has its duties as well as its rights, they might have retorted that, in Ireland, government had not fulfilled its duties as severely as it had enforced its rights.[127]

O'Connell inevitably was impressed by Drummond. There was a 'lot of gossip in London clubs' to the effect that O'Connell was to be offered the post of Chief Baron or Master of the Rolls. F. D. Finlay of the *Northern Whig* told the *Spectator* in July 1838 that O'Connell had turned down

125 'Illustrations of Whiteboyism in Ireland', *Westminster Review*, 34 (1839), 79.
126 'The Late Thomas Drummond', *Edinburgh Review*, 126 (Oct. 1867), 524–40.
127 W. O'Connor Morris, *Ireland from 1798 to 1898* (London, 1989), 124.

these positions at 'great pecuniary sacrifice'.[128] In August 1838 O'Connell did accept, with a display of reluctance, a less-than-radical settlement of the tithe question, connecting tithes to a rent charge and scaling down the amounts payable. The radical and much-debated principle of appropriation was quietly dropped:[129] Lord Stanley felt he had saved the Irish Church,[130] O'Connell claimed that he had saved the people from assault by a reactionary establishment.[131]

In *Ireland Under Lord Mulgrave*, an anonymous London pamphleteer had cooed with delight: 'Where now is the Repealer? The Government of Lord Mulgrave, by an equally firm and mild administration of justice, making the law respectable and truly formidable, has hushed the wild Irish cry for a domestic legislature.'[132] But was the 'wild Irish cry' for a 'domestic legislature' hushed? To some observers, O'Connell appeared to have been seduced. According to the *Freeman* in August 1838: 'O'Connell, however, is not a Repealer. He has said over and over again, and his policy during the last three years proves it. He will only become a Repealer again on compulsion.'[133]

Even the Whig government's deeply conventional and Anglocentric handling of the Irish poor law did not shatter O'Connell's strategy. The Irish Poor Law Commission, with Archbishop Whateley as its chairman, presented its first report in 1835. It differed from its English counterpart in that it attempted (rather ambitiously) to prevent destitution rather than merely soften the effects of poverty. It suggested a range of proposals, including reclamation of waste lands, and a general plan for economic development. The commissioners accepted that the state should not become directly involved in providing outdoor relief. But they clearly felt that the government should intervene to reduce the level of poverty in Ireland. The government was exasperated—'This comes of appointing university professors to great office',[134] observed the Prime Minister, Lord Melbourne, with some acidity—and proceeded to set up an inquiry which would have a more acceptable outcome. On the basis of a quick, nine-week tour of Ireland, an English Poor Law commissioner, George Nicholls, delivered what was required. Nicholls advocated a deterrent workhouse system 'as a

[128] *Spectator*, 2 July 1838.
[129] The *Dublin Evening Mail* gleefully cackled: 'If paper could blush, says our correspondent, it would assuredly do so, on finding itself, after all that had occurred, impressed with an Irish Tithe Bill wearing the name of Lord John Russell and containing not one single syllable of an appropriation clause.'
[130] Vincent (ed.), *Disraeli, Derby and the Conservative Party*, 224.
[131] *Spectator*, 6 Oct. 1838.
[132] *Ireland Under Lord Mulgrave* (London, 1837), 41.
[133] *Freeman's Journal*, 2 Aug. 1838.   [134] Macintyre, *The Liberator*, 213.

first step towards effecting an improvement in the characters, habits, and social conditions of the people'.[135] This, it was piously hoped, could restore order and peace while at the same time making Ireland more attractive to English capital. Nicholls was well aware of the inherent limitations of his proposals. He certainly did not expect an immediate sharp improvement in the condition of Ireland. He explicitly warned that, in the event of famine, no poor law could prove adequate. His scheme was, however, predictably accepted by the government, becoming law in 1838: the country was henceforth divided into poor law districts, each with a workhouse under a board of guardians, and with the levying of a poor rate to be paid, half by the landlords, half by the tenants.[136]

'Morty' O'Sullivan, the highly intelligent Orange critic of O'Connell, always insisted that O'Connell was essentially indifferent to the material issues raised by the Irish poor law debate.[137] This, it can easily be said, is an unfair charge from a partisan source. But Father Thaddeus O'Malley, a Repealer and communitarian radical, also clashed sharply with O'Connell on the issue: in particular, O'Malley disliked O'Connell's denial of any right of the poor to relief.[138] The Liberator could never bring himself to believe in the efficiency of any poor law: 'A poor law will no more relieve the ills of Ireland than rubbing oil upon a broken bone.'[139] The poor law question did not then have the capacity to disrupt the Lichfield House compact.

Repeal, in short, seemed to be slipping into the background. When O'Connell seemed to be evoking repeal sentiment orthodoxy in a Dublin speech in 1839—'I pledge myself to the honest men of St Catherine's

[135] George Boyce, *Nineteenth-Century Ireland: The Search for Stability* (Dublin, 1990), 71.

[136] D. Norton, 'Lord Palmerston and Irish Famine Emigration: A Rejoinder', *Historical Journal*, 46:1 (2003), 158; Mandler, *Aristocratic Government*, 174–5.

[137] *Speech Delivered by the Rev Mortimer O'Sullivan at a meeting of the Protestant Conservative Society of Ireland Held at their Rooms, Grafton St, Dublin, on the 9th September 1834, Rt. Hon. the Earl of Roden in the Chair* (Dublin, 1834), 5. For further information on O'Sullivan and the lesser-known brother Samuel see Patrick O'Sullivan, 'A Literary Difficulty in Explaining Ireland: Tom Moore and Captain Rock, 1824', in R. Swift and S. Gilley (eds.), *The Irish in Britain 1815–1839* (London, 1989), 239–74.

[138] F. D'Arcy, 'Religion, Radicalism and Liberalism in Nineteenth-Century Ireland: The Case of Thaddeus O'Malley', in J. Devlin and R. Fanning (eds.), *Religion and Rebellion* (Dublin, 1997), 101.

[139] *Freeman's Journal*, 21 Nov. 1836; for O'Connell's complex views on the Poor Law, see A Macintyre, *The Liberator*, 201–26; F. O'Ferrall, *Daniel O'Connell* (Dublin, 1981), 95–8. O'Hagan, in his laudatory address, presents O'Connell's position on the Poor Law as one of his few mistakes: 'He was led—I think, and the event has proved mistakenly—to oppose the introduction of poor laws into Ireland, though the popular sentiment interpreted by the illustrious Bishop of Kildare was very strong against him.'

parish, that if I do not get justice for Ireland, I will raise the standard of repeal among you'[140]—the *Northern Whig* felt that the real meaning was fairly obvious. Repeal was being used simply as a rhetorical device to extract more reforms from the government; indeed so: O'Connell extracted one more substantial measure out of the Whigs—municipal reform, which passed through Parliament in August 1840. At last the Protestant monopoly of corporate rights and control of the administration of justice was ended.[141] Even before that date, however, O'Connell, anticipating the decomposition of the Whig administration, had formed in April the National Association of Ireland—to be renamed the Loyal National Repeal Association on 13 July.

In this context, O'Connell's trip to Belfast in January 1841 was to be of major significance. His repeal speech on 18 January was striking for its weaknesses as much as its strengths. While he did address fears of religious persecution, acknowledging that the reign of 'Bloody Mary' gave some ground for Protestant concern, he insisted that Irish Catholics were fundamentally tolerant: 'There is not a Protestant more opposed to Catholic ascendancy than I am.'[142] His arguments against the union—achieved by force and fraud and economically exploitative of Ireland—failed to address a single characteristic Belfast argument in its favour. In Protestant Belfast the view was that O'Connell had learned nothing since the celebrated parliamentary encounter with Emerson Tennent in 1834.

O'Connell's silence allowed Dr Cooke and Emerson Tennent to repeat those themes. Above all, the economic triumph of Belfast was stressed—'When I was myself a youth, I remember it almost a village. But now he noted our manufactories lifting themselves on every side.' For Cooke this was a tribute to the union, but also to Protestantism. 'In one word more, I have done with my argument—look at Belfast and be a Repealer—if you can.'[143] O'Connell seemed to welcome a growing polarization of Irish politics: 'Before long, every Whig must become a Conservative or a Repealer.'[144] This was a sentiment which can only have worried the delegation of leading Belfast liberals, led by R. J. Tennent and R. Grimshaw and McNamara, who waited on O'Connell at his hotel. They knew that their clever, highly intellectual Conservative opponent Emerson

[140] *Northern Whig*, 28 May 1839.
[141] O'Ferrall, *O'Connell*, 94; Macintyre, *The Liberator*, ch. 7.
[142] *Northern Whig*, 21 Jan. 1841.
[143] See Patrick Maume's important introduction in The Classics of Irish History series (Dublin, 2003) to William McComb, *The Repealer Repulsed: A Correct Narrative of the Repeal Invasion of Ulster: Dr Cooke's Challenge and Mr O'Connell's Declinature Tactics and Flight* (Belfast, 1841), 193.
[144] *Northern Whig*, 23 Jan. 1841.

Tennent would exploit that argument by simply agreeing with it.[145] They urged O'Connell to respect the peculiarities of Belfast liberalism—nonsectarian, in their view, but also anti-repeal—otherwise Tennent would simply seduce the 'liberal Protestants' of Ireland. Emerson Tennent's approach was taken up by Cooke, who even brought himself to praise Montgomery. Nonetheless, the *Whig* remained hostile to the intimidatory tone of the rhetoric at the Conservative meeting which followed on the heels of O'Connell's Belfast trip. George Dawson, who had been shouted down himself by a Protestant mob on the emancipation issue in 1828, now said he would participate in an 'Orange' mob to 'hoot and hiss O'Connell'.[146] There is a purely personal dimension to these remarks. Dawson was paying O'Connell back for a perceived political betrayal, when, in the 1837 general election, he had offered Dawson support for the Londonderry seat and then withdrawn it.[147] The *Whig*, nonetheless, was appalled by Dawson's words in what was, after all, an address to Her Majesty; in particular, it was appalled by the loud, enthusiastic applause his words received.[148]

O'CONNELL AND THE PEELITE CHALLENGE, 1841–1846

The general election of July 1841 marked the end of almost a decade of continuous Whig rule. The new Conservative government of Sir Robert Peel had a majority of between eighty and ninety seats; O'Connell was marginalized: only nineteen out of Ireland's 105 members seemed to have been repealers, a setback which O'Connell attributed to a drop in clerical support.[149] Some of O'Connell's early exchanges with Tory ministers were surprisingly civil.[150] The organ of Dublin Toryism, the *Evening Mail*, noted in early March 1842: 'He is neither shaking the government, nor rattling the rent boxes, nor stirring the populace.'[151] Such satisfaction was, however, misplaced—change was coming. On 23 April 1842 Daniel O'Connell wrote to his lieutenant T. M. Ray from London. O'Connell argued that Ireland desperately needed repeal, but 'the cause of repeal is now placed on a double basis: fixity of landed tenure and the abolition of the tithe rent charge'.[152]

145 *Belfast News Letter*, 22 Jan. 1841; Maume (ed.), *The Repealer Repulsed*, 113.
146 *Belfast News Letter*, 22 Jan. 1841.   147 Macintyre, *The Liberator*, 87.
148 *Northern Whig*, 23 Jan. 1841.   149 Lecky, *Leaders*, ii. 230.
150 *Dublin Evening Mail*, 7 Mar. 1842.   151 Ibid.
152 *Northern Whig*, 28 Apr. 1842.

The *Northern Whig* was impressed, while intelligent Conservatives in Dublin Castle worried about the explosive potential of the land question.[153] The *Whig* could not forbear from reminding O'Connell that he had himself supported the imposition of a rent charge as the solution of the tithe issue; it noted with satisfaction that the Repeal Society's activities were now confined to two issues, and of repeal itself 'we hear little'. The *Whig*'s fear of 'repeal' had a certain objective basis. The newspaper would have been horrified by the tone of O'Connell's private letter the following month to Dr Paul Cullen, Rector of the Irish College in Rome: in it O'Connell insisted that 'repeal of the union would be an event of the most magnificent importance to Catholicity, of an importance so great and valuable that I am prevented from presenting it in its true colours to the British people lest it should have its effect in increasing their hostility to that measure'.[154] In this letter O'Connell appears, in substance, to take the view that Protestantism was simply the self-serving ideology of a privileged caste, not a proper religion; remove those privileges and Protestants would naturally become Catholics. This O'Connell–Cullen correspondence informed rather precisely the fear expressed by Cooke. The cosy sectarianism of this discussion was to be challenged in October 1842 by the foundation of *The Nation* newspaper, devoted to non-sectarianism and passionate nationalism, in Dublin—Charles Gavan Duffy, John Blake Dillon, and the Protestant Thomas Davis were the original guiding talents.[155] But they were joined by others, notably the Ulster Unitarian John Mitchel and Thomas Francis Meagher, over the next few years.

There is a massive contrast between the tone of the O'Connell–Cullen correspondence and the preface, written by John Mitchel, to his book on Hugh O'Neill, a book dedicated to Thomas Davis. Mitchel argued, in effect, that Ireland should turn her back on the historic injustices of the sixteenth and seventeenth centuries: 'The struggle is over, and can never, upon that quarrel, be renewed. Those Milesian Irish as a distinct nation (why not admit it?) were beaten—were finally subdued as the Firbolgs were before them, as the ancient Kymry were in Britain, and afterwards *their* conquerors, the Saxons.'[156] Mitchel conceded that the origins of the Established Church of Ireland were 'too sanguinary', but added, 'yet, *now*, amongst the national institutions, amongst the existing forces that make up

---

[153] K. Nowlan, *The Politics of Repeal* (London, 1965), 33.

[154] O'Connell (ed.), *The Correspondence of Daniel O'Connell*, vii. 184–5, 9 May 1842, O'Connell to Cullen.

[155] For the tone see B. Clifford (ed.), *The Nation: Selections 1842–1844* (Aubane, 2000).

[156] Preface, *The Life and Times of Aodh O'Neill, Prince of Ulster* (Dublin, 1845), 22 Sept. 1845.

what we call an Irish nation, the church, so far as it is a spiritual teacher, must positively be reckoned.'[157] Mitchel concluded:

When Irishmen consent to let the past become, indeed, history, not party politics, and begin to learn from it the lessons of mutual respect and tolerance, instead of endless bitterness and enmity, then, at last, this distracted land shall see the dawn of hope and peace, and begin to renew her youth and rear her head amongst the proudest of nations.[158]

The Nation defined itself by a romantic critique of modernity which was much influenced by Thomas Carlyle.[159] The Young Irelanders seem to have been impressed by Carlyle as early as 1839, with the publication of his *Miscellanies*. In 1840 Carlyle published his volume on Chartism, with his important chapter on Ireland, expressing sympathy for the condition of Ireland, but also a degree of contempt. Carlyle wrote: 'There is one fact which statistic science has communicated, and it is a most astonishing one ... Ireland ... has not for 30 weeks a year as many third-rate potatoes which will satisfy.'[160] In a passage of some emotional power, Carlyle declared: 'All men, we must repeat, were made by God and have immortal souls in them. The *sanspotatoe* is of the self-same stuff as the finest Lord Lieutenant.'[161] Carlyle acknowledged gloomily: 'England is guilty towards Ireland and repents, at least, in full measure the first of 15 generations of wrong doing.'[162] It is easy enough to see why such passages should attract the enthusiastic admiration of Young Ireland.

But other aspects of Carlyle's discourse were rather disconcerting. He was less than impressed by the current state of the Irish national character: 'Unmethodic, headlong, violent, mendacious. What can you make of the wretched Irish? "A finer people never lived", as the Irish lady said to us, only they have two faults. They do generally lie and steal.' Most outrageous of all, Carlyle concluded: 'The time has come when the Irish population must either be improved a little or else exterminated.'[163] The Young Irelanders chose, at first, to ignore such passages, and instead warmed to the humanity of the Carlylean critique of industrial capitalism. Karl Marx acknowledged the power of Carlyle's rhetoric. The young Thomas Davis rejected the alienation perceived to be at the heart of the new bourgeois civilization with the same vigour as the young Marx: but for Davis, the countervailing force was not the international proletariat but the plain people of Ireland,

---

[157] Ibid., p. x.   [158] Ibid., p. xi.
[159] *The Nation*, 29 Oct. 1842; Roger Swift, 'Thomas Carlyle and Ireland', in D. George Boyce and Roger Swift (eds.), *Problems and Perspectives in Irish History Since 1800* (Dublin, 2004), 135–6.
[160] Thomas Carlyle, *Chartism* (London, 1840), 25.
[161] Ibid. 28.   [162] Ibid. 26.   [163] Ibid. 29.

who as yet stood outside and against the values of the emergent new order. Thomas Davis defined his thinking in a letter to Daniel O. Madden:

Modern Anglicanism, i.e. utilitarianism, the creed of Russell and Peel as well of the Radicals, this thing, call it Yankeyism or Englishism, which measures property by exchangeable value, measures duty by gain, and limits desires to clothes and respectability; this damned thing has come into Ireland under the Whigs, and it is equally the favourite of the Peelite Tories. It is believed in the political assemblies of our cities, preached from the pulpits; and it is the very apostle's creed of the professions and threatens to corrupt the lower classes, who are still faithful and romantic.[164]

Davis allowed himself to consider that repeal might lead to 'papal supremacy', but argued that it would collapse after twenty years, leaving the people 'mad' but not 'mean'.

Given O'Connell's greater sectarianism and greater pragmatic utilitarianism, *The Nation* group worked surprisingly well alongside the Liberator. But they were, after all, the principal beneficiaries of the relationship. The repeal movement provided the 'Young Irelanders' with a space to operate in. Repeal activists acted as an effective distribution agency for the *Nation* in the country. This was a priceless asset. In his later biography of Thomas Davis, Charles Gavan Duffy cited Charles (later Sir Charles) Trevelyan, who had accurately ascribed to the paper 'all the good writing, the history, the poetry and the political philosophy, such as it was, of the party'.[165] But such praise, implying as it did a certain intellectual deficiency in the O'Connell camp itself, could be embarrassing; O'Connell, indeed, made a point as early as 1843 of denouncing Trevelyan as possessing anti-Irish prejudice.[166]

It is difficult to avoid feeling a certain sympathy for O'Connell; clever, impatient young men are not always an unqualified benefit for an older political leadership, one which was rather set in its ways and fully aware of its responsibilities. William Cooke Taylor noted: 'O'Connell showed unusual hesitation in opening his last repeal campaign.'[167] Cooke Taylor speculated that

if Lady de Grey, the wife of the Lord Lieutenant, had not given some unnecessary provocation, the nature of which has never been explained, it is possible that Peel might have had an opportunity of developing that liberal scheme of policy which he did not formally profess, but on which he steadfastly acted.[168]

---

[164] P. J. Smyth, 'Young Ireland', *Fortnightly Review*, 34 (Dec. 1880), 703–4.
[165] Charles Gavan Duffy, *Thomas Davis*, Aubane Historical Society, Cork (Oct. 1843), 125.
[166] *Belfast News Letter*, 24 Oct. 1843.
[167] 'A Munster Farmer', *Reminiscences of Daniel O'Connell*, 84.   [168] Ibid.

It is also possible that the Lord-Lieutenant's decision to restore Mansergh St George—one of those legal officers purged in the Drummond era—to the Commission of the Peace would have infuriated O'Connell.[169] But O'Connell's calculations probably had a more profound basis. In considering O'Connell's state of mind at this juncture, W. E. H. Lecky laid great stress on his reply to the Earl of Shrewsbury's critique of his politics. John Talbot, the sixteenth Earl of Shrewsbury and seventh Earl of Waterford (1791–1852), was a scion of one of the oldest Catholic families in Britain, who had managed to retain most of their estates. In O'Connell's view, an English Catholic like Lord Shrewsbury was in his debt—even Shrewsbury had at times acknowledged it—and had no right to criticize the Liberator. O'Connell, as Lecky pointed out, disfigured his pamphlet reply with 'coarse abuse', 'exaggerated emphasis', 'tawdry sentiment', and 'vulgarity', but nonetheless, 'with all its defects, this pamphlet contains pages of admirable reasoning, supported by a vast array of well selected and well arranged facts, and it is one of the best defences of his political position'.[170] The union, O'Connell insisted, was 'a barefaced mockery, and resembles in nothing a real union'.[171] Ireland had a right to her own parliament. The union had been perpetrated by a mixture of force and fraud. It had denied Catholic emancipation for a generation. It denied prosperity and political equality to the Irish people—Cork, with close to the same population as Wales, had but 3,000 votes; Wales, on the other hand, had 36,000. Shrewsbury was moved to reply at even greater length: O'Connell's forty-eight-page pamphlet provoked a volume of 322 pages of text and 107 pages of appendices. He criticized O'Connell's style rather than the policy of repeal. Shrewsbury had one key point: O'Connell's militant and demagogic modus operandi was, in effect, self-defeating within the United Kingdom framework.[172]

O'Connell's New Year letter of 1843 continued to operate within the terms set out by his letter to Ray, but he was being steadily pushed back towards the theme of repeal by *The Nation's* pressure on the one hand, and the Tory regime in Dublin Castle on the other. The idea of a formal public debate—so popular in the 1820s—was revived in February 1843, with the great contest in the Dublin Corporation between the repealers, led by O'Connell and the unionists, led by the interesting figure of Isaac Butt. Isaac Butt was born in Glenfin, Co. Donegal, in 1813, the son of the

---

[169] *Dublin Evening Mail*, 27 May 1842. The Lord-Lieutenant, it was reported, had overruled the Chief Secretary.

[170] Lecky, *Leaders*, ii. 232.

[171] Daniel O'Connell, *Observations on Corn Laws, on Political Pravity and Ingratitude* ... (Dublin, 1842), 37.

[172] *A Third Letter to Ambrose Lisle Phillippe*, 21.

rectory. He was educated at Trinity College, Dublin, where he displayed a remarkable academic brilliance. He was the first Professor of Political Economy at Trinity, from 1836 to 1841; he also found time to found the *Dublin University Magazine* in 1833, edit it from 1834 to 1836, and practise at the bar. Butt openly wore Orange insignia,[173] and in 1836 he was actively involved in writing for the *Ulster Times* (strongly pro-Church and Tory in tone) based in Belfast.[174] Perhaps significantly, he was also known in Dublin social life as a brilliant amateur actor—particularly adept at the game of charades:[175] more profoundly, although friendly with Dublin's scientific elite, he did not share its characteristic world outlook, being inclined instead to a certain religious mysticism.

The *Dublin University Magazine* was strongly opposed to O'Connellism.[176] But nonetheless, it was also imbued with a 'certain Irish sentiment'. An Irish-American nationalist magazine was to pose the question: 'What more powerful agency could be devised against the annihilation of Ireland by the union than the culture of home life, home romance and home genius?'[177]

Butt had opposed, in 1840, the democratization of Dublin Corporation and argued that it should remain under the control of a Protestant elite. He claimed 'that the bodies to whom it is now proposed to confide the rights and powers which are forcibly torn from their present possessors, will be dangerous to the peace of the country, hostile to the Protestant religion and the British authority in Ireland'.[178] But as early as 1841 rumours circulated, both in Ireland and England, that the 'fraternization' of Butt and O'Connell on the issue of home manufactures presaged 'some extraordinary political conjunction'.[179] In 1843 (28 February–2 March), in the celebrated 'repeal' debate with O'Connell at the Dublin Corporation, Alderman Butt defended the union in classic Burkean-Pitt style: 'I believe with Pitt that no one can speak as a true Englishman who does not speak

---

[173] W. McCullagh Torrens *Twenty Years in Parliament* (London, 1893), 232. 'I remember having seen him wearing the Orange insignia after he was called to the bar.'

[174] A. Albert Campbell, *Belfast Newspapers, Past and Present* (Belfast, 1921), 9; Terence de Vere White, *The Road of Excess* (Dublin, 1946), 29.

[175] Valentine Ball, *Reminiscences and Letters of Sir Robert Ball* (London, 1915), 15. 'Nothing could exceed the brilliance of Isaac Butt's acting.'

[176] Joseph Spence, 'Isaac Butt, Irish Nationality and the Conditional Defence of the Union, 1833–1870', in D. George Boyce and Alan O'Day (eds.), *Defenders of the Union* (London, 2001), 67.

[177] *Donahue's Magazine*, 1:1 (July 1879).

[178] *Irish Corporation Bill: A Speech delivered at the Bar of the House of Lords on Friday, the 15th May 1840, in Defence of the City of Dublin, or the Order for Young into Committee, on the Irish Corporation Bill, by Isaac Butt, Esq.*, (Dublin, 1840), 13.

[179] *Evening Mail*, 20 Jan. 1841, 'The Butt–O'Connell Cross'.

as a true Irishman; or as a true Irishman who does not speak as a true Englishman.'[180] O'Connell, nonetheless, on the basis of some keen personal intuition, predicted that this would not always be Butt's position, and that some day he would join the popular cause.

O'Connell had correctly perceived a common ground with Isaac Butt. Indeed, in the 1870s Butt became one of the great defenders of O'Connell's reputation and policies. But there was no point in O'Connell confining the case to repeal to set-piece Dublin events. He now judged that it was time to take the case to the country. On 19 April 1843 he held his first great repeal rally at Limerick. The strain on the 'Liberator' was immense. John Locke, a highly intellectual local Presbyterian farmer, observed in his diary the Limerick demonstration.

From 30,000 to 40,000 assembled. No rioting nor drunkenness. But the repetition of these vast assemblages must end in bloodshed and civil war. They were incompatible with social order and contravene the spirit, if not the letter, of the law. O'Connell, in the midst of his glory, looked harassed and broken.[181]

The agitation now took on the most striking public manifestation: monster meetings upon historic sites—hundreds of thousands would come to listen to thundering speeches, and then, to demonstrate the Liberator's power, disperse peacefully. O'Connell addressed crowds at Mullingar (150,000 was the claimed attendance), Mallow (400,000), Lismore (400,000), and Tara on 15 August, where the crowd was said to be between 800,000 and 1 million: although sceptical newspapermen from outside the nationalist tradition could always be relied on to offer significantly lower figures, nobody doubted that there were immense crowds. It was a mobilization so widespread and intense that inevitably it excluded as much as it included. The Duke of Wellington might have had it said to an Irish audience that he thought himself Irish, but O'Connell did not. The message at Mallow was unequivocal: 'Who calls him an Irishman? If a tiger cub were dropped in a fold, would it be a lamb?'[182]

There was, as always with O'Connell, a degree of inconsistency. Sometimes his language was passionate indeed: 'Where was the coward who would not die for such a land?'[183] There are other startling examples of emotionally extreme language. Amazingly, O'Connell, who had, on his own account, taken himself to the tranquil county of Kerry during 1798,[184] now insisted at a Repeal Association meeting on 13 February 1843 that

---

[180] Joe Spence, 'Isaac Butt and Irish Nationality', in Boyce and O'Day (eds.), *Defenders of the Union*, 69.
[181] NLI Ms 3566, Locke diary, 19 Apr. 1843.   [182] *The Pilot*, 14 June 1843.
[183] Gavan Duffy, *Young Ireland, Part 1, 1840–5* (Dublin, 1892), 12.
[184] *Sessional Papers (8)*, 4 Mar. 1825, p. 117.

Napoleon's 'great mistake' had been his neglect of Ireland in favour of his Egyptian campaign.[185] On 21 May 1843, at Cork, speaking to an audience some estimated to be of half-a-million people, O'Connell warned Peel against an 'attack'. He evoked a poor Irish emigrant in England being told: 'Your father was cut down by a dragoon, your mother was shot by a policeman; and your sister—but I will not say what has happened to her. She is now a wandering maniac.' O'Connell concluded by asking Peel—in such a context—to contemplate 'how many fires' would 'blaze' in the 'manufactories of England'.[186]

A former ally, Eneas McDonnell, pointed out that O'Connell's broader assessment of the English people was hardly conciliatory. Even away from the excitement of the public platform, in the quiet of his study, O'Connell could be brutally frank: 'The bad passions of the English people which gave an evil strength to the English government for the oppression of Ireland still subsist, little diminished and less mitigated.'[187] The response O'Connell's language provoked was equally harsh. One well-connected aristocrat sneered:

Every step the agitator takes, more and more illustrates that the Irish response to the call of self-government are no more fit for self-government than the wildest tribes of the coloured races of Africa. History furnishes no example of a civilised people, being moved by such continuous untruth, as seems to be imbued on the minds of the misguided for attending republican gatherings.[188]

But when a young Protestant repealer seemed to take O'Connell's emotive talk seriously and talked of shedding his 'blood for repeal ... on the scaffold', O'Connell was rather more circumspect: 'I confess, I do not go as far as my excellent friend.'[189] Friedrich Engels, who had taken up with an Irish working-class woman, Elizabeth Burns, watched the renewed repeal agitation with a mixture of admiration and exasperation. On the one hand, he was contemptuous of O'Connell and his 'petty middle-class objectives' combined with his 'egoism and vanity': the politics of the repeal leader were dismissed as 'stale obsolete rubbish' and old 'fermenting junk'. But, on the other hand, Engels could not but be impressed by the scale of the

[185] John Flanedy (ed.), *A Special Report of the Proceedings: The Case of the Queen Against Daniel O'Donnell MP* (Dublin, 1844), 125.

[186] Eneas McDonnell, *Moral Force Agitation*, Kensington, 3 Aug. 1843, p. 15; John Flanedy (ed.), *A Special Report of the Proceedings in the Case of the Queen against O'Connell* (Dublin, 1844), 130.

[187] 'A Memoir of Ireland', quoted in McDonnell, *Moral Force Agitation*, 46.

[188] Viscount Wellesley, *The Irish Question Considered in its Integrity* (Dublin, 1844), 81.

[189] *Belfast News Letter*, 30 June 1843.

mobilization: 'A triumphal procession lasting a fortnight such as no Roman Emperor ever experienced.'[190]

There was good reason to back up Engels's belief: the level of co-operation between the Whigs and O'Connell's friends in the House of Commons was striking, coinciding as it did with the most intensive phase of the repeal agitation in Ireland. Even Palmerston was prepared to back Russell in his critique of Peel's Irish policy.

The noble Lord, the member for North Lancashire had told the House the other evening, in discussing a Bill on the subject of Canada, that it was not possible that this country should maintain the Connexion [*sic*] which now existed between Canada and England if it was to be maintained by the sword and not by the affections and good feeling of the people.[191]

But, declared Palmerston, if this was true of Canada's relationship with Britain, it was all the more true of Ireland. In the spring of 1843 the government had signalled its determination to pass an Irish Arms Act. This required the legalization of firearms and placed restrictions on the manufacture and importation of arms and ammunition. Thomas Wyse wrote to George Wyse: 'the Bill will appear as a Bill for disarming the Catholics and leaving the Orangemen armed.'[192] Between 23 June and 27 July Irish MPs forced no fewer than fifty-one divisions on the Arms Bill. It was, as Palmerston told his brother, an interesting example of how 'a compact' group, even if small, might 'obstruct' the working of Parliament.[193] English Whigs, however, were queasy about the arms issue. Russell in particular was identified with support for the principle of the government's legislation.[194] But on 9 July, while the Arms Bill was painfully struggling through committee at hardly the rate of a clause a day, W. Smith O'Brien put down a substantive motion for a committee on the state of Ireland. This motion, which *was* supported by Lord John Russell and the Whig leadership, led to a debate lasting eight days.

Engels was convinced that O'Connell merely wished to 'embarrass' the Tories and put the Whigs back into office.[195] He acknowledged the spectacular and moving nature of an agitation which drew on a sense of historical resentment so deep that O'Connell was able to make himself an intimate

---

[190] Karl Marx and Friedrich Engels, *Ireland and the Irish Question* (Moscow, 1971).

[191] Palmerston on the Arms (Ireland) Bill, 23 June 1843, *Hansard*, 3rd ser., vol. 70, col. 2990.

[192] Robert Sloan, *William Smith O'Brien and the Young Ireland Rebellion of 1848* (Dublin, 2000), 85.

[193] Malcolm MacColl, *Reasons for Home Rule* (London, 1886), 7.

[194] 'Outlines of the History of Ireland', *Quarterly Review*, 83:166 (Sept. 1848), 589.

[195] Marx and Engels, *Ireland and the Irish Question*, 33–7; 'Letter from London', published in *Der Schweizerische Republikaner*, no. 39, 27 June 1843.

presence in the minds of huge numbers of his countrymen: the lowest possible attendance of the 1843 repeal meetings gives a total of 1.5 million—a quarter of the population of Munster, Leinster, and Connaught.[196] In one matter O'Connell and his allies were totally consistent—Engels to this extent also had a serious point. They were steadfastly opposed to agrarian secret societies and, indeed, agrarian radicalism in general. In September 1843 the agrarian radical William Conner, Arthur O'Connor's illegitimate son and first cousin of the Chartist Fergus O'Connor,[197] put O'Connell under pressure in an extraordinary moment of confrontation at a meeting of the Dublin Repeal Association. Conner insisted that the Repeal Association support a complete rent strike; indeed, a strike on all payments by the rural poor. O'Connell quickly moved to reassert the priority of a purely legal strategy and block 'this attempt to violate the law'.[198] But Conner was moved by a vision of imminent catastrophe and would not be restrained: 'Next summer millions of men, women and children will be starved by the want of crops.'[199] At this point, amidst great uproar, Conner's intervention was brought to an end.

The repeal agitation was set to peak with the election of a council of 300, a de facto Irish parliament, which was set to meet in Dublin—before Christmas, according to O'Connell at Baltinglass in August[200]—to 'enact' a Repeal Bill. At Mullaghmast, at the beginning of October 1843, O'Connell appeared to be more vague about timing, but still insistent on the proposal: 'When we have it arranged, I will call together 300 as the *Times* called them "bogtrotters", but better men never stepped on a pavement. But I will have 300, and no thanks to them.'[201] He insisted: 'We will be obedient to the Queen, but we must have our own parliament.' This language provoked the anger of Thomas Carlyle, *The Nation*'s great ideological patron: 'Monster meetings, O'Connell eloquence and Mullaghmast caps can not change the state of the fact, can not alter the laws of the universe; not a whit; the universe remains precisely what it was before the Mullaghmast cap took shape amongst the headgear of men.'[202] Carlyle even more brutally declared

---

[196] Gary Owens, 'Nationalism without Words: Symbolism and Ritual Behaviour in the Repeal Monster Meetings of 1843–5', in James S. Donnelly Jr. and Kerby Miller (eds.), *Irish Popular Culture* (Dublin, 1998); Maura Cronin, ' "Of One Mind?": O'Connellite Crowds in the 1830s and 1840s', ch. 5 in Peter Jupp and Eoin Magennis, *Crowds in Ireland 1790–1920* (London, 2000).

[197] George O'Brien, 'William Conner', *Studies* (June 1923), vol. 12, p. 283.

[198] *Belfast News Letter*, 22 Sept. 1843.   [199] Ibid.

[200] Eamon Kane (ed.), *Daniel O'Connell: Rath of Mullaghmast* (Castledermot, 1993), p. v.

[201] Ibid. 22–3.

[202] 'The Repeal of the Union', in Percy Newberry (ed.), *Rescued Essays of Thomas Carlyle* (London, 1892), 40.

that Tipperary contributed nothing to the resources which had made the British Empire great: 'No, it was out of other regions than Tipperary, by other equipments than are commonest to Tipperary, that England built up her social condition, wrote her literature, planted her Americas and even Tipperary will be made to know it—by terrible schooling, if mild will not serve.'[203] Carlyle felt that such tough language was required to puncture what he called the 'inextinguishable Irish self-conceit'.[204] For Carlyle, Catholic Ireland contributed nothing ('close to zero')[205] to the greater British project, but, for strategic reasons, had to be kept secure. Given that Britain could not allow repeal, the best course was to force the Irish to come to terms with realities. 'The Celt of Connemara and other repealing finest peasantry are white and not black; but it is not the colour of the skin that determines the savagery of a man.'[206] The Catholic Irish must either accept the realities of the modern world and the rules and behaviour necessary to achieve progress or face extermination.[207]

Both O'Connell's rhetoric and Carlyle's angry commentary rather suggested that matters were coming to a head. When Sir Robert Peel's government banned his great climatic meeting for 8 October at Clontarf near Dublin, O'Connell gave way. The *Freeman's Journal* loyally explained the apparent climb-down: 'Prudence, the desire to put the enemy in the wrong and above all, respect for human life, caused the leader of the repeal move ment to abandon the project of the meeting.'[208] This retreat, followed as it was by the arrest of O'Connell and other leaders on charges of conspiracy, is perceived to have brought about the collapse of the agitation. But the reality was more complex: O'Connell may well have intended Clontarf to be his last monster demonstration anyway, and his new status of martyrdom brought

---

[203] Ibid. 40.   [204] Ibid. 22.   [205] Ibid. 39.   [206] Ibid. 50.

[207] From this point onwards, the relationship between Carlyle and the Young Ireland intellectuals became more fraught and complicated. The tensions of Carlyle's essay on 'the finest peasantry in the world' in his *Chartism* text of 1840 appeared increasingly to be resolved in an 'anti-Irish' way. On 27 April 1845 a rather edgy evening ensued when a group of Young Ireland intellectuals—Duffy, J. E. Pigot, and John O'Hagan—called at the Carlyle home in Chelsea. Pigot raised the issue of the passage in *Chartism* referring to the alleged Irish propensity to 'lie and steal'; Jane Carlyle wondered why her young Irish visitors had bothered to come. John Mitchel, in *The Nation* in January 1846, condemned the Irish sections of Carlyle's book on Cromwell, published in 1845. Nonetheless, something of a mutual attraction persisted: even alongside the striking harshness of some of Carlyle's commentary on Ireland, he was capable of expressing a personal (even protective) sympathy for the spirit of the Young Irelanders or even a demand that the government extend public works during the famine. Charles Gavan Duffy, for example, remained a friend throughout Carlyle's life. Even Duffy, however, exploded when told that Ireland had brought her troubles on herself by refusing the Protestant reformation. I am indebted to discussions on this subject with C. D. C. Armstrong.

[208] *Freeman's Journal*, 9 Oct. 1843.

many new political opportunities. The British government may be said to
have broken the repeal movement in 1843 by a resolute combination of
indifference, force, and law.[209] But O'Connell was not finished, not by any
means—even Young Ireland backed his retreat with some obvious reluctance. *The Nation* took succour in the impact of mobilization on the people:

Look among the peasantry for its influence. You will find a new class of men,
created within 20 months, as distinct from the old as the teetotallers from the
drunkards. Where are the sullenness, the apathy, the slavish condescension to rank,
which were too often found amongst them? They are gone forever—they died of
the agitation ... Scarcely the French revolution, certainly none other, effected so
miraculous and electric a change in the character of the people.[210]

One important new aristocratic recruit now rushed to O'Connell's side. On
20 October 1843 William Smith O'Brien, who had been leaning in this
direction, finally joined the Repeal Association: the Clontarf proclamation
was cited as the decisive factor.[211] At a Limerick banquet O'Brien made
it clear, despite his family's obvious dislike of his new stance, that he did
not see himself as a class renegade. He spoke about the need to remove
the Protestant population and the landlords, adding with a cagey double
negative: 'I do not think, with a perfect, universal national union, you could
not expect to obtain a repeal of the union.' He noted also that he was glad
O'Connell had agreed to drop the use of the derogatory word 'Saxon'—'I
never could understand the term'.[212]

The government now resolved to prosecute O'Connell for sedition. But
it was a problematical task. John Flanedy, an ardent repealer, observed in
the preface to his volume on the proceedings of the O'Connell trial, that the
government faced an obvious difficulty in proving the existence of a crime:

It is legal to repeal the act of union, but the means by which it was intended to be
accomplished are charged as illegal. Now what was the mode attempted to establish
this charge? First, a number of overt acts were offered to the jury, perfectly harmless
in themselves; and in order to make their evidence, the jury was called upon to
imagine a conspiracy.[213]

John Flanedy was *parti pris* on the matter, but the same can not be said for
the liberal unionist editor of the Belfast *Northern Whig*. Yet he too reported
from Dublin: 'But what the Attorney-General has to prove, it occurs to me,

---

[209] H. C. G. Matthew, 'Gladstone, O'Connell and Home Rule', in R. W. Comerford
and Enda Delaney (eds.), *National Questions: Reflections on Daniel O'Connell and
Contemporary Ireland* (Dublin, 2000), 13.
[210] *The Nation*, 21 Oct. 1843.   [211] Sloan, *William Smith O'Brien*, 104.
[212] *Limerick Reporter*, 10 Nov. 1843.
[213] John Flanedy (ed.), *A Special Report of the Proceeding of the Queen Against Daniel
O'Connell Esq MP* (Dublin, 1844), p. v.

is not merely that these objectionable and seditious things have been spoken and written, but that there has been an undoubted conspiracy to sever the union by force—by a recourse to war.'[214]

At Mullaghmast O'Connell had, after all, finally solved the problem created by his own rhetorical inconsistency on the subject of fighting and dying for Ireland:

> Oh, my friends, it is a country worth fighting for (loud cheers)—it is a country worth dying for (renewed cheering), but above all, it is a country worth being tranquil, determined, submissive and docile for; disciplined as you are in obedience to those who are breaking the way, trampling down the barriers between you and your constitutional liberty.[215]

Personal factors entered into the conduct of the case. The Attorney-General, Thomas Berry Cusack Smith (1795–1866), the second son of William Cusack Smith, conducted the prosecution in an all-too-obviously hot-tempered fashion, even challenging a defence counsel to a duel.[216] Cusack Smith claimed that he was being accused of launching the prosecution for personal and dishonourable motives. How far was Cusack Smith influenced by O'Connell's treatment of his father?[217]

After a three-week trial, O'Connell was convicted on 10 February 1844. During the interval between trial and sentence he received a standing ovation from the opposition as he entered the Commons Chamber. On 16 February an emergent young Tory politician, Benjamin Disraeli, insisted that the oppression of Ireland was so great that Britain could only meet it by a revolutionary policy of reform from above.[218] O'Connell was the hero of banquets and public displays of support in London, Birmingham, Wolverhampton, and Liverpool. The sentence handed down on 30 May was for a fine of £2,000 and one year of jail. Lord John Russell pointedly sided with O'Connell during the early session of 1844. The *Annual Register* noted: 'To Mr O'Connell', in the aftermath of his sedition conviction, 'Lord John paid a high tribute.' He strongly reproached Sir Robert Peel 'for having filled Ireland with troops and with not governing but militarily occupying the country'.[219] On 25 June the *Freeman's Journal* pointed out: 'In the days of monster meetings the repeal rent never rose to £3,000 in any month but once, and only on rare occasions came up to £2,000.' But now,

---

[214] *Northern Whig*, 28 Jan. 1844.
[215] Kane, *Daniel O'Connell*, 26.   [216] Ball, *Irish Judges*, ii. 288.
[217] For Cusack Smith's explosion at the trial, see Flaneny, *O'Connell's Report*, 300–2, and for his parliamentary apology, see *Hansard*, vol. 72, 21 Feb. 1844, cols. 1331–3. Peel greatly admired the grace of his apology.
[218] J. A. Froude, *The Earl of Beaconsfield* (London, 1890), 104–6.
[219] 'Outlines of the History of Ireland', 590.

in the fourth week of his conviction, the total raised was already £11,587. John Anster of the *North British Review* was not alone in acknowledging a feeling that O'Connell had not had fair play—there had been tampering with the jury—and that the bench was prejudiced against him.[220] O'Connell now had a new source of advice. Infuriated by the British state's authoritarianism, the new Irish Catholic legal elite (men like O'Loghlen and O'Hagan) returned to O'Connell's side. But as 'men of the world', they felt the need to push O'Connellism along more practical lines. They urged a new policy of federalism. Federalism meant the creation of a local executive and legislative that would deal solely with domestic affairs and would remain subordinate to the Westminster Parliament. For a moment, and for a few key figures, federalism seemed the obvious sensible middle position between repeal and the existing Act of Union.

But how would O'Connell react? Incarcerated in a suite in the governor's house in Dublin's Richmond Jail, he discussed matters with his many visitors. There was much talk of federalism—to which O'Connell was sympathetic anyway.[221]

On 4 September the House of Lords reversed the judgment and O'Connell, the Liberator, was freed. O'Connell now made his federalist leanings known:

Repeal may possibly be dispensed with … if the people of England joined with him in achieving justice. I promise them the lion's heart and sinewy arm of Ireland. I promise them the acute wit to advance their glory and prosperity. I promise them the congregation of virtues which ennoble and dignify the character of the people of Ireland—virtue, temperance, morality, religion—I promise them love unbounded and fidelity unpurchaseable.[222]

Some in Young Ireland were appalled; Gavan Duffy created a great stir on the issue, though Thomas Davis was clearly more sympathetic. Federalism contained, at least, the possibility of reducing Protestant fears, but under pressure O'Connell dropped it. *The Nation* eventually took the view, after the death of Davis, that a federal solution would be more demeaning to Ireland than the status quo.[223]

By 1844–5 the scale of O'Connell's achievement was clear. He had failed to achieve repeal, but he had brought the Irish question back to the centre of British politics. The British government was convinced that the Catholic clergy provided the organizing intelligence of the movement, and Peel,

---

[220] 'Trials in Ireland', *North British Review*, 9:18 (Aug. 1848), 547.

[221] Angus Macintyre, 'Home Rule for Ireland: A Failure of Federalism?', in Preston King and Andrew Bosco (eds.), *A Constitution for Europe: A Comparative Study of Federal Constitutions and Plans for the United States of Europe* (London, 1991), 250.

[222] *Northern Whig*, 19 Sept. 1844.   [223] *The Nation*, 25 Oct. 1845.

concerned lest the union between O'Connell and the clergy might eventually result in the disintegration of the union, made the weakening of this 'powerful combination' the core of his Irish policy.[224] O'Connell rightly claimed that the Devon Commission, appointed in November 1843 to examine the Irish land question, had been conceded because of the repeal agitation.[225] There were, of course, other pressures.

The British journalist Alexander Somerville claimed that his exposé of landlord malfeasance in Bennet's Bridge, Kilkenny, had been the decisive moment in Peel's decision to create the Devon Commission; certainly, while the Commission sat, other sharp critics of Irish landlordism, such as Sir Matthew Barrington, felt free to communicate their views to the Prime Minister.[226] Also while the commission sat, 'GHQ' published *Confessions of a Whitefoot*, an influential and sympathetic account of a suffering peasantry. At the beginning of 1845 the Devon Commission reported. It was a wistful, cautious, limited document. Strikingly, Devon noted that in those areas of the country where 'life and property ... are systematically rendered insecure', it must be 'regarded as beyond the hopes of such amelioration as it suggests'.[227] But it did reflect on the O'Connellite theme of land reform: at Mullaghmast he had declared: 'We will recollect that the land is the landlord's, and let him have the benefit of it, but we will also recollect that the labour belongs to the tenant, and the tenant must have the value of his labour, not transitory and by the day, but permanently and by the year.'[228] In response, the Devon Commission officially placed the tenant's perception of his own insecurity at the heart of the Irish land question. The Devon Report recommended only a Compensation for Improvements Bill; it sidestepped the thornier issue, raised most obviously in Ulster, but also in other relatively prosperous parts of Ireland, of whether or not the tenant had a right of free sale.[229] Legalizing the Ulster custom, or, indeed, any variant of tenant right, would be an unthinkable abrogation of the 'just rights of property', but on the other

---

[224] Donal Kerr, *Peel, Priests and Politics* (Oxford, 1982), 108.

[225] Kevin B. Nowlan, *The Politics of Repeal: A Study in the Relations between Great Britain and Ireland 1841–88* (London, 1965), 59.

[226] K. D. M. Snell (ed.), Alexander Somerville, *Letters from Ireland During the Famine of 1847* (Dublin, 1994); Joseph Fisher, *The History of Landholding in Ireland* (London, 1877), 120.

[227] *Report from Her Majesty's Commissioners of Enquiry into the State of the Law and Practice reltaing to the Occupation of Land in Ireland* (Dublin, 1845), *Sessional Papers (19)*, 43.

[228] Kane, *Daniel O'Connell*, 23.

[229] The classic exposition given to the Devon Commission by Lord Lurgan's agent, Neilson Hancock, insisted: 'The disallowance of tenant right, as far as I know, is always accompanied with outrage.' See W. F. Bailey, 'The Ulster Tenant Right Custom: Its Origins, Characteristics and Position under the Land Acts', *Journal of the Statistical and Social Inquiry Society of Ireland*, 10:1 (Sept. 1894), 6.

hand, social turmoil would 'result from any hasty or general disallowance of it'.[230] Radicals like W. D. Conner and his personally supportive ally J. S. Mill were disappointed: 'It were well, if the delusion of "Ulster tenant right" and "tenants" improvement protection",' Conner said, 'were gone into the same dark oblivion.'[231]

Nevertheless, the Peelite government's tacit acceptance of the Devon Commission's approach, not simply on issues such as free trade on land but also on security for improvements,[232] must have given O'Connell some satisfaction as he worked on a repeal subcommittee with William Smith O'Brien and Thomas Davis to press the case for further change.[233] The important truth to grasp is that the Devon Commission's Report fully endorsed the view that there were important differences between Irish and English landed society, and these differences tended to weaken the moral case of Irish landowners. The Devon Commission stated bluntly:

It is well known that in England and Scotland, before a landlord offers a farm for letting, he finds it necessary to provide a suitable farmhouse, with necessary farm buildings, for the proper management of the farm ... In Ireland, the case is wholly different. The smallness of the farms as they are usually let, together with other circumstances, to which it is not necessary to advert, render the introduction of the English system extremely difficult, and in many cases impracticable.[234]

This frank admission alone guaranteed that the Devon Commission Report had an important long-term significance: it became a major source for those arguing for land reform later in the nineteenth century.

It is also important to note the way in which Sir Robert Peel's thinking about Ireland was undergoing a profound change. From the earliest years of his engagement with Ireland, Peel's excellent Irish library, built up for him by Shaw Mason, had contained works—such as those of J. B. Trotter and J. C. Curwen—which were obsessed with Burke's legacy.[235] At first

---

[230] Martin W. Dowling, *Tenant Right and Agrarian Society in Ulster 1600–1870* (Dublin, 1999), 277.

[231] William Conner, *A Letter to the Tenantry of Ireland* (Dublin, 1850), 11. As Bruce Kinzer observes, the vigour of Mill's agrarian radicalism at this point is striking: 'J. S. Mill and Irish Land: A Reassessment', *Historical Journal*, 27 (1984), 115–16. In his case against Ulster tenant right, Conner enters the case of a Mr Berwick, a tenant of the Marquess of Downshire's at Lisnabree, Co. Down, who paid £1,000 for the incoming tenant right and a further £800 on improvements, but was then, at the end of his lease, set a rent which forced him to leave the farm.

[232] Peter Gray, *Famine, Land and Politics: British Government and Irish Society 1845–50* (Dublin, 1999), 84.

[233] T. P. O'Neill, 'The Irish Land Question, 1830–50', *Studies*, 44 (1955), 331–2.

[234] P. G. Cambrai, *Irish Affairs* (London, 1911), 173.

[235] N. D. Palmer, 'Sir Robert Peel's Select Irish Library', *Irish Historical Studies*, 6 (1948–9), 113.

they appear to have had little impact on Peel, but by 1834 the terms of Peel's defence of Judge Cusack Smith sharply implied that for Peel Burke had, indeed, made an important contribution to the Irish political debate. By the time Peel formed his government in the 1840s, he had come to the view that Burke was central to any proper understanding of the requirement of Ireland. In his 1847 Tamworth manifesto Peel treated his electors to lengthy quotations from Burke's letter of 1792 to his son, and added:

It was with reference to that state of Ireland, and with reference to such considerations as those to which Mr Burke has adverted, that the government with which I was connected brought forward measures which constitute no precedent for any other part of the United Kingdom, but are specially applicable to the peculiar condition and structure of society in Ireland.[236]

To the initial surprise of Catholic leaders, the British government was now sending the message that it was keen to deal with specifically Catholic grievances, where possible: on 11 February 1844 Peel told the Cabinet: 'I know not what remedy there can be for such an evil as this but the detaching from the ranks of Repeal, agitation and disaffection of a considerable portion of the respectable and influential Roman Catholic population.'[237]

On 18 June 1844 Peel made his opening gambit of a new strategy: the first reading of the Irish Charitable Donations and Bequests Bill. The intention was to facilitate endowment of the Catholic Church. Sir James Graham, making a very obvious deliberate effort to control his Protestant prejudices, piloted the Bill through the House of Commons in a conciliatory manner. Nevertheless, the bruised nature of Irish public opinion, combined with the inherent technical complexities of the issue, threatened to destroy government policy. But despite the strongly expressed views of a majority of Irish Catholics, both clerical and lay—who feared that the government was attempting to manipulate the Catholic Church—three Catholic bishops agreed to serve on the board set up by the new Act.[238] In return, the government officially recognized the prelates by their full titles for the first time, it was remarked, since the penal laws.[239] On 4 February 1845 Peel made clear his intention to increase substantially the grant in Maynooth College. In March the anonymously published work of Charles Greville, clerk to the Privy Council, *The Past and Present Policy of England Towards Ireland*, was published.[240] It encouraged the idea that the Maynooth grant was the thin end of the wedge and that the Church of Ireland establishment was doomed. Gladstone, who had argued vigorously in 1838 that the state

---

[236] *Dublin Evening Mail*, 19 July 1847. [237] Kerr, *Peel, Priests and Politics*, 117.
[238] Ibid. 127. [239] Ibid. 190.
[240] P. Morrell (ed.), *Leaves from the Greville Diary* (London, 1929), 5 Mar. 1845, p. 469.

should stand by the maintenance of Protestant grants only, felt compelled to resign from government.[241] On 3 April Peel introduced his Maynooth College Bill into the House of Commons. He had decided to treble the Maynooth grant. The Carlton Club was in a 'state of insurrection' afterwards and full of 'fury'.[242] O'Connell reminded everyone of his original poor view of Peel: 'But perhaps as he is growing older, he is growing wiser and better. I think I must fall in love with him (laughter), for nothing was ever more fair, manly and excellent in all its details than his plan regarding Maynooth.'[243] Peel delivered on his Maynooth proposal—surviving a diehard Protestant revolt within his own party. But with Whig rather than Tory support, Peel successfully passed the Maynooth measure.

Two letters of Lord Palmerston to correspondents with Irish concerns explain precisely the Whig calculations. Palmerston was cautious, noting that: 'One does not like to expose sentiments offensive to the majority of the Christian world, for such the Catholics unquestionably are.' He felt that Catholicism was a backward form of religion—'absurdities and superstitions'—which had negative effects on Irish economic and social development: 'It is unfavourable to industry, morality and liberty.' He devoutly wished that Irish Catholics would convert to Protestantism: 'I should be rejoiced if there were no Catholics in Ireland or if we could convert the Irish Catholics to Protestantism.' But the fact remained that there were 6 million Irish Catholics who adhered to their religion as steadfastly as English Protestants. In such a context, it was preferable to create a better-educated Catholic priesthood, tied to England by emotions of gratitude.[244] 'We may decide if they be ignorant or enlightened Catholics.' To the Revd Francis Gervis of Cecil Manor, Co. Tyrone, on 15 December 1845, Palmerston argued that he would not withhold state support or payment from the Catholic clergy simply because Catholicism was 'a modification of Christianity different from that which I myself prefer'. It was essential, he declared, that Catholic priests should be rescued from their 'material dependence on their flocks'.[245]

There were, however, to be decided limits to the O'Connell–Peel rapprochement, as became clear when the government introduced the Irish

---

[241] E. R. Norman, 'The Maynooth Question of 1845', *Irish Historical Studies*, 15 (1966–7), 410.

[242] Morrell (ed.), *Leaves from the Greville Diary*, 469.

[243] *Northern Whig*, 10 Apr. 1845; 6 Apr. 1845.

[244] NLI Ms 22,977, Palmerston to A Brewin, 13 Apr. 1845.

[245] NLI Ms 24,987. For Francis Gervis and his bitter conflicts with local Catholic interests, see PRONI D2697/4/5. For a good general discussion of Palmerston's view on these matters, see John Wolffe, 'Lord Palmerston and Religion: A Reappraisal', *English Historical Review*, 120: 488 (Sept. 2005), 907–36.

College Bill in May 1845. Peel's objective was to found an adequate system of middle-class education. Colleges would be established in Cork, Belfast, and Galway, liberally endowed by the state to provide a purely secular education. The government made it clear that it had been much influenced by the ideas of Thomas Wyse, Liberal MP for Waterford, and very knowledgeable about Irish education.[246] The Young Ireland leader Thomas Davis was excited by the prospect of mixed-denominational higher education, and reacted very positively. For Davis, a path was being almost magically opened up, leading to the triumph of a civic, liberal patriotism. A minority of the Catholic bishops, led by Archbishop Murray, were attracted to the possibility of gaining greater educational advantages for the Catholic middle class. But a majority of the bishops, led by the vigilant Archbishop McHale, saw the scheme as a proposal for 'godless colleges', and denounced Peel's project. O'Connell decided to accept episcopal direction; in May 1845 Davis clashed publicly with him—O'Connell responded by implicitly accusing Davis of a latent Protestant sectarian prejudice, to the fury of the latter's Young Ireland Catholic friends. The whole exchange ended in a moment of pure tragic farce. Davis burst into tears, O'Connell quickly seized the moment to effect a reconciliation: 'Davis, I love you.'[247] There was, however, to be no end to the actual controversy, and the O'Connellite press continued to abuse Davis.

It is easy to make a good case in defence of O'Connell's position. Thomas Davis disingenuously claimed that the Catholic bishops were in favour of 'mixed education' in principle; though, if he had made the same claim about O'Connell's previous views on the subject, he would have had a good enough point. O'Connell had talked to the Select Committee in 1825 about how he had wanted to send his eldest son to Trinity College, Dublin, despite the acrimonious atmosphere. He added: 'I am sure it would be very much the wish of the Catholic laity to see the clergy of the three principal persuasions at the same university, as it is very desirable that the laity of all persuasions should be educated together.'[248] It has seemed to some that O'Connell himself might have accepted mixed education with separate religious education, but he had already conceded to the Catholic Church the right to control the education of Catholics. But the fact cannot be denied that for those in Irish society who looked in on this debate

---

[246] Angela Clifford, *The Godless Colleges and Mixed Education in Ireland* (Belfast, 1992), 53.

[247] Denis Gwynn, *O'Connell, Davis and the Colleges Bill* (Cork, 1948); Geraldine Grogan, 'The Colleges Bill 1845–9', in M. R. O'Connell, *O'Connell, Education, Church and State* (Dublin, 1992), 19–34; Clifford, *Godless Colleges*, 109.

[248] *Reports (brought to the Lords) viz On the state of Ireland, 3 February to 6 July 1825*, vol. 9, 9 Mar. 1825, O'Connell evidence, 11 Mar. 1825, p. 157.

from the outside, as it were, it confirmed doubts about the cosmopolitan 'liberalism', so visible in other respects, of the O'Connell movement. The *Northern Whig* scathingly observed:

This liberal and liberalising man—the 'liberator' of Catholics from sectarian bondage—now desires to rear up and foster sectarian collegiate monopolies; and that being effected, if another Newton were to appear and offer himself to Galway College or Cork College, he would have slight chance of being chosen to teach science, unless his religious creed happened to be of the right sort, which Newton's was not.[249]

Conor Cruise O'Brien, in a celebrated phrase, has pointed out that O'Connell was both 'a strong Catholic and a strong Liberal'. Oliver Mac-Donagh has described O'Connell as one of the great carriers of the historic liberal tradition of the 'Enlightenment'. Fergus O'Ferrall has written:

If we wish to get to the heart of the Irish democratic and liberal tradition, we must begin with O'Connell. He displayed a strong commitment to political equality, to humanitarian reform, to anti-imperialist and anti-racialist politics. O'Connell, uniquely among Catholic statesmen of his period, espoused the complete separation of church and state and the struggle to establish religious liberty upon a general principle which would give religious freedom to all, whether Jew, Muslim, Christian, Catholic or Protestant.[250]

R. V. Comerford has pointed out that some of O'Connell's thinking prefigures modern concepts of power-sharing along religious lines, as, for example, in his support for rotation of office at municipal level.[251] Yet here is the difficulty: on the veto controversy O'Connell's position put him at odds with other celebrated Catholic liberals like Shiel or Thomas Moore. In the aftermath of the achievement of emancipation, he failed to maintain a sustained working relationship with the emancipationist wing of Presbyterian liberalism: although there were to be some moments of political co-operation, they were never to be sustained. In 1842 O'Connell privately told Cullen that repeal would destroy Irish Protestantism because Protestantism was more an ideology of superiority and a patronage machine than a genuine religion. In 1845 he adopted a sectarian stand on higher-educational questions which dismayed Young Ireland.

In the late twentieth century it has become conventional to stress unproblematically O'Connell's liberal, democratic credentials. In 1875

[249] *Northern Whig*, 15 May 1845.
[250] For a fascinating discussion of these liberal 'readings' of O'Connell, see Fergus O'Ferrall, 'Liberty and Catholic Politics 1790–1990', in Maurice O'Connell (ed.), *Daniel O'Connell: Political Pioneer* (Dublin, 1991), 43. O'Connell paid a real political price, it should be noted, on account of his opposition to slavery in the USA. See Kevin Kenny, *The American Irish: A History* (London, 2000), 85.
[251] *Inventing the Nation: Ireland* (London, 2003), 160.

Lord O'Hagan, in fact, initiated this interpretation of O'Connell's career: 'History will tell that O'Connell used his power for pure and generous purposes, in no spirit of poor self-seeking or of insular narrowness or of exclusive sectarianism—but with a true and liberal sense of his public duty and a firm resolution to discharge it.'[252] O'Hagan added: 'The union of Irishmen was always among the fondest aspirations of O'Connell.'[253] That shrewd commentator William Cooke Taylor, however, struck a different, more critical, note in his 1847 study. Cooke Taylor acknowledged that it was unfair to claim, as O'Connell's enemies did, that he deliberately heightened sectarian feeling to increase his own power: 'We know that he was activated by no such mean and mercenary motives.' But, Cooke Taylor added: 'Through life he believed that the purity of the Catholic religion in Ireland could only be maintained by keeping the Irish Catholics distinct and apart from the Irish Protestants.' A fusion between the liberal and enlightened men of both churches would, he feared, generate a cold latitudinarianism, such as prevails in France, and this he dreaded as little better than infidelity.[254] For Cooke Taylor, this dread of 'fusion' explained his position on the 'Godless colleges', which so dismayed Thomas Davis. The long-term consequences for the quality of Irish intellectual life were, however, as significant as Davis feared. Dr Walter MacDonald, later Professor of Theology at Maynooth, described the culture of higher education experienced by Irish Catholicism in the latter half of the nineteenth century: 'We were educated in a fool's paradise, as if we were still in the eighteenth or even the sixteenth century. Darwin was then revolutionising thought, but we overturned him in two or three sentences.'[255] But in May 1906 the *Freeman's Journal*, then the voice of mainstream nationalism, took a different view:

It will be for the historian of the future to tell that the two decades of years that followed the foundation of the Queen's Colleges coincided with the period of militant Darwinism in European universities. Who can say what has been saved to Irish Catholicism by its resolution to battle against godless education at that time?[256]

Who can doubt that the mature Daniel O'Connell, who was in revolt against the modernistic religious ideas of his youth, would have endorsed this verdict of the *Freeman*?[257] There was to be a significant ideological cost.

[252] The Rt. Hon. Thomas, Lord O'Hagan, *The O'Connell Centenary Address* (Dublin, 1875), 34.

[253] Ibid. 41.

[254] 'A Munster Farmer' (William Cooke Taylor), *Reminiscences of Daniel O'Connell*, (London, 1847), 51.

[255] J. Chartres Molony, *The Riddle of the Irish* (London, 1927), 129.

[256] 'The Catholic University School of Medicine', *Freeman's Journal*, 12 May 1906.

[257] See Sean McGraw and Kevin Whelan, 'Daniel O'Connell in Comparative Perspective', in *Eire–Ireland*, 40: 2 (Spring–Summer 2005), 66–89.

As late as 1908, Thomas Sinclair, the leading figure of liberal Presbyterian unionism, recalled the Davis–O'Connell controversy in order to rehearse the stand of Davis against denominational education. The issue helped liberal unionists to bury their doubts about their illiberal Orange allies in a 'harmonious denunciation of catholic designs'.[258]

[258] Graham Walker, *A History of the Ulster Unionist Party: Protest, Pragmatism and Pessimism* (Manchester, 2004), 26.

5

The Politics of Hunger, 1845–1850

Had our own parliament ruled us, the landlords would not have had their tyrannies sanctioned and increased in licence till the suffering people were reduced down to the lumper potato for a wretched and alas a fatally precarious subsistence.

(Address of the Repeal Association to the electors of Ireland, John O'Connell, *Freeman's Journal*, 14 June 1847)

The Population in Ireland in April 1846 was eight million and a half: in 1851 it was six million and a half. So great a diminution of population in so short a time is not to be found in the history of any civilised people, and fills the mind of the statesmen with almost appalling thoughts.

(Benjamin Disraeli, *Lord George Bentinck* (1852), 258)

An Irish catholic bishop said bitterly to me that every death lay at England's door. England, it seemed, was expected to work a miracle like the multiplication of the bread at the sea of Galilee. Yet, what the bishop said was true after all. The condition of things which made such a calamity possible was due essentially to those who had undertaken the government of Ireland and had left Ireland to her own devices.

(J. A. Froude, *The English in Ireland* (1895), iii. 571)

In September 1845 the distinguished Paris professors Payon and Pouchet warned Dr William Buckland, a scientist of Oxford and friend of Robert Peel, of a serious danger to the potato crop in Europe.[1] On 9 September 1845 the *Dublin Evening Post* reported the arrival of the potato blight. But for a while, at least, the full significance of this was not clear. Nationalist Ireland was first to be transfixed instead by another tragic event. On 16 September Thomas Davis died in Dublin of scarlatina: a severe blow not only to *The Nation* group, but also, and even more profoundly, to 'a vision of Irishness to which Protestant as well as Catholic might pledge

[1] PRONI T330/16/1/4a, William Buckland to Sir Robert Peel, 14 Nov. 1845, *Oxford University City and County Herald*, 15 Nov. 1845.

allegiance':[2] Davis had, uniquely in Irish politics, a gift for holding and making friends across divides. An ardent Young Irelander, he nonetheless retained friendly relations with liberal Protestants outside the Young Ireland ranks—members of the Whig administration like David Ross,[3] MP for Belfast, W. Cooke Taylor, and Torrens MacCullagh. He had a decided impact on Samuel Ferguson.[4] He was close to Grey Porter, an Anglican who had supported Stanley's Legislation Bill, and his friendship with Daniel O. Madden—a Catholic who had converted to Protestantism and also a rather cynical view of O'Connellism—led him into difficulties with O'Connell himself. He even inspired John Tyndall, the great scientist, close friend of Carlyle, and later ardent unionist. Dame Dehra Parker, later an Ulster Unionist Cabinet Minister and grandmother of James Chichester-Clark, Unionist Prime Minister from 1969 to 1971, confessed to having had an 'ardent admiration' for the poetry of Thomas Davis in her youth.[5] As *The Nation* group mourned the loss of their brilliant colleague, it had also to come to terms with the full horrendous implications of the potato blight.

Following the death of Thomas Davis, the task of writing *The Nation* editorials fell to John Mitchel. Mitchel's temperament, northern, abrasive, and absolutist, now emerged in full power—unaffected by the softening influence of Davis. Stephen Gwynn wryly observed that Mitchel, like many an Ulster Presbyterian, knew his Bible, from which he learned how to curse. The implication of Mitchel's writing was clear enough: a massive human tragedy was just around the corner, but also a tragedy which had implications for 'normal' economic and social relationships in Ireland. At the beginning of November O'Connell made a call to the government to provide employment on railway construction.[6] On 3 November Dr William Buckland gave a paper in Oxford, arguing that the 'destruction to the potato means food will be fearfully expensive', and warning that 2 million people in Ireland were dependent on the crop. Buckland believed that 'the blessings of providence' will fall on those who 'themselves help' in this crisis: he urged Peel to take rapid remedial action.[7] On 5 November 1845 Peel wrote to the Queen that he felt 'it would be his duty not to withhold from Her Majesty the expression of his apprehension that there are important differences of opinion in the Cabinet in respect of the measures to be adopted in consequence of the

---

[2] Gerry Kearns, 'Time and Good Citizenship: Nationalism and Thomas Davis', *Bullan: An Irish Studies Journal*, 5: 2 (Spring 2001), 237–9.

[3] Thomas Davis to Thomas Wyse, 10 July 1843, NLI Ms 15026(2), Wyse papers.

[4] Eve Patten, *Samuel Ferguson and the Culture of Nineteenth-Century Ireland* (Dublin, 2004), 99–130.

[5] G. C. Duggan, *Northern Ireland: Success or Failure* (Dublin, 1950), 13.

[6] *Irish Times*, 4 Nov. 1845.   [7] PRONI T330/66/1/4a.

apprehended scarcity in Ireland'.[8] The next day he expressed his 'relief' that there appeared to be 'some exaggeration' in the reports coming from Ireland. On 10 November Peel, on his own responsibility, ordered the purchase in America of £100,000-worth of Indian corn for shipment to Ireland. The government, at least, was now taking some action to alleviate suffering.

But what of nationalist Ireland? How did it respond to the growing humanitarian crisis? What is striking here is the way in which, both for O'Connell and, more particularly, Young Ireland, politics remained in command. For Young Ireland there was to be no question of subordinating everything to a massive humanitarian effort, because this involved becoming supplicants upon English generosity. Young Irelander Richard O'Gorman impressed O'Connell with a speech at the Repeal Association at the end of October 1845: 'They had plenty of means for the support of their people. They wished not to appear as beggars, as they did in 1822, when England preserved from perishing in the west three or four thousand persons.'[9] The decisive message here is the rejection of any concept of dependence on Britain, even if British aid saved Irish lives. The political imperative of maintaining Irish national self-respect was considered to be more important than the actual feeding of the Irish people.

A week later *The Nation* repeated the point, a day before Peel's decision to purchase the Indian corn. *The Nation* saw the oncoming famine as a tragedy generated by the absence of Irish self-government:

Changes, indeed, are coming and more than the poor need to be up and watching. And gracious Heaven! To think that these evils might be mitigated or turned aside, if this country were governed by its own people—governed by men who knew its resources and would willingly come together in brotherly love to save it, by willing labours and sacrifices.

To lament the absence of self-government is conventional enough. But the implication here is stronger: the absence of self-government meant that the evils of the famine could not be addressed. It was not possible that these evils be mitigated in the context of the union.

In fact, *The Nation* went on, the London government only had the capacity to make things worse for *all* the Irish social classes: 'And black hell! To think that they will be aggravated by a foreign parliament—ignorant, vain, headlong, insolent and selfish, who will take no heed of anything

[8] Royal Archives, C 44/2, 5 Nov. 1845.
[9] *The Nation*, 1 Nov. 1845. For a discussion of some of the authorship of *Nation* essays, see Kevin McGrath, 'Writers on the Nation 1842–45', *Irish Historical Studies*, 6: 23 (Mar. 1949), 189–223. See also Melissa Fegan, *Literature and the Irish Famine, 1845–1919* (Oxford, 2002), 45.

that is Irish—who will treat landlord and peasant, merchant and artisan, with indiscriminate insolence.' The most striking and original aspect of *The Nation*'s thinking echoed Richard O'Gorman rather precisely. Appeals to British charity were to be rejected for an essentially political reason: they undermined the case for Irish self-government. 'But let us have no begging appeals to England—no gathering eleemosynary help, to be distributed for the use of paupers—no feeding of our people with alms and as mendicants. For who could make men and freemen of a nation so basely degraded?'[10]

The message here is unambiguous. The famine was so threatening precisely because Ireland lacked self-government. But in the absence of self-government—the only real answer to the country's problems—there should be no unmanly appeals to England for assistance. Such appeals would in themselves indicate Ireland's unfitness for self-governance and thereby merely guarantee the perpetuation of a deeply unsatisfactory situation. The implication of such a view was unavoidable: the normal business of nationalist organization should carry on as before. Logically, therefore, on 21 October 1845 John Power and Cornelius MacLoghlin announced the simultaneous collection for the O'Connell Tribute of 1845 to be made in all the parishes of Ireland on Sunday, 16 November: 'Again the Irish people are called upon to testify their gratitude to their great Benefactor—their pride in his wonderful ability, and their appreciation of his unexampled services.' The O'Connell Tribute was a major endeavour; a moderately sized town like Clonmel had sixty active sponsors for the Tribute. As the words of the Tribute declaration stated: 'The grateful Irish people are eager once more to manifest their enthusiastic attachment. They feel it is not so much their duty as their interest, to sustain their matchless champion, and they will do it nobly and universally more.'[11] *The Nation* fully supported the O'Connell Tribute:

The O'Connell rent is a claim which has ever been recognised by Irishmen, not only as a public tribute, but as a private and individual debt affecting each of us personally and burthening every man's conscience until it is discharged—we need scarcely say that there shall be no repudiation either of that or of any other just claim to which the Irish people are liable.

To make matters absolutely clear, *The Nation* insisted: 'Such a claim as this is one which must not be postponed to *any* other charge whatever—from which the country must not be frightened either by monetary panic, food-panic or the vile and mercenary hoard of the people's well known and unrelenting enemies.'[12]

---

[10] *The Nation*, 8 Nov. 1845.   [11] Ibid.   [12] Ibid., 15 Nov. 1845.

Nor can these remarks be seen as reflecting a moment when it was possible to believe that the impending crisis might have been limited in effect. These sentiments were sustained throughout the winter of 1845 and into the following spring,[13] by which time the scale of the tragedy was widely grasped. Inevitably, those who found themselves outside the ranks of Irish repealers were less than impressed. Outsiders saw a rather chimerical, political project being given a priority over the alleviation of a humanitarian tragedy. The widespread perception was that an actual and real crisis was being downgraded in favour of a somewhat abstract political agenda. In Belfast the liberal unionist *Northern Whig* was astounded: 'Would Grattan, when he saw the advancing steps of gaunt famine, have consented to send out the announcement that his rent was to be collected? Impossible! But Grattan was a patriot, an honourable, high-minded man.'[14] In London the *Examiner* asked even more brutally of O'Connell: 'But what cares he? If thousands are doomed to perish by famine or pestilence.' There were several Orange ballads on the subject. J. W. Croker, in the *Quarterly Review*, was even more brutal in denouncing 'Repeal rent and O'Connell tribute at a moment and in places where the miserable people are dying in frozen ditches for want of food'. The *Review* concluded bitterly that O'Connell was exhibiting 'a wanton and outrageous defiance of the good feelings and common sense of mankind'. Even at this early stage in the famine, the impulse towards a generous response in the rest of the United Kingdom was being curbed by rising irritation with perceived Irish political self-indulgence. The fact is that English public opinion was annoyed by the Tribute and O'Connell's means of personally financing himself at the best of times. The Dublin Castle press regularly commented sourly upon it. In 1843 an 'English Traveller', on a visit to the 'Wild West' of Ireland, expressed amazement that O'Connell should 'be able to wring from the poorest people in the

---

[13] Ibid., 28 Mar. 1846, speaks of 'our deep anxiety to assist as much as possible in ensuring to the present collection for this commanding claim the universal support of the country'. NLI, Ms 3143, Daniel O'Connell to T. M. Ray, 2 May 1846, discusses the collection of the rent without any reference to the public controversy.

[14] *Northern Whig*, 15 Nov. 1845. The *Whig*, it is interesting to note, accepted O'Connell's defence of his own conduct as a landlord against the charges made by T. Campbell Foster of *The Times* in the autumn of 1845; *The Nation*, 29 Nov. 1845. For this incident, see Lesley A. Williams, *Daniel O'Connell, the British Press and the Irish Famine* (Ashgate, 2003), 145; Maurice O'Connell defended the situation on the O'Connell estate by acknowledging that his father had, in fact, allowed destitute tenants from neighbouring estates to settle on his land. 'Is it for not evicting these people ... that he is censured? Or is it for not applying some Malthusian anti-population check? Was no feeling of pity to be shown towards them?'

world an immense amount of money, not only for personal expenses, but for all sorts of absurd and unimaginable reasons for which he renders no account whatever'.[15] The repealers responded justly enough that those who were, or had been, the recipients of tithes and rents were in no position to complain. Nevertheless, to many in England the continuation of the Tribute in the famine period seemed to be an affront to any code of decency.

While O'Connell and *The Nation* agreed on the necessity of the Tribute—famine not withstanding—they were, nonetheless, moving towards a decisive split. As the Peelite ministry collapsed under the weight of the Corn Law crisis, O'Connell's instincts were drawing him towards a renewed Whig alliance. On 6 December 1845 Peel, having failed to win over his Cabinet to the need for repeal of the Corn Laws, resigned. On 8 December the Queen asked Russell to form a government: but would it be possible? One key issue for Russell was the degree of O'Connellite support he could expect. On 15 December O'Connell addressed the Loyal National Repeal Association at Conciliation Hall on the subject. The formal disclaimer, of course, was that: 'Am I for giving up Repeal (no, no)? No such thing (cheers).' But Russell's eye was bound to fall on another, crucial passage: 'The new administration will be wanting us, and they shall have us if they do good for the Irish people (cheers). There is a little bird that always whispers to me—get something good for Ireland.'[16] The British press interpreted these remarks reasonably enough; the way was now clear for Russell to form a ministry with Irish support. William Smith O'Brien wrote nervously to O'Connell, advocating 'a strict neutrality between the two great English factions'.[17]

Daniel O'Connell did not seem to feel the same way. The *Sun*, one of O'Connell's favourite London journals, commented approvingly: 'O'Connell prefers food for the people to Repeal.'[18] *The Nation* was furious: 'O'Connell prefers food for the people to Repeal!' *The Nation* claimed: 'We have yet to learn that well-fed men will be in a worse condition to achieve Repeal than starving ones.' But the problem in Ireland was the relative absence of well-fed men. *The Nation* continued angrily:

What *gobe-mouches* [simpletons] be these English! When will they understand that O'Connell is not Repeal? That O'Connell cannot undo what has been done—that

[15] *A Visit to the Wild West by an 'English Traveller'* (London, 1843), 27.
[16] *The Nation*, 20 Dec. 1845.
[17] Maurice O'Connell (ed.), *The Correspondence of Daniel O'Connell*, vol. 7, *1840–45* (Blackwater, Dublin, 1972–80), 349. For O'Connell on the *Sun* see *O'Connell Correspondence*, iv. 197, O'Connell to Robert White, 16 Aug. 1830: 'I am particularly anxious to have the *Sun*. It is the best daily London paper.'
[18] *The Nation*, 20 Dec. 1845.

powerful (and justly powerful as he is) he *cannot* (even if the bare speculations of these newspapers as to his intentions were well founded) he cannot bid us to forego the noble struggle on which the heart of Ireland is set. O'Connell is not a traitor, and if he were, Irishmen are not idiots.[19]

On 18 December Russell, nonetheless, failed in his attempt to form a Cabinet. O'Connell was disappointed, telling Smith O'Brien on 22 December that Russell was in favour of a 'Bill for the extension of the suffrage in Ireland without delay ... If we could have managed to play our cards well in Lord John's government, we should have *squeezed out* a great deal of good for Ireland without for one moment merging or even postponing Repeal but, on the contrary, drawing on that measure.'[20]

Young Ireland was hardly convinced. Edgily *The Nation* asked O'Connell to clarify his position at the next Conciliation Hall meeting, which fell also on 22 December. O'Connell observed again the proprieties on the subject of Repeal: 'Our cause is the cause of Ireland—we are on our majestic search for nationality and the changings and shiftings of administrations only exhibit the throes and struggles of that species of political tyranny that would debase us by dividing us and separating us one from the other.' But when a voice cried out 'It is nothing', in answer to O'Connell's rhetorical question about the state of play within British high politics—'Well, now, what is that to Ireland?', O'Connell responded immediately: 'It is a good deal—it animates our hopes—it raises our expectations—it gives us the certainty of success.'[21] O'Connell was watching keenly the divisive effect of the Corn Law issue on the Tory administration of Sir Robert Peel. In the eyes of his critics and even some of his friends, he was clearly hoping to re-establish a Lichfield House type of arrangement with an English Whig government. In a key phrase he declared: 'I call upon the ministry to bid for the Irish people against me.' *The Nation* grouping was not satisfied. Fully in the grip now of *politique du pire*, *The Nation* insisted that the deeper the catastrophe, the better, because it would, in the end, be for Ireland. It editorialized coldly: 'Had the destruction of the people's food been, to any extent, complete as was apprehended on the very commencement of the season, it would be so much the better for the poor.'[22]

The government, rather than *The Nation*, had the responsibility of alleviating the impending crisis. The government's preferred mode of relief was employment by public works. On 23 January 1846 the Public Works (Ireland) Bill, the first of a series of measures, was introduced in the House

---

[19] *The Nation*, 20 Dec. 1845.   [20] *O'Connell Correspondence*, vii. 353.
[21] *The Nation*, 27 Dec. 1845.
[22] Ibid., 'Eighteen Hundred and Forty-Four!', 27 Dec. 1845.

of Commons.[23] In proposing a motion that the House employ a committee to consider the famine, on 17 February 1846 O'Connell told Parliament that the famine was not the fault of the Irish people: 'It is owing to a dispensation of Providence which man can not control. Our duty is to submit to the will of an all disposing power and to perform the part of charitable Christians, by endeavouring to mitigate the evils as they arise.'[24] The tone of the government's response was, however, reassuring; O'Connell reciprocated by withdrawing his motion.

One point, however, is worth noting at this stage. From the earliest moment of the famine crisis, English public opinion was predisposed to blame Irish landlords. On 13 March 1846 300 tenants were evicted on the Gerrard estate at Baltinglass. It was a particularly harsh case: the tenantry claimed in press interviews to be willing to pay rent, but that the Gerrards wanted the land for grazing bullocks.[25] With mounting excitement *The Nation* editorialized on 'The Agrarian War', listing in particular the Gerrard case. The English press was also shocked.[26] *The Times* declared angrily that the Gerrard affair showed that 'blatant indifference to social conditions, of which no one but an Irish landlord is capable'.[27] In liberal unionist Belfast the *Northern Whig* was similarly angry:

The man who is the owner of land is entrusted by the state, with a responsible office, which, whilst he is to be protected in his own interest, he is bound to fill with a due regard for the interests of the community, and if he fails in the later respect, he fails in his duty, and the state is injured. Mr Gerrard and others like him have evidently so failed.[28]

On 26 June 1846 Peel finally achieved the objective of repealing the Corn Laws, at the price, however, of splitting his own party. There is little doubt that, in his own mind at any rate, Peel's Irish policy was connected to Corn Law policy; which is not to deny the many other reasons for the long-term shift of his policy on this matter. It was impossible in his view to vote public money to sustain the Irish poor while maintaining in operation the existing restriction on the import of cheap grain.[29] John Mitchel argued

---

[23] Peter Gray, *Famine, Land and Politics: British Government and Irish Society* (Dublin, 1996), 133.

[24] *Northern Whig*, 2 Feb. 1846.

[25] *Freeman's Journal*, quoted in *Northern Whig*, 28 Mar 1846.

[26] *The Nation*, 28 Mar. 1846.

[27] *The Times*, quoted in *Northern Whig*, 9 Apr. 1846.

[28] *Northern Whig*, 9 Apr. 1846.

[29] I. McLean, *Rational Choice and British Politics* (Oxford, 2001), 39. Brian Jenkins, 'The Chief Secretary', in D. G. Boyce and Alan O'Day (eds.), *Defenders of the Union: A Survey of British and Irish Unionism Since 1801* (London, 2001), 44.

that Ireland exported enough food to England in 1846, 1847, and 1848 to avert famine twice over, but trade statistics suggest that the exported grain would have filled only one-seventh of the gap left by potatoes.[30] Peel's last major speech in office spoke in especially warm terms of the Irish need for equality, but what, critics asked, did he really mean? The fact remains that Peel now became a surprisingly popular politician in Ireland. The *Cork Examiner*, in January 1847, acknowledged a 'charm' in the name of Sir Robert Peel.[31] In September 1847 the *Cambridge and Oxford Review* carried 'Notes of an Irish Tour by an English MP', which found it 'very amicable' to recount Irish rumours of Robert Peel's conversion to Catholicism.[32] Lord John Manners found the same rumours to be widespread.[33]

THE WHIGS IN POWER

The fall of the Tories was welcomed by O'Connell. He made it clear that he was anxious to re-establish his alliance with the Whigs and promote a policy of 'justice' for Ireland.[34] More generally, Russell was firmly in the Burke–Fox tradition of sympathy for Ireland, though this was limited by the nature of some of his religious views; O'Connell correctly identified in Russell an 'anxious abhorrence of Popery'.[35] Russell was also considered to have relatively broad-minded views on Irish agrarian issues.[36] In 1844 he had accused Peel of failure to govern Ireland and instead going for a policy of 'military occupation'. In April 1846 he had opposed Peelite coercion by calling for a new landlord–tenant measure.[37] In particular, Russell's distribution of the subordinate Irish offices was interesting. Thomas Redington, from a Galway Catholic gentry family,

---

[30] C. O'Grada, *Black '47 and Beyond: The Great Irish Famine in History, Economy, and Memory* (Princeton, 1999), 124.

[31] *Cork Examiner*, 'Meeting of Parliaments—Opposition Tactics—The Doomed Landlords', 4 Jan. 1847. A second editorial in the same issue, 'Famine and Death in the West of Ireland', adds: 'There is no excuse for Lord John Russell.'

[32] *Oxford and Cambridge Review*, 4: 23 (Sept. 1847), 333; see also Christine Kinealy, 'Was Ireland a Colony? The Evidence of the Great Famine', in Terrence MacDonough (ed.), *Was Ireland a Colony? Economics, Politics and Culture in the Nineteenth Century* (Dublin, 2005), 58.

[33] Lord John Manners, *Notes of an Irish Tour* (London, 1849), 101.

[34] Christine Kinealy, *The Great Irish Famine: Impact, Ideology and Rebellion* (London, 2002), 36.

[35] D. Kerr, *'A Nation of Beggars': Priests, People and Politics in Famine, 1846–1852* (Oxford, 1994), 8.

[36] Gray, *Famine, Land and Politics*, 58.

[37] *Cork Examiner*, 8 Dec. 1847, 'The Whigs and the Country'.

and a repealer when at Cambridge University, was chosen as the first Irish Catholic to hold the post of Under-Secretary.[38] William Torrens MacCullagh (a college friend of Thomas Davis) was appointed Private Secretary to Henry Labouchere, the new Chief Secretary, whilst Corry Connellan became the Lord-Lieutenant, Bessborough's Private Secretary. Bessborough himself (formerly Duncannon) was probably O'Connell's best ally and most sincere friend amongst senior Whigs: he had been the first Protestant member of an aristocratic family to join Daniel O'Connell's Catholic Association.[39] The law offices and legal appointments went to O'Connell's perceived allies—Pigott, Moore, Brady, and Monahan.[40]

Daniel O'Connell was privately very satisfied: he was now even more anxious to work with the Russell government. But Russell had sharply criticized *The Nation* as a grouping which 'exerts every species of violence' and 'regards separation from Britain as its end'; O'Connell, as he was publicly to admit, was worried by Russell's remarks.[41] He decided to give a very public signal of his own moderate intent. In July 1846 O'Connell declared: 'I appeal to the people of England. I ask them whether they will continue the injustice of inequality between the two countries.'[42] O'Connell was particularly exercised by the proposed legislation on arms importation. Privately he wrote to Pigot on a matter of immediate concern: 'For heaven's sake, get rid of the Arms Bill or mitigate it exceedingly.'[43] The right to bear arms was seen as a basic liberty of the British Constitution, and the restriction placed on it in Ireland a mark of second-class citizenship. 'Practical justice' to Ireland would prove 'to demonstration' that the repealers were 'wrong'. O'Connell,

[38] Gray, *Famine, Land and Politics*, 149.

[39] Dorothy Howell-Thomas, *Duncannon: Reformer and Reconciler* (Norwich, 1992), 115.

[40] For Redington's repeal views at university, see Ged Martin, *The Cambridge Union and Ireland 1815–1914* (Edinburgh, 2000), 163–4. Torrens MacCullagh's friendship with Thomas Davis is noted in Helen Maloney, *Thomas Davis* (London, 2003), 25; he served in the Thomas Davis Memorial Committee, *The Nation*, 25 Oct. 1845.

[41] J. Savage, *'98 and '48: The Modern Revolutionary History of Ireland* (New York, 1856), 282.

[42] *Northern Whig*, 21 July 1846.

[43] MacDonagh, *O'Connell*, 579. The impact on British opinion of Irish agitation on the arms issue should not be underestimated. The evangelical Earl of Shaftesbury, once seriously considered as a possible Peelite Irish lord–lieutenant, was deeply moved by the famine. On 7 October 1846 he wrote in his diary: 'Give orders that no more potatoes should be bought for the house. We must not, by competing on the market, raise the cost on the poor man.' But on 12 December 1846 Shaftesbury noted angrily: 'We expend money for their maintenance at a rate of £127,000 a week; and the starving peasantry can save from this effort of mercy and munificence enough to purchase arms to a greater extent than was ever before known for the assault and overthrow of their benefactors': Edwin Hodder, *The Life and Work of the Earl of Shaftesbury*, vol. 2 (London, 1887), 183.

urged on by his loyal lieutenants T. M. Ray and Tom Steele, was now clearly challenging 'Young Ireland' to accept his pragmatic leadership. Within a few days he received his reply from Young Ireland; it was not an encouraging one. While O'Connell was out of the country, his son John entered into a prolonged dialogue with the Young Irelanders, a dialogue designed to re-establish their fidelity to the Liberator. This dialogue did not go well. O'Connell—worried by Russell's critical comments on *The Nation* group—urgued that all members of the Repeal Association adopt a pledge repudiating physical force in any and all circumstances. Towards the end of the second day of a long drawn-out meeting, passions finally erupted on 28 July 1846. The 23-year-old Thomas Meagher, speaking in a pronounced English public-school (Stonyhurst) accent, launched into a calculated oratorical effort with a carefully phrased defence of the potential role of physical force in the achievement of national liberation.[44] The speech won loud applause, but John O'Connell and his allies would have found it difficult to take such a rhetorical attack—and from such a presumptuous, inexperienced young man—with any degree of seriousness. John O'Connell rose and declared the utterance of such a sentiment was a danger to the existence of the whole repeal organization. In a memoir of Meagher, written twenty-one years later, John Mitchel noted: 'We all knew that this meant that his father would break up the Association.'[45] Mitchel added, with an interesting display of tactical caution and concern for the political 'blame game': 'It might have been better if we had allowed him to do so, but O'Brien took his hat, saying: "No, let *us* go rather!"—We all walked out, a large number of the people in the hall came away also, and never entered it again.' The split with Young Ireland was now formalized. On 3 January 1847 the Young Irelanders established a rival organization, the Irish Confederation, of which William Smith O'Brien accepted leadership. As a symbol of the gap between Young and 'Old' Ireland, on 19 January 1847 O'Connell's loyal aide, Tom Steele, wrote to Patrick Lalor, the ranking O'Conellite leader in Queens County: 'A memorial adapted for presentation to the Lord Chancellor by the Liberator, soliciting your appointment to the Magistracy of Queens County. Send to me, directly here, and I will take care of it.'[46] At the very same time Lalor's son James Fintan, was moving towards an involvement with Young Ireland which would land him in jail and probably shortened his life.

---

[44] Denis Gwynn, *Thomas Francis Meagher*, O'Connell Lecture delivered at University College, 17 July 1961, National University of Ireland, p. 14; John M. Hearne, 'The Sword Speech in Context', *Decies Journal of the Waterford Archaeological and Historical Society*, 59 (2003), 56.
[45] M. J. McManus (ed.), *Thomas Davis and Young Ireland* (Dublin, 1945), 85.
[46] NLI Ms 8362.

O'Connell's wager on the Whigs was to prove to be ultimately unsuccessful; but it is hardly surprising that he expected Lord John Russell might be an ally: certainly Orange sentiment in Belfast was alarmed.[47] Indeed, Russell made one remarkable and controversial gesture in his favour. He allowed O'Connell to announce, at a Dublin repeal meeting on the morning of 17 August 1846—before the formal public announcement—that Peel's Arms Bill was not to be renewed. The government, said O'Connell, in a striking phrase, had 'withdrawn the measure in compliance with the wishes of the Irish people'.[48] Nor was there any reason as yet to fear any radical erosion of the paternalist impulse which had characterized the Peel government. When the Whigs returned to power in the summer of 1846, they were opposed to any interference with the market. This laissez-faire attitude was the inevitable result of the crisis over the repeal of the Corn Laws which had brought the Whigs back to power. But they were also predisposed to favour the interventionist policy of public works as a means of providing famine relief.[49]

Charles Trevelyan, the senior Treasury official, designed a new set of relief measures for the Whig administration. The new policy sought to achieve relief through a revamped, more efficient system of public works, combined with a new and vitally significant reluctance to interfere with the grain trade. Indeed, agricultural exports were allowed, and this inevitably contributed to the steady rise in Irish food prices between September and the end of the year.[50] On several occasions before 1845 a public-works policy had served as an effective means of defence against local famines. But the application of 'the same remedy' in this style in the apocalyptic context of autumn and winter 1846–7 was proved to be a serious mistake. Professor Cormac O'Grada has pointed out that requiring 'masses of half-starving and poorly clothed people to build roads and break stones in all weathers, often for less than a subsistence wage, was no way to minimise mortality'.[51] More recently, Dr Pat McGregor has argued that the administration correctly attempted to set the target wage at subsistence level, but failed to achieve it, because they were unable to forecast prices correctly.[52]

---

[47] C. Kinealy and G. McAtasney, *The Hidden Famine: Poverty, Hunger and Sectarianism in Belfast* (London, 2000), 54–5.

[48] 'Ministerial Measures', *Quarterly Review*, 'Outlines of the History of Ireland', 83: 166 (Sept. 1848), 592–3.

[49] George L. Bernstein, 'Liberals, the Irish Famine and the Role of the State', *Irish Historical Studies*, 29: 116 (1995), 534; *Northern Whig*, 30 July 1846; for Meagher, see W. F. Lyons (ed.), *Brigadier-General Thomas Francis Meagher: His Political and Military Career: With Selections from his Speeches and Workings* (New York, 1870), 9–12.

[50] James S. Donnelly Jnr., *The Great Irish Potato Famine* (Stroud, 2001), 64.

[51] C O'Grada, *Black '47 and Beyond*, 66.

[52] 'Insufficient for the Support of a Family: Wages on the Public Works During the Great Irish Famine', *Economic and Social Review*, 25: 2 (2004), 219.

Those charged with the administration of the scheme had their own, rather different complaints. Lieutenant Inglis reported for Limerick that the relief committees were giving relief to visibly undeserving cases, whilst the normal 'agricultural operations of the country' were being 'dreadfully neglected'.[53] Father Mathew, the great temperance campaigner, complained that many relief works were leading to an increase in drunkenness.[54] He objected to payment in money instead of food. Most of the relief committees simply wanted to employ as many people as possible, regardless of any consideration of efficiency. The 'interest point' of the potential for roadmaking had been reached.[55] Nearly half-a-million persons were supported by labour for the Board of Works, but the appalling truth remained: 'The famine is increasing; deaths become more frequent; and the prospect may well appal the heart.'[56] The core of the problem was clear enough. 'The palpable evil in these localities is the absolute want of cheap food, and the prospective want of food itself, even at high prices.'[57] Indeed, by the end of 1846 the government finally realized that its scheme of public works was failing to check the loss of life, and 'a new system of relief designed to deliver cheap food directly and gratuitously to the destitute masses was gradually put into place'.[58] But the damage was already done: most dramatically in south-west Cork.

On 7 January 1847 the *Cork Examiner* reported on 'Skibbereen', a whole village, a 'theatre of famine, disease and death', conveying the plight of the Irish poor:

How can the labourer work? He has a wife, perhaps an old father or bed-ridden mother and three or four children in his cabin; he strains and toils for them—for the sickly wife and the youngest darling, whose once round cheeks are now pale and shrivelled, resting on the mother's fleshless breast; he thinks of them, and toils on—but every blow he gives is at his heart strings—he is sounding his funeral knell—every effort of that starving man, who hides the hunger that is gnawing at his entrails that he might spare a morsel for those he loves is hurrying him to the coffinless grave and the shroud of rags.

This was an appalling account, yet even in Skibbereen the hotel was serving fine fare at the height of the famine.[59] The *Spectator* later noted: 'A middling prosperity has been in the very midst of starvation.'[60] But it was hardly surprising. West Cork achieved world notoriety, not because it was 'a

---

[53] BPP 1847 (764), *Correspondence Relating to the Measures Adopted for the Relief of Distress in Ireland, Board of Works series (First Part) ... 1847, Famine Ireland 6* (Shannon, 1970), 292 and 353, Reports of Lieut. Inglis on Limerick, 15 Nov. 1846 and 5 Dec. 1846.
[54] Ibid. 304.　　　[55] Ibid., Trevelyan to Father Matthew, 30 Nov. 1846, 517.
[56] Ibid. 527.　　　[57] Ibid.　　　[58] Donnelly, *Great Irish Potato Famine*, 80.
[59] W. J. McCormack, ed. William Hanbidge and Mary Ann Hanbidge, *Memoirs of West Wicklow 1813–1939* (Cork, 2005), 57.
[60] *Spectator*, 2 Dec. 1848.

poor backward district, engaged in subsistence agriculture on the edge of nowhere', but 'because potato failure had devastated a commercial crop in a community that had lived by agricultural trade and handicraft production for generations'.[61]

A. M. Sullivan, who hailed from south-west Cork, described the shocking, demoralizing impact of famine. Sullivan, a Young Ireland activist, was for a time clerk of relief works and knew the realities.

The doomed people realised but too well what was before them. Last year's suffering had exhausted them; a sort of stupor fell upon the people, contrasting remarkably with the fierce energy put forth a year before. It was no uncommon sight to see the cottier and his little family seated on the garden fence, gazing all day long in moody silence at the blighted plot that had been their last hope. Nothing could arouse them. You spoke, they answered not. You tried to cheer them, they shook their heads. I never saw so sudden and so terrible a transformation.[62]

W. S. Chenevix Trench reported on 'Three Days at Schull' for *Fraser's Magazine*. In this account horror was piled upon horror. Trench's narrative contained one particularly dreadful moment:

In a sort of hutch there lay four skeletal children ... All these children were death-stricken. Had they been removed at this moment to go to the Queen's palace, they could not have lived. We turned to go, but the mother, starting up from another bed, holding out to us an empty bowl in both her hands, cried out with frantic eagerness that we should not go without giving her some drink ... As she half rose from the bed, the little covering which she had, fell off; and our eyes could hardly have perceived a ghastlier anatomy than was shown to them ... [63]

What was the reaction in the metropolis to such stories of horror? The tone of British public opinion was uncertain. *The Times* commented in the middle of December 1846:

We can understand how the cottiers must have been affected by the potato rot; but how, except indirectly, this can have made the superior middleman and the [comfortable farmer] suffer, we do not see ... They have been exporting abundantly, too, and selling fairly, if not dearly, in the English market. Yet now they are petitioners to the English people, for what, under the circumstances, must be called superfluous alms.[64]

In a more generous spirit, in the same month, the *Cambridge and Oxford Review* insisted on the 'Ills of Ireland': 'To the attention of Christian

[61] David Dickson, *Old World Colony: Cork and South Munster 1680–1830* (Cork, 2005), 499.
[62] *New Ireland* (Dublin, 1878), 59.   [63] *Fraser's Magazine*, 36: 301 (July 1847).
[64] *The Times*, 16 Dec. 1846.

men its [Ireland's] claims are irresistible. *Homo sum: humanis nihil a me alienum puto.* The familiar sentiment of a heathen philanthropist must not be despised in the foremost nation of Christendom.'[65] The *Review* was particularly repelled by the idea that God had sent the famine.[66] The *Spectator* declared: 'In the present temper of the English people, there is no need to cheat them into assisting the Irish people.'[67] But it wanted the Irish to see and acknowledge with thanks the full scale of English assistance. The inevitable nationalist political point was, however, also forcibly made. 'And this in a Christian country!—This under the proud banner of British sway!—This is a land united to England by a union considered sacred as a holy covenant, so much so that the thought of severing it is regarded as profanation, a sacrilege.'[68] Those words were to have a profound impact, destined to be repeated again and again by angry Irish commentators. A. M. Sullivan's remarks were less dramatic, but achieve a certain effect because of their patent attempt to be fair: 'It would be utter injustice to deny that the government made exertions which, judged by ordinary circumstances, would be prompt and considerable. But judged by the awful magnitude of the evil then at hand or actually befallen, they were fatally tardy and inadequate.'[69]

At the beginning of 1847, in recognition of the failure of the public-works policy, the government decided to adopt a new policy based on the provision of a number of specially established soup kitchens. Such a move constituted a decided break with the conventional orthodoxy, which asserted that the provision of gratuitous relief was both ideologically flawed and hopelessly expensive.[70] In a compensating move, Trevelyan insisted on a rapid reduction of public-works schemes, even in areas when soup kitchens were not operative.[71]

Russell now explained that the Irish question was a question not of money but of food. 'My Lords, supposing it had been a question of money, I am quite prepared to say that there is no sum of which it would not have been the duty of government to have proposed to Parliament for the extraction of people from so great an evil.' But the fact was that the government could not intervene in the grain market. Suppose it offered to spend £10 million, then

---

[65] *Cambridge and Oxford Review*, 3 (July–December 1846), 522.   [66] *Ibid.* 557.

[67] *Spectator*, 30 Jan. 1847.

[68] *Cork Examiner*, 6 Jan. 1847; on this theme see also Patrick Hickey, *Famine in West Cork: The Mizen Peninsula, Land and People 1800–52: A Local Study of Pre-Famine and Famine Ireland* (Cork, 2002), 207.

[69] *New Ireland*, 60.

[70] Christine Kinealy, *The Great Irish Famine: Impact, Ideology and Rebellion* (London, 2002), 41–2.

[71] *Ibid.* 42.

rapidly £20 million would be required because prices would rise dramatically. The government had to accept the natural limitations to its role: it was the 'worst cultivator, the worst of manufacturers and the worst of traders'.[72] According to Russell, half-a-million people were being employed on public works. But there was evidence of 'idling' on good wages—farmers were unable to get labourers for harvest work. Solid and even substantial farmers were putting their sons on the relief works. Hence the need for a new strategy—local committees under the direction of Sir John Burgoyne were to establish soup kitchens. The work of the Quakers in Ireland had given credibility to the soup-kitchen concept. One Irish newspaper, the *Northern Whig* in Belfast, was deeply impressed: 'The English certainly are a noble-minded people.'

But this was, as the same newspaper soon admitted, to be rather too generous a conclusion. In January 1847 Russell had also signalled his government's determination that outdoor relief should be paid for out of local rates. While soup kitchens gradually replaced the failed public works in the early months of 1847, the Whig government was advancing the legislation which became the Poor Law Amendment Act, a measure eventually passed in June. The initiative behind the radical departures agreed in January 1847 came primarily from the professional administrators of the Board of Works, who argued that labour and relief should be kept conceptually and practically apart.[73] The Soup Kitchens Act of February 1847 was an unprecedented and remarkable innovation; a break with the key principle that the poor should only eat by the sweat of their brows. But the assumption remained that the responsibility for the crisis lay with the Irish landlords, and that they should be made to meet the costs. This assumption explains Parliament's decision to rely on the Poor Law as soon as the 'exceptional' season ended—as soon as it could plausibly be said that the potato blight had ended. The Poor Law system was made responsible for both preventative and temporary relief. The workhouses built after 1838 had a capacity for 110,000 paupers. To cope with their extended role in relief provision, additional workhouses were built and, subject to strict conditions, outdoor relief was allowed. 'For the government, the advantage of this change was that it made the landlords responsible for relief in their own localities, both through management of the workhouses and by payment of rates to finance the constitutional relief system.'[74] This law, in short, shifted the burden of providing relief away from the British

---

[72] *Northern Whig*, 30 Jan. 1847.

[73] Peter Gray, 'The Triumph of Dogma: Ideology and Famine Relief', *History Ireland*, 3: 2 (Summer 1995), 31.

[74] Christine Kinealy, *A New History of Ireland* (Stroud, 2004), 164.

Treasury, instead placing it squarely on the shoulders of Irish landlords and tenants. It was also this same law which drastically increased the weight of that burden by authorizing relief outside the workhouses in a broad array of circumstances.[75]

John Stuart Mill was allowed to write to all the leaders on Ireland in the radical *Morning Chronicle*, from 5 October 1846 to 17 January 1847.[76] It is, therefore, no surprise that the *Chronicle*, whose owner was a leading Whig, Sir John Eastwood, published on 10 March 1847 a powerful editorial denunciation of government policy.[77] It drew attention to the telling conflict of opinion and confusion of leading government spokesmen when they expounded the basis of policy. The debate concerning new relief measures took place against a backdrop of industrial recession and monetary crisis in Britain. Russell clearly believed that his new approach was popular in such a context, but, as the *Morning Chronicle* pointed out:

If the experiment of outdoor relief proves unsafe, and if the whole machinery of the extended Poor Law breaks down, as it will certainly do in the west and south of Ireland, it will be no defence that the government took the step, not because they considered it to be wise, but because they knew it to be popular.

The *Chronicle* insisted that the key flaw in the government's plans—'the small amount of property which Ireland possesses in proportion to its population'—was a fatal one, because 'the capacity of a country clearly depends upon the proportion which her property bears to the numbers which become chargeable as paupers'. But if Ireland was compared with England, a startling fact became clear: Ireland, with a population of 8 million against the 16 million of England, had a rateable property value of £13,500,000 as against £65,500,000—in other words, Ireland, with half of the population, had not more than one-fifth of the means of supporting those who might become chargeable under a poor law. Professor Michael de Nie has pointed out that much of the British press accepted this analysis by the autumn of 1849. 'An English-style poor law, which supposedly worked well in a nation with one fifteenth of its population as paupers, simply could not work in a country whose paupers accounted for no less than one third of the population.'[78] It is possible to give individual meaning to this general crisis. Let us consider Lord Palmerston's extensive estates in north Sligo. In a powerful article—based on recently opened archives—Desmond Norton

[75] Donnelly, *The Great Irish Potato Famine*, 92.

[76] Bruce Kinzler, *England's Disgrace: John Stuart Mill and the Irish Question* (Toronto, 2001), 144.

[77] *Dublin Evening Mail*, 12 Mar. 1847.

[78] Michael de Nie, *The Eternal Paddy: Irish Identity and the British Press, 1798–1882* (Madison, Wisc., 2004), 114.

has demonstrated that Palmerston was a 'humane landlord', who took a serious interest in the condition of his tenantry: not the stereotype of the hard-hearted absentee.[79] Lord Palmerston's agent in the parish of Ahamlish, Co. Sligo, calculated that he would be liable to pay £10,000 for seven months when the legislation went into effect. This would have exceeded Palmerston's entire rental from north Sligo in a normal year; perhaps unsurprisingly, emigration and assisted passage was advocated as the best way out.[80]

But as British policy slipped into a harsher mode, how did the friends of Ireland within the Whig establishment react? Lord Morpeth was a leading figure here; as Chief Secretary in Dublin, he had been the decisive supporter of Thomas Drummond and his reform programme. Morpeth prided himself on his sympathy for Catholic Ireland (he had got into trouble in Yorkshire for saying Irish women were more chaste); so much so that he stated firmly that he could not accept a purely strategic rationale for the union: he acknowledged that Irish independence could lead to a situation where Britain was threatened on both sides by 'adverse' republics in Ireland and France, deriving support from United States republicans.[81] Even so, Morpeth insisted that he would accept Irish independence, so long as he was convinced it was for Ireland's own good. He was convinced, however, that 'in the long run' the union had the effect of neutralizing animosities. 'Does not every field of discovering—does not every exploit of science and every achievement of art—show us the identity of our pursuits and forbid the scheme of our separation?'[82] The Irish might dream, he said, of French or United States aid, but who else would really give the £10 million granted over the past two years from the English Exchequer? Morpeth declared: 'These churlish Saxons are actually feeding about 200,000 of the destitute inhabitants of Ireland.'[83] When Morpeth spoke, in spring 1847, these words still had a certain grip on reality: by the autumn it was harder to defend the humanitarian record of the government.

[79] Desmond Norton, 'On Lord Palmerston's Irish Estates in the 1840s', *English Historical Review*, 119: 484 (Nov. 2004), 1254–74.

[80] Thomas Power, 'The Palmerston Estate in County Sligo: Improvement and Assisted Emigration Before 1850', in P. J. Duffy (ed.), *To and From Ireland: Planned Migration Schemes c. 1600–2000* (Dublin, 2004), 120. Desmond Norton shows that Palmerston displayed considerable concern that 'his' emigrants should have a comfortable passage. Palmerston wrote 'that if the terms were not sufficient to treat *his people* well, to rescind them and put in a higher tender to get the best entertainment on board the ships'. He paid attention to detail, every man and woman was to be given a hot tumbler of the best Jamaican rum punch after Sunday dinner and the captain was to be given £ 10 to induce him to be kind to Palmerston's people. Desmond Norton, *Landlords, Tenants, Famine: The Business of an Irish Land Agency in the 1840s* (Dublin, 2006), 53.

[81] *Hansard*, vol. 98, 11 Apr. 1847, col. 215.   [82] Ibid., col. 218.

[83] Ibid., col. 217.

On 20 September 1847 Lord John Russell was to write to T. C. Anstey, the Youghal MP with Repeal and Young Ireland connections:

I am deeply concerned at the prospect of distress in East Schull, in the county of Cork. It appears to me that the owners of property in Ireland ought to feel the obligation of supporting the poor who have been born on their estates and have hitherto contributed to their yearly incomes. It is not just to expect the working classes of Great Britain should permanently support the burden of Irish poverty.

The *Evening Mail* offered an accurate translation:

I am sorry I can not arrest the progress of famine, or prevent the remaining population of Schull from following their neighbours, who have gone last winter before them to their grave. I can not allay their hunger without being unjust to those working classes—therefore, I must leave the sufferers of Schull to their fate. But I may as well take this opportunity of informing the owners of property in the rest of Ireland what my intentions are towards them. I consider them to be under an obligation to support the poor that have been born on their estates, and my intention is to compel them to do so.[84]

The Cork landlords protested that they had worked hard to help the starving poor and the poor had never been a material asset to them, but to no avail. The *Dublin University Magazine* concluded flatly that the 'real property, as held by the Irish owners, is not ample enough to provide for the new demands which the law has placed upon it'.[85] The Russell Cabinet was in the grip, observed the *Mail* with telling force, of 'anti-Irish' 'English middle-class feeling'.[86]

The *Morning Chronicle* apart, most segments of English opinion moved into a more hard-hearted mode. The 'Gregory' clause, which excluded those holding more than one-quarter of an acre of land from relief, was a significant part of the new legislation.[87] Some Poor Law Guardians seem to have taken the harshness of the legislation a step further than was intended—by privately advising the Relieving Officer to refuse relief to 'miserable applicants until their houses are given up along with their land'.[88]

The Dublin *Evening Mail*, the voice of Irish Tory opinion, denounced the drift of London policy.[89] Many Irish Tories admired the paternalist, protectionist Tory leader Lord George Bentinck (1802–48), employing Benjamin

[84] *Dublin Evening Mail*, 24 Sept. 1847.
[85] *Dublin University Magazine*, 20: 184 (Apr. 1848; January–June 1848), 'The Irish Crisis: The Poor Law', 538.
[86] *Evening Mail*, 4 Oct. 1847.   [87] O' Grada, *Black '47 and Beyond*, 70.
[88] *Cork Examiner*, 23 Feb. 1848.
[89] *Dublin Evening Mail*, 26 Mar. 1847; James S. Donnelly, 'British Public Opinion and the Great Irish Famine', in C. Morash and R. Hayes, *Fearful Realities: New Perspectives on the Famine* (Dublin, 1996), 68.

Disraeli as a kind of political lieutenant, who challenged the outlines of government policy in early 1847. Bentinck's programme centred on investment in a railway scheme, and included endowment of the Catholic Church, tenant compensation, and taxes on absentee landlords.[90] It was a remarkable early venture in constructive unionism. The railway plan, by which Treasury loans of £16 million, repayable over thirty years, were to be made to railway companies, was designed both to give employment to 100,000 people and to provide Ireland with a modern transport system. The Treasury, however, found the economics of Bentinckism were entirely unacceptable.

The *Evening Mail* in Dublin expressed a not dissimilar traditional conservatism—always militant in support of measures to repress 'crime' in Ireland, but horrified, nonetheless, by the ethos of liberal capitalism and its effect on famine policy.[91] The *Mail* saw *The Times* as the voice of the heartless British establishment. 'We can only say in return for the information of the *Times* that Irishmen of all ranks and parties have begun to ponder again the analogous question—"Of what use is this union to Ireland?"'[92] Deprived of Thomas Davis—who had a gift for crossing divides—*The Nation* missed the moment for an alliance cutting across traditional oppositions without apparently realizing the opportunities presented.[93]

The *Mail* suggested a concession to repeal: a revolving parliament meeting one year in Dublin, one in Edinburgh, one in London. The *Mail* agreed with *The Nation*'s denunciation of the French celebrity chef Alexis Soyer's supposedly helpful visit to Dublin with his demonstration soup kitchen. 'Suffice to say, the whole affair was ridiculous and very contemptible, conducted in a style of Gallic pageantry that was quite unsuited to the object and a very bad taste on the occasion.' But the *Mail* was shocked by *The Nation*'s extravagant catatrophism; when *The Nation* proposed that the English cities should be turned into 'charnel houses' of 'our dead', the *Mail* was horrified by this proposal for a game of 'shuttle cock with our paupers'.[94]

In July of 1847 the *Spectator*, full of good sentiment in the beginning of the year, reviewed William Bennett's *Narrative of a Recent Journey of*

---

[90] *Spectator*, 13 Feb. 1847.

[91] Martine Faraut, *Études Irlandaises* (Spring 2003), no. 28, 'Les Tories, la famine et l'Irlande: une lecture de Blackwoods'.

[92] *Dublin Evening Mail*, 24 Feb. 1847. But on 28 July 1847 the *Dublin Evening Mail* supports Clarendon: 'It is impossible for a nation to subsist on state alms.'

[93] There is no hint of this material in Gavan Duffy's account: Gavan Duffy insisted that the *Mail* regarded the fear of famine as exaggerated and insisted only that landlords should collect rents as before: *My Life in Two Hemispheres* (London, 1903), i. 197. Davis himself had earlier picked upon the 'patriotic' tone of the *Evening Mail* in his essay 'Orange and Green': Mulvey, *Thomas Davis*, 237. Although Duffy had later access to the *Mail*'s private papers and published files, he never seems to have got the point.

[94] *Dublin Evening Mail*, 12 Apr. 1848.

Six Weeks in Ireland. A Quaker liberal, Bennett (1804–73) had painted a horrific picture of human suffering. He tried to force an emotion of empathy upon his English readership:

The loss of a parent, of a child, we know what it is in any of our own families. If the causes are, or appear to have been, in any way within the reach of neglected assistance, or of human control, we know how manifold the agony is increased. Multiply this on to all the cabins, the populous waysides, the far-off solitary mountain hamlets—vivify the details of famine, and we may have some idea of the voice of anguish and lamentation that now ascends from her whole land.[95]

The *Spectator*, however, entered a mode of reserve, noting that Bennett's most dramatic evidence came from Kerry and Cork. It stated: 'Mr Bennett will perhaps think us hard-hearted, but we must confess that his book induces us to suspect not the intensity of partial distress, but its national effect.'[96] Even Chenevix Trench's ghastly account of suffering in Cork had acknowledged that the scale of the suffering was not visible to him when he first reached that county. The Viceroy's levees and other social events of the Dublin season carried on as normal, even as the Viceroy worked hard on famine relief. Nor was this just a matter of prosperous Protestant indulgence; in many places Catholic middle-class pleasures continued undisturbed. Colm Tóibín and Diarmaid Ferriter have observed that the expensive work on the 'sumptuous' building of the Catholic Cathedral in Enniscorthy was supported by the local Catholic middle class during the famine years.[97]

Throughout the famine *The Times*[98] insisted on the culpability of the Irish landlord class:

We know of nothing to which we can compare the situation of an Irish peasant in the hands of a griping or, still worse, a good-natured careless landlord. If, through their own criminal carelessness, or for the purpose of creating faggot votes, the Irish landlords—the grandfathers and fathers of the present men—either produced or suffered such a state of things to be produced, who shall say that their descendants come into court with clean hands?[99]

The *Spectator* agreed: 'The Irish landlords as a class have shown no capacity for the business of landlords.'[100] The *Westminster Review* insisted that Irish landlords would not employ labour in their localities unless they were

[95] William Bennett, *Narrative of a Recent Journey of Six Weeks in Ireland* (London, 1847), 134; see also, for Bennett, Glen Hooper (ed.), *The Tourist's Gaze: Travellers to Ireland 1800–2000* (Cork, 2001), 79.
[96] *Spectator*, 24 July 1847.
[97] Colm Tóibín and Diarmaid Ferriter, *The Irish Famine: A Documentary History* (London, 1998), 6.
[98] *The Times*, 31 Aug. 1847.   [99] *The Times*, 31 Aug. 1847.
[100] *Spectator*, 30 Jan. 1847.

allowed to plunder Treasury funds at the same time.[101] In vain the *Quarterly Review* rejected the charge.[102]

In principle, this meant that the answer lay in changing the landlords, not opening up old historical sores, for there was no current blame to be placed at the door of Westminster:

Without returning to Clontarf or Tara, or the time when Spenser wrote, we freely admit that in the days of our forefathers a policy was pursued in Ireland such as it was then supposed would best lead to the subjugation of the country. Stern and inexorable enough at the best of times, it was neither better nor much worse than passages in the history of contemporary Europe.[103]

But there was nothing now to be done about these old wounds.

The implication was clear enough. Irish society, particularly its landlord element, was to blame for the crisis; England, happily, was not responsible. Even Belfast liberalism—in many ways more locked into laissez-faire values than Dublin Conservatives—found this rhetoric very frustrating. The *Whig* seized angrily on the new callous tone: it noted that English journalists were in 'a state of great satisfaction' as they contemplated the forthcoming crisis of Irish landlordism. Under the operation of the new Poor Law, it was being said, the 'trial of Irish pauperism and property will begin in earnest'. But, noted the *Whig*, few seemed prepared to measure the consequences of the new tough-mindedness: 'They see us like so many animals in a cage; whether they destroy or be destroyed, they take comfort from the conviction that England, at least, is safe.'[104]

The *Cork Examiner* described the agony of the country with even more direct and vivid language:

Reader! Glance your eyes on our columns this day, and what meets your eye wherever it turns! Hideous facts, more startling in their woe and horror than any fiction—death in every paragraph—desolation in every district—whole families lying down in fever—hovels turned into charnel houses—entire villages prostrate in sickness, or hushed in the last sleep.[105]

THE ROLE OF PROVIDENTIALISM AND CHARLES TREVELYAN

How could Britain allow such a tragedy to happen? In recent years it has become commonplace for historians to lay great emphasis on the alleged

101 *Westminster Review*, 4 (Jan. 1849), 449.
102 *Quarterly Review*, 74: 157 (Sept. 1848), 'State of Ireland'.
103 *The Times*, 31 Aug. 1847.   104 *Northern Whig*, 21 Sept. 1847.
105 *Cork Examiner*, 8 Sept. 1847.

role of a cruel, punishing providentialism at the heart of British policy. It has been argued that Charles Trevelyan, Secretary of the Treasury and the most important force in British famine policy, believed that God was punishing the Irish for their fecundity and sloth. In fact, Trevelyan did not believe that God was punishing the Irish. In October 1846 he had written to Father Mathew: 'With you I regard the prospect of Ireland with profound melancholy; but I fear much less from the judgement of God than from the aggravation of men owing to the ignorance, the selfish and evil passions of men!'[106] Trevelyan's letter, widely taken as the key source for the view of Trevelyan as a punishing providentialist, simply does not support this interpretation. Trevelyan wrote again to Father Mathew on 5 October 1847: 'I have come to Dublin for a few days in the prosecution of my labours in the cause of old Ireland in whose service I am proud to find myself employed.' But how well did he 'labour' in the 'cause' of 'old Ireland'? The crisis was deepening all the time. On 6 October 1847 Jeremiah O'Callaghan reported from Bantry:

The hunger screams of the famished infants, blended with the suppressed moans of the suffering parents, were calculated to awaken the sympathy of the most obdurate ... the resources of the union are exhausted ... Let ministers no longer deceive themselves by vainly imagining that the local resources of any union in Ireland would be sufficient to maintain its poor; if they regard us as fellow subjects and wish to snatch us from the jaws of death, let them interfere without loss of time and not permit, by their indifference, the entire island to be converted into a frightful charnel house.[107]

Trevelyan was, indeed, well aware that the 'local resources' of the Poor Laws would not suffice to meet the crisis. In response, Sir John Burgoyne

---

[106] Trevelyan Ms, University of Newcastle Library. This letter was misread by Jennifer Hart, who transcribed it thus: 'Trevelyan believed that the Irish famine was the judgement of God on an indolent and unself-reliant people, and as God had sent the calamity to teach the Irish a lesson, that calamity must not be too much mitigated': 'Sir Charles Trevelyan at the Treasury', *English Historical Review*, 75 (1960), 99. Many distinguished scholars were misled by Hart. Boyd Hilton, in his brilliant volume *The Age of Atonement: The Influence of Evangelicanism on Social and Economic Thought 1785–1865* (Oxford, 1988), 351, argues 'that many politicians followed Trevelyan as seeing the hand of God as directed against the Irish themselves for their philoprogenetiveness and sloth'. It can be seen that, while many politicians did hold to this view of the Irish, they were most definitely not following Trevelyan. See Paul Bew, 'A Case of Compassion Fatigue', *Spectator*, 13 Mar. 1999, for the correct text of Trevelyan's letter; and now, Robin Haines, *Charles Trevelyan and the Great Irish Famine* (Dublin, 2004), 3–26. The influence of Hart's analysis has been considerable: see Robert Romani, 'British Views on Irish National Character, 1800–1846', in his *National Character and Public Spirit in Britain and France 1750–1914* (Cambridge, 2002), 224. I am indebted also to the archivist of Newcastle University Library for allowing me to consult these Trevelyan letters.

[107] *Cork Examiner*, 6 Oct. 1847.

and Charles Trevelyan issued a joint statement, calling for a 'great effort' of 'humane exertion': in short, a great display of English private charity. In an accompanying letter dated 7 October 1847, Charles Trevelyan wrote from the Salt Hill Hotel, Dublin, to *The Times*:

I hope you will do justice to those who have appointed a general collection in the churches on 17 October [the day of Thanksgiving] and still more in pity to the unhappy people in the western districts of Ireland, who will again perish by the thousands this year if they are not relieved. Publish the accompanying statement which has been prepared by Sir John Burgoyne for the purpose of explaining why another effort of this sort is necessary.[108]

Burgoyne and Trevelyan insisted, with complete honesty:

Absolute famine still stares whole districts in the face, and we must not allow ourselves to become callous to the horrors of such an evil, because we have here had it before us for any given period. It may be assumed, perhaps, that the people having gone through the periods of dearth for the last two years ought to be sufficiently provided for by the abundant produce of the present season ... the special hand of Providence has been thus mercifully extended toward the relief of the people in manners that will greatly mitigate the general distress; but it still leaves a large amount absolutely requiring a great extent of human and humane exertion.[109]

Trevelyan insisted that a good end was in sight, but private English charity was required to help in the short term:

The change from an idle, barbarous potato cultivation to corn cultivation, which enforces industry, binds together employers and employed in mutually beneficial relation and requiring capital and skill for its successful prosecution, supports the existence of a class of substantial yeomanry who have an interest in preserving the good order of society, is proceeding as fast as can reasonably be expected under the circumstances.

Trevelyan insisted, however, that 'the rich and highly favoured portions of the Empire gave some further temporary assistance to those distressed sections of our population, to enable them to tide over the shoals upon which they have fallen, the harbour will ere long be attained'. But while Trevelyan fully supported Burgoyne's plea for charity, he also insisted that the new Poor Law would be enforced in Ireland 'to the utmost extent of the power of the government'. Trevelyan claimed:

No assistance whatever will be given from national funds to those unions which, whether they have the will or not, undoubtedly have the power of maintaining their own poor and ... the collection of the rates will be enforced so far as it can, even in those distressed western unions in which some assistance from some source or other must be given.

108 *The Times*, 12 Oct. 1847.   109 *Spectator*, 16 Oct. 1847.

Reactions differed to Trevelyan and Burgoyne in ways that were not entirely predictable. Irish opinion was divided. In his book, largely devoted to an indictment of British attitude and policy towards Ireland, Aubrey de Vere nonetheless praised Burgoyne and Trevelyan for their intelligence and generosity.[110] De Vere's assessment, however, was not mirrored elsewhere. Elizabeth Smith, the conservative wife of a Wicklow landlord and Burgoyne's cousin, exploded on the publication of the Trevelyan–Burgoyne letter: 'One would suppose stones were scarce in Ireland and her rivers dry when no one hoots such drivellers out of the country. We want no charity. We want a paternal government to look a little after our interests, to legislate for us *fairly* ... '[111] *The Nation*'s response to the letter was an angry one, full of predictable injured national pride.

> We tell our countryman that a man named Trevelyan, a Treasury Clerk—the man who advised and administered the Labour Rate Act—that this Trevelyan has been sent to Ireland that he, an Englishman, may send over from this side of the channel a petition to charitable England. We are to be made to beg whether we will or no.

The Nation (John Mitchel's pen is evident) insisted that the real problem was the export of food to England:

> We repudiate this Trevelyan and his begging letter. We entreat our countrymen to read the account we give in another page of the rate at which Irish wealth is floating from our shores upon every tide. *Twenty steamers* go from Ireland to England *every day*, laden with the choicest of wheat and oats, beef and butter to feed the alms-giving English.

The Nation rejected the 'benevolence' of 'individual' Englishmen—it was these same Englishmen who devoured the anti-Irish propaganda of *The Times*: 'We scorn, we repulse, we curse all English alms. Give us our rights and keep your charity',[112] while the *Freeman's Journal* agreed: 'We do not want alms. We want our rights.'[113] Rather more significant was the reaction of English public opinion. The *Morning Chronicle* echoed some of the Irish arguments to the effect that the Trevelyan–Burgoyne approach was inadequate and a mere sop: 'It is an attempt to throw on private individuals a responsibility which properly belongs to the government.'[114]

But the really striking development was the strongly expressed view of some key opinion-formers that Trevelyan–Burgoyne were *too* generous in their sympathy for the Irish. The leading role here was played by

---

[110] Aubrey de Vere, *English Misrule and Irish Misdeeds* (London, 1848), 29.

[111] David Thomson and Moyra McGusty (eds.), *The Irish Journals of Elizabeth Smith* (Oxford, 1980), 17 Oct. 1847, p. 158.

[112] 'More Alms for the "Destitute Irish"', *The Nation*, 16 Oct. 1847.

[113] *Freeman's Journal*, 14 Oct. 1847.

[114] Quoted in *Cork Examiner*, 18 Oct. 1847.

T. Campbell Foster of *The Times*, who explicitly accused Trevelyan of attempting to 'thwart' the 'Providence of God' under the name of charity. Campbell Foster played a critical role in helping to generate a more anti-Irish mood within English public opinion. In tones which reflect an assumption that God was indeed teaching the Irish a much-deserved lesson, he declared:

What then do we, in our mistaken humanity, want people to do? With stupid blindness to the character of the people under the name of charity to the poor Irish, we would thwart the Providence of God, we would lighten the necessity under the pressure of which to meet, they alone will work ... [115]

The *Spectator* felt that Trevelyan and Burgoyne were 'too close to the wretched people' and perhaps too influenced by 'a natural feeling of compassion'. But the fact was that Campbell Foster was a guide to much feeling in England: 'The Irish flattered in their suicidal weaknesses, have made their case impracticable and exhausted the patience of the English.' The *Spectator* concluded bitterly: 'Thank you for nothing is the Irish thanks for ten million.'[116]

In Ireland the Campbell Foster attack on Trevelyan and Burgoyne was noted. 'Oh, let every man who loves Ireland sternly refuse to advance her one penny, and compel her, in spite of herself, to do more than "labour very little" to convert into many sources of wealth her almost boundless natural advantages',[117] he had said. Some were simply shocked. John Mitchel, of course, was delighted: 'Cordially, eagerly, thankfully we agree with the English *Times* in this one respect—there ought to be no alms for Ireland.'[118] *The Times* 'has denounced and is demanding an end for all assistance to be derived from England in the shape of voluntary aid from the benevolent rich of England'.[119] The *Cork Examiner* exploded with anger:

The first duty of every government is to look to the safety of the people committed to its charge. All things else are secondary ... The English portion of the contract has been violated. In our prosperity, we are an integral portion of the British Empire—in our adversity, we are the Irish difficulty, and are flung upon 'our own resource'.[120]

That, however, is not how matters were seen on the other side of the Irish Sea. The *Spectator*, too, believed that the union was weakened by the operation of a double standard, but it was one imposed by Ireland, not by

[115] Quoted in *the Spectator*, 16 Oct. 1847.
[116] Ibid., 20 Nov. 1847, 'The Best Result for Ireland'.
[117] *The Times*, 13 Oct. 1847.
[118] P. A. Sillard, *The Life of John Mitchel*, 2nd edn. (London, 1901), 54; cf also Richard Davis, *The Young Ireland Movement* (Dublin, 1985), 194–5.
[119] *Cork Examiner*, 15 Oct. 1847; *The Times*, 13 Oct. 1847.
[120] *Cork Examiner*, 15 Oct. 1847.

England. 'The union must be thoroughly carried out—all must be done for Ireland that would be done for a part of England, and no less expected from Ireland—or Ireland must cease to be a part of the same kingdom: there must be an English measure of repeal.'[121] 'But,' observed the *Spectator*, 'England knew that her aid was wasted, perverted—almost embezzled.' When the economist W. T. Thornton advanced peasant proprietorship as the solution for Irish evils, the *Spectator* doubted whether the Irish peasantry, so associated with 'dishonesty' and 'fraud',[122] was endowed with the 'necessary virtues' to make such a system work. English sentiment had been further soured by the mounting evidence of corruption in the administration of relief in Ireland. Jonathan Pim, the hard-working, charitable Quaker—even John Mitchel called him honest—acknowledged: 'In many cases the relief committees, unable to prevent maladministration, yielded to the torrent of corruption, and individuals only sought means to benefit their own dependants.'[123] The pressure on relief committees was considerable: it was well known that those from a relatively comfortable farming background, who were denied a place on public-works schemes, were capable of turning to violence.[124] Some nationalists tended to agree that the food was not reaching the right people, but still blamed the government. The *Cork Examiner*, for example, claimed that if £10 million, as the government claimed, had been spent in 1846–7, 'the expenditure of such an enormous sum, without producing any results, could only be the effect of ... incredible incompetence'.[125]

All this throws more light on English attitudes. As the distinguished political economist Nassau Senior declared in the *Edinburgh Review*: 'The English resolved that Ireland should not starve. We resolved that for one year at least we would feed them. But we came to a second conclusion, inconsistent with the first, that we would not feed them for more than one

[121] *Spectator*, 20 Nov. 1847.   [122] Ibid., 19 Feb. 1848.

[123] Jonathan Pim, *The Condition and Prospects of Ireland* (Dublin, 1848), 77. On p. 97 Pim adds: 'The following is given on the authority of a gentleman of landed property, as showing the manner in which a Roman Catholic clergyman was abused for refusing the unreasonable demands of some of the more powerful of his parishioners: "I know of the most shocking instance of this, where shameless, worthless farmers came in bodies, and compelled the priest by threat to give them the meal intended for the poor. In this very parish, a scene occurred truly scandalous. The British Association gave our parish priest three tons of meal. On its arrival the riotous conduct of the population was such, I had to go out, and the priest begged of me to take in the meal and store it for him. I did so. On the third day after, he took it to the parish chapel, where a scene occurred that baffles description; and in the end this donation was totally misapplied, as the destitute got nothing and those well off got everything".' According to Disraeli, in one fortnight in Co. Clare, 5,000 such cases of abuse by relatively well-off farmers were uncovered, B. Disraeli, *Lord George Bentinck: A Political Biography* (London, 1852), 232.

[124] *Dublin Evening Mail*, 22 Oct. 1847.   [125] *Cork Examiner*, 11 Oct. 1847.

year.'[126] But if public opinion became callous as compassion-fatigue set in, this does not fully explain the position of the administrative elite. Although it did not believe that Providence was punishing Irish fecklessness, it did believe that a divine judgement had been registered against a particular form of agrarian, potato-based social order, and perhaps a particular form of agrarian social relationship. Charles Trevelyan in particular believed that the day of the cottier and small-farmer based Irish public economy was over. The position occupied by these classes was, he felt, no longer tenable, and it was necessary for them to become substantial farmers or to live by the wages of their labour. As Patrick McMahon, in the *Dublin Review*, sarcastically observed at the same time, Trevelyan believed in a 'wise and merciful Providence', which confirmed 'Anglo-Saxon discovery in economic science'.[127] The Irish, in McMahon's view, were treated like Negroes—for much the same reason: they accepted the treatment.[128]

THE IMPACT OF ANTI-IRISH RACISM

This remark poses the problem, how far did the English political class assume the existence of an Irish ethnic inferiority or laziness? Professor Michael de Nie has written that 'Paddy's aboriginal laziness and hatred of regular labour were taken for granted by England's middle class'.[129] In 1847 the *Cork Examiner* proclaimed: 'They [the English] have a political theology, and the great divine truth they attest to is the industrial energy of the Englishman and the reckless improvidence of the Irishmen.'[130]

There is certainly some evidence of a disdainful anti-Irish tone in British public debate. *The Times*'s activist proprietor, John Walters, MP for Nottingham, told the House of Commons on 7 December 1847:

I have always considered that one of the best tests of the capacity of a people for self-government was the possession of business habits; and of these habits, one of the most important was the habit of keeping to any question under discussion. Now, if I were to apply that test to the people of Ireland, I should say that, after the

[126] N. W. Senior, *Edinburgh Review*, 'Relief of Irish Distress', 139: 89 (Jan. 1849), 230. See also Peter Gray, 'Nassau Senior: The *Edinburgh Review* and Ireland 1843–49', in Tadhg Foley and Séan Ryder (eds.), *Ideology and Ireland in the Nineteenth Century* (Dublin, 1998), 130–43; William Graydon, *Relief for Ireland, Prompt and Permanent ... A Letter to Lord John Russell* (London, 1847), 14.

[127] *Dublin Review*, 27 (1850), 399.

[128] 'Measures for Ireland', *Dublin Review* (Sept.–Dec. 1848), 285.

[129] 'The Famine, Irish Identity and the British Press', *Irish Studies Review*, 6: 1 (Apr. 1998), 31.

[130] *Cork Examiner*, 10 Sept. 1847.

course which was pursued by the Irish members during this debate, they were about as fit for self-legislation as the blacks. The House may not be aware of it, but it is, nonetheless, a fact that the blacks have a proverb that 'If nigger were not nigger, Irishman would be nigger'.[131]

Making allowance for a particularly discursive debate on the subject of repeal—in which, in typical Irish style, much old family business was worked out, this was a vile moment. (Fergus O'Connor, Chartist leader, Walters's fellow MP for Nottingham, and the nephew of United Irishman Arthur O'Connor, claimed that Grattan had been a United Irishman in 1798, much to the rage of his son.) In a striking tribute to the power of the press, Walters was censured neither by the Speaker nor by members of the Cabinet who were present: John O'Connell called Walters 'a buffoon', but the lacerating contempt of Walters's language left a deep impression.[132] Yet, Walters did not speak for mainstream English opinion.

Sir Robert Peel specifically rejected the concept of Paddy's 'aboriginal laziness' in his analysis of the famine.[133] *The Times* was capable of writing bitterly of the need to free England from 'the drag chain of Irish improvidence',[134] but it also pointed out: 'How is it that we hear of Irish enterprise and Irish industry in every quarter of the globe but in Ireland? Transplant the peasant from Kerry, Roscommon or Sligo to Philadelphia, New York or Upper Canada, and instantly his whole nature undergoes a metamorphosis.'[135] The *Spectator* asked: 'How is it that the Irish, who are so idle and barbarous in Ireland, so readily become civilised out of their native land? At home they prefer starvation and murder; abroad, peace and industry; what makes the difference?'[136] The answer is blunt: 'The rough and ready teaching of the adult school abroad.' A raft of intellectual and political authorities could all be cited to the same effect. Harriet Martineau had reported in her *Letters from Ireland* (1852): 'There seems to be no room for a theory of constitutional indolence here.'[137] The historian Henry Thomas Buckle (1821–62) opined, in his *History of Civilisation* (1857–61): 'We should not hear so much about the idleness and levity of the Celtic race ... Even in 1799 it was observed that the Irish, as soon as they left

---

131 *Hansard*, 3rd ser., vol. 95, col. 791.

132 Lady Ferguson, *Sir Samuel Ferguson and the Ireland of his Day*, i. 250.

133 William Edward Hearn, *The Cassell Prize Essay on the Condition of Ireland* (London, 1851), 5.

134 *The Times*, 25 Jan. 1847; Williams, *Daniel O'Connell*, 199.

135 *The Times*, 3 September 1847.

136 'The Root of Evil in Ireland', *Spectator*, 22 Jan. 1848. A month later the *Spectator* returned to the issue: 'It is not denied that Irishmen are possessed of brilliant qualities', but their, 'great individual successes' were achieved outside the country.

137 Glenn Hooper (ed.), *Harriet Martineau: Letters from Ireland* (Dublin, 2001), 81.

their own country, became industrious and energetic.'[138] Sir Charles Lyell (1797–1875) reported the assumption that the 'Irish are most willing to work hard'. American capitalists had been decidedly impressed.[139] Lord John Russell's speech in the House of Commons on 25 January 1846 is the most striking example:

There is no doubt ... I must say, of the strength and industry of the inhabitants. The man who is loitering idly by the mountain-side in Tipperary or in Kerry [where he has nothing to do], whose potato plot has furnished him merely with occupation for a few days in the year, whose wages and whose pig have enabled him to pay his rent and eke out afterwards a miserable subsistence—that man, I say, may have a brother in Liverpool, or Glasgow, or London, who by the sweat of his brow, from morning to night, is competing with the strongest and steadiest labourers of England and Scotland, and is earning wages equal to any of them. I do not, therefore, think that either the fertility of the soil of Ireland, or the strength and industry of its inhabitants, is at fault.[140]

Palmerston agreed: 'It is quite a mistake to suppose that the Irish are an idle race, unwilling to labour and not prepared to make great exertions for the sake of accomplishing any legitimate object.'[141] The evangelical Shaftesbury chimed in: neither religion nor race was the cause of Irish poverty, as was proven by Irish success outside the island.[142] The cause of Irish poverty, it was widely believed, was the specific nature of the social arrangement within Ireland: in particular, the landlord system.

Sir George Cornewall Lewis (1806–63) had devoted his early life to a study of Irish social conditions; later he held three senior positions in Palmerston's Cabinet:

Before I went to Ireland, I had very strong opinions as to the influence of *race* on the Irish character. [But he had changed his mind.] *Ceteris paribus*, I would sooner have a German than a Celt, and a Protestant than a Catholic; but I have no doubt that a peasantry of Catholic Celts may be so governed, and placed under such moral influences as to be peaceable, industrious and contented; and I have no doubt that a peasantry of Protestant Germans might, if properly oppressed and brutalised, be made as bad as the Irish.[143]

The implications of this survey of the commentary is unavoidable: England did have a minority of thinkers whose attitude towards the Irish was

---

[138] *A History of Civilisation*, 68 n.
[139] Sir Charles Lyell, *A Second Visit to the United States* (London, 1849), i. 187.
[140] Ibid. 68.   [141] Ibid., 187.
[142] Hodder, *Life and Work of the Seventh Earl of Shaftesbury*, diary entry, 5 Jan. 1849, p. 277.
[143] *Letters of the Rt. Hon. Sir George Cornewall Lewis, Bart to Various Friends* (London, 1870), 49–50.

explicitly racist, but mainstream writers insisted on Irish qualities of hard work and intelligence, proved, above all, by Irish success outside the island, especially in the United States; an assumption of ethnic Irish laziness is not the decisive clue to English attitudes during the famine. England certainly did believe, however, that Irish landlordism was much at fault, though England could not be blamed for this legacy of history.

The British government's response to the famine was a product in the main of the standard nineteenth-century view that the state's role in society was a strictly limited one—as Trevelyan put it, merely to 'mediate' the relations between classes. Trevelyan believed, above all, that the poor should work to live: only 'in the sweat of their faces' shall men 'earn' their 'bread until their return into the ground', was a favourite theme. It was vital not to undermine the self-reliance of the poor: these were views he held to, both in the English and the Irish context.[144] *Fraser's Magazine* summed up the position of the Prime Minister: 'Lord John Russell wished, as a Christian statesman, to preserve the lives of famishing Irishmen; but he also wished to preserve the interests of trade. He regarded his fellowmen much; but he regarded the principles of political economy more.'[145] On 8 September 1848 Russell received a deputation from the nobility and gentry of Galway: they requested support for a Dublin–Galway railway. Russell replied that the government had no funds: 'The Exchequer being low, he would not hold out any hope that negotiations for a loan would be entertained, and without the sanction of Parliament, he could do nothing.'[146]

THE IRISH REACTION: JOHN MITCHEL AND THE GENOCIDE THESIS

British policy during the famine achieved precisely what O'Connell failed to do—it made Sharman Crawford a repealer. He accepted that Britain had 'mitigated' distress, but could not accept a verdict of 'noble generosity': rather, British rule was the source of Ireland's woes.[147] Maria Edgeworth, the Anglo-Irish novelist critic of her own order—*Castle Rackrent* (1800); *The Absentee* (1812)—expressed the widespread Irish gentry frustration with the working of the Whig government:

---

[144] See Trevelyan's letters to *The Times*, 27 May, 1 and 2 June 1870; W. L. Burn, *The Age of Equipoise: A Study of the Mid-Victorian Generation* (London, 1964), 125. I owe this reference to C. D. C. Armstrong.

[145] *Fraser's Magazine*, 'Famine in the South of Ireland', 25 (Apr. 1847), 493.

[146] *Spectator*, 16 Sept. 1848.   [147] *The Irish Felon*, 1 July 1848.

'The fatalism of the economists,' she remarked, 'will never do in a great trial like this'; and she read us a letter from Lord John Russell, complimentary and courteous, but refusing to listen to certain projects of relief. 'He is true,' she wittily said, 'to the motto of his kind; but *che sara, sara* is the faith of the infidel'.[148]

From an Irish point of view, this was appalling. Commenting on a recent academic defence of political economy, the *Freeman's Journal* noted:

What matters it, for instance, to the hundred thousand peasants who died months ago of starvation because Indian corn was at 76s. a quarter (though the Government could have imported at 23s.) that the operations of the private merchants may, in the long run, introduce the commodity at a cheaper rate than it could be bought by the state?[149]

The best way to measure the full impact of the famine is to note the decline in the number of inhabitants in each square mile of arable land. Taking Ireland as a whole, the epoch saw a major change: from 335 inhabitants per square mile in 1841 to 231 in 1851, a drop of 104. Taking the provinces: in Leinster the figure had fallen from 247 to 189; in Munster, from 332 to 218; in Ulster, from 406 to 280; whilst in Connaught it had fallen from 335 to 231. In Leinster, therefore, the drop was 58; in Munster, 114; in Ulster, 126; and in Connaught it was 104.[150]

The disappearance of the rural poor produced a complex societal reaction. The old pre-famine Ireland had been characterized by an intense fear of the poor, often felt as acutely by the Catholic middle strata as the Protestant. The Callan, Co. Kilkenny, author Amlaoibh Ó Suilleabháin (1780–1837), the outstanding Irish-language writer of this period, exhibited an 'almost obsessive' fear that social order and discipline might collapse:

The poor are pulling the potatoes out of the edges of the ridges or lazy beds. Stark famine is upon them. It is hard to say that God will avenge it on them; but nevertheless, it is a bad habit; for, if the poor begin with petty pilfering, the danger is that they will go on pilfering on a larger scale, to thievery, robbery, plunder, rapine and brigandage. If a man violates one commandment, there is no knowing where he will stop.[151]

One village schoolteacher in Donegal summed it up brutally:

[148] W. O'Connor Morris, *Memoirs and Thoughts of a Life* (London, 1895), 105; for Maria Edgeworth's impressive and humane activism during the famine, see Michael Hurst, *Maria Edgeworth and the Public Scene* (London, 1969), 140–73. See also Margaret Kelleher, 'Maria Edgeworth and the Great Famine', *Eire–Ireland*, 32: 1 (Spring 1997), 41–62.

[149] *Freeman's Journal*, 6 May 1847.

[150] Ibid., 13 Sept. 1856, 'The Census of Ireland'.

[151] Gearóid Ó Tuathaigh, 'Amlaoibh Ó Suilleabháin as Historical Witness', in Liam P. Ó Murchú (ed.), *Cinnlae Amaloibh uí Shúileabháin*, Irish Texts Society, subsidiary ser. 14 (Dublin, 2004), 17.

Arising from death, emigration and desperation, the population soon dwindled away. And indeed, I hope it will not be any way uncharitable to say [it, but] with the multitude also disappeared many turbulent and indifferent persons and characters who were only a disgrace to the good, the honest, the well-doing, and if there was poverty, there was peace, too.[152]

There was also a kind of revolutionary resentment against those who died, shown by Michael Davitt, whose family just avoided being swallowed up by the famine: 'As the peasants had chosen to die like sheep rather than retain that food in a fight for life, to live or die like men, their loss to the Irish nation need not occasion many pangs of racial regret.'[153]

The famine was a heavy blow to the Irish language, already under pressure arising from the success of the national schools. The national system had grown from 789 schools with 107,042 pupils in December 1833 to 3,637 schools with 456,410 students in December 1846.[154] Nevertheless, on the eve of the famine it is likely that a third or more of the population could speak Gaelic. In 1851 still a third admitted to speaking some Gaelic, but monoglot Gaelic-speakers were now only 5 per cent[155] of the total. Gaelic-speakers had been concentrated in the lower social strata, among the cottiers, labourers, and servants; they were especially concentrated also in the west—thus they were, as a group, especially vulnerable to the ravages of the famine.[156] These figures also dramatically disprove the notion that Ulster was a province unaffected by the famine. In fact, Donegal saw the sharpest reduction in the population per square mile, from 472 persons to 231, a loss of 241 persons, while Tyrone (136) stood close in the tragedy lists with Leitrim (132), Galway (144), and Sligo (116), and was far more seriously affected than Roscommon (77).[157]

At the beginning of March 1849 Sir Robert Peel, during a debate on the Irish Poor Law, attempted to lay out both a new diagnosis and a proposed cure for the ills of Irish society. He insisted that it was impossible to continue in the old way. 'Do you mean to rely on the potato? Will you again run the risks of such a reliance?' It was the duty of the House, said Peel, to consider any means which might improve the condition of Ireland. But then, very dramatically, he made reference to the time of James I

[152] H. Dorrian, *The Outer Edge of Ulster: A Memoir of Social Life in Nineteenth-Century Donegal*, ed. Breandan MacSuibhne and David Dickson (Dublin, 2001), 223.

[153] *Fall of Feudalism* (New York, 1904), 66.

[154] W. Cooke Taylor, *Atheneum*, 1035 (28 Aug. 1847), 901.

[155] L. Kennedy, Paul S. Ell, E. M. Crawford, and L. Clarkson, *Mapping the Great Irish Famine* (Dublin, 1999), 102.

[156] Garret FitzGerald, 'Irish Speaking in the Pre-Famine Period: A Study Based on the 1911 Census Data For People Born Before 1851 and Still Alive in 1911', *Proceedings of the Royal Irish Academy*, 1030: 5 (2003), 200–4.

[157] *Freeman's Journal*, 13 Sept. 1856, 'The Census of Ireland'.

and the plantation of Ulster, when a 'large quantity of land was forfeited'. Peel suggested that it might be possible—this time 'without injustice' and allowing 'no religious distinction'—to effect a similar transformation in the mid-nineteenth century. Even more dramatically, Peel called for a developmental commission, which would have a general controlling influence over improvements, public works, and the operation of the Poor Law in the west.[158] On 26 April he returned to the theme, calling for a massive new investment of capital, which would constitute an 'invasion'. Peel's remarks excited considerable interest in the House of Commons and outside. The Encumbered Estates Act was passed in 1849—designed to create a new, more efficient landlord class. The great agriculturist James Caird set off for the west of Ireland, inspired by Peel's initiative.[159]

The *Spectator* reflected upon Peel's analysis:

> Brutalities like Irish society as founded on the late potato—ought not to be allowed to lie under the title of human ... What the fall of Louis Philippe and the street barricades of Paris have been to Europe, the ruin of the potato has been to us. Frightful enough, yet not without some consoling features.[160]

The patriotic, neo-Mitchelite *Irishman* journal (run by Denis Holland) picked up on Peel's speech in a most interesting way: 'The question to be solved is simply this: are we to barter nationality, and all the proud hopes which it retains amongst us, for provincial prosperity? If we despair of liberty—if so, let us have Sir Robert Peel as a saviour.'[161]

In his powerful essay 'Constructing the Memory of the Famine, 1850–1900', James S. Donnelly has drawn attention to the predominant meanings immediately attached within Irish culture to the famine. The unfeeling British Parliament and public opinion were blamed; Ireland, deprived of a native parliament, was presumed to have been especially vulnerable to the ravages of the potato blight. The Irish landlords were blamed—in particular those who had carried out mass evictions. This condemnation was especially bitter amongst those forced to emigrate to America; a bitterness given an extra tinge by the harshness of US conditions for poor emigrants. Even those who—and they were many—were able and lucky enough to adapt successfully to America now embraced a democratic culture which made the social and political hierarchy of Irish life apparently even more absurd. The Catholic Church was criticized by

[158] Peter Gray, 'Famine and Land in Ireland and India, 1845–50: James Caird and the Political Economy of Hunger', *Historical Journal*, 49: 1 (2006), 193–215.
[159] James Caird, *The Plantation Scheme for the West of Ireland: A Field of Investment* (Edinburgh, 1850).
[160] *Spectator*, 20 Jan. 1849, 'Ireland and Sir Robert Peel'.
[161] *The Irishman*, 7 July 1849.

some nationalists for its political passivity; but the enduring theme was the memory of the struggle of ordinary priests to ameliorate the suffering of the poor.[162]

This was a compelling story. It contained significant elements of the truth. But, as Donnelly acknowledges, this orthodox nationalist interpretation inevitably suppressed important aspects of reality. Heavy food imports beginning in 1847, and the role of the British government in bringing this about, faded from the popular memory; instead, John Mitchel's account—which exaggerated the role of food exports in causing mass death and insisted that there was a deliberate British policy of starvation and emigration—was widely accepted.

In John Mitchel's classical argument, England's ruling elite—disturbed by the massive repeal mobilization of 1843—were psychologically predisposed to believe that a sharp reduction of the Irish population levels might be in their interests. Mitchel stated: 'In 1844 the surplus population of Ireland had become truly alarming to English politicians. At the call of O'Connell it had paraded in masses half a million strong.'[163] The implication was clear: 'The necessity of thinning it became more than ever apparent and urgent.'[164] This underlying assumption, Mitchel believed, was the clue to British half-heartedness in famine relief. Britain had, he acknowledged, spent £10 million on relief during the whole five years of the famine. But he claimed: 'If double that had been advanced in the first years, there would have been little famine even that year, none at all in following years.' Thousands of exiled Irish-Americans were convinced by such arguments; they have a genuine credibility. It is, however, worth pointing out that John Mitchel's own position at the time was entirely different; he opposed any Irish appeals for relief from the British Exchequer.

Patrick MacMahon, in the *Dublin Review*, argued:

For years past every heartless noodle, who aimed at attaining the character of a profound philosophical and statesmanlike writer or speaker on our affairs, has uniformly expatiated on the superabundance of our number, that by force of constant and uncontradicted repetition the notion that we are too many by millions has become part of the popular faith of Great Britain and is at the heart of every selfish expedient proposed for our relief and acts as one of the direct causes of the clearance system.[165]

[162] John Boyle O'Reilly's poem 'The Priests of Ireland' (Boston, 1878), 116.
[163] *An Apology for the British Government in Ireland* (Dublin, 1882), 6.
[164] Ibid. 19.
[165] Patrick MacMahon, *Dublin Review*, 'Measures for Ireland: Tillage, Wastelands, Fixity of Tenure', 25 (Sept.–Dec. 1848), 285.

In 1849 the English authority Joseph Kay claimed that 50,000 evictions took place during the famine.[166] But John Mitchel gave this thesis a particular cutting edge. His original claim was that Britain, frightened by the sight of the huge crowds mobilized by O'Connell, had decided that the Irish population needed to be 'thinned'. All those speeches stressing the large unrepresented population of Cork had inspired a secret fear. This is the core of his genocide thesis, in support of which it is possible, at first sight, to cite Charles Trevelyan's trip to Ireland in October 1843, resulting in newspaper articles under the pen-name of 'Philalethes' (lover of truth), 'conveying in dramatic and hyperbolic terms his belief that an uprising was imminent'.[167] The fact remains that the same key English policy-maker, Charles Trevelyan, was not primarily motivated by any desire to reduce the Irish population, but was, indeed, criticized during the famine for his failure to support mass emigration as the obvious solution.[168] The strong influences on policy seem to have been rather different. An initially relatively benign English public opinion pursued various measures of varying effectiveness—interference in the market for corn; public works and soup kitchens—until mid-1847, when a more unsympathetic mood took over. This more hard-hearted sentiment had a number of sources. Some important opinion-formers—though not those who were actually applying government policy—believed that God *was* punishing the Irish for idleness, fecklessness, and promiscuity. Others believed that the Irish landlords were to blame, and somehow they, not the virtuous English taxpayer, should be made to meet the costs of the disaster. Such 'tough-mindedness' was greatly assisted by certain developments within Ireland itself: O'Connell's decision to continue to collect his personal tribute long after the potato-blight effects were evident; Young Ireland's aggressive insistence that English help was not wanted because the problem was, in essence, one of the lack of self-government; the reports from reliable sources that strong farmers were exploiting the crisis, while others were effectively 'embezzling' relief. There were reports also that Ireland faced a localized calamity but not a national disaster; so why were the more prosperous parts of Ireland not doing more? The Irish obsession with the ownership of arms in 1846, and worse still, the attack on landlords in the winter of 1847[169]—some of whom, at least, were seen as progressive and humane in England—did not help.

[166] *Social Conditions and Education of the People*, i. 315–18, quoted in the *Roscommon Herald*, 26 Nov. 1921, 'England's Policy Always the Same. Extermination and Evictions for the Irish'.
    [167] Robin Haines, *Charles Trevelyan and the Great Irish Famine* (Dublin, 2004), 53.
    [168] 'A Semi Official Manifesto against Irish Emigration', *Spectator*, 25 Dec. 1847.
    [169] R. J. Scully, *The End of Hidden Ireland: Rebellion, Famine and Emigration* (Oxford, 1985), 35.

Within government, however, a different mindset was to be found. A cruel God was not punishing the Irish for their sins, rather a benign God was moving Ireland towards a more modern English type of agricultural economy, reducing its abject dependence in the 'potato'. There were human costs of this process, of course, and it was the duty of the state and private benevolent English opinion to play a charitable role. Naturally, there were definite limits to the state's role. The problem of Irish society was that somehow it lacked the springs of self-activity: there was a culture of dependence. Trevelyan repeated the old quip that an Irish gentleman seemingly could not marry his daughter without asking for help from a committee at Dublin Castle.[170] There was much meaning lying behind this sardonic joke. The English in general could not quite fathom how the disordered political and social relations within a society might leave it unable to unite to fight a human disaster. But Jonathan Pim was able to grasp the point:

Ireland appears to labour under the difficulty of having aristocratic social institutions, without an aristocracy; and the mechanism of a popular government, inapplicable to its present social condition; because it does not possess an educated middle class by whom these popular institutions might be worked. The great mass of the rural population have no respect for the laws relating to the tenure of land, because they consider them unjust.[171]

The state's role, in Trevelyan's view, was limited: 'The government holds the balance between the contending parties.'[172] Irish society was so flawed, that it required decisive remedial change. Trevelyan made generalized reference to the 'social revolution'[173] in precisely this context: 'Two cardinal principles' of British policy, 'strict adherence to the rules of political economy'[174] and an insistence that the whole administration of famine relief be a government concern, fit with this account. But Mitchel went further than other critics by insisting that *all* of Britain's actions with regard to Ireland were entirely malign and designed for the purpose of marginalizing, demoralizing, dividing, or otherwise weakening Irish interests. He appears to have gone so far as to believe that the Colleges Bill of 1845 was deliberately designed to foster division within Ireland between Young Ireland and O'Connell.[175]

Against such hyperbole, Professor Hugh Kearney's judgement—offered some fifty years ago—still has interest; the British government 'may

---

[170] *The Irish Crisis*, 188.   [171] Pim, *Condition and Prospects of Ireland*, 190.
[172] Ibid. 149.   [173] Ibid.
[174] John Mitchel, in Patrick Maume (ed.), *The Last Conquest of Ireland (Perhaps)* (Dublin, 2005), 107.
[175] Ibid. 77.

have lacked foresight and generosity. They may have been guilty of underestimating the human problems, but it was not guilty of either criminal negligence or of deliberate heartlessness.' Professor Kearney added decisively: 'The tale is not one of deliberate extermination.'[176] In spite of this, there is evidence from the summer of 1847 onwards of heartlessness. By early 1849 the *Spectator* defended the Prime Minister against Disraeli's charge that he had no plan. Russell, in the *Spectator*'s view, had a plan, but it was a thoroughly bad one:

> Short of incidental details, the principles of his plan are two in number. One is that Irish property shall support Irish poverty; the other—intended as a corrective to the first—that in no case shall the legal provision for the Irish poor exceed a certain percentage of the valuation of the land. Comprehensive enough, beyond all manner of doubt, the first establishes a distinct nationality for Ireland; the second negatives the existence of a 'right to relief'. Both, although to a certain extent neutralising each other, are pregnant with consequences of the deepest importance.

The *Spectator* concluded: 'Ireland must support her own poor, because England must support her own poor.' But England, in that sense, did not support her own poor; each parish supported its own poor, hence Russell's new rate-in-aid proposals of 1849 asked the more prosperous parts of industrialized Ulster to bear a burden in a way that was not characteristic of the English model. The Ulster rate-payers would have to be 'very ardent philanthropists' to accept the role of 'whipping boys'. 'The reasoning sounds plausible to a mob or to a House of Commons rendered frantic by anti-Irish prejudice.'[177]

Mitchel was profoundly correct in one important respect. His powerful description of how Ireland and England faced each other in 1847 cannot be improved upon: 'In Ireland, a vague and dim sense that they were somehow robbed, in England, a still more vague and blundering idea that an impudent beggar was demanding their money with a scorch in his eye and threat upon his tongue.'[178] It is striking that Mitchel could evoke such a mood with such brilliance without, in any way, acknowledging Young Ireland's role in creating it. Nor, of course, were British publicists willing to accept the impact of their language on the Irish. The *Cork Examiner* observed icily: 'When the *Times* takes to damning the union, and shouts aloud that shovelling out the Celts would be a happy riddance, it revealed a foregone conclusion—the present Act of Union is doomed.'[179] Yet, for all

---

[176] H. F. Kearney, 'The Great Famine', *Studies*, 46 (1957).
[177] 'The Premier's Plan for Ireland', *Spectator*, 24 Feb. 1849. See also James Grant, 'The Great Famine and the Poor Law in the Province of Ulster: The Rate-in-aid Issue of 1849', *Irish Historical Review*, 27: 105 (1990), 30–47.
[178] *Last Conquest*, 107.   [179] *Cork Examiner*, 17 Apr. 1848.

Mitchel's profound influence on the Irish popular mind, it is worth noting that a different, non-Mitchelite reading of the famine and its implications found its way into Irish national consciousness. Justin McCarthy provides a most striking example. As a young man McCarthy's first job in journalism was with J. C. Maguire's *Cork Examiner*.[180] The *Cork Examiner*, along with the *Southern Reporter*, probably more than any other provincial newspapers, gave the most graphic coverage of the horrors of the famine: McCarthy himself grew terribly familiar with the frequent sight of death in some of its most heart-rending shapes.[181] He covered sympathetically the state trial of William Smith O'Brien at Clonmel.[182] In 1849 McCarthy even joined for a while the '1849 movement', a secret conspiracy organized by youthful veterans of 1848. The talented McCarthy then moved into the world of London journalism, becoming editor of the *Morning Star*. He began to mix with English liberals like John Bright and John Stuart Mill; in the 1860s Bright gently chided him for not offering more support in the *Morning Star* to the Fenians.[183] McCarthy became increasingly aware of the depth of English liberal sympathy for Irish nationalism. John Mitchel, however, insisted in 1860 that for 'British statesmen their absolute duty was to prevent a Celtic peasantry from having any proprietary interest in the land, and to this end they are bound to resist all movements in favour of tenant right'.[184]

In the autumn of 1868, though, Justin McCarthy met John Mitchel in New York. McCarthy passed on his assessment of the genuinely reformist nature of English liberalism: Mitchel was shocked and irritated. To McCarthy's surprise, 'he told me gravely that Gladstone and Bright were the worst enemies Ireland ever had'.[185] In 1879 McCarthy, by then the leading Parnellite, was to write: 'Terrible as the immediate effects of the famine are, it is impossible for any friend of Ireland to say that, on the whole, it did not bring much good with it.'[186]

Perhaps even more tellingly, the dominant nationalist account excluded all issues of class conflict; except, of course, where these involved the landlords and the peasantry: Mitchel's own defence of many resident landlords was forgotten.

---

[180] Justin McCarthy, *An Irishman's Story* (London, 1904), 9.
[181] Eugene J. Doyle, *Justin McCarthy* (Dundalk, 1996), 8.
[182] *An Irishman's Story*, 72–7.
[183] Justin McCarthy, *Reminiscences* (New York and London, 1910), i. 71.
[184] John Mitchel, *An Apology for the British Government in Ireland* (Dublin, 1882), 31.
[185] Ibid. 389. See on this general topic G. Kearns, ' "Educate that Holy Hatred": Place, Trauma and Identity in the Irish Nationalism of John Mitchel', *Political Geography*, 20 (2001), 885–911.
[186] Quoted in C. Morash, *Writing the Irish Famine* (Oxford, 1995), 149, also gives us a most interesting discussion of McCarthy's writing on this subject.

Irish landlords are not all monsters of cruelty. Thousands of them, indeed, kept far away from the scene, collected their rents through agents and bailiffs and spent them in England or in Paris. But the resident landlords and their families did, in many cases, devote themselves to the task of saving their poor people alive.

But the famine clearances directly benefited significant sections of the Irish Catholic middle class. Decades later police reports took a malicious delight in noting that prominent nationalist families owed their prosperity to land acquired during the famine. Indeed, clearances had pre-dated the famine, as William Connor embarrassingly pointed out in the case of the prominent Lalor family. Hugh Dorrian observed at the time how the

> miserly narrow-living class of people, those who were little thought of before, crept up in the world and became possessors of land such as never was in the tribe or family before ... some did undermine and injure their poorer neighbours and got property without paying a farthing ... Oh! The hypocrisy, the wickedness of some who are under the mask of a false face now.[187]

Even more problematic of all, the dynamic of Irish social life—the post-famine transition from arable farming to pasture—put this question of a double standard right at the heart of political life.

In fact, in a county like Meath the consolidation of holdings, evictions, and the switch from tillage to grazing were initiated in the 1830s. Famine conditions were 'particularly desperate' in Kells, but not because the area was overpopulated or remote; rather, it was at the heart of an already commercialized agriculture. In 1847 and 1848 the graziers who dominated the area refused to break up their land and provide employment.[188] During the period of the famine there occurred, in the words of the preface to the 1850 agricultural returns, 'an immense alteration in the numbers and wealth of different classes of farmers'.[189] In the throes of the crisis many small or medium farmers died in the west, while others left or were forced to give up their holdings. The land was then consolidated and re-let in larger holdings: the number of small and medium tenancies declined sharply. The role played here by famine clearance is not in doubt. George Poulett Scrope wrote in the *Westminster Review*: 'A deep-seated and general feeling has come to be entertained by the owners of the soil of the sister island that Ireland must be largely cleared of the Irish, as a first step towards the

---

[187] For Mitchel on the resident landlords see *Last Conquest of Ireland*, 115; for Dorrian on the land-grabbers see *The Outer Edge of Ulster: A Memoir of Social Life in Nineteenth-Century Donegal*, 228.

[188] Peter Connell, *The Land and People of County Meath, 1750–1850* (Dublin, 2004), 247.

[189] David Seth Jones, 'The Transfer of Land and the Emergence of the Graziers During the Famine Period', in Arthur Gribben (ed.), *The Great Famine and the Irish Diaspora in America* (Amherst, Mass., 1999), 86.

improvement of their prosperity—the only means of saving it from being eaten up by paupers.'[190] Between 1845 and 1851 the total extent of land comprising holdings of 200–499 acres increased by nearly 1 million acres, a rise of 45 per cent. For holdings of 500 acres and above, the increase was estimated to be 700,000 acres, a rise of 53 per cent. Scrope described this as an 'extraordinary social revolution', claiming that the 'total diminution of the aggregate number of the occupiers of land is more, on the whole, than a quarter of a million, with their families probably comprising one and a half million souls'.[191]

The great bulk of the land on these large holdings was devoted to pasture. Even before the famine graziers were already a numerous and economically powerful group in Meath, Westmeath, and Kildare; it was, however, the famine which expanded dramatically the opportunities for the development of such farming in the western counties of north Munster and Connaught.[192] The implications of this profound socio-economic reality for the development of post-famine nationalism were immense.

THE YOUNG IRELAND REVOLT

On 15 May 1847 Daniel O'Connell, who had been in poor health for three years, died on his way to Rome at Genoa. His heart was buried in Rome. Catholic opinion throughout Europe, and Irish Catholic opinion in particular, was deeply moved. The Westminster Parliament—much to the annoyance of the O'Connellite Dublin press—displayed a marked lack of emotion.[193] The *Spectator* in London was also more cool:

The O'Connell who won that prize [emancipation] was a far lesser man than the O'Connell whom that achievement created. He obtained an influence over his race commensurate with that of great historic personages—Moses, Epaminondas, Mohammed, Napoleon. What did he do with all that power? What remains? Nothing but the first deed—still Catholic emancipation. Like great historic men in the extent of his power, he has proved unlike them in the smallness of its use. His great deed was always in the future—to be performed.[194]

Young Ireland, John Mitchel in particular, was in full agreement with such an analysis. The *Dublin University Magazine* suggested that if O'Connell had spent one-tenth of the energy devoted to repeal on the reclamation of waste land, 'Ireland would have been a far better place'.[195] But as the *Spectator*

[190] G. P. Scrope, 'Irish Clearances and Improvement of Waste Lands', *Westminster Review*, 4 (Oct. 1848), 164.
[191] Ibid. 164.   [192] Jones, 'Transfer of Land', 86.
[193] *Dublin Evening Mail*, 14 June 1847.   [194] *Spectator*, 29 May 1847.
[195] *Dublin University Magazine*, 32 (July–Dec. 1848), 237.

admitted, the perception of O'Connell held by most Irish people was rather different: 'By affection, he was, after all, one of the common "Irish", the wild Irish—without the pale—the "liberator" of his people.' But just as the famine had sealed the fate of the potato-based Irish agricultural economy, the *Spectator* now hoped that O'Connell's death would terminate the 'drain' of repeal and other such delusions of 'separating the interests of the Celt over the Anglo-Saxon'. Here, of course, the Young Ireland analysis parted company with the *Spectator*: after O'Connell's death, Young Ireland felt even more keenly the challenge to act decisively. John O'Connell's address to the Repeal Association had stressed the 'myriads of fresh graves' as final condemnation of the union and vindication of the repeal cause.[196] The actual election results in August 1847 revealed 'a considerable increase in the velocity and power of the popular movement'[197]—in part, it was widely felt, because the moderating influence of Daniel O'Connell was no longer available to protect Whig candidates from successful repeal assaults in seats like Dundalk, Waterford, Youghal, and New Ross. The repealers' share of the vote rose from over twenty seats won in 1841 to thirty-six, while the liberals dropped forty-two seats, to twenty-five.

In the vacuum created by O'Connell's death political leadership passed to other hands. The leader of the 1848 rebellion, William Smith O'Brien (1803–61), was an unlikely revolutionary. His instincts were decidedly conservative; he was, as the Liberator's son John O'Connell pointed out, 'almost an anti-agitator'.[198] Born into a Protestant gentry family, O'Brien inherited estates at Cahirmoyle, Co. Limerick. He was sent to school at Harrow and then on to Trinity College, Cambridge. At Cambridge Smith O'Brien became a member of the 'Apostles' (a self-conscious intellectual elite with whom he retained his connections in later life) and president of the Cambridge Union.[199] 'Educated in England, I associated on equal terms with my own rank and class', he reminded his new friends at the moment of his conversion to repeal. It was true. His university friend Richard Monckton Milnes (later Lord Houghton) wrote home: 'O'Brien is fascination itself. Did neither Papa nor you know his mother Edwina Noel?'[200] Smith O'Brien was elected MP for Ennis in 1828 as a Tory, but he supported Catholic emancipation and generally evolved in an independent 'liberal' direction. In this he was not alone amongst Irish MPs—but what *did* make him stand out was the most intense (even by Irish standards) form

[196] *Dublin Evening Mail*, 14 June 1847.   [197] Ibid., 9 Aug. 1847.

[198] *Dublin Review*, 29 (Sept.–Dec. 1848), 333.

[199] Ged Martin, *The Cambridge Union* (Edinburgh, 2000), 183; W. C. Lubenow, *The Cambridge Apostles 1820–1914* (Cambridge, 1988), 226.

[200] T. Wemyss Reid, *The Life, Letters and Friendships of Richard Monckton Milnes, First Lord Houghton* (London, 1891), i. 92.

of family pride.[201] This foible was rather visible. He gave the impression that he believed in his heart that the old kingship of the O'Briens might be revived in his person, in the form of a ruler of a 'free Irish nation'.[202] There were, therefore, ludicrous aspects to Smith O'Brien's conversion to 'repeal': in particular, his claim that, as a descendant of Brian Boru, he was compelled to respond to the humiliation of Clontarf.[203] But even cynical northern critics accepted that he was a man 'who can not fail to secure respect'[204], though it was widely accepted that his Limerick estate was as chaotically run as O'Connell's at Derrynane.[205] When he embraced repeal he did not embrace class or sectarian war: 'So long as the Protestant population and the landed proprietary are as a mass opposed to us ... I do not think without a perfect, universal national union, you could expect to obtain a Repeal of the union.'[206] 'I was ready to give my life in a fair fight for a nation's rights,' he said a year later, 'but I was not willing to lead a Jacquerie.'[207] In this socially conservative approach William Smith O'Brien was strongly supported by Charles Gavan Duffy. Duffy wrote to O'Brien on 26 December 1846:

As to the future, our chance of effecting anything important depends on your continuing as our recognised leader. You seem to be providentially gifted with qualities and attributes for the time and place. The Protestants and the landed gentry must be won—and you [as] a man of property and family and a Protestant, can, and will, win them. What chance of their listening to young men, most of whom are Catholics, and all of them springing directly from the trading classes?[208]

O'Brien still insisted, as late as March 1848:

Now with respect to the landlords of this country, I have been disappointed by the course they have taken, with reference to the national affairs during the last twelve months. There are some of them who don't seem capable of generous emotions, yet we must endeavour to win this class to us.[209]

This attitude or cast of mind was, however, to be strongly challenged within the Young Ireland movement by Fintan Lalor and John Mitchel in early 1847. By the beginning of 1847 Mitchel had been prepared to advocate

201 Richard Davis, *The Rebel in his Family: Selected Papers of William Smith O'Brien* (Cork, 1998), 213.
202 O'Connor Morris, *Memories and Thoughts of a Life*, 113.
203 *Northern Whig*, 9 Dec. 1843.   204 *Northern Whig*, 8 July 1843.
205 Faraut, 'Les Tories, la famine et l'Irlande'. Cf. also Alexander Somerville's savage comments on the state of his estate.
206 *Limerick Reporter*, quoted in *Belfast News Letter* (1843).
207 Sullivan, *New Ireland*, 87.
208 Robert Sloan, *William Smith O'Brien and the Young Ireland Rebellion of 1848* (Dublin, 2000), 175.
209 William Smith O'Brien, 15 March 1848, quoted in *Cork Examiner*, 17 May 1848.

political alliance with moderate landlords, if any could be persuaded to take up the cause of repeal. By the beginning of 1848, however, James Fintan Lalor had convinced Mitchel that Young Ireland should embrace the land question: the struggle of the tenantry against the landlord. Lalor insisted that he could not support national independence, if national independence did not include repeal of the historical confiscation which gave the soil of the country to strangers and enemies; though he also claimed to believe that a generous Ireland would 'reconfirm' the titles of those landlords who sided with the people during the crisis.[210] There had been some stirring of agrarian radicalism in the north. James McKnight played a key role in establishing an Ulster Tenant Right Association at a meeting in Derry,[211] chaired by the mayor. The Down landowner and MP for Rochdale Sharman Crawford pushed the issue of Irish land reform back onto the floor of the House of Commons. On 16 June 1847 Sharman Crawford's Bill was defeated by 112 votes to 25 in the House. But the *Northern Whig* drew comfort from the 'almost complete' assumption that 'some such measure' was necessary.[212]

By the autumn, though, there was still no sign of government action. This helped Fintan Lalor in his project. Lalor called a public meeting in September 1847, to be held at Holy Cross, Tipperary. The concept behind this meeting was the formation of a new league of tenant farmers, determined to resist landlord attempts to extract rent. Ominously, Lalor publicly declared: 'The question between the landlord and the tenant must now at last be fully and finally settled. It shall be settled. It shall be settled in Holy Cross, Sunday, on 19 September.'[213] It is little wonder that Dublin Castle was worried by the aggressive tone of Lalor's placard, combined as it was with an upsurge in agrarian violence in Tipperary.[214] At Holy Cross Lalor did manage to have a resolution passed which asserted that, as 'a natural right, or the grant of God, the soil of Ireland belongs to the people of Ireland', and that 'the people of Ireland have been for ages deprived of their natural right' and that 'right' required to 'be asserted, enforced and established': the right of sufficient subsistence was superior to 'every other claim', including rent. But the audience of 4,000 farmers—considerable numbers of them 'apparently comfortable farmers'—was also treated to a rather more moderate discussion from the platform, suggesting that Ulster tenant right be recognized in Tipperary; so moderate, in fact, that Lalor was attacked from the left by W. D. Conner, who called tenant right a

[210] T. P. O'Neill, *James Fintan Lalor* (Wexford, 2003), 79–80.
[211] *Northern Whig*, 29 May 1847.   [212] Ibid., 19 June 1847.
[213] *Dublin Evening Mail*, 'Progress of Tenant Right', 10 Sept. 1847.
[214] Clarendon Ms, Bodleian Library, Oxford, Clarendon to Lord Chancellor, 10 Sept. 1847; *Dublin Evening Mail*, 10 Sept. 1847, 'The Tenant Right of Tipperary is Terror'.

'delusion'.[215] Gavan Duffy observed that the 'meeting ended in confusion', and Lalor's attempt to popularize his concepts had failed utterly. 'Here was another significant lesson in the feasibility of Lalor's theories, for all those who understood the philosophy of facts.'[216] 'To me Lalor's theory seemed a phantastic dream,' Gavan Duffy added, 'his angry peasants, chafing like chained tigers, were creations of the imagination.'[217] To be fair to Lalor, Mitchel was probably closer to the 'chained tiger' concept than he was. Mitchel, up to that point, had never been in Munster, but instead of simply backing Lalor's proposal for a rent strike, he went a step further, arguing for a strike against the poor rate. Duffy commented icily: 'Mitchel's scheme would starve the people whom he desired to save—for during a famine the poor rate was the peasant's income.'[218] Duffy presents a picture of Mitchel as a mind almost unhinged: he notes that at this moment Mitchel began to state his pro-slavery positions (which were very unpopular within Young Ireland) and denounced the emancipation of the Jews as a sin against God.

The *Cork Examiner* denounced the new ultra-leftism: 'We are told that the "only trustworthy, pure heroic and patriotic class" left, by which the country is to be saved, is that termed the mass, the people in a word—the peasantry.' But, insisted the *Examiner*: 'The middle-classes are not cowardly, they are not corrupt.'[219] Anyway, the whole project was deeply flawed: 'But could you get the peasantry? No? Could you wield them? No.' Prophetically enough, the *Examiner* concluded: 'Without the priest the people will not come.' The anticlericalism of some of the Young Irelanders worried respectable opinion: J. F. Maguire, the *Examiner* proprietor, had, after all, been prepared to enter into a local alliance with them, but now he felt they were going too far. After a speech in which T. F. Meagher asked 'Do not the gentry of Ireland recognise, among the young Catholics of Ireland, a spirit that will bend to no clerical authority beyond the sanctuary?', the *Cork Examiner* insisted that Irish circumstances—of injustice to the poor—required the priest to be a political leader. Why did the Young Irelanders not accept this?[220] But Mitchel carried on, undaunted.

Mitchel did feel, however, the need for a new journal; it was hardly fair to associate Gavan Duffy with an agrarian leftism he disowned. On 2 February 1848 the first number of a new Dublin weekly, the *United Irishman*, edited by John Mitchel, Thomas Devin Reilly, and John Martin, was published.

[215] *Freeman's Journal*, 20 Sept. 1847.
[216] Gavan Duffy, *Young Ireland, Part II* (Dublin, 1892 edn.) 178.
[217] Ibid. 170.   [218] Ibid. 175.
[219] *Cork Examiner*, 24 Jan. 1848, 'How Repeal May Not, and How It May Have Carried'.
[220] Ibid. 29 Sept. 1847.

The published principles of the *United Irishman* were unambiguous: 'That no Irishman has any legal "rights" or claim to the protection of any law and that all "legal and constitutional agitation" in Ireland is a delusion. That every free man, and every man who desires to become free, ought to have arms and to practice the use of them.'[221] But few were prepared to heed such a strong injunction to revolution. The *Cork Examiner* described Devin Reilly as a young man riddled with conceit, and as fit for a leader as a lighted match is 'fit company for a powder magazine'.[222]

Then an external factor intervened. Between 22 and 24 February popular demonstrations in Paris escalated into a rising which forced the sudden abdication of Louis-Philippe. A. M. Sullivan later remarked:

A fierce contagion seemed to spread all over the continent. The Holy Alliance was in the dust, and a thousand voices from Milan to Berlin proclaimed that the deliverance of subject peoples was at hand. Ireland could not escape the fever of the hour. It found her in circumstances that seemed to leave her little choice but to yield to its influence.[223]

The Duke of Wellington was worried by reports he had received that Irish revolutionaries were gaining technical advice in barricade construction from Paris. So worried, in fact, that the 'Iron Duke' drew up a military plan for the defence of Dublin Castle—based as it was on his recollection of a city he had not visited for forty years—and sent a copy to Sir Edward Blakeney, commander of British forces in Ireland.

In a celebrated article ('The French Fashion') in the *United Irishman* on 4 March 1848, Devin Reilly wrote: 'To master Paris was to master the existing government of France; and if we seized Dublin, we hold in our grip English rule in Ireland, its head and body and limbs—to choke it or let it off again as we pleased.' A year later, rereading a reprint of Devin Reilly's article 'The Sicilian Fashion', the now disillusioned Young Irelander Charles Hart recalled:

The whole tide of feeling came back again to my mind: the strong parallel between the supposed condition of Sicily and the Sicilians and Ireland ... the example of Paris, Milan, Berlin, where, tho' the people were more military and intelligent, their attempts followed by such considerable successes, seemed to be impulsive and without organisation.

These remarkable occurrences conduced to the belief that there was going on in the world a general uprising of 'suffering and downtrodden people', however 'previously humbled and broken-spirited they were'.[224]

---

[221] *Cork Examiner*, 21 Jan. 1848.   [222] Ibid., 9 Feb. 1848.
[223] *New Ireland*, 83.
[224] Brendan Ó Cathaoir (ed.), *The Young Irelander Abroad: The Diary of Charles Hart* (Cork, 2003), 66 (15 Apr. 1845).

In February 1848, for example, Meagher was still a reluctant constitutionalist, launching an unsuccessful parliamentary campaign in Waterford city, following Daniel O'Connell junior's resignation and acceptance of a post as Consul in France.[225] But in March Reilly's rooms at Mosipher Lodge in the suburbs of Dublin became the hiding-place for scores of belts, cartridges, and bayonets. The money for this enterprise came from Thomas Meagher; it was actually the money received from his wealthy merchant father at the beginning of 1848 to qualify him as a parliamentary candidate. Meagher also set about personally supplying the poorer members of his own club (the Grattan) with rifles.[226] The similarity with Emmet's abortive rising in 1803 is striking; for Emmet too relied on his father's legacy to finance an attempted revolution. Looking back some thirty-three years later, Richard O'Gorman commented:

The queerest part of this affair as it then seemed to me was that Dublin was at the time fully garrisoned by British troops, perfectly armed and equipped, occupying every point of vantage within the city and that none of the popular party had, with the exception of some incompletely armed clubs, organisation of whatever kind.

But even the relatively cautious O'Gorman's memoirs recalled 'the electricity of revolt which seemed in the air'.[227] In this new and more militant atmosphere, John Mitchel was able to repair his relationships with the rest of Young Ireland: relationships which had been weakened by his embrace of agrarian revolutionary themes. On 15 March 1848, at a meeting of the Irish Confederation at Music Hall, Dublin, both William Smith O'Brien and Thomas Francis Meagher advocated physical force. Privately the authorities regarded Dublin as 'surprisingly quiet',[228] , but requiring action to keep it that way. The Attorney-General presented the Music Hall meeting as an attempt 'to excite the people to rise in rebellion against their lawful sovereign'. In late March Mitchel, Smith O'Brien, and Meagher were arrested on charges of sedition. On 18 March the *United Irishman* bitterly criticized the British Parliament's negative attitude towards 'just and reasonable' land-reform proposals, but rapidly Mitchel radicalized and denounced any legal tenant-right agitation as a hopeless distraction.[229]

---

[225] Eugene Broderick, 'From the Shadow of his Father: "Honest Thomas Meagher"', the Father of an Irish Patriot', in John M. Hearne and Rory T. Comish (eds.), *Thomas Francis Meagher: The Making of an Irish-American* (Dublin, 2005), 56–9.

[226] *The Emerald* (New York), 28 Nov. 1868.

[227] NLI Ms 5896. This is a memoir prepared in 1881 for Charles Gavan Duffy (for use in Duffy's own memoirs).

[228] PRONI D 3078/3/35/4, letter from Corry Conellan, Private Secretary to the Lord-Lieutenant, the Duke of Leinster, 17 Mar. 1848.

[229] Sillard, *John Mitchel*, 107.

On 3 April 1848 Smith O'Brien, Meagher, and O'Gorman presented a fraternal address of the Irish Confederation to Alphonse de Lamartine in Paris. Lamartine, who was not a newcomer to politics, made a noncommittal reply.[230] O'Brien returned to Dublin to face trial. The charge called him a turbulent seditious person, and the Attorney-General argued that he had attempted to mobilize the people against their lawful sovereign. The conservative lawyer Isaac Butt made a classic speech in his defence:

Why is the country in the state it is? Why is Ireland a byword among nations? Because Irishmen have been divided—because Protestant was opposed to Catholic. I would be ashamed if I allowed political differences to prevent me from recognising sincerity and patriotism of mind.[231]

Butt added, in a celebrated passage:

Did you read the other day that in a country of justice it was proved, that in this Christian land, a mother—within a day's journey of the throne of the greatest monarch on earth—a woman with a mother's feeling, strong in the throbbing heart, kept the corpse of her dead infant, that she might satisfy upon it the cravings of her ravenous hunger. (An awful shudder at this moment pervaded the audience, which it was positively painful to contemplate, and it was observed that more than one of the jurors seemed to be affected to tears).

O'Brien's most recent biographer considers that he was probably guilty, but one of the jurors (who included three Catholics and a Quaker) refused to convict, and the jury was discharged.[232] On 22 April 1848 the government passed the Treason Felony Act. The government was determined to act decisively—even to the extent of arming the Orange Lodges as a defence against a rising. Attempting to woo the northern Protestant community away from the government, John Mitchel was now in full rhetorical flow: 'I am one of the Saxon Irishmen of the North, and you want that race of Irishman in your ranks more than any others.'[233] He broke with O'Connellism, he claimed, because it was corrupt, money-gathering, and hypocritical, but especially because it was sectarian. More worryingly for the government, at the beginning of May 1848 he stated firmly: 'I believe the time for conciliation of the landlord class is past. I believe rights of property as they are termed must be invaded—in short, I believe the national movement must become a movement also—or it will stand still.'[234]

On 13 May John Mitchel was arrested and tried under the new repressive legislation. On 25 May he was convicted as charged under the Treason Felony Act, and the following day was sentenced to fourteen years

[230] D. N. Petler, 'Ireland and France in 1848', *Irish Historical Studies*, 24: 96 (Nov. 1985), 502.
[231] *The Irishman*, 14 Apr. 1848.   [232] Sloan, *William Smith O'Brien*, 229.
[233] *United Irishman*, 29 Apr. 1848.   [234] Ibid., 6 May 1848.

transportation. Before a startled Baron Lefroy, who had once attracted the romantic interest of Jane Austen, Mitchel was allowed one last act of defiance. The *Irish Felon* reported Mitchel's last plea: 'The Roman who saw his hand burning to ashes before the tyrant promised that 300 should follow at his enterprise. Can I not promise?' The *Felon* continued: 'He was interrupted by a fierce outburst of enthusiasm from his friends round about. Several voices in the vicinage simultaneously cried with arms outstretched: "Yes, Mitchel, for thousands".'[235] There then followed scenes of intense emotionalism. The police feared a renewed attempt to rescue Mitchel was imminent. They flung themselves on Mitchel and brought him down to the hold: troops hurried up to the scene and no rescue was attempted. A. M. Sullivan's judgement is hard to dispute: 'It may be pronounced that in that moment the Irish insurrectionary movement of 1848 was put down.'[236] In his diary, Charles Greville rather doubted whether the multitudes allegedly ready to step into Mitchel's shoes for martyrdom would appear. But he added with sober realism: 'So far as the type of terror is concerned, which is the only one we can now employ, it is a great and happy event, but it will [not] contribute to the regeneration of the country, and will probably augment the fund of accumulating hatred against the English connection.'[237] In June and July the number of Confederate clubs increased from forty to around 225, as thousands flooded in to join the new movement.[238]

The government was faced with a steadily escalating challenge. On 24 June Fintan Lalor, the son of a Queens County gentleman farmer, tithe warrior, and O'Connellite MP, repeated again his message that the land question, not the national question, famously contained the material for victory:

You may think it a pity to crush and abolish the present noble race of landowners ... what! Is your sympathy for a class so great and your sympathy for a people so small? It is a mere question between a people and a class—between a people of 8,000,000—and a class of 8,000. No one has a higher respect for the rights of property than I have, but I do not class among them the robber's right, by which the lands of this country are holden in fee of the British Crown.[239]

[235] The report is to be found in *Irish Felon*, 24 June 1848. This drama is more cynically described by Elizabeth Smith as a 'slight blustering among his friends within the court, and disturbance but no rioting without', *The Irish Journal of Elizabeth Smith, 1840–50*, a selection edited by David Thomson with Moyra McGusty (Oxford, 1980), 186.

[236] *New Ireland* (1878), 89.

[237] P. Morrell (ed.), *Leaves from the Greville Diary* (London, 1929), 579.

[238] Gary Owens, 'Popular Mobilisation and the Rising of 1848: The Clubs of the Irish Confederation', in L. M. Geary (ed.), *Rebellion and Remembrance in Modern Ireland* (Dublin, 2001), 55.

[239] *Irish Felon*, 24 June 1848; *North British Review*, 18: 120 (1 Aug. 1848), 544.

For Lalor, while the blight was a visitation of God, 'the landlords made the famine'. The landlords were a garrison who should be summarily expelled: 'They or we must quit this island.'[240] On 1 July Lalor openly opined: 'We have determined to set about creating a military organisation of which the *Felon* Office shall be the centre and citadel.'[241] But Lalor himself was hardly a credible military leader, if only on account of his visible physical weakness.

On 8 July 1848 John Mitchel's close friend and radicalized future brother-in-law John Martin published an open letter to Lord Clarendon:

Oh God! Inspire the Irish people with enough courage and virtue to resist this blasphemous foreign tyranny—in the rebellion of right against wrong, of truth against the devil's lies, of every human feeling of honour and interest against such debasement as only Ireland can exhibit ... The British Empire is doomed.[242]

On the same day a warrant was issued for his arrest, and he surrendered himself to the police. Before his arrest Martin had also addressed the 'Orangemen of Co. Down'. He told them: 'It [the union] is ruining you Orangemen. It is making beggars and slaves of you.' The Orangemen showed no sign of accepting this analysis. In 1845 legislation against party processions had expired; the Order reorganized itself, but it was not until 1848 that the Orangemen resumed their traditional 12 July parade. Orange speeches in July were full of pleasure at the sight of the 'respectable', who had kept aloof from the Order, suddenly giving it a renewed cachet. The *Belfast News Letter* commented in July 1848: 'It is manifest of late that the Orangemen so far from having their ranks thinned and their loyalty deadened by the recent monster growth of Republicanism and disaffection, had been spurred on by it.'[243]

The Revd Theophilus Campbell, speaking at Carrickfergus on the '12th', proclaimed happily: 'The name of Orangemen, which he said was never in itself, or justly, a term of reproach, was now held in honour as proof of which he referred to the presence of men on that platform who, 12 months ago, would not have ventured to appear at a meeting of Orangemen.'[244] There was, in fact, a widespread perception that the government was pleased by the Orange remobilization. In fact, Clarendon's private attitude was more complex: he felt the Protestants were the only real supporters of the British

---

[240] Terry Eagleton, *Saints and Scholars in Nineteenth-Century Ireland* (Oxford, 1999), 37.

[241] *Irish Felon*, 1 July 1848.

[242] Ibid., 8 July 1848. At the beginning of April 1848, Martin had insisted: 'I am opposed to insurrection against the usurping government. I do not approve of French intervention in our national affairs', *United Irishman*, 1 Apr. 1848.

[243] *Belfast News Letter*, 14 July 1848.   [244] Ibid.

government, but worried about displays of 'excessive loyalty'.[245] But not all of Clarendon's servants were so fastidious: the pro-Dublin Castle press tended to praise the Orangemen unreservedly.[246] Both Russell and Clarendon discussed the idea of arming the Orangemen. They decided not to do so. Even so, Russell cautioned Clarendon '*in extremis* not to rebuff offers of help from Orange associations, and to envisage arming the Protestants'.[247] In fact, the *Dublin Evening Herald* later reported that the Castle had, through the agency of its counter-insurgency chief—the Major Sirr *de ses jours*—Major Turner, transferred funds to the Orange Order to allow the acquisition of weapons.[248] Such reports were bound to affect the public perceptions of the government's role.

The *Northern Whig* was altogether more gloomy. The *Whig* reported, as the *News Letter* did not, an unsuccessful attempt to raise tenant-right issues from the floor of this Orange meeting. It editorialized gloomily that the repealers had once coquetted pointlessly with the Orangemen, but now their activities 'were giving a new impulse to Orangemen, long a source of bitter evil in this country'.[249] But regardless of the failure of their appeal to the Orangemen, the Young Ireland mobilization continued. On 21 July a war directory, consisting of Dillon, Reilly, O'Gorman, Meagher, and Father Kenyon, was appointed, and the following morning O'Gorman started for Limerick, Doheny for Cashel, and O'Brien for Wexford, to prepare the circumstances. The clubsmen felt themselves to be indeed 'sheep without a shepherd' when the snow shuts out the sky.[250] John Locke caught sight of O'Gorman preaching sedition 'enthusiastically' on 25 July.[251]

Some believed that this decision to move into the countryside was a mistake. Thomas D'Arcy McGee claimed that the 'township organisation consisted of 50 clubs, in the total of 30,000 men of fighting age, half of them armed'.[252] The most recent scholarly estimate places the total membership of the clubs at 45,000. While there was strong support in Tipperary and Cork, the clubs were particularly weak in the poorest region of the country, Connaught.[253]

---

[245] Maxwell, *Clarendon*, 289, Lord Clarendon to George Cornewall Lewis, 4 May 1848.

[246] *Dublin Evening Mail*, 19 Oct. 1848, 'Lord Clarendon and the Orangemen'.

[247] Kinealy, *The Great Irish Famine*, 199; Larcom Papers, 75161.

[248] *Dublin Evening Herald*, 25 Oct. 1849; *Dublin Evening Mail*, 26 Oct. 1849; Mitchel, *The Last Conquest*, 178.

[249] *Northern Whig*, 15 July 1848.   [250] *The Emerald*, 28 Nov. 1868.

[251] Diary, John Locke, NLI Ms 3566.

[252] *New York Morning Herald*, 17 Oct. 1848.

[253] Owens, *Popular Mobilisation*, 56–7.

D'Arcy McGee and Devin Reilly shared an assumption that the Dublin clubs were a real threat; Richard O'Gorman took a more sceptical view. The *Dublin Evening Mail* agreed with O'Gorman: 'The club organisation in Dublin and other prominent towns consisted more of the braggart display of men who walked in military array and talked in military slang, than in any strong or formidable organisation; ... a company of grenadiers would have sufficed any day to disperse them.'[254] But it did not follow that Young Ireland's project was any more secure in the countryside. Richard O'Gorman concluded that

we were wholly misinformed as to the conditions of the people in the remote localities. They were not sufficiently informed of the issue presented to them, and they were by no means prepared for the energetic action we expected. In short, they did not mean to fight—they were dissatisfied—but not spurred by that noble rage which drives men to face great odds and prefer even death to a life of misery.[255]

Young Irelanders were lost when they attempted to spread revolution to the countryside, as long as the Catholic clergy remained opposed. Donal Kerr estimated that the trauma of the famine created a context in which a score or more Catholic clergymen used militant language; this represented a small percentage out of 3,000 priests, even if many others more quietly shared the anger of the militants.[256] Clarendon himself was in no doubt as to the 'bitter hostility' of the priesthood to the government, elsewhere speaking of the priests' democratic views.[257] But they did not give their active support to Young Ireland, and that was the decisive reality. T. F. Meagher has left us a tragicomic account of his adventures with the asthmatic Lalor, dressed in 'a brown dressing gown with white spots, which showed his small and singular form to no great advantage ... His travelling garb was as outlandish as the most outlandish of the aesthetic costumes of the present day'.[258] Lalor complained that 'the young men around him seem to know little or nothing of his writings, not to speak of their total deficiency in their critical perception of the finer features of the composition'.[259] Meagher reported Tipperary peasants saying dismissively: 'Here comes *critheen* Lalor to get up

254 *Dublin Evening Mail*, 3 Nov. 1848.   255 NLI Ms 5896, O'Gorman Ms.
256 *Dublin Evening Mail*, 3 Nov. 1848; Donal Kerr, 'Priests, Pikes and Patriots: The Irish Catholic Church and Political Violence from the Whiteboys to the Fenians', in S. J. Brown and D. W. Miller (eds.), *Piety and Power in Ireland 1760–1960* (Belfast and Notre Dame, 2000).
257 Clarendon to Russell, 28 Aug. 1847; Clarendon Papers, Bodleian Library, Oxford.
258 *Irish Nation*, 28 Jan. 1882. Lalor was treated by Richard Dalton Williams, the Young Ireland doctor-poet. See the *Poems of Richard Dalton Williams*, 4th edn. (Dublin, 1879).
259 *Irish Nation*, 28 Jan. 1882.

a rebellion.'[260] The government continued to be frightened. Recalling the mood of apprehension, the barrister John Ball, who had travelled widely in the south and west, recalled the 'incredulity' of that 'able, diplomatist liberal',[261] when he explained to Clarendon that it would take little effort to defeat Young Ireland.

The denouement was at hand. On 29 July William Smith O'Brien, Terence Bellew MacManus, James Stephens, and about 100 confederates engaged about forty police at Bonlagh Commons, near Ballingarry, Co. Tipperary—the 'battle of the Widow MacCormack's cabbage patch'. O'Brien's proud but ultimately hollow battle-cry was typical: 'I shall never retreat, Sir, from the fields where my forefathers reigned as kings!'[262] The police had refused to surrender, safe in the knowledge that the widow's spacious, well-built, two-storey, isolated house, which dominated a garden enclosed by a perimeter wall, was actually a better defensive position than most barracks. The rebels had to act quickly, as they were well aware that British army and police reinforcements would soon arrive upon the scene. Poorly armed—only twenty of the 100 or so rebels had rifles—they decided on a direct assault. The results were predictably bad. After some casualties the attack—ingloriously—was called off.

In the week after Ballingarry, it is worth noting that the people harboured William Smith O'Brien; he disappeared without trace for several days before deciding, in effect, to give himself up.[263] One of John Martin's jail visitors informed him that the people of Clare and Limerick were expecting to fight, even after Ballingarry, had O'Brien kept himself free from the clutches of government.[264] At his trial for high treason at Clonmel, witnesses were happy to perjure themselves. Young Ireland sympathizer Father Kenyon wryly observed: 'The Irish peasantry have proved they have, at least, the instinct to perjure themselves rather than give evidence against their leader.'[265] Kenyon had hidden himself away at the critical moment—for fear of his bishop, as much as of the authorities.

Along with Terence Bellew McManus, Thomas Francis Meagher, and Patrick O'Donoghue, O'Brien was sentenced to death. He and his colleagues spent a year in an Irish jail before learning that the actual punishment was to be transportation for life to Van Diemen's Land. In the year which immediately followed, the waters closed over the Young Ireland; its leaders dispersed and the legacy appeared to be—at best—simply an image of

[260] Ibid., 31 Dec. 1881. *Critheen* means 'hunchbacked'.
[261] Daniel O'Connell, *Macmillan's Magazine*, 28 (July 1873), 222–37.
[262] Sloan, *William Smith O'Brien*, 279.   [263] Ibid. 283.
[264] PRONI D560/1/p6, The Diary of John Martin, 7 Nov. 1848.
[265] *Irish Nation*, 11 Feb. 1882.

noble, high-minded, if impractical, idealism; at worst, the undignified absurdity of the widow's cabbage patch. A successful royal visit in the summer of 1849 seemed to close the chapter. William Smith O'Brien's fellow Cambridge apostle and close friend, Richard Monckton Milnes, noted icily on 17 August 1849: 'The Queen's reception in Ireland has been idolatrous, utterly unworthy of a free, not to say ill-used, nation. She will go away with the impression it is the happiest country in the world and doubt in her own mind whether O'Connell or Smith O'Brien ever existed.'[266]

Yet the vast circulation of Young Ireland literature carried on. Over a longer period of time the Young Ireland movement had a profound effect: there can be no denying the intellectual impact of Mitchel, for example, on John Devoy or Arthur Griffith, the leading ideologue of Sinn Fein.[267] There were also more strictly military lessons which were to be drawn from the fiasco. The words of Thomas D'Arcy McGee (1825–68) were to be internalized by a later generation in the twentieth century. On 17 October 1848 he observed:

The people are not to blame that there has not been a revolution. Next time they must trust in local leaders like the Raparees and the Catalonian chiefs—fierce men and blunt, without too many ties binding them to the peace. They must choose, too, the favourable, concurrence of a foreign war, an event which is likely to precede the settlement of the newly awakened races of the continent.[268]

In 1844 James Grant had noted that he would not be surprised if English government policy drove the *Dublin Evening Mail*, ultra-Tory though it was, to join the ranks of the repeal cause. The *Mail* never seriously contemplated going so far, but it did raise itself to protest in a strikingly

---

[266] Reid, *Life, Letters and Friendships of Richard Monckton Milnes*, i. 438.

[267] Patrick Maume, 'Young Ireland, Arthur Griffith and Republican Ideology: The Question of Continuity', *Eire–Ireland*, 34: 2 (Summer 1999), 155–74. The *Daily Telegraph* obituary of Griffith makes this point well and, interestingly, the work of Peter Hart suggests Young Ireland ideas had more influence on the IRA of 1918–21 than the more recent Gaelic revival.

[268] *New York Morning Herald*, 17 Oct. 1848. Ironically, D'Arcy McGee, like Gavan Duffy, was to play a distinguished role in mainstream Imperial politics outside Ireland: he played a prominent part in guiding Canada towards Dominion status, was president of the Council of the Legislative Assembly (1862–4) and Minister for Agriculture and Emigration (1867). Ironically, he was to fall victim himself to the kind of ferocity he advocated: following his denunciation of Fenian raids in Canada, he was assassinated in Ottawa on 7 April 1868. But D'Arcy McGee was to be a prototype for those Irishmen in North America who were to play an increasing role in the politics of the USA and Canada: he was regarded as emblematic by President J. F. Kennedy. See R. B. Burns, 'D'Arcy McGee and the Fenians', in M. Harmon (ed.), *Fenians and Fenianism* (Dublin, 1968), 68–81.

'patriotic way'.[269] The *Dublin Evening Mail*'s final summary of the epoch was the most impressive indictment of all:

England has for fifty years had in her hands the supreme authority over Ireland. She has not been restricted in the exercise of her power, even by the shadow of an Irish representative system; for those who are elected Irish members of Parliament, seldom bring with them to Westminster the slightest tincture of national feeling; and even if the whole hundred and five were to join in opposition to the Minister's Irish policy (as they may be said to have done in opposing the poor law), still their united voice would not be heard amid the clamour of five hundred and fifty-three opponents. Well, what has England done for Ireland during the half century now closing ... According to Downing Street ... Ireland is, for her own good, passing through a purgatorial time, which is to eventuate about the time of the millennium in a state of freshness and hope.[270]

England, of course, did not accept this negative verdict. Contemplating the history of the Union after five decades, Sir Digby Neave declared 'Englishmen of this century will never admit the right of anyone, however his veins may swell with the purest Celtic blood, to say that they have not near their hearts the welfare of their western sister whom God and nature have placed by each one's side.'[271] For Charles Trevelyan, the famine had brought the public opinion of England and Ireland to a place of closer and more intimate connection. For Trevelyan, contemplating his role in the feeding of hundreds of thousands, this could only be a benign development; Ireland now knew how much England cared. For many in Ireland, however, that was precisely the problem.

In the immediate post-famine era, public debate in Ireland was particularly sour and sectarian. Some Protestant zealots had seen the famine as an opportunity sent by God, which would weaken Irish attachment to Catholicism.[272] Against this, Catholic Ireland reinterpreted the Catholic deaths of the famine as a return of religious martyrdom. In his history of those who had suffered for their faith in Ireland, Myles O'Reilly gave pride of place to those who resisted conversion in famine times and thus achieved a place in heaven 'by a death of hunger'.[273]

Further evidence of an apparently intensifying sectarianism came on 12 July 1849, when a murderous Orange–Ribbon clash took place at Dolly's Brae, Co. Down. The Orangemen were to blame for the bulk of the

---

[269] James Grant, *Impressions of Ireland and the Irish* (London, 1844), 276.
[270] 'The Result of English Government in Ireland', *Dublin Evening Mail*, 12 Oct. 1849.
[271] *Four Days in Connemara* (London, 1852), 14.
[272] *Irish Intelligence: The Progress of the Irish Society of London* (London, 1848), i. 3.
[273] Myles O'Reilly, *Memorials of those who Suffered for the Catholic Faith in Ireland* (London, 1878), pp. xv–xvi.

violence. Walter Berwick's report for the Lord-Lieutenant condemned a 'work of retaliation ... reflecting the deepest disgrace on all by whom it was perpetuated and encouraged'. A 70-year-old woman had been murdered and a 10-year-old boy been shot. Clarendon dismissed Lord Roden from the magistracy in punishment for his apparent acquiescence. Clarendon was in close contact with *The Times*, which fully supported his action: '[We] have proscribed every form of political sectarianism ... You may starve, shoot down, even corrupt, a generation of Mitchels and O'Briens, but with Rodens still reminding the people that they are a conquered and contemptible race, your pains are worse than fruitless.'[274] In 1850 Clarendon pushed through the Party Procession Act, directed against displays of Orange triumphalism. But there were others not slow to accuse Clarendon of hypocrisy, recalling Dublin Castle's willingness to arm the Orangemen in 1848. The atmosphere appeared irredeemably rancid.

[274] *Evening Herald*, 25 Oct. 1849; *Dublin Evening Mail*, 20 Oct. 1849; 19 Oct. 1849; Tom Morley, 'The Arcana of that Great Machine, Politicians and the *Times* in the Late 1840s', *History*, 72: no 273 (Feb. 1988), 43; Christine Kinealy, 'A Right to March: The Conflict at Dolly's Brae', in D. G. Boyce and Roger Swift (eds.), *Problems and Perspectives in Irish History Since 1800* (Dublin, 2004).

6

The Fenian Impulse

A restless craving for some visionary kind of self-assertion against the power of England.

('English Democracy and Irish Fenianism', *Quarterly Review*, Jan. 1867)

Listen to what they say; read what they wrote; look at what is going on in this very year [1863], one of the calmest, one of the most happy that Ireland has known.

The language of hate is the habitual language of the party which forms the largest portion of the people.

(Jules de Lasteyrie, 'L'Irlande et les causes de sa misère', *Revue des Deux Mondes* (Aug. 1863), 967)

Such is the Fenian ideal—the ideal of an Irish Republic existing by virtue of an undying hostility to Great Britain without any other *raison d'être* or aspiration.

(G. C. Brodrick, *Political Studies* (1879), 348)

THE LEAGUE OF NORTH AND SOUTH?

'When the nineteenth century had reached its midway, no crux in the tangle of Irish politics seemed more hopeless than to combine the north and south for any public end', recalled Sir Charles Gavan Duffy in 1886.[1] Yet, for a time, it seemed—against all the odds—that it was indeed possible to rise above sectarian differences. This development owed everything to an unusual friendship between two rather different and very remarkable men, Charles Gavan Duffy (1816–1903) and Dr James McKnight (1801–76). They had met at a difficult and apparently exceptionally unpropitious moment: the young Monaghan man Gavan Duffy, then only 23 years old, had been

---

[1] *The League of North and South: An Episode in Irish History, 1850–84* (London, 1886), 2.

asked to edit the *Vindicator*, an O'Connellite newspaper designed to appeal to the Belfast Catholic community, launched in May 1839. During Duffy's term as editor O'Connell, on Duffy's advice, paid his ill-fated visit to Belfast in January 1841. All the windows in the *Vindicator*'s office were smashed by an Orange mob while the police did nothing.[2] Duffy, a son of a prosperous Catholic family with—he stressed—some history of intermarriage with Protestants, brought with him to Belfast a strong sense of resentment over the historic ill-treatment of Irish Catholics in general, and Ulster Catholics in particular. His editorials in the *Vindicator* reflect his sense of outrage; in turn, the *Vindicator* exasperated the established Protestant journals in the city. On a celebrated occasion in 1842, the *Vindicator* was reprimanded by the national Repeal Association for describing the Protestant Church as an 'insignificant heresy'.[3] But Duffy was a complex figure; along with his strong resentment he retained a willingness to be impressed by other strong and talented personalities, regardless of their political background.

Shortly after his arrival in Belfast he met Dr James McKnight, an ardent Presbyterian, then editor of the *Belfast News Letter*, at 'Jenny McAlisters' (in Graham's entry, between High St. and Rosemary St.), a favourite rendezvous for men of business, young professional men, and journalists. At first there was an inevitable tension in the relationship: the young 'repeal'-oriented editor of the first Catholic newspaper in Belfast meeting the Unionist and Presbyterian editor of the city's oldest 'Protestant' organ. McKnight, after all, had been a supporter of O'Connell's great opponent Emerson Tennent in the 1830s.[4] Duffy recalled: 'We viewed each other at the onset with initial caution, but at bottom we desired the same thing, we advanced by degrees from armed neutrality to a friendly pact.'[5] A crucial fact of Duffy's background may have been decisive. His ambitious family took the decision to send the young Duffy to the non-Catholic Classical Academy, run by the Revd John Budeley in Monaghan town. It was a tough experience for Duffy, but he survived it. Dr Gerard O'Brien has acutely noted that Duffy was 'able to relate to protestants and Presbyterians in a way which would never be learned by many catholics, even of his own class'.[6] Over time the two men became close friends—though McKnight never shared Duffy's

---

[2] Gavan Duffy, *My Life in Two Hemispheres* (London, 1903), i. 51.

[3] Catherine Hirst, *Religion, Politics and Violence in Nineteenth-Century Belfast* (Dublin, 2002), 58.

[4] Peter Brooke, *Ulster Presbyterianism* (Dublin, 1987), 156.

[5] Charles Gavan Duffy, *Thomas Davis* (Aubane, 2000), 19.

[6] Gerard O'Brien, 'Charles Gavan Duffy 1816–1893: Rebel and Statesman', in G. O'Brien and P. Roebuck (eds.), *Nine Ulster Lives* (Belfast, 1992), 90. Suggestively Duffy attended night classes at the largely Presbyterian Academical Institution while in Belfast.

political Irish nationalist sympathies. He wrote to Duffy: 'I have too much Milesian blood in me not to be right glad to have a genuine Irishman, and to treat him as a friend, even though I should not adopt any of his opinions.'[7] McKnight had been born into a Presbyterian farming family in Rathfriland, Co. Down. His father, unusually, could speak the Irish language and was fond of singing Irish songs to his child. As Duffy acknowledged explicitly in the portrait of McKnight to be found in his history of the tenant movement: 'By birth he was descended from the Ulster settlers with a strain of native blood, of which he was proud; in opinion he was a Nationalist of the Scotch pattern, eager to foster the native music, manners and literature of the country, but disposed to leave its politics to the Imperial Parliament.'[8] Duffy acknowledged that McKnight was 'frightened by the spectre of a Popish ascendancy, but he had a contempt for greedy landlords and the retinue of mean Whites [sectarian bigots] with which the Orange Lodges so often furnished them'.[9] There was, therefore, a certain common ground, a certain set of shared values and assumptions. McKnight maintained that the current landed proprietors were drawing enormous revenues from estates created exclusively by tenant capital and tenant labour.[10] Whilst he articulated a doctrine of Ulster tenant right, MacKnight did not make a local fetish of it, but supported land reform for *all* Irish farmers. The importance of fixity of tenure was paramount: 'All legislation of tenant right is delusive without fixed tenure, secured occupancy so long as the rent is paid, and an independent tribunal for limitations of rent.'[11]

McKnight, having moved from the increasingly uncongenial *News Letter*[12] to the *Banner of Ulster* in 1846, made his new journal the focus of agitation in the late 1840s. He was involved in a large, 15,000-strong tenant-right demonstration at Dungannon in March 1848; Catholic priests and Presbyterian clergy happily adorned the platform. McKnight also spoke at a similar non-sectarian meeting in Lurgan at the end of March.[13] Even

---

[7] PRONI T1143/1, McKnight to Duffy, 11 Nov. 1847.

[8] *The League of North and South*, 33.   [9] *My Life in Two Hemispheres*, ii. 203.

[10] James McKnight, *The Ulster Tenants' Claim of Right, or Landownership a State Trust; the Ulster Tenant Right an Original Grant from the British Crown, and the Necessity of Extending its General Principle to the other Provinces of Ireland Demonstrated in a Letter to Lord John Russell* (Dublin, 1848), 50. Not everyone was impressed by McKnight's radicalism: John Mitchel discussed McKnight dismissively in 'The Letter from John Knox Junior', *United Irishman*, 11 Apr. 1848, 'Tenant Right of Ireland'.

[11] See the *Banner of Ulster*'s little pamphlet, *A Catechism of Tenant Right* (Belfast, 1850), para. 3; see also McKnight to Duffy, 28 June 1847, in Duffy, *My Life in Two Hemispheres*, ii. 203.

[12] In 1840, he was, for example, excluded from the printing room by workers who disliked his 'liberal' writing, *Northern Whig*, 11 Apr. 1840.

[13] *Belfast News Letter*, 28 Mar. 1848.

when he did not speak, as at the Tandragee meeting, a month later it was clear that other Presbyterian clerical speakers had fully absorbed McKnight's historical thesis.[14] The *Cork Examiner* noted: 'The south should take example by the north. Why should not the protestants, catholics and Presbyterians of Munster stand together on a platform and advocate the tenant right of all Ireland?'[15] John Mitchel, however, regarded this new movement with contempt: 'The principles it contended for—rent fixed by the state and permanent tenure—could never be accepted by the House of Commons. Never, never.'[16]

In the south a number of local tenant-protection societies had attempted to use the weapon of collective rent resistance to force landlords to reduce rent levels. The Tenants Protection Society, founded by Father O'Shea in October 1849 in Callan, Co. Kilkenny, inspired other societies in Kilkenny; societies appeared in Tipperary, Limerick, and Waterford. Although there was a degree of support for the concept of a tenant movement in the poorest province of Connaught, Gavan Duffy, in a striking phrase, made it clear that there was a significantly greater impact in 'Meath, Westmeath and Wexford, where a still prosperous population were in a better condition to maintain a contest with the landlords'.[17] In fact, compared to its serious participation in the repeal movement of 1843, Connaught's participation in the Tenant League was to be strikingly restrained, weak indeed, to the point of being almost non-existent.[18]

It should not be surprising, then, that the agrarian programme of the Tenant League, decided after its founding conference on 6 August 1850 was attended in cordial harmony by Presbyterian and Catholic clergymen, was decidedly radical. Rents, it was declared, must be fixed by a valuation of the land; and the power of raising them at will or recovering a higher rent than the rent so established taken away from the landlords. The tenant must have a fixed tenure and not be liable to disturbance, so long as he paid the rent settled by the proposed valuation. If he chose to quit, or if he could not pay the rent, he must have the right to sell his interest for the highest market value. This is the first formulation of a tenant-right programme known as the three Fs—fair rent, fixity of tenure, and free sale.[19] Underpinning the agrarian rhetoric was a more subtle—albeit largely unregistered—appeal to English self-interest: in this conception, the tenant-right movement was

---

[14] *Belfast News Letter*, 28 Apr. 1848.   [15] *Cork Examiner*, 3 May 1848.

[16] *United Irishman*, 11 Apr. 1848.

[17] Duffy, *The League of North and South*, 21; Paul Connell, *The Diocese of Meath under Bishop John Cantwell* (Dublin, 2004), 170–3.

[18] K. Theodore Hoppen, *Elections, Politics and Society in Ireland 1832–85* (London, 1984), 480.

[19] Duffy, *The League of North and South*, 53–4.

presented as the last chance to bring Ireland, alienated and humiliated by the famine, within the fold of the United Kingdom. As the *Cork Examiner* argued: 'It may not yet be too late' to make Ireland a secure part of the Empire, 'a barrier against invasion and a terror to the foe. Give the Celt an interest in the soil he toils.'[20]

The tenant movement was interested in a parliamentary strategy. In these early discussions the idea of an independent parliamentary party surfaced in a significant way: the conference passed a resolution stating that the new league would support only

representatives who will give a written pledge that they will support in and out of a parliament a tenant law, based upon and carrying into effect, the principles adopted by the Irish Tenant League; and that they will withhold all support from any Cabinet that will not enhance these principles ...[21]

But at first all seemed to be plain sailing for the new movement. Duffy was to claim: 'Within two months 30 constituencies had pledged themselves to return only tenant right representatives; the Moderator of the General Assembly and a large number of Presbyterian ministers, several bishops, and the mass of the catholic clergy, gave their adhesion to the new organisation.'[22] The Tenant League was able, in the autumn of 1850, to dominate the public agenda in Ireland. Dozens of Presbyterian clergymen, hundreds of priests, and most important of all, thousands of tenants rallied to its banner. Although these meetings never approached the scale and size of the remarkable repeal rallies, they were nonetheless an impressive achievement, remarkably ecumenical by Irish standards.[23]

Suddenly, out of the blue, the Prime Minister, Lord John Russell, to the surprise of friend and foe alike, ignited the fires of political Protestantism. The context is clear. On 29 September 1850 Pope Pius IX had announced the re-establishment of the Catholic hierarchy in England and Wales: Cardinal Nicholas Wiseman (born in Seville of Irish parents and with strong Irish political connections), Archbishop of Westminster, issued an allegedly triumphalist pastoral letter. When Parliament met in February 1851, the Prime Minister introduced a Bill to make illegal the assumption by Catholic prelates of titles taken from anywhere in the United Kingdom. The Whigs had apparently convinced themselves that the authority claimed by the Pope was not merely spiritual but a political right to interfere in the affairs of the United Kingdom.

[20] *Cork Examiner*, 28 Jan. 1852.
[21] J. H. Whyte, *The Independent Irish Party 1850–9* (Oxford, 1958), 12–13.
[22] *Dublin Evening Mail*, 20 Aug. 1855.
[23] Richard Pigott, *Personal Recollections of an Irish Nationalist Journalist* (Dublin, 1883), 45.

On 4 November Russell issued his letter to the Bishop of Durham denouncing the superstitious and anti-intellectual nature of Catholicism. Russell's intervention came as an unpleasant shock to his Irish administration, which, once the turbulence of 1848 passed, had been increasingly cool towards Orange-Protestant interests and, indeed, friendlier towards the Catholic hierarchy.[24] Not surprisingly, Clarendon refused to accept, at first, that the Prime Minister could really have acted in this way: 'Whenever Lord Clarendon [then viceroy] first heard of the Durham letter, and had it read to him, he expressed admiration at the cleverness of the forgery, nor, until proof arrived, would he admit it to be genuine.'[25] Once compelled to face this unpleasant reality, Clarendon made it all too visible in Dublin that he was 'lukewarm in the cause',[26] and urged Russell to mollify his Catholic Under-Secretary Redington in every way possible. Redington was persuaded to stay in office, but his credibility as a political Catholic never recovered.[27]

Revealingly, when the Orange Order rushed in to support the government campaign against papal aggression by sending a pledge of support to the throne, the government—happy to accept similar Orange protestations in the context of the 1848 revolt—refused to allow the presentation to be made.[28] But the fact remained that Russell's move was bound to infuriate the Irish Catholic body politic, invoking the worst historical memories: rejection of 'penal' legislation became the theme of the day.

The Ecclesiastical Titles Bill, introduced into the House of Commons in February 1851, hugely complicated life for the Tenant League. The Bill reinforced the prohibition under which territorial titles already used by Protestant dignitaries could not be assumed by any other ecclesiastics, and it also voided any bequests made to such persons as illegal designations. The Russell government was clear in its own mind that it was merely responding to a series of Catholic actions which it saw as hostile to British liberalism: the appointment of the inflexible Paul Cullen as Archbishop of Armagh, the convocation of the Synod of Thurles, and most significantly of all, the refusal to withdraw papal condemnation of the Queen's Colleges.[29] But Irish Catholic MPs simply could not accept this argument.

---

[24] Murphy, *The Redingtons of Clarinbridge*, 196.

[25] J. R. Vincent (ed.), *Disraeli, Derby and the Conservative Party: The Political Journals of Lord Stanley, 1849–69* (Hassocks, 1978), 40.

[26] 'The Roman Catholic Movement in Ireland', *Dublin Evening Mail*, 15 Nov. 1850.

[27] Murphy, *Redington*, 198; even to the extent that he was defeated by a Tory in New Ross in 1856.

[28] *Dublin Evening Mail*, 12 Mar. 1851.

[29] George L. Bernstein, 'British Liberal Politics and Irish Liberalism after O'Connell', in *Piety and Power in Ireland, 1760–1960: Essays in Honour of Emmet Larkin* (Belfast and Notre Dame, 2000), 51.

A large group of Irish Liberal MPs now began to denounce the government, and, more importantly, given the government's weak parliamentary position, vote against it regularly. From early March 1851 this group—whose leading figures included an old friend of Cardinal Wiseman, the Mayo Catholic gentry figure George Henry Moore, John Sadleir, and the Peelite Catholic William Keogh—was known as the 'Irish Brigade'. In August 1851 they established the Catholic Defence Association in Dublin.

There were now two distinct bodies—the Tenant League and the Catholic Defence Association—both claiming to be committed to the policy of independent opposition. Sharman Crawford, now MP for Rochdale, made himself the indispensable linkman. Crawford was the principal voice of tenant right in Parliament, but he considered the Tenant League's proposal to be too radical to have any remote chance of acceptance. He persuaded the Tenant League leadership to moderate its proposal by dropping security of tenure, at the same time persuading the Catholic Defence Association to adopt Crawford's own tenant-right proposals. But what were the prospects for the alliance which Crawford had created? How many of its supporters genuinely believed in independent opposition? Then again, liberal Presbyterians—the *Northern Whig* and MacKnight, for example—disapproved of Russell's handling of the ecclesiastical titles question, but they were also fearful of an increasing Catholization of the public sphere.

By the spring of 1852 a general election was clearly in the offing: in public, at least, a certain unity of purpose remained. A contest had been created which maximized the attraction of even a superficial unity; everyone had an interest in going with the flow. The Irish Brigade/Tenant League approached the contest with a certain optimism. Their candidates were pledged to a vaguely defined policy of remaining aloof from British parties unless offered substantial agrarian and religious concessions. In an act of considerable political daring and ambition, Sharman Crawford resigned his Rochdale seat to contest the Co. Down constituency. This was undoubtedly the most significant of all the electoral contests fought on the island. It was to be a decisive test—was there really a 'League of North and South'?

Crawford had set himself a formidable task. Unlike those in the south and west, many northern landlords had emerged relatively unscathed from the famine, with their social functions and prowess preserved, possibly even enhanced.[30] The principal target of Sharman Crawford was the electoral power of Lord Downshire, but his supporters could claim that during the famine 'Lord Downshire ... lived with the people and had provided work for 600 to 1,000 men between October 1846 and the spring of 1847'.[31]

---

[30] Frank Wright, *Two Lands on One Soil* (Dublin, 1996), 107.
[31] *Belfast News Letter*, 7 July 1847.

The nominations took place in Downpatrick on 21 July 1852, in the midst of an appalling riot. Several thousand people took part in these affrays, 'which were not so much bouts of mindless brutality, as a raw, unfranchised counterpart of the poll'.[32] It was also a turbulent polling day: 'It is necessary to say', recorded the *Downpatrick Recorder*, 'that with all this voting, collision and trampling of dragoons, no little bodily injury was sustained.'[33] The result was a bitter blow for Crawford. Lord Edwin Hill obtained 4,654 votes, David Stewart Ker won 4,117, while Crawford received only 3,113. Crawford's supporters insisted that their man had the support of a majority of the electorate, but that intimidation — 'sheer brute force'[34] — had kept some 2,000 of his supporters from the polls. Certainly, lives were lost, as Orange 'bludgeon men' — who had also prevented Crawford's last election meeting — tried to stop tenant-right supporters getting through to the polling stations. The Tories insisted that Crawford had entered into an alliance with 'Ribbonmen', and only their countermeasures had allowed frightened Conservative supporters to register a vote. The tone of the election was bitterly sectarian. The victors celebrated with a sumptuous lunch at Downpatrick, eaten at a single table, at the head of which a significant 'bunch of Orange lilies raised their ... gorgeous heads'.[35]

There was also a key role played by a realistic tenant fear of land-lord power. The tenants of Alexander R. Stewart of Newtownards were deprived of a rent abatement if they had voted for Sharman Crawford.[36] Similarly, John Malcolm of Corcraney was evicted by the Marquess of Downshire — from a farm which had been in his family for over a century. Malcolm's 'sin' had been to vote for Crawford; other tenants with similar arrears problems were allowed to stay in place.[37] Only one Presbyterian tenant-righter, William Kirk of Newry, was elected in Ulster. The League was now essentially a southern phenomenon, with some northern allies.[38] At the time the *Freeman's Journal* was more upbeat but less realistic: the *Freeman* acknowledged the 'disappointments' in the 'northern counties': 'They are discouraging but not disheartening.' But it noted realistically: 'No candidate has ever yet been returned for a northern county save by the aid of landlord influence.' The old Parliament had but one 'apostle' of tenant

---

[32] Peter Carr, *Portavo: An Irish Townland and its People: Part 2, The Famine to the Present* (Belfast, 2005), 389.

[33] *Belfast News Letter*, 26 July 1852.   [34] *Northern Whig*, 24 July 1852.

[35] Carr, *Portavo*, 393. James McKnight had warned Gavan Duffy that he did not fully understand the strength of reaction in the north: S. Knowlton, *Popular Politics and the Catholic Church: The Rise and Fall of the Independent Irish Party* (New York and London, 1992), 126.

[36] *Northern Whig*, 9 Dec. 1852.   [37] *Ibid.*, 2 Apr. 1853.

[38] John Whyte, *The Independent Irish Party, 1850–59* (Oxford, 1958), 31.

right, Sharman Crawford—'in the new Parliament there will be many such apostles'.

In this assessment, the major disappointment in Down aside, the broad picture after the 1852 election was still not unpromising for Irish supporters of 'tenant right'. For, if the landlords had revealed the vitality of their power in the north, then so had the catholic clergy in the south. Nearly half the Irish representation was now Catholic.

Frederick Lucas and the *Tablet* stated it bluntly: 'The priests have interfered, and by their active exertions between 30 and 40 seats have been secured to represent the feelings and wishes of the bulk of the people of this island, which otherwise would have been submerged in the general flood of English representation.'[39] Some of the language employed was remarkable: at Tralee, the Revd Father Maw thundered that any Catholic who voted for the English enemy was 'wretched' and 'corrupt'; so 'wretched' and corrupt, in fact, that the good priest would be reluctant to extend the last rites to such a person, and having done so—in line with his duty—he would do so with little hope. 'I would fear that my mission would be fruitless, that I could have no hope of converting a heart so lost to every sense of duty, and religion, as to vote in support of those who would trample on the Lord's Hosts.'[40] Mainstream English opinion was shocked. The new Derby government was anxious to achieve a better era in Anglo-Vatican relations, but this was largely with a view to mollifying English, not Irish, Catholics; indeed, a new papal concordat was perceived as a means of bringing pressure 'from the highest spiritual authority'[41] to bear on over-zealous and politically intimidatory priests.

In Ireland, however, the Tenant League remained resolute. On 8–9 September 1852 the Tenant League conference in Dublin, attended by forty-one liberal MPs, adopted a policy of independent opposition to any government not taking up the tenant-right question. On 16 December 1852 Irish votes brought down Derby's government on the budget; on 19 December Aberdeen formed a new coalition government, which remarkably included members of the independent Irish party, John Sadleir and William Keogh. Perhaps surprisingly, there was a genuine sense not just of annoyance but of shock. The *Cork Examiner* insisted: 'The country had not the slightest idea that there was any intention to reverse a policy of complete parliamentary independence.'[42]

[39] *Tablet*, 21 Aug. 1852.
[40] James Lord, *Popery at the Hustings: Foreign or Domestic Legislation* (London, 1852), p. viii.
[41] Vincent (ed.), *Disraeli, Derby and the Conservative Party*, 79.
[42] *Cork Examiner*, 3 Jan. 1853.

Political debate became less political in character: one Independent Irish bubble pricked in Parliament, the focus switched to themes of economic and social reconstruction. In May 1853 the Irish industrial exhibition attracted huge crowds, and William Dargan, the farmer's son who had made himself a great entrepreneur, so admired by royalty, was said to be the new hero of the Irish people who had displaced the memory of O'Connell. Unworried by what came to be seen as a rather anti-Irish budget of W. E. Gladstone, the Chancellor of the Exchequer in 1853 and 1854, economists hailed a new agricultural prosperity. John Mitchel, who escaped from Van Diemen's Land in July 1853, resisted such talk in his *New York* journal: 'All that had happened was that a large proportion of the population being destroyed so that the survivors got more to eat of the food that England leaves them.'[43] The fact remains that Irish life seemed to be improving. Lord Houghton, who had been contemptuous of the Queen's visit in 1849, took a different, much more positive view of her attendance at the exhibition, which attracted over 'a million souls'.[44] There was further dispiriting news for those who supported Mitchel's agenda.

The outbreak of the Crimean War in March 1854 had seen brisk recruiting in Ireland; in the war itself a large number of Victoria Crosses were awarded[45] to Irishmen serving in a British army which, for the first time since 1798, granted Catholic chaplains official status; Cullen happily saw the Crimean War as principally a Catholic crusade. This Irish reaction to the Crimean War had a decisive and depressing effect on Gavan Duffy. Explicitly lamenting that the doctrine that 'England's difficulty was Ireland's opportunity' appeared to be dead,[46] he left for Australia, where he developed a major career as an imperial statesman. John Mitchel, as usual, disagreed with Duffy's assessment: Irish 'disaffection' was as 'intense' and 'profound' as ever it had been: 'There is no trusting to appearances.'[47]

On 6 February 1855 the revelation of military weakness in the Crimea made Palmerston, now 70 years old, Prime Minister. It is conventional wisdom to assert that the Palmerston years (1855–8; 1859–65) were a

---

[43] *The Citizen*, 7 Jan. 1854. Thomas Lough, *England's Wealth: Ireland's Poverty* (London, 1896), 49–51, 74–5, for a discussion of Gladstonian monetary policy and its impact on Ireland.

[44] T. Wemyss Reid, *The Life, Letters and Friendships of Richard Monckton Milnes, First Lord Houghton* (London, 1891), i. 484; Alan C. Davies, 'Ireland's Crystal Palace, 1853', in J. M. Goldstrom and L. A. Clarkson (eds.), *Irish Population, Economy and Society: Essays in Honour of the Late K. H. Connell* (Oxford, 1981), 249–70.

[45] D. Murphy, *Ireland and the Crimean War* (Dublin, 2002), 227–9.

[46] *Dublin Evening Mail*, 20 Aug. 1855.

[47] PRONI D249/1, Mitchel to Miss Thomas, 1 Nov. 1855.

missed opportunity for British policy in Ireland.[48] In fact, Palmerston had serious Irish concerns when he took office,[49] and even, as Karl Marx rightly detected, certain Irish sympathies. Marx even saw some of Palmerston's Irish Catholic appointees as a kind of revival of the Lichfield House compact;[50] more subversively, Marx saw this as a cover for the triumph of large-scale British capitalism within Irish agriculture. But even this was only very partially true;[51] as the country stabilized after the shock of the famine, it proved very difficult to transform the local economy. But why did Marx get it wrong? Was he not merely describing government policy?

Addressing the Royal Agricultural Improvement Society of Ireland at the banquet following the great annual cattle show at Athlone, the Lord-Lieutenant, Earl Carlisle (formerly Lord Morpeth), declared on 13 August 1856:

How can I be debarred, even by the golden promise of these harvests which now gladden our eyes from urging you to bear in mind what nature in her wise economy seems especially to have fitted this island for is to be the mother of flocks and herds—to be, if I may, be the larder and dairy of the world—to send rations of beef and bales of bacon to our armies wherever they are.[52]

Carlisle noted that more than 'one million people had been subtracted from the population', but did not discuss the reason. This was the classic statement of what became known as the 'flocks and herds' doctrine. W. O'Connor Morris, then a young friend of the Lord-Lieutenant, commented darkly in his memoirs, written in old age as a protectionist Tory, that Carlisle was 'hinting, not obscurely, that all could be well if the whole island became a thinly-peopled sheepwalk'.[53] Morris added for good measure that Lord Carlisle was a 'Whig economist at bottom, though he concealed its harsher phrases, and like all the leading statesmen of the time, he encouraged Irish landlords to dispossess their tenants—advice unhappily followed by a

---

[48] The point is well expressed in Matthew Potter, 'The Life and Times of William Monsell, first Baron Monsell of Tervoe', unpublished Ph.D thesis, National University of Ireland (2001), 84; 'The Lord Palmerston of today is more hostile to tenant industry than the Lord Palmerston of ten years ago', *Freeman's Journal*, 18 Sept. 1856.

[49] E. D. Steele, *Irish Land and British Politics* (Cambridge, 1974), 37.

[50] 'Ireland's Revenge', 16 Mar. 1855; K. Marx and F. Engels, *On Ireland* (London, 1971), 74–6.

[51] Ellen Hazelkorn, 'Some Problems with Marx's Theory of Capitalist Penetration into Agriculture: The Case of Ireland', *Economy and Society*, 10: 3 (Aug. 1981), 284–7.

[52] Mansion House Banquet, *The Vice-Regal Speeches and Addresses, Lectures of the Late Earl of Carlisle, KG*, ed. J. J. Gaskin (Dublin, 1865), 159.

[53] *Memories and Thoughts of a Life* (London, 1895), 193.

242   *The Fenian Impulse*

few'.[54] But at the time the young O'Connor Morris was one of those who agreed that Ireland was poised to undergo a benign transformation.[55] It had certainly become fashionable for English writers to advertise the positive prospects for such a transformation.[56] At first the signs were said to be good. On 20 March 1852 the *Saunders Newsletter* celebrated 'the perfect success so far of the Scotch settlements in different parts of Ireland'.[57] But other matters became decidedly more complex. In the years 1854–7 Allan Pollock, a Galway landlord and 'new man', who had bought land under the Encumbered Estates Act, attempted to clear part of his 500-tenant estate. He sought to introduce tenure for one year only, 'unknown in any part of Ireland'.[58] Pollock immediately ran into a storm. He faced pressure, exercised through direct violence (the burning of his house), clerical denunciation, resistance, and even became the subject of a parliamentary debate. *The Times*, in London, exploded with anger: 'This gentleman appears to be seized with a perfect mania for eviction ... Here is a case where every feeling of our nature is enlisted on the side of the poor tenants.' *The Times* concluded with some dramatic force: 'It shocks every feeling of humanity. It is a reproach to the civilisation of the age, and by so signally illustrating the abuses of property itself, the groundwork of human society, the bond that holds communities together.'[59]

Pollock was forced to pay considerable sums to the outgoing tenantry: he ended up leaving at least 200 tenants on his estates, holding their small farms. The Pollock affair has a deep symbolism: not only was the Pollock estate one where an advanced, cattle-based husbandry coexisted with a more traditional farming sector, a symbol of post-farming Irish agriculture[60] as a whole—Pollock, after all, might be said to be have been carrying out Peel's policy of a new benign plantation and modernization of the west; but in doing so he was not only resisted by the locals—hardly surprising—but also denounced by the principal organ of the English establishment.[61]

But even if the hard-nosed capitalist agenda of a man like Pollock was blocked, there was a broad sense of increasing prosperity, as advertised

[54] *Memories and Thoughts of a Life* (London, 1895), 193.
[55] 'The Land System of Ireland', in *Oxford Essays* (Oxford, 1856), Morris, *Memories and Thoughts*, 201.
[56] Glenn Hooper, *Travel Writing and Ireland, 1760–1860: Culture, History, Politics* (London, 2005), 144–89.
[57] Patricia Pelly and Andrew Tod (eds.), *The Highland Lady in Dublin 1851–56* (Dublin, 2005), 77.
[58] *Freeman's Journal*, 22 July 1856.   [59] *The Times*, 3 May 1856.
[60] P. G. Lane, 'The Attempt at Commercial Farming in Ireland after the Famine', *Studies*, 401 (Spring 1972), 54–66.
[61] Barbara Lewis Solow, *The Land Question and the Irish Economy, 1870–1903* (Cambridge, Mass., 1971), 89–90.

by the political economists. Others detected a fundamental change in the culture of Ireland. G. W. Asplen said that the 'rollicking recklessness of ould Ireland'[62] was gone, and the *Ballymena Observer* claimed that the new gentry were interested in 'rotation of the crops' rather than 'rotation of the bottle'.[63] In 1858 the *Northern Whig* claimed that the national Presbyterian liberal agenda of 1798 had triumphed, in the sense that the British state in Ireland was now committed to policies of progress and toleration.[64] The *Whig* was worried by the serious outburst of sectarian rioting in Belfast in 1857, and worried again by what it saw as the irrationalism of the 1859 religious revival in rural Ulster,[65] but it remained fundamentally optimistic about the future. The *Ulster Magazine*, moderate conservative in tone, agreed: 'Tipperary emulates Down in the peaceable habits and determined industry; Galway has put aside its rage and recklessness, and along the entire line of the Shannon, all ranks of the people have settled down from the wild vagaries of theoretic patriotism to the cool and healthy pursuits of self-exertion.'[66]

But was the *Ulster Magazine* right in its belief that Ireland had put aside 'theoretic patriotism'? Was there perhaps some evidence to support the *Ulster Magazine*'s view? In 1858 even Cardinal Wiseman, who had so infuriated Lord John Russell in 1850–1, took up the subject of the famine: the wonderful material progress of Ireland proved, he declared, that 'dreadful scourges' were 'often the mere chastenings of a father', in short, a 'benefit' of the 'wonderful ways of God'.[67] Lord George Hill had argued this first in 1853; but to have it said by a Catholic archbishop of Irish parentage was striking indeed.[68] The *Freeman* declared that the history of the famine could probably never be written.[69] However, memories persisted, and could lead to difficult moments.

[62] *A Lively Sketch of a Trip to Killarney* (London and Cambridge, 1858), 36.

[63] *Ballymena Observer*, 22 Aug. 1857.   [64] *Northern Whig*, 6 Feb. 1858.

[65] Janice Holmes, 'Transformation, Aberration or Consolidation? Explaining the Ulster Revival of 1859', in Niall Ó Cósáin (ed.), *Explaining Change in Cultural History* (Dublin, 2005), 120–39.

[66] 'Modern Ulster', *Ulster Magazine*, 1: 1 (1860), 43–9.

[67] 'Impressions of a Recent Visit to Ireland', given to an audience of 2,000–3,000 persons in Hanover Sq, London, in *The Sermons, Lectures and Speeches Delivered by His Eminence, Cardinal Wiseman, Archbishop of Westminster, During his Tour of Ireland in August and September 1858, with his Lecture Delivered in London on the Impressions of his Tour* (Dublin, 1859), 386. Cardinal Cullen was believed to have regarded the famine as a dispensation of Providence, intended to enable the Irish to spread the faith abroad. Joseph Hone, *The Moores of Moore Hall* (London, 1939), 161.

[68] *Facts from Gweedore*, a facsimile reprint of the 1887 edition, with an introduction by E. Estyn Evans (Belfast, 1981), 9.

[69] *Freeman's Journal*, 18 Sept. 1856.

In 1848 Gavan Duffy had seen, on the streets of Galway, crowds of creatures 'more debased than the yahoos of Swift—creatures having only a distant a hideous resemblance to human beings'.[70] Ten years later, the waiter serving the roast lamb and wine in a Galway hotel recalled the scene and broke down in tears:[71] a telling reminder that not everyone could forget or, indeed, forgive.

THE REBIRTH OF THE IRISH REVOLUTIONARY TRADITION

By the first week of October 1858 the Catholic clergy were aware of the existence of a new, oath-bound, secret armed conspiracy, the Phoenix Society.[72] Father John O'Sullivan, parish priest of Kenmare, Co. Kerry, spoke on the subject at mass, and next day sent a copy of the oath to the authorities. On 30 October 1858 *The Nation*—since 1858 controlled by the 'patriotic', pious Catholic and nationalist brothers A. M. Donal and T. D. Sullivan—warned the young militants that they were in great danger of arrest,[73] but drilling activities continued under the direction of an Irish-American officer. In fact, a young Irish speaker, O'Donovan Rossa (1831–1915), and others were arrested in December; much to the relief of the prisoners,[74] *The Nation* then threw itself into the defence of the alleged conspirators—such legal luminaries as Thomas O'Hagan QC offered their services. A pattern was early established. The actual activity of the new movement was easily quelled by the authorities, but subsequent arrests and allegedly high-handed judicial behaviour led to an outpouring of sympathetic, liberal and patriotic—and even in this early case—loyalist sentiment. The government, in effect, retreated and allowed the release of those it had arrested.

But who were the new revolutionaries? They had, at any rate, a self-appointed leader. A Kilkenny man, James Stephens (1824–1901), the son of John Stephens, an auctioneer's clerk, had been impressed and magnetized by *The Nation* newspaper in the 1840s. In 1848 Stephens, then a young civil engineer, threw in his lot with William Smith O'Brien at Ballingarry, where he was wounded. After six weeks on the run, James Stephens escaped

---

[70] *Conversations with Carlyle* (Belfast, 2006), 147.

[71] An Oxonian, *A Little Time in Ireland* (London, 1859), 50.

[72] T. D. Sullivan, *A. M. Sullivan: A Memoir* (Dublin, 1885), 17.

[73] T. D. Sullivan, *Recollections of Troubles Times in Irish Politics* (Dublin, 1905), 38–9.

[74] See the letter signed from the self-styled 'political prisoners' to the editor of *The Nation* offering profuse thanks, J. O'Sullivan, etc. to T. D. Sullivan, 28 Feb. 1859.

to a new life as a revolutionary exile in Paris, studying philosophy at the
Sorbonne, giving English lessons, and generally inserting himself, alongside
a comrade, John O'Mahony, into the revolutionary subculture of the Latin
Quarter, staying in the bohemian boarding house immortalized by Balzac in
Le Père Goriot. Stephens returned to Ireland in late 1855: he earned a living
by teaching French in aristocratic Dublin households, whilst also touring
the country extensively. A conviction formed in his mind: any future Irish
uprising must be the work of a secret revolutionary organization under
his own personal autocratic control. This new organization must mobilize
Irish-American resources in anticipation of an international crisis that would
create a powerful anti-British ally. For all his arrogance and pomposity,
relentlessly satirized even by his political friends, Stephens, nonetheless,
had the kind of self-belief essential to revolutionary leadership, and—more
important—to the task of inducing others, notably Irish-Americans, to
accept that leadership. The Stephens-led movement, it should be stressed,
flourished amongst recent Irish emigrants in Britain as well as America,
and, for much the same reason, it gave identity and self-respect to those
who felt themselves to be otherwise marginalized and despised by their host
society.[75]

Fenianism, as the new movement came to be called, was the decisive
proof that a greater Ireland beyond the seas now existed. It linked the
concerns and passions of patriotic young men in the homeland with the
Irish-born of America and of England and Scotland. At the beginning
of the first major book to be published on Fenianism, John Rutherford
noted that the Irish emigrants carried with them a predilection for secret
association, hatred of the 'Saxon', and an undying sense of wrong combined
with a passionate desire for vengeance, 'if not in his own person, at least
in the persons of his children'. Rutherford drew particular attention to
a parliamentary intervention by Grattan's son. Speaking in the House of
Commons in July 1848, Henry Grattan, member for Meath, related the
following anecdote:

Being at one of the Irish seaports in 1847, I entered into a conversation with a man
about to emigrate to America. I advised him to remain at home. 'No, Sir,' said he,
'I will go to the land of liberty'. 'But consider your sons,' was my reply. 'Oh! They
will come back,' was the response, 'and when they do come back, it will be with
rifles on their shoulders'.[76]

The 'land of liberty' provided many opportunities for Irish advancement,
but at the same time it assaulted Irish sensibilities. The Irish emigrants

[75] W. J. Lowe, *The Irish in Mid-Victorian Lancashire: The Shaping of a Working Class
Consciousness* (New York, 1989), 190–1.
[76] John Rutherford, *The Fenian Conspiracy* (London, 1877), 15.

of the famine generation and their successors after 1850 were bringing with them, to the 'most militant Protestant nation in the world', a highly distinctive and energetic variant of Catholicism.[77] In 1858 the 'know-nothing' party, bitterly anti-Irish Catholic, won a majority of the New York state legislature.[78] Father Boyce, the interesting Irish novelist resident in Worcester, Massachusetts, has one of his characters say in an 1859 novel that the Orangemen in Ireland were a decent lot compared to the American variant.[79] Part of the Irish response to such contempt was to attempt to reassert national pride.

In 1857 John O'Mahony and Michael Doheny in America sent Stephens a message to ask if he would set up a revolutionary organization in Ireland with which the American exiles would co-operate.[80] Stephens responded by saying that he demanded total control and serious American money. This was accepted. On St Patrick's Day 1858 Stephens, having won the argument to his satisfaction, founded the Irish Revolutionary Brotherhood or Irish Republican Brotherhood, designed to 'make Ireland an independent republic' and 'to preserve inviolable secrecy regarding all the transactions of this secret society'. It absorbed the Phoenix Society. Britain, it was claimed, would never concede self-government to the force of argument, but only to the argument of force.

In April 1859 the American counterpart, the 'Fenian Brotherhood', was organized and gave its name in popular parlance to the whole movement; the name 'Fenian' was derived from the *Fianna*, the legendary warriors of Irish mythology. The preservation of secrecy was to prove an impossible task. Stephens was, nonetheless, adept in playing on the air of crisis created by the American Civil War and subsequent Anglo-American tensions: some external event, it was hoped, would occur to destroy the superficial stability of the union. The pattern of organization espoused by Stephens was the familiar continental model. A super-efficient organizer of civilians, there was little sign that he possessed military judgement. A circle, commanded by a centre, theoretically consisted of 820 men, organized in multiples of nine. Under each centre was one 'B' or captain, and under each 'B'

---

[77] Mike Davis, *Prisoners of the American Dream: Politics and Economy in the History of the US Working Class* (London, 1986), 23.

[78] Thomas N. Brown, *Irish-American Nationalism 1870–90* (Philadelphia and New York, 1996), 22–3

[79] Patrick Maume, 'Father Boyce, Lady Morgan and Sir Walter Scott: A Study in Intertextuality and Catholic Polemics', in J. H. Murphy (ed.), *Catholics and Evangelicals in Nineteenth-Century Ireland* (Dublin, 2005), 167; Christopher McGimpsey, 'Internal Ethnic Friction: Orange and Green in Nineteenth-Century New York', *Immigrants and Minorities*, 1: 1 (Mar. 1982), 39–59.

[80] Mary C. Lynch and Seamus O'Donoughue, *O'Sullivan Burke Fenian* (Midleton, 1999), 90.

were nine 'C's or sergeants, each of whom commanded a unit of nine men or 'D's. In practice, this most methodical arrangement—reflecting the scientific training of Stephens—was never fully implemented. Circles varied enormously in size.[81] For the first 'six or seven years' Fenianism was strongest in, first, Leinster and secondly Munster, thirdly Connaught, and finally Ulster: 'The Orangeism of Ulster was a stubborn obstacle in parts; nearly as stubborn was the Ribbonism of Connaught.'[82] Fenianism was exceptionally popular amongst the bored young men of urban and small-town Ireland (artisans, clerks, and shop-assistants), but a good deal less popular amongst the farming classes who constituted the great majority of the community. There is voluminous evidence that fraternization in a recreational setting was at the heart of much Fenianism in the early and middle 1860s.

The only serious military experience of most Fenians—drill—became their mode of social life par excellence.[83] Fenianism is a fine example of patriotism as past time, but this should not obscure the existence of a highly motivated core of activists who believed in a revolutionary solution to the evils of nineteenth-century Ireland, and were 'prepared to risk their lives to attain it'.[84] There were, indeed, many striking examples of revolutionary zeal and self-sacrifice. In Connaught, the militant consumptive Ned Duffy (1840–68) threw himself heart and soul into the task of bringing Ribbonmen into the new movement.[85] Duffy at least laid down the initial basis for a new Fenian radical agrarian tradition which was to prove to be of some importance.

The newspaper of this new movement, published quite openly from 1863, was the *Irish People*. The *Irish People* had a cadre of relatively talented individuals at its helm: as well as the novelist Charles Kickham, there was Thomas Clarke Luby (1822–1901), the son of a Church of Ireland priest and a Catholic mother. Luby was a Trinity College, Dublin, graduate. It was Luby who recruited Ned Duffy in Dublin. John O'Leary (1830–1907), was a former Young Irelander, an intensely proud man who later caught the imagination of the poet W. B. Yeats. O'Leary was a literary, middle-class Catholic from Tipperary town, a medical doctor manqué, who combined slightly snobbish but sophisticated literary tastes with a romantic nationalist

---

[81] E. R. R. Green, 'The Beginnings of Fenianism', in T. W. Moody (ed.), *The Fenian Movement* (Cork, 1968), 19.

[82] John Rutherford, *The Fenian Conspiracy* (London, 1877), i. 86.

[83] R. V. Comerford, *The Fenians in Context: Irish Politics and Society 1868–82* (Dublin, 1985), 111.

[84] Mairead Maume, Patrick Maume, and Mary Casey (eds.), *The Galtee Boy: A Fenian Prison Narrative* (Dublin, 2005), 8.

[85] John O'Leary, *Fenians and Fenianism* (London, 1896), i. 132; Liam Swords, *A Dominant Church: The Diocese of Achonry 1818–1960* (Dublin, 2004), 121–76.

desire to convert the Protestant gentry.[86] He had studied in Paris and was recruited by Stephens, who made him one of his key lieutenants. The most formidable Fenian leader of all, however, was the young John Devoy, who was charged by Stephens with the task of infiltrating the British army.[87] Devoy was to place himself at the centre of Irish nationalist politics for the next six decades. Able though they were, the Fenian intelligentsia, with the exception of O'Leary, never achieved the level of friendly recognition granted by the English metropolitan intelligentsia to Young Ireland. It may, however, be of significance to point out that their writing had as much, if not more, influence within Ireland itself.

The Fenians were, at any rate, just as much in revolt as Young Ireland had been against the prevailing conditions in Ireland, even if the horrors of the 1840s had given way to the mediocrity of the 1860s. There was also a sense in which the Fenians were regarded as dangerously *declassé*. Commentators regularly stressed the 'tone' of Fenianism, and felt it was related to the changed class basis of Irish political nationalism. The nationalist Justin McCarthy felt that, unlike previous Irish patriotic movements, Fenianism had no upper-class appeal: 'The Fenian movement, on the other hand, had sprung from the very soil and from the streets ... it was a movement created ... by the harsh and exceptional conditions to which the Irish peasantry were subjected.'[88] There was truth in this observation—nonetheless, comfortable farmers displayed less activism than the urban artisans and clerks who flooded into the movement, creating a striking imbalance in a largely rural country. Karl Marx, in his notes for an undelivered speech on Ireland, went as far as to claim Fenianism was a 'socialist lower-class movement'. Marx later added: 'Socialistic ... in a negative sense directed against the appropriation of the soil.'[89] There were, in fact, some links between the Fenians and the First International. Indeed, John Devoy's organ, the *Irish Nation*, declared on the death of Karl Marx: 'Whatever Irishmen may think of the general policy of Karl Marx, it must never be forgotten that he was a sincere friend to Ireland. To him as much as any man of the century it is due that the cause of Ireland is now heard

---

[86] For a discussion of O'Leary's memoirs and self-image, see Amy E. Martin, 'Nationalism as Blasphemy: Negotiating Belief and Institutionality in the Genre of Fenian Recollections', in James H. Murphy (ed.), *Evangelicals and Catholics in Nineteenth-Century Ireland* (Dublin, 2005), 123–35.

[87] Terry Golway, *Irish Rebel: John Devoy and Ireland's Fight for Ireland's Freedom* (New York, 1998), 49–50.

[88] Justin McCarthy, *Reminiscences* (New York, 1910), i. 96.

[89] E. Strauss, *Irish Nationalism and British Democracy* (London, 1951), 145–7; Gearóid Ó Tuathaigh, 'Ireland under the Union: Historiographical Reflections', *Australian Journal of Irish Studies*, 2: 2 (2002), 10.

on the continent of Europe through other than an English medium.'[90] Fenianism had a decided whiff of social radicalism, although its principal focus was sharply political in a decidedly nationalist sense.

The early years of Fenianism coincided with an agrarian depression, which put in doubt the successful reconstruction of post-famine Ireland.[91] While Dr Neilson Hancock, almost the official economist of government in this period, argued that the causes of the depression were temporary and short-term,[92] the Fenian *Irish People* argued that the real crisis of Irish development was more fundamental and rooted in the 'patterns of development imposed by British rule'.[93] There is little doubt that frequent reports of growing rural hardship stimulated support for Fenianism. The *Freeman's* influential special correspondent in the west concluded his reports: 'The holders of four, six, eight or ten acres are heavily in debt … and have no means whatsoever of clearing their liabilities.'[94] It was articles like these, rather than the deliberations of more optimistic economists, which caught the Irish public's attention: 'None of the essentials of famine are present,' acknowledged the *Freeman's* leader writer, 'yet such is the state to which the deep-rooted malady has reduced the mass of the population that they suffer many of the evils which are felt in other countries only in times of famine.'[95] As a solution to rural hardship, the Fenian newspaper the *Irish People* trenchantly advocated peasant proprietorship and the destruction of the landlord system. *The Nation* observed: 'The Fenians think that if they are to fight at all, the battle may as well be for the ownership as for the tenancy [of the land].'[96] But as James Stephens later recalled: 'It is true that in the columns of *The Irish People* several articles were written advocating peasant proprietorship; but national independence was certainly put forward as the point to be gained first.'[97] Fenianism, therefore, was in favour of agrarian radical objectives, but these objectives were considered only to be attainable *after* the achievement of self-government. Nevertheless, the social themes of the *Irish People* reflected a kind of nascent populist

---

[90] *Irish Nation*, 14 Mar. 1883.   [91] Rutherford, *Fenian Conspiracy*, 198.

[92] W. N. Hancock, *Report on the Supposed Progressive Decline in Irish Prosperity* (Dublin, 1863), 83; for an important discussion of Hancock and his influence, see Peter Gray, 'The Peculiarities of Irish Land Tenure 1800–1914: From Agent of Impoverishment to Agent of Pacification', in D. Winch and P. K. O'Brien, *The Political Economy of British Historical Experience* (Oxford, 2002), 147–8; id., 'The Making of Mid-Victorian Ireland? Political Economy and the Memory of the Great Famine; in id. (ed.), *Victoria's Ireland: Irishness and Britishness, 1837–1901* (Dublin, 2004), 151–96.

[93] *Irish People*, 28 May 1864 and 8 Oct. 1864.

[94] *Freeman's Journal*, 17 Jan. 1863.   [95] Ibid., 20 Jan. 1863.

[96] Oliver P. Rafferty, *The Church, the State and the Fenian Threat 1861–75* (London, 1999), 90.

[97] Desmond Ryan, *The Fenian Chief* (Dublin, 1967), 65.

consensus as to the definition of agrarian justice. The Fenian spokesmen broadcast social criticism that was concerned with the whole pattern of post-famine Irish development. There was a widely based hostility towards consolidation, and the increased emphasis on pasture as opposed to tillage: a transition which had strengthened a culture of 'grazierdom' amongst Irish farmers.

The transition to pasture was resisted on the grounds that it encouraged emigration and was, even in its own narrow economic terms, less than triumphantly successful. Between 1841 and 1871 the total number of cattle grew from 1.8 million to 4 million, while the population fell from 8.2 million to 5.4 million, so that the ratio of cattle to people rose from 22 per 100 to 74 per 100 in the course of thirty years.[98] Underpinning such a critique was an underlying popular tendency to deny full legitimacy to the Irish land system. It was a system rooted in acts of confiscation—acts which were graphically recalled in nineteenth-century historical works; *The Times* (24 October 1865) favourably reviewed J. P. Prendergast's *The Cromwellian Settlement of Ireland*, noting the 'fraud' and 'bribery' attendant upon that 'squalid process', and rejected also J. A. Froude's effort in 1872 to rehabilitate the Cromwellian mission. Landlords were, in fact, increasingly religiously mixed—in the 1861 census 48 per cent were Church of Ireland and 43 per cent were Catholic[99]—but most of the largest landlords were Protestants, so a religio-ethnic division served for many as a sharp reminder of historical grievances.

The *Irish People* critique of 'grazierdom' fitted easily into a broadly held populist view in the Irish countryside which defined the main trends in post-famine agriculture in highly negative terms. In this version, Ireland was undergoing a process of depopulation in which the Irish people were being replaced by cattle and sheep. This process was driven, it was claimed, by British and landlord self-interest: cheap food for British cities and easy profit for landlords and their local allies, graziers. Karl Marx, in the first volume of *Capital*, published in 1867, noted the 'depopulation' which had thrown 'much of the land out of cultivation', combined with the greater area devoted to 'cattle breeding'.[100] It was a perception felt all the more keenly in Ireland itself.

There was a particular popular sympathy for those tens of thousands of tenants whose hard labour over many years—the so-called 'reclamation

    [98] B. M. Walsh, 'Marriage Rates and Population Pressure: Ireland, 1871 and 1911', *Economic History Review*, 22 (Apr. 1976), 157–8.
    [99] W. E. Vaughan, *Landlords and Tenants in Mid-Victorian Ireland* (Oxford, 1994), 11.
    [100] *Capital* (London, 1867), i. 703.

tenantry'—had created the value of the land itself; in general, Irish landlords were exposed because their record as investors in Irish land improvement was, at best, patchy. Landlord expenditure on improvement in the period 1850–75 did not exceed £7 million or £8 million, perhaps 3 per cent of gross rental received over these years. There is no question that the tenant had a superior record as a sole improver in nineteenth-century Ireland.[101] Absenteeism was often seen as the greatest vice of the Irish landlords: some absentees, in fact, owned the lowest-rented estates. Nevertheless, perhaps one-quarter of the total rental of Ireland went to landlords who traditionally lived outside their country.[102] All these anti-landlord resentments were, of course, reinforced by another common-sense observation: in the absence of alternative industrial employment—except in the north-east corner of the island—the Irish peasantry could hardly be expected to endure a vulnerability more tolerable in England, where tenants had greater alternative opportunities.

Charles Kickham's most celebrated novel, *Knocknagow*, presented a picture of a people denied 'security', and thus a vital element of self-respect and personal autonomy, by an unjust land system which had 'cleared' so many from the country and driven them to America: the origin of such a tragedy lay in English selfishness and self-interest.[103] The speeches of the Earl of Carlisle had a long afterlife in nationalist recollection. A character in the novel declares: 'The English Viceroy tells us that Providence intended Ireland to be the fruitful mother of flocks and herds. That is why our people are hunted like noxious animals, to perish in the ditchside or in the poorhouse.'[104]

The *Cork Examiner* protested that the object of tenant-right supporters was to win for the farmer 'some security that the fruits of his labour and capital ... will remain for himself to keep and not to go to fill the coffers of some person who had contributed nothing'.[105] Kickham's characters picked up this theme of 'security' and set it in a broader context. ' "It is a remarkable illustration," said the doctor of the saying, "give a man security and he'll turn it into a garden".' *Knocknagow* contains as the ultimate elaboration of the theme much argument in favour of a 'Peasant Proprietary'. ' "I hope we

---

[101] Cormac O'Grada, 'Agricultural Head Rents, Pre-Famine and Post-Famine', *Economic and Social Review*, 5: 3 (Apr. 1974), 390.

[102] N. D. Palmer, 'Irish Absenteeism in the 1870s', *Journal of Modern History*, 12 (1940).

[103] Charles Kickham's novel, *Knocknagow: In the Homes of Tipperary*, first published in 1870.

[104] *Knocknagow* (Dublin, 1887 edn.), 592. For a similar attack on Carlisle, see O'Leary, *Fenians and Fenianism*, i. 261.

[105] *Cork Examiner*, 22 Apr. 1865.

may live to see the day," Dr Kiely observed, "when freeholders will be more numerous than they are in Ireland". "Sure you don't think the English Parliament would do that for us, Sir?" "I'd rather have it done by an Irish Parliament," replied the doctor.[106] This last point was decisive. The novelist Charles Kickham puts it obliquely; the politician Charles Kickham insisted more bluntly that an Irish parliament was the only route for a peasant proprietorship. Kickham had involved himself in tenant-right politics in the early 1850s, but by the early 1860s he believed that such a reformist parliamentary project could not work.[107] The landlords were too strong, and they had allies amongst the strong peasantry—'shoneens'—willing to assist them. The Fenians satirized the Catholic graziers as 'boors in broadcloth', who lacked the social refinement of the real gentry.[108] In consequence, it was useless for the people to waste their strength on struggling for anything but 'the one thing'—national independence. An editorial in February 1864 contained the passage: 'We have insisted over and over again, there is but one way in which Irishmen can benefit themselves fundamentally, and that is by regaining their lost independence, and at the same time reconquering the land for the people.' In September 1865 Kickham penned another editorial, 'Priests in Politics', which advised priests to stay out of anti-national politics and called for revolution: 'Our beautiful and fruitful land will become a grazing farm for the foreigners' cattle, and the remnant of our race wanderers and outcasts all over the world if English rule in Ireland be not struck down. Our only hope is revolution.'[109] The Fenians, therefore, had a social philosophy, a leaning towards social radicalism, but it was subordinated to nationalist principles: with the result that for many in his target audience the message was a little abstract.[110]

Like any other such movement, Fenianism required inspiring examples of self-sacrifice and bravery as a source of inspiration. However, in 1860

---

[106] Knocknagon, 489.

[107] R. V. Comerford, Charles J. Kickham: A Study in Irish Nationalism and Literature (Dublin, 1979), 37.

[108] Irish People, 30 July 1864.

[109] Frank Rynne, 'Focus on the Fenians: The Irish People Trials, November 1865–January 1866', History Ireland, 13: 6 (Nov.–Dec. 2005), 42.

[110] The former Parnellite and League activist J. P. Hayden recalled: 'Once I was told by a Fenian organiser of his experience when he was endeavouring to enlist a Donegal farmer into his organisation. He had been talking to him about misgovernment and oppression by a foreign government. This man had said that the only government he knew came from the "Big House", to which he pointed, where the landlord lived and reigned, had his minions, and held and exercised all power over the countryside.' ' "Impressions of Memory": Memories of John P. Hayden', Co. Roscommon Historical and Archaeological Society Journal, 10 (2006), 83.

the most obvious display of Irish manly valour came from the 1,000-strong Papal Irish Brigade of St Patrick, fighting in Italy under the command of the gallant and educated gentleman farmer Major Myles O'Reilly (1825–80), who had been much involved with John Henry Newman in running the affairs of the Catholic University, opened in 1854.[111] The Papal Irish Brigade was explicitly inspired by the ideal of Irish Catholicism rather than Irish nationalism.[112] The Papacy was considered by British liberals to be a reactionary *ancien régime* locked in battle with the forces of a progressive Italian nationalism. In September 1860 the battalion of St Patrick bravely defended Spoleto against Piedmontese troops, who were repeatedly repulsed before O'Reilly's final inevitable surrender. But in Ireland the resonance of his conflict were rather different. Charles Kickham, whose first cousin was an Irish brigadier, composed the 'address' to the Tipperary men of the Irish Brigade.[113] Cardinal Cullen insisted in 1862: 'Every day there are new proofs that the Brothers of St Patrick [the Fenians] are nothing more or less than Irish Mazziniani.'[114] But the reality was more complex. Some priests refused to accept Cullen's version of Fenianism; of particular importance here was Father Patrick Lavelle. Lavelle was also significant because he, like his friend and ally Canon Ulick J. Bourke, kept alive an interest in the Irish language on the fringes of Fenianism as elsewhere politicians and churchmen accommodated themselves almost unreservedly to the exclusive use of English for public purposes.[115]

Father Patrick Lavelle was essentially right. The Fenians were not anticlerical in the continental European ('no priests in politics') sense—for all that Cardinal Cullen believed them to be so. Charles Kickham, for example, did not believe that priests should not express political opinions. As Francis Hackett observed: 'The tenderness which the common Irish feel for the priests is a deep and heartfelt tenderness. It was conceived in the mutual experience of the penal laws. It throbs through the novels of men like Kickham ... who were close to the country people and knew their hearts.'[116]

---

[111] Colin Barr, *Paul Cullen, John Henry Newman and the Catholic University of Ireland, 1845–65* (Leominster, 2003), 148.

[112] Myles O'Reilly, *Memorials of Those Who Suffered for the Catholic Faith in Ireland in the Sixteenth, Seventeenth and Eighteenth Centuries* (London, 1868), p. ix.

[113] Comerford, *Charles J. Kickham*, 51.

[114] E. Larkin, *The Consolidation of the Roman Catholic Church, 1860–70* (Chapel Hall and London, 1987), 88.

[115] Kevin Collins, *Catholic Churchmen and the Celtic Revival in Ireland 1848–1916* (Dublin, 2002); 'Old Gaelic Culture', *Westminster Review* (1888), 154. See, for the best treatment, Gearóid Ó Tuathaigh, 'Language, Ideology and National Identity', in Joe Cleary and Claire Connolly (eds.), *The Cambridge Companion to Modern Irish Culture* (Cambridge, 2005), 44–5.

[116] Hackett, *Ireland: A Study in Nationality*, 277.

Kickham's novels are marked by a sympathetic attitude towards Catholic clergy expressing a nationalist world-view. Rather, Kickham believed that priests deserved no special privileges in the political sphere, in particular when they opposed the nationalist message.

In January 1861 Terence Bellew MacManus, a Young Ireland exile, died in California. MacManus (born 1811/12), who came from a recently impoverished Catholic gentry background, had been one of the more decisive Young Irelanders. In October 1848 he had been sentenced to death alongside Smith O'Brien, Thomas Francis Meagher, and Patrick O'Donaghue. Transported instead to Van Diemens Land (now Tasmania), he escaped to San Francisco, where, after an unsuccessful decade, he died and was buried. Months later he was disinterred for reburial in Ireland.

The idea of burying Terence MacManus in Dublin originated in Irish circles in California. James Stephens himself was initially opposed to it, apparently fearing that some hoped to use the funeral as a signal for a premature rising.[117] But Stephens soon moved decisively to take over the arrangements; he was greatly helped here by the activism of Thomas Clarke Luby. The opportunity for a great political funeral was created, evoking religious and national symbolism. At first, various nationalist groups worked together to repatriate MacManus's remains for burial; but once the remains arrived in Dublin, the Fenians took control of the arrangements. Cardinal Cullen prohibited the use of the Dublin churches, but nevertheless a massive crowd of some 50,000 people followed the coffin through the streets of Dublin to Glasnevin—the crowd heaved with emotion when it passed historic sites such as those associated with Robert Emmet's execution. At Glasnevin Father Patrick Lavelle's sermon was a scarcely veiled Fenian appeal.[118] In the *Irish People* it was proudly declared:

In the funeral of Terence Bellew Macmanus we have the struggle for the independence of Ireland forefigured. We see the people taking the initiative. We see the 'leaders' holding aloof from them, or endeavouring, in vain, to stop their onward march. We see them pre-organised, disciplined and obedient to authority. We see them in a word depending upon themselves alone, and assuming so proud an attitude that men of all classes fall into the ranks with them, and even genteel heads are uncovered as the cortège passes the spot where the head of Robert Emmet fell under the axe of the executioner. We saw all this while the people bore the dead patriot to the grave. So shall it be when they lift the living land to her rightful place

---

117 Joseph Denieffe, in Sean Ó Luing (ed.), *A Personal Narrative of the Irish Republican Brotherhood* (Shannon, 1969), 64.
118 Gerard Moran, 'The Radical Priest of Partry: Patrick Lavelle', in Gerard Moran (ed.), *Radical Irish Priests* (Dublin, 1998).

among the free nations of the earth. But woe to the people if they do not depend upon *themselves alone.*[119]

During the six months following the MacManus funeral the IRB doubled its numbers, and James Stephens worked hard to build up a revolutionary momentum. Despite the huge impact of the MacManus funeral, John O'Mahoney, the key figure of American Fenianism, felt that the American Civil War, which had begun in April 1861, imposed an inevitable delay on any plans for an insurrection in Ireland. But from November 1863 Stephens formed an alliance in Chicago with a more activist group of American Fenians; he went on a dramatic American political tour from March to August 1864, taking in many camps in the Union army, and won over many new recruits by his oratory. But Stephens was also preparing his own downfall: he was now arousing hopes of an imminent insurrection that he was in no position to satisfy. In particular, he fell into the habit of telling hardened Irish-American soldiers that in Ireland itself there was a serious Fenian military force prepared and ready to strike.

The Fenian threat was now giving the government serious cause for concern. The Irish Chief Secretary Sir Robert Peel's administration probably helped the Fenian cause. In the public mind Peel became associated with government heavy-handedness, leading to violence following the Longford by-election on 6 March 1862, which saw Myles O'Reilly returned to Parliament. The Dragoon Guards were employed, unnecessarily, some felt, to disperse a mob who were rather excited ('a great deal of exultation manifested')[120] by the victory of Major O'Reilly. On 7 April 1862 Chichester Fortescue, a rising star of Irish liberalism, recorded in frustration in his diary: 'Dined with the D of Newcastle. Talked Irish politics. He let out the idea which is Peel's—if he has any—that the true policy for the Govt is to gain the Irish Conservatives, a vain idea as I told him.'[121] The departure of Carlisle as Lord-Lieutenant, and the arrival in Dublin in November 1864 of the highly intelligent Lord Wodehouse (later the Earl of Kimberly, 1826–1902), was seen by some as a harbinger of a new conciliatory impulse. With the reappearance of violent separatism, it had become more important than ever for the Church to assist the development of a form of constitutional politics likely to generate popular support, and thus inoculate the more restless section of the laity against revolutionary—and

---

[119] Quoted in J. J. Rutherford, *The Secret History of the Fenian Conspiracy* (London, 1877), i. 175.

[120] *Irish Times*, 6 Mar. 1862.

[121] Osbert Wyndham Hewett, … *and Mr Fortescue, A Selection for the Diaries from 1851 to 1862 of Chichester, Fortescue, Lord Carlingford KP* (London, 1958), 157–64.

politically anticlerical infections of various kinds. The Church-inspired National Association of 1864 was the outcome of such preoccupations, and its programme of disestablishment, mild agrarian reforms, and better funding for Catholic education, represented 'a compromise between clerical ideals and the politics of the possible'.[122] The National Association's 'Great Aggregate Meeting' of December 1864 saw the launch of this new reformist venture, designed to marginalize Fenianism. The Great Aggregate meeting was attended by seven Catholic prelates and headed by Cardinal Cullen. Prominent liberals were present: Peter Paul MacSwiney, the Lord Mayor of Dublin; John Blake Dillon, a former Young Irelander and, after the 1865 general election, Liberal member of Parliament for Tipperary; W. J. O'Neill Daunt, one of O'Connell's secretaries and now a widely respected political figure; Sir John Gray, the Protestant proprietor of the *Freeman's Journal*, which was strongly pro-Catholic in its sympathies, and Liberal member for Kilkenny from 1865. Also present was J. F. Maguire, member for Cork and owner of the *Cork Examiner*. A letter was read from John Bright, suggesting that English Liberals were disposed to support church and land reform in Ireland.[123]

But still towering over the scene was the figure of Palmerston. In February 1865 the Premier offered his last major statement of Irish policy. He was still full of sympathy for the hard-working Irish: 'It is impossible for any man to know anything of the Irish people without wishing them every happiness, which can be confirmed among them. They are a light-hearted, warm-hearted race, they are most industrious too.'[124] But he insisted that tenant right would not have the 'slightest effect' in improving Ireland's fortunes. 'I may be allowed to say that I think it equivalent to landlord wrong. Tenant right, as I understand it, to be proposed would be little short of landlord confiscation.'[125] This formula, though not without a little ambiguity, was infuriating to Irish land reformers. More importantly, Palmerston offered his analysis of Irish woes: British capital was discouraged by the sectarian rhetoric of Irish society. Sadly, British capital did not fully realize that Ireland was a safe place to invest in and a country with substantial material and moral resources. However worthy Palmerston's ideas, they were certainly not the basis for a legislative programme.

Even with Palmerston gone, the relationship between British liberalism and Irish Catholicism was never an easy one. Cullen's dislike of Fenianism is obvious. He was even at times critical of the British government for treating

---

[122] K. Theodore Hoppen, *The Mid-Victorian Generation* (Oxford, 1998), 584.
[123] E. R. Norman, *The Catholic Church and Irish Politics in the Eighteen Sixties* (Dundalk, 1969), 9–10.
[124] *Hansard*, vol. 177, 24 Feb. 1865, col. 826.   [125] Ibid., col. 824.

the movement too leniently.[126] But Cullen also heartily disliked cosmopolitan liberal Catholics. This is the key to understanding why he disapproved of the ex-Young Irelander Bishop Moriarty's famously ferocious denunciation of the movement. Cullen was even prepared to commend privately Father Patrick Lavelle's critique of Moriarty;[127] remarkable indeed, when Cullen's disapproval of Lavelle's crypto-Fenianism is recalled. 'Catholics who mix with Protestants,' Cullen wrote privately in July 1865, 'are all hostile to us.'[128] In Cullen's mind, one great principle prevailed: 'The nationality of Ireland means simply the Catholic Church.'[129] Cullen was an opponent of secular nationalism, but he was himself a nationalist from a nationalist family. His uncle and namesake was shot in the wake of the 1798 rising, and his father, Hugh, was imprisoned in 1803 after Robert Emmet's rising, but acquitted by court martial.[130]

Cullen's farming father had been a tithe-resister in Kildare, and his uncle, the Revd James Maher, was an active political priest.[131] Cullen's pastoral of January 1868 could, after all, have been lifted from an editorial in the *Irish People*.

The country has lost more than three million inhabitants who have been obliged to brave the dangers of the wide Atlantic, in order to save themselves and their families from starvation. About 400,000 cottages of the poor have been levelled to the ground, lest they should ever again offer shelter to their former inmates. Many villages have been completely destroyed, and several towns, once busy and prosperous, are now almost abandoned and falling into ruin.

In the first flush of renewed enthusiasm for Irish reform, especially Irish church reform, English liberals preferred not to think about the underlying emotions which motivated their clerical allies.[132]

But despite the effort to reinvigorate constitutional reformism, for a while events moved in favour of Stephens. The ending of the American Civil War in April 1865 raised Fenian hopes of an imminent Anglo-American war. On 8 September 1865 Stephens sent out the message that 'this year—and let there be no mistake about it—must be the year of action'.[133] Yet, not all tempers were calmed. At the beginning of October 1865 Lord

---

[126] Cullen to Gladstone, 12 Mar. 1870, BL Ad Ms 44,425, f. 423.
[127] D. Bowen, *Paul Cardinal Cullen and the Shaping of Modern Irish Catholicism* (Dublin, 1983), 219–20.
[128] Ibid. 131.
[129] James Macaulay Fox, *Ireland in 1872: A Tour of Observation* (London, 1872), 81.
[130] Barr, *Cullen, Newman and the Catholic University*, 137.
[131] Desmond Keenan, *Ireland 1800–1850* (Philadelphia, 2002), 233.
[132] 'The Irish Church', *Quarterly Review*, 124: no 247 (Apr. 1868), 543.
[133] Frank Rynne, ' "Focus on the Fenians": The *Irish People* Trials, November 1865–January 1866', *History Ireland*, 13: 6 (Nov.–Dec. 2005), 44.

Lismore encountered the son of one of his tenants, who had returned home after twelve years in America. This man, now a colonel in the American army, possessed excellent revolvers of the latest design—provoking Lord Lismore's envy—and plenty of money, and was thought to be on a Fenian mission. It was a typical edgy moment: a vignette of Fenianism's subversive possibilities—'the whole conversation is of the Fenians, whether there will be a real outbreak'.[134] On 15 September the government decided to take action against the most obvious public target, the *Irish People*. The police raided the offices of the newspaper and arrested most of the key contributors—including Kickham, Luby, O'Leary, and O'Donovan Rossa. Stephens, however, was arrested at Sandymount on 11 November. He was lodged in Dublin's Richmond Prison on a charge of high treason. But within two weeks he had escaped, thus gaining a temporary aura of invincibility.

He made his way to New York, where he exploited his own enhanced prestige to raise expectations even higher. He also provoked a degree of ridicule by paying extravagant prices for hotel accommodation.[135] In February 1866 the government suspended the Habeas Corpus Act in Ireland and made hundreds of arrests, sapping the morale and efficiency of home-based Fenianism beyond repair. In April 1866 John O'Mahony, against his better judgement, reacted to divisions within Fenianism by permitting a Fenian escapade in North America, which backfired badly: an unsuccessful attempt to occupy, on behalf of the United States, the disputed island of Campo Bello in the Gulf of St Laurence. This was foiled by US forces without serious fighting. At the end of May 1866 a second Fenian assault was made on Canada by O'Mahony's factional rivals. A Fenian army under Colonel John O'Neill crossed the Niagara from Buffalo on 31 May; but they were forced to withdraw on 3 June. The authorities had been forewarned of the whole affair by Henri le Caron, who now established himself as the premier British spy within Fenian ranks.[136] Also in June 1866, the Reform Bill crisis brought the Tories into power in London until February 1868: with Derby as Prime Minister and Lord Naas (Earl of Mayo in 1867) as Chief Secretary, the Fenians faced even tougher adversaries. Michael Morris, a clever Catholic lawyer, elected in Galway, became Irish Solicitor-General. Fenianism was now facing failure on two fronts. No international crisis intervened to weaken Britain; a somewhat beleaguered

---

[134] Arthur Irvin Dasent, *John Thadeus Delane: Editor of the Times* (London, 1980), 146.

[135] *New York Tribune*, 1 Jan. 1867.

[136] Henri le Caron, *Twenty-Five Years in the Secret Service: The Recollections of a Spy* (London, 1893), 29–33.

Stephens was now forced to tell New York Fenians in December 1866 that another postponement was necessary. He was immediately deposed—the victim of the very expectations he had so sedulously raised. The 'teasing schizoid leadership' of Stephens ended in a 'welter of personal abuse'.[137] Even at such a moment of loss of face in Fenian affairs, it is worth noting that Chichester Fortescue wrote to J. T. Delane, the editor of *The Times*, on 6 December 1866: 'Conceive the curse it would be to have a body of moral force Fenians or Nationalists returned to Parliament.'[138] It was a sharp insight, in effect accepting both the degree of political support for Fenianism and its potential as an open activist movement rather than a military conspiracy. But the military conspirators were in the ascendant. The new leadership group was dominated by Thomas Kelly, a former captain in the US federal army, who had the rank of colonel in the American Fenian roster. In January 1867 Kelly and a number of supporters went to England, where they made contact with other impatient groups of Fenians, including the Mayo men, O'Connor Power and Michael Davitt. On 11 February there was an unsuccessful attempt to seize arms at Chester Castle: 1,000 English-based Fenians had turned out. The authorities had received advance warning from an Irish-American soldier and informer, J. J. Corydon—one of Stephens's most trusted agents, high in the confidence of the conspirators and deep in the pay of the government.[139] One detachment of Fenians, led by Michael Davitt (1846–1906), quickly grasped the fact that the authorities were forewarned and quietly and effectively melted away. There was also a premature Fenian outbreak in the Iveragh peninsula: an outbreak which incidentally provoked fear as well as support from the local population.[140] On 5 March 1867 the main Fenian rebellion at last began, met by the worst snowstorm in fifty years. But the leadership did, at least, manage to issue the Fenian proclamation of 1867. It expressed with great clarity a nationalist, democratic, and agrarian radical message:

[All] men are born with equal rights, and in associating to protect one another and share public burdens, justice demands that such associations should rest upon a basis which maintains equality instead of destroying it. We therefore declare that, unable any longer to endure the curse of Monarchical government, we aim at founding a republic based on universal suffrage, which shall secure to all the intrinsic value of their labour. The soil of Ireland in the possession of an oligarchy belongs to us, the Irish people, and to us it must be restored. We declare also in favour of absolute liberty of conscience, and complete separation of Church and State.[141]

---

137 Jackson, *Ireland 1798–1998*, 99.   138 Dasent, *Delane*.
139 A. M. Sullivan, *New Ireland* (London, 1877), 276.
140 'The Iveragh Fenians in Oral Tradition', in Maurice Harmon (ed.), *Fenians and Fenianism* (Dublin, 1968), 32.
141 Alan O'Day, *Irish Home Rule* (Manchester, 1998), 8.

There is little doubt that the anti-British monarchy and anti-landlord messages were popular; perhaps less so were the themes of separation of Church and State. The *Cork Examiner* editorialized: 'The numbers who actually rose were not large, but it would be the idlest farce to deny that they carried with them the sympathies of the masses.'[142] The *Spectator* in London admitted: 'The lower class, partly upon a worthy national feeling, partly from the base hopes excited by the Fenian promise to redistribute the soil, may be regarded as sympathising with the insurgents.'[143]

By the time of the March rising the authorities were more than adequately prepared: troop levels in Ireland had been increased and the necessary dispositions made. Regiments which had been infiltrated to any degree by the Fenians were moved out of the country. On the evening of 5 March 1867 poorly armed Fenians started heading out of Dublin towards Tallaght; the plan was to draw the military and police out into the mountains and then seize the city. Simultaneously, Fenians began to move from Cork City towards Limerick Junction. The plan here was to tear up the rails at Limerick Junction and seize the telegraph. The next step was to telegraph America, where a ship, *Erin's Hope*, filled with soldiers and arms, was to set sail for Ireland. The Fenians were unlucky with the weather: 'A perfect tempest of hail and snow swept the land.' The coincidence grimly reminded some of the 'historic records of the storm that wrecked the Spanish Armada and the hurricane that swept the French fleet out of Bantry Bay'.[144]

By the morning of 6 March both groups had either scattered or been taken prisoner. In Dublin, some men who had been arrested were released by the orders of the Lord-Lieutenant, the Duke of Abercorn. There were a few sporadic outbursts of physical-force activism elsewhere in the country, but most Fenians behaved as if they were there to bear witness of their loyalty to their comrades and to their cause; they did not act as people who seriously believed—in the absence of foreign aid or seriously complicating international factors—that they could take on the British army in Ireland. 'The insurrection, or attempted insurrection, of 1867 was one of those desperate and insensate proceedings into which men involved in a ruined cause sometimes madly plunge, rather than bow to the disgrace and dishonour of defeat without a blow.'[145]

In March 1867 the Fenians faced an enemy who possessed overwhelming advantages.[146] The British forces numbered some 50,000 men, including the police: they knew Ireland, and, indeed, many of the Fenian plans

---

[142] *Cork Examiner*, 20 Mar. 1867.   [143] *Spectator*, 9 Mar. 1867.
[144] Sullivan, *A. M. Sullivan*, 107–8.   [145] Sullivan, *New Ireland*, 273.
[146] S. Takagamli, 'The Fenian Rising in Dublin 1867', *Irish Historical Studies*, 39: 15 (May 1995), 362.

intimately, and they possessed that military self-confidence which comes from repeated victory in the field. If this was not enough, the British army had artillery; their opponents had not. A. M. Sullivan's brother, T. D. Sullivan, summarized the situation with some accuracy:

The rising, so long prepared and planned, and about which for a period of four or five years so great a noise had been made, perished without the occurrence of anything that could be dignified with the name of a battle against the military forces of the crown. This was not owing to any want of courage or determination on the part of the men who had taken the field ... They would have delighted and gloried in the chance of making a fight for Ireland, if it had been given to them. But they got no chance: they lacked every requisite of success except physical strength and courage; and it is simply absurd to suppose that under such circumstances any set of men can be got to stand up against the well equipped, thoroughly disciplined and skillfully led troops of a modern army. There are some things that are too much to expect from human nature, and this happens to be one of them.[147]

FENIANISM: FROM MILITARY ELITISM TO POPULAR POLITICS

Fenianism, in essence, was more of a socio-political protest movement than an insurrectionary army;[148] put to a military test, despite its cadre of tough Irish-American officers, it inevitably failed—1,000 Fenians fled, for example, in the face of fourteen armed and disciplined policemen at Tallaght. To prevent escape, the Fenians captured at Tallaght had their belts and braces cut; they presented an image of dejected humiliation when they arrived in the centre of Dublin, each holding up his trousers with both hands. Cardinal Cullen wrote to Archbishop Leahy in Cashel and expressed relief that the police had acted before troops arrived, probably saving many lives.[149] Simultaneously, thousands of Cork Fenians, who had set out for Limerick Junction, were scattered. In the following days there were minor incidents in counties Limerick, Tipperary, Clare, Louth, and Queen's County, but these were soon brought rather easily under control.

---

[147] Sullivan, *A. M. Sullivan*, 108.

[148] R. V. Comerford, 'Gladstone's First Irish Enterprise', in W. E. Vaughan (ed.), *A New History of Ireland*: vol. 5, *Ireland Under the Union* (Oxford, 1989), 439. For a critique of Comerford's important work, however, see John Newsinger, *Fenianism in Mid-Victorian Britain* (London, 1994), 83–90.

[149] Dom Mark Tierney (ed.), 'Calendar of the Papers of Dr Leahy, Archbishop of Cashel', NLI Ms' Cullen to Leahy, 14 Mar. 1867. Cullen's concerns were not unreasonable; Froude noted 'the exhortation of a leading Liberal journal to make an example of the rebels in the field, because executions afterwards were inconvenient', J. A. Froude, *Lord Beaconsfield*, 3rd edn. (London, 1890), 201.

In June, however, Thomas Larcom, a highly experienced official at Dublin Castle, was still writing nervously to the Lord-Lieutenant, the Duke of Abercorn: 'Things are on the surface quiet enough here—and the happy public begin to think Fenianism a thing of the past. It would be cruel to deceive them, and our effort must be vigilance to keep the enforced calm which now presides.'[150]

Larcom's letter to Abercorn implies a sense of an underlying latent political strength of Fenianism, even in the aftermath of military defeat. How strong was the Fenian movement, even at its high point? Stephens himself frequently claimed 100,000 members; but more realistic American Fenians acted as if the true figure was not more than 50,000.[151] Even on the basis of this reduced figure, Fenianism represented a formidable mass nationalism by any serious comparative European criteria. Some 1,600 Fenian members of the British army were brought before 150 courts martial in 1866. As a movement, Fenianism decidedly lacked weaponry. The largest possible number of firearms possessed by the Fenians in the summer of 1865 was 6,500. Formally a secret, oath-bound military conspiracy, it functioned rather differently. When T. C. Luby went to Britain on an organizational tour, he found himself speaking to large groups in public halls, but even at home in Ireland the organization was loose, porous, fraternal, and social in a way that made it easy for spies to penetrate. Even defined principally as a political-social mass movement, Fenianism had obvious deficiencies: in particular, it had too narrow a social basis. It appealed to a newspaper-reading, self-educated young male culture in the cities and small towns of Ireland; but it did not have quite the same appeal to the mass of the Irish people who lived on the land. When Disraeli succeeded to the premiership in place of the ailing Derby in February 1868,[152] he appointed Lord Naas Viceroy of India and replaced him with Colonel John Wilson Patten (later Lord Winmarleigh), despite, or perhaps because of, Patten's desperate plea that he neither deserved nor was qualified for the Irish post.[153] It all implies a certain confidence that the Fenian military threat was over. None of this should distract from the broader popular

---

[150] PRONI, T2549/VR/168, Larcom to Abercorn, 20 June 1867.

[151] This was the view, in July 1865, of the Irish-American Gen. F. F. Millen—soon to become a British spy. See Christy Campbell, *Fenian Fire* (London, (2002), 57.

[152] *Freeman's Journal*, 16 Mar. 1868; Sam Clark, *Social Origins of the Irish Land War* (Princeton, 1979), 203, gives an analysis of the occupational breakdown of a sample of Fenian suspects from a government index between 1866 and 1871. In this sample 8.5% were farmers or farmers' sons: 10.6% were general agricultural labourers—artisans and non-farm labourers constituted 44.7%. The British government was well aware of this fact, see *Freeman's Journal*, 16 Mar. 1868.

[153] H. J. Hanham, *Elections and Party Management: Politics in the Time of Disraeli and Gladstone* (Brighton, 1978), 297. I owe this reference to Dr Patrick Maume.

resonance achieved by the Fenian movement. A British government which failed to appreciate this was a government living in denial. Many Fenians throughout displayed an exemplary Catholic devotion: Irish public opinion was inevitably impressed. Peter O'Neill Crowley, the Fenian fatal casualty at Kilclooney, died, it was later claimed, with the following words on his lips: 'Father, I have two loves in my heart—one for my religion, the other for my country. I am dying today for my Fatherland. I could die as cheerfully for the Faith.'[154] The *Cork Examiner* at the time noted 'One of the stories mentioned in connection with the story of the Fenians' supposed residence in the woods—that they recited the Rosary every evening and that Edward Kelly, although a Protestant, joined in the prayers'.[155] One Fenian memoir records the reaction of the Cork crowd to the arrival of arrested Fenian prisoners in the city: 'Cheer after cheer, loud, long and enthusiastic, burst forth from the multitude mingled with voices such as "God bless the prisoners".'[156]

The *Spectator* offered a relatively sympathetic analysis when it declared: 'The mass of the Fenians are, no doubt, dupes, and ridiculous as it may seem that 103 linendraper's assistants should have quitted Dublin to declare war on the British Empire, still, there must be in men who risk life and liberty for an idea an element of nobleness.'[157] But one darker aspect of the Fenian legacy should not go unmentioned. Fenianism intensified sectarian animosities in Ulster, where it had a significant appeal to the Belfast Catholic working class.[158] Belfast was growing dramatically in the 1860s—from 121,602 inhabitants to 174,412, the largest increase since the first decade of the century. This expansion was based on the linen industry; the cotton famine generated by the American Civil War allowed linen to enter new markets. The shipbuilding industry, which by 1914 was responsible for almost 8 per cent of world output, had opened for business.[159] Belfast was characterized by a rather arrogant, albeit successful, industrial bourgeoisie: they provoked a desire in Fenians to prick their grand pride, a desire which, for some, was irresistible. The *Northern Whig*,

[154] John Devoy, *Recollections of an Irish Rebel* (Dublin, 1929), 216–17; but see also L. Broin, *Fenian Fever* (London, 1971), 161.

[155] *Cork Examiner*, 8 Apr. 1867, 'The Recent Affray in Kilclooney Wood'. Edward Kelly was buried in the Mount Hope Cemetery in the Roxbury district of Boston, where John O'Boyle Reilly erected a monument in the form of a round tower to his memory. Kelly had been a printer in New York.

[156] Casey, *The Galtee Boy*, 61.   [157] *Spectator*, 9 Mar. 1867.

[158] C. Hirst, *Religion, Politics and Violence in Nineteenth-Century Belfast* (Dublin, 2002), 98–103. See also T. McKnight, *Ulster As It Is* (London, 1896), i. 57; Frank Wright, *Two Lands on One Soil: Ulster Politics Before Home Rule* (Dublin, 1996), 274–83.

[159] F. Geary and W. Johnson, 'Shipbuilding in Belfast, 1861–1986', *Irish Economic and Social History*, 16 (1989), 43.

on 31 August 1865, carried a threat posted by C. M. O'Keefe, one of the more demagogic Fenian *littérateurs*: 'The moment the British government, at the suggestion of your paper, or at any other suggestion, suspends the Habeas Corpus Act, or seizes the leaders of the Irish Fenians, that moment the linen of Belfast will blaze to the skies of New York.'[160] Inevitably, the reaction of Belfast public opinion was one of outrage.

Despite the military collapse of the insurrection itself, Fenianism managed to generate a sense not only of anger, but also of fear in Belfast and throughout the United Kingdom. The growth of Fenianism was the essential 'backdrop' for the dramatic revival of loyalist activism in the North in the mid- and late 1860s. William Johnston emerged as the populist voice of this new assertiveness; forming an opportunistic alliance with the local liberal elite, he topped the poll in Belfast in 1868. Since the MacManus funeral in 1861 Johnston had gained political credibility by asking one question: 'If Nationalists are allowed such mobilisation, why were loyal Orangemen not to be allowed to march freely?'[161] In the end it was to prove a winning argument; in 1872 the Liberal government dropped the Party Processions Act.

But by this point the militarily defeated movement of Fenianism had also shown a marked resilience and capacity to affect the agenda. On 11 September 1867 Colonel Thomas Kelly and a fellow Fenian officer, Timothy Deasy, were arrested in Manchester. On 18 September they were taken in a police van from their jail in order to make a short, formal court appearance. This gave the Fenians the opportunity to attempt a dramatic rescue; the rescue-bid, while successful, was to have the most profound consequences. Thirty Fenians were involved in an operation which freed Kelly and Deasy but killed one of the prison guards. Twelve Fenian suspects were charged with involvement in the crime; in the end, three of the rescue party—Allen, Larkin, and O'Brien—went to the gallows on 23 November. The British government had avoided having Fenians sentenced to death in Ireland, but it was felt an example had to be made of those operating in England. At last, the Fenians had what the men of '48 lacked: martyrs, men whose bodies were destroyed by the British state, acting in cold blood. Irish popular sentiment was less than magnetized by the fate of the unfortunate Sergeant Brett, but insofar as the fate of the policeman was considered, it could easily be said that his death was an accident caused by a bullet fired at a

---

[160] T. D. Sullivan, *Recollections of Troubled Times in Irish Politics* (Dublin, 1905), 64–5.

[161] Sean Farrell, 'Recapturing the Flag: The Campaign to Repeal the Party Processions Act, 1860–1872', *Eire–Ireland*, 321 (1997), 55–8; PRONI, T 3314/1/92a Thomas Morris document, 30 July 1869, for a classic statement of the 'right to march doctrine'.

lock rather than at his person. It became a commonplace assumption of Irish nationalist public life that the actions of Allen, Larkin, and O'Brien did not constitute murder, but those of the British state did. The dignity and courage of the young Irishmen was contrasted scornfully with the degraded English crowd outside the prison, which had come to cheer their execution.[162] The song 'God Save Ireland', composed by their opponent T. D. Sullivan, was to become one of the most celebrated nationalist anthems. On 20 November Richard O'Sullivan Burke, who had organized Fenianism in the army of the Potomac before planning the Manchester rescue of Colonel Kelly, was arrested—a heavy blow to the movement.[163] The attempt to rescue O'Sullivan Burke was to have profound consequences.

On 13 December an explosion occurred at a House of Detention in the Clerkenwell suburb of London: the explosion failed in its objective of freeing O'Sullivan Burke and another Fenian held there. The authorities, who had advance knowledge of the plot, did enough to ensure that the two Fenian prisoners did not escape, but they incompetently allowed the bombing expedition to go ahead, with the result that the explosion not merely blew down the wall of the jail, but also demolished tenement houses on the opposite side of the street.[164] Twelve people were killed and 120 were maimed. Four people were arrested, one—Michael Barrett—was subsequently hanged for the bombing. The commander of the Fenian rescue party was a young Kerryman and Irish-speaker, Jeremiah O'Sullivan, who had been living in London for six years. O'Sullivan, a very fit 22-year-old, outran his police pursuers over five miles, finally escaping them by leaping across a stream; shortly thereafter he was smuggled away to the United States, where he was to die long afterwards in the Bronx at the age of 77.[165]

The initial reaction to Clerkenwell was one of shock. Even traditional sympathizers with the Fenians were alienated: and British reactionaries naively believed that, at last, all shades of British opinion would agree to a strictly repressive policy.[166] On 14 December 1867 Karl Marx wrote to his friend Friedrich Engels:

The last exploit of the Fenians at Clerkenwell was a very stupid thing. The London masses, who have shown great sympathy for Ireland, will be made wild by it and

---

[162] Gary Owens, 'Constructing the Martyrs: The Manchester Executions and the Nationalist Imagination', in Lawrence W. MacBride, *Images, Icons and the Irish Nationalist Imagination* (Dublin, 1999), 21–4.

[163] Lynch and O'Donoghue, *O'Sullivan Burke Fenian*, 132.

[164] Sir Robert Anderson, *Sidelights on the Home Rule Movement* (London, 1906), 74–9; *Gathorne-Hardy, First Earl of Cranbrook: A Memoir with Extracts from his Diary and Correspondence*, edited by the Hon. Alfred E. Gathorne-Hardy (London, 1910), 221–2.

[165] *Weekly Freeman*, 23 Dec. 1922; Campbell, *Fenian Fire*, 78–9.

[166] S. M. Ellis (ed.), *The Hardman Papers* (London, 1930), 298.

driven into the arms of the government party. One can not expect the London proletarians to allow themselves to be blown up in honour of the Fenian emissaries.

For Marx, however, Clerkenwell was no mere accident, but a tragedy rooted in the nature of Fenianism: 'There is always a kind of fatality about such a secret, melodramatic conspiracy.'[167] Engels agreed in a reply on 19 December: 'The stupid affair in Clerkenwell was obviously the work of a few specialised fanatics; it is the misfortune of all conspiracies that they lead to such stupidities because after all, something must happen, after all, something must be done.'[168]

The explosion threw London into an exaggerated state of panic: within a month over 50,000 special constables were recruited. One Irish counter-terrorism expert, Sir Robert Anderson, working in London, drily observed:

The teetotalers, their enemies say, throw off all restraint when they give way to a debauch; and the same remark applies to Englishmen when they give way to a scare. Even the Private Secretaries at Whitehall carried revolvers. And staid and sensible men gave up their evening engagements, and their sleep at night, to take their turn at 'sentry-go' as special constables. The lives of many of them were seriously imperilled, but it was by London fogs and not by Fenian plots.[169]

The Clerkenwell effect was not confined simply to one of widespread panic. Despite, or perhaps because of, all the moral outrage, there was a political dividend for the 'popular' cause in Ireland. W. E. Gladstone had, in the weeks before Clerkenwell, stated his firm desire to bring about the disestablishment of the Irish Church. Nevertheless, in his famous Midlothian campaign he openly proclaimed that it was the Clerkenwell explosion which brought that question within the sphere of practical politics.[170] Liberal MPs began to talk more loudly about the need for radical land reform in Ireland.[171] The bomb, which Marx and Engels saw as simply a self-inflicted disaster for Fenianism, was, in broader political terms, no such thing, for all the misery it brought down on the heads of the London Irish community.

Sir Robert Anderson recorded that the Fenians themselves initially were horrified by Clerkenwell, but soon changed their minds when they saw its impact: 'But when they discovered that by exploding a cask of gunpowder, they could throw not only the government but the country into hysteria, they rallied from their flight and got themselves profit by the lesson.'[172]

---

[167] Marx to Engels, 14 Dec. 1867: Marx and Engels, *On Ireland*, 149.
[168] Ibid.   [169] Anderson, *Sidelights*, 78.
[170] Charles Townshend, *Political Violence in Ireland: Government and Resistance Since 1848* (Oxford, 1983), 37.
[171] *Spectator*, 28 Dec. 1867.
[172] Robert Anderson, *The Lighter Side of my Official Life* (London, 1910).

English liberal opinion had been stirred. It did not like 'the spy system' which the collapse of insurrectionary Fenianism had revealed. In some cases, at least, liberals were confident that it amounted to a form of entrapment.[173] It hated the urban mob assaults on Irish communities in British cities which characterized the Fenian excitement: 'We think Bohemians and Wallachians infamous for their treatment of the Jews, but in what are they worse than the Englishmen, who sack a street because people of the same faith as its inhabitants have broken the law.'[174] The capriciousness of fear induced by Fenianism was said to reflect neatly the capriciousness of English rule in Ireland. Fenianism, therefore, was 'retributive'.

Nobody would be astonished to hear of an attempt in Balmoral, or that Mr Disraeli had been seized at Hughenden Manor, and spirited away from among his devoted farmers and labourers, or that a *coup d'état*, organised by Fenians, had occurred in New Zealand, or that the Irish Republic had been proclaimed in Sark.[175]

The divide between the main parties on the issue appeared to deepen. Lord Stanley argued that Ireland and England 'are inseparable now',[176] but Gladstone's tone was quite different: he began to talk about governing Ireland according to Irish ideas.[177] He was later to tell his Irish Lord-Lieutenant: 'I admit ... that the Fenian outrages and their overflow into England have had a very important influence on the question of the time for moving upon great questions of policy for Ireland.'[178] There were those in liberal England who felt they were being justly punished for a historic crime:

We confess there is something which strikes us as retributive ... Nothing can be more arbitrary and capricious than the English government there once was; and even now all its sins, or nature, all its deficiencies, partake of the same fault. The Irish tenant still complains that he has no security, no guarantee against the caprice of the landlord. The Irish priest complains justly enough that we capriciously apply one rule to the education of the English people and another to the education of the Irish.[179]

Even the conservative *Quarterly Review* was in self-critical mood: 'Ireland is the problem of problems to the English statesman.' The *Review* added grimly: 'No one can present its present condition as satisfactory. No one can consider its treatment up to Catholic emancipation as just.'[180] It called for a 'closer union' and rejected all colonial attitudes towards Ireland,

---

[173] *Spectator*, 24 Aug. 1867.
[175] Ibid., 21 Dec. 1867.
[177] Ibid., 30 Jan. 1868.
[179] *Spectator*, 21 Sept. 1867.

[174] Ibid., 22 June 1867.
[176] *Freeman's Journal*, 14 Jan. 1868.
[178] BL 44536 f. 152, 18 Apr. 1869.
[180] *Quarterly Review*, 124: 247 (1868), 257.

while worrying that Fenian disposition was a preference for Ireland to 'be governed badly by themselves'[181] rather than well by Englishmen. This argument was, naturally enough, reiterated in Ireland. Care was taken to disassociate the Irish sense of grievance from Fenianism, even though Fenianism had effectively highlighted it. According to the constitutionalists, 'In opposition to Fenians we say Ireland will be peaceful, happy and loyal if these wrongs be addressed'. It was simply a matter apparently of applying principles already applied in the rest of the United Kingdom:

Let Ireland be treated as Scotland was treated in the matter of religion and much will be done. Give Irishmen whose landlords pursue a far different system from that which is followed in England, a suitable adjudication of the existing tenure, and more will be done. Give Ireland an educational system on the English plan and still more will have been effected towards mutual good will between the countries.[182]

The rules of a new political game were slowly being formulated.

Gladstone had voted against Irish Church disestablishment in 1865; but in 1867 he now claimed that the Irish Church represented an injustice of which he had long been aware. Even his daughter Mary felt that there was inconsistency here, and later reproached her father on the point. His reply was instructive: 'He said that was quite different. Irish Church rotten, but nobody thought about it, dearth of political energy before Palmerston's death, if Palmerston had lived, Irish Church might not have been disestablished for years.'[183] It was, of course, the perfect issue to bind Liberals together[184] following the tactical defeats on electoral reform inflicted on them by Disraeli in 1866–7. As was often the case with Gladstone, self-proclaimed, long-term intellectual convictions turned out to be strikingly compatible with short-term tactical advantage. While Disraeli was still in office, Gladstone pushed motions on disestablishment through the Commons in 1868. Gladstone's opponents stressed the dangerous nature of this radicalism, and tried to insist that it was not a mere Irish clerical issue. Lord Redesdale declared:

It is the Church of a minority. Granted, but are the endowments which have belonged to it for centuries, to be disregarded because they belong to minorities? The land of the United Kingdom belongs to a minority smaller in proportion than that of the Churchmen of Ireland. Houses belong to a minority. All property

---

[181] *Quarterly Review*, 124: 247 (1868), 267.   [182] *Freeman's Journal*, 8 Jan. 1868.

[183] J. R. Vincent (ed.), *The Diaries of Edward Henry Stanley, 15th Earl of Derby 1826–1893, between 1878 and 1893* (Oxford, 2003), 817, diary entry for 22 Oct. 1885.

[184] Jonathan Parry, *Democracy and Religion: Gladstone and the Liberal Party 1867–75* (Cambridge, 1986), 269; P. M. H. Bell, *Disestablishment in Ireland and Wales* (London, 1969), 198–9.

belongs to a minority. The argument, if insisted on as sound, is destructive to the rights of property.[185]

Regardless, Gladstone built up a coalition of liberal Anglicans, Catholics, and British Nonconformists which swept all before it (outside Orange Lancashire) in the general election. As Thomas MacKnight pointed out: 'The country had been opposed on the question by Gladstone's opponents, and it returned him with a majority of 112 to support Irish disestablishment. The fact could not be gainsaid.'[186] For the British Nonconformists it was a remarkable example of a successful displacement of their complaints against the Church of England; for Irish Catholics (and even Irish Nonconformists) the issue was more substantive, a major source of irritation was removed. Gladstone's passionate Anglicanism—'he can not endure coarse creeds and Irish Catholicism is unquestionably a coarse creed'—was, in effect, turned against the Irish Protestant establishment. Precisely because the Prime Minister was perceived to be so sound theologically, his logical critique of the Irish Church's position was rendered all the more formidable: precisely because Disraeli had produced insufficient public evidence of deep religious conviction, he was less able to defend the Irish Church with effect.[187] Gladstone's May 1867 speech on the subject in the House of Commons was regarded as a classic: 'No speech ever made here shows more completely the triumph of the statesman over the natural bias of theological propaganda and social prepossession.'[188] Gladstone argued that a state church is properly the church *either* of the majority of a nation, or, if there be no such unity of faith among an absolute majority, then even of the majority of the poorest class of the nation. There was only one special purpose for which the religious endowments of Ireland were devoted—they were devoted to the Protestants of Ireland, who were well able to pay for their own teachers and teaching. Significantly, Gladstone refused to consider notions of concurrent endowment (providing state cash for a number of denominations) favoured by some Whigs and, at least, one liberal Irish Catholic bishop, Moriarty of Kerry, who feared that simple disestablishment would intensify sectarian animosity within Ireland.

The Church of Ireland lost some £16 million, though £10 million was returned. One remarkable aspect of the settlement was the decision to make available the 'balance' for non-religious causes: the relief of poverty, agricultural improvement, and higher education.[189] More important was

[185] Lord Redesdale, *Some of the Arguments by which Mr Gladstone's Resolutions are Supported Considered*, National Protestant Union (London, 1863), 1.
[186] MacKnight, *Ulster As It Is*, 184.   [187] Parry, *Democracy and Religion*, 271.
[188] *Spectator*, Irish Church debate, 11 May 1867.
[189] Bell, *Disestablishment in Ireland and Wales*, 110–212.

the psychological impact: the Archbishop of Dublin, Richard Whately, had warned as early as 1850 that an alienation of feeling was opening up between the Established Church in England and Ireland.[190] This was positive proof that he had been right to have such a fear.

Cullen licked his lips in anticipation of the long-term outcome, as he saw it, of disestablishment: 'If the plan now proposed to Parliament, and already adopted by the House of Commons, be put into operation, in 30 years we shall not have many Protestants in Ireland.'[191] It was, of course, precisely such anticipations that led the Revd Henry Cooke and the Orange forces into their last great campaign against disestablishment; but Irish liberalism, as well as English liberalism, held firm and the Gladstone measure became law on 26 July 1869.

Gladstone's conversion to the cause of disestablishing the Irish Church dismayed Trinity College, Dublin, generating a great sense of betrayal. However, one of Trinity's most able products, Isaac Butt, had produced his own solution to the crisis of patriotic Irish Toryism: in the autumn of 1868 Butt made his long-anticipated formal commitment in the cause of nationalism. The famine had visibly weakened Butt's unionism. His text, the *Famine on the Land* (1847), had argued bitterly that Irish property was being asked to carry the burden of Irish poverty—a clear impossibility: that the union meant Ireland shared the costs of an empire but was separate when the benefits were handed out.

In 1848 the *Cork Examiner* carried a story—derived from the *Evening Herald*—that Butt was 'about declaring himself Repealer'.[192] Butt certainly continued to modify his old Orange political tone. As a lawyer, he defended prominent Young Irelanders, including William Smith O'Brien and Gavan Duffy, with immensely suggestive language: 'I would be ashamed if I allowed political differences to prevent me from recognising sincerity, patriotism and truth ... The object of Mr Duffy's political life was this—to unite and combine all classes, creeds and denominations of Irishmen—to restore the Constitution of 1782.'[193] Later he added, even more decisively: 'We were told, when the union was carried, if an Irishman went off to England, he would be received there with great cordiality, all the distinction of race being forgotten. Is it so? You know that is not ... since the period of the union, the [national] character ... has deteriorated.'[194] He was now refuting in public the Burkean unionist language of his 1843 debates with O'Connell.[195] In the 1850s Butt was still, however, trapped within the coils of a romantic

    [190] PRONI T2772/2/6/47B, Beresford Papers, Whateley to the Archbishop of Canterbury, 12 Dec. 1850; also Froude, *Disraeli*, 206–7.
    [191] E. Larkin, *The Consolidation of the Roman Catholic Church in Ireland 1860–70* (Chapel Hill and London, 1987), 89.
    [192] *Cork Examiner*, 5 Apr. 1848.   [193] Isaac Butt, *The Irishman*, 14 Apr. 1849.
    [194] *Cork Examiner*, 17 May 1848.   [195] Ibid.

Toryism: not to mention personal, financial, and sexual problems. It was the Fenianism of the 1860s that gave the decisive impetus to his political transformation. In 1865 Butt, on the eve of losing the Youghal seat to Sir Joseph McKenna, declared in the midst of the Fenian crisis: 'I am not a rebel; I am loyal, but I would fling my silk gown to the wind if I was told that I could not sympathise with a man who would die for Ireland.'[196] Sympathy for Young Irelanders might be excused in a gentleman; sympathy for Fenians placed Butt far more decisively outside the bounds of social acceptability. As with Young Ireland, he used his legal skills to defend Fenians before the courts and then threw himself into the agitation for an amnesty, with the foundation of the Amnesty Association in 1870. Later he was to say: 'Mr Gladstone said that Fenianism taught him the depth of Irish disaffection. It taught me more. It taught me the depth, the passionateness and sincerity of the love of liberty and of fatherland which misgovernment had turned into disaffection.'[197]

On 12 November 1868 Isaac Butt presided over an amnesty meeting at the Mechanics Institute (later the Abbey Theatre) in Dublin. Behind Butt there stood the formidable figure of John Nolan, Secretary to the Amnesty Association, a former journalist, clerk, trade-unionist, and a member of the IRB Supreme Council. The skill and organizing power of John Nolan had built up 'a mass movement of strength unknown in Ireland since O'Connell'.[198] The government was soon aware of the mood of Irish public opinion. At the beginning of the new year 1869 Lord O'Hagan, the Irish Lord Chancellor, wrote to Lord Spencer urging that he consider a programme of early release for Fenian prisoners.[199] Gladstone wished to see a more rapid release of Fenians, but was to be frustrated by the more cautious attitude elsewhere in Dublin Castle.[200] The key here was Spencer's attitude. At the end of 1869 he wrote to the Duke of Cambridge, the Commander-in-Chief, that 'there is very general disaffection and uneasiness in the country'. He was concerned that Fenianism still existed as an organization. The Fenians suffered from a serious lack of weaponry and another rising 'would be the act of lunatics, but they are not much more reasonable'.[201] As long as the lingering fear of another insurrection persisted—a fear strong

[196] Ibid., 8 July 1865.   [197] Ibid., 19 Nov. 1873.
[198] P. S. O'Hegarty, introduction to *Devoy's Post Bag, Vol. 1*, ed. W O'Brien and Desmond Ryan (Dublin, 1948), 1; Owen McGee, *The IRB: The Irish Republican Brotherhood from the Land League to Sinn Fein* (Dublin, 2005), 40.
[199] PRONI D-2777/8/6, O'Hagan to Spencer, 7 Jan. 1869.
[200] P. Bull, 'Gladstone, the Fenian Prisoners and the Failure of his First Irish Mission', in Philip Francis (ed.), *The Gladstone Umbrella: Papers Delivered at the Gladstone Centenary Conference* (Hawarden, 2002), 98–114.
[201] NLI Ms 241889, Spencer to the Duke of Cambridge, 30 Nov. 1869.

enough to lead to a significant strengthening of the Crown forces in Ireland in late 1869[202]—the prospect for early release of the 'military' Fenians, at least, was bound to be prejudiced, though 'non-militant' Fenians were amnestied from February 1869 onwards. Spencer retained this caution well into the autumn of 1870.[203] In fact, thirty-three important prisoners, such as John Devoy, O'Donovan Rossa, John O'Leary, Thomas Clarke Luby, Dennis Downing Mulcahy, and William Mackey Lomasney, were not released until January 1871.

Less threatening figures were, however, released. On 22 February Chichester Fortescue announced an amnesty for forty-nine of the eighty-one non-military Fenian convicts; in March 1869 this group, including C. J. Kickham, J. F. X. O'Brien, and James O'Connor, were freed. At the banquet for this first batch of Fenian prisoners at Hood's Hotel in Dublin, Butt made a stunningly effective, highly emotional speech. He appealed to the released Fenian leaders to give him a chance to try other methods. Butt added that, if he failed, 'his arm and his life' would be placed at their service. Not surprisingly, he then had to plead with a young cub reporter from Cork, William O'Brien, to burn his notes of the speech.[204] Butt's caution was fully justified. At a Cork banquet given for two released Fenian convicts on 27 April, the Mayor of Cork, Daniel O'Sullivan, attributed 'noble' and 'patriotic' feelings to the Fenians executed in 1868 for an attack on the Duke of Edinburgh, son of the Queen, in Sydney: on 11 May the unfortunate O'Sullivan felt compelled to resign, as in the ensuing furore the House of Commons moved towards legislation to disqualify him. Within days of Gladstone's letter of reproof censuring the ongoing agitation to Butt in November 1869, a convicted Fenian felon, O'Donovan Rossa, won a Tipperary parliamentary seat on 27 November. As Thomas MacKnight observed, the election of O'Donovan Rossa was a significant reply to the Prime Minister's letter. For Denis Caulfield Heron, this must have been an ironic moment. He had, after all, excellent anti-establishment credentials; but in this election he was seen as the establishment Whig candidate. Heron had been a Catholic scholarship boy, in 1843 refused by Protestant Trinity College, who had then successfully sued the college. He was then notably pro-land reform, a defender of tenant-right ideas against the tide of the 1850s,[205] and a critic of Hancock's post-famine economic optimism. Yet

---

[202] NLI Ms 241889, Spencer to the Duke of Cambridge, 27 Dec. 1869.

[203] Sean McConville, *Irish Political Prisoners 1848–82* (London, 2003), 242–3.

[204] William O'Brien, *Recollections* (London, 1905), 138.

[205] D. Caulfield Heron, *Should the Tenant of Land Possess the Property of the Improvements Made By Him?*, a paper read before the Dublin Statistical Society on Friday, 23 April, and on Monday, 17 May 1852 (Dublin, 1852), 7; Peter Gray, 'Political Economy and the Memory of the Great Famine', in id. (ed.), *Victoria's Ireland*, 160.

he now found himself on the wrong side of 'popular' feeling. William O'Brien, a young nationalist radical, has recorded his own surprise that 'the sober-sided farmers of Tipperary should face the anger of their priests' by returning O'Donovan Rossa, 'who was that evening forced to consume his supper while his hands were chained behind his back' in an English police station.[206] But, surprising or not, Rossa won by 1,131 votes, to 1,028 for Heron: 'The most startling event of modern Irish history', declared the *Irish Times*.[207]

Interestingly, in 1869 the meetings held to demand amnesty for Fenian prisoners were heavily concentrated in Munster (twenty-seven meetings with 595,000 attending) rather than Connaught (seven meetings with only 94,000 attending).[208] Perhaps because he felt that he was not confronted by a truly 'national movement', Gladstone remained convinced that he could yet control Irish public opinion. But, in truth, he had little reason for such optimism. When Denis Caulfield Heron finally defeated a new Fenian candidate, Charles Kickham, *The Times* noted realistically on 1 March 1870 that Kickham's health was to blame: 'Had Kickham only been able to show himself among the people prior to the election, he would have been the member for Tipperary by a considerable majority.'

Gladstone, however, hoped that a judicious land reform might transform the public mood. In the late 1860s it was widely and conventionally argued that the Irish tenantry lacked security of tenure. But how did this square with realities in rural Ireland? As post-famine society stabilized, the number of evictions had dropped radically: in 1866 there were 596, and in 1869 some 309.[209] On 2 December 1868 the Earl of Dufferin, a prominent liberal Irish landlord, wrote to the Duke of Argyll: 'There is a slight decrease in the number of smallholdings in Ireland ... There is no doubt a certain amount of consolidation going on, but it is effected with great caution and has ceased, I think, to form an item in the accusations brought against the landlords.' Why, then, the popular focus on insecurity of tenure? In part because, as Isaac Butt observed in a direct riposte, Dufferin could not actually prove that the process of consolidation had reached a 'terminus';[210] in part also, the theme of insecurity remained as a means of maintaining a critical focus on the absolute power which, in theory, the Irish landlord

---

[206] O'Brien, *Recollections*, 104.   [207] *Irish Times*, 26 Nov. 1869.
[208] K. Theodore Hoppen, 'Landlords, Society and Electoral Politics in Mid-Nineteenth Century Ireland', in C. H. E. Philpin (ed.), *Nationalism and Popular Protest in Ireland* (Cambridge, 2002), 288.
[209] W. E. Vaughan, *Landlords and Tenants in Mid-Victorian Ireland* (Oxford, 1994), App. 1, pp. 230–1.
[210] Isaac Butt, *The Irish People and Irish Land* (Dublin, 1807), 134–6; PRONI D1071/18/13.

possessed. As *The Nation* acknowledged in 1870, it was a matter of the 'extremes' of legal tyranny rather than actual practice.[211] In Butt's words, the Irish peasantry carried a burden greater than 'the heaviest yoke of feudal servitude':[212] they were serfs to those regarded as alien in blood, religion and sentiment.[213]

In an influential series of letters in the *Spectator*, J. J. Murphy argued: 'The agrarian difficulty consists in this, that the descendants whose property in the land of Ireland was confiscated at the time, or in most cases before the time of William III', do not accept the 'justice of the present settlement of property', but dream of 'reconfiscation'.[214] Those who opposed the reformist path in Ireland rejected such arguments. Lord Redesdale declared: 'It is false and unjust to the Irish people to hold that they are slaves to the sentimental nonsense of being a conquered race.' But even Redesdale added: 'That feeling does not trouble them, unless they are told by their leaders that they should cry about it to serve a political purpose.'[215] The point being, of course, that this was precisely what Irish 'leaders' were telling their people. An anonymous landlord contributor to the *Country Gentleman's Magazine* put it more sharply, when he described the mentality and culture of the Irish tenant: he is told that 'he was born for better things; that the blood of the O'Hagan or O'Flaherty flows in his veins, and that, when right and justice to Ireland are established, every man will have his acre to enjoy'.[216] The English system of land was tolerable in England, because the aristocracy was in 'normal' harmony with the people. In Ireland, however, matters were very different. J. J. Murphy concluded:

I will only remember that the question can not be solved if you persist in supporting the landlords' views of the rights of property. They will cling with desperate tenacity to the right of arbitrarily evicting the tenants and confiscating his improvement: few of them do this, but they will not voluntarily give up the power of doing it, and it is the possibility of this being done that makes the tenants' position so unhappy.[217]

It was a matter of limited possibility, not probability, but it was a sore point for all that.

J. S. Mill published *England and Ireland* in February 1868, helped by his Irish friend J. E. Cairnes; it constituted a firm statement of the need

---

[211] *The Nation*, 4 June 1870.   [212] Ibid. 8.   [213] Ibid. 11.

[214] *Spectator*, 16 Nov. 1867.

[215] *Some of the Arguments by which Mr Gladstone's Resolutions are Supported Considered*, 3.

[216] *Country Gentleman's Magazine* (Oct. 1868), a practical view of the Irish land question in five chapters, ch. 2, p. 330.

[217] *Spectator*, 16 Nov. 1867.

for reform.[218] Mill, like Cairnes, remained a firm believer in the union: 'It is my conviction that the separation of Ireland from Great Britain would be undesirable for both, and that the attempt to hold them together by any form of federal union would be unsatisfactory while it lasted, and would result either in reconquest or complete separation.'[219] But such a consideration implied the necessity for British politicians to meet the Irish peasantry's needs, before they allied with the British working class to support some dangerous destabilizing project.

When a country has been so long in possession of full power over another as this country has had over Ireland, and still leaves it in the state of feeling which now exists in Ireland, there is a strong presumption that the remedy required must be much stronger and more drastic than any which has yet been applied ...

Mill told the House in March 1868.[220] Even more importantly, Sir Charles Trevelyan passed on to Gladstone George (later Sir George) Campbell's privately printed pamphlet on Irish land, a pamphlet which utilized Campbell's Indian experience of customary tenures to convince Gladstone that custom could be a basis for his Land Bill. Campbell, even more convincingly than Mill, argued that a truly responsible policy in Ireland involved recognizing the force and virtuousness of the peasantry's historic sentiments towards the land.

George Campbell argued that Irish landlords were only 'in theory' absolute owners; both in the north, but also in the south of Ireland, landlords had been compelled to recognize a kind of tenant interest in the soil, an interest which had a tacit monetary exchange value.[221] Campbell stated that a defining moment had been reached in Ireland's agrarian history:

In the last few years the process of what may be called consolidation has reached its limits—the demand for land has again become great—the tenant right has become as valuable as ever, or more valuable than ever—landlords can no longer get rid of tenants or get possession of land on easy terms—any attempt to get rid of the occupiers otherwise than by buying them out, at very onerous rates, is very fiercely resisted.[222]

The point endlessly reiterated was that it was necessary to end the sense of uncertainty: although evictions were rare, the fact remained that 'there seems to be on many estates a constant struggle between a growing tenant

[218] E. D. Steele, *Irish Land and British Politics: Tenant Right and Nationality* (Cambridge, 1974), 55.
[219] Quoted in Peter Kerr-Smiley, *The Peril of Home Rule* (London, 1911), 68.
[220] Stefan Collini, *Public Moralists: Political Thought and Intellectual Life* (Oxford, 1991), 164.
[221] G. C. Campbell, *The Irish Land* (London, 1869), 8, 117.   [222] Ibid. 40.

right and a desire of the landlords to get the whip hand over the tenants'.[223] 'Rare as evictions now are, there seems to be present in every Irishman's mind the image of the typical case: a peasant farmer who has built his home, improved the land, begotten children, and is then turned out on the roadside at the arbitrary will of a landlord.'[224] Campbell, in fact, was a little disappointed by Gladstone's legislation; this reflected the impact of Chichester-Fortescue, the Irish Chief Secretary, who was more cautious on the land issue. There is no doubt, however, that the Prime Minister had been influenced, as he publicly acknowledged, by Campbell's book.[225]

What was the basis of Gladstone's engagement, and why was it possible to invest such hope in the 1870 legislation? The thinking behind the 1870 Act was intense and serious. Gladstone had become emotionally involved in the issue. His letters to Cabinet colleagues on the subject were 'eloquent', but also displayed a 'huge pressure of feeling'.[226] Gladstone argued, correctly, that a form of tenant right had come to be respected over large parts of Ireland, not just Ulster.[227] The Poor Law Inspectorate of 1869 had confirmed the Devon Commission's view on the point: departing tenants sold their tenant right to the incoming purchaser. In Gladstone's theory, legislative respect for tenant right could so enhance the value of the land by stimulating better cultivation that higher levels of rent and tenant-right values would be likely. Argyll was sceptical that a small farming economy like Ireland would have the capacity to achieve such a dramatic expansion of production. Certainly, free sale of tenant right was largely irrelevant to the small farmers in many areas of the west. These appear to have been more anxious to cling to their holdings at any cost, than to secure a 'free sale' of their interest, even where tenant right existed.[228] But there was now no stopping Gladstone—who was further pushed along the path by a persuasive article by John Cairnes; John Bright made sure the Premier saw it.[229]

There was certainly much hope invested in the new legislation. In May 1870 W. E. H. Lecky, for example, thought that to 'pass Gladstone's Land

[223] G. C. Campbell, *The Irish Land* (London, 1869), 126.   [224] Ibid. 102.
[225] Campbell, *The Progress of the Land Bill* (London, 1870), 3–5, Gray, *The Peculiarities of Irish Land Tenure*, 155.
[226] PRONI D1071/18/13/C05, Argyll to Dufferin, 4 Dec. 1869.
[227] Steele, *Irish Land and British Politics*, 9. James McKnight, the great advocate of Ulster tenant right, explained to Gladstone that 'Ulster custom' was simply the outgoing tenant's 'prescriptive right' to dispose of his interest to any tenant purchaser, McKnight to Gladstone, 11 Mar. 1870, Ad 44,425, p. 238.
[228] Joseph Lee, 'Gladstone and the Landlords', *Times Literary Supplement*, 9 May 1975.
[229] H. G. C. Matthew (ed.), *The Gladstone Diaries: With Cabinet Minutes and Prime-Ministerial Correspondence*, vol. 7 (Oxford, 1982), 5 Jan. 1870, p. 212.

Bill is now the best thing to be done and that the country be left alone to right itself'.[230] Lecky wrote to his cousin Charles Bowen on 14 March 1870:

Of course, this Bill interferes a great deal with that freedom of contract which political economists have preached, though not at all more than the English Factory Bills, which have been among the most successful branches of modern legislation. But I think the majority of people have come to the conclusion that the social, political and agricultural condition of Ireland is such that some special and, if you like, paternal legislation for Ireland is necessary; and, if this postulate be granted, I think, the present Bill as a whole is moderate, honest and comprehensive.[231]

The Landlord and Tenant (Ireland Act) 1870 in Section 1 gave the force of law to the customary tenant of Ulster and Section 2 legalized similar rights elsewhere in the country. It provided for compensation for disturbance of tenants evicted other than for non-payment of rent, and made provision for compensation for improvements in the case of a departing tenant. At John Bright's insistence, 'some mouse-like clauses were added, providing assistance for those wishing to purchase their holdings'.[232]

The ninth clause of the 1870 Land Act turned out to have a major important implication—one that was not fully visible for a decade. It offered a limited protection for small tenants paying an annual rent of £15 or under. In such a case, provided that it could be said that the 'eviction has arisen from the rent being an exorbitant rent', then the landlords could be challenged in the courts as guilty of 'disturbance'. But most small tenants, of course, lacked the funds to go to the courts—until, that is, the advent of the Land League in 1879 and its team of lawyers, financed by Irish-American cash. John Morley accurately described the long-term meaning of the 1870 Act: 'What seemed so simple, and what was so necessary, marked in truth a vast revolutionary stride. It transferred to the tenant a portion of the absolute ownership and gave him something like an estate in his holding.'[233] Gladstone was so pleased with his handiwork that he began to fear that the Fenians would be driven to make a 'real attempt'[234] simply to thwart the benign effects of his legislation.

The years after the 1870 Act did see some reduction in the level of eviction: in the decade 1860–9 there were 9,671 evictions; in the decade 1870–9 there were 6,857. There was one clear advantage which accrued to the tenantry: of the 3,625 tenants evicted between 1871 and 1876, about

230 NLI Ms. 18490, Robert McDonnell, Ms Lecky note dated 20 May 1870.
231 Elisabeth Lecky, *A Memoir of W. E. H. Lecky* (London, 1909), 66.
232 Hoppen, *The Mid-Victorian Generation*, 596.
233 John Morley, *Life of Gladstone* (London, 1903), ii. 294.
234 BL Add MS 44538 f. 79, Gladstone to Spencer, 17 Feb. 1871.

one-third got some sort of compensation—about £86 each on average.[235] Landlords insisted that the fact that the Act had so little impact on rural realities showed that it was irrelevant for advancing the public good, whilst on the other hand it had decisively weakened the necessary rights of property. Lord Derby, who had expected the Act actually to increase the pace of consolidation in 1870, sold his Irish estate in 1872 because he became convinced that it was becoming impossible to influence the behaviour of tenants on even small matters, due to the 'general disaffection'.[236] Tenants and their spokesmen, however, insisted that experience merely proved the inadequacy of the 1870 legislation: that it was all too easy for landlords to evade the spirit of the legislation by raising rents or introducing new restrictive leases. Nevertheless, having pushed through legislation which breached the absolute rights of property in an important and symbolic way, Gladstone began to show the first signs of a certain war-weariness on the Irish issue: an irritation, at least, with apparent Irish ingratitude and insatiability. For it soon became clear that Ireland did not regard the 1870 Act as a final settlement. Irish disaffection continued to be a fact of life; Gladstone was aware that some (including the Queen) exploited the continuing malaise to question the whole basis of his reforming policy. Agrarian crime affected Westmeath and parts of Longford, Meath, and Kings' County in the early 1870s, provoking much alarmed commentary on Ribbonism.[237]

ISAAC BUTT AND THE CASE FOR HOME RULE

In April 1870 George Henry Moore died suddenly at his home, Moore Hall, leaving Butt centre-stage, with no real rival for the constitutionalist nationalist political leadership. Butt reached his final political resting-place and launched the Home Rule movement at a private meeting the following month at Bilton's Hotel in Dublin. But even as he moved forward, Butt reached backwards toward the elements of his own political past. Butt was desperately keen to see Protestants of substance rally to his cause. He could count on old-style Protestant nationalists like John Martin (elected Member for Meath in 1871 against a clerically supported Catholic gentry

[235] Vaughan, *Landlords and Tenants in Mid-Victorian Ireland*, 100–1.

[236] J. R. Vincent (ed.), *The Diaries of Edward Henry Stanley, 15th Earl of Derby, 1826–1893*, between September 1869 and March 1878 (London, 1994), entries for 16 June 1870, p, 62; 1 Jan. 1872, p. 95.

[237] Brian Griffin, *Sources for the Study of Crime in Ireland* (Dublin, 2005), 37; A C Murray, 'Agrarian Violence and Nationalism in Nineteenth-Century Ireland: The Myth of Ribbonism', *Irish Economic and Social History*, 13 (1986), 71; Froude, *Disraeli*, 211.

opponent) to join the cause, but he hoped also for new recruits, based on novel elements in the political conjuncture.

Butt hoped to capitalize on Protestant resentment against Gladstonian reforms such as disestablishment and land reform; but this was always an issue of ambiguity. In effect, Butt was asking Protestants—annoyed by Gladstone's reforms—to take a grand leap towards acceptance of the idea that their best interests were best served by close collaboration with that very Irish Catholic democracy which had pushed Gladstone into these reforms. Colonel King-Harman later recalled the early days of the Home Rule movement as attracting 'a substantial group of leading merchants and magistrates—bankers and men who had a good deal at stake in the country, men, who, one and all, scouted the idea of separation'.[238] It was easier and more imperative for the intellectual and social elite of Protestantism—those conservative newspaper-owners, Trinity College professors, and *engagé* landowners—who did attend the private meeting in Bilton's Hotel to grasp the Home Rule concept than it was for more plebeian loyalists. But, of course, not everyone involved with Home Rule did 'scout' the idea of separation. O'Connor Power, who was on the Supreme Council of the IRB, persuaded that body to allow parliamentary action a trial.[239] The influential J. J. O'Kelly also supported the new policy.[240] J. G. Biggar, who was on the same body, supported Power, and they were followed by John 'Amnesty' Nolan into Parliament. However, the IRB appears to have regarded this as a trial period of only three years. Butt seems to have given such an understanding in 1873, and therefore his time-limit expired in 1876. Hostile Fenians broke up a meeting held by O'Connor Power and his ally, Joseph Biggar, in Manchester in that year, and in August 1877 both men were formally expelled from the IRB.[241] Many Fenians continued to operate in the 'open' political sphere. The Home Rule movement was an unstable 'mix', the 'respectable' and eventually conservative mixed up with more radical, even subversive, elements: even Colonel King-Harman, soon to return to a more conventional Toryism, allowed the Fenian Patrick Egan to write his election manifesto in 1870.

Gladstone was increasingly exasperated. He insisted that no one had explained how a Home Rule parliament could pass good legislation for Ireland, which the Westminster Parliament could not pass with equal effect

---

[238] *Evening Standard*, 2 June 1886.

[239] 'Memoirs of an Old Mayo Fenian in Colorado', *Irish Tribune*, 30 Apr. 1926.

[240] James McConnell, 'Fenians at Westminster: The Edwardian Irish Parliamentary Party and the Legacy of the New Departure', *Irish Historical Studies*, 24: 133 (May 2004), 49.

[241] *The Speaker's Handbook on the Irish Question*, by an Irish Liberal (London, 1890), 14.

and satisfaction.[242] This was his message when he accepted the freedom of Aberdeen in July 1871. Gladstone's speech at Aberdeen infuriated Irish nationalists. He had pointed out, for example, that more Welsh than Irish spoke the Celtic tongue. The Prime Minister dismissed the concept of Home Rule as 'very unintelligible' and 'superfluous': 'The momentary sympathy of a particular constituency.' But such language utterly failed to demoralize the leaders of the new movement; in fact, it opened the door to an obvious rebuttal—what if Home Rule proved to be more than the momentary sympathy of a particular constituency? John Francis Maguire MP declared: 'Once let the number of Irish members *pledged to home rule* reach the figure of 70—and Mr Gladstone will ... be very likely to make the "delusion" a Cabinet question.'[243]

Butt was elected for Limerick City in a by-election in September 1871. On 14 November 1871 he formally replied to Gladstone in Glasgow: 'A nation, as Mr Gladstone tells you, and as all experience tells you, does not complain for nothing. It ought to be the first element in all political philosophy that, when a nation is universally discontented, its government must be wrong, and the only remedy from that discontent is to alter the government that creates it.'[244] R. P. Blennerhasset, a Protestant squire and home-ruler just down from Oxford, defeated a Catholic Liberal candidate, backed by Moriarty, in a Kerry by-election in February 1872. One observer later recalled: 'I can still hear the pretty academic drawl of the candidates' "Howm Rule for Ayland" and the full-mouthed, full-hearted "Howm Rool" which was shouted back by the multitude in the delightful music of the broad Kerry Doric.'[245] There was little doubt that the tide was flowing Butt's way. Why? Undoubtedly some Protestant 'gentlemen' were stimulated by the disestablishment of the Church to move towards Home Rule politics. But the real causes were deeper and rooted in the anomalous nature of the union itself. In a powerful article in *Fraser's Magazine*—which was widely reprinted in Ireland—James Anthony Froude insisted that 'Gladstone's system has broken down'.[246] He argued that Home Rule deserved to be taken seriously and that Ireland was capable of self-government. Gladstone himself was largely unaware of such a possibility. He told John Martin in the House of Commons that he was confident he could defeat him in the favour of his fellow countrymen.[247]

[242] O'Brien and Ryan (eds.), *Devoy's Post Bag*, i. 76.
[243] John Francis Maguire, *Home Government for Ireland: Being a Series of Articles reprinted from the Cork Examiner* (Dublin, 1872), 37–8.
[244] *Speech of Isaac Butt Esq. MP at Glasgow, 17 November 1871 on Home Rule for Ireland* (Dublin, 1871), 7.
[245] O'Brien, *Recollections*, 143.   [246] Repr. in *Cork Examiner*, 4 Sept. 1873.
[247] O'Brien, *Recollections*, 147.

Froude was displaying a more acute insight here. The very moderation and social conservatism of Isaac Butt's proposals for Home Rule have drawn attention away from the radicalism of his critique of the working of the union. Butt was a conservative rather than a liberal; a federalist, and not even remotely a separatist. But he grasped, in a way which Gladstone failed to grasp, the depth of the crisis of the union experiment, made all the more clear, in some ways, as Butt himself pointed out, by the way in which Gladstone's undoubted good intentions towards Ireland had done nothing to alleviate Irish alienation. Butt reminded English readers that the union had arisen out of the crisis of 1798, in which apparent Irish disloyalty posed serious questions for the security of Britain. But this problem of security still existed as acutely as ever. In 1871 Butt observed: 'We were told the union would render an invasion of Ireland impossible, but would an enemy be worse received by many of the people now than in 1798?'[248] In 1874 he returned to the point:

But one thing I do know, that if a war, such as it is at least possible, does arise, and if England does go into that war with the guilt of Ireland's oppression hanging like a millstone around her neck, and the cause of Irish disaffection weakening her arm, the boldest may well look with trembling to the effect on her greatness of that struggle.[249]

Butt effectively set out to answer the question posed by J. W. Croker's celebrated article in the *Quarterly Review* of 1848: why was Britain perceived to be such a failure in Ireland, given its good intentions and close ties? He provided an answer which Croker might well have accepted. The Anglo-Irish 'community of social interest' or the 'community of property' (to use two of Croker's phrases) which underpinned the attempt to create a political community under the union had been shattered by the 1832 Reform Act. The automatic grip of landed property on political power was decisively weakened; the impact of such a development being, however, considerably more profound in Ireland than Britain. In this sense, Croker had been right to say that the Reform Act made Irish separation inevitable.[250] Butt acknowledged Croker's point that there had, indeed, once been a community of social interest and 'property' which linked the politics of the two countries, but it had now dissolved.

Sir Robert Peel was not less of an English statesman, because he first took his seat for the Irish borough of Cashel; neither was Lord John Russell, because he was

---

[248] *Speech of Isaac Butt Esq. QC MP at Glasgow, 14 November 1871, on Home Rule for Ireland* (Dublin, 1871), 4.
[249] *Irish Federalism: Its Meaning, its Objects and its Hope*, 4th edn. (Dublin, 1874), 45.
[250] 'Ireland', *Quarterly Review*, 83 (June and Sept. 1848), 596.

nominated by the Duke of Devonshire for Bandon. The governing classes in whom power was vested before the Reform Bill, were nearly identical in the two countries. They had common interests, sympathies and feelings.

But after 1832, according to Butt, matters changed utterly:

> With the extension of popular power created by the Reform Bill—and even more than this, with the new questions raised, and the new passions stirred by the impulse given to popular ambition—a wholly new order of things was created. An entirely different assembly took the place of the old House of Commons.[251]

Butt pointed out with some clarity:

> To anyone who studies the history of English politics since the union, it will be evident that, since the Reform Bill, the illegitimate action of the Irish element in the House of Commons has exercised a very decisive influence over their course. Before the Reform Bill, it was not felt, partly because governments were then stronger and did not depend so much as they do now upon the management of sections in the House—partly because in the days of nomination boroughs, there was not the line of demarcation between Irish members and English members which there is now.[252]

Butt's strategy here is to argue that English interests would be better served by a purely English House of Commons, hence his rather surprising use of the word 'illegitimate' to describe the activities of Irish members. For their own selfish reasons, the English would do well to give the Irish their own parliament.

Butt drew attention to the way in which a separately constituted Irish 'popular' interest had played a significant role in determining the fate of British ministers. In 1835 the Lichfield House Compact had displaced the ministry of Sir Robert Peel and handed over the guidance of English affairs to Lord Melbourne. In 1851 and 1852, Butt also pointed out, the Whig ministry was shaken by the votes of Irish MPs anxious, above all, to punish Lord John Russell for his Durham letter and his role in the ecclesiastical titles controversy. In 1852 the ministry of Lord Derby was displaced by a compact between the opposition and the Irish Party, who were at least notionally pledged to support tenant right.

In all these cases, the continuance or fall of the ministry depended upon the arrangement they or their opponents were able to make for Irish support, and that support was given or withheld, not with any view to English interests or English questions, but with reference to the bargain which was made as to Irish affairs.[253]

---

[251] Butt, *Irish Federalism*, 48.   [252] Ibid. 48.   [253] Ibid. 47.

The arrangements of the union had been subjected to a new test, one totally unexpected by those who had brought it into being. It is easily intelligible that a system which might have worked in blending together two sets of members drawn from the unreformed constituencies, would altogether break down when it was applied to another, and a wholly different, state of things. The moment the Irish vote appeared as a distinct power in the House, detached from, and uninterested in, the questions of English policy, then the system of intrigue and bargains and compacts became the inevitable result—and from that moment the House of Commons was incapable of fulfilling, even for England, the true functions of the representation of the people. In fact, Butt's arguments drew partially on the arguments of writers like Croker and Froude, who stressed the way in which inter-party competition at Westminster undermined the coherence of Westminster rule in Ireland.[254] Both main parties frequently engaged in a policy auction, designed to win Irish support, and anyway, since Catholic emancipation, significant sections of the Irish representation were 'outsiders' in terms of the traditional power elite. The political rules of the game which underpinned the project of the union had been in gradual decay since 1832.

To counterbalance the radicalism of this criticism of the union—which clearly, on this account, was inevitably dysfunctional—Butt then offered a vision of Home Rule which was equally profoundly moderate and even conservative. Butt's vision was federalist and not remotely separatist: he drew heavily on the federalist moment of 1844–5. Butt noted that, in the face of judicial oppression of O'Connell—Thomas O'Hagan, now the Lord Chancellor in Gladstone's Cabinet, and several other moderate men who were supposed to 'be rather Whiggish, came down to the Repeal Association and joined it, guarding themselves by saying they were Federalists'. Federalism was then firmly started.[255] Butt did not stop by calling attention to the Irish moderates who were drawn in support of federalism in the mid-1840s; he even suggested that the Whig elite had been supporters of his policy. 'There are men who do not hesitate confidently to assert that, had Lord Bessborough and O'Connell both lived,

---

[254] Ibid. 48. Butt was here echoing the serious arguments of Croker and Froude, but how absolutely valid were they? Derby, who along with Carlyle had encouraged Froude to begin his work in Irish history, was disappointed by the result. Derby argued that laws of 'extreme severity' in Ireland were impossible because 'such laws require to be executed by offcials or private persons resident among the persons against whom they are directed—and the personal contact of man with man produces a state of feeling which necessarily mitigates the law and its final application.' Vincent (ed.), *Derby Diaries* (London, 1994), 15 Mar. 1870, p. 55; (Oxford, 2003), 2 Sept. 1880, p. 268.

[255] *Cork Examiner*, 19 Nov. 1873.

and O'Connell kept his power, a federal constitution for Ireland would have been among the Cabinet measures of the ministry which succeeded to that of Sir Robert Peel.'[256] In this way, federalism became a policy which the British ruling class had not opposed, but merely mislaid. This was Butt's central point. He was, he felt, avoiding the dangerous ambiguities of repeal, which thus gave room for 'Protestant alarm and apprehension'. In his *Irish Federalism*, first published in November 1870, Butt insisted that his object was not to stimulate the desire for national independence, but to point out how it was possible 'to realise that independence without breaking up the unity of the Empire, interfering with the monarchy or endangering the rights or liberties of any class of Irishmen'.[257] Federalism, Butt asserted, was preferable to repeal because it devolved the internal power on Ireland but maintained a formal link with Great Britain and continued the current Irish role at Westminster. Federalism could also be justified as a patriotic Irish response to changed circumstances—since 1800 Britain had expanded its empire, and Ireland had a direct interest in that and, therefore, required continued representation at Westminster to protect that interest. Simple repeal would eliminate such an option and thus be a betrayal of those 'exiles of the Irish race' who had settled in the colonies.[258] John Martin, MP for Meath, did not assert the 'federalist' theme in the same way as Butt, and was more happy to stress a continuity with repeal and Young Ireland, but even he noted in this context: 'Clearly it is quite possible for Irishmen to live happily and prosperously and honourably under the English crown and in connection with the English nation.'[259]

By November 1873 the Home Rule Conference was supported by a requisition which included twenty-six MPs, three bishops, and 20,000 local worthies. At this conference Butt outlined the methods of obtaining self-government: if he were asked by what means he hoped to carry a federal arrangement such as he proposed, he believed it would be carried if Ireland, at the next election, sent eighty men faithfully to press the case of the Irish nation for Home Rule.[260] The achievement of the conference, which was attended by some 800 delegates, was that it provided the new movement with a programme, an organizational structure, and a leader,

---

[256] Butt, *Irish Federalism*, advertisement to the 1st edn. (1870), p. A2.

[257] Spence, 'Isaac Butt and Irish Nationality and the Conditional Defence of the Union, 1833–70', in D. George Boyce and Alan O'Day (eds.), *Defenders of the Union: A Survey of British and Irish Unionism since 1801* (London and New York, 2001), 70.

[258] Alan O'Day, *Irish Home Rule 1867–1921* (Manchester and New York, 1998), 30–1.

[259] PRONI D1/16/D23/pp99–102, Home Rule League Letter Book, D. Martin to E. Murphy, 11 Dec. 1874.

[260] O'Day, *Irish Home Rule 1867–1921*, 35.

Isaac Butt: former Fenian activists, some disgruntled Protestant gentlemen, and Catholic Whigs all accepted his leadership. Butt was well aware of the latent fears of his Protestant supporters. Would the Fenians and Romanists be content with nothing less than separation? He decided to tackle the issue head on: 'It is we—it is our nation, our desertion of the people and the country, the abdication of the positions and duties, that have cast these men into the eddies and whirlpools of rebellion.'[261]

The Home Rule Conference claimed for Ireland the privilege of managing her own affairs by a parliament composed of the Queen, Lords, and Commons of Ireland. The conference proposed to adopt the federal arrangement under which the right of legislating on all matters relating to the internal affairs of Ireland would be vested in the Irish Parliament, leaving to the Imperial Parliament—in which Ireland was to retain her existing representation—the power of dealing with all questions affecting foreign affairs, the government of the colonies, Imperial taxation, and the military and the naval forces. The resolutions further demanded for Ireland a separate ministry, responsible to the Irish Parliament, and it was also proposed to insert in the federal constitution articles supplying the amplest guarantees that no change shall be made by the Parliament in the present settlement of property in Ireland, and that no persons should be subject to disabilities on account of their religious opinions.[262]

There was, however, a degree of controversy on two issues, both reflecting Butt's not so latent conservatism: some did not want to see Irish peers forming a part of the new legislature; others—a clearly related matter—resisted Butt's benign version of Irish history, which suggested that Catholics could expect, at least, a measure of justice from the Protestant upper classes. Butt strongly argued on behalf of the retention of an Upper House of peers, on the grounds that it would 'help to destroy class prejudices' and add 'a new element of strength for the nation'.[263] But he added a further safeguard to protect Protestant interests: an Irish House of Lords, with a veto power which could be employed to defend the interests of the Protestant minority.

I should be very sorry to suppose that the Irish House of Lords would ever set itself against the deliberate opinion of the Irish nation. I do not believe it ever could. But in checking a measure of injustice—if any one should unhappily pass the House of Commons—I believe, the veto of the Lords could never be overcome.[264]

Most importantly for Butt, though, personally the greatest safeguard of all was the religiosity of the Irish people: 'Above all, we have not a population

---

[261] Sullivan, *New Ireland*, 344.
[263] Ibid., 19 November 1873.

[262] *Cork Examiner*, 11 Nov. 1873.
[264] Butt, *Irish Federalism*, 39.

outgrowing the means of religious instruction and living in a state of heathenism.'[265] In the revised 1903 edition of his *Leaders of Public Opinion*, first published in 1871, Lecky made it clear that he still opposed the claims of the Buttite movement, but he had to concede a certain retrospective sympathy. Looking back somewhat wistfully, Lecky recalled of Butt in the early 1870s:

However, the days were not yet when all power was to be taken out of the hands of the educated and propertied classes, and he was still sanguine enough to hope that some measure of local government in which these classes should have a predominant influence, might be possible. As he said in his introduction: 'To call into active political life the upper class of Irishmen, and to enlarge the sphere of their political power, to give, in a word, to Ireland the greatest amount of self-government, that is compatible with the unity and security of the Empire, should be the aim of every statesman'.[266]

Shrouded with uncertainties as it was, Butt's movement seemed set to make progress, helped to some degree by the 1872 Ballot Act,[267] introducing the secret ballot, which further reduced gentry power, perhaps more particularly in the north of Ireland.[268] 'The democratic Orange tenant right cry under the Ballot [Act] is a much more potent form of mischief than I had imagined', the Earl of Belmore was told.[269] Butt was potentially able to cut even more effectively into the constituency of Catholic Whiggism, some of the resources of landlord power, even if others were best suited to the task of defeating Orange Toryism. In such a context, Gladstone attempted the great Irish reform of the 1868–74 ministry.

In a 1873 pamphlet, *The Intellectual Resources of Ireland*, R. B. Lyons, Vice-President of the Royal College of Physicians in Ireland and a Professor of Physiology and Pathology from 1856 to 1886 at the Catholic School of Medicine, pleaded for the endowment of a Catholic university, and pointed to the buoyant demand among the Catholic middle class for third-level education. There was, he claimed, one graduate to every 3,095 people in Ireland, compared to one in 6,486 in England, but he argued that the desire for university education among the Catholic middle classes had not yet been exhausted. Lyons claimed that he had been speaking to J. H. Newman

---

[265] Butt, *Irish Federalism*, 62.

[266] Lecky, *Lecky: A Memoir*, 76–7; Donal McCarthy, *W. E. H. Lecky: Historian and Politician, 1838–1903* (Dublin, 1994), 82–3.

[267] See Michael Hurst, 'Ireland and the Ballot Act of 1872', *Historical Journal*, 8 (1965), 326–52.

[268] J. W. E. McCartney stood in the Tyrone by-election in 1873 as an independent Orange–Tory type with a 'progressive' stand on land: he did well in 1873 and actually took the seat in 1874 with Catholic support.

[269] PRONI D3007/P/117, James Greer to the Earl of Belmore, 9 Apr. 1873.

'of the most unsuperable difficulties under which Catholics laboured in Ireland in their attempts to cultivate science', and the consequent dearth among them of men of high-class attainment in the physical sciences. Lyons said that Newman had felt that, if necessary, non-Catholics could be appointed to do some of the teaching at the Catholic University: prompted by the Irish bishops, Newman soon retracted this suggestion.[270] This episode pointed up both the political opportunity which existed and the difficulties in the way of resolving it. The Catholic University had simply not solved the problem of providing higher education for Catholic Ireland. But it also revealed that the problems were not simply those of money.

By 1860 the Catholic bishops had all been agreed that neither control by the state nor mixed education between Catholics and Protestants was desirable. The real question of the 1860s, therefore, had been how the bishops were to gain and maintain control over the Irish education system in all its aspects, while at the same time making it purely denominational.[271] As Gladstone wrote to Lord Spencer: 'We are pledged to redress the Roman Catholic grievance, which is held to consist in this, that a Roman Catholic educated in a college or a place where his religion is taught can not, by virtue of that education, obtain a degree in Ireland.'[272] But there were always underlying obstacles. In 1872 the O'Keefe case brought the issue of priestly control over education and, indeed, that of papal interference in politics, into the consciousness of liberal British public opinion, and throughout 1873 it continued to cause indigestion.[273] In 1871 Cardinal Cullen had ensured that Father Robert O'Keefe, school manager of the Callan Academy, was suspended as a priest; on 29 April O'Keefe was removed from his position as manager and workhouse chaplain. Father O'Keefe responded by taking civil proceedings against the local curates and bishops for slanders he alleged they had issued during a power struggle between his local national school and a nearby Christian Brothers school. Father O'Keefe's Callan Academy had a board of management, with a former model-school headmaster as principal. It offered a wide range of subjects and, unusually, was affiliated to the Department of Science and Art, South Kensington. Was this a petty local squabble or an example of ultramontane anti-intellectual authoritarian treatment of a progressive educationalist? British liberals tended to agree

---

[270] Greta Jones, 'Catholicism, Nationalism and Science', *Irish Review*, 20 (Winter–Spring 1997) 48.
[271] Larkin, *The Consolidation of the Roman Catholic Church in Ireland*, p. xvii.
[272] Gladstone to Earl Spencer, 26 Sept. 1872, p. 216.
[273] Parry, *Democracy and Religion*, 350–1, 370–1; Colin Barr, 'An Irish Dimension to a British *Kulturkampf*', *Journal of Ecclesiastical History*, 56: 3 (July 2005), 473–96.

with Father O'Keefe's view that he was the victim of clerical intolerance. Gladstone spent some sympathetic hours with him on 3 September 1872.[274] 'I can not but think he has been wrongly used', Gladstone wrote to Richard Dowse, the Irish Attorney-General.[275] Some weeks later, Gladstone told R. P. Blennerhasset, the Protestant Home Rule MP for Kerry, that the dominant party in the Catholic Church was nothing less than awful.[276] The issue for Father O'Keefe's supporters was a simple one: why was it assumed that the state recognized that the position of manager of the National School in Callan depended on the approval of the Catholic hierarchy? For example, although most schools had clerical managers, this was not always the case. The appointment of a person as manager was supposed to be made because in theory that person was supposed to 'represent the feeling of the people in the locality'.[277]

Lord John Russell defended O'Keefe in his *Essays on the Rise and Progress of the Christian Religion in Western Europe*: for Russell, O'Keefe had been caught in the many 'snares the Jesuits had prepared'.[278] The Irish Lord Chancellor, Thomas O'Hagan, prepared a riposte to this, arguing that Russell misunderstood the facts of the case and overstated its sectarian dimension.[279] On 22 October 1875 Lord Russell wrote to the Duke of Abercorn in Dublin Castle: 'Is it true, nothing has been done to save O'Keefe's house from destruction? Do the ultramontanes or does the Queen govern Ireland?' Russell included a private letter from James Macaulay: 'England is ready to go to war with China and Burmah for the protection of citizens and allows a British subject within a day's journey of London to be at the mercy of a foreign potentate, who is said to have no power in this realm.' Russell concluded: 'I gave £10 to Father O'Keefe, I should give no more—but call on you to protect life and property in Ireland as in England and Scotland.'[280] By late 1875 it was clear that British liberal opinion could not prevent the deployment of canon law in Ireland against one who had freely submitted to it: in 1879 O'Keefe signed an unqualified apology and was granted a small pension.

[274] Gladstone to R. Dowse, Irish Attorney-General, in H. G. C. Matthew (ed.), *The Gladstone Diaries: With Cabinet Minutes and Prime-Ministerial Correspondence*, vol. 8 (Oxford, 1972), 3 Sept. 1872, pp. 205–6.
[275] Ibid. 206.   [276] Ibid., 19 November 1872.
[277] James Macaulay, *Ireland in 1872: A Tour of Observation, with Remarks on Irish Public Questions* (London, 1873), 186.
[278] Russell, *Essays on the Rise and Progress of the Christian Religion in Western Europe* (London, 1873), 324.
[279] PRONI D2777/9/6/A/36, O'Hagan papers, contains O'Hagan's draft critique of Russell's book; see also Norman, *Catholic Church and Ireland*, 431–46, for the O'Keefe episode.
[280] PRONI T/2541/VR/375.

It was in an atmosphere poisoned by such concerns that, early in 1873, Gladstone finally brought forth his Irish University Bill. Those Irish Liberals, like J. E. Cairnes, who passionately believed in non-sectarian liberal education, were disappointed;[281] but, given that the measure was designed to meet a specifically Catholic grievance, it was of more immediate importance that the Irish bishops should not dislike it. To please the bishops, Gladstone had made major concessions on matters of intellectual freedom.

His plan was to separate Trinity College from the University of Dublin, which was to become a purely examining body, to which teaching institutions would be affiliated. Three of these would be denominational: Magee College in Ulster for the Presbyterians, and Maynooth and a college to be established in Dublin for the Catholics. The teaching of religion was to be separated from secular education (this was calculated to appease the Nonconformists).[282] In the Catholic institutions certain areas of secular teaching would be under strict reservation; and a certain 'controversial' area would not be examinable. Gladstone argued that the well-being of Ireland depended ultimately on the 'moral and intellectual culture of her people'. But when he disclosed restrictions as to teaching and examining—there were to be no chairs in theology, philosophy, and modern history in the denominational colleges—he provoked laughter in the House of Commons. These so-called 'gagging clauses' became the subject of much debilitating controversy within the liberal constituency. Where would it end, asked Thomas Sinclair, the Belfast liberal: 'Who can tell, but one day it will be announced that even Professor Tait's Quarternions have a dangerous affinity to the Roman guardians of St Peter?'[283]

It was perhaps inevitable that Gladstone's plans for Irish university reform should fail. On the one hand, he never really convinced the Irish hierarchy that he could be trusted. Cardinal Cullen feared that 'Mr Gladstone intends giving professorships to distinguished Germans and Frenchmen who will bring Hegelism and infidelity with them'.[284] On the other hand, classical Irish liberals like J. E. Cairnes were disappointed, not just by Gladstone's compromises, but also by J. S. Mill's tacit acceptance of them—compromises which, they felt, undermined some vital principles of intellectual freedom.[285]

---

[281] Bruce Kinzler, *England's Disgrace: J. S. Mill and the Irish Question* (Toronto, 2001), 120–63.

[282] Richard Shannon, *Gladstone: Heroic Minister* (London, 1999), 122–3.

[283] *Considerations on the Irish University Education Bill with some Remarks upon the Nature and Functions of a University* (Dublin, 1873), 12.

[284] E. Larkin, *The Roman Catholic Church and the Home Rule Movement in Ireland 1870–74* (Dublin, 1990), 164.

[285] Kinzler, *England's Disgrace*, 120–63.

The Catholic hierarchy concluded that Gladstone's scheme was one that 'Catholic youth can not avail themselves of without danger to their faith and morals'.[286] Gladstone saw his proposal narrowly defeated, and naturally blamed the influence of the Catholic hierarchy over the Irish members. Writing to Archbishop Manning on 13 March 1873, the Prime Minister bitterly stated: 'Your Irish brethren have received in the late vote of Parliament the most extravagant compliment ever paid to them. They have destroyed the measure which was otherwise safe enough.'[287] But the strictly political influence of the hierarchy had reached its zenith with this victory.

At the general election of 1874 a party of sixty home-rulers were duly returned. The Irish liberal share of the vote fell from fifty-five seats to twelve, partly in consequence, and Gladstone fell from office. The modest reduction of landlord influence evident in 1868 was now more marked. William O'Brien's description of the new Buttite party, however, was true: 'They formed an incongruous and barbaric mosaic, held together by no discipline, and a not much larger quantity of principle.'[288] On 2 February 1874 the former Young Ireland intellectual J. Cashel Hoey (1828–92) wrote to William Monsell that the Buttite party, 'though home rule in the carnal part, [were] still good Liberals at the heart'.[289] The novelist Anthony Trollope, who had considerable Irish experience, was equally dismissive: 'The professors of the doctrine do not believe it themselves.'[290] On 18 March 1874 Spencer conveyed to Dufferin a similar view: 'About ten of [the Buttite MPs] were genuine in their desire to get an Irish parliament in Dublin.' But Spencer was, nonetheless, relieved that Disraeli had won decisively in 1874 and could 'afford to suck his fingers at home rule'.[291] Spencer's relief vindicated Butt's arguments that Irish parties could act as serious independent pressure-groups in the House of Commons.

Spencer's letter expressed this sense of relief, in part also because some Liberals regarded Disraeli as unreliable on Ireland. There was no telling what he might have done if the home-rulers had held the balance of power, in Spencer's view. Butt, after all, regarded Disraeli's pro-Irish speech of 1844 as entirely sincere.[292] Disraeli had reprinted his 'Irish' speech in a collection of his speeches published in 1869 and again in 1874, and, indeed, had publicly defended it in March 1868.[293] But once installed in power with a very large majority, Disraeli took a conventional stance. He rejected Home Rule, as leading to 'the destruction of the empire'. There were hints

286 Larkin, *Roman Catholic Church and the Home Rule Movement*, 165.
287 *Gladstone Diaries*, viii. 302.   288 O'Brien, *Recollections*, 147.
289 Thornley, *Isaac Butt*, 203.   290 *Autobiography* (Oxford, 1999), 73.
291 PRONI D1071/H/BC/476/33.
292 Butt, *The Irish People and the Irish Land*, 263.
293 Malcolm MacColl, *Reasons for Home Rule* (London, 1886), 18–19.

of some of Disraeli's old Hibernophilia: why did the Irish people, 'gifted with so much genius, so much talent, such winning qualities',[294] constantly describe themselves as a conquered nation? The English had historically been more conquered than the Irish. Why such Irish harping on a theme 'so deficient' in 'self-respect'? Disraeli made it clear that he disliked the mass emigration Ireland had suffered: 'I do not share the feelings of all in the House on that subject. I can not say that I view without emotion the immense emigration of the people.'[295] His private commentary was, nonetheless, smug in its satisfaction with the heavy parliamentary defeat (458 votes to 61) suffered by Butt's Home Rule motion on 2 July. In a letter to Lady Bradford on 3 July 1874, Disraeli spoke of Home Rule having received its *coup de grâce*, adding that Butt was 'left without a shred on his shoulders'.[296] Disraeli did, however, indicate a willingness to visit Ireland to see things for himself. In late September the *Freeman* in Dublin reported with optimism: 'Disraeli is the first Prime Minister of England who, holding that great office, came to Ireland as a visitor.'[297] In fact, illness prevented Disraeli's visit, and the trip was never made.

But one politician defied illness to make an important trip to Ireland some months later. In February 1875 John Mitchel returned to Ireland, perhaps surprisingly, in view of his stated objections to all parliamentary reformism, to fight the Tipperary by-election. William O'Brien found him very weak, and noted: 'Whatever was the design with which Mitchel returned to Ireland from his long exile, he really came back to die.' Mitchel allowed others, including O'Brien, to write his electoral address. But for all the physical weakness of the candidate, the symbolism of the occasion was, nonetheless, intense. 'The evening of his arrival at the Limerick function, there was a scene of volcanic enthusiasm, more like the outburst of a revolution than the sequel of a parliamentary election.'[298] There was a significant side-effect: it was now possible for those Fenians who intensely admired Mitchel to argue that he was not a rigid opponent of all parliamentary activity. Mitchel was elected unopposed on 16 February, but then unseated as a convicted felon by the House of Commons on 18 February. On 12 March he was returned again as MP for Tipperary, but died in Newry on 20 March: John Mitchel 'had died a member for Tipperary'.[299] The great Irish revolutionary pragmatist Devoy's assertion was not an unreasonable one. Mitchel made it

---

[294] *Hansard*, 3rd sers., vol. 225, 2 July 1874, col. 959.   [295] Ibid., col 956.

[296] Marquess of Zetland (ed.), *The Letters of Disraeli to Lady Bradford and Lady Chesterfield* (London, 1929), i. 111–12.

[297] *Freeman's Journal*, 23 Sept. 1874.   [298] O'Brien, *Recollections*, 112.

[299] Devoy's public letter on this point, dated 11 Dec. 1879, is reprinted in the text of P. H. Bagenal, *The Irish Agitator in Parliament and on the Platform* (Dublin, 1880), see esp. p. 123.

clear at the time that, if elected, he would not sit in Parliament. But he did publish a letter in the *New York Herald*,[300] saying that he intended to stand for county after county, to show the Irish people how 'they may gradually shake off the oppression of a pretended parliamentary franchise'. Home Rule MPs would gain from this, because ministers would think it better to yield 'something of the demand of those moderate and loyal gentlemen'.

In the autumn of 1874 the full cost of the failure of Gladstone's university reform became very apparent. Professor John Tyndall's Belfast address, given before the British Association for the Advancement of Science in 1874, referred to a memorandum which briefly circulated in November 1873 from staff and students of the Catholic University, asking for more attention to be given to science in its curriculum. It was, Tyndall claimed, 'the plainest and bravest remonstrance ever addressed to their spiritual pastors and masters'.[301] Tyndall's proudly Darwinian address, however, horrified mainstream Dublin Catholic opinion. The *Freeman's Journal* spoke for many when it editorialized: 'These phantoms will disappear like last visions of the night, and the Darwinian theory and the doctrine of evolution will be placed in the well filled museum, where are deposited the Dreams of Errors of the over wise.'[302] But the son of John Blake Dillon, the young John Dillon, for example, was sufficiently intrigued by Tyndall's address to raise his concerns with the recently formed Literary and Historical Society of the Catholic University.

What can it avail to keep a student in ignorance of such theories as those of Darwin, Huxley and Herbert Spencer, when, on leaving University, he must find the intellectual atmosphere full of the opinions and writings of these men? Is it not likely that he will look with contempt on the teachers who made it part of their task to keep him in ignorance of much that is true and wonderful, while they professed to offer him every kind of knowledge?[303]

John Dillon felt it wise subsequently to send a letter to the *Freeman*, pointing out that he had had no intention of criticizing the Catholic University. Isaac Butt weighed in on the side of those who disliked Tyndall:

---

[300] Repr. in the *Irish Times*, 12 Mar. 1875.

[301] G. Jones, 'Catholicism, Nationalism and Science', *Irish Review*, 20 (Winter–Spring 1997), 48.

[302] *Freeman's Journal*, 24 Sept. 1874.

[303] Greta Jones, 'Catholicism, Nationalism and Science', *Irish Review*. (Winter–Spring 1997), 5. See also Greta Jones, 'Darwinism in Ireland', in David Attis and Charles Mollan (eds.), *Science and Irish Culture* (Dublin, 2004), 115–39; David Livingstone', Darwin in Belfast: The Evolution Debate', in John Wilson Foster (ed.), *Nature in Ireland: A Scientific and Cultural History* (Dublin, 1997), 387–448; John Wilson Foster, *Recoveries: Neglected Episodes in Irish Cultural History 1800–1912* (Dublin, 2002).

It could be said that he [Butt] was an ultramontane, in league with Cardinal Cullen and the Jesuits, because he advocated the union of religious with secular education. Not so. This was the mere voice of bigotry. If ever religion was essential to education, it was now, when the contest was closing, not between one religion and another, but between a low materialism which would degrade man below the beast and the benign doctrines of Christianity.[304]

This was a fairly conventional position for a conservative Anglican in England, but few accepted this logical implication in Ireland: it was an index of Butt's ideological consistency, if nothing else. The debate in the *Freeman* continued, however. The *Freeman* itself admitted in November: 'The literary side of the national character has always been stronger than the scientific, and the triumphs of our countrymen in invention and contrivance have been quite poor.'[305] But it did not change its decided view that Ireland should keep the new intellectual materialism at arm's length.

In 1874 also Gladstone published his *Vaticanism: An Answer to Replies and Proofs*, arguing that Catholicism was incompatible with loyalty to the state. The former premier included a passage attacking the illiberal evolution of the Catholic Church in Ireland.[306] Gladstone was widely perceived to be acting out of a kind of spite—a delayed revenge for Cullen's sabotaging of higher-educational legislation. It is but fair to add that Catholic authoritarianism had been troubling the Liberal leader for quite some time.

The *Freeman's Journal* reflected mainstream Irish Catholic opinion in its response to Gladstone, which verged on disbelief: Gladstone, it said, had adopted the language of the 'No Popery' zealots: 'And what a falling off is here?' The *Freeman* continued by employing a language of mounting anger:

There was a time when Mr Gladstone's name was a loved and honoured name to the people of Ireland. Mistaken policy created between him and them a wide gulf. There were those who entertained hopes that it might be bridged over. He has himself made it yawn to such a width as to sever him from the Irish heart and confidence forever. Many things can be forgiven, but amongst them is not the act of the man who places his hand to the juggernaut of English fanaticism.[307]

Even the Ulster liberals, who had a well-deserved reputation for Gladstone worship, were shocked. The *Northern Whig* editorialized: 'Does

---

[304] *Freeman's Journal*, 27 Oct. 1874.   [305] Ibid., 18 Nov. 1874.
[306] Bowen, *Cullen*, 208.
[307] *Freeman's Journal*, 30 Sept. 1874. Gladstone's 'theological diversion' certainly enhanced his popularity with English Nonconformity: T. A. Jenkins, *Gladstone, Whiggery and the Liberal Party* (Oxford, 1988), 36.

anybody seriously question the loyalty of our Roman Catholic fellow countryman, whether in England or Ireland?'[308] The attempt to launch a new liberal Catholic movement in 1875—at the great O'Connell centenary celebrations of that year—were easily broken up by supporters of the Fenians or home-rulers. But it was Gladstone himself who, more than any single individual, destroyed the prospects of such politics in the mid-1870s.

Lord Acton, a former MP for Carlow, had attempted to dissuade Gladstone from publication.[309] As early as 1870, Acton had 'ceased to be sanguine that the English could govern Ireland successfully'.[310] Nonetheless, he was a critic of the Catholic hierarchy's educational stand in 1873–4,[311] and his advice was of some weight. The world of Irish liberalism was shattered by what was seen as the crudity of Gladstone's intervention. 'Did it not take your breath away? It did mine, though I was better prepared for it than any other Papist at all events—not counting Acton, of course', J. Cashel Hoey wrote to Chichester Fortescue, Lord Carlingford, on 19 November 1874. Despite having received advance warning from Gladstone, Hoey was hugely unimpressed: Irish Catholics, in adherence to a tradition 'running back to St Patrick', had been made ultramontanes by 'the statute book' which had described them as Papists. But since English government in Ireland had become less hostile to Catholicism, the Catholic Church in Ireland 'in proportion had asserted … political loyalty to the crown, greatly against the grain of their people, and not without injury to its influence'.

Gladstone's anti-papal pamphleteering activity was one of many factors which complicated his historiographically neglected visit to Ireland in 1877. Despite his broad reputation as a unionist and reformer, he could not count on an unreserved rapport with large sections of either mainstream Catholic or Protestant opinion. His Liberal supporters were desperately keen to fête him in the north—but even here there were some fears of Orange counter-demonstrations because of Gladstone's role in disestablishment. Mainstream Dublin Tory opinion had not forgiven this—or Gladstone's policy on Irish land and educational issues. Catholic opinion had not forgiven the intellectual outrages of *Vaticanism*. Gladstone proposed to avoid public reference to contentious political topics, but, of course, this was quite beyond him. In an impromptu oration at Trinity College, Dublin,

[308] *Northern Whig*, 25 Feb. 1875; MacKnight, *Ulster As It Is*, i. 303.
[309] PRONI T3314.
[310] James V. Bryce, 'The Letters of Lord Acton', *North American Review*, 178: 5 (May 1904), 702–3. For the Gladstone–Acton relationship, see also Owen Chadwick, *Acton and History* (Cambridge, 1998), 151.
[311] Seamus Deane, *Foreign Affections: Essays on Edmund Burke* (Cork, 2005).

he assured his listeners that he had only disestablished the Irish Church out of love.[312]

A longer formal speech at a gathering of Dublin notables deserves some analysis as indicating rather precisely the mindset of mid-Victorian English liberalism on the Irish issue at a difficult, ambiguous, but by no means explosive moment in Anglo-Irish relations. Echoing the classical thought of an earlier Liberal premier, Lord John Russell, Gladstone attacked the over-centralization of government, stressed local initiative, but remained a firm unionist:

We have been abridging local institutions (hear, hear) and taken powers which were formerly local into the hands of the central authority (hear, hear). In my opinion, we have been moving in that sense in the wrong direction. Central control undoubtedly must accompany the grant of public money to local institutions; but, instead of abridging the power of these local institutions, we ought to seek to extend it, and this is the principle which, in my opinion, lies at the root of all sound policy (applause) and is allied indeed to a fundamental principle which, I do not believe anyone will question or deny. I am persuaded that we are at one in holding that these Three Kingdoms should be one nation in the face of the world (hear)—one nation for every purpose of duty and of power—and that one Imperial Parliament should give effect to that principle in all things that fall legitimately within its scope.[313]

Most profoundly, he touched on the famine and painful topics of Irish depopulation and mass emigration. Here his tone was entirely sympathetic and warm-hearted—he found this history 'painful and mournful in the highest degree'. He hoped it was time that this epoch was now drawing to a close, and that Irish population numbers were stabilizing. Nevertheless, it was 'by a severe dispensation of Providence' in the 1840s that 'instead of eight millions of a population you now have less than five and a half millions'. Furthermore, in Gladstone's view, 'the sufferings have been suffered—the ties have been snapped—the ocean has been crossed', and the important thing to concentrate on now was the steady improvement of Irish prosperity within the United Kingdom, backed up by all the latest available figures. These latter remarks reflected the continuing influence of the Irish liberal economist Professor W. Neilson Hancock on Gladstone at this moment. This was hardly, of course, the view of Irish America.

It is clear, however, that Gladstone now rejected the notion of an English model for Irish development. Large-scale capitalist tenant-farming agriculture was the reality of English life. 'I—for one—am not very anxious that small proprietors should be greatly multiplied in England,' but, 'I attach

---

[312] *Daily News*, 23 Oct. 1877. This was 'a scoop' for Andrew Dunlop, who was the only journalist tracking the premier.
[313] *Dublin Evening Express*, 8 Nov. 1877.

a great importance to it in Ireland.' In Ireland, insecurity on the land was almost a norm. 'You have had in this country—unfortunately too much warranted by history—a very sharp division between the interests of the cultivator and the capitalist, or proprietor. The best cure for this is that in a good and appreciable number of instances, the same man shall be cultivator and proprietor.'

This willingness to contemplate a specifically Irish path of development—peasant proprietorship—should be noted, even if, as Gladstone admitted, he could not spell out precisely how it might be achieved. In the rest of his speech he expressed his warmth for Trinity College, Dublin, and the disestablished Church of Ireland—both of which institutions felt, in recent years, that they had suffered at Gladstone's hands. He had acted in their best interests, he remarked—as defined by himself, of course—and they would come to see that. Needless to say, this priggishness infuriated some in his audience. Finally, he reviewed the political situation: he noted sadly that in the 1874 general election the Home Rule gain of fifty seats had been at the expense of Irish Liberalism, which fell from fifty-five seats to twelve, and not of Toryism (from thirty-eight seats to thirty-one), and hinted strongly, with a clear reference to Daniel O'Connell, that Irish home-rulers and English Whigs were liberal brothers under the skin.[314] These were the themes of an English liberalism facing difficulties in Ireland—but difficulties which were, at this point in 1877, felt to be surmountable by the extension of broad measures of local government and land reform.

These illusory assumptions did not stand the test of time. A steady volume of agitation in the Irish countryside had raised much concern about the working of the 1870 Act. Much of this activity was moderate and respectable, but aspects of it were militant and decidedly more threatening. Agrarian crime figures rose from 135 incidents in 1875 to 201 in 1876, and then in 1877 up to 236; at the same time emigration fell sharply—the two-year average of 90,000 emigrants a year fell to 37,000 in 1876 and 38,000 in 1877.[315] Ireland in the mid-1870s was a country which appeared to be reluctant to employ the traditional safety-valve for social tensions—emigration—whilst at the same time becoming steadily more turbulent.

It became conventional wisdom in the Irish countryside that the 1870 Land Act had failed. At the Limerick and Clare Farmers Club in September 1874, 'The speeches added that the fatal defect of the Act was that it did not

---

[314] There is a striking difference between the tone of Gladstone and that of other leading Liberals such as the Marquess of Hartington on this subject: Jenkins, *Gladstone, Whiggery and the Liberal Party*, 113.

[315] *Donahue's Magazine* (Mar. and June 1879), 266.

give any facility and chance for the obtaining of two great boons for which they sought—namely a fair adjustment of rent and fixity of tenure'.[316] Later that year, at the Farmers Club Conference, held at Mallow, 'a speaker expressed not only the views of the delegates present but the unanimous opinion of the tenant farmers of Ireland, when he declared the Land Bill of 1870 to be defective because it failed to give security of tenure'.[317] How was it possible to 'read' all this? Edward Smith O'Brien, William Smith O'Brien's son, wrote to Robert McDonnell as early as New Year's Day 1876 that:

it appears to me that only two courses are open to those who wish for a thorough settlement of the land question—either to throw themselves into the popular movement, go with it in the direction in which it is setting and trying to control as wisely as may be along that course; or else to take their stand on the principles of the 1870 Land Act.[318]

It was a shrewd comment, which captured much about the political choices of the mid-1870s.

In the western province of Connaught—building on the earlier work of Ned Duffy—local Fenians began to involve themselves heavily in the affairs of the Tenants' Defence Associations in Galway, Mayo, and Roscommon.[319] In May 1876 a senior Fenian, Matthew Harris, published a lengthy pamphlet on the reclamation of waste lands addressed to Benjamin Disraeli. Michael Malachi O'Sullivan also provided his exceptional organizing skills. Isaac Butt was a prominent supporter of the cause of land reform: 'The more I study and reflect on the Irish land question, the more I am convinced that it can not be settled except by a measure that will provide fixity of tenure and an equitable adjustment of rents.'[320] For the time being, though, agricultural prices remained high and attendance at land reform meetings relatively low.[321] The gross capital figures appeared to show a marked improvement. The accumulated capital per head of population in 1846–50 was £12, while in 1876 it was £49.[322] Lecky claimed: 'For 15 or 20 years before 1876, I believe, Ireland was steady and rapidly improving. The proportion of comfortable to infinitesimal farms steadily increased, and the people, judged by every possible test (houses, clothes, wages, savings bank deposits, criminal statistics) were steadily advancing.'[323] On the other

---

[316] *Freeman's Journal*, 29 Sept. 1874.   [317] Ibid., 10 Dec. 1874.
[318] NLI Ms 18,490, 1 Jan. 1876.
[319] *Connaught Telegraph*, 13 May 1876; 11 Nov. 1876.
[320] Ibid., 23 Sept. 1876; McGee, *The IRB*, 55.
[321] See the admission of Malachy O'Sullivan in *Connaught Telegraph*, 16 Dec. 1877.
[322] Irish Land Committee, *The Land Question in Ireland no V. Arrested Progress* (London and Dublin, Jan. 1881).
[323] Lecky, *A Memoir*, Lecky to O'Neill Daunt, 15 Oct. 1880, p. 147.

hand, Matthew Harris even gave evidence to the Shaw Lefevre Committee on the working of the 1870 Land Act. In his view, Ireland was facing a stark choice between a countryside dominated by a system of large grass or small tillage farms.[324]

In 1875 Patten Smith Bridge, who administered the estate of Nathaniel Buckley (a Lancashire manufacturer and former Liberal MP, who had acquired property on the Cork–Tipperary border under the Encumbered Estates Act), obtained damages from local ratepayers after two attempts on his life. For Patten Bridge, the blame lay with outside agitators. John Sarsfield Casey, a Fenian activist who had been deported to Australia from 1867 to 1870, now denounced Patten Bridge in the *Cork Examiner* and *Freeman's Journal*, arguing that Bridge had brought unpopularity on himself by exorbitant rent increases. Casey gave examples of large-scale rent increases on smallholdings in the Galtee mountain district at Skeheenarinka, where the tenants had literally created their farms by bringing up soil from the valleys. Casey's local knowledge was excellent—some of these tenants were his relatives, others were customers in his father's shop. With the publication of Casey's letters, the 'reclamation tenantry' as a potent example of extreme oppression had entered the stage of history. Bridge promptly sued for criminal libel. Casey performed solidly, even if he did not win, in a parliamentary by-election in Tipperary against Edward Dwyer Gray of the *Freeman's Journal* in May 1876. Isaac Butt supported Gray, but after the election he offered to defend Casey as he had done in the Fenian trials—this time with more success, as the case effectively collapsed in late December 1877.[325] But then, thanks largely to a brilliant young reporter with Fenian connections, William O'Brien of the *Freeman's Journal*, public attention had focused ever more sharply in late 1877 on this particularly touching case of peasant hardship,[326] where 517 tenants farmed 22,000 acres of mountain and lowland. Isaac Butt, seizing the opportunity to act as counsel for the defendant, examined several tenants, and the tenants told stories of hardship, of unremitting toil, of the carrying of lime and manure on the backs of men and boys up the steep mountainside to fertilize land which had paid little or no rent in the recent past. In what became a celebrated example of campaigning journalism,[327] William O'Brien conveyed the story of the peasants in the Galtee Hills, who,

---

[324] Report from the Select Committee appointed to inquire into the workings … of the Irish Land Act 1870 [Shaw Lefevre Committee], 271 [HC 1878], (249), XV 313, QS5805.

[325] Maume, Maume, and Casey (eds.), *The Galtee Boy*, 3–4.

[326] *Connaught Telegraph*, 29 Dec. 1877, 'Christmas in the Galtees'.

[327] O'Brien, *Recollections*, the Revd Dr Delany to William O'Brien, 14 May 1878, p. 145.

by carrying soil and manure, created the very farms upon which they were rackrented. The reclamation tenantry became the iconic figure of the suffering Irish peasant who had a direct access to the heart of the English liberal.[328] The Galtee story had everything. The wealthy English manufacturer Nathaniel Buckley had bought the land in the Encumbered Estates Court; he had evaded the provisions designed to protect smallholders in the 1870s Land Act by doubling and trebling rents on the tenants' own improvements.[329] Only when two Tipperary men (Ryan and Crowe) married into their midst did the stimulated Galtee tenantry resist physically. Crowe was hanged for the murder of a bailiff. Even 'Orangemen of the deepest tint'[330] were moved by such injustice and sent subscriptions for the relief of the destitute tenantry. The Galtee case was *the* extreme example of Irish agrarian injustice, but the fact that it could happen at all acted as a powerful de-legitimization of the landlord system.

Events were now to prove decidedly unmanageable: a shattering crisis awaited, a crisis which had both economic and political dimensions. Ireland was deeply implicated in the transformation of the world economy which took place in the third quarter of the nineteenth century. Between 1800 and 1840 world trade increased by 100 per cent, and some 1.5 million people left Europe; between 1850 and 1870 world trade increased by 260 per cent, and more than a million people left Europe, a vastly disproportionate share of them being Irish, nurturing a bitter resentment about the governance of their homeland. By 1840 there were 4,800 miles of railway laid on the planet; by 1880 there were 228,400 miles. Between 1840 and 1880 the area under crops increased by half—from 500 million acres to 750 million acres.[331] Europe was freed from the threat of mass subsistence crisis which had last threatened it in the 1840s, most dramatically in Ireland, but it was also the case that these changes posed a challenge, in particular, to the smaller and less efficient sectors of European agriculture. In a *Fortnightly Review* article, 'The Railroads of the US and their Effects on Farming in that Country and Britain', Edward Atkinson argued that the consequences for British agriculture would be dramatic and inevitably destroy the rent relationship.[332] Many felt that the really

[328] George Bernard Shaw, *John Bull's Other Ireland*, Penguin edn. (Harmondsworth, 1984), 111–16.

[329] O'Brien, *Recollections*, 188–97.

[330] Ibid. 145, the Revd Dr Delany to William O'Brien, 14 May 1878.

[331] Gareth Stedman Jones, 'Society and Politics at the Beginning of the World Economy', *Cambridge Journal of Economics*, 1: 1 (Mar. 1977), 79–82.

[332] 'The Railroads of the United States: The Effects on Farming and Production in that Country and in Great Britain', *Fortnightly Review*, 30 (July 1880), 83–104.

exposed element in the United Kingdom's agriculture system was in Ireland, where impoverished rent-paying smallholders in the west particularly found themselves locked into a new world of international competition, combined, as bad luck would have it, with a series of bad seasons from 1877 to 1879: the value of the seven major crops was depressed by an average of 30 per cent for three years.[333]

J. A. Blake, Home Rule MP for Waterford County, argued that Atkinson, whom he had met in Boston, had overstated the case, but he still believed that the effects of the Irish landlord system on the value of Irish land would be dramatic: 'So convinced am I of what I state that if an estate were now offered me, let at full rents, considering present prices to good tenants, at 15 years purchase, on condition that I should retain it as a permanent investment, I would not accept it.'[334] But, of course, economic realities are always embedded within a political context: in this case, the Irish-American journal *Donahue's Magazine* put it thus in 1880:

Independent of the effect which the products of the vast free lands of America and other favoured countries must have in competition with the produce created under rent-tied and paralysing conditions in Ireland, almost all the evils under which her people suffer, are referable to a land system glaringly antagonistic to the first principles of justice, and fair government, which place the good of the greatest number above the privileged gratification of the few.[335]

This comment underlines an important reality: America's destabilizing impact on Ireland was not just economic but also political. As Earl Spencer, a Gladstonian grandee, was to opine:

The Irish peasantry still live in poor hovels, often in the same room with animals, they have few modern comforts; and yet, they are in close communication with those who live at ease in the cities and farms in the US. They are also imbued with all the advanced political notions of the American republic and are sufficiently educated to read the latest political doctrines in the press which circulates among them. *Their social condition at home is a hundred years behind their state of political and mental culture* [my italics].[336]

---

[333] For interesting accounts of the agricultural crisis, see Sam Clarke, *Social Origins of the Irish Land War* (Princeton, 1979), 225–45; Michael Turner, *After the Famine: Irish Agriculture 1850–1914* (Cambridge, 1996), 215.

[334] *The Effect of American Agricultural Competition on the Value of Land in Great Britain and Ireland* (London and Dublin, 1881), 3; Frederick Engels, 'American Food and the Land Question', *The Labour Standard*, 2 July 1881, in Ellen Hazelkorn, *Marx and Engels: On Ireland: An Annotated Checklist*, Bibliographical Series, no. 15, American Institute for Marxist Studies (1981), 13.

[335] 'Here Stands Ireland: Appeal to the Irish Race', *Donahue's Magazine*, 22 (Jan. 1880), 93.

[336] Earl Spencer, introduction to J. Bryce (ed), *The Handbook of Home Rule: Being Articles on the Irish Question*, 2nd edn. (London, 1887), p. xi.

'Terence McGrattan' spelled out the implications concisely: 'To the Irish landlord the year 1879 will present itself in the time to come as one of the saddest in his history.'[337] The signs of long-term decline for the Irish landlord class were all too obvious. 'Politically' as well as 'economically', Irish landlords were in a 'very vulnerable position by the 1880s'.[338] Happy but rare, indeed, was the aggressive Irish land speculator who could report that he could cope with the loss of rent at home in the 1880s because he had bought land in Texas in the 1870s.[339]

---

[337] Terence McGrath (H. A. Blake), *Pictures from Ireland* (London, 1880), 1.

[338] T. Dooley, *The Decline of the Big House in Ireland* (Dublin, 2001), 210.

[339] PRONI T3314, Carlingford Papers, Mrs J. G. Adair to Lord Carlingford, 12 Aug. 1881/4(?), bemoaning the 'success of socialist agitators ... With these troubles here we were lucky to have bought land in Texas when we did three years ago. It has turned out an extraordinary success.' For Adair, see W. E. Vaughan, *Sin, Sheep and Scotsmen: John George Adair and the Derryveagh Evictions 1861* (Belfast, 1983).

7

Parnellism: 'Fierce ebullience linked to constitutional machinery'

> Broadly speaking, although the revolutionary forces were headed by a
> Protestant landlord, the revolution was an attempt to take from the
> Protestants a considerable part of what they possessed in money and
> power.
>
> (Stephen Gwynn, *Ireland* (1924))

> The question of property in Ireland is curiously complicated with the
> question of nationality: and socialist talk which would not be accepted
> on its merits, is justified to the Irish mind where the parties against
> whom it is directed are English—that is, foreigners and enemies.
>
> (J. R. Vincent (ed.), *The Diaries of Edward Henry Stanley, 15th
> Earl of Derby, 1826–1893* (2003), entry for 23 Nov. 1879)

One Irish political leader, Daniel O'Connell, dominated the Catholic
emancipation crisis of the 1820s; in like fashion, Charles Stewart Parnell dominated the Home Rule controversy of the 1880s.[1] But, powerful
charismatic leaders as they both were, Parnell and O'Connell, the populist
Catholic 'Liberator', were radically different in their political personalities. O'Connell loved heated, overblown rhetoric, even abuse, whilst
David Bennett King, an astute American academic, described Parnell in
1881 in Parliament as 'mild, hesitating, as though at a loss for words
to express accurately his thought, cold and unimpassioned, yet plausible and gentleman-like'.[2] McCullagh Torrens, who knew both men,
observed: 'O'Connell was accustomed to sway the multitude alternately

---

[1] Oliver MacDonagh, *O'Connell and Parnell*, Magdalene College Occasional Papers,
no. 11 (1993). MacDonagh here insists upon the 'essential similarity of O'Connell's
operation to Parnell'. For a suggestive similar view see Alan O'Day, 'Max Weber and
Leadership: Butt, Parnell and Dillon: Nationalism in Transition', in D. G. Boyce and
Alan O'Day (eds.), *Ireland in Transition 1867–1921* (London, 2004), 2.
[2] David Bennett King, *The Irish Question* (New York, 1882), 112.

by his eloquence and humour. Charles Parnell possessed neither.'[3] Parnell impressed unsympathetic English audiences in a way never achieved by O'Connell. One highly intellectual English opponent of Home Rule, Professor T. H. Huxley, rated Parnell as superior to the Liberal leaders of his day: 'Mr Parnell has great qualities. For the first time the Irish Nationalists have a leader who is not eloquent and is honest, who knows what he wants and faces the risks involved in getting it. Our poor right honourable rhetoricians are no match for this man, who understands realities.'[4]

Parnell's most recent biographer has observed: 'A Protestant landlord, scion of an ascendancy vilified in national demonology as the "west British" backbone of the English garrison, he was the unlikely object of popular veneration.'[5] Gladstone, who was the only person in public life at Cabinet level to have dealings with both of them—indeed, in Cabinets that sent them both to jail—preferred O'Connell. Gladstone, in fact, developed a rather sentimentalized image of 'the Liberator', whilst regarding Parnell as a more ruthless, even dangerous, political operator.[6] But where did this particular political capacity emerge from? What was the background and belief of this unusual figure?

D. F. Hannigan's 'Parnell and Cromwell: A Dialogue between Two Ghosts', has Cromwell say: 'Am I not right in assuming the Parnells were a Cheshire family?' Parnell replies: 'Certainly.' 'And there was a Parnell on the Commonwealth side?' asks Cromwell; Parnell replies: 'There was indeed. A son of his removed to Ireland after the restoration, and that was how I came to be born on Irish soil.'[7] Charles Stewart Parnell's grandfather, William Henry Parnell (1780–1821), who inherited the Avondale estate in 1795, was, however, a major figure: the genuinely liberal patriotic MP for Wicklow from 1817 to 1820. William Parnell addressed his own class with eloquence:

I would repeat once again to the remnant of that once important class of men, the Irish country gentleman, that neither their dignity, nor their interest, nor their happiness, can ever consist in setting themselves up as a party opposed to the mass of the peasantry and the majority of the nation.[8]

---

[3] W. McCullagh Torrens, *Twenty Years of Parliamentary Life* (London, 1893), 245.

[4] *Evening Standard*, 13 Mar. 1886.

[5] Alan O'Day, *Charles Stewart Parnell* (Dundalk, 1998), 8.

[6] H. C. G. Matthew, 'Gladstone, O'Connell and Home Rule', in R. V. Comerford and E. Delaney (eds.), *National Questions: Reflections on Daniel O'Connell and Contemporary Ireland* (Dublin, 2000), 24.

[7] 'Parnell and Cromwell: A Dialogue between Two Ghosts', *Westminster Review*, 202 (Sept. 1899), 243.

[8] R. F. Foster, *Charles Stewart Parnell: The Man and his Family* (Hassocks, 1976), 23.

William Parnell published *An Inquiry into the Causes of Popular Discontents in Ireland, by an Irish Country Gentleman* in Dublin 1804; his brother, Henry Parnell, published a work of similar, if more restrained, tone, *A History of the Penal Laws against the Irish Catholics from the Treaty of Limerick to the Union*, in Dublin in 1808. There was also, however, a strain of fervent Protestantism in the family: a great-uncle, Thomas Parnell, was an anti-Catholic zealot who, incidentally, made life miserable for a nervous recent convert from Catholicism, William Carleton, in the mid-1820s.[9] Parnell's father, John Henry, though a rather strict Protestant, had mildly held political views and no public ambitions; he was the first of the line for five generations not to become an MP. In fact, his son's parliamentary colleague Frank Hugh O'Donnell made a point of describing the Parnell home as 'idle' and 'uncultured', like so many gentry homes of this period. When the *Freeman's Journal* asked Parnell to offer titles for a list of the best 100 Irish books, Parnell failed to come up with any suggestions, but he had definitely read his grandfather's works, and their influence is clear in his speeches.[10]

Sir Richard Temple described Parnell as 'a handsome man, with fine head and face and commanding stature. He has nothing Irish about him, though, of course, he poses as an Irishman. He looks what he is—an English-American.'[11] He stood well in the estimation of his own class, was regarded as a retiring country gentleman of politically rather conservative tendencies, noted as an improving landowner who played an important part in opening the south Wicklow area to industrialization. In 1874 he also became High Sheriff of Co. Wicklow and was chosen as a member of the General Synod of the disestablished Church of Ireland. While he was to drop away from formal church attendance in later years, he always held genuine, if rather vague, religious convictions. His attitude to Catholicism was inconsistent: he once told Andrew Kettle: 'I believe the Catholic religion is the only spiritual religion in the world. It seems to connect this world and the next in a more positive way than the doctrines of any other church.'[12] Following his spell in Kilmainham Jail in 1882, however, he left all the Roman Catholic devotional material sent to him by well-wishers with the prison governor. At other times he seemed even less enthusiastic.

---

[9] Carleton, *Autobiography* (Belfast, 1996), 199.

[10] Paul Bew, 'The Chief: A Republican Revolutionary or a Tory Landlord', *Sunday Tribune*, 23 June 1996; Michael MacDonagh, 'With Parnell at Avondale', *Irish Daily Independent*, 11 Oct. 1941.

[11] *Letters and Sketches from the House of Commons: Home Rule and other Matters* (London, 1912), 137.

[12] L. J. Kettle (ed.), *Material for Victory: Being the Memoirs of Andrew Kettle* (Dublin, 1958), 96.

'At dinner ... Parnell happened to observe that he was a Protestant, upon which my friend remarked: "But I hope you won't die one, Mr Parnell". Parnell at once flushed up and said: "Certainly I will, most certainly".'[13] Another account suggests that his eyes 'blazed with indignation' in response to a similar proposition from an Irish party MP.[14]

'What were the motives that brought this human enigma to espouse the case of the Irish tenants?'[15] He was a country gentleman, brought up on the 'prejudices of his class', his tenants were treated 'no better and no worse' than most others. Parnell had never 'brooded over Irish wrongs'; he had not read deeply in Irish history, he had not 'shared the woes' of the people or travelled amongst them. Boredom might, in fact, have played a key role in pushing Parnell towards a political career: boredom, and a sense of the importance of the family name. The Irish political scene in the mid-1870s was dominated by Isaac Butt's Home Rule League, which had been formed in 1873. Butt and the majority of his followers devoted their energies to a polite parliamentary campaign to advance the Irish case for a moderate degree of self-government. Whatever his reservations about this style of politics, Parnell, on deciding to enter politics in the nationalist interest, had little choice but to attempt to become a Home Rule MP.

Parnell, it should be stressed, was an upper-class gentleman, with much of the assurance—and occasional toughness—of his class. At times, the assurance became laziness: his speeches were always stronger when dealing with character and motivation, and weaker when it required a mastery of details or statistics.[16] He had a more than healthy respect, as Michael Morris, the Catholic Lord Chief Justice, pointed out, for serious Irish revolutionaries, but he was disdainful in his attitude towards his more run-of-the-mill nationalist colleagues.[17] As James Mullin's memoirs recorded, on matters of social life he lied casually and badly.[18] A favourite trick was to pay more attention to his beautiful red setter Grouse than to the political conversation at his host's dinner table.

There is something more than faintly shocking about Parnell's bad manners. 'In Mr Parnell's nature, the moral element was imperfectly developed', wrote James Bryce. Bryce added:

He seemed cynical and callous; and it was probably his haughty self-reliance which prevented him from sufficiently deferring to the ordinary moralities of mankind.

---

13 Patrick Maume (ed.), *The Story of a Toiler's Life, 1921* (Dublin, 2000), 191.
14 J. Valentine, *Irish Memories* (London, 1928), 10.
15 Sir William Butler, *The Light of the West* (Dublin and Waterford, 1909), 52.
16 Temple, *Letters and Character Sketches*, 137.
17 W. H. Hurlbert, *Ireland under Coercion* (Edinburgh, 1889), 55.
18 Maume (ed.), *Story of a Toiler's Life*, 188–9.

His pride, which ought to have kept him free from the suspicion of dishonour, made him feel himself dispensed from the usual restraints. Whatever he did was right in his own eyes, and no other eyes need be regarded.

In a final attempt to sort out the muddle of this aspect of Parnell's character, Bryce concluded:

Mr Parnell was a gentleman ... He had the bearing, the manners, the natural easy dignity of a man of birth who had always moved in good society. He rarely permitted anyone to take liberties with him, even the innocent liberties of familiar discourse. This made his departures from what may be called the inner and higher standard of gentlemanly conduct all the more remarkable.[19]

Parnell once told John Morley 'his favourite place was a small shooting lodge of his in the Wicklow Hills, originally planted as a barrier to the rebels of 1798'.[20] It was the small group of MPs who visited him there who were to prove to be the most loyal—his relationship with the party's intelligentsia was to prove somewhat less enduring. Perhaps that is not a surprise. James Bryce noted: 'His general reading had been scanty, and his speeches show no acquaintance either with history beyond the commonest facts, or with any other subject connected with politics ... Nor did he ever attempt to give them the charm of literary ornament.' In an important passage, Bryce added: 'Yet, he never gave the impression of being an uneducated man. His language, though it lacked distinction, was clear and grammatical. His taste was correct. It was merely that he did not care for any of those things which men of ability comparable to his usually do care for.'[21]

Parnell's early impact on the House of Commons was slight. On 22 April 1875 he took his seat in the House as member for Meath—a seat he had secured in part through the good offices of John Martin its late MP, who had first met Parnell at the unveiling of the Grattan monument in 1868. Four days later he made his first speech, opposing a committee on a Bill for the preservation of peace in Ireland. He maintained that 'in the neglect of the principles of self-government lay the root of all Irish trouble' and 'that Ireland was not a geographical fragment, but a nation'.[22] On fourteen other occasions he spoke during the session, but made no particular impression. Barry O'Brien recorded that he remained 'chiefly a calm spectator of the proceedings of the House of Commons, watching, learning, biding his time'.[23] In 1876 he caught the public eye

---

[19] *Studies in Contemporary Biography* (London, 1903), 238.

[20] John Morley, *Recollections*, vol. 1 (London, 1917), 253.

[21] *Studies in Contemporary Biography*, 231.

[22] *Hansard*, ser. 3 (1878), cols. 1643–6; see Stephen Gwynn, *Dublin Old and New* (London and Dublin, 1937), 35.

[23] R. B. O'Brien, *Life of ... Parnell* (London, 1895), 85.

by declaring that the Fenians, who had accidentally killed a policeman in Manchester while attempting to rescue two of their comrades, had committed no murder. This was almost a conventional cliché in nationalist Ireland, but Parnell had had the nerve to say it while interrupting the Irish Chief Secretary. In the parliamentary session of 1877 Parnell had thrown himself into the project known as 'obstruction'. In itself there was nothing particularly original about the idea of delaying parliamentary business by prolonged and irrelevant speechmaking during debates. Palmerston had noted the Irish danger as early as the 1840s. 'Mere loquacity is not an offence of which Parliament can take notice', noted Lord Derby in precisely this context.[24] Even Isaac Butt had employed the practice in 1875 on the occasion of an Irish Coercion Bill.

However, despite Butt's reproofs, Parnell and his allies, the Belfast pork merchant Joseph Gillis Biggar and the pockmarked 'workhouse boy' John O'Connor Power (both of whom were under sentence of expulsion from the Irish Republican Brotherhood at this time for their participation in constitutional politics), did not restrict themselves to blocking Irish legislation, but widened the scope of the tactic to cover Imperial concerns. On 13 April Butt, driven to distraction, openly criticized Parnell.[25] This defiant activity reached its high point in July 1877 with a twenty-six-hour sitting on the South Africa Bill. The effect on the House of Commons was remarkable: a senior Tory like Gathorne Hardy, for example, was compelled to stay in the House for nearly twenty hours. He was pleased that, in the end, the Bill was pushed through and that 'if the Recusants had not yielded, the House was becoming ready for the strongest steps ... I hope, we produced an effect, but Parnell, Biggar, O'Donnell and worst, Nolan, are made of impenetrable stuff'.[26] But in March of the following year life had not improved. 'Mutiny Bill, on till after one o'clock, so that but to snatch a mouthful, I never left my seat. Reiterations of O'Donnell, Parnell, O'Connor Power, over and over again.'[27] Exchanges between Parnell and Butt became more and more strained. Butt was even more convinced that Home Rule was being weakened by the alienation of moderate MPs.

Thanks to such work it was clear by mid-1877 that Parnell was the effective leader of the Irish in England and Scotland. Suggestively, Parnell was more popular than John O'Connor Power, the Mayo MP: yet O'Connor

---

[24] J. R. Vincent (ed.), *The Diaries of Edward Henry Stanley: 15th Earl of Derby, 1826–1893* (Oxford, 2003), 7, entry for 15 Apr. 1878.
[25] Nancy Johnson, *The Diary of Gathorne Hardy* (Oxford, 1981), 13 Apr. 1877, p. 315.
[26] Alfred E. Gathorne Hardy, *Gathorne Hardy: First Earl of Cranbrook: A Memoir*, vol. 2 (London, 1910), 27, diary entry for 1 Aug. 1877.
[27] Ibid. 55, diary entry for 26 Mar. 1878

Power had greater intellect and patriotic credibility as an organizer of the Chester Castle escapade and as a keen supporter of the amnesty movement.[28] Parnell's deposition of Butt as president of the Home Rule Confederation of Great Britain in the autumn merely ratified this situation; though Butt was still, at this point, capable of organized resistance in Ireland itself.[29]

Shortly after Butt's death, Lord Derby discussed his career with two other great Irish political lawyers, Lord Cairns and Lord O'Hagan. 'They agreed in considering him the most effective Irish orator of his time.' The conversation, however, helps to explain Butt's vulnerability to Parnell's offensive:

Poverty and absence of self-respect led him into some questionable transactions with Indian princes, to whom he has been more than suspected of selling his parliamentary influence: from that he became impossible as an official personage, and his necessities increased until he had come to the habit of borrowing small sums from any chance acquaintance.[30]

The fact was that Butt was almost overwhelmed in the 1870s by problems arising out of his irregular sexual and financial life. Drink, too, was taking its toll. Despite his considerable scholarly achievements, he was 'blackballed' by the Royal Irish Academy in 1876,[31] a strange snub, which may well have hurt. He could still command surprisingly strong personal loyalty in Catholic bishops like Nulty and O'Dwyer, for example, but he certainly did not inspire fear in young parliamentary lieutenants.

Obstruction, therefore, did not disappear during 1878. Its force was, however, muted by the ministry's promise of legislation on Irish intermediate education. That subject was then left for consideration until late in the session. Ireland would receive this boon if time remained. It was incumbent upon the 'obstructionists' to restrain delaying procedures or face losing an Irish reform. By mid-1878 relations between Butt and Parnell had, nonetheless, reached a nadir; each sought to claim that the education legislation had been enacted because of his own tactics. Parnell reiterated that his was not a policy of obstruction at all; it was really a policy of independent and strenuous opposition to the government of the day 'all along the line' upon every question. The emphasis on 'independent' opposition carried, of course, the implication that somehow Butt was co-opted by the government. This high-profile defiance of the British government

[28] *Weekly Freeman*, 1 Mar. 1919, 'Mr O'Connor Power dies in London: Feud with Parnell'.
[29] Alvin Jackson, *Home Rule: An Irish History* (London, 2003), 332.
[30] Vincent (ed.), *Derby Diaries*, 7 May 1879, p. 124.
[31] Lady Ferguson, *Sir Samuel Ferguson in the Ireland of his Day*, vol. 1 (Edinburgh, 1896), 31.

and moderate home-rulers in the House of Commons naturally attracted favourable attention from the Fenians.

Parnell's active flirtation with Fenianism was linked to a series of private meetings with Irish republican leaders. As early as August 1877 in Paris he had managed to make a very favourable impression on a prominent figure, James J. O'Kelly, who declared to John Devoy: 'He has many of the qualities of leadership—and time will give him more. He is cool—extremely so and resolute.'[32] Two weeks later O'Kelly added: 'Butt is a little frightened by Parnell's popularity.'[33] By the beginning of 1878 Parnell had managed to convince Dr William Carroll of Philadelphia, a Presbyterian doctor and separatist leader, of his adherence to the principle of absolute independence while avoiding any commitment to the Fenian movement as such. In fact, the increasing hopelessness of the traditional militarist dream of an armed uprising to drive out the English predisposed the more realistic separatists to give him a good hearing. Not that he was saying much. At a second meeting in March 1878 he remained largely silent. He could afford to. The separatists were gradually dropping the idea of making Parnell one of their number. Instead, they were beginning to think in terms of how they could most profitably assist him in the task of transforming the tone of Irish popular politics.[34]

THE NEW DEPARTURE

John Devoy was the most capable and serious of the Irish-American militants. He had been the director of a great tactical success, the *Catalpa* rescue of Fenian prisoners in Australia in 1876: a real achievement, which soon assumed mythic proportions.[35] He now became involved with Parnell by sending a public telegram on 25 October 1878, when he offered Parnell the 'New Departure' package. Parnell had just been re-elected president of the Home Rule Confederation of Great Britain with Fenian support, and Devoy felt—wrongly, as it turned out—that this was a moment of crucial importance. However, the important thing to note is that he offered Parnell the support of American militants on certain conditions: abandonment of Butt's federal demand and substitution of a general—that is, undefined—demand in favour of self-government;

---

[32] W. O'Brien and D. Ryan (eds.), *Devoy's Post-Bag* (Dublin, 1948–53), 267–8.
[33] Ibid., 21 August 1877, pp. 269–70.
[34] Terence Dooley, *The Greatest of the Fenians: John Devoy and Ireland* (Dublin, 2003), 89–90.
[35] Philip A. Fennell, 'History with Myth: The Catalpa's Voyage', *New Hibernia Review*, 9: 1 (2005), 770–4.

vigorous agitation of the land question on the basis of a peasant proprietary, while accepting concessions tending to abolish arbitrary eviction; exclusion of all sectarian issues from the platform; collective voting by party members on all Imperial and home questions; the adoption of an aggressive policy; energetic resistance to coercive legislation; and advocacy of all struggling nationalities in the British Empire or elsewhere.

The 'New Departure' package was a dagger to the heart of Buttism. Federalism was Isaac Butt's core principle, his deepest belief, and much of the point was that it could be precisely defined and did not deny a supreme authority to Westminster. Furthermore, Butt's land reform politics were focused on security of tenure and franchise rather than peasant proprietorship. Parnell made no public response to this offer. A few days later he decided to accept an invitation from the Ballinasloe Tenants' Defence Association to speak in the west of Ireland. Poor harvests in the late 1870s and falling agricultural prices had created the preconditions for such gatherings. Shrouded as he was in an aura of republican conspiracy, it is hardly surprising that Parnell had yet to become a completely respectable figure in Irish politics. Outside Meath, the clergy regarded him warily. As James Kilmartin, the president of the Ballinasloe Tenants' Defence Association, later recalled: 'The priests would not then identify with Parnell. None of them would take the chair, and only two took places on the platform.'[36]

At Ballinasloe Parnell defended the 'energetic' section of Irish MPs and declared himself in favour of a peasant proprietary as a principle. He could afford to do so in this general way: after all, Gladstone's speech in Dublin in 1877 had advocated the multiplication of small agricultural properties in Ireland. Two weeks later, however, Parnell addressed the Kerry Tenants' Defence Association at Tralee, at their invitation. Parnell continued to defend his parliamentary policy against that of Isaac Butt. He strongly implied that the seductions of London had subverted the integrity of Irish members. 'A man might be the best man in the world in Tralee,' but when 'got over to London among his new-found acquaintances,' somehow or other 'his patriotism was diluted.'[37] But while continuing to attack 'Buttism' on the issue of obstruction, he now became surprisingly deferential on the subject of land reform. While still in favour of the peasant proprietorship, Parnell seemed to accept that, as a practical strategy, the moderate Buttite approach, which laid greatest emphasis on fair rents and fixity of tenure, was the way forward. *The Nation* reported Parnell's careful words that

unless they went in for a revolution, he confessed he did not see how they were going to bring about a radical reform of the system of land tenure in this country.

[36] Paul Bew, *C. S. Parnell* (Dublin, 1980), 25.   [37] *The Nation*, 23 Nov. 1878.

For his own part ... he was disposed to devote his energies to endeavouring to obtain a settlement on the basis laid down by Mr Butt's Fixity of Tenure Bill as introduced in 1876.[38]

The meeting was infused by a tone of moderation, though the presence of more militant themes cannot be denied. A voice from the crowd challenged Parnell: 'The land is ours.' He replied carefully: 'We do not wish to interfere with the proprietorial rights of the landlord ... there are many good landlords.' Another voice cried out: 'Aren't you a landlord yourself?' Someone replied from within the crowd: 'He is, and a good one.' A 'somewhat exhilarated' individual called out: 'Butt to the devil', but was promptly 'silenced'. Another voice called out for 'total separation'—and provoked a chorus of 'No, No' and 'Yes, Yes'. William O'Brien, the young reporter, later to be a Parnellite lieutenant, noted in his diary of this Tralee meeting: 'Parnell addressed a rough-and-tumble meeting, half farmers, half Fenians, with several tipsy interrupters, and a preliminary alarm that the floor was giving way. He spoke under cruel difficulties, but fired them all before he sat down.'[39] Parnell was clearly still keeping his options open. O'Brien concluded: 'The country is with him in a half-hearted way, so far as it has any heart in anything.' But, in the midst of all this manoeuvring, the Kerry speech did contain one key theme which was to represent the core element of consistency in Parnell's approach to the problem of the relationship between the land and the national question:

He had heard some people say 'Oh, I am not a Home Ruler—I am a Tenant Righter'. He had to say to such a man: 'I don't care what you are' ... there was no antagonism between them, and there could be none. Settle the land question on a firm basis, give the tenant farmers the right to live on their farms, level the barriers that divided class from class, and there would be no interest sufficiently strong to retain English misgovernment, and they would then have Home Rule (cheers).[40]

Everything that Parnell said at Kerry was pervaded by one key assumption: it was possible to win land reform, even peasant proprietorship, by pressure on the British Parliament. 'They will give us nothing', said a voice in the crowd; but this was not Parnell's message.

At this moment the idea was taking shape that the nation's Farmers' Clubs and Tenants' Defence Association should coalesce and form a Farmers Union for the whole country.[41] But the 'neo-Fenians' continued to work to

[38] *The Nation*, 23 Nov. 1878.
[39] Michael MacDonough, *The Life of William O'Brien* (London, 1920), 50.
[40] Ibid.
[41] XYZ, 'The Irish Land Question, being extracts from a pamphlet', *England and Ireland: Together with a Few Words on the Means of Obtaining the Settlement* (Dublin, 1879), 13.

their own, more radical, Mitchelite agenda. John Devoy published another letter at the end of 1878, defending Fenian support for land reform: 'But I will be told that no English parliament will do any of these things. Then I say these things must wait until our Irish parliament can do them better,'[42] he said in a public letter at the end of 1878. At a secret meeting in March 1879 in Claremorris, the Fenians decided to support an agrarian movement, provided that they retained control of its county and provincial organization.[43] It is clear, too, that they acted on a key strategic assumption: the British Parliament was a 'parliament of landlords'—it would not, therefore, sponsor serious land reform. Any substantial mass Irish peasant agitation would, therefore, at some stage have to challenge the framework of the union, either by insurrection or, at least, secession of MPs from Westminster.

Not surprisingly, in the face of these currents, Parnell's early involvement in the land agitation was marked by an obvious hesitancy. Even after the success of the first Land League meeting held at Irishtown, Co. Mayo, on 20 April 1879 had indicated the obvious potential, he still held back. He noticed that O'Connor Power, a former Fenian and a popular MP for Mayo, 'did not make exactly a Land League speech'.[44] Parnell must have felt he should be careful. It required a special effort of persuasion from Michael Davitt, at that time a separatist activist recently released from prison and beginning his involvement in land reform, to persuade him to attend the second key meeting at Westport, Co. Mayo, on 8 June 1879.

Even then he was not fully committed. This is hardly surprising: Malachy O'Sullivan's speech at Westport was suffused with explicit revolutionary sentiment and attended, for good measure, with a '98 pike', making 'significant flourishes in the air'.[45] O'Sullivan asked rhetorically: 'Do you expect tenant right from a parliament of landlords?' They were to combine and offer a fair rent, and if that was not accepted, pay none. If they followed his advice, 'Before long you'll own your lands (great cheering). A voice—three cheers for the revolution.' O'Sullivan concluded: 'The rulers of your own country.' Parnell's speech at Westport was quite different in tone: he insisted that 'I am as confident as I am of my own existence that if you had men of determination or some sort of courage and energy representing you, you could obtain concessions'. He also suggested that the 'breaking down of barriers' between classes in Ireland by means of a

[42] Devoy, quoted in *Irish Nation*, 26 Nov. 1881.   [43] *An Phoblacht*, 8 Mar. 1930.
[44] *Weekly Freeman*, 1 Mar. 1919, 'A Famous Orator: O'Connor Power dies in London'.
[45] *Connaught Telegraph*, 14 June 1879.

'good Land Bill' would assist the cause of self-government. He had said earlier in the year: 'If you had the land question settled on a permanent basis, you would remove the great reason that now exists to prevent the large and influential class of Irish landlords falling in with the demand for self-government.'[46]

The new movement exploited Ireland's past to generate a strong sense of historical legitimacy. The Land League Convention at Castlebar on 16 August 1979 insisted that before the English conquests of the sixteenth and seventeenth centuries the people knew nothing of absolute property in land.[47] Lord Derby's shrewd diary note of 29 September 1879 summarises both the scale of Parnell's opportunity and the problems posed by the potential radicalism of the new movement.

> The anti-rent agitation in Ireland continues and is bearing fruit ... Even fixity of tenure is now thought not to be enough ... in truth, the object is to get rid of the landlord altogether: the Irish peasantry have never ceased to hold that the land belongs to them, and has been taken away by violence and confiscation. Which, as is historical fact, is in most cases true.[48]

Michael Davitt's cousin and close political ally, John Walshe, insisted: 'Did they believe that any man who held over a title from Oliver Cromwell, who came to the country and butchered their fathers and mothers because they were Irish—did they believe that any man holding land by that title had a first title to land?'[49] As Professor J. J. Lee has argued, the League offered tenants 'retrospective shares in a Gaelic Garden of Eden, a powerful incentive for agitation'.[50] It was a powerful source of encouragement for popular mobilization.

William O'Brien, one of Parnell's brightest lieutenants, was later to explain:

> While the confusion of the last three centuries has little or nothing to distinguish the child of the chief from the child of the lowliest clansman, the course of our history gives to the Irish poor the consolation of thinking that the more complete their present poverty, the more probably it was earned by some heroic ancestor who preferred a bold dash for liberty against Cavan or Cromwell to broad lands and apostate English titles. This is no inconsiderable heritage for a nation. Fancy a dumb yokel in the fens of Lincolnshire being able to pick out his progenitor among the squadrons of the battle of Hastings as formally as any Howard or de Winton of them all.[51]

[46] *Freeman's Journal*, 4 Feb. 1879.
[47] Michael Davitt, *Fall of Feudalism* (London and New York, 1904), 160.
[48] Vincent (ed.), *Derby Diaries* 171.
[49] *Freeman's Journal*, 30 Aug. 1880; Bernard O'Hara, *Davitt* (Westport, 2006), 36.
[50] J. J. Lee, *The Modernisation of Irish Society, 1848–1918* (Dublin, 1973), 44–6.
[51] 'The Influence of the Irish Language', *Irish Ideas* (London, 1893), 51–3.

In fact, it was not until early November, some days after the Irish National Land League was set up in Dublin on 21 October 1879, that Parnell, as the organization's president, committed himself fully to such a highly charged movement. He did this by signing a militant Land League address, which left no doubt that he stood with the new movement. At the age of 32, after four-and-a-half years in Parliament, he had put into place a political coalition without precedent in Irish politics. It was not an easy position for a young Protestant landlord to take up.

THE LAND LEAGUE EXPERIENCE

The outbreak of the land war in Mayo was accompanied by a dramatic eruption of Catholic religious passions: these passions were not autonomous but intimately linked to the political crisis.[52] On 21 August 1879, on a wet Thursday evening, a vision appeared on the church gable at Knock, Co. Mayo. 'The wall beautifully illuminated by a white flickering light, through which could be perceived brilliant stars, twinkling as on a fine frosty night.'[53] Mary McLoughlin, the 45-year-old housekeeper to the parish priest, Father Cavanagh, saw the Blessed Virgin. Filled with excitement, she gathered together a small group of family members and friends, who all claimed later that they too had seen the Blessed Virgin, flanked by St Joseph on her right side and St John the Evangelist on her left. At first a little reluctant to accept the story, Father Cavanagh soon endorsed the apparition. But it was only when the *Tuam News* gave a summary of the event that the local population started to attach to it any degree of credibility.[54] On the second Sunday after the apparition, Mrs P. J. Gordon of Claremorris brought her 12-year-old daughter Delia to attend mass at Knock, 5 miles from Claremorris. Delia had been suffering from intense pains in her ears. During mass Delia was again afflicted, and began to cry. Her mother took her out to the gable wall and told her to pray: she also took a piece of cement from the gable wall and placed it next to

---

[52] ' "A Vision to the Dispossessed?": Popular Piety and Revolutionary Politics in the Irish Land War, 1879–82', in Judith Devlin and Ronan Fanning, *Religion and Rebellion* (Dublin, 1997), 136–51; Tom Neary, 'A Short History of Knock', in Donal Flanagan (ed.), *The Meaning of Knock* (Dublin, 1997), 7–27. Neary repeats the claim that Delia was cured of deafness, and this seems to have been Father Cavanagh's view, but it is not the claim made by Delia's mother at the time, *The Nation*, 2 Feb. 1880.

[53] 'Apparition of the Blessed Virgin at the Chapel of Knock near Claremorris', *Tuam News*, repr. in *The Galway Vindicator* and *Connaught Advertiser*, 14 Jan. 1880.

[54] *Donahoe's Magazine*, 3: 4 (Apr. 1880), 'The Apparitions of the Blessed Virgin Mary, St Joseph and St John in the Parish of Knock, Co. Mayo', p. 400.

her daughter's ear. Happily, Delia was cured and never troubled again.[55] This first 'miraculous' cure opened the way for the arrival of thousands of pilgrims who came to Knock seeking cures. By the end of the year the 'greater part' of the gable wall was 'much disfigured', reported the *Tuam News*, 'by persons breaking off portions of the cement, some of which, following the good example of the pious people we also carried off with us'. Why not, indeed, as the report continued: 'many cures have already been worked through the apparition of the Blessed Virgin Mary and by the application of the cement taken from the garden wall.'[56] Incidentally, this created a fortunate business opportunity for a former papal soldier,[57] P. J. Gordon, who provided the carriages to convey visitors from Claremorris to Knock. Most important of all, however, were the political implications. A Fenian, Gordon was a key Land League organiser and activist, at the sharp edge of local militancy, and well known to Parnell himself.[58] His wife had designed the 'Land for the People' banner at the Irishtown land meeting, in association with Mrs P. J. Sheridan.[59]

Father Cavanagh had been a rather well-known conservative priest, very much disliked by agrarian radicals and neo-Fenians in Mayo. But somehow he now became a local patron saint for Land League activists—whether an anticlerical revolutionary like P. J. Gordon or a more moderate figure like Thomas Sexton, who covered Knock journalistically for T. D. Sullivan's *Nation* and *Weekly News* newspapers. This is not to say that all previous differences were swept away in a wave of religio-national enthusiasm. The Land Leaguers did not take over completely the Knock experience. The next 'miracle' cure, a Mrs Bourke, who unfortunately died within weeks, was brought to Knock by her brother, Colonel Walter Bourke, a local Catholic landlord who was deeply unpopular with the local agrarian activists, including P. J. Gordon, and who was, indeed, eventually murdered by them in June 1882.[60] But the fact remains that the most prominent local Leaguers

[55] Neary, 'A Short History of Knock', 7–27.

[56] *Tuam News*, quoted in *Galway Vindicator*, 14 Jan. 1880.

[57] Owen McGee, *The IRB: The Irish Republican Brotherhood from the Land League to Sinn Fein* (Dublin, 2005), 76. Gordon was not alone in making the transition from papal soldier to Fenian, see Patrick Maume, 'Fenianism as a Global Phenomenon: Thomas O'Malley Baines, Papal Soldier and Fenian Convict', in Leon Litvak and Colin Graham (eds.), *Ireland and England in the Nineteenth Century* (Dublin, 2006), 148–60.

[58] Bew, 'A Vision to the Dispossessed', 145; Katharine O'Shea, *Charles Stewart Parnell* (London, 1914), i. 170.

[59] Patrick Maume, 'Rebel on the Run: T. J. Quinn and the IRB/Land League Diaspora in America', *Working Papers in Irish Studies* (2000), 2; W. Flanagan, *Parnellism and Crime* (n.p., n.d.), 10.

[60] Fergus Campbell, *Land and Revolution: Nationalist Politics in the West of Ireland* (Oxford, 2005), 77.

were the guiding spirits. Parnell knew, therefore, that he was placing himself at the head of a popular movement at a moment when intensive and combined religious, national, and agrarian passions had been unleashed.[61] He may well have assumed (correctly) that the neo-Fenians, including Michael Davitt, were actively supplying guns for the west of Ireland.[62]

On 22 November 1879 there came a pivotal moment in the League's early history. The planned eviction of Fenian Anthony Dempsey on Loonmore mountain was stopped by a crowd of thousands, led by Parnell but organized in semi-military style on a parish basis by the IRB: for example, the Aughamore men surrounded the house, while the Knock men occupied the only available cover. The Crown forces had to make a humiliating withdrawal, and Parnell told the crowd they had broken the 'back of landlordism'.[63] On 10 December the forces of the state returned and successfully carried out the eviction. The League then paid Anthony Dempsey's rent and costs in order to prevent the demoralizing effect of putting Dempsey out of his house by Christmas.[64]

The limits of mass mobilization were revealed clearly: the importance of money was also underlined. In December 1879 Parnell left for the United States to obtain financial support for the new movement, while the neo-Fenians organized a series of mass demonstrations and other confrontations with landlord power in the west of Ireland. The scale of these confrontations—in one celebrated example an entire village, Carraroe in Co. Galway, turned out in December to resist an eviction—depended both on the special poverty of the smallholders of the west and the local organizational strength of Fenianism. Inevitably, violence and assassinations against those—landlords, agents, or backsliding tenants or labourers—who opposed the 'popular' will accompanied this movement. But there was also much Land League-financed activity in the Connaught law courts, utilizing the elements of Gladstone's 1870 Land Act designed to protect smallholders threatened with eviction. These legislative provisions assumed a much greater significance now, and the affected families did not have to rely on

---

[61] *Connaught Telegraph*, 23 July 1881; contemporary Irish reportage in the *Tuam News*, *Mayo Examiner*, 17 May 1880, and *The Nation*, for example, were respectful of the Knock phenomenon, see Marie-Louise Legg, *Newspapers and Nationalism The Irish Provincial Press 1850–1892* (Dublin, 1994), 154–5; Andrew Dunlop, 'The Alleged Miracles in Ireland', *Daily News*, 28 Feb. 1880; for classic Irish-American endorsements see *Donahoe's Magazine*, 3: 5 (May 1880), 597; and 5: 5, 'Are the Wonders of Lourdes and Knock Illusions?', 393–400. Gordon was charged with others in July 1881 at the Castlebar Crown Court that 'he did encourage others to kill Walter Bourke' (*National Archives: Irish Crime Records 1881–2*, ii. 40)

[62] Paul Bew, *Land and the National Question in Ireland 1858–82* (Dublin, 1978), 93.

[63] Maume, 'Rebel on the Run', 2.

[64] Chief Secretary's Office, Registered Papers, 1880/12061.

their own resources to pay legal fees. Money from America was an important factor here. Parnell addressed a sparsely attended House of Representatives and had an audience with the American President on 4 February. He spoke in sixty-two cities to largely Irish-American audiences. Parnell had actually arrived at the moment when Irish-America was beginning to feel that it had survived the worst ravages of anti-Catholic discrimination and was now gaining a respected place in American life.[65]

This, if anything, enhanced the level of support for self-government for Ireland. John Boyle O'Reilly, ex-Fenian and celebrated Boston literary figure of the 1880s, put it very well: 'Irishmen can not become mere provincials. Everything about them indicates distinct nationality. They may consent to change as we are doing in America, joyfully and with pride, but the Irishman in Ireland can never be made into a West Briton.'[66] He added: 'We must work so that Ireland shall not be oppressed, ridiculed and patronised, so that our Catholic nature should have equal honour with all men's names in America.'[67] Hardly surprisingly, Parnell allowed himself a few rhetorical indulgences in America: most notably when, in Cincinnati on 20 February, he spoke of breaking the 'last link which keeps Ireland bound to England'.[68] He never quite embraced revolutionary methods, but he often came close. In Boston he declared he was not in favour of revolutionary methods, provided other means worked. In Rochester he said he was in favour of revolutionary methods, provided other means did not work.[69] In later years he recalled this tour with loathing, and by implication discounted some of the rhetoric. At the time, however, he was clearly anxious to retain Fenian support. In a conversation with a New York journalist on the outward voyage, Parnell insisted that, while personally he could not join a secret society, he nonetheless needed the support of Fenianism.

The announcement of the general election of April 1880 brought Parnell's labours in America to an abrupt end. He hurried home. Overall the election saw the triumph of Gladstone's Liberal Party over the Conservative government. Parnell achieved the personal triumph of being returned for three seats in Cork, Mayo, and Meath. He chose to sit for the Cork seat. However, most of the notable successes for Parnell's supporters were obtained in the province of Connaught. It was clearly revealed that the

[65] Eric Foner, 'Class, Ethnicity and Radicalism in the Gilded Age: The Land League and Irish America', *Marxist Perspectives*, 1: 2 (Summer 1978), 7.

[66] *Boston Herald*, 12 Oct. 1886.

[67] Ibid., 12 May 1887; for Michael Davitt's similar understanding, see T. N. Brown, *Irish-American Nationalism 1870–1890* (Philadelphia, 1966), 24.

[68] The balance of evidence suggests that Parnell did use these disputed words, see F. S. L. Lyons, *Charles Stewart Parnell* (London, 1977), 111–12.

[69] Donal McCartney, 'Parnell and the American Connection', in *The Ivy Leaf: The Parnells Remembered* (Dublin, 2006), 38–55.

Land League was still very much a Connaught phenomenon and that, while Parnell had personal influence in the other provinces, it was still limited. On 17 May he was elected leader of the Irish Parliamentary Party, but by a mere twenty-three votes to eighteen. There were, it should be remembered, a total of fifty-nine nominal Home Rule MPs.

W. E. Forster, the new Irish Chief Secretary in a new Gladstone government, as a young man and Quaker activist, at considerable risk from disease, had played a distinguished role alongside James Hack Tuke in famine relief; he had natural sympathy for the tenantry. Intended by Gladstone to be a 'message for peace in Ireland', he had broken down in tears when an Irish priest wrote to him as a friend of Ireland.[70] If he expected any broader political sympathy from Irish nationalists, though, he was to be disappointed—J. G. Biggar crassly declared that Forster's 'probable motive' in famine relief had been to 'take pleasure in human suffering'.[71]

In August 1880 the House of Lords seemed to set its face against even mild land reform in Ireland by rejecting a very moderate Compensation for Disturbance Bill. Gladstone argued with some force that this legislation was entirely consistent with the logic of the 1870 Act—particularly its protection for smallholders.[72] The action of the House of Lords reflected not strength and certainty on Ireland but rather confusion. Lord Derby reported in his diary a significant conversation with a former Irish Chief Secretary:

Much talk with Lord Winmarleigh on Irish affairs, as to which I find his ideas perplexed to the last degree. He is a good deal alarmed, thinks an outbreak must come, thinks we ought to concede every reasonable demand, and even go beyond what is reasonable, in order to show our moderation—etc, etc, but in the same breath says that small holdings are fatal to the chance of improvement, that they ought to be discouraged, that it would be a good thing to subsidise emigration on a great scale, that the one thing most wanted is the introduction of English capital—all true, but exactly the reverse of the ideas which the agitators are trying to work out. His mind seemed to be in utter confusion: yet he has been Irish Secretary, has been 50 years in Parliament and is fairly clear-headed in ordinary life.

[70] T. W. Moody and R. A. J. Hawkins (eds.), *Florence Arnold-Forster's Irish Journal* (Oxford, 1988), 11 July 1881, pp. 197 and xxi.

[71] Vincent (ed.), *Derby Diaries*, 11 Mar. 1882, p. 456.

[72] Gladstone to Argyll, 14 June 1880, in *Duke of Argyll, Autobiography and Memoirs*, vol. 2 (London, 1906), 352. The Duke of Argyll accepted Gladstone's argument. Referring specifically to the case of Carraroe he declared: 'You had in that case at the mercy of the landowner a whole population of upward of 500 souls who under the existing dispensation would have been evicted without one shilling of compensation, without one shilling to carry them to America, because they were evicted for nonpayment of rent.' For this reason Argyll, a consistent critic of Irish nationalism, urged the Lords to pass the Compensation for Disturbance Bill. Sir Charles Russell, *Speech Before the Parnell Commission* (London, 1889), 158.

He might have added that Winmarleigh's experience of Ireland went back to 1835, when, as John Wilson Patten, he had chaired the Select Committee on Orangeism. Derby noted that Winmarleigh's 'usual good nature, combined with a certain timidity', made him want to 'agree with everybody', but tellingly he concluded, 'in the present case his perplexity is not greater than that of society in general'.[73]

Ireland prepared for a turbulent winter. The scene was set for the League's expansion into the more prosperous regions of Leinster and Munster. But how to achieve such an expansion? The problem which faced the League in the summer of 1880 was in essence a simple one. The methods of mobilization which had worked amongst a relatively impoverished tenantry in Connaught had considerably less resonance in the considerably more prosperous regions of East Munster and Leinster:[74] only smallholders, for example, were protected by the 1870 Land Act in ways which the Land League could exploit in the court. The cautious sense that the Irish farmer had something to lose in a conflict with the landlord was much stronger in the south and east of Ireland. But the Land League had to achieve a national basis. The alternative was to accept the limited view of the problem put forward by the landlords' intellectual front, the Irish Land Committee, which argued that the Irish land problem was essentially the problem of the minority of small, uneconomic farmers: 'It is not too much to say that an improvement in the condition of 100,000 families or less than 500,000 persons, whichever way it ought to be brought about, would go far to solve the Irish economic problem.'[75] W. Bence Jones insisted: 'It is these small refuse farms which are the cause of the trouble, nothing else.'[76]

For the League, it was essential to prove the existence of a national problem by a national mobilization. Pragmatically, the League leadership

[73] Vincent (ed.), *Derby Diaries*, 26 Sept. 1880, p. 273.

[74] Bew, *Land and the National Question*, 115–216; L. P. Curtis, 'On Class and Class Conflict in the Land War', *Irish Economic and Social History*, 3 (1981), 86–94. For important local studies, see Donald E. Jordan, *Land and Popular Politics in Ireland: Co. Mayo from the Plantation to the Land War* (Cambridge, 1994), 264–82; J. W. H. Carter, *The Land War and its Leaders in Queens County* (Portlaoise, 1993); and cf. also work of D. Marnane, unpublished Ph.D thesis on Tipperary land war, 'Land Ownership in South Tipperary, 1849–1903', University College, Cork (1991); Gerard Moran, 'James Daly and the Fall of the Land League in the West of Ireland', *Irish Historical Studies*, 29: 114 (Nov. 1994), 211. Irish land was held by two classes of tenants—the small farmers who paid £1 to £20, and the comparatively large farmers who paid rent from £20 upward. Of the first class there were 536,000, averaging £6 each; of the second class there were 121,000 holdings, averaging £56 each: *Fall of Feudalism*, 506. The League's problem in the summer of 1880 was to appeal to this better-off group, which was more significant outside the west.

[75] Irish Land Committee, *The Land Question in Ireland: Arrested Progress* (Dublin and London, 1881), 24.

[76] 'What Can Be Done For Ireland?', *Macmillan's Magazine*, 254 (Dec. 1880), 140.

hit on a solution. In August the League Treasurer, Patrick Egan, argued that the Land League 'should compel the landlord to collect rents at the point of the bayonet as the tithe rents were formerly collected'.[77] Egan, the revolutionary, made it clear that he was here outlining a compromise; the compromise fell short of the more revolutionary policy of a general strike against all rent, which he would himself have preferred.

But for all that, this was a striking moment: instead of adopting a new radical strategy, the Land League was instead harking back to one of the traditional forms of struggle—'rent at the point of the bayonet'—much beloved of stronger farmers during the tithe war conflicts of the 1830s. It was a policy which had been invented not by the agrarian radical Fintan Lalor, but by his much more moderate father, Richard. It was a policy which allowed senior Catholic clerics like Archbishop Croke of Cashel to give their blessing to the League. Farmers typically selected a sum they were willing to pay—Sir Richard Griffith's valuation of Irish land was often selected for this purpose, because by 1880 it was well below the rental value—and then refused to pay the full rent, which was perhaps 30 per cent or 40 per cent more.[78] The level of risk—or to put it another way, real martyrdom—was sharply reduced for a farmer who defied his landlord by refusing to pay his full rent with the proviso that if the landlord actually managed to bring sufficient pressure to bear—through, for example, sheriff's sale of the farmer's stock—the tenant might, at the least, 'at the point of the bayonet', pay not only his debt, but the costs incurred. Such a strategy could only be fully effective against a weak and demoralized landlordism, with no support from government; a landlord class which attained any level of organizational effectiveness would be likely to be able to expose the strategy as a 'sham', and an expensive 'sham' at that, as farmers turned to the League expectant of financial support with their legal expenses.[79]

The language of Matthew Harris, the neo-Fenian and senior Land League organizer, is very revealing here. It exposes fully the tensions at the heart of the movement. He had spoken, in April 1880, of an alliance of the grazier and the small farmer as being an alliance of the shark with the prey. In August 1880 he expressed irritation that the provinces

---

[77] *Freeman's Journal,* 11 Aug. 1880.

[78] As early as 4 January 1860, Sir Richard Griffith had written that 'the fair letting value of the land should be from 12 per cent to 16 per cent over the valuation; between 1860 and 1880 the price of agriculture doubled and in some cases trebled'. Bernard Fitzpatrick MP, *The ABC of the Irish Land Question* (London, 1881), 13.

[79] Jane La Côte, *Fanny and Anna Parnell: Ireland's Patriot Sisters* (Dublin, 1991), 194; A. Pole, 'Sheriff's Sales During the Irish Land War 1879–82', *Irish Historical Studies*, 24: 136 (Nov. 2005), 386–403.

of Leinster and Munster were leaving the sole burden of the struggle to Connaught. In November 1880 he softened his tone. Whether it was through 'sincerity or through policy', a great number of the grazier class were now siding with the people. In December he happily announced that in Limerick the 'wealthy graziers' had joined the cause. But by February 1881 Harris had now returned to his more traditional view: only small farmers really deserved nationalist support. By April 1881 his public hostility to the graziers as false friends of the people was again clear.[80]

There were personal, as well as socio-political, contradictions at the heart of Parnellism. In July 1880 Parnell had met Mrs Katharine O'Shea (1845–1921), the wife of a somewhat 'Whiggish' member of Parliament for the Home Rule Party, Captain William Henry O'Shea (1840–1905). She was a woman well connected with the Liberal Party, being the niece of Lord Hatherley, Gladstone's first Lord Chancellor, and the sister of Sir Henry Evelyn Wood, who achieved the rank of field marshal.[81] By 17 October Parnell was writing to her as 'My dearest love'.[82]

Did O'Shea know of his wife's liaison, which was a subject of gossip in London political circles from 1881? Was he, in short, a wittol? In an able series of letters, he later denied that he had firm knowledge of his wife's *affaire*. But it is unlikely that he was telling the whole truth and, indeed, appears to have calculated that his wife's new relationship could be turned to his political advantage.

However, in the early weeks and months the O'Shea liaison was of little political importance. Much more important was the fact that Parnell was swept along by what became a truly national agitation. Moreover, while the bulk of the newly attracted stronger farmers in the south and west were supporters of legalistic forms of struggle—some of it highly expensive and rather ineffective, as his activist sister Anna pointed out in her intelligent book, *The Tale of the Land League: A Great Sham*, serialized first in the *Irish People* in 1907—agrarian outrage grew from 863 incidents in 1879 to 2,590 in 1880. In 1880 there were seven agrarian murders—the most noted being that of Lord Mountnorres at Cong. By March 1881 it became obvious that where the landlords were prepared to finance agents—the most celebrated was Norris Goddard of the Property Defence Association—to bid for the interests of farmers' cattle and other goods sold at sheriff's sales, they could unnerve the tenantry. Patrick Egan later told General Patrick Collins that the League's costs on this policy often reached £2,000 a week,

[80] Bew, *Land and the National Question*, 134–6.
[81] J. L. Hammond, *Gladstone and the Irish Nation* (London, 1938), 296.
[82] Jane Jordan, *Kitty O'Shea: An Irish Affair* (Stroud, 2005), 29.

when their means were only a few hundred.[83] Parnell agreed publicly with his sister's analysis at Carrick on Suir in October 1881, when he denounced 'rich farmers' who allowed 'hard-working Irish and American people, many of whom work ten times as hard as many Irish farmers', to finance their struggle.[84] But he nevertheless remained the figurehead of an organization packed with revolutionary organizers, violent assassins on the fringe, and a solid core of opportunist farmers looking to exploit the misery of the poorer neighbours by making gains out of the reduction in landlord power. Serjeant Sullivan noted acutely that 'the threat to his power, levelled by the combination of Fenianism and the Land League, compelled him to associate with men of a social and intellectual order that he must have disliked'. But he also noted that this was precisely 'the dispensation'—'hard to understand' though it was—by which Parnell became the 'hero of the bourgeoisie'.[85]

Parnell never accepted the revolutionary premises of his neo-Fenian allies. He believed in the possibility of a major land reform; he aspired to satisfy the tenantry on terms which were not disadvantageous to the landlords—the whole process to be subsidized by a generous contribution from the British taxpayer. He wanted to bring the younger and more progressive landlords into the Home Rule movement so as to give it sufficient social cachet to convince British legislators in London: a cachet that was absent in 1880.[86] But he was not able to set the limits of a popular agitation: his advocacy of the boycott and other forms of social ostracism did not satisfy his most militant supporters. Interestingly, however, the unionist *Irish Times* insisted that while Parnell committed a 'flagrant injustice' against his 'own social class', the fact that the land movement fell into 'extremes' was due 'less to the leader's incapacity than the madness of portions of those that followed him'.[87]

---

[83] Egan to Collins, Burns Library, Boston, 29 Mar. 1882; see also the correspondence addressed to Egan's close ally, Thomas Brennan, on this topic, NLI Ms 17,693. For example, the heavy list of costs submitted by Father Thomas Cummins of Scotstown.

[84] *Munster Express*, 8 Oct. 1881.

[85] A. M. Sullivan, *Old Ireland* (London, 1927), 47.

[86] 'Talking of Ireland, I said that much of the soreness of the Irish MPs, I thought, arose from the feeling that in Parliament they were not treated socially as equals. This Vernon Harcourt confirmed, saying that most of those who took the lead were not gentlemen, nor persons with whom it was possible to associate—Biggar, Callan, Sullivan etc.—in fact, these men brought in contact with English society feel themselves in a foreign country and one where they are not welcome. Hence their animosity': Vincent (ed.), *Derby Diaries*, 1 Feb. 1880, p. 210. In fact, in the 1880s there is evidence of a growing Irish ability to operate within the left liberal ambience of British politics (see Alan O'Day, *The English Face of Irish Nationalism* (Dublin, 1979)), but this passage in the *Derby Diaries*, nonetheless, throws light on the perception of senior English politicians that while Parnell might be 'respectable' (Derby's word), his collegues were not.

[87] *Irish Times*, 8 Oct. 1891.

But, whatever the personal responsibility of Parnell, Dublin Castle did feel the land movement was out of control. In late 1880 the rate of increase of agrarian outrages was remarkable: of the 2,590 listed for 1880, nearly 1,700 were committed in the last three months of the year. Exclusive of the threatening letters, there were 717 'actual' agrarian outrages in Ireland in the period from October to December 1880. Forster was increasingly perplexed. He was restrained both by a strong sense of the need for land reform and a strong sense also that some in the Cabinet were opposed to any form of repression. In particular, Gladstone appeared to be reluctant.

On 15 November Forster finally told another member of the Cabinet with special interest in Ireland, Joseph Chamberlain, of his intention to propose the suspension of habeas corpus; in other words, to take the power of arbitrary and preventive arrest of those allegedly involved in agrarian terror.

But while not denying that a widespread system of rural intimidation was in place, Gladstone wondered if it was quite so bad as to justify such extreme action by the executive. On 16 November he wrote to Forster that such a suspension should be based on a danger of life, which was not the defining feature of the present agitation. 'Statistics', he had noted in pencil beside Forster's claim that the government was failing in its duty to protect the person: between October and December 1880 there were only two actual agrarian murders in Ireland.[88] Charges of seditious conspiracy were laid by the Irish Attorney-General against Parnell and the Land League executive in November 1880, and their trial began in Dublin in December 1880. The trial was obviously a farce. Parnell noted that P. J. Gordon broke a leg and stopped turning up, but no one seemed to care. After a hearing of nineteen days the jury failed to agree on a verdict, and the case was dismissed. In such a context, Forster was finally able to convince the Cabinet of the case for coercion. The government brought in a 'Coercion Bill' on 24 January 1881. This practically suspended the Habeas Corpus Act and opened the way for mass internment of some 1,000 'suspects'. Admittedly, the regime was less than harsh. One police source accurately noted that Forster's special prisons were 'nothing more than fairly comfortable clubs, where the prisoners wanted for nothing but their liberty'.[89]

The coercion debates of February 1881 were notable primarily because they had a remarkable effect in helping to transform the Irish Parliamentary Party into a specifically Parnellite party. The Irish MPs who opposed the

[88] Bew, *Land and the National Question*, 146, 206; Vincent (ed.), *Derby Diaries*, 16 June 1882, p. 432: 'Walk with Dalhousie ... He says that Gladstone disavowed the Coercion Bill of last year, as ascribing it entirely to Forster and saying that it was against his wish: which seems strange.'

[89] Stephen Ball (ed.), *A Policeman's Ireland: Recollections of Samuel Waters RIC* (Cork, 1999), 50.

legislation had no hope of ultimate success, but they fought their corner admirably. Not only did Parnell find himself working with more Irish representatives than ever before, but also a new level of parliamentary unity and combativity was attained. Irish parliamentary orators, who were a little unsure on agrarian platforms, found it easier to defend the constitutional liberties of Irishmen. It was a field in which these men—many of them budding lawyers—were natural experts. It was, for the young Parnellite lieutenants, an intoxicating experience in which they decisively proved themselves. Meanwhile, in Ireland itself, Michael Davitt denounced the thirteen moderate home-rulers, led by William Shaw, who refused to support Parnell as traitors to the national cause.[90] As Stephen Gwynn later put it: 'What was new in Parnell's movement was the linking of fierce ebullience to a constitutional machinery.'[91] A fierce ebullience, which, it might be added, destroyed a part of the old constitutional machinery of the House of Commons.

Obstruction now reached its climax and imploded as a strategy: the Speaker on 2 February brought a debate, which had lasted forty-one hours, to an end. By the application of the closure he ensured that the House divided, and the first reading of the Bill was thus passed. A significant moment in the history of the House of Commons had been reached—the Speaker's action was widely described by parliamentarians as a *coup d'état*, in recognition of the fact that he had gone beyond the powers he was previously believed to have held. But the mainstream English parties were relieved that at last something had been done which allowed the House 'to carry out its business'. Not that there was to be an immediate end to chaos. On 3 February the government revoked Davitt's ticket of leave and arrested him in Dublin. When the news reached the House on that day, thirty-six Irish MPs, led by Parnell and Dillon, were suspended amidst scenes which 'could hardly have been exceeded if a revolution was in progress'.[92] In the midst of all this clamour, Parnell himself made major attempts to explain to British politicians the relatively conservative ethos that lay behind his apparently aggressive public announcements. Not surprisingly, his efforts were greeted with incomprehension: tellingly, however, in Paris on 4 February Parnell resisted efforts by lieutenants to radicalize the agitation and stressed the value of parliamentary work.

Why was Parnell able to impose such a moderate course? The revolutionary left wing of the League, Davitt, Dillon, Egan, Brennan, and Harris, wanted Parnell to return to America to collect funds. This would

90 T. W. Moody, *Davitt and Irish Revolution* (Oxford, 1981), 460.
91 *Freeman's Journal*, 29 Sept. 1906.
92 Vincent (ed.), *Derby Diaries*, 303.

have given the neo-Fenians and their allies control of events in Ireland itself. But at this point only Andrew Kettle actually argued for a policy of Irish withdrawal from Parliament. Kettle had emerged from the world of land reform politics rather than Fenian conspiracy. It seems that his arguments carried little weight. Kettle later wrote: 'The trouble about the whole thing seemed to be that the revolutionary policy of the Land League movement was being pushed by an outsider.'[93] Kettle's intervention came, as he put it, 'like a blizzard for which they were not prepared'.[94] Parnell, in the end, unified all factions by arguing that, following the first arrest under the Coercion Act, Irish MPs should return to their constituencies and lead a general strike against rent. This sounded very radical, but it stopped short of a withdrawal from Parliament. Why were the neo-Fenians so moderate (by their own standards) during these discussions? No doubt their greater experience in these matters taught them to be more careful of inviting government oppression. They were also, perhaps, too confident that they had built up momentum and were, as a small inner directing force, in control of the movement. They had hopes that reactionary forces in the British Parliament would block Gladstone's projected measure of land reform. It might be noted here that Parnell's close knowledge of the balance of forces within the Liberal government—much remarked upon by British contemporaries—gave him an edge when it came to political calculations.[95]

For, as Parnell grasped more surely than other Irish leaders, the British government was obsessed with a settlement of the land question. There was little belief that repression alone would do the trick. The *Westminster Review* summarized a mood amongst Liberals. It denounced attempts at character assassination of the Irish. There were no 'innate tendencies' of Irish character; for example, Irishmen outside Ireland rarely invested in land but were among the 'most enterprising merchants and speculators'.[96]

What does a Mayo peasant know about the law? He has a vague notion that the law took away the land from some old Irish and Anglo-Irish families, whose name is still great in the countryside: that the law will support the landlord, that the law is purposely framed to confuse him with technicalities and saddle him with heavy costs if he attempts to improve his position.[97]

One prominent Liberal Irish landlord, the Marquess of Dufferin, home on leave from his duties in the St Petersburg embassy, joined the discussion

[93] L. J. Kettle (ed.), *Kettle: Material for Victory* (Dublin, 1958), 39.
[94] Ibid. 48.
[95] *Quarterly Review*, 151: 301 (Jan. 1881), 'The Truth about Ireland', p. 265.
[96] Ibid. 107.
[97] *Westminster Review* 115 (1881), 'The Irish Land Question', p. 107.

in December 1880. Dufferin had no doubt as to the underlying political reality: 'It is quite evident that no government—I don't care whether Conservative or Liberal—will risk losing the entire Irish vote, and making enemies of the whole Irish nation, merely for the purpose of saving the property of the Irish landlords.'[98] Dufferin had noted the way in which Ulster Conservative, even Orange, members had moved into the agrarian radical camp.[99] Broad political considerations now dominated everything—the Bessborough Commission's assumption that a rent which had been paid regularly should be assumed to be fair rent, was about to be summarily dismissed by government.[100] Dufferin, therefore, regarded major land reform on the '3Fs' (fair rents, free sale, fixity of tenure) model as inevitable, but he fully understood that any such concession would inevitably be expanded in practice: 'Any so-called qualifications or qualifications by which the application of the infamous 3 Fs may be limited, would be swept away during the course of ten years.' But some shrewd judges did not get the point. W. E. H. Lecky felt sure that events were set on a much more gentle course: 'The Land Bill, I believe, will be very moderate. Curiously enough, Gladstone, on this question, is much more conservative than most of his party. I hear that he is for one "F" only—fair rents—ie some court of arbitration.'[101] By mid-January 1881, however, Forster and Gladstone had settled on the 3Fs as the only possible solution, but Gladstone never faced up to the full implications of his own actions. The difficulty lay in the fact that, in 1870, he had defined the principle of fixity of tenure as pure confiscation. In a perhaps necessary act of self-deception, he convinced himself (mainly by defining fixity of tenure as permanent tenure in all circumstances) that he had not broken with a key principle of market economics and conceded fixity of tenure![102] Lecky observed with some coldness:

As was his usual custom on such occasions, he pitched his tone very high and appealed in noble language to the loftiest of motives. 'Justice, Sir, is to be our guide; and it has been said that love is stronger than death, even so, justice is stronger than

---

[98] Sir A. Lyell, *The Life of the Marquis of Dufferin and Ava* (London, 1905), i. 190.

[99] Hammond, *Gladstone and the Irish Nation*, 216–17; Margaret O'Callaghan, *British High Politics and a Nationalist Ireland: Criminality, Land and the Law under Forster and Balfour* (Cork, 1994), 54; *The Witness*, 3 Dec. 1880. 'Ulster has been carried by O'Reilly, Dillon, Kettle, Sheridan and Jordan', Davitt wrote to Devoy on 16 Dec. 1880: *Devoy's Post Bag*, ii. 22.

[100] W. E. H. Lecky, *Democracy and Liberty*, vol. 1 (London, 1896), 188.

[101] Elisabeth Lecky, *W. E. H. Lecky: A Memoir* (London, 1909), Lecky to Booth, 17 Jan. 1881, p. 149.

[102] See Gladstone's speech, *Hansard*, vol. 260, col. 915 (7 Apr. 1881). Dublin Castle (Forster and Cowper) and even Hartington were more openly radical than Gladstone on this issue. See Henry Vane, *Affair of State* (London, 2004), 138.

popular excitement, stronger than the passions of the moment, stronger even than the grudges, the resentments and the sad traditions of the past. Walking in that light, we can not err. Guided by that light—the Divine Light—we are safe'.[103]

Even now, Gladstone still, in some corner of his mind, wished to assimilate Irish to English land tenure: for this reason he deprived future tenants of the advantages of his Bill, which gave every present tenant an interest in his holding, regardless of whether he made improvements or not.[104] These future tenants were to hold the land on a pure contract basis. Ironically, but quite unintentionally, Gladstone had fashioned a weapon against the League: farmers began to fear they would lose out if they followed radical courses by losing the rights they held as present tenants under the 1881 Act. The subversive radicalism of Gladstone's land legislation was nonetheless profound. Consider the case of R. J. Mahoney, one of a minority of activists and improving landlords in the south-west of Ireland.[105] His *A Short Statement Concerning the Confiscation of Improvements in Ireland Addressed to the Rt Hon W. E. Forster by a Working Landowner*[106] argued against the confiscation of money spent by him on his land as part of a broader 3Fs settlement. Mahoney noted with great perception: 'If Great Britain and Ireland are to remain a united kingdom, then surely a property in Kerry, managed on similar principles to a property in Devonshire, should be subject to the same legislation.' Mahoney added: 'If a law is passed on the assumption that the tenant is the only improver, it is manifest that the so-called owner is thereby relieved of all responsibility to make improvements himself.' Some were slow to get the message. In mid-April Lecky was still prepared to assume the essential moderation of the legislation: 'As far as I can judge, the Land Bill will greatly increase the probability of regular payment of rents in Ireland (and this Gladstone himself strongly holds), and I think it will also raise the price of Irish land.'[107] Lecky did, indeed, meet with Gladstone on 28 April 1881; but the meeting failed to prevent a sudden rapid disillusionment on Lecky's part with the Prime Minister.[108] Lecky's eventual description of the 1881 Act is striking, and has stood the test of time: 'Landlords who possessed, by the clearest title known to English law, the most absolute ownership of their estates have been

[103] Lecky, *Democracy and Liberty*, i. 196.

[104] W. O'Connor Morris, *Ireland from 1798 to 1898* (London, 1989) 253; W. H. Kisbey, *The Irish Land Act 1881* (Dublin, 1881), p. v.

[105] For Mahoney see Gerard J. Lyne, *The Lansdowne Estate in Kerry under W. S. Trench 1849–72* (Dublin, 2001), 404.

[106] (Dublin, 1880).

[107] Lecky, *Lecky: A Memoir*, Lecky to his stepmother, 15 Apr. 1881, p. 155.

[108] H. C. G. Matthew (ed.), *The Gladstone Diaries*, vol. 10, *January 1881—June 1883* (Oxford, 1990), 59.

converted into rent chargers.'[109] It is perhaps hardly a surprise that when Engels came to write his celebrated article 'Social Classes—Necessary and Superfluous' in August 1881, he located Irish landlords in the 'superfluous' category.[110] One young landlord writer, George Moore, in *Parnell and his Island* described Irish landlordism 'as a worn-out system, no longer possible in the nineteenth century, and one whose end is nigh'.[111]

The implication is clear: legislation such as the 1881 Land Act weakened the union and demoralized the best elements in Irish landlordism. Yet, even Mahoney, despite his forcefully argued pamphlet, was subject to conflicting emotions. Derby found Mahoney more flexible than his published text—which Derby had absorbed—implied.

But I find on enquiry that he thinks many rents are fixed at too high a rate in his part of the country by the small owners and should not be averse to see a court established which should limit the amount of rents. I could not, however, get him to say by what process a fair rent was to be fixed: he seemed to think that according to Irish practice, there would be no great difficulty in the matter.[112]

When the government unveiled its new legislation, it gave full recognition to tenant right throughout Ireland and established a new tribunal, a land court, to fix 'fair rents'. Parnell immediately recognized in private that Gladstone had done enough, but in public he maintained a critical stance before Gladstone's proposal became law in August. Parnell had relatively few problems in dealing with it. To maintain agitation was the easiest way of ensuring amendments to make the legislation even more favourable to the tenants. Prominent Irish-Americans were told by Patrick Egan that, 'in all probability', the Bill would not get through Parliament.[113] Egan had, after all, plenty of 'movement work' to engage in: in June he employed Land League funds to establish a nationalist newspaper, *United Ireland*, under the editorship of firebrand William O'Brien. The more staid T. D. Sullivan and his organ, *The Nation*, were unceremoniously pushed aside; Sullivan, although a member of the Land League executive, was

---

[109] W. E. H. Lecky, 'Ireland in the Light of History', in *Historical and Political Essays* (London, 1910), 79.

[110] 'The Labour Standard in August 1881', in Karl Marx and Friedrich Engels, *Articles on Britain* (Moscow, 1971), 384 ff.; for the controversy which surrounds this essay, see Étienne Balibar, 'Self-Criticism: An Answer to Questions from Theoretical Practice', *Theoretical Practice*, 7–8 Jan. 1973, p. 72.

[111] Carla King (ed.), *Parnell and his Ireland: George Moore* (Dublin, 2004), 3; see also Adrian Frasier, *George Moore 1852–1933* (New Haven, 2000), ch. 3.

[112] Vincent (ed.), *Derby Diaries*, 285.

[113] Burns Library, Boston College, Collins Mss. 86–38, Patrick Egan to P. A .Collins, 3 May 1881.

told nothing about the interesting use of Land League funds.[114] It was a suggestive example of the revolutionary elitism to be found at the heart of the League's affairs. However, with the passing of the Act (which Gladstone intended to undercut the League) the context changed. Parnell's refusal to wind down the agitation implied the risk of his own imprisonment and the loss of 'moderate' support in Ireland. On the other hand, refusal to maintain the agitation would have alienated Irish-American feeling and the radical wing of the Land League. Parnell presided at a League convention at which it was resolved that the Act should be 'tested' by selected cases. He was present thereafter at several large Land League demonstrations in opposition to it, and on 13 October he was arrested and conveyed to Kilmainham Jail.

On the occasion of his arrest at Morrison's Hotel in Dublin, Parnell behaved, as the authorities acknowledged, 'like a gentleman'. He was surprised but perfectly composed, and asked leave to post three letters. One, of course, was to Mrs O'Shea: 'Politically it is a fortunate thing for me that I have been arrested, as the movement is breaking fast, and all will be quiet in a few months when I shall be released.'[115]

In Kilmainham, William O'Brien drafted, and Parnell, Dillon, Kettle, Brennan, and Thomas Sexton all signed, the celebrated 'No Rent Manifesto'. It called on Irish farmers to pay no more rent until the government abandoned its policy of coercion. The 'No Rent Manifesto' merely served to weaken clerical support for the Land League. Fanny Parnell naively believed that the senior pro-Land League prelate Archbishop Croke, on her brother's arrest, should have stepped into Parnell's place. The Land League, in fact, made an immediate request to Croke to 'act as President'.[116] Instead, Croke, according to Fanny, 'issued a bullying and ignorant letter' denouncing the 'No Rent Manifesto'.[117] Croke's letter, his biographer, Dom Mark Tierney, observes, fell like 'a bombshell upon the Kilmainham party'.

Parnell, with some astuteness, believed that his arrest had been made certain on account of a by-election defeat suffered a week earlier. On 7 September, in Tyrone, a Gladstonian Ulster Liberal, T. A. Dickson, received 3,168 votes, the Conservative 3,081, and Parnell's candidate only 907. Following this somewhat fortuitous Liberal by-election victory, Gladstone still believed in an Irish 'middle way'.

---

[114] NLI Ms 8237, T. D. Sullivan note, dated 16 July 1881, recounting his confrontation with Parnell on this topic; It also contains Sullivan's neglected correspondence with Davitt.
[115] Katherine O'Shea, *Charles Stewart Parnell* (London, 1914), i. 207.
[116] Burns Library, Fanny Parnell to Gen. Collins, 10 Nov. 1881.
[117] Mark Tierney, *Croke of Cashel: The Life of Archbishop Thomas William Croke 1832–1902* (Dublin, 1976), 130.

If Ireland is still divided between Orangeism and law haters, then our task is hopeless, but our belief and contention always is that a more intelligent and less impassioned body has gradually come to exist in Ireland. It is on that body and its precepts and example that our hopes depend, for if we are at war with a nation, we can not win.[118]

Gladstone's position on Home Rule was increasingly an unstable one, dependent on distinctions more real to him than to others. Gladstone, on 9 February 1882 and again on 16 February 1882, acknowledged that no one would doubt the Irish capacity for self-rule, but he would not grant Home Rule. Neither Butt nor O'Connell had formulated a scheme whereby Ireland could enjoy autonomy without weakening the British Empire. Yet, both had formulated such federalist schemes, and the 'new departure' was built on a denial of them. The Prime Minister himself could not see any authority capable of deciding the limits of the Irish jurisdiction, save the will or whim of the sovereign.[119] To set these February comments alongside the dramatic private declaration—'If we are at war with a nation, we can not win'—is to place them in their context. John Devoy, in his American-based paper the *Irish Nation*, was quite correct to suggest that nationalists should take hope from Gladstone's remarks. At this very moment, Gladstone recorded a private discussion with his son: 'Conversation with HJG on home rule and my speech for the subject has probably a future.'[120]

Parnell was probably right in his view that without the unfortunate election defeat in Tyrone he would not have been imprisoned. But Forster, in a sense the wiser man on this issue, already knew that Ireland was divided between 'Orangeism' and 'law haters', and that any attempt—as suggested by Gladstone—to recruit a new non-sectarian body of Irish constables would fail. He told the premier bluntly: 'In the South and West we can not get them, and in the North, Orangemen would offer themselves, and we would have to put a policeman on the side of every Special [constable] to keep them in order.' Forster knew how dark the reality was; but he still felt compelled to soldier on rather than allow a victory to law-breakers. Forster, in short, was prepared reluctantly to bear the moral cost of repression, even if at 'war with a nation'. The Prime Minister, on the other hand, told an incredulous Earl of Derby that he believed 'the Irish people as a body to be loyal', and that there were not more than '10 or 12 really disaffected Irishmen in the House'.[121] The divergence of outlook between the Prime Minister and his Irish Secretary became more and more obvious.

---

[118] Hammond, *Gladstone and the Irish Nation*, 246.
[119] Matthew (ed.), *The Gladstone Diaries*, x. 208–11; *Irish Nation*, 28 Feb. 1883.
[120] Matthew, *The Gladstone Diaries*, introduction to vols X and XI, p. cxix.
[121] Vincent (ed.) *Derby Diaries*, 28 Oct. 1881, 367.

The management of a mass agitation is no easy business. Parnell had to retain a notion both of the lines of fissure in the British Cabinet and within the Irish tenantry. This he did, never allowing himself to be deluded by the rhetoric of the former or the latter. In March 1882 even John Devoy conceded that the Land League was losing momentum. Quite apart from the political tensions within the leadership, many farmers now wished to grasp the benefits of the 1881 Land Act—offering real promise of rent reductions of 20 or 25 per cent—whilst the poorest peasantry now intuited that their hopes of land would not be fulfilled. John Devoy acknowledged that 'the Land League is in an internal crisis greater than any the British Government has been able to put on it'.[122] But he also now offered a less-than-Mitchelite explanation of the whole project since 1879. Gesturing back to the original revolutionary hopes, 'a satisfactory settlement ... could not be achieved under English rule'. So far, so Mitchelite; but then he revealed the real logic of the Land League movement, as opposed to the revolutionary hopes of its neo-Fenian leadership. 'They knew that although the question could not be finally settled, the power of the landlord class would be broken—and the people considerably strengthened by organisation, combination and passive resistance among the rural population.'[123]

Whether part-rationalization or not, Devoy's words have the ring of truth. As early as 6 March 1882 the most senior Irish Tory, the Belfast lawyer Earl Cairns, was convinced that the only possible strategy was to create a peasant proprietorship in Ireland with state support.[124] By April 1882 Lord Salisbury had declared his public support for peasant proprietorship.[125] With the Tories moving so fast in their thinking on Ireland, the Liberals did not like to stand still. Parnell was well aware that members of the Liberal Cabinet—in particular Joseph Chamberlain—had doubts about the new policy of mass internment of suspects. Through Captain O'Shea, Parnell kept open his lines of communication to Chamberlain. Partly in consequence, he was released on parole on 10 April 1882, having been given permission to visit Mrs O'Shea, who placed his dying child Claude Sophie (b. 16 February 1882) in his arms. This can only have increased his desire to get permanently out of prison and return to Mrs O'Shea's side. This was made very much easier by the growing isolation within the Cabinet of Chief Secretary Forster and his policy of repression. The predicted improvement in social conditions in Ireland never seemed to materialize. Coercion was increasingly distasteful to the Liberal Party, especially now that it did not appear to be working.

[122] *Irish Nation*, 4 Mar. 1882.   [123] Ibid., 11 Mar. 1882.
[124] Vincent (ed.), *Derby Diaries*, 6 March 1882, p. 405.
[125] Philip Bull, *Land Politics and Nationalism: A Study of the Irish Land Question* (Dublin, 1996).

THE KILMAINHAM TREATY

In the early spring of 1882 the mood of Gladstone's circle turned decisively against coercion. On 26 March 1882 Gladstone's Secretary, Edward Hamilton, recorded in his diary: 'My own belief is that the present means of coercion have wholly failed as regards shutting up permanent political agitators. For these the Act was not really intended; while for those who are committed to outrages such kid-glove confinement is a pleasant change.'[126] One of the reasons for the change in Gladstone's thinking was the ineffectiveness of the Crown legislation in reducing actual murder, the most serious crime. Between October 1880 and the end of March 1881—the Peace Preservation (Ireland) Act of 1881 was passed on 21 March—there were three agrarian murders in Ireland. Between April and June 1881 the figure rose to seven; between July and September 1881 there was a drop to one, but in the autumn the figure rose dramatically again. Between October and December 1881 there were eight murders; this upsurge in crime continued into March 1882; between January and March 1882 there were six murders.

On 6 April Herbert Gladstone recorded in his diary: 'Father... is accepting my view of the Irish situation, ie that the "No rent" manifesto has failed and that crime is more revolutionary in its character; and outrages committed to prove the Government wrong in coercing.'[127] Parnell later remarked of Gladstone to Davitt: 'You know he put us in prison, and we were called upon to strike back so as to deter others from resorting to like methods again.'[128] For the government's area of success—the Land Act and the defeat of the 'No rent' manifesto—to be fully capitalized upon, it was necessary to abandon a Coercion Act which was, to use Herbert Gladstone's word, 'inoperative' for the suppression of crime and, in fact, very often the cause of it.

At this moment Parnell intervened with a new political initiative: he contacted the government through Captain O'Shea. Parnell informed O'Shea that if the government settled the arrears question on the lines he proposed, he and his colleagues had every confidence that they would be able to exert effective influence against outrages. On 30 April O'Shea met with Forster: during this interview, O'Shea gave the Chief Secretary a copy

---

[126] Sir E. W. Hamilton, in D. W. R. Bahlman (ed.), *The Diary of Sir Edward Walter Hamilton*, 2 vols. (Oxford, 1972), i. 242.

[127] A. B. Cooke and J. R. Vincent (eds.), 'Herbert Gladstone, Forster and Ireland 1881–2', *Irish Historical Studies*, part 2, 18: 69 (Mar. 1972), 77; Vincent (ed.), *Derby Diaries*, 2 May 1882, p. 420, confirms the point.

[128] *Fall of Feudalism*, 481.

of a letter from Parnell, dated 28 April, stating his terms for a settlement with the government and (as recorded by Forster) declared on behalf of Parnell that 'the conspiracy which has been used to get up boycotting and outrages, will now be used to put them down and that there will be a union with the Liberal Party', providing that Parnell's land programme could be carried out, and with the hope that further coercion would be shelved.[129] In a succeeding paragraph, he told the Cabinet that the arrangement would 'enable him to cooperate cordially for the future with the Liberal Party in forwarding liberal principles'.[130] To promote the settlement of the west of Ireland, Parnell urged that Sheridan and Boyton, organizers of the League in the west, should be given a free hand by the government to carry out the work of pacification. Soon after the arrest of Parnell, Sheridan had been released from jail because of his wife's illness: in December 1881 a warrant was issued for his rearrest, but he escaped to Paris. In 1882 he paid several clandestine visits to Ireland, disguised as a priest; he distributed relief to evicted tenants and helped organize the struggle.

For Forster, Parnell was admitting that his lieutenants controlled the level of crime; for Gladstone, however, the key point was that Parnell was now offering to stop that crime. On 30 April Gladstone told Forster: 'I can not help feeling indebted to O'Shea.'[131] Accordingly, on 2 May 1882 Gladstone informed the House of Commons of the release of Parnell, but also of the resignation of Forster. On 3 May Florence Arnold-Forster recorded the consensus of the Forster family in her diary: 'Mr Parnell, according to Mr O'Shea, would undertake not only in a vague way to discourage outrage, but to cause Mr Sheridan, the Land League organiser, to do the same.'[132] On 4 May Gladstone, after a somewhat disturbed night, wrote in his diary: 'Arrest was for intentions, which placed us in the midst of a social revolution. We believe the intentions now are to promote law and order.' In such a context, 'continued internment was an absurdity. Had Parnell declared in October what they declare now, we could not have imprisoned him'.[133] It is worth noting that even within the Forster camp there was an acceptance that the Parnellites had moderated their position.[134]

[129] Moody and Hawkins (eds.), *Florence Arnold-Forster's Irish Journal*, 465.
[130] Bew, *Land and the National Question*, 57.   [131] BL Add Ms 44160, f. 160.
[132] Moody and Hawkins (eds.), *Florence Arnold-Forster's Irish Journal*, 472.
[133] Matthew (ed.), *The Gladstone Diaries*, x. 251.
[134] Moody and Hawkins (eds.), *Florence Arnold-Forster's Journal*, 27 Apr. 1882, p. 460: 'It must be allowed that, the 'New Departure' is not only on the side of the government.' As late as 30 April, Forster's daughter (p. 468) wrote of her father's view that Parnellite acceptance (via Healy's Bill) of the 1881 Act showed that 'the government has triumphed in establishing the law of the land as opposed to the law of the Land League'.

Gladstone always denied that there had been a 'Kilmainham treaty', though he accepted that 'we have obtained information'. It was a distinction which made little sense, even to close colleagues;[135] but it is worth noting that a Rubicon had been crossed. For the first time a British prime minister had attempted to co-opt the political leadership of a violent nationalist movement (the Land League) by a process of secret negotiation and concession. It is true that the Whigs attempted to co-opt O'Connell via the Lichfield House Compact of 1835: but O'Connell was not linked, as Parnell was, to figures like Sheridan, who famously declared: 'We'll give the landlords what they got from the French revolution—twelve feet of rope, but always in a strictly constitutional manner.'[136] More than this, the exposure of the deal, whilst it led to serious heart-searching and high-level resignations, did not lead to prime-ministerial collapse. As Derby noted: 'In fact, it is a new departure, founded on partial alliance with the Land League and on an emphatic repudiation of the policy of coercion which has been accepted as necessity up to this date by parliament and the public.'[137]One Gladstonian Liberal and Ulsterman, James Bryce, driving home from the House in a hansom cab with G. J. Goschen, was told: 'If Disraeli had been living, we would have risen to say "The House has just witnessed the humiliating spectacle of the Prime Minister of England defending a bargain of dishonour with the suspects of Kilmainham".' But as Bryce added:

Gladstone used afterwards to express his surprise at the reproaches made to him. He would say he had no right to keep the men in prison when that was no longer needed for the peace of the country. There was no bargain in the matter. When anyone of his colleagues inadvertently talked of the Kilmainham Treaty, he did not conceal his displeasure.[138]

The significance of the release was well understood by Forster, who argued that the Parnellites were being recognized as the 'representatives of Ireland': 'Such a course would be a tremendous step towards Home Rule. It would be equivalent to admitting that these men are what they claim to be, and the Government releases them in order to effect what it can not accomplish itself—the pacification of Ireland and the maintenance of law and order.'[139] Lord Derby agreed, despite an intensive personal effort by Gladstone to persuade him otherwise. The

    135 Vincent (ed.), *Derby Diaries*, 2 May 1882, p. 420.
    136 William O'Brien, *Evening Memories* (Dublin and London, 1920), 73.
    137 Ibid.
    138 H. A. L. Fisher, *James Bryce: Viscount Bryce of Deechmount*, vol. 1 (London, 1927), 206.
    139 *Florence Arnold Forster's Journal*, 460.

Westminster Review later aptly summarized what became the conventional view: 'Surely never in the history of English administration did a cabinet so completely cry *peccavimus* ['we have sinned'], as the cabinet did, which ordered the release of Parnell.'[140] On 15 May Forster effectively forced the revelation in the House of Commons that Parnell had offered to support the Liberals in the House as part of the deal.

No such deed goes unpunished: Forster was, of course, right, but 'Forsterism' soon became a shorthand Gladstonian phrase for crude authoritarianism.[141] But despite these condemnations, Forster continued to haunt Gladstone; the GOM's failure to make any public comment on Forster's death in 1886 was seen by some as evidence of a meanness of spirit.[142] Gladstone, however, felt rather differently; even after Forster's death and the publication of his official life, Gladstone thought it worthwhile to make a highly critical assessment of his years in Ireland.[143]

Parnell, at this moment, did not quite share Gladstone's supreme self-belief. In fact, Parnell appears to have been concerned that radical nationalists would feel that he had made a discreditable deal with the enemy. Immediately upon his release, Parnell may have met by chance with P. J. Sheridan in Dublin. On the suppression of the Land League in 1881 Sheridan had fled to Paris, but in 1882 he returned to Ireland and travelled widely disguised as a priest.[144] One later report records that Parnell had allowed that mild-mannered fanatic to swear him into the Irish Republican Brotherhood in the incongruous setting of the library of Trinity College, Dublin, on either 2 or 3 May. Parnell had offered to join the brotherhood at least once before, in conversation with Patrick Egan, but this time he may have actually taken the oath, on condition that his doing so would be kept a secret during his lifetime.[145] Parnell may well have wanted to control the hard men. The father of one of the Invincible murderers, Joe Brady, told Frank Hugh: 'Do ye think there could be 500 Land Leaguers in Kilmainham, with everybody free to see his friends, and not one of them

[140] 'Parnell', *Westminster Review*, 151 (Jan. 1899), 10.

[141] H. C. G. Matthew (ed.), *The Gladstone Diaries*, vol. 11, *July 1883–December 1886* (Oxford, 1990), 151, Gladstone to J. Bright, 28 May 1884.

[142] W. Hart Westcombe, *The Irish Question: Its Essence, Cause, Solution and the Issues it involves for Ireland and for England* (London, 1886), 35.

[143] Allen Warren, 'Forster, the Liberals and New Directions in Irish Policy', *Parliamentary History*, 6: 1 (1987), 118. See also Dudley W. R. Bahlman, *The Diary of Sir Edward Hamilton* (Hull, 1993), 80–3.

[144] 'Memories of Stormy Days', *Weekly Freeman*, 16 Feb. 1916; P. J. Sheridan and a *Times* overture.

[145] Patrick Maume, 'Parnell and the IRB Oath', *Irish Historical Studies*, 29: 115 (May 1995), 363–70.

to tell Parnell that brave men had their knives waiting to kill Forster and coercion?'[146]

Sheridan was certainly one of the hard men. In acting as a go-between with Gladstone, Captain O'Shea had stated categorically that Sheridan's influence could put down crime in the west, if the warrant for his arrest was withdrawn. Parnell, therefore, had every incentive to reassure Sheridan and thereby enhance his hold over him. But then events took a sudden and unexpected turn, which placed such calculations in a very different light. Hard on the heels of this incident, on 6 May 1882, Lord Frederick Cavendish, Forster's replacement as Chief Secretary, along with his permanent Under-Secretary, Thomas Burke, was stabbed to death in Phoenix Park by the Invincibles, a group of nationalist assassins. Of particular concern to Parnell was the fact that P. J. Sheridan was later to claim a leading role in this body.[147]

All accounts agree that Parnell—'white and broken with horror and despair, the knives had gone close to his heart too'[148]—was shaken to the core, and beyond, by the assassination, even to the extent of writing to Gladstone offering to resign as an MP. James Bryce observed that Parnell's characteristic 'undismayed fortitude only once forsook him and that was in the panic which was suddenly created by the Phoenix Park murders in 1882'.[149] But Parnell's genuine sense of revulsion, even fear, worked to his advantage. When he rose to speak on the Phoenix Park murders in the House, the initial mood of some MPs was hostile, but the mood changed when it was found that he was speaking with scarcely less feeling than Mr Gladstone himself, and in an even more 'faltering tone'.[150] Gladstone refused his offer to resign, and a different course was resolved upon: Parnell and Gladstone were to work more closely together.

On 23 May 1882 Parnell opened up a correspondence with Gladstone via Mrs O'Shea, which was to last for some years. At the beginning of June 1882 Mrs O'Shea met Gladstone in Thomas's Hotel in London: she told him that after his Kilmainham experience Parnell was now 'quite a different

[146] F. H. O'Donnell, *A History of the Irish Parliamentary Party* (London, 1910), ii. 131.

[147] Le Caron records Luke Dillon, the legendary hardest man of all in Fenian circles, saying: 'It was undoubtedly true that it was money which was subscribed for Land League funds, which was made in payment of the assassins of Burke and Cavendish, although he doubts if Parnell knew of the affair beforehand, prior to the act, although he says Egan declares that Parnell did know and would neither countenance nor discountenance the perpetration of the act.' Entry dated 10 Dec. 1888 in Le Caron's report, in the possession of the antiquarian bookseller Peter Rowan of Belfast. For Le Caron's career see J. A. Cole, *Prince of Spies: Henri le Caron* (London, 1984).

[148] O'Donnell, *Irish Parliamentary Party*, ii. 122.

[149] Bryce, *Studies in Contemporary Biography*, 236.

[150] Aaron Watson, *Newspaper Man's Memoirs* (London, 1927), 151.

man'. Gladstone replied that he had 'carefully studied Parnell' and that he considered him now a 'conservative force' in Ireland, and that from that point onwards, he would not attack Parnell, even though he accepted that Parnell would have to attack him.[151] This is the starting-point of one of the most surprising collaborations in Victorian political history. The two men were hardly natural soulmates. Gladstone had a profound knowledge of history, exalted culture, and was possessed by a deep religious seriousness. Parnell had a gloomy temperament, was generally ignorant of literature, and given over to curious superstitions. Neither man had a gift for personal friendship, but both had the capacity to be clear-sighted in pursuit of a political objective. The Phoenix Park assassinations, which at first glance seemed likely to blow away the Gladstone–Parnell new departure, actually strengthened it: it did so because, to Gladstone, a contrite Parnell now appeared to be a considerably more malleable figure. While some in the Cabinet fondly believed that Gladstone now was in a position to 'escape',[152] the alliance with Parnell was, in fact, placed on a more stable basis. As usually happens in such cases, officials tended to agree and exaggerate the evils which had been averted by the new policy; Edward Hamilton apparently believing that it had averted a 'general strike' against rent and the union of Ulster with the rest of Ireland.[153]

The fact remained that, if the basic policy was right, the murder changed nothing: it was certainly not carried out at Parnell's command. In fact, the popular disapproval of the murder in Ireland gave Parnell the necessary accretion of political strength he required to follow the Kilmainham strategy.[154] The old Irish hand G. S. Shaw Lefevre had fully expected to be offered the Irish Chief Secretaryship in the aftermath of the Cavendish assassination. But, he told Professor Hancock, his previous support for coercion, and his public hostility to the 'No Rent Manifesto', counted against him. Instead the job went to G. O. Trevelyan, who took care to break with Forster's characteristic tone and approach.[155]

[151] F. E. Hamer (ed.), *The Personal Papers of Lord Rendel* (London, 1931), 1 and 173, note dated 2 Mar. 1889. Gladstone placed this meeting in May, but it took place on 2 June. O'Shea, *Charles Stewart Parnell*, i. 269.
[152] Vincent (ed.), *Derby Diaries*, 10 May 1882, p. 433.
[153] *The Diaries of Sir Edward Hamilton* (Oxford, 1972), 11 June 1882, vol. 1, p. 281.
[154] Sir Robert Anderson, *The Lighter Side of my Official Life* (London, 1910), 103.
[155] NLI Ms 18,972. G. Shaw Lefevre to Prof. W. Neilson Hancock, 18 May 1882; cf. also his letter on his attitude to coercion, same to same, 17 Jan. 1884. In fact, Gladstone's first choice was the senior Ulster Liberal lawyer J. L. Porter, son of the Revd William Porter of Limavady, one of Montgomery's Liberal allies within the Presbyterian Church, known as 'Papist Billy' to his local Orange enemies. Porter's refusal (on health grounds) marked a final closure for the prospects of that particular Liberal Unionist tradition.

TOWARDS HOME RULE?

It should not be thought that the new course was an easy and unproblematical one for senior Liberals. On 6 June 1882 a Catholic landlord, Colonel Walter Bourke, was murdered in east Galway. It was widely believed that another landlord, John Shawe-Taylor, witnessed the murder but was too afraid to give evidence.[156] The police strongly suspected the involvement of P. J. Gordon, one of Parnell's fellow traversers at the state trial. But when in mid-June 1882 Parnell spoke in the House, denouncing evictions, Trevelyan made no mention of the Bourke affair, simply saying that Parnell had spoken with 'perfect correctness',[157] and adding that official opinion agreed that these were cases of great hardship. Nevertheless, it has to be said that a letter from O'Shea, stressing Parnell's power of 'control' in the countryside, moved Spencer to tell Gladstone: 'I can not but reflect on the position of Parnell in connection with those who plot murders such as Burke's.'[158]

Nor should it be thought that somehow the politics of violent threat had ended simply because Parnell was now claiming to be in a position to control it. The reverse is actually true. From this moment onwards, fear of assassination entered the lives of senior British politicians. George Trevelyan, for example, was a visibly frightened man in Belfast in August 1882:

During his short visit to the North, Mr Trevelyan was evidently suffering from extreme anxiety about his children, whom he had left in Dublin, and several times during the day telegrams arrived, informing him of their safety. He was impressed with the idea that no official of the Crown, nor any connected with any official, was safe.[159]

The fear moved to London when Irish-American extremists such as O'Donovan Rossa established a 'Skirmishing Fund' to promote dynamite explosions in England. In the period from 1881 to 1885 explosions took place at the Tower of London, Scotland Yard, and the Houses of Parliament, and at railways and underground stations. On 13 December 1884 a serious attempt was made to blow up London Bridge, which led to the self-destruction of the bombers, the Lomasney brothers and John Fleming; William Lomasney was a particularly well-known Fenian cadre whose

---

[156] For this case, see Fergus Campbell, *Land and Revolution: Nationalist Politics in the West of Ireland 1891–1912* (Oxford, 2005), 77–8.
[157] *Hansard*, 14 June 1882, cols. 1175–6.
[158] Gordon, *Red Earl*, Spencer to Gladstone, 18 Sept. 1882, p. 222.
[159] Thomas MacKnight, *Ulster As It Is* (London, 1896), ii. 21.

activities went back to 1865 in Cork. Amongst those arrested for bombing activities was Thomas J. Clarke (1858–1916), who was imprisoned under very harsh conditions until 1898.[160] Both the Secret Service and the Scotland Yard Special Branch were formed in the attempt to contain the Fenians, and government awareness that the Fenian–Irish Parliamentary Party relationship was both close and complex[161] led to surveillance of the lives of elected Irish parliamentarians. The British were aware also, from their spy Henri Le Caron, that the Fenians had been testing a submarine in the United States.[162] Parnell was to be fortunate, however, in that after the Phoenix Park murders those Land Leaguers who had the most pronounced connections with extremist violence—men such as the treasurer Patrick Egan, the secretary Thomas Brennan, and the organizers M. M. O'Sullivan, P. J. Sheridan, and Michael Boyton—fled to the United States. In effect, this flight of the radicals made much less visible the links which existed between Parnellism and crime.

For a while Gladstone became obsessed with security and intelligence: a tough new Crimes Act was passed. At this point Gladstone regarded Francis P Dewees's *The Molly Maguires: The Origin, Growth and Character of the Organisation* (Philadelphia, 1877) as 'throwing more light on the case of Ireland than anything I have read'.[163] The 'Molly Maguires' were presented by Dewees as inherently evil Irishmen who had terrorized the anthracite coalfields of Pennsylvania for two decades before being brought to justice by the heroic exploits of James McParlan, an Ulster Catholic-born Pinkerton detective.[164] But Gladstone, unbothered by the moral simplicities of this account, saw it 'as [presenting] a case of Ireland over again and even something more, all worked by the Irish'. Impressive intelligence and detective work had destroyed this 'murderous organisation'; he noted: 'Surely there were lessons to be learnt for Ireland itself?'[165]

But gradually Gladstone's thoughts returned to a broader political focus. Young Liberal MPs who thought they were talking career risks by criticizing coercive legislation found instead that the GOM smiled upon

---

[160] K. R. M. Short, *The Dynamite War: Irish-American Bombers in Victorian Britain* (Dublin, 1979), 200–8.

[161] Ibid. 82, 171, 189–90, 229.

[162] W. Garrett Scaife, 'John Philip Holland: Father of the Modern Submarine', in David Attis (ed.), *Science and Irish Culture* (Dublin, 2004), 89.

[163] Matthew (ed.), *The Gladstone Diaries*, x. 302, Gladstone to Harcourt, 21 July 1882.

[164] Kevin Kenny, *Making Sense of the Molly Maguires* (Oxford, 1998), esp. 3, 41, and 57.

[165] Matthew (ed), *Gladstone Diaries*, x. 303, Gladstone to Lord Spencer, Lord-Lieutenant of Ireland, 2 July 1882.

them.[166] Bryce has described the mood of Gladstonian Liberal members in this era. The experience of 1881 had been a souring one—the House had devoted itself massively to Ireland with its coercive and agrarian legislation, but 'at the end of a long session, devoted entirely to her needs, we found her more hostile and not less disturbed than she was at the beginning'. But 1882 was the decisive year. 'It is from this year 1882 that I date the impression that we found that home rule was sure to come. "It may be a bold experiment," we said to one another in the lobbies, "there are serious difficulties in the way ... but if the Irishmen persist as they are doing now, they will get it".'[167] In his 1882 essay 'The Incompatibles', Matthew Arnold still insisted optimistically that Ireland could be 'blended' with England 'in the same way as Scotland, Wales and Cornwall'—but it was a view that was increasingly challenged. Derby noted on 1 March 1883: 'The common talk I am told in London is that the Irish are irreconcilable, that home rule, or government by mere force are the alternatives.'[168] But mere force had little appeal to Liberal MPs. Bryce also noted that the comparatively quiet session of 1883 did nothing to weaken the force of the gathering Liberal pro-Home Rule consensus. There was, on the contrary, a steady increase in the numbers of nationalists returned from Irish seats, and a growing habit of co-operation between the Tories and Irish members. Liberal MPs began to fear a Tory–Irish deal to their disadvantage if they did not act first. On 8 October 1883 Gladstone talked privately to Derby about Ireland: 'He talked about the prejudice and timidity of the English mind where Ireland was concerned, and said that he would never agree to anything that would destroy the supremacy of the Imperial parliament, but as to this he was very vague, and, I think, did not wish to be otherwise.'[169] Before the end of 1883 other experienced Gladstone-watchers like Chichester Fortescue claimed to have become convinced that Gladstone's ambiguous language on the subject gave a strong hint of a conversion to Home Rule.[170]

Parnellism itself had been changing in ways which made it more acceptable to Westminster opinion. In the autumn of 1882 Parnell replaced existing national structures with a new, highly centralized body, the Irish National League, which, at Parnell's insistence, laid great emphasis on its legal and constitutional character; also agrarian objectives were downplayed in favour of the pursuit of Home Rule. Tim Healy reported to General

---

[166] Fisher, *Bryce*, i. 207–8.   [167] Ibid. i. 199.
[168] Vincent (ed.), *Derby Diaries*, p515.   [169] Ibid. 594.
[170] *Home Rule: A Reprint from the Times of Articles and Letters, in Continuation of the Previous Volume* (London, 1886), 43; but see also A. B. Cooke and J. R. Vincent (eds.), *Lord Carlingford's Journal* (Oxford, 1971), 106–7, entry for 28 May 1885.

Patrick Collins that the agrarian left was on the defensive: 'Davitt did not suggest one line on the constitution of the new League. Parnell drew up the land clause, O'Brien the labour, and I did the others.'[171] Parnell devoted more and more of his time to Westminster: indeed, he spoke only once in the west of Ireland between October 1881 and January 1885, in marked contrast to the frequent visits of 1879–81. It became known early in 1883 that Parnell was in financial difficulties and that his Co. Wicklow estates were heavily mortgaged. This was by no means simply on account of his involvement in the Irish cause: he had been in debt long before his entry into politics. However, the sentiment developed that the Irish people ought to reimburse Parnell for his troubles. By May papal disapproval for this scheme (influenced by British contacts at the Vatican) was announced. The result was the opposite of that intended. Subscriptions soon flooded in, key leaders of the Irish Church, such as Archbishop Croke, ignored the papal prohibition, and Parnell received in December a cheque for over £37,000 from the Lord Mayor of Dublin. The source of the money is interesting. Mayo, the radical stronghold of the Land League, contributed a mere £174. 4s. 3d., whilst the more prosperous Meath offered £1,454; Connaught managed some £1,796, whilst Leinster and Munster each gave just under £12,000[172]—clear proof of how Parnell had become, in Serjeant Sullivan's classic phrase, 'by a dispensation hard to understand ... the hero of the bourgeoisie'.[173] Parnell's acceptance speech was rather graceless, but his popularity seems to have suffered little. True to the traditions of the Anglo-Irish gentry, Parnell always refused to take money (especially other people's) seriously. The Quaker nationalist Alfred Webb, otherwise a loyal Parnellite, complained of Parnell's 'autocratic management' of 'funds', a style which provoked his resignation from the post of treasurer of the League.[174]

In February 1884 Gladstone sought leave to introduce a Bill to extend the franchise: the Bill, which extended the right to vote to the agricultural labouring poor in Ireland, was passed on 6 December. It was yet another decisive step along the path to Home Rule policy for British liberalism. H. A. L. Fisher, Bryce's biographer, observed that the grant of self-government to Ireland became inevitable after the passage of the Franchise Bill in 1884. Irish loyalists proclaimed that property and money were being sacrificed to a mud hut franchise; not only because henceforward the Irish Nationalists were inevitably destined to hold the balance in English politics,

---

[171] Burns Library, Boston College, Collins Ms, Healy to Collins, 4 Nov. 1882.

[172] *Parnell a National Tribute: An Analysis of Subscriptions* (Dublin, 1884).

[173] *Old England* (London, 1927), 47.

[174] Marie-Louise Legg (ed.), *Alfred Webb: The Autobiography of a Quaker Nationalist* (Cork, 1999), 49.

but because, in the face of so large a parliamentary party as the Irish had now become, it was impossible to govern Ireland on the 'crown colony plan'.[175]

The erosion of liberal support for the traditional version of the union was taking place not only at Westminster but also in Dublin. Earl Spencer's administration was relentlessly presented as coercion and tyranny by William O'Brien and Tim Healy. The handling of justice in cases such as the murder at Maamtrasna, Co. Galway, of five members of the Joyce family in August 1882 became disputed and damaging to the authority of government. Timothy Harrington MP devoted himself to arguing that the executed man, Myles Joyce, was innocent, while the organizer of the massacre, who remained free, received enormous subsidies from the Crown all the time that the wrong men were being hanged.[176] As William O'Brien declared: 'The cries of dying protestations of innocence from the scaffolds gave rise to investigations here, there and everywhere, which filled the country with a sickening suspicion of the methods by which convictions had been secured.'[177] The railing against the Castle and its methods even included the exposure of a homosexual scandal at the heart of the administration. William O'Brien's *United Ireland* contained a celebrated article, 30 August 1884, proposing that Earl Spencer 'should be raised a step in the peerage with the appropriate title of the Duke of Sodom and Gomorrah'.[178] Spencer made a point of saying in later years that he disregarded this type of abuse, but he was certainly not indifferent to the difficulties his administration faced in attempting to implement a strong law-and-order policy in Ireland: interestingly, Sir Robert Hamilton, who replaced the murdered Thomas Burke as permanent Under-Secretary, became a strong advocate of Home Rule and had a significant influence on Gladstone.[179]

In his speech of 1 May 1884 William Shaw, whom Parnell had defeated narrowly for the leadership of the Irish Party, predicted that, in the forthcoming general election, in three out of four Irish provinces 'it would hardly be worthwhile to contest those constituencies' against 'what was called the active Irish Party'. Shaw appeared to accept that, as a 'moderate', he could not win against an activist, but also to be happily resigned to such a fate: 'He looked upon the settling of the Irish question as so great that he would vacate his seat tomorrow, and give it to any gentleman who would come into that House in order to make a party to bring that question to

---

[175] Fisher, *Bryce*, i. 199.
[176] O'Brien, *Evening Memories*, 34.   [177] *Ibid.* 33.
[178] O'Donnell, *Irish Parliamentary Party*, ii. 177.
[179] Michael J. F. McDonnell, *Ireland and the Home Rule Movement* (Dublin, 1908), 224.

an issue.' Shaw added, in a passage which definitely caught Gladstone's ear: 'This was not a question which they could let drift from year to year.'[180] The Prime Minister wrote to his Irish Lord-Lieutenant in September 1884: 'The most remarkable Irish speech of the last session was perhaps that of Shaw, in which this really (as I believe and hope) constitutional man expressed his belief that the agitation would go on and his desire that it should go on. This is hardly a question for me, but it is sure to be one for you.'[181] The hint that the Home Rule question would probably come to a head after Gladstone's retirement hardly obscures the meaning of the passage as far as the evolution of Gladstone's own personal view. In June 1885 Gladstone again addressed Spencer, whose mind was moving along the same lines, on the topic: 'No one, I think, can doubt that, according to all present appearances, the greatest incident of the coming election is to be the Parnell or Nationalist majority. And such a majority is a very great fact indeed. It will at once shift the centre of gravity in the relations between the two countries.'[182]

But such 'flexible' thinking in Ireland was not confined to the Liberals. On 8 June 1885 Gladstone's government was defeated by Irish votes on the coercion issue and replaced by a minority Tory coalition. Lord Carnarvon took charge in Dublin Castle. On 17 July his ally, Lord Ashbourne,[183] Lord Chancellor of Ireland, introduced an Irish Land Purchase Bill in the Lords—what was to become known as the Ashbourne Act—which provided the first workable scheme to facilitate purchase by tenants of their farms. On 1 August 1885 Carnarvon met Parnell alone. Parnell offered a decidedly conservative version of the Home Rule conception. He even went so far as to say that the issues around the land question should remain at Westminster. Parnell said that 'some form of central body, council or board, was essential for reasons of sentiment', but a body which simply dealt with education, railway regulation, drainage and fisheries might be initially acceptable. He also argued the case for protection for native Irish industries.[184] Carnarvon, it is clear, accepted the need for an Irish parliament, and was impressed by Parnell's conservatism.[185] Andrew Kettle noted the sudden appearance of protectionism in the Chief's oratory in Wicklow in November 1885, and asked for an explanation. Parnell replied

180 *Hansard*, ser. 3, vol. 297, 1 May 1884, col. 111.
181 *Gladstone Diaries*, xi. 209, Gladstone to Lord Spencer, Viceroy of Ireland, 17 Sept. 1884.
182 Ibid. 366, to Lord Spencer, 30 June 1885 (private).
183 A. B. Cooke, introduction to *The Ashbourne Papers, 1869–83*, compiled by A. B. Cooke and A. P. W. Malcolmson (Belfast, 1974), p. xvi.
184 Andrew Roberts, *Salisbury: Victorian Titan* (London, 1999), 349–50.
185 Vincent, *Derby Diaries*, 21 Mar. 1886, p. 832; 5 May 1886, p. 834.

that he was preparing to break with 'Free Traders'. 'He then explained the project of aristocratic home rule and the colonial right to protect our industries against English manufacture.' He went on to explain that it was not from a sense of justice or generosity that the Conservative Party were making their proposals:

Inspired chiefly by Lord Randolph Churchill, the upper classes in Britain were afraid that if the Irish democratic agitation were to continue in conjunction with the English radicals, class rule might be overturned altogether. So, to save themselves, they are going to set up a *class* Conservative government in Ireland, with the aid and consent of the Irish democracy or, in other words, with our assistance, having no connection with England, but the link with the Crown and an Imperial contribution to be regulated by circumstances.[186]

Parnell called Michael Davitt down to Avondale to tell him the same story: Davitt was dubious—he particularly feared the impact of protectionist talk on the free-trade Liberal Joseph Chamberlain. But Davitt and Kettle were clear that Parnell was ideologically predisposed in favour of a conservative deal.

Having urged the Irish voters in Britain to vote against the Liberals, Parnell then turned his energies towards the electoral campaign in Ireland itself. Here the expected nationalist electoral triumph was achieved. Parnell won every seat outside eastern Ulster and the University of Dublin. He now had eighty-six MPs at his back, 'pledged' to 'sit, act and vote' with the party and to resign if a majority of the party felt that the obligations had not been fulfilled. For the first time, a very large majority of the Irish electors had clearly and unambiguously declared for Home Rule. Parnell was in an exceptionally strong moral position. But what was the reaction of the leadership of the two main British parties? To put it briefly, the Conservatives turned against the Irish, while the Liberals moved towards them.

The overall result of the election could hardly have suited the Irish purpose better. Outside Ireland the Liberals won eighty-six seats more than the Conservatives, but since eighty-six was also the number of Parnellite MPs, the nationalists were close to holding the balance of power. But they did not actually hold it, because the Ulster Tories would certainly have revolted if Salisbury had led the Tories towards an alliance with Parnell. The Conservatives were quick to end any flirtation with him. Lord Salisbury's government announced to the new parliament in January 1886 that a return to coercion in Ireland was in prospect. By combining with the Liberals, Parnell immediately threw them out of office.

---

[186] Kettle, *Material for Victory*, 63–4; *Fall of Feudalism*, 478. Parnell's talk of protection also seriously alarmed northern Protestant opinion: 'Ulster and Home Rule', in *Home Rule: A Reprint from 'The Times'* (London, 1886).

By November 1885 Gladstone had now resolved in his own mind the doubts that he had expressed in early 1882 about the nationalist conception of self-government. In 1882 he was still troubled by Parnell's apparent ambitions on this point—but by late 1885 he had satisfied himself there was no danger to the authority of the Westminster Parliament:

The main questions are, does Irish Nationalism contemplate a fair division of Imperial burdens, and will it agree to just provisions for the protection of landlords. I do not think that on the other hand sufficient allowance has been made for the *enormous* advantage we derive from the change in the form of the Nationalist demands from repeal of the union (which would reinstate a parliament having *original* authority) to the form of a Bill for a democratic chamber acting under Imperial authority. The whole basis of the proceeding is hereby changed.[187]

Meanwhile, Gladstone's son Herbert had, in December 1885 (after the election was over, but before Parliament had met), flown the famous 'Hawarden kite': a press declaration by Herbert that his father was moving towards Home Rule. Gladstone's colleagues were given absolutely no warning of this Home Rule 'balloon'. Even loyal Gladstonians were shocked: Edward Hamilton, whose job it was to convey to Gladstone the dismay of the Cabinet, later noted: 'It certainly was extraordinary behaviour.' He added later: 'J. M. [John Morley] has come to the conclusion, he says, that the machinations of December 1885 strike him more and more "the most absolutely indefensible thing in Mr G's career. They drove him wild".'[188] But, in fact, the premier had been moving steadily and fairly openly—as far as Cabinet colleagues were concerned—to this conclusion.

On 1 February 1886 Gladstone saw the Queen and explained his intention of introducing a Home Rule measure. On 4 February he made a public statement, which was perceived to be a commitment to some form of autonomy for Ireland. A Liberal government, depending on the votes of Parnell's Parliamentary Party and generally believed to be intending a measure of Home Rule, was now in office.

THE HOME RULE DEBATE

It was at this propitious moment for the Irish leader that a remarkable episode occurred, which threatened to impair fatally the unity of his party, both in Parliament and in the country, for Parnell announced his intention

---

[187] Matthew (ed.), *The Gladstone Diaries*, xi. 433, 18 Nov. 1885.
[188] D. W. R. Bahlman (ed.), *The Diary of Sir Edward Walter Hamilton, 1885–1906* (Hull, 1993), 2 July 1902, p. 421.

to support Captain O'Shea as an 'unpledged' parliamentary candidate for the vacant seat of Galway City. It was a surprising move; everyone knew that O'Shea was an unprincipled opportunist and job-seeker—he had, for example, sought the position of Thomas Burke's replacement as Under-Secretary in Dublin Castle.[189] For the first time Parnell's liaison with Mrs O'Shea appeared to have forced its way onto the political stage. Why did Parnell act as he did? The implication must be that O'Shea was again blackmailing Parnell and that the threat of exposure was responsible for Parnell's dictatorial action.

But there was a price to be paid. In the course of riding roughshod over opposition, he publicly put down one of his lieutenants, Tim Healy, and disoriented the two most significant ones, John Dillon and William O'Brien. Michael Morris, Irish Lord Chief Justice, analysed the crisis in striking fashion:

Parnell comes of the conquering race in Ireland, and he never forgets it, or lets his subordinates forget it. I was in Galway when he came over there suddenly to quell the revolt organised by Healy. The rebels were at white heat before he came. But he strode in among them like a huntsman among the hounds—marched Healy off into a little room, and brought him out again in ten minutes, cowed and submissive, but filled, as anybody can see ever since, with a dull smouldering hate which will break out one of these days, if a good and safe opportunity offers.[190]

Michael Davitt noted, with an air of vindication, that the Galway contest had served 'to bring home to even the intolerant lieutenants what their advocacy of Mr Parnell's pontifical power was leading to'.[191] In short, Galway was a harbinger of the fatal crisis to come. Such a price was only justifiable on the assumption that Parnell's leadership was an absolute necessity. This, indeed, seems to have been accepted by Parnell and his party, with only Biggar in opposition. Just as Parnell's greatest contribution to Irish nationalism had been to bring unity to previously divided forces, so that unity, once established, became the greatest reason for keeping him in the leadership.

Having survived the Galway crisis, Parnell was able to return to London to study the unfolding of Gladstone's hand. It was a supreme test: Parnell was now unchallenged as party leader, but how would he stand up as a statesman? Gladstone's guiding concept was to link his planned Home Rule Bill with a Land Bill, and thus to deal with the political and social questions simultaneously.[192] He had moved to the point where he accepted

189 D. W. R. Bahlman (ed.), 20 Aug. 1882, p. 327.
190 W. H. Hurlbert, *Ireland Under Coercion* (Edinburgh, 1889), 55.
191 *The Fall of Feudalism*, 468.
192 Alan O'Day, *Parnell and the First Home Rule Episode* (Dublin, 1986), 232–82.

Parnell's view that somehow conditions had to be created in which the gentry could emerge, purged of their 'bad' history, as the natural leaders of the people.[193] The premier had to bear in mind the difficulties of setting up a subordinate legislature. In this area alone there was a difficult question: how to preserve the sovereignty of Westminster and yet make Irish autonomy a worthwhile proposition? (This presented particular difficulties in the fiscal sphere.) But he also had to think about the future social order and peace of Ireland. He had, in particular, to think of ways of reconciling the substantial Protestant and unionist minority in Ireland to the new arrangements. This in itself divided into two parts. In the south the Protestants were a privileged minority with heavy representation in the landlord class; in the north-east they were a majority and well represented in all the social classes, including the tenantry. It was probably impossible to produce a legislative proposal that could embrace satisfactorily all these problem areas. It is certain that it was impossible to do so when hindered by the spirit of financial caution which was the hallmark of Gladstone's party.

But despite these disputes over financial matters, the thought of Parnell and Gladstone was converging on one fundamental matter: the future of the land question. Both wanted to find a way out for the Irish landlords. In a document concerning a land-purchase proposal, which Mrs O'Shea passed on to Gladstone, Parnell wrote:

A communication, the substance of which I append, has been forwarded to me by the representatives of one of the chief landlord political associations in Ireland. It is thought that if this arrangement were carried out, there would remain no large body of opinion amongst the landowning class against the concession of a large measure of autonomy for Ireland, as the Protestants, other than the owners of land, are not really opposed to such concession.[194]

This clearly reveals that Parnell was in contact with Irish landlord leaders. It reveals also, of course, a rather foolish reduction of the problem of the Protestant minority to that of the problem of the landlord minority. But the main thing to note is Parnell's determination to reach some workable compromise with the Irish landowners. He wanted to get them out of their difficulties on the best possible terms. It certainly impressed some of the Whig grandees like Spencer and Granville—Granville, who believed that 'if the question were not settled ... Irish landlords would be in a bad way' and that 'Parnell would show himself very conservative as an Irish

[193] D. G. Boyce, 'Gladstone and the Unionists of Ireland 1868–1893', in David Bebbington and Roger Swift (eds.), *Gladstone: Centenary Essays* (Liverpool, 2000), 198.
[194] Bew, *Parnell*, 81.

statesman'.[195] Bryce agreed: 'He [Parnell] did not desire the extinction of landlordism and would probably have been a restraining and moderating force in any Irish legislature.'[196]

On 8 April 1886 Gladstone introduced his Government of Ireland Bill, better known as the Home Rule Bill. His object was to establish an Irish legislature, although large imperial issues were to be reserved to the Westminster Parliament. It was a moment of high drama in modern parliamentary history. Public excitement was intense, and huge crowds gathered outside Westminster, despite dreadful weather. Reputedly, as much as £1,000 was offered for the mere privilege of watching the proceedings from the visitors' gallery.[197]

The Home Rule debate still possesses an inherent fascination. At one extreme Gladstone, at this moment 'transfixed by the Irish charm, its wit, grace and intelligence',[198] and at the other G. J. Goschen, transfixed by the thought that Britain was the first country in the history of the world ready to betray its 'own people'. Professor Michael de Nie has recently stressed the presence within British popular culture of a discourse which stressed the inferiority of the Irish and essentially denied 'the capacity of the Irish to govern themselves'.[199] But at parliamentary level it has to be said that the debate was dominated by a rather more subtle historical and constitutional argumentation on both sides. Even Goschen insisted that the Irish were no more violent than any other people. The most serious opponents of Irish Home Rule wished above all to avoid the charge of ignorant 'prejudice'. John Bright told Barry O'Brien that the moral character of the Irish people was no better and no worse than that of any other people. Indeed, he did not fear religious persecution, but this oldest and most consistent 'friend of Ireland' in the House of Commons, still opposed Home Rule. 'I object to this Bill. It either goes too far, or it does not go far enough ... It would lead to constant friction between the two countries.'[200] In fact, the analysis of Irish discontents, it was argued, should be conducted

without having recourse to any theory of race, and without attributing to Irishmen either more or less of original sin than falls to the lot of humanity, to see how it is that imperfect statesmanship—and all statesmanship, it should be remembered,

[195] Vincent (ed.), *Derby Diaries*, 2 Mar. 1886, p. 832.
[196] Bryce, *Studies in Contemporary Biography*, 246.
[197] Alan O'Day, *Parnell and the First Home Rule Episode*, 178.
[198] Mark Bonham Carter (ed.), *The Autobiography of Margot Asquith* (London, 1995), 101; Bew, *Parnell*, 86.
[199] Michael de Nie, 'Pigs, Paddies, Prams and Petticoats: Irish Home Rule and the British Comic Press, 1886–1893', *History Ireland* (Jan.–Feb. 2003), 47.
[200] O'Brien, *The Life of Charles Stewart Parnell*, ii. 145–52; A. D. Elliott, *The Life of Lord Goschen 1831–1907*, vol. 2 (London, 1911), 48–9.

is imperfect—has failed of obtaining good results at all, commensurate with its generally good intentions.[201]

Sir John Lubbock, an opponent of Home Rule, wrote to *The Times* on 18 March 1887, nonetheless, citing the anthropologist John Beddoe to argue that the racial components of English, Scottish, Welsh, and Irish society were present in all but predominant in or peculiar to none. Arthur Balfour adopted a similar stance in his case against Home Rule. There was, he wrote, 'no sharp division of race at all' between England and Ireland. 'We must conceive the prehistoric inhabitants both of Britain and of Ireland as subject to repeated waves of invasion from the wandering peoples of the Continent.'[202]

On the Home Rule side, Edmund Burke was the icon of icons. The Chancellor of the Exchequer (W. V. Harcourt),[203] Lord Granville[204] and Gladstone all invoked Burke in support of their argument. The opponents of the Bill were hardly surprised by this tactic. Hartington reacted somewhat wearily: 'I have no doubt before the end of these debates we shall hear a good deal of Mr Burke and Mr Burke's sayings.'[205] Hartington and the Duke of Argyll insisted[206] that conditions had changed a great deal since Burke's time. The union today was now a liberal conception. The Gladstonian utilization of Burke's language was entirely inappropriate. Professor Huxley publicly was even more forthright in his repudiation of Gladstone's 'Burke'. 'Is there among us a man of the calibre of Burke ... who will stand up and tell his countrymen that the disruption of the union is nothing but a cowardly wickedness, an act base in itself, and fraught with immeasurable harm, especially to the people of Ireland.'[207]

The home-rulers remained loyal to 'their' Burke. When Gladstone, for example, attacked William Johnston's assumption of an innate loyalty of the Ulster Protestant, he made Burke his witness. Gladstone—a little inappropriately, as Johnstone was an Anglican—recalled the radicalism of Ulster Presbyterianism in the late eighteenth century. He quoted Burke:

It [disaffection] has cast deep roots in the principles and habits of the majority of the lower and middle classes of the whole Protestant part of Ireland. The Catholics who are intermingled with them are more or less tainted. In the other parts of Ireland, some in Dublin only excepted, the Catholics who are in a manner the whole people,

---

[201] A. V. Dicey, *England's Case against Home Rule*, 3rd edn. (London, 1887), 74.
[202] J. C. D. Clark, *Our Shadowed Present: Modernism, Postmodernism and History* (London, 2003), 108.
[203] *Evening Standard*, 2 June 1886.
[204] Ibid., 8 May 1886, 'Lord Granville in Manchester'.
[205] Ibid., 15 April 1886.
[206] *Irish Nationalism: An Appeal to History* (London, 1893), 264.
[207] *Evening Standard*, 13 Apr. 1886.

are as yet sound, but they may be provoked as all men may easily be out of their principles.[208]

This text gave Gladstone his theory of Irish history. 'The Protestants, not having a grievance to complain about, have become loyal', while the Catholics were provoked into 'disloyalty'.

There was a more pragmatic Home Rule argument: simply a case that Home Rule was the only way to give Ireland stable government. Here the voice of two former lord-lieutenants was vital. The Earl of Kimberley (who had been so contemptuous of the Fenians) observed:

When he held the office of Lord-Lieutenant [as Lord Wodehouse], he said on the occasion of the suspension of the Habeas Corpus Act, he felt strongly that they would never succeed in dealing with the land question of that country until they had touched the hearts of Irishmen and brought them into sympathy with the people of this country.

Kimberley added: 'The question was who was to apply that force? Was it to be applied by the Irish government under the influence, and with the consent of, the Irish people, or was it to be applied by what they termed an alien government?'[209]

Another former lord-lieutenant, Lord Spencer was a reluctant and slow convert. In mid-September 1885 he could see the case for Home Rule as an act of Anglo-Irish reconciliation. But it required a benign resolution of both the Ulster question and the land question, both of which were rather hard to obtain. By the end of the year, however, aversion to the 'old and unsatisfactory' way of running Ireland had won out, and Home Rule was accepted as a lesser evil to 'that wretched and doomed policy'.[210] In explanation for his final conversion, Earl Spencer, speaking at Newcastle, took the same position as Kimberley. Only an Irish government could control Irish society. 'It will be one of the first and perhaps one of the most difficult duties which Mr Parnell, if he becomes Minister for Ireland, will have to perform, but it is one which I am sure he will do with vigour—namely to put down these extreme rebels and fanatics in Ireland.'[211] It should be noted that the presumption that Parnell would want to do this lay at the heart of much liberal pro-Home Rule thinking. Parnell's conservatism was a reassuring reference point for this constituency. Canon Malcolm MacColl wrote: 'Mr Parnell would be its first Prime Minister,

---

[208] *Evening Standard*, 8 June 1886 'Government of Ireland Bill'. Gladstone even attempted to convince a sceptical J. G. Swift MacNeill, a Home Rule MP, on the evidence of the speech by Burke's friend, Dr French Lawrence in January 1799, that Burke would have opposed the union. *What I Have Seen and Heard* (Boston, 1925), 248.

[209] Ibid.   [210] McKnight, *Ulster As It Is*, i. 136.

[211] *Evening Standard*, 22 Apr. 1886.

and his interest and inclination would be to induce the gentry of Ireland to become members of parliament.'[212]

The Ulster question also appeared on the scene in a decisive way. A proletarian unionism forced its way on to the stage. In Belfast, the anti-Home Rule and anti-police riots of the summer of 1886 claimed the lives of at least thirty-one people, more than the combined total of all the Irish rebellions of the nineteenth century. Colonel Saunderson, the future Ulster Unionist leader, appeared to the metropolitan eye as 'the very pink and type of Ulster pugnacity'.[213] Saunderson's speech reflected the analysis he had advanced in his pamphlet *Two Irelands: Loyalty versus Treason*.[214] These 'two Irelands' were not defined geographically but by sentiment. Publicly, Saunderson declared in Froude-like mode: 'No nation was free' until she was 'strong' enough and 'brave' enough to extract 'her freedom from the dominant nation'. When William O'Brien called out, 'You would not let us possess arms', Saunderson replied that if all the police were removed from Ireland, there could be a conflict between loyalists and home-rulers which the Parnellites would not win. Referring to Chamberlain's idea of separate treatment for Ulster, he added: 'There was a suggestion that Ulster should be excluded from this Bill, or be treated in a different way from the rest of Ireland (Mr Gladstone shook his head). On the part of Ulster, he repudiated such an exclusion. They were determined to stand or fall with every loyal man in Ireland.'[215] Behind the scenes, however, in Belfast more bourgeois liberal unionist elements were already contemplating partition.[216] But there were, of course, two communities in Ulster, and both were represented in the House. Charles Russell, the Attorney-General and an Ulster Catholic, gave full voice to the alienation and resentment of Ulster's Catholic community.

Does the House know that with the management of Ulster estates, the Catholic had no chance of getting a farm if a Protestant or Presbyterian could be had as a tenant, and the result was that the worst land, and in the worst places, fell to their lot? In

---

[212] *Reasons for Home Rule* (London, 1886), 23.

[213] Temple, *Letters and Character Sketches*, 160.

[214] Alvin Jackson, *Colonel Edward Saunderson: Land and Loyalty in Victorian Ireland* (Oxford, 1995), 55–7.

[215] *Evening Standard*, 13 Apr. 1886.

[216] MacKnight, *Ulster As It Is*, ii. 382–3. 'Col. Saunderson, Dr Kane, and some other Orangemen have declared themselves opposed to the separate Ulster which Gladstone, in introducing his first home rule bill had intimated that, if it were the wish of the Unionist population in whole or in part, he was not indisposed to grant. But the feeling expressed by Colonel Saunderson and Dr Kane in the words "We won't desert under any circumstances our brethren in the South" is not general, or is certainly not sympathised with by the Liberal Unionists, and by the commercial classes in Belfast and the north of Ireland.'

the north of Ireland to this day, and in the south of Ireland, the Catholics were known by the name of mountainy men, because they had been driven to the rude, barren land of the mountain to try and push fertility up the hills.[217]

One major sub-theme of the debate was that of Conservative bad faith. Spencer claimed that Tory softness towards nationalism when in office had convinced him that a new departure was required. The settled policy of *all* previous governments had been fatally undermined. Parnell reminded the House of his conversations with Carnarvon.[218] Carnarvon's reply insisted that his discussion with Parnell did not involve any offers or promises on his part. 'Both of us left the room as free as when we came into it.'[219]

By the end of May it was clear that opposition from the radical and 'Whig' wings of the Liberal Party was sufficiently strong to prevent the Bill passing the Lower House. On 28 May Gladstone announced that the Bill, even if passed, would be withdrawn and reintroduced with important amendments. In June the Home Rule Bill was defeated by forty votes on the second reading. Despite this setback, it was clear that Parnell's leadership had advanced dramatically a cause which had been drifting aimlessly in the mid-1870s at the moment when he entered Parliament. Home Rule was now endorsed by a Liberal premier, and it seemed that its eventual triumph was certain, even if the Liberal split now returned the Tories temporarily to power.

THE POLITICS OF ANTICLIMAX, 1886–1891

After a glimpse of the promised land, Parnell now had the task of keeping together a movement and a country through a period of powerlessness dominated by a sense of anticlimax and disappointment. He needed to keep the Gladstonian Liberals, now in opposition following their election defeat in July 1886, to their bargain, while mitigating as best he could Unionist opposition to Home Rule. That opposition was intensifying rather than diminishing. Home Rule was now *the* polarizing issue for the political class[220] in British politics, that which separated Gladstone's Liberals from the Tories and their allies. In Ireland Unionist resistance, especially in

[217] *Evening Standard*, 13 Apr. 1886.   [218] Ibid., 8 June 1886.

[219] Ibid., 9 June 1886. For this episode, see L. P. Curtis, *Coercion and Conciliation in Ireland 1880–1892* (Princeton, 1963), 449–53.

[220] But not necessarily the electorate, see A. B. Cooke and J. R. Vincent, *The Governing Passion: Cabinet Government and Party Politics* (Brighton, 1974), 20. Cecil Spring-Rice, an intelligent young Irishman recently arrived at the Foreign Office, assessed the role of the Home Rule issue rather cynically: 'the fact is that people just want a peg to hang abuse of Gladstone on, as an excuse for turning Tory which they have been in their hearts for years.' Stephen Gwynn, *Letters and Friendships of Sir Cecil Spring-Rice* (London, 1929), i. 38–9.

Ulster, became increasingly organized. Parnell pursued a moderate and conciliatory policy on land purchase, and still hoped to retain a significant landlord presence under Home Rule. Parnell, therefore, opposed any ideas which jeopardized the Home Rule movement's newfound respectability, as when William O'Brien, a political lieutenant, launched a renewed land agitation, the 'Plan of Campaign', designed to unsettle the Tory and Unionist government which had been returned in the general election of July 1886.

The 'Plan of Campaign' was first published in William O'Brien's paper *United Ireland* on 24 October 1886.[221] Ironically, it drew its inspiration from a remark made by Parnell in his radical heyday. In the aftermath of the failure of the 'No rent' manifesto of 1881, Parnell had said that he would never again lead an agrarian movement unless the tenants lodged 75 per cent of their rents in a common fund. This was the core idea of the new agitation: it was sharply emphasized that under no circumstances should tenants pay legal costs.[222] The Catholic clergy played an enhanced role in looking after the funds.

In December 1886, when the Plan of Campaign was still in its infancy, Parnell summoned William O'Brien. The two men met behind Greenwich Observatory, which was cloaked in thick fog. Parnell pointed out to O'Brien the risks involved in the plan, and suggested that he limit it to the estates where it was already in operation. Parnell exploited his sick and haggard appearance to win O'Brien's confidence and sympathy—even, rather erratically, taking the decision to dine with him in a very public venue, having first called the meeting at a spot designed to preserve secrecy. On 12 December Parnell saw Morley and told him that he had parted with O'Brien on 'the understanding that the meeting would be dropped, and the agitation calmed as much as could be'.[223] But Parnell took out some insurance in case the agitation was, in fact, maintained. O'Brien had said: 'Why on earth should you not get some lady of your family to come over and take care of you?'[224] At the moment when the Plan of Campaign was proclaimed, Parnell let it be known publicly that he was recovering from serious illness in the company of his mother. *The Law and the League*, an Irish Loyal and Patriotic Union (ILPU) pamphlet, noted that 'Mr Parnell became as invisible, as inarticulate and unapproachable as the veiled prophet of Khorastan'.[225] In Thomas Moore's 'Lalla Rookh' the veiled prophet is a

---

221 For the full text see Laurence M. Geary, *The Plan of Campaign 1886–1891* (Cork, 1986), App. 1, pp. 144–50; see also J. J. Cleary (ed.), *Mr Dillon and the Plans of Campaign* (London, 1887), 23–6.
222 Geary, *Plan of Campaign*, 23.
223 W. O'Brien, *The Parnell of Real Life* (London, 1926), 135.   224 Ibid. 140.
225 (Dublin, 1887), 5.

'false chief', who betrays his 'dupes', revealing his malevolent, hideous face to them only at the moment of their destruction.[226]

It was reported that 'Mr Parnell was not aware that the Plan of Campaign had been devised or was going to be proposed until he saw it in the newspapers'.[227] He would not give a view until he was well enough to travel to Ireland to make a full analysis of the conditions on the ground. The *Pall Mall Gazette* was less than impressed. It accepted that Parnell had been ill, but refused to accept that he knew so little, so late, of the plan: 'The situation is not helped by make-believe that could not deceive a Kerry cow.'[228] Rather darkly, the *Gazette* observed: 'What with Olympian religions at Hawarden and Eleusinian mysteries at Eltham, our composite party seems to be in a bad way.' Everyone, it seems, knew the real truth. The ILPU opined confidently: 'Mr Parnell knew all about the plan, disapproved of it, but feared to say.'[229]

Coercion of the plan might create some bad publicity for the Conservative government, but it was far more likely that an intensive anti-rent agitation would place great strain on the Liberal–nationalist alliance. Michael Davitt, interestingly, accepted Parnell's view that the plan was a violation of the terms of the Kilmainham Treaty and, at his request, had little to do with it.[230] In the end the plan, while quite effective on a small scale, only directly affected a mere 1 per cent of the Irish estates.[231] The enforcement of law and order when Arthur Balfour was Chief Secretary (March 1887–November 1891) combined with the plan's deficiencies of organization to limit its impact. Balfour's Crimes Act in the latter half of 1887 was effective even in tough areas such as West Kerry: 'the National League's position as the dominant authority rapidly disintegrated.'[232] The most notorious event of the Plan of Campaign took place on 9 September 1887: the police, vastly outnumbered by an angry crowd, killed two nationalists in Mitchelstown, Co. Cork. 'Remember Mitchelstown', Gladstone's tense comment, became the slogan of the hour for both Liberals and nationalists. A young lawyer, Edward Carson, a legal officer of the Crown, was one of the spectators at Mitchelstown. Balfour 'made' Carson by giving him responsibility in these high-profile cases, but 'Mitchelstown' also 'made' Balfour: he was given an opportunity to display an unflinching coolness of demeanour in the face of an angry outcry, both inside and outside the House of Commons.[233] Balfour

[226] *The Poetical Works of Thomas Moore* (Paris, 1827), 20.
[227] *Evening Standard*, 20 Dec. 1886.   [228] *Pall Mall Gazette*, 22 Dec. 1886.
[229] *Coercion plus Lying*, (Jan. 1888), 77.   [230] *Fall of Feudalism*, 519.
[231] Geary, *Plan of Campaign*, 140–1.
[232] Donnacha Séan Lucey, *The Irish National League in Dingle, Co. Kerry, 1885–1892* (Dublin, 2003), 55.
[233] Curtis, *Coercion and Conciliation*, 197–9.

was the beneficiary of a broad unease generated by the moral ambiguities of the Kilmainham Treaty. Parnell turned away from such confrontation by making it clear that, as far as he was concerned, the political objective of Home Rule was far more important than any agrarian considerations. Parnell's moderation and relative inactivity were no protection against his enemies. As the Liberal leadership insisted that no Irish political leader had been connected to agrarian crime, the Tories became all the more determined to link Parnell with the unacceptable violent face of Irish nationalism. In the spring of 1887 the attack came. On 18 April *The Times*, at the end of a series of articles on the theme of Parnell's links with crime, published a letter purporting to have been written by Parnell, seeking to excuse, under the plea of necessity, his public condemnation of the Phoenix Park murders. The amazing document, dated 15 May 1882, ran as follows:

Dear Sir
I am surprised at your friend's anger, but he and you should know that to denounce the murders was the only course open to us. To do that promptly was plainly our best policy.
But you can tell him and all others concerned that though I regret the accident of Lord F. Cavendish's death, I cannot refuse to admit that Burke got no more than his deserts.
You are at liberty to show him this, and others whom you can trust also, but let not my address be known. He can write to House of Commons.
Yours very truly,
Chas S. Parnell

The government set up a special commission of three judges to inquire into the allegations made in *The Times*. Parnell was not particularly alarmed by the letter, which, after all, he knew to be forged. But he was alarmed by reports that *The Times* had successfully offered P. J. Sheridan in Colorado a sufficient cash incentive to testify. Sheridan may well have been close to so much—and certainly gossiped, accurately or otherwise, about Parnell's 'swearing' in at Trinity College, Dublin. He claimed a role in the Phoenix Park murders, and indeed, Walter Bourke's murder a month later involved men close to him—so that he could have been an explosively destructive witness. Only when Thomas Brennan and Michael Davitt discovered that Sheridan was only 'playing' *The Times* and had no intention of publicly testifying, did Parnell calm down. The government used its resources to help *The Times*; it even kept Parnell himself under daily surveillance.[234]

---

[234] Margaret O'Callaghan, 'New Ways of Looking at the State Apparatus and the State Archive in Nineteenth-Century Ireland: "Curiosities from that Phonetic Museum"—Royal Irish Constabulary Reports and their Political Uses, 1879–91', *Proceedings of the Royal Irish Academy*, 104: 2 (2004), 51–3.

But such activities, highly questionable though they were, hardly served to criminalize Parnellism. Parnell's evidence before the Special Commission was moderate and relaxed in tone: 'Mr Parnell spoke of compromise, talked not unkindly of the landlord garrison, the starvation of which was supposed to be the purpose of the League's existence.'[235] He made much of how the state had come round to accepting the need for a transformation of Irish agrarian life. The surveillance reports are principally interesting for the evidence they give of his style of party management. Despite his imperfect health in the late 1880s, Parnell seems, nonetheless, to have devoted significant time to party strategy at Westminster. He spent time cajoling impoverished members to 'remain at their posts' in London when it was clear that some of his parliamentary colleagues wished to slip back to their constituencies and local business concerns.[236] There was a tendency in these reports to play up Parnell's estrangement from his left wing,[237] while presenting other developments, such as Parnell's acceptance of a cheque in July 1888[238] from the Imperial Federalist Cecil Rhodes, as signs of an exciting new moderation. It is striking how government surveillance was not used to strike a crippling blow: for example, there do not seem to have been any attempts to spread stories about Parnell's private life.

Let us take the case of the so-called 'Prince of Spies', Henri le Caron. As his time in America, spying on the Fenians, drew to a close, Luke Dillon, the legendary 'hardest man of all', told Henri le Caron that Patrick Egan had told him that Parnell knew in advance about, but did not support, the Phoenix Park murders. In December 1888 le Caron filed this report to his spymasters in London. At the beginning of February 1889 le Caron told the *New York Herald* that Parnell had been a genuine revolutionary, but his imprisonment had changed the Irish leader: being behind bars had had 'a singularly happy effect on moderating his views'.[239] Le Caron's evidence to the Special Commission hurt the Parnellites, but he did not repeat the Dillon–Egan story. In his later memoir le Caron mentions Egan's claim that 'Parnell was all right as a revolutionist', without discussing his claim to Luke Dillon about Parnell and the Phoenix Park. It is most likely that le

[235] John MacDonald, *The 'Daily News' Diary of the Parnell Commission*, 31 Oct., p. 112.

[236] PRO 30/60/13/2/70987, dated 7 June 1888, Maj. Gosselin's report. Gosselin was judged to be a 'keen patriot' by his friend the Protestant home-ruler Augustus B. R. Young, *Reminiscences of an Irish Priest, 1845–1920* (Dublin, 1931), 57–100.

[237] Ibid., 6 June 1888, Davitt and Parnell were said to be upon 'terms of mock friendship' only.

[238] Donal McCracken, 'Parnell and the South Africa Connection', in Donal McCartney (ed.), *Parnell: The Politics of Power* (Dublin, 1991), 129.

[239] *New York Herald*, 6 Feb. 1889.

Caron simply did not accept Dillon's story, and like Gosselin, believed in Parnell's moderation.[240] The final collapse of any policy of 'criminalization', such as it was, came with the exposure and suicide of Richard Pigott (1828–89). Pigott had forged the original Parnell letters apparently endorsing the Phoenix Park murders, and then, via Thomas Maguire, a Catholic Unionist don at Trinity College, Dublin, sold the letters to *The Times*. Pigott had broken down under the cross-examination of Charles Russell and then fled to Madrid, where he committed suicide at the end of February 1889. News of the sudden death of Dr Thomas Maguire of Dublin broke almost simultaneously.[241] These tragic events decided the issue in Parnell's favour; he must, nevertheless, have been privately grateful that all the efforts made to get P. J. Sheridan to testify before the Special Commission had met with failure.[242] The Liberals were delighted by the turn of events. On 8 March 1889 Parnell attended the Eighty Club to receive the homage of a vastly relieved Liberal alliance. He symbolized the Parnell–Liberal alliance publicly by shaking hands with Lord Spencer, the Lord-Lieutenant of Ireland at the time of the Phoenix Park murders.

All that remained, it seemed, was for Parnell and Gladstone to work out the details of a new Home Rule Bill to set against the day when the Tories inevitably fell from office. Gladstone discussed these matters at two meetings with Parnell, in London on 8 March 1888 and at Hawarden on 18–19 December 1889. On each occasion Parnell's demands were entirely within the accepted parameters of Liberal thinking. After the first conversation Gladstone noted: 'Undoubtedly his tone was very conservative,' and after the second: 'He is certainly one of the best people to deal with that I have ever known.'[243] Parnell discussed the meeting the next day with a friend, Edward Byrne of the *Freeman's Journal*, and gave no hint of any unease.[244] But such confident pre-eminence was not destined to last. Four days later Captain O'Shea petitioned for divorce. Parnell won time for himself by assuring his colleagues that he would not be damaged in any way.

In the early months of 1890 Parnell still had the confidence to advance a position on the land question which offended substantial sections of his

---

[240] Henri le Caron, *Twenty-Five Years in the Secret Service* (London, 1893), 168.

[241] T. P. Foley, 'Thomas Maguire and the Parnell Forgeries', *Journal of the Galway Archaeological and Historical Society*, 40 (1994), 173–96; see also Stephen Ball (ed.), *A Policeman's Ireland: Recollections of Samuel Waters RIC* (Cork, 1999), 67.

[242] *The Times*, 7 Mar. 1887, repr. in *Parnellism and Crime or the Bloody Work of the Two Leagues*, revised edn. (n.p., n.d.), 10–17, shows itself fully aware of Sheridan's potential significance.

[243] Matthew (ed.), *The Gladstone Diaries*, vol. 12 (Oxford, 1994), 311.

[244] Frank Callanan (ed.), *Parnell: A Memoir* (Dublin, 1991), 14.

own party, because he now appeared to be concerned to defend the interests of the middling gentry and, as far as the tenantry were concerned, to be in favour of discriminating in favour of the smaller tenants. But soon his capacity to direct the nationalist movement along these lines was to be fatally undermined.

This was to be a matter of some significance. Parnell's growing and viable conservatism on land might have allowed closer co-operation with a Tory government, now moving into 'compassionate' mode on Irish land questions. On 26 October 1890 Balfour had started out on a tour of the impoverished districts of the west. On his return, on 19 November, he delivered a speech in Liverpool 'throbbing with sympathy and an intense desire to relieve the distress of the Irish people'.[245] Balfour was not naturally an emotional speaker—to say the least—and his speech clearly presaged some form of action. In 1891 the 'Balfour Act' constituted a Congested Districts Board, with powers and resources to enable it to amalgamate holdings and to aid migration and emigration, agriculture, and industry in the areas defined as congested. The Board undertook a small number of schemes which would set a model for purchase of grasslands and very poor estates, where redistribution of holdings was desirable.

Parnell, however, was not to be in a position which enabled him to respond to a new epoch in Tory thinking. The divorce case began on 15 November 1890. No defence was entered, and the trial lasted a mere two days. The evidence presented the two lovers in the most squalid light: most ludicrous of all, it was alleged that Parnell had on occasions evaded the Captain by departing rapidly down the fire escape. A decree nisi was granted on 17 November. On the following day the Dublin branch of the National League passed a resolution upholding Parnell's leadership. The meeting of the party to elect their sessional leader, the technical title of the Irish leader, was fixed for Tuesday, 25 November. Meanwhile, everyone held their breath. Then events took a sudden twist.

Parnell was at the height of his power, and it was difficult for any Irish force to move against him. The bishops were silent, some of them explicitly declaring the issue to be purely political, a fact Parnell was to exploit in 1891, when the bishops rediscovered their capacity for moral leadership. It was rather the 'Nonconformist conscience' in England which first openly rebelled against Parnell. The Liberal leader, Gladstone, found that a large proportion of his own supporters would no longer support an alliance with the Irish if the Irish were to continue to be led by Parnell.

[245] Bernard Alderson, *Arthur James Balfour* (London, 1903), 94. See also Ciara Breathnach, *The Congested Districts Board of Ireland, 1891–1923: Poverty and Development in the West of Ireland* (Dublin, 2005), 170.

Gladstone then sent for Justin McCarthy, generally regarded as Parnell's second-in-command, and, while paying tribute to Parnell's work, told him that Parnell's retention of the leadership would mean the loss of the next election and would mean also the putting off of Home Rule until a time when he (Gladstone) would no longer be able to lend a hand in the struggle. In order to avoid the charge of 'dictation', Gladstone had resolved not to convey this directly to Parnell himself, but he authorized McCarthy to pass on these opinions when he next saw him. McCarthy attempted to contact Parnell, but without success, or, at any rate, impact.

On 25 November Parnell managed temporarily to control his party. It re-elected him to the chair, but at this stage the members did not know of Gladstone's assessment of the situation. When this became clear, angry party members pressed for a new meeting. In retaliation, on 29 November Parnell issued a manifesto, *To the People of Ireland*. Its theme was a simple one: a section of the Irish Party had lost its independence. The Liberal alliance, Parnell said, had been desirable, but this had evolved into a fusion. He then, rather unprofessionally, attempted to make damaging revelations about his visit to Gladstone at Hawarden in December 1889, when, he said, Gladstone had confided to him the details of the Home Rule proposals which the next Liberal administration would introduce.

These included, according to Parnell, in a rather different version from Gladstone's carefully documented record, the reduction of the Irish representation in the Imperial Parliament from 103 seats to thirty-two; the reservation to the Imperial Parliament of power to deal with the land question; and the maintenance under Imperial control of the constabulary for an indefinite period and of judges for ten to twelve years. With so much reserved to the Imperial Parliament, Parnell was unwilling to consent to a reduction of the Irish representation at Westminster. He had told Gladstone that he would try to 'reconcile Irish opinion' on the constabulary and judges, but he dissented from the reduction of representation and from the absence of a land settlement. The feeble nature of the Liberal proposals had a definite implication. The Irish Party must retain its independence at all costs. Even if an 'independent' policy led to the defeat of the Liberals at the next general election, 'a postponement would be preferable to a compromise of our national rights by the acceptance of a measure which would not realise the aspirations of our race'.[246]

On 1 December the 'requisitioned' meeting of the party opened a new debate on the leadership in Committee Room 15 at Westminster. The ensuing split tore the country apart. Parnell vehemently insisted that the independence of the Irish Party could not be compromised either

[246] Bew, *Parnell*, 116.

by Gladstone or by the Catholic Church. Healy counter-attacked with a devastating series of polemics in which he attacked Parnell ('Mr Landlord Parnell') and Katharine O'Shea with a chauvinistic, moralizing virulence.[247] In articulating an aggressively Catholic nationalism, he defined one of the dominant idioms of modern Irish politics. Parnell, on the other hand, insisted, in a major speech in Belfast: 'It is undoubtedly true that until the prejudices of the [Protestant and Unionist] minority are conciliated ... Ireland can never enjoy perfect freedom, Ireland can never be united.'[248] The bitterness of the split did not abate with the death of Parnell on 6 October 1891. His supporters were inconsolable: the writings of W. B. Yeats and James Joyce bear witness to the intensity of their allegiance in the split.

Stephen Gwynn's conclusion is striking: 'Hatred is a fish that haunts slow, stagnant waters. It can hunt in packs, too. I have heard of a sick salmon being devoured alive by eels. Parnell's last months were like that.'[249]

---

[247] Frank Callanan, *The Parnell Split* (Cork, 1992) and *Tim Healy* (Cork, 1996), are the classic studies. Parnell replied sourly, 'I have not chosen eight members of the Parliamentary party. Everybody has chosen my colleagues except myself.' 'The Times', *The Parnellite Split* (London, 1891), 49.

[248] *Northern Whig*, 23 May 1891.

[249] Stephen Gwynn, *Fond Opinions* (London, 1938), 39.

8

Squelching, 'by way of a *hors d'oeuvre*': Conflict in Ireland, 1891–1918

> If they [Sinn Fein] can get an independent republic, and sepa-
> rate this country completely from England, and by way of a *hors
> d'oeuvre*—squelch Carson and the Ulsterman (laughter) they will be
> very remarkable men …
>
> (John Dillon, *Weekly Freeman*, 14 Dec. 1918)

Parnellism as an independent force, representing one-third of nationalists, and an ideology survived the death of Parnell. John Redmond developed a distinctive, almost conservative approach to the issues of the day.[1] When the second Home Rule Bill was vetoed by the House of Lords in 1893, Redmond refused to support a broad radical campaign within the 'British democracy' to break the power of the Lords. Rather, he insisted that priority should be given to a campaign which broke down sectarian divisions in Ireland, and thus gave British public opinion sufficient confidence to implement Irish self-government.

In short, Redmond tried to maintain an affinity with the relatively conciliatory themes of the later Parnell. It has to be said that this took considerable political courage. Many Parnellites in Dublin were naturally inclined to support a more radical nationalism.[2] The Gaelic League's dramatic emergence after 1893—in 1892 William O'Brien publicly assumed that interest in the Irish language was low amongst even patriotic young men[3]—changed the tone of debate also in an implicitly separatist direction.[4] The Parnellite press

---

[1] Ex-MP, 'Parnellism and Practical Politics', *Westminster Review*, 149 (1899), 45. Henry W. Lucy wryly noted Redmond's 'grotesquely assumed attitude of patron of Her Majesty's Government'. *A Diary of the Unionist Parliament, 1895–1910* (London, 1901), 97.

[2] Matthew Kelly, *The Fenian Ideal and Irish Nationalism* (Woodbridge, 2006).

[3] 'The Influence of the Irish Language', *Irish Essays* (London, 1893), 47.

[4] Sydney Brookes, *The New Ireland* (London and Dublin, 1906), 33; Philip G. Cambrai, *Irish Affairs and the Home Rule Question* (London, 1911), 126–7; Tom Garvin, *Nationalist Revolutionaries in Ireland 1858–1928* (Oxford, 1987), 95.

had picked up on the way in which a weary Gladstone seemed prepared to concede a partition settlement,[5] while everyone noted the playful, patronizing tone of the Tory leader Lord Salisbury, the dominant political figure of the era. In April 1893 Salisbury addressed a confident Irish Unionist gathering at Hatfield:

> We are told, I do not know with how much truth—that we unionists regard the majority of the people as something less than human. Well, at all events, we regard you representatives of the minority as, at least, human (laughter and cheers)—and I believe, you will be human enough to rejoice that we are bound together by ties of sympathy but also by ties of self-interest.[6]

All these developments made it difficult for a leader who wished to maintain a consensual course.

In 1898, however, William O'Brien revived anti-landlord, anti-grazier agitation in the shape of the United Irish League, which attracted some of Redmond's formerly loyal Parnellite colleagues, especially in the west of Ireland. In 1900 Redmond was compelled to accept that Parnellism was fading as an independent force: but the price imposed for a new unity of the parliamentary bloc was his election as chairman. It is clear that Redmond instinctively did not believe in the desirability of the revival of agrarian class conflict, and ironically, by 1902 William O'Brien had come to agree with him.[7] O'Brien had discovered, in particular, that it was difficult to maintain traction when so many prominent nationalists were themselves involved in grazing. O'Brien, having taken agrarian radicalism as far as it could go—in his own view—became a sudden and complete convert to the doctrines of dialogue and conciliation. When landlord spokesmen, led by Lord Dunraven and the dashing Captain Shawe-Taylor—the same Shawe-Taylor who had once witnessed Colonel Bourke's murder[8]—suggested a conference on the land issue with tenant leaders, they responded positively.

At the Land Conference of 1902 both landlord and tenant representatives had wanted to see a bold measure which would facilitate the sale of holdings on estates to the occupying tenants by means of state loans, to be repaid through purchase annuities. The Wyndham Land Act substantially conceded this ground: the state now moved to subvent the process of land purchase in Ireland as a healing measure. It was precisely the policy which Parnell had enunciated in the 1880s: Parnell, had he lived, would have been 57 years of age.

---

    [5] *Northern Whig*, 5 May 1893; *Irish Independent*, 5 May 1893.
    [6] *Irish Times*, 25 Apr. 1893.
    [7] Paul Bew, *Conflict and Conciliation in Ireland: Parnellites and Radical Agrarians 1890–1910* (Oxford, 1987), 94–5; *John Redmond* (Dundalk, 1996).
    [8] See Fergus Campbell, *Land and Revolution* (Oxford, 2005).

Charles Johnstone, in the *North American Review*, declared: 'that a nation, having lost its land by invasion, conquest and confiscation, should buy that land by instalments is a thing unprecedented in history.' But did this allow, as Parnell had hoped, the younger and more progressive landlords to play a broader political and social role in Irish society?[9] Charles Johnstone assumed that this development implied a new and better relationship between the gentry and their neighbours. William O'Brien agreed: he told Harold Begbie: 'Why keep up the old estrangements? Why insist on the very letter of your demand? Why not try conciliation, a seeking of agreement, a give and take, an amicable undertaking?'[10] Redmond undoubtedly agreed with this assessment, but the bulk of the Irish Party—following the lead of John Dillon and Michael Davitt—refused to consider such an option. Davitt told his friend T. D. Sullivan, who had backed the O'Brien line: 'I think you are wrong in favouring the conciliation policy. How many policies of that kind have you seen tried in your time, with but the uniform result? These landlords will *never* reciprocate advances of that kind.' He added: 'It is impossible to convert them.'

Emboldened, however, by the success of the Land Conference, Lord Dunraven—with the tacit support of George Wyndham, the Chief Secretary in Dublin Castle—called for Ireland to be given more extensive powers of self-government: while not Home Rule, these ideas could be seen as a significant step in that direction. But such a policy failed to gain sufficient popular nationalist support: John Dillon dismissed the new proposals. Meanwhile the Ulster Unionists—also worried by internal social conflicts, both urban[11] and rural[12]—responded by establishing the Ulster Unionist Council in 1905, an organization designed to enhance their local effectiveness and vitality. For Dillon, devolution was not enough; for the Ulster Unionists, it was a Trojan horse for Home Rule. A pattern was beginning to establish itself: relatively sophisticated attempts to establish a *via media* in Irish politics were rejected both by nationalists and unionists. Related to this was the emergence within Irish nationalism of new voices, both militant and eloquent, outside the party.

One of the new voices of radical nationalism, Arthur Griffith, regarded Britain as the most selfish of nations—devoted to the commercial domination of the world. By the Act of Union, according to Griffith,

---

[9] *North American Review*, v 177 (1903), 555–6.

[10] Patrick Maume (ed.), Harold Begbie, *The Lady Next Door 1914* (Dublin, 2005), 53.

[11] Henry Patterson, 'William Walker, Labour, Sectarianism and the Union, in Fintan Lane and Donal Ó Drisceoll (eds.), *Politics and the Irish Working Class* (London, 2005), 160.

[12] Alvin Jackson, 'Irish Unionism and the Russellite Threat', *Irish Historical Studies*, 25: 100 (Nov. 1987), 387.

Britain had degraded Ireland from its potential role as co-ruler of the Empire to the level of an agricultural colony. This view was, of course, widespread within nineteenth-century nationalism; Griffith's originality lay elsewhere. By 1902 he had devised a programme for the parliamentary withdrawal of Irish MPs to Ireland, the declaration of an Irish state, using the 'existing powers and resources of Irish local government'.[13] In 1904 he wrote *The Resurrection of Hungary: A Parallel for Ireland*, in which he set out his ideas on Irish independence under a dual monarch. These two terms became key elements of the political programme of *sinn fein* (self-reliance) as a political movement on 28 November 1905. Sydney Brooks, an English admirer of Sinn Fein, was highly impressed by the potential of the new movement. He declared of Sinn Fein policy that, 'if Ireland were to adopt it and stand by it, British rule in its present form and, indeed, in any effective form, would disappear from the country in less than 20 years'.[14]

Sinn Fein, it has to be said, did not present itself at this moment as notably more tolerant and pluralistic than the Irish Party; rather the reverse, in fact. In January 1904 Father John Creagh, a senior Limerick City priest, delivered a wide-ranging denunciation of Jews in history (including accusations of ritual murder) and alleged contemporary usurious practices. The Jews, according to Father Creagh, had come to 'our land to fasten themselves on us like leeches and to draw our blood'. The sermon had an immediate impact—that night there was an immediate backlash of mob violence against Limerick's small Jewish community. There followed a week of unrest, during which Creagh's call for a boycott of Jewish traders and shops was widely supported. Facing economic collapse, the Jewish community in Limerick dispersed and never recovered.[15] Throughout the crisis prominent nationalists like Michael Davitt defended the rights of the Jews, but Arthur Griffith took up a very different position. His journal, the *United Irishman*, reacted to the news of the Limerick events by noting: 'No thoughtful Irishman and Irishwoman can view without apprehension the continuous influx of Jews into Ireland.'[16] He later defined the Limerick crisis as amounting to no more than 'a few charges of common assault'.[17] 'The Jew,' he insisted, 'is in every respect an economic evil ... is ever and always an alien.' A week later, the Jews were 'these vultures'.[18]

---

[13] Thomas Hennessy, *Dividing Ireland: World War I and Partition* (London, 1998), 37.

[14] *The New Ireland*, 3.

[15] Dermot Keogh and Andrew McCarty, *Limerick Boycott, Anti-Semitism in Ireland* (Cork, 2005), 51.

[16] *United Irishman*, 31 Jan. 1904.   [17] Ibid., 23 Apr. 1904.

[18] *Ibid.*, 30 Apr. 1904.

Griffith's emergence as a serious nationalist polemicist in the early 1900s coincided with the emergence also of James Connolly, a proletarian patriotic Marxist with an equally sharp pen. Connolly at first was, however, to be frustrated by the subaltern role Irish nationalism granted to the urban working class. He was well aware of the meaning of the history of the Land League and the United Irish League: 'The tenant farmers dominated the thought of the country and made the fight of their own class for its rights identical with the idea of Irish patriotism.' Every farmer who battled for a rent reduction had been presented not just as fighting for 'his own purse, but for his country'; a 'land grabber' was a traitor to Ireland. 'The agricultural labourer had no concern in it; indeed, he invariably got better terms from the landlord than from the tenant farmer.' Connolly argued that the 'working class of Ireland' should define itself as the hegemonic class which alone had the right to define public struggles as patriotic or not.[19] It was to be no easy task in an overwhelmingly rural country; within a month of the publication of this article, the *Workers' Republic* suspended publication.[20] But formidable figures now existed outside the boundaries of official nationalism: *novi homines*, who regarded the existing leadership elite with more than a touch of contempt.

The Liberal landslide in 1906 led to a further flirtation with devolution, supported by James Bryce (appointed in December 1905) and then his successor as Chief Secretary in 1907, Augustine Birrell. Redmond was obviously tempted, but in May 1907 gave way to internal pressure and rejected the government's proposal. Bryce put the defeat down to an 'unusual combination of priests, Sinn Feiners and Irish Americans'. Why had no one 'courage enough' to see that the scheme would have given a tremendous lift to Ireland and enable the people to turn the Castle 'inside out'?[21] W. F. Monypenny felt justified in concluding: 'Whatever the merits or demerits in the abstract may be, devolution is the line of greatest, not the line of least resistance in Irish politics. It is despised and rejected by both the Irish nations.'[22] Birrell's reaction was, however, revealingly fatalistic and defeatist. One of the key figures in forcing Redmond to drop devolution was the radical agrarian MP Laurence Ginnell, who now launched a highly disruptive campaign of cattle-driving in the

---

[19] 'Unpatriotic?', *Workers' Republic* (May 1903), in Aindrias Ó Cathasaigh (ed.), *The Lost Writings of James Connolly* (London, 1997), 64.
[20] C. Desmond Greaves, *The Life and Times of James Connolly* (London, 1972), 165.
[21] NLI Ms 15070, J. V. Bryce to Alice Stopford Green, 23 May 1907.
[22] *The Two Irish Nations* (London, 1912), 52.

countryside. Bryce had regarded Ginnell as 'half crazy',[23] but in contrast, Augustine Birrell told Cherry: 'Were I an Irishman, I would agree with Ginnell.'[24]

In June 1907, however, C. J. Dolan, a young Irish MP dismayed by the continued 'moderation' of party policy, had resigned his seat and joined Sinn Fein. By 1908 Sinn Fein had reached the point where it could offer a significant, but not in any way decisive, challenge to the IPP machine in a North Leitrim by-election. Dolan, having resigned his seat as an IPP member, lost the by-election, polling 1,157 votes against F. Meehan the official Irish Party candidate's 3,103.[25] It is worth noting that the victory of Meehan, while solid enough, was won without the support of half the electorate he represented: in short, the victory was not of the scale which would destroy Sinn Fein factionism forever.[26]

On 9 February 1909 O'Brien was shouted down at the United Irish League National Convention, which he later furiously termed a 'baton convention', by Joe Devlin's Ancient Order of Hibernians and midland cattle-drivers. (The Ancient Order of Hibernians constituted a strong all-Catholic pressure-group within the Irish Party—its Catholic exclusivity leading to much criticism from both liberal nationalists and unionists.) There were shouts, directed at his wife, of 'Down with the Russian Jewess and her moneybags!'[27] At the same convention John Dillon opposed the Gaelic League's campaign to establish Irish as a compulsory matriculation requirement for entry into the new National University.[28] But, as a Unionist writer pointed out—despite the opposition of Dillon and some Catholic bishops—the League employed its muscle and financial pressure through county councils to win this argument.[29]

The language movement provided a new reference point, a new world of meanings and a potential basis for the constitution of new hierarchies: it was all the more necessary because Irish Unionism had the support of so many

---

[23] PRONI D2166/3/1/2A–D, Bryce to R. R. Cherry, 26 Dec. 1907.

[24] PRONI D/2166/3/1/10 n.d.

[25] Ciaran Ó Duibhir, *Sinn Fein—The First Election 1908*, North Leitrim History Series, no. 4 (Manorhamilton, 1993), 81–2.

[26] Ibid. 90.

[27] P. Maume, *The Long Gestation* (Dublin, 1999), 99. See also Patrick Maume's forthcoming *DIB* entry on Sophie Raffalovich O'Brien, which reveals her passionate Catholicism. For the Hibernians—whose Catholic sectarianism infuriated William O'Brien, see A. C. Hepburn, 'Catholic Ulster and Irish Politics: The Ancient Order of Hibernians, 1905–1914', in *A Place Apart: Studies in the History of Catholic Belfast* (Belfast, 1996), 157–74.

[28] *Weekly Freeman*, 20 Feb. 1909; A. C. Hepburn (ed.), *Ireland 1905–25: Documents and Analyses* (Newtownards, 1998), 74.

[29] Philip G. Cambrai, *Irish Affairs and the Home Rule Question* (London, 1911), 125.

eminent and internationally renowned Irish-born scientists who could not be dismissed as privileged layabouts of the Ascendancy.[30] The emotional intensity of Irish-language activists was, in part, designed in part to block out the prestige of men like the scientist and unionist John Tyndall;[31] a contributor to the journal *Sinn Fein*, in 1907, insisted that Tyndall was simply *not* Irish.[32] Irish nationalism in 1909–10 was in less than exciting shape.

Its victories seemed only to be victories for vested interests, while its idealists seemed only to contribute to internal divisions and allegations of small-mindedness and bigotry. Lawrence Ginnell's attempts to revive rural militancy during the ranch war of 1906–10 had served—as Ginnell himself acknowledged—to remind many of how far the rural *embourgoisement* of nationalism had progressed; more precisely, it revealed how many nationalists were themselves ranchers. Meanwhile, British welfare reform—in particular the old-age pensions legislation—evoked an enthusiastic Irish popular response which worried nationalist purists.

But suddenly Redmond and the official Irish Party were given a new boost: developments in the rest of the United Kingdom raised his prestige when the 1910 general election gave Redmond the balance of power at Westminster.[33] The key issue became—how should he employ it? Unionists reminded him of his language of the 1890s, when he derided the use of a British parliament to coerce them, as opposed to a policy of conciliation. But how realistic was it to hope that he could turn down the new opportunities?

Patricia Jalland has argued that the immediate exclusion of part of the north from the operation of the Home Rule Bill might have defused Unionist opposition and opened the way to the successful enactment of Home Rule.[34] The senior Tory and Unionist politician Walter Long wrote in his memoirs: 'To this day I marvel that the government did not take

---

[30] Greta Jones, 'Catholicism, Nationalism and Science', *Irish Review*, 20 (Winter– Spring 1997); and the same author's 'Scientists Against Home Rule', in D. George Boyce and Alan O'Day (eds.), *Defenders of the Union* (London, 2001), 188–208.

[31] For Tyndall see Thomas MacKnight, *Ulster As It Is* (London, 1896), ii. 252–3; see also Jones, 'Catholicism, Nationalism and Science', 54; compare with the modern Irish attitude which embraces such men, Richard Kearney, *Post Nationalist Ireland: Politics, Culture and Philosophy* (London, 1997), 159–77.

[32] It is worth noting that both James Joyce and George Bernard Shaw went out of their way to satirize catholic anti-scientific philistinism. See Joyce, *Ulysses*, the Danis Rose edition (London, 1997), 149, 159, and 627; see also the celebrated stage direction of Shaw's *John Bull's Other Island* (Harmondsworth, 1989), 97: 'FATHER DEMPSEY: A Theory? Me! [Theories are connected in his mind with Professor Tyndall and with scientific scepticism.]'

[33] G. R. Searle, *A New England? Peace and War 1886–1918* (Oxford, 2004), 417.

[34] Patricia Jalland, *The Liberals and Ireland: The Ulster Question in British Politics to 1914* (Aldershot, 1993), 65. For a recent critique, see Cornelius O'Leary and Patrick Maume, *Controversial Issues in Anglo-Irish Relations 1910–1921* (Dublin, 2004), 17–18.

some step in this direction.'[35] But instead, Ulster Unionism was encouraged to mobilize.[36] What was the ideological basis of that mobilization? In April 1912 Asquith introduced the Home Rule Bill: there followed much heated and unusually intemperate rhetoric inside and outside Parliament. On 'Ulster Day', 28 September, a quarter-of-a-million people signed the Solemn League and Covenant pledge to resist Home Rule. Nevertheless, the third reading of the Home Rule Bill was carried by 367 votes to 257 in January 1913. In response, the Ulster Volunteer Force was formed and began to drill at the end of the month: a clear escalation was thus marked, and was further compounded when, in September, Sir Edward Carson announced in Newry that a provisional Ulster government would be set up in the event of Home Rule coming into effect.

The unionists regarded the nationalist movement with both fear and suspicion. They saw the policies of the Catholic Church in the *ne temere* decree (1908) on mixed marriages, insisting in effect that the children of mixed marriages should be raised as Catholics, and its practical outworking in a number of controversial cases, as a denial of the validity of their own religious tradition. In this, a senior Liberal home-ruler like Augustine Birrell tended to agree with them. They saw the growing support for compulsion in Irish-language policies as presaging a form of cultural oppression. In this, John Dillon, who talked about gross oppression of the 'Protestants', agreed with them.

The uneven development of Irish capitalism had created a gap in basic outlook between Belfast and the rest of the island. The *Financial Times* supplement of 1914 glowed with praise for the 'premier shipbuilding centre of the entire world'.[37] Francis Hackett rejected the unionist view of the Irish Party as 'too ferociously unfriendly', but admitted that the Irish Parliamentary Party never had a genuine economic policy outside land purchase.[38] Lecky observed that north-east Ulster, 'alone in Ireland', had reached the full vigour of 'British industrial civilisation',[39] and Philip Cambrai added: 'Today [Belfast] is one of the biggest, most energetic and commercially successful cities of the Empire.'[40] Unionists argued that their

---

[35] The Rt. Hon. Viscount Long of Wraxall (Walter Long), *Memoirs* (London, 1923), 213.

[36] A. Jackson, *Home Rule: An Irish History* (London, 2003), 11.

[37] *Financial Times*, 28 Mar. 1914; John Lynch, *An Unlikely Success: The Belfast Shipbuilding Industry 1880–1935* (Belfast, 2001), 58; id., *Forgotten Shipbuilders of Belfast: Workman Clark 1880–1935* (Belfast, 2004), p. vi. For a fuller discussion of the ideological dimension of the Home Rule crisis, see Paul Bew, *Ideology and the Irish Question* (Oxford, 1994).

[38] Hackett, *Ireland*, 331.   [39] *Historical and Political Essays* (London, 1910), 80.

[40] Cambrai, *Irish Affairs*, 89.

complex modern achievement could not be governed by men rooted in an agrarian past.

Above all, it was a matter of the imagined community to which the unionists felt they belonged. In the late eighteenth century it was possible for a significant section of the Protestant political class in the north to have a natural primary identification with 'Ireland'. Yet, all the key developments of the nineteenth century had weakened that identification: the development under O'Connell of a form of Catholic nationalism which disregarded the concerns of Protestant liberals; the dramatic industrialization of Belfast, locked into a Belfast–Glasgow–Liverpool triangle of economic interconnectedness which contrasted with the relative weakening of economic links with the rest of the country;[41] and last but not least, the willingness of the British state until, at least, the 1880s to regard the Protestants as a potential garrison against Catholic revolt: more positively, the removal of the various grievances affecting Dissenting congregations throughout the nineteenth century further integrated Protestant Ulster within the rest of the United Kingdom.

In 1886 Gladstone had explicitly announced a preference that Belfast should rediscover its late eighteenth-century 'Irish' identity: his statement came as a profound shock to both conservative and liberal Belfast. But given the choice between separating from Britain and separating from the rest of Ireland, the unionists still chose to separate from the rest of Ireland. The Ulster Protestant community resolved to stay locked into the parliament of what Daniel O'Connell, after all, had called 'the most intellectual and commercial nation on the face of the world ... a mighty empire, upon whose limitless dominion the sun never sets'.[42] Lockean constitutional theory was marshalled to say that the principle of consent did not allow government to expel a settled community who wanted to remain within the polity. In less exalted fashion, a language of threat entered mainstream politics embodied in the Ulster Volunteer Force: senior Tories as well as Ulster Unionists connived at illegal gun-running.[43] It can be said that this was an extreme form of the politics of theatre, and that the danger of civil war was always more apparent than real[44]—but there is no question that nationalist Ireland felt mightily provoked. The unionists having borrowed some Fenian methods, the nationalists, in turn, took them back: in such

[41] Philip Ollerenshaw, 'Industry 1820–1914', in Liam Kennedy and Philip Ollerenshaw (eds.), *An Economic History of Ulster* (Manchester, 1985), 95.

[42] *Northern Whig*, 11 July 1837.

[43] Jackson, *Home Rule: A History*, 117; Jeremy Smith, *The Tories and Ireland: Conservative Party Politics and the Home Rule Crisis* (Dublin, 2000).

[44] J. A. Spender and Cyril Asquith, *Life of Herbert Henry Asquith: Lord Oxford and Asquith*, vol. 2 (London, 1932), 39.

a context, Parnell's and Redmond's hopes for a domestic reconciliation of creeds and classes were destroyed.

Such activity in Ulster was now creating a response in nationalist Ireland. Carson declared: 'I am not sorry for the armed drilling of those opposed to me. I certainly have no right to complain of it; I started this with my friends.'[45] James Connolly's language was typical in urging his supporters to follow Carson's example.[46] Carson advocated armed resistance, and nationalists took the hint. The Irish National Volunteers, founded on 25 November 1913, a smallish organization under Eoin MacNeill, dominated by nationalist independents and Sinn Feiners, had managed to build up a membership of 7,000 or so by the end of March 1914. In mid-June Redmond moved to establish official party control of the Volunteers.

In frustration, the Prime Minister, H. A. Asquith, gave his consent to a plan proposed by Winston Churchill and Colonel Seely, the Secretary of State for War, to overawe the Ulster Volunteers by swift and decisive military action. This was not intended to be a direct attack, but military manoeuvres were employed to emphasize that such a crackdown was possible.

Carson, in fact, was privately increasingly nervous: he was well aware that there were those in the British government who favoured decisive action against his movement. General Sir Arthur Paget publicly declared—and was praised in the nationalist press for so doing—that, if ordered north, the British army would act without question.[47] He could not have been more wrong. On 20 March 1914, at the Curragh Camp, Co. Kildare, Paget explained that any northern operation was likely to lead to bloodshed: in response, fifty-seven (out of seventy) cavalry officers, led by their brigadier, Hubert Gough, declared that they would resign if ordered north.[48] Although it was later to be correctly claimed that no orders had been disobeyed, this was, nonetheless, 'a kind of pre-emptive mutiny'.[49]

All the key events of 1914 appeared to presage further confrontation. On 24–5 April the unionists pulled off the coup of a substantial gun-running operation out of the port of Larne. Unionist gun-runners, it should be noted, relied on a degree of collusion on the part of customs officers and police. On 21–4 July a conference at Buckingham Palace failed to achieve an agreement based on Ulster's exclusion from Home Rule. On 26 July the nationalist

---

[45] Hugh Martin, *Ireland in Insurrection* (London, 1921), 51–2.

[46] Padraig Yeates, *Lockout: Dublin 1913* (Dublin, 2000), 21.

[47] Maume, *The Irish Independent and the Ulster Crisis*, 213.

[48] From Sir Hubert Gough's notes, it is evident that at the meeting with General Paget upon the 20th the officers were told that the operations were likely to lead to bloodshed. Henry Maxwell, *Ulster Was Right* (London, 1935), 119–31.

[49] Keith Jeffery, *Field Marshal Sir Henry Wilson: A Political Soldier* (Oxford, 2006), 124.

reply to Larne came: the Howth gun-running—in this case an open, not a secret, operation, leading to a confrontation between the British army and protestors which left four of the latter dead at Bachelor's Walk, Dublin. On 3 August, however, one event overshadowed all these dramatic events: the outbreak of war between Britain and Germany. It soon became clear that Redmond was keen to support the British war effort. His reasoning was simple: constitutional nationalists had always promised loyalty to Britain in an international crisis, and he wanted to live up to that pledge. He also hoped that his action would lessen unionist–nationalist divisions in Ireland itself: at any rate, it would prevent Ulster Unionists gaining all the benefits of their professions of loyalty to the British state. Redmond's actions were, however, a direct challenge to more radical nationalists. On 9 September 1914 a conference took place at the Gaelic League Library in Dublin, involving mainly members of the secretive Irish Republican Brotherhood, which discussed the possibility of exploitation of the European war to organize an insurrection in Ireland: the attendance included Thomas James Clarke (presiding), Eamonn Ceannt, Sean MacDermot, Joseph Mary Plunkett, Patrick Pearse, Sean T. O'Kelly, John MacBride, Arthur Griffith, Thomas MacDonagh, and William O'Brien (of the Labour Party).

Despite angry Unionist objections, Home Rule was placed on the statute book on 18 September 1914. The Prime Minister attempted to mollify the Unionists by suspending the operation of the Bill until the end of the war and undertaking to bring in an amending Bill before the implementation of Home Rule. Redmond signalled in Parliament on 15 September that he did not believe in coercing any county in Ireland into accepting a Home Rule settlement, though he hoped that the unity generated by a common effort in wartime would help to create a genuine emotional unity in Ireland. On 24 September MacNeill and other members of the original committee of the Irish Volunteers issued a manifesto repudiating the leadership of Redmond. Significantly, the cult of Emmet now revived in advanced nationalist circles, as men considered how best to foil Redmond's Anglophile strategy.

Herbert Pim, in his influential pamphlet *What Emmet Means*, in 1915 described the 1803 rising as a 'spiritual triumph': a view shared by other advanced nationalists such as Patrick Pearse, Sean MacDiarmada, and Terence MacSwiney. In his essay on *Robert Emmet: Irish Fundamentalist*, MacSwiney called special attention to the passage of Emmet's manifesto, which had cited Castlereagh's words that 'Ireland never had, and never could enjoy under other circumstances, the benefit of British connexion; that it necessarily must happen when one country is connected with another, that the interests of the lesser will be borne down by those of the greater'.[50]

[50] University College, Dublin, Archives, pp. 48(b), 319 (13).

Many nationalists began to feel the force of this observation. It seemed that Ireland was being asked to make a huge blood sacrifice for a British war without sufficient return. The backdrop of historical suspicion was great indeed, even amongst those close to Redmond. Redmond was asked to join the British Cabinet. Symptomatically, when the emissaries from Dublin Castle came to his' country house, saying they 'wanted Mr Redmond', the door was slammed on them by Redmond's cook, who feared they had come to arrest the Irish leader![51] Redmond, perhaps unwisely, turned down the offer—and lost a degree of visible sway over policy as it affected, in particular, Irish recruits. Nationalist public opinion saw only apparent impotence and yet another British display of double standard, especially when Carson joined the Cabinet in May 1915. Even so, Redmond's lieutenant Joe Devlin, dining with Lord Basil Blackwood in June 1915, remained 'very keen about recruiting',[52] and the Irish Party won the Dublin College Green by-election in the same month.

The Irish Party's electoral performances in the period between the outbreak of the First World War and the Easter Rising require some analysis; there were five contested seats, each possessing considerable political interest; in addition, two seats—Wicklow West in August 1914 and Galway East in December of that year—fell vacant and were uncontested, and Sir James Browne Dougherty, the former Under-Secretary, took Londonderry City as a Liberal pro-home-ruler. But what do the five contested seats reveal about the evolution of nationalist opinion?

The conclusion of any analysis of wartime by-elections in nationalist Ireland is clear enough. The Irish Party won all five of the contested seats, as well, of course, as retaining the non-contested ones. The *Weekly Freeman's Journal* was quite correct to criticize the separatists for their failure to put up candidates: 'There were vacancies in the South, in the West, in the East and in the North. They could have tested their views in Tipperary, in Galway, Kings County or Derry, but they did not budge.'[53] The two seats where separatists stood—College Green and North Louth—were won by the Irish Party. Nevertheless, there is clear evidence of the weakness of the IPP's structures. As a powerful study of regional grass-roots sentiment concludes: 'Redmond's political leadership had for years been placed rather uncomfortably at the head of the less compromising Nationalism of the mass of his followers.'[54] In general, the rural results were better than the urban: in Tipperary, given a choice of three parliamentarians, the electors selected the candidate

[51] *Weekly Freeman's Journal*, 10 July 1915.
[52] PRONI D1231/G/5/281, Lord Basil Blackwood to his mother, Hariot.
[53] *Irish Times*, 1 Oct. 1915.
[54] Michael Wheatley, *Nationalism and the Irish Party* (Oxford, 2004), 266.

closest to Redmond's personal philosophy; in Dublin Harbour, in the same situation, they did not. But even in rural areas there was evidence of a correspondingly low level of involvement in the Irish Party's apparatus. This was due in significant measure to the fading resonance of the land question. A new 'mosquito' press developed, expressing the views of Dublin's revolutionary subculture. In February 1915 Sean Doyle launched the *Spark*. On 19 June Arthur Griffith launched a new title, *Nationality*: British intelligence estimated a real circulation of 8,000.[55] In May James Connolly relaunched the *Workers' Republic*. In December 1915 the military council of the IRB was formed: MacDermot, Clarke, Pearse, Joseph Mary Plunkett, and Eamonn Ceannt. In January 1916 the Supreme Council of the IRB decided to launch an insurrection at the earliest opportunity: on 19–22 January they were joined in their counsels by James Connolly.

The mood of the insurgent press is instructive. In October 1915 Arthur Griffith, in *Nationality*, insisted on his traditional theme: 'Ireland's economic oppression is within the British Empire. Ireland was the most heavily taxed country in the history of nations since the fall of the Roman Empire.'[56] The *Workers' Republic*—whose moving spirit was the Marxist James Connolly—drew on a strong 'faith and fatherland' sentiment: 'Now or never ... are you going to oblige John Bull, the butcher of your priests and people, by remaining quiet till he is in a position to finish you off?'[57] The *Spark*, anti socialist and obsessed with the conversion of England, rightly insisted that *Workers' Republic* was compatible with its own credo: an explicit Catholic nationalism.[58]

Redmond, who sought out the quietness and solitude of rural Wicklow when he spent time there, had little feeling for the proletarian passions of Dublin. Michael MacDonagh noted:

Redmond looked upon this as play-acting by nobodies—a manifestation of the histrionic side of the Irish character by persons of no consequence. He was without fear for his position in Ireland. Had not his influence over the coalition saved Ireland from the threatened disruption of its civil life by conscription? And had not the South and West voluntarily joined the colours to the number of 45,000? That, indeed, was a remarkable response, everything considered. Looking to the future, Redmond saw the reconciliation of North and South, and home rule established by general consent, at the victorious conclusion of a terrible war, out of which all came softened by suffering.[59]

It was a vision which the men of 1916 were determined to thwart.

---

55 Charles Townshend, *Easter 1916: The Irish Rebellion* (London, 2005), 81.
56 *Nationality*, 2 Oct. 1915.
57 *Workers' Republic*, 19 Feb. 1916.   58 *Spark*, 16 Apr. 1916.
59 Emily Lawless and Michael MacDonagh, *Ireland*, 3rd edn. (London, 1923), 446.

PLANS FOR A RISING

The original plan for the 1916 Rising involved an elaborate county-by-county rebellion, which would have depended for its success on a German-backed invasion, with the landing being at Limerick.[60] This was the basis of the proposal put by Joseph Plunkett and Sir Roger Casement to the Germans in 1915. By January 1916 this proposal had been modified. Dublin was now more explicitly the centrepiece of the Rising: 'The activity in Dublin was intended as a trigger for the rest of the country. The provincial rising would be started in the west and assisted now by the anticipated arrival of a large German arms shipment.'[61] In January 1916 the Supreme Council of the IRB decided to launch an insurrection at the earliest opportunity. With this objective in mind, James Connolly conspired with the IRB Military Council at Dolphins' Barn, Dublin. On 16 March Dublin Castle was told: 'Things look as if they are coming to a crisis, each man has been issued with a package of lint and surgical dressing.'[62] Even allowing for the Chief Secretary Augustine Birrell's reluctance to spend time in Dublin,[63] with this sort of information to hand it is difficult to comprehend the inactivity of the authorities. But it must be recalled that the Volunteers periodically took over central Dublin for military exercises and that the separatist press would publish fantasies about a successful German invasion. It was exceptionally difficult to disentangle dream and play actions from fact: the Dublin Castle authorities resolved that the 'seditious bodies' would not venture unaided to 'break into insurrection'. Instead, they believed that the insurrectionaries were 'prepared to assist a German landing'. Thus, in such thinking, the key element in British strategy was the successful prevention of the arrival of significant German military assistance. But such thinking made no allowance for the type of military calculation on the Irish nationalist side, which was determined to offer up a kind of 'blood sacrifice' in any case. The fact, too, that the hard core of revolutionaries (Pearse, Connolly, and the former dynamitard of the 1880s, Tom Clarke) were an elite within an elite, with a different agenda, made it even harder for the British system. The existence of genuinely divided counsels within the insurrectionary movement did more to disable the Dublin Castle authorities

---

[60] '1916 Invasion Plans are Found', *Sunday Press*, 31 Mar. 1991.
[61] Michael Foy and Brian Barton, *The Easter Rising* (Stroud, 1999), 25.
[62] PRO CO 904/23/128.
[63] 'Report of the Royal Commission on the Rebellion in Ireland 1916', in David Coates (ed.), *The Irish Uprising 1914–21: Papers from the British Parliamentary Archive* (London, 2000), 112.

than, in the end, it actually weakened the insurrectionaries. The willingness of the militants to deceive their own chief-of-staff (Eoin MacNeill), also helped to deceive the governmental system. On 3 April Padraig Pearse, as director of organization, issued orders to the Irish Volunteers for a three-day march and field manoeuvres throughout Ireland, to begin on Easter Monday. On 20 April the *Aud* arrived in Tralee Bay from Germany with a cargo of arms for the Irish Volunteers; it, however, was arrested by a British naval vessel. On 21 April Sir Roger Casement, a British diplomat turned radical Irish nationalist, landed from a German submarine on a mission to warn Eoin MacNeill that the expected German aid, even if received, would be insufficient for insurrection.[64] Casement was, however, arrested shortly after landing, but not before he had instructed a Volunteer from the neighbouring town of Tralee to rush to Dublin and tell the leaders that the German offer of support was negligible. Eoin MacNeill received this communication on Easter Sunday and thus resolved to call off the Rising.

But others in the leadership were imbued with an overriding principle—that of sacrificial patriotism. In Michael MacDonagh's phrase: 'They would offer themselves up as a holocaust for their country.'[65] They assumed that the British response would be both 'rapid' and 'hard':[66] sufficiently severe to make it clear that government from London was a form of imperial occupation, 'brought about and sustained by force'.[67] For romantic nationalists—Padraig Pearse, Thomas MacDonagh, and Joseph Plunkett—the idea of blood sacrifice had a significant appeal. For Pearse in particular, religion combined with nationalism: he acted as he did partly in conscious emulation of Christ's sacrifice on the cross—in following His example he would redeem the Irish nation.[68] On 22 April Chief-of-Staff Eoin MacNeill issued a countermanding order, cancelling activities planned for the next day. O'Neill's order was published in the *Sunday Independent* on 23 April. On the same day, the Military Council of the Irish Volunteers met at Liberty Hall, the veteran republican Tom Clarke in the chair. They unanimously decided to strike next day (Easter Monday) at noon. The proclamation of the revolutionaries, *The Provisional Government of Ireland to the People of Ireland*, signed by Clarke and six others, was printed at Liberty Hall.

On 24 April the General Post Office and several other buildings in Dublin were seized by the Irish Volunteers and citizen army, led by Pearse

---

[64] B. L. Reid, *The Lives of Roger Casement* (New Haven and London, 1976), 351.

[65] Lawless and MacDonagh, *Ireland*, 453.   [66] Townshend, *Easter 1916*, 181.

[67] Matthew Kelly, 'The Myths of 1916', *London Review of Books*, 27: 273 (1 Dec. 2005), 7.

[68] Brian Barton, *From Behind a Closed Door: Secret Court Martial Records of the 1916 Rising* (Belfast, 2002), 5.

and Connolly. 'The day before the Easter Rising was Easter Sunday, and they were crying joyfully in the churches "Christ has risen". On the following day, they were saying in the streets "Ireland has risen". The luck of the moment was here.' These are the opening words of James Stephens's *The Insurrection of Dublin*, a text by a skilled writer, published in November 1916, which was never revised and has thus retained the sense of immediacy, which makes it the classic eyewitness account: 'Today [Easter Monday] our principal city is no longer peaceful; guns are sounding, or rolling and crackling from different directions.' 'What chance have they?' James Stephens asked an admirer of Connolly. The reply was terse but accurate. 'None,' he replied, 'and they never said they had, and they never thought they would have any.'[69] Alfred Fannin, a Dublin businessman and opponent of the Rising, noted at eight o'clock in the evening on 25 April: 'Short of a German invasion of England at the same time on a big scale, the whole thing was doomed to failure.' But he added: 'All the same, after 36 hours rebellion, the rebels hold nearly all the points they have taken.'[70] A brave effort had, at last, been made; Dublin, a city which had long listened to the rhetoric of nationalist revolutionaries, but had experienced nothing but fiascos (1803, 1848, and 1867), now experienced an altogether more serious event. On Easter Tuesday a veteran of the nineteenth-century British intelligence operation against Irish revolutionaries recalled, with his friend the Revd. Augustus Young, the humiliation of the beltless Fenians in 1867. Gosselin clearly understood that he had lived to see a rather different event. Connolly knew this well, telling his daughter: 'It was a good clean fight, the cause can not die now. It will put an end to recruiting. Irishmen now realise the absurdity of fighting for the freedom of other countries while their own is enslaved.'[71]

The cost was heavy and not only, or even mainly, to the Volunteers; some 450 people were killed in the Rising. British military losses were 116 dead, while sixteen policemen were killed. The remaining figures do not distinguish between Volunteers and civilians, for whom the combined figure was 318 dead. They also do not convey the impact of certain crimes by the British forces—as when the pacifist Francis Sheehy-Skeffington and two others were summarily executed at Portobello military barracks on 26 April. Interestingly, however, a roll of honour, which was compiled out of later records, showed sixty-four rebels as having died, out of a grand

[69] Stephens, *The Insurrection of Dublin* (Dublin, 1916), 47.
[70] Adrian and Sally Warwick Haller, *Letters from Dublin, Easter 1916: Alfred Fannin's Diary of the Rising* (Dublin, 1995), 23.
[71] Nora O'Brien, 'Easter', *Atlantic Monthly*, 118 (1919), 684.

total of 1,558 insurgents.[72] The rebels, in a sense, had it both ways. Since 1867 Dubliners had lived alongside an underground Fenian tradition, but a tradition which had resulted only in some ugly crimes and, in the nineteenth century at least, was well penetrated by informers.[73] Now the conspirators had covered themselves in glory by showing a willingness to die for their country, but the great majority actually survived and were—after a period which began on 1 May 1916, when 400 were sent to Britain only to return, in most cases, after a few months—the sanctified focus of a new resistance to British rule.

In the General Post Office they had issued a document which was to cost its signatories their lives—the Proclamation declaring an Irish republic. The text eloquently declared that Ireland was now at last regaining control of its destiny. The revolutionary elite—with some presumption—proclaimed: 'The Irish Republic is entitled to, and hereby claims, the allegiance of every Irishman and Irishwoman.' While there was reference to 'gallant allies in Europe' (the Germans), the deepest thrust of the Proclamation was on the willingness of the insurrectionaries 'to sacrifice themselves for the common good'. After Pearse had finished reading, Connolly shook his hand, saying: 'Thanks be to God, Pearse, that we live to see this day.'

The leaders of the Rising, knowing that they had little chance of conventional military success, acted, instead, in a mood of passionate exhilaration. Constance Markievicz, a leading figure among the Easter revolutionists, later recalled this moment in a description of James Connolly:

I never saw him happier than on Easter Monday morning, when he came downstairs with the other members of the Provisional Government of the Republic. We parted on the steps of Liberty Hall for the last time. He was absolutely radiant, like a man who had seen a vision. The comrade of Tone and Emmet, he stood on the heights with them, his spirit one with theirs. The rapture that comes only when the supreme sacrifice is made intentionally and willingly in a man's heart, was his. The life of the flesh was over for him: the spirit life had begun.[74]

But for all the raw emotional power of the proclamation, the Easter Rising did not claim the united support of the majority of the nationalist 'family'. In fact, the reference in the Proclamation to the 'secret organisation' (the underground IRB) was, after all, a reference to a body which, after

---

[72] Foy and Barton, *Easter Rising*, 211.

[73] David Fitzpatrick, *Harry Boland's Irish Revolution* (Cork, 2003), 18–24, contrasts the career of Harry Boland (1887–1922), an insurgent of the Easter Rising period, with that of his father and uncle, ardent republican conspirators also, but whose lives were dominated by murky and ambiguous activities in a Dublin underworld characterized by intrigue and betrayal.

[74] *Mayo News*, 1 June 1935.

'more than half a century in existence, had achieved no political result whatsoever'.[75] Stephen Gwynn, in his *Observer* article ten years later,[76] felt sure that the British decision (supported by Redmond, at least in the four most prominent cases) to execute the leaders had played a key role in changing the sympathy of the populace. Some 700 rebels took up arms on Easter Monday, though as news of the revolt spread others joined in and the numbers at least doubled. Nevertheless, this total composed less than 1 per cent of the total number of Irishmen who served in the British army during the war.[77] This had created other loyalties, other connections, for many Irishmen. A letter from an Irish soldier and college contemporary of Eamon de Valera, one of the Easter week commandants, made the point very forcefully: 'While Mr de Valera stood on Mount Street Bridge commanding the rebels, four Britishers helped me to carry across No Man's Land at St Julien the dying, some of whom sat on the same benches with us at school.'[78] For a moment at least, it seemed as if Irish public sympathy was torn.

How far did the British response to 1916 determine the subsequent political outcome? Was it possible for the British to have viewed the bulk of the insurgents in a more lenient light? When W. T. Cosgrave—he had fought as a senior officer at the South Dublin Union—was being court-martialled, the prosecuting counsel at the courts martial of the captured leaders, W. E. Wylie, records asking if 'he had any defence, and he said he had never "heard of the rebellion until he was in the middle of it"'. 'He assured me,' Wylie continued, 'that when he marched out on Easter Monday, he thought he was merely going out for a route march.'[79] Stephen Gwynn was referring to Cosgrave, later the Irish premier, when he noted:

Everyone of the men who were in that rising, Mr Cosgrave not least of them, admits that if the rank and file—many of whom had no idea for what purpose

[75] Leon O'Broin, *Revolutionary Underground: The Story of the Irish Republican Brotherhood* (Dublin, 1976), 140.

[76] *Observer*, 26 Apr. 1926.

[77] Michael Laffan, *The Resurrection of Ireland: The Sinn Fein Party 1916–23* (Cambridge, 1999), 44.

[78] *Weekly Freeman*, 24 Nov. 1917. Ben Novick has recently pointed to the 'connexion between the Ireland that fought in the Somme and Gallipoli, and the Ireland that rose at 1916. The two Irelands are inextricably linked.' *Conceiving Revolution: Irish Nationalist Propaganda During the First World War* (Dublin, 2001), 17. Stephen Gwynn observed: 'In scores of Catholic families the elder brothers were with some Irish regiment; the younger were training with the Volunteers to become part of the Irish Republican Army. Kevin O'Higgins, for example, had a brother serving in France.' *Dublin Old and New* (Dublin and London, 1937), 133.

[79] Barton, *From Behind Closed Doors*, 59.

they had been mobilised on Easter Sunday—had been dismissed contemptuously to their homes and the leaders treated as lunatics, the whole thing would have been over.[80] But instead, by 1 May over 400 insurgents had been sent to Britain for internment. Within days of their surrender prisoners were being court-martialled. James Stephens recalled: 'Nobody believes there will be any mercy shown ... the belief grows that no person who is now in the insurrection will be alive when the insurrection is ended.'[81] A total of fifteen men were shot by firing squad—including Padraig Pearse, Tom Clarke, James Connolly (wounded and strapped to a chair), and Eamonn Ceannt. These men all died as good Catholics. Pearse was enormously relieved when he heard that Connolly, the Marxist, had made his peace with the Church: even more remarkably, Connolly, at the last, requested that his Protestant wife Lily convert to Catholicism.[82] Ceannt, who had once piped 'O'Donnell Abu' before the Pope in the Vatican,[83] fell under a hail of bullets, clutching his blood-spattered crucifix.[84] Such a powerful symbolism compelled the Irish people to identify the insurgents as representative Irishmen with whom they shared much—not crazed subversives: not as 'partly socialistic' and 'partly alien', as the *Irish Catholic*, an authoritative voice, had been tempted to call them in the week after the rising.[85] As Redmond's nephew L. G. Redmond Howard, in his *Six Days of the Irish Republic*, published in 1916, shrewdly noted: 'Once the link of race had been appealed to, of course, every attack that reflected in any way upon the character of the fighters, was resented by the whole nation as a matter of honour.'[86] Ceannt was certain that, in 'the years to come, Ireland will honour those who risked all for her Honour at Easter in 1916'.[87] His confidence was absolute and absolutely justified. The *Catholic Bulletin* soon took a very pro-rebel line, giving, for example, great prominence to the account of Father John Flanagan, unofficial chaplain of the garrison in the GPO, who stressed the pious Catholicism he found here.[88] Finally, on 3 August, Sir Roger Casement, who at the last converted to Catholicism, was hanged in Pentonville

[80] *Observer*, 26 Apr. 1926.   [81] Stephens, *The Insurrection of Dublin*, 64.

[82] John Newsinger, *Rebel City: Larkin, Connolly and the Dublin Labour Movement* (Dublin, 2004), 148.

[83] William Henry, *Supreme Sacrifice: The Story of Eamonn Ceannt* (Cork, 2005), 23.

[84] Ibid. 131.

[85] David Miller, *Church, State and Nation in Ireland 1898–1921* (Dublin, 1973), 324.

[86] L. G. Redmond Howard, *Six Days of the Irish Republic* (Cork, 2006 edn.), 70.

[87] Henry, *Supreme Sacrifice*, 127.

[88] Keith Jeffery (ed.), *The GPO and the Easter Rising* (Dublin, 2006), 157–63.

Prison, London. Those who were executed were 'unofficially but popularly beatified'.[89]

One of the best descriptions of the effect of the executions came from the pen of James Malone, a captured insurgent:

> But the most of the people had real hatred in their hearts for the Irish volunteers. We were often insulted on the journey. On our way through Dublin city, we were insulted in every street and attacked fiercely. Stones and bottles were thrown at us. Were it not for the guards, I am certain that we would have been injured or killed. It was not only the followers of the British army who were the cause of it, but all the inhabitants of the city. If I hadn't seen it with my own two eyes, I would not have believed it.[90]

But Malone immediately adds, in a striking passage: 'Three weeks later, when we were on our way to England, the very same people were praising and blessing us, waving the Tricolour and shouting. Seventeen of our comrades had been executed in the meantime. Pearse was right when he said that nothing would awaken the spirit and courage of the people but bloodshed.' Professor Michael Laffan has concluded: 'Far more men were killed than was necessary to remove dangerous revolutionary leaders, but too few to deter future rebellions.'[91]

The *Freeman's Journal* later observed: 'The executions of the men of 1916 would, under any circumstances, have profoundly moved the people and inflamed them against the executioners.' But it added that the history of the Home Rule crisis was also of great significance; the presence within the British coalition government of Tories and Unionists who had helped to unleash anarchy in Ireland powerfully delegitimized the official response. The *Freeman* declared: 'The fact that the insurgents were sent to death by a government largely composed of the men who had set in motion the process of demoralisation that had ended in the bloodshed, utterly revolted the conscience of the country.'[92] This was the profound conviction of most Irish constitutional nationalists.

When the apostles who preached the 'Grammar of Anarchy' for their gospel let themselves loose in Ireland to teach the people that the established authority had no moral rights unless it derived from the people that it was governing, it converted

---

[89] Jonathan Githens-Mazer, *Myths and Memories of the Easter Rising: Cultural and Political Nationalism in Ireland* (Dublin, 2006), 144.

[90] Patrick J. Twohig (ed.), *Blood on the Flag: Autobiography of a Freedom Fighter* (Ballincollig, 1996), 38. This volume is a translation from the Irish of James Malone's memoir *B'Fhiu an Braon Fola*, more closely translated as 'The Drop of Blood was worth it': an implied criticism of O'Connell's dictum that the resolution of Ireland's ills did not justify the loss of a single life.

[91] Laffan, *Sinn Fein*, 49.

[92] *Weekly Freeman*, 20 Sept. 1919, 'Coercion and Distrust'.

the government of Ireland in the eyes of large masses of the people into a sort of organised immorality, engaged in war upon the people.[93]

Within constitutional nationalism, only Stephen Gwynn insisted that their own tradition was partly to blame, because it had failed to concede the principle of consent quickly enough and unambiguously enough.

A RETROSPECTIVE VALIDATION FOR EASTER WEEK? IRISH POLITICS, 1916–1918

The British government's political response to the Rising consisted in a serious, if flawed and ambiguous, effort to revive the Home Rule project. Many Irish Unionists were surprised and dismayed: Carson had to send James Craig out on an educational tour. It was explained that the Cabinet was 'quite unanimous'.[94] The Foreign Minister, Sir Edward Grey, wanted the new policy because of American pressure. But others noted the view of such wartime allies as the ex-Boer leader, now South African premier, Louis Botha; also the existence of 'Home Rule' enthusiasm within the Empire. Most of the erstwhile Unionist press in London supported the new line. Asquith insisted that, despite all appearances, there was reason for optimism and that the rebellion might, indeed, act as a spur to efforts to resolve the Irish question. Between May and July 1916 Lloyd George intensified his contacts with the Irish parties. The key issue, of course, remained, as before the war: the issue of partition. It has been argued that the discussion here was dogged by Lloyd George's duplicity. The Irish Party was given the impression by Lloyd George that any exclusion of north-eastern counties would be temporary. The Unionists were told in writing—in words that were not without ambiguity, however—that Ulster's exclusion would be permanent. The public statements of the government on this topic were actually quite consistent. On 27 May 1916 H. H. Asquith, who had just returned from Ireland, said: 'The Government of Ireland Act in the statute book has not and would not, so far as I know—and I have said so repeatedly—ever desire to induce any coercive application by one set of Irishmen against another.' Two months later, on 25 July, Lloyd George said: 'Under no conditions did the present government or any member of it ever contemplate bringing in a measure to force the six counties into a home rule government for Ireland against their will.'[95] Behind the scenes, the

[93] Ibid., 5 July 1919, 'The Irish Peace'.

[94] PRONI D627/429/46, Hugh de Fellenberg Montgomery to Charles Montgomery, 9 June 1916.

[95] *Weekly Northern Whig*, 26 Jan. 1918, 'Sir Edward Carson's Resignation'.

senior Tory politician Walter Long played a significant part in sabotaging Lloyd George's scheme; his inflexibility contrasted with Carson's relative flexibility. On 6 May 1916 Carson wrote to Sir Arthur Conan Doyle, a friend of the constitutional nationalists. While he insisted that it was an 'utter fallacy' for the economically incompetent south and west of Ireland to wish to rule the North, he added, nonetheless, that if partition was established he would urge southern unionists to work positively with the new dispensation. He would wish to reserve for north-east Ulster the right to join the South of its free own will.[96] Even the temporary exclusion of a large part of Ulster was difficult for the Redmond leadership to sell to its base. Northern nationalists living in the north-east alongside large unionist majorities tended to be pro-compromise on the issue, whilst those living in nationalist majority areas of Derry, Tyrone, and Fermanagh were opposed to any concession. Eventually, however, a Belfast convention of northern nationalists, on 23 June 1916, agreed by a majority of 475 to 265 to the exclusion of Antrim, Down, Armagh, Fermanagh, Tyrone, and Londonderry from the operation of the Home Rule Act.

At this point, and at a huge price, Ulster Unionism gained a new credibility within British political life. The exploits of the Ulster Division at the Battle of the Somme—its first major engagement—'rapidly achieved legendary status'.[97] Going over the top on 1 July 1916, the division suffered terrible casualties on Thiepval Ridge and the supposedly impregnable Schwaben Redoubt. The commander of the 36th Division, General Sir Oliver Nugent, who sometimes felt exasperated by a perceived narrowness of the Ulster Unionist world-view, on 2 July wrote to his wife: 'My dearest, the Ulster Division has been too superb for words. The whole army is talking of the incomparable gallantry shown by officers and men.'[98] Captain Wilfrid Spender, an English officer—but one who had totally embraced the Ulster cause—took the opportunity to pen anonymously a widely reprinted article for the press: 'I am not an Ulsterman, but yesterday, as I followed their amazing attack, I felt I would rather be an Ulsterman than anything else in the world. They changed over the two frontlines of the enemy's trenches, shouting "No surrender, boys!" '[99] This was Ulster Unionism which Britain could identify with; it was all the more difficult at such a moment for Britain to 'betray' it. As in 1798, the Orange Order

---

[96] 'Conan Doyle's Bestseller is Unearthed', *Irish News*, 22 May 2004. For the background to Carson's thinking see Jeremy Smith, 'Sir Edward Carson and the Myth of Partition', in R. Swift and C. Kinealy (eds.), *Politics and Power in Victorian Ireland* (Dublin, 2006), 178–91.

[97] Keith Jeffery, *Ireland and the Great War* (Cambridge, 1998), 55.

[98] Nick Perry, 'General Nugent', *Military History Society* (forthcoming 2007).

[99] Jeffery, *Ireland and the Great War*, 55.

abandoned its Boyne commemoration processions on 12 July, and, at the suggestion of the Lord Mayor of Belfast, five minutes silence was observed on noon of that day.[100] But, of course, nationalists also counted the losses of many, many brave men, notably the 10th Division at Gallipoli and the 16th at the Somme in late July, where Andrew Kettle's son, Tom Kettle, died.

But if, in fact, the Irish political elites had reached an understanding on the basis of the principle of consent in 1916, it was probably already too late. Sinn Fein would not have accepted that deal, making the whole project unsustainable. It is worth noting that from the point of view of northern nationalism there was one key advantage in a constitutionalist approach. The legislation for the 'excluded' area in the north-east clearly envisaged continued direct rule by London, but with a decidedly green tinge through the pressures exerted both by an Irish Parliament within the United Kingdom and those Irish MPs staying at Westminster. In Redmond's assessment, this Irish representation could, in principle, after the implementation of Home Rule, provide United Kingdom Cabinet members. These arrangements, on the face of it, constituted a strong potential defence of the interests of the Catholic and nationalist minority in the north-east; they were certainly perceived at the time to be superior (from a nationalist point of view) to later proposals for a local Protestant state which gained ground after Easter 1916.[101] This was a point understandably harped upon in later years by Redmond's close supporters, such as J. P. Hayden's newspaper, the *Roscommon Messenger*, which pointed out in August 1921: 'The policy of optional exclusion was quite different to that which gives the cut-off area all the machinery of legislation.'[102]

Just before Christmas 1916 the British released from Frongoch and Reading jails the remaining untried Irish political prisoners. On their return to Ireland, most threw themselves into activist politics. Good, but not spectacular, results in by-election contests against the Redmondite party were achieved by Sinn Fein in 1917. In Roscommon North, in February, thanks above all to the campaigning priest Father Michael O'Flanagan,[103]

---

[100] Ibid. 57.

[101] Eamon Phoenix, *Northern Nationalism: Nationalist Politics, Partition and the Catholic Minority in Northern Ireland* (Belfast, 1994), 23–7; *Weekly Freeman*, 28 Sept. 1917.

[102] 'The Peace Movement', *Roscommon Messenger*, 5 Aug. 1921. The editorial continues with a phrase which has a precise resonance in the language of the Downing Street Declaration of 1993: 'It was with the false cry of partition that the ferocity of the attack on the Irish Party grew. Partition in real earnest and full operation must now be faced. It is evident from his pronouncements that Mr de Valera is quite prepared to accept it in principle, provided that it comes from an Irish, not a British, authority.'

[103] Kathleen Hegarty Thorne, *They Put the Flag Aflying: The Roscommon Volunteers 1916–23* (Eugene, Oreg., 2005), 13.

George Noble Count Plunkett beat the Redmondite Thomas Devine decisively, but the next by-election, South Longford in May, was only won when the returning officer had a recount of Sinn Fein votes (for J. P. McGuinness, then in Lewes Jail), perhaps encouraged at pistol point.[104] John Redmond was privately well aware that South Longford was a decisive negative turning-point for his fortunes: in Longford town the Redmondites still had a militant following and considerable local clerical support, but it had been overwhelmed by rural voters. In desperation, Redmond contemplated a mass resignation of MPs as the only possible way to regain the initiative, but the idea had come too late to be of any utility.[105] On 16 June 1917 the British released the remaining Irish prisoners, including Joe McGuinness and Eamon de Valera. The idea was to help Redmond with a final conciliatory effort—the Irish Convention—attended by Unionists, but de Valera immediately achieved a slashing victory in the East Clare by-election. Worse was to follow: Thomas Ashe, one of those released in June, was rearrested and sentenced to two years jail in August: he died, as a result of force-feeding on hunger strike in pursuit of political status, on 25 September. Bishop Fogarty of Killaloe issued a public letter, in which he stated that Ashe had become a martyr for the Irish cause and that his death would increase the hatred for the British government.[106] Certainly, the Bishop of Killaloe's own statement fanned the flames of that hatred:

This is the sort of cruelty we are accustomed to hear of as possible only in the ancient Bastille, or the dungeons of Naples, but as altogether impossible under English rule. We have no need to wait for the future to inform us: the world sees

[104] T. P. Coogan, *Michael Collins* (London, 1990), 67. Coogan's account is unsubstantiated elsewhere. Joe Good, *Enchanted Dreams: The Journal of a Revolutionary* (Dingle, 1996), 109, simply says that Joe McGrath of Sinn Fein demanded a 'recount' and 'to our amazement McGuinness was declared elected for Sinn Fein by a majority of 37 or thereabouts'. In her essay 'Michael Collins: The Granard Connection', Margot Gearty does, however, record: '"Vote early, vote often" was the catchphrase of this election, and I believe Kitty [Kiernan] and Maud encouraged others to do just that. An old gentleman here in Granard tells me he remembers them coming to borrow his sick father's voting card, so they could do some personation in favour of McGuinness.' Gabriel Doherty and Dermot Keogh (eds.), *Michael Collins and the Making of the Irish State* (Cork, 1998), 41. Marie Coleman, in her *County Longford and the Irish Revolution* (Dublin, 2003), 65, is inclined not to accept Coogan's version. 'It is an account which does not figure prominently in any other commentary on the election and was not referred to by anyone else who was involved.'

[105] T. Wilson (ed.), *The Political Diaries of C. P. Scott 1911–1928* (London, 1970), 290.

[106] Jerome Aan de Wiel, *The Catholic Church in Ireland 1914–1918: War and Politics* (Dublin, 2003), 188.

already in these hideous atrocities what the triumph of English culture means for small nationalities.[107]

The reference to Naples conjured up Gladstone's support of Italian liberalism, while the reference to culture recalled the theme of German *Kultur*, by which the Germans—as alleged by the British—justified their war crimes. Who were the British, the senior cleric was saying, to lecture Europe in matters of political morality?

On 25–6 October the tenth Sinn Fein *Ard Fheis* (conference) was held at the Mansion House, Dublin; de Valera, the sole surviving commandant of the Easter Rising, was elected president on the first day. On 27 October he was also elected president of the Irish Volunteers. It was already clear that Sinn Fein had a genuine popular appeal. The new movement also differed from the Easter Rising insurgency in that it was not so much recruited from the towns and was not entirely led by townsmen. The farmers, their sons, and labourers were in it. Further, it embraced, far more than the Easter Rising had, the professional and commercial classes.[108] Shortly afterwards, at the convention of the Irish Volunteers on 27 October 1917, de Valera said:

There had already been too much bloodshed without success, and he would never advocate another rebellion without hopeful chances of success. They could see no hope of that in the near future ... They must continue to drill, in spite of all opposition. They would try to avoid coming into conflict with the military and at the same time continue, in a passive way, to keep their cause before the world until the peace convention. Before the war was over, England would be softening. The Allies would not win ... [109]

Some of the delegates wanted an immediate attempt at rebellion. De Valera replied that there was now nothing to be gained by a wild or hot-headed outbreak; it would be a foolish move. The blood that had been spilled was enough to show the world that they were in the fray.

De Valera was here signalling a political battle with the Irish Party. The Irish Party desperately tried to defend itself by stressing its record on the land issue. John Dillon declared:

'One of the new doctrines preached by Sinn Feiners is: "Don't recognise English law" (laughter). I would like to ask you this—how do you hold your farms? Are they not held under the Land Acts? Where were the Land Acts passed? If the principle

[107] Ibid. 155, 'Done to Death: Behind the Walls of Mountjoy—Letter of the Bishop of Killaloe'.

[108] Lawless and MacDonagh, *Ireland*, 468.

[109] PRO CO 904/24/1, secret crime branch special information received from a reliable source, 20 Nov. 1917.

were logically and honestly enforced, not one of you today would have any right to your farms, because the only title you have is under English law.[110]

Eaten bread is, however, soon forgotten in the world of popular politics.[111] The Irish Party might denounce the ingratitude of its erstwhile supporters, but the fact remained that the party's previous services on the land issue constituted absolutely no block to any farmer from switching his vote from the constitutionalists to Sinn Fein. Indeed, a policy of withdrawal from Westminster was economically more attractive, now that an increasingly 'piratical'[112] Westminster might wish to tax the comfortable rural propertied elements in society to finance urban social reform. British government policy in Ireland since 1885 had sought to foster a conservative kulak class, but in Ireland, as in Russia, the wager on the kulak as the decisive bulwark against revolution failed; though, it has to be said, for very different reasons.

In Ireland, a socially conservative farming community found its social conservatism to be largely compatible with the world of nationalist emotionalism from 1916 to 1921. The 'check' on the Dublin-based and radical-, even Marxist-inspired Rising of 1916—widely hoped for by British policymakers—thus never actually materialized. This is not to suggest that there were no tensions between Sinn Fein and the Irish rural bourgeoisie. Michael Collins told a favourite lieutenant, James Malone, that he would be wasted as an activist in his native midlands. According to Collins: 'The people of the Midlands lacked the will for soldiering—they were too slow, too dead in themselves. The land is too rich.'[113] There was never a complete meeting of minds, and when Sinn Fein eventually split, some farmers, especially better-off farmers, were glad of the opportunity to take a step away from militant nationalism, but there was enough affinity with the countryside, particularly the young sons of the farming community, to sustain the new movement.

Much of the Irish Party's remaining popular strength was in the north. It is interesting that the party suffered more for its apparent weakness on partition in the south as opposed to the north. Northern nationalists appeared relatively unenthusiastic about Sinn Fein: de Valera was less than pleased, claiming after the Armagh by-election defeat at the hands of the Irish Party in February 1918 that the 'melt has been broken in

[110] *Weekly Freeman*, 3 Nov. 1918.
[111] Ibid., 23 Nov. 1918 reprints an Irish Party leaflet, recalling the Irish Party's services to the farmers: all to little avail.
[112] Raymond Crotty, 'The Irish Land Question', *The Tablet*, 7 Nov. 1981; Tom Garvin, *The Evolution of Irish Nationalist Policy* (Dublin, 1981), 212.
[113] Twohig, *Blood on the Flag*, 95–6.

these people'.[114] The Irish Party replied that Sinn Fein's treatment of the northern issue was hardly a proof of consistency or unity of purpose. Most Sinn Fein speakers denounced the party for its feebleness on the Ulster issue. Again and again, it was stated that the party had given way to British, or worse still, Orange pressure to deny the national rights of the Catholics of the north and, indeed, the rightful place of Ireland within the firmament of nations. Yet, Sinn Fein contained voices, such as Arthur Clery and Father Michael O'Flanagan, who did not accept the Sinn Fein party line and who, indeed, dissented radically from the nationalist conventional wisdom in the north.

Throughout 1916 and 1917 Sinn Fein vice-president Father Michael O'Flanagan, the hero of the Roscommon by-election triumph in February 1917, insisted in the most explicit terms that there were two nations in Ireland, both with a right to self-determination.

If we reject home rule rather than agree to the exclusion of the Unionist Party of Ulster, what case have we to put before the world? We can point out that Ireland is an island with a definite boundary ... National and geographic boundaries hardly ever coincide ... if a man were to try and construct a political map of Europe out of its physical map, he would find himself groping in the dark. Geography has worked hard to make one nation of Ireland; history has worked against it. The island of Ireland and the national unit of Ireland simply do not coincide.[115]

The following month the pro-Sinn Fein *Irish Opinion* published the views of 'RJS', who argued from a pro-Sinn Fein stance that the Irish Party had failed to grasp the 'true inwardness of Ulster Unionism'. He stated bluntly: 'If Irish unity is to be a new experiment and not a historical restoration, it ought to be asked humbly as a favour and not demanded proudly as a right.'[116]In September of the same year O'Flanagan argued: 'I agree that the "homogeneous Ulster" of the Unionist publicists is a sham and a delusion. But if there be no homogeneous Ulster, how can there be a homogeneous Ireland? A more accurate description of Ireland for the past 200 years would be an economic and social duality.'[117]

A year later, in early September 1917, O'Flanagan gave a further exposition of his views. This was of particular significance, because his earlier statement of 1916 on the Ulster issue pre-dated his emergence to a position of national importance in 1917. But in the course of a lecture entitled 'Orange and Green' at Town Hall, Omagh, in one of the heartlands of anti-partitionist sentiment, O'Flanagan showed that he had lost none of the old heterodoxy. Indeed, his speech may well have been

[114] *Roscommon Herald*, 6 Feb. 1918. [115] *Freeman's Journal*, 19 June 1916.
[116] *Irish Opinion*, 15 July 1916. [117] *The Leader*, 2 Sept. 1916.

perceived as a veiled comment on de Valera's aggressive stance. Following a rather unconvincing attempt to distance himself from O'Brien's doctrine of conciliation, O'Flanagan came to the nub of the matter using the analogy of Ireland under the union.

> Now, is there any other method we could try on the Orangemen? I confess I don't like the word coercion, whether it be applied in Ireland or in Belgium or in any other part of the world. Forty million of [British] people have tried to coerce four millions, and they have failed. The relative proportion of the forces was ten to one, and the ten failed to coerce one—so, also I believe that if three million tried to coerce one million, they would fail, too. Therefore I can see no hope of solution in coercion. You might try to get along, but in the end, if the process was coercion, it would fail; and I for one hope to God that it would (applause).[118]

The Irish Party did everything it could to draw attention to Father O'Flanagan's arguments. It attempted to start a debate: where did Sinn Fein really stand, with the coercionists or with O'Flanagan? Yet, the debate really never started. O'Flanagan's popularity, based on his record as an outspoken agrarian radical, was untouched. Archbishop Walsh, for example, still felt it right to denounce the Irish Party on the partition issue on the day of the Longford by-election, a serious blow.[119] The party leaders were reduced to contemplation of the basic injustice, as they saw it, of such a rebuke, when the only possible beneficiary was Sinn Fein, which did not have a credible policy on the issue.

The momentum moved much more radically in Sinn Fein's direction in 1918; especially after the so-called 'German plot', an intelligence fiasco which led to mass arrests of leading Sinn Fein members.[120] On 17–18 May seventy-three prominent Sinn Feiners were detained, and more were lifted in the course of the next few days. Those 'lifted' included de Valera, Griffith, and W. T. Cosgrave—detainees were again deported to England. The government alleged (and appears to have sincerely believed) that there was evidence that Sinn Fein cadres had renewed seditious contacts with the Germans. But the evidence produced in public was unimpressive and hardly likely to convince a highly sceptical Irish public opinion: indeed,

---

[118] *Fermanagh Herald*, 8 Sept. 1917.

[119] Jerome van deWaal, *The Catholic Church in Ireland 1914–18, War and Politics* (Dublin, 2004), 175.

[120] PRO CO 904/24/1. This is the most recently released file on the government's decision-making process, but does not contain any significant new evidence. This document, marked 'Secret' and '10 February 1917' claims: 'Germany still hopes to invade Ireland and arms will be brought by submarines if the extremists pay for them.' It is also marked, somewhat ambiguously, 'Corroboration' in the margin. It is not clear whether this means that the writer believes that 'corroboration' of this claim did or did not exist; see also R. B. McDowell, *The Irish Convention 1917–18* (London, 1970), 191.

even a note on the most recently released file papers refers ambiguously to the nature of the evidence.

Suddenly, in the spring of 1918, the issue of conscription began to dominate the Irish political agenda. Following the Bolshevik surrender at Brest-Litovsk, 1 million German soldiers were taken from Russia and placed on the western front: Paris now appeared to be under threat. The British government was forced to increase the draft, by raising the age of conscription from 41 to 51. In such a context, Ireland's exemption from conscription appeared (to British public opinion) to be all the more indefensible. Ireland was enjoying the subsidized fruits of old-age pensions and the wartime boost of agricultural profits—why did it not contribute more to the survival of the state? The Cabinet was told that the introduction of conscription in Ireland would provide 200,000 new recruits for the army. Of course, this was true only in theory, and rather abstract, nebulous theory at that. When the new Military Service Bill was introduced, all shades of nationalist opinion—from moderate constitutionalist to clerical and revolutionary—were horrified and united in their intense opposition. Hundreds of thousands signed the anti-conscription pledge. It soon became obvious that it would require so many troops to enforce it that Irish conscription would be an entirely self-defeating move for the British government. Lloyd George realistically took the decision to delay the application of the military service law to Ireland, but not before Sinn Fein had received a further boost to its strength against an ailing Irish Party.

Young people were easily caught up in a wave of mutually reinforcing national and religious emotion. Sean Clancy later recalled:

I became acquainted with the Volunteers during the conscription crisis of 1918, and the whole country was against it, and we had all kinds of parades and Novenas and everything in the evenings in the local churches. And the Volunteers used to call in after the Novenas. I was only a schoolboy. I was allowed to fall in with them anyhow.[121]

The issue of conscription also allowed the downplaying of certain social tensions with nationalism. The *Freeman's* midland correspondent noted on 19 September that, in the course of 1918, Sinn Fein had garnered electoral support in the Irish farming community, but he added: 'This was due to the conscription menace, and they [the farming classes] do not take kindly to what they regard as the close alliance of Labour and Sinn Fein, and the indications that they see of a future aggressive policy in which their interests would be anything but identical with the promoters.'[122]

---

[121] 'Memoirs of Michael Collins', *The Village*, 8–14 July 2005.
[122] *Weekly Freeman's Journal*, 19 Sept. 1918.

Within nationalism, Sinn Fein achieved a dramatic victory in the 1918 general election; the party received a popular vote of 485,105 and won nearly all (seventy-three against six) of the old Irish Party seats. In terms of actual votes, on the other hand, the result was less impressive, perhaps even less so when the boasts of IRA men in later years to have voted frequently are taken into account. Kevin O'Higgins handsomely defeated P. F. Meehan at the polls—13,452 votes to 6,480—but the Meehan family recalls to this day serious instances of intimidation during the campaign. The Irish Party retained the loyalty of 237,393 electors: the 'total anti-Republican vote', including Unionists, was 557,435.[123] Against this, it has to be said that some twenty-five seats out of 105 were not fought, most of them likely handsome Sinn Fein victories. Was this a vote for a thirty-two-county republic achieved by force, whether Ulster Unionists consented or not? Given the position of the Unionists, the pro-consent positions of the Irish Party, and even of some in the Sinn Fein leadership, it seems hard to argue this. Was it a vote for a twenty-six-county republic? This is a considerably more serious argument; while some, like the Revd Walter MacDonald, argued that the Sinn Fein vote should not be seen as a pro-republican vote, because so many contingent factors—including an intuition that, 'when driving a bargain, one must try for a good deal more than one means to take'[124]—played a role in generating it, it is clear that a majority of the votes in the twenty-six counties, formally at least, endorsed a separatist rather than devolutionist version of Ireland's future.

It does not, however, follow that there was a mandate won for violence; no such mandate was explicitly sought by Sinn Fein candidates, who simply did not talk openly about a forthcoming campaign of armed struggle. In a lengthy address at a Sinn Fein meeting in Mohill, Co. Leitrim, on 18 November 1917, de Valera had said: 'We can work according to the will of the Irish people, working by peaceful methods if you will.' In the same speech, he declared: 'In a time past it was necessary to strike, even if you knew you had to strike again, but that necessity is past, and as long as this nation is true to itself, there would be no need.'[125] The public might reasonably have concluded that the view of the Sinn Fein president remained in force—in the absence of any explicit repudiation. There were undoubtedly references made to the possible use of force. The Sinn Fein manifesto of 12 October set the objective of achieving an Irish republic by the withdrawal of the Irish representation from Westminster, the using of every means to render impotent the power of England to hold Ireland in

---

[123] R. Kee, *The Green Flag: Ourselves Alone* (London, 1989), 53.
[124] *Ethical Questions of Peace and War: A Postscript* (London, 1920), 22.
[125] *Weekly Freeman*, 24 Nov. 1917: Eamon de Valera on 'Need of Sacrifice'.

subjection, the establishment of a constituent assembly, and an appeal to the international post-war Peace Conference. Force presumably was one of the means by which English power in Ireland could be made impotent, but was it the actual use of force or its implied latent threat which Sinn Fein sold to the electorate?[126] On 24 November 1918 Sinn Fein held twenty open-air meetings in Dublin. Sean T. O'Kelly, Sinn Fein candidate for College Green, told a meeting at Blessington Street: 'Independence could not be achieved in a foreign parliament but by demanding it at the Peace Conference which would soon be assembling.'[127] Speaking later at College Green, O'Kelly's message was more ambiguous: 'Sinn Fein intended to ask that Ireland be freed from slavery, and if they did not obtain it that way, they would obtain it by other means.' O'Kelly warned Irish Labour that social issues must await the establishment of a republic. Sean O'Callaghan, speaking on behalf of Desmond FitzGerald, the candidate for the Pembrooke division, declared: 'Sinn Fein stood by the policy of Parnell.' Michael Brady, speaking for J. V. Lawless, then Sinn Fein candidate for the Harbour division, declared of Easter 1916: 'They were prepared to carry out the programme of that flag that was hoisted upon that occasion.' The *Freeman* reported icily: 'The different speakers managed to deliver themselves of a sufficient number of contradictory views and policies to demonstrate the peculiar elasticity of Sinn Fein principles.'

But, in fact, there were two serious discussions on the role of extra-parliamentary agitation, including the role of threats of force in Irish and British politics that endorsed that threat, but none of the examples given had actually required the transformation of the politics of threat into actual armed struggle. P. J. Little, Sinn Fein candidate for Rathmines, referred to the British 'Labour Party and the benefits they gained ... by persistent agitation outside parliament'. The other examples employed by Little were more local: 'Carson had made his movement such as it was, successful not by parliamentary action, and in Grattan's days it was the pressure of the Volunteers that formed the one hope for his countrymen. In the same way O'Connell won emancipation before he entered Parliament.' Of course, this particular history lesson had an obvious moral: neither Carson nor Grattan nor O'Connell had resorted to the actual use of force to achieve their objectives. J. V. Lawless gave an even more telling example of the same process: he argued that the threat of the rifles of the Volunteers had defeated the Conscription Act. 'De Valera went to Maynooth with the programme and with his back to the wall, told the Bishops he was prepared to go to the hillsides against the force of England if conscription was put in place.'

---

[126] Ibid., 28 Dec. 1918.   [127] Ibid., 30 Nov. 1918.

In short, it was the latent threat of force, but not its actual application, which Sinn Fein offered the Irish electorate in 1918. Dillon charged that a vote for Sinn Fein was a vote for a new insurrection; de Valera rebuked him. One outspoken product of a celebrated parliamentary nationalist family, Serjeant A. M. Sullivan, made the point forcefully: 'Many murderers were elected, but they had not stood as murderers.'[128] As the *Irish Times* put it: 'Sinn Fein has swept the board, but we do not know—does Sinn Fein itself know what it intends to do with the victory?'[129] The Ulster Unionists had employed the politics of armed threat from 1912 to 1914, but most of their leaders knew that it had decided limitations: who, after all, were they to fight? The British army?—impossible for unionists. But then, one was locked into an obviously 'dirty war'. Sinn Fein now faced a problem that was in some respects similar. They could attack British forces and retain nationalist credibility, but how would a dirty war against Catholic Irish police be received? Understandably, there was a moment of hesitancy before militants took control.

[128] Serjeant A. M. Sullivan, *Old Ireland* (London, 1927), 237.
[129] *Irish Times*, 30 Dec. 1918.

9

The Politics of the Gun or a 'Saving Formula', 1919–1923

The wickedness of conquest was enacted with English soldiers shouting 'Halt' to Irishmen as in the days of Elizabeth, and English mercenaries burning houses and murdering prisoners as in the days of '98 ... And the Irish Republican Army fought back.

(Francis Hackett, *The Story of the Irish Nation* (1922), 386–7)

Generous recognition for differing interests without regard to their numerical strength is the saving formula for Ireland.

(Stephen Gwynn, *Observer*, 2 Apr. 1922)

In January 1919 the Sinn Fein members, having met in Dublin and proclaimed themselves Dail Eireann, the Parliament of the Irish Republic, reaffirmed the Easter Rising declaration of 1916, adopted a provisional constitution, and appointed delegates to attend the Peace Conference of the Allied Powers in Paris. The Sinn Fein executive invited all 105 elected members to attend the Assembly in Dublin on 21 January, but unsurprisingly, both Unionists and nationalists ignored the call. The first meeting lasted just two hours, and the proceedings were largely conducted in Irish. The Dail unanimously adopted documents prepared by Sinn Fein committees—the Declaration of Independence, with its triumphant declaration: 'The elected representatives of the ancient Irish people ... ratify the establishment of the Irish Republic' and 'a state of war existed, which could never end until Ireland is definitively evacuated by the armed forces of England'.[1] A provisional constitution was drawn up, which did not mention the word 'republic' but—significantly—provided for a parliamentary system, with a cabinet, based on a single elected chamber. The Dail also endorsed a democratic programme, enunciating a humane social programme—such as the protection of all children from hunger, lack of clothing or shelter,

---

[1] For the impact of this statement on activists, see Tom O'Neill, *The Battle of Clonnult: The IRA's Worst Defeat* (Dublin, 2006), 15.

and the right of a proper education. As Professor O'Leary and Dr Maume have recently observed, this was in advance of the existing concerns of Irish political life, not just at that moment, but for four subsequent decades.[2]

In early January 1919 the *Freeman's Journal* was still impressed by the peaceful, moderate language of Sinn Fein activists, but on 21 January a dramatic destabilizing event took place. Seamus Robinson, Sean Treacy, Dan Breen, and six other Irish Volunteers ambushed a cart carrying gelignite at Soloheadbeg, Co. Tipperary, killing two policemen, whilst a group of quarry-workers, who had been warned beforehand to stay silent, watched in horror. Breen later made it clear that for him the purpose of the operation was to kill the policemen rather than get the gelignite.[3] Thomas Fennell, a retired Royal Irish Constabulary man with very strong nationalist sympathies, concluded:

No dispassionate reader of the published accounts of the ambush will believe that these men were not shot down before they got time to think or realise that they were in a death trap. They had no reason to fear any trouble, for once they saw the explosive delivered to the quarry official, their duty was finished, and they would have returned to their station. Possession of the gelignite could then, or at some other time, have been got, doubtless with little trouble.[4]

But even now, all did not appear to be lost: Soloheadbeg did not, in itself, signal an irreversible break with the past. It seems clear, after strong clerical condemnation of the murders, that the Volunteer leadership, including Michael Collins, gave serious consideration to a plan which would have removed the attackers to a safe haven in the United States. This reaction harked back to the strategy of secret society assassins of the Land League era; but the militants involved refused to participate.[5]

The Sinn Fein leadership clearly did not seek an escalation at this moment. Lord French, the Lord-Lieutenant, in Dublin Castle struck out on a surprisingly conciliatory course; it is clear that by February 1919 he had decided to release the remaining Sinn Fein prisoners. In March, even more reassuringly, Harry Boland repudiated any suggestion that a recent interview (given to an American journal) by Mr de Valera was offering any support for violence.[6] Less reassuringly, later in the month a young medical

[2] Cornelius O'Leary and Patrick Maume, *Controversial Issues in Anglo-Irish Relations, 1910–21* (Dublin, 2004), 79.

[3] Joe Ambrose, *Dan Breen and the IRA* (Cork, 2006), 9.

[4] Rosemary Fennell (ed.), *Thomas Fennell, The Royal Irish Constabulary: A History and Personal Memoir* (Dublin, 2003), 161.

[5] Mitchell, *Revolutionary Government* (Dublin, 1995), 734; Joost Augusteijn, *From Public Defiance to Guerrilla Warfare: The Experience of Ordinary Volunteers in the Irish War of Independence* (Dublin, 1996), 88.

[6] *Weekly Freeman*, 24 Mar. 1919.

student, M. Farrell, appeared in court charged with being in possession of a pamphlet entitled *Ruthless Warfare*, composed by Ernest Blythe, a northern Protestant republican, which argued against 'passive resistance' and advocated, instead, a fight with utter ruthlessness and ferocity.[7] What did these conflicting signals mean? What was the lie of the land? Sean Treacy had remarked at the end of 1918: 'If this is the state of affairs, we'll have to kill someone and make the bloody enemy organise us.'[8] Professor Michael Laffan has argued that 'the resumption of fighting was the action of a small and unrepresentative minority'.[9] Cathal Brugha, Dr Laffan has pointed out, dismissed Ernie O'Malley's claim that the people had not been consulted and pointed out that, 'if so, we would never have fired a shot. If we gave them a good strong lead, they would follow.' Ernie O'Malley, anyway, was a profound believer in the viability of this sort of 'revolutionary galvanism'.[10] In the end, Brugha's prediction was to prove accurate—at least for a majority of the nationalist population—but not without an intense labour of mutual provocation: this provocation produced an inevitable security response and thus gradually wore down the resistance of those who had opposed the initial acts of escalation. It all happened surprisingly quickly. In May 1919 an attempted rescue by the Irish Republican Army (as the Irish Volunteers came to be known) of two of their colleagues at Knocklong led to the death of two policemen. Within months, ballads celebrated this attack as well as Soloheadbeg.

Senior British politicians sought to ameliorate the situation. Walter Long's Cabinet Committee on 4 November 1919 recommended, in a 'well-drafted paper',[11] the creation of two parliaments, one in Belfast for the nine Ulster counties, and the other in Dublin. While Long was absolutely clear that Britain could not impose Irish unity, it was felt that such a nine-county partition, coupled with a Council of Ireland, would facilitate a development towards Irish unity. Redmondites could have been forgiven a snort of irritation—Long, an old opponent of Irish Home Rule, had now embraced it. James Craig effectively then lobbied the Cabinet for six-county partition, and the subsequent Bill received its third reading on 23 December 1920.[12] Hugh Pollock, later Northern Ireland's Minister of Finance, told Wilfrid Ewart: 'The present Act of Parliament is the only

---

[7] Ibid. 29 Mar. 1919.

[8] Laffan, *The Resurrection of Ireland* (Cambridge, 1999), 271.   [9] Ibid.

[10] Richard English, *Ernie O'Malley: IRA Intellectual* (Oxford, 1998), 78.

[11] John Kendle, *Walter Long, Ireland and the Union 1905–1920* (Dublin, 1992), 183.

[12] P. N. S. Mansergh, 'The Government of Ireland Act 1920: Its Origins and Purposes in the Working of the "Official" Mind', in *Nationalism and Independence: Selected Irish Papers by Nicholas Mansergh* (Cork, 1997), 64–92.

form of home rule acceptable to us. We never asked for the Government of Ireland, but in my opinion it is a good Act, and we mean loyally to work it, whatever happens. In doing that, we're only carrying out the law.' For Ulster Unionism, the days of mobilization against government in London was over; it was now a matter of attempting (somewhat nervously) to work with the grain of British policy, now apparently based on the principle of the necessity of Ulster Unionist consent for unity. It also involved an important public willingness to keep the door, at least theoretically, open for Irish unity, providing, of course, that the rest of Ireland did not follow an openly republican course. This concession allowed Pollock's interesting reply to Ewart's next question: 'Does it make for the ultimate unity of the country in your opinion?' 'Through the Council of Ireland, yes. North and South would be brought into constant contact, and the possibilities of ultimate union are, on the whole, great.'[13]

Mainstream nationalist Ireland was, however, not interested in these ethereal possibilities. The Long Committee's proposal, variously described by its advocates as federal, semi-federal, and Dominion—'a most peculiar blend'—was dissected by the *Irish Independent* to show how far it fell short of Dominion status held by Canada or Australia. The proposed Council of Ireland was dismissed as a 'mere academic debating society', and the proposals put forward by Long to heal the 'chronic wound of Irish discontent' were described as 'a poison ... called partition ... slightly diluted and [christened] self-determination'.[14] The Better Government of Ireland Bill was 'such a negation of the principles of self-government and democracy that the Irish people, unless devoid of all self-respect and dignity, could not give it a moment's serious consideration'. The Council of Ireland would give 'a permanent veto to the Carsonites designed to divide and conquer Ireland ... they, who agreed with the proposal of President Wilson, that the world be made safe for democracy, accede to the claim of a privileged Irish minority to rule the majority'; the financial provisions were 'a swindle upon Ireland'.[15] The provisions of the Long Committee Report were a dead letter in southern Ireland, but by removing the new Northern Irish political entity from the equation, it opened the way for the eventual Dominion settlement of the 1921 Anglo-Irish Treaty. In the end, nationalists were to find it possible to make gains on the sovereignty, but at the price of losing on partition.[16] This was always a likely, but not absolutely inevitable,

[13] Wilfrid Ewart, *A Journey in Ireland 1921* (London, 1922), 157.

[14] Mansergh, 'The Government of Ireland Act 1920', 64–92; Patrick Maume, 'The *Irish Independent* and the Ulster Crisis', in D. G. Boyce and Alan O'Day (eds.), *The Ulster Crisis, 1885–1921* (London, 2005), 224.

[15] Maume, 'The Irish Independent and the Ulster Crisis', 224–5.					[16] Ibid.

outcome, but in the short term the important reality was the failure of the British government's plan to soften antagonisms 'on the ground'.

As early as September 1919 the RIC inspector-general had acknowledged that 'the general public is prepared to suffer rather than openly condemn the criminal acts of the republican fanatics'.[17] By the end of the year *The Times* noted, with some considerable insight, that 'the population in southern Ireland is between two coercions, laws imposing restrictions upon ordinary liberty … of the two powers Sinn Fein has the more terror. That perhaps should be neglected. The serious part is that, on the whole, Sinn Fein has more moral authority.'[18]

At first the build-up of IRA military activity was relatively slow. There were some shocking moments of public horror. Sergeant John D. Barton, a big Kerry man recently transferred to Dublin, was shot down: 'I am dying, get me a priest,' onlookers heard him cry as he fell.[19] Yet, all operations of the Dublin Volunteers together led to 120 casualties among the Crown forces prior to 1920. By the end of 1919 only eighteen policemen had been killed throughout the country.[20] But such pressure was quite enough to initiate major changes in the environment. In late 1919 the police began the process of abandoning hundreds of rural facilities to consolidate shifting ranks in fewer, fortified stations. The pressure exerted directly on RIC men, their families and friends and those who did business with them, resulted in unfilled vacancies arising out of casualties, resignations, and retirements. The Lloyd George government, however, insisted that defeating the IRA was a policeman's job—albeit with military support; to do otherwise would have been to concede belligerent status to Dail Eireann. Faced now with the need for a new type of policing, the government hastily increased RIC numbers by recruiting Great War veterans throughout the United Kingdom. From early 1920 through to mid-1921, 13,732 new police recruits were added to the nearly 10,000 members of the old and increasingly demoralized RIC. The new recruits stood out in RIC ranks anyway, but an initial shortage of complete bottle-green constabulary uniforms resulted in the temporary use of military khaki and the name that stuck: 'The Black and Tans.'[21]

While Collins organized the violence at home, de Valera tried to work the political track in the United States. On 6 February 1920 the *New York Globe* published an interview given by de Valera on Anglo-Irish relations. De Valera's intention was to offer the British government a form of reassurance

---

[17] Laffan, *The Resurrection of Ireland*, 274.   [18] Ibid. 276.
[19] *Co. Cork Eagle*, 6 Dec. 1919.
[20] Conor Kostick, *Revolution in Ireland: Popular Militancy, 1917–1923* (London, 1996), 50.
[21] W. J. Lowe, 'Who were the Black and Tans?', *History Ireland*, 12: 3 (Autumn 2004), 47.

on the subject of any strategic vulnerability which might arise from Irish independence. He argued that the United States safeguarded itself from the possible use of the island of Cuba for an attempt by a foreign power by stipulating 'that the Government of Cuba shall never enter into a treaty or other compact with a foreign power to obtain, by colonisation of the military or naval purposes or otherwise, lodgement control over any portion of the said island'.[22] De Valera had asked: 'Why doesn't Britain do thus with Ireland as the United States did with Cuba? Why does not Britain declare a Monroe doctrine for the two neighbouring islands?' Irish-Americans, in particular, were infuriated: they knew full well how the United States treated Cuba. But it did appear, for a moment, that de Valera was now willing to accept less than complete unfettered sovereignty for Ireland. For some, this was the first chink of light.

But de Valera's moderate mood had no impact on the course of the IRA campaign. March 1920 was a dreadful month. Assassinations of Robert Marsh, a Cork auctioneer, and Captain Shawe-Taylor, a brother of Mr Shawe-Taylor of the Land Conference of 1903, all took place at the beginning of the month. An IRA prisoner confessed also that he had shot Mrs Gillian Morris at her house.[23] Then came a 'portent of gravest evil'.[24] On 19 March 1920 Constable Murtagh of Cork was shot seven times by the IRA and killed: Murtagh was a veteran officer unpopular with local republicans.[25] Several hours later, in the early morning of 20 March, a group of anonymous men appeared at the Blackpool house of Tomas McCurtain, the Lord Mayor of Cork and commandant of the 1st Cork Brigade of the IRA. Rushing past his wife—who was pregnant and later lost the twins she was carrying[26]—they shot McCurtain three times in the chest and killed him. The police did not attempt to investigate the crime, while government lawyers concentrated on defending the police and Dublin Castle blamed rogue IRA gunmen.[27] Few were convinced: the coroner later ruled that it had been a police murder. J. L. Hammond of the *Manchester Guardian* had no doubt it was the work of the state forces, which he encountered 'washing black cork off their faces, in high spirits, in his own hotel'.[28] The *Freeman*

---

[22] Patrick Murray, 'Obsessive Historian: Eamon de Valera and the Policing of his Reputation', *Proceedings of the Royal Irish Academy*, 101 C: 2 (2001), 59, 5, 65.

[23] *Weekly Freeman*, 6 Mar. 1920.   [24] Ibid., 17 Mar. 1920.

[25] J. Borgonovo, *Spies, Informers and the Anti Sinn Fein Society: The Intelligence War in Cork City* (Dublin, 2006), 105.

[26] 'Events of Easter Week—And After: The First Martyred Lord Mayor of Cork', *Catholic Bulletin*, 12 (Jan.–Dec. 1922), 329.

[27] Peter Hart, *The IRA and its Enemies: Violence and Community in Cork, 1916–23* (Oxford, 1998), 78.

[28] Stewart A. Weaver, *The Hammonds: A Marriage in History* (Stanford, 1997), 169.

denounced the 'foul murder of the Lord Mayor of Cork'. It concluded: 'Anarchy is in sight when the zealous supporters of the government betake themselves to the methods of the criminal vendetta under the delusion that by their crimes they are assisting the public powers.'[29] Even more significantly, the constitutional nationalist press insisted that there was no conceivable connection between Constable Murtagh's murder and that of McCurtain.[30]

This was clear evidence of the selective condemnation of political violence which was essential to sustain the momentum of the IRA cause. An emotional hardening had taken place. The McCurtain murder 'anticipated the degeneration of the conflict into tit-for-tat killing and reprisals'.[31] But the horrors of the month were not exhausted. One counter-terrorist old hand, Alan Bell, was killed by the IRA on 26 March 1920; Sir Nevil Macready was appointed GOC Irish Command on 29 March. A new broom was set to brush clean. Within days it became clear that Sir John Taylor,[32] the senior figure in Dublin Castle, who, like Bell, had decades of experience of fighting Irish 'subversives', had been dismissed. In mid-February the *Irish Bulletin* of Sinn Fein had denounced him as the 'real ruler' of Ireland,[33] but now the *Limerick Leader* noted with some satisfied brutality that Sir John Taylor had 'in effect been cashiered'.[34]

On 14 April, two days after a general strike called in support of hunger-strikers in Mountjoy Prison, political prisoners were released. The potential power of the hunger-strike weapon had been revealed again. Warren Fisher, head of the London civil service, initiated the clear-out and shift of policy.[35] Lord French, employing a telling phrase in an interview with an English journalist on 6 April 1920, had said: 'I totally disagree with Dublin Castle methods.'[36] French let slip the new policy: 'That a split in Sinn Fein will eventually lead to their undoing.'[37] On 12 April Sir Hamar Greenwood was appointed Chief Secretary in Ian MacPherson's place. Any remaining officials who expressed sympathy for the *ancien régime* were marginalized or, like Somerset Saunderson, son

---

[29] *Weekly Freeman*, 27 Mar. 1920.   [30] *Limerick Leader*, 22 Mar. 1920.
[31] Michael Hopkinson, *The Irish War of Independence* (Dublin, 2002), 28.
[32] *Irish Statesman*, 1 May 1920; *Young Ireland*, 14 Aug. 1920; Charles Townshend, *The British Military Campaign in Ireland* (Oxford, 1979), 176. Taylor, whose mother's maiden name was Keely, was believed correctly by some of these sources to be Catholic, but as a former aide of Walter Long his removal was widely welcomed in the nationalist press.
[33] 'Facts concerning the real ruler of Ireland', *Irish Bulletin*, 26 Feb. 1920.
[34] *Limerick Leader*, 23 Apr. 1920.
[35] Eunan O'Halpin, *Head of the Civil Service: A Study of Warren Fisher* (London, 1989), 86–7.
[36] *Ulster Guardian*, 10 Apr. 1920.   [37] Ibid., 18 Apr. 1920.

of the former Unionist leader, simply had to accept that 'a new clique was created which governed policy'.[38] A network was instituted, involving 'flexible' Irish officials like W. E. Wylie,[39] a law officer, and G. C. Duggan of Dublin Castle, and above all new English officials like Sir John Anderson and Andy Cope, now the driving force in Dublin Castle. Duggan later recorded approvingly, in his unpublished memoir, that 'Anderson and Cope carried matters to the approved end, which was the extraction of the army from Ireland'.[40] They were joined by Mark Sturgis, who left an excellent diary record. This group worked closely with Philip Kerr[41] in the Prime Minister's office, Sir Basil Thomson at Scotland Yard, and C. J. Phillips, Chief Assistant to the Foreign Secretary, Lord Curzon. More surprisingly, they also worked closely with Sir James Craig, the Ulster Unionist leader in 1921.

This group had a clear picture of the likely settlement from the outset and a confidence in their ability to deliver, in the end, the Prime Minister. Friendly journalists were told to disregard all superficially hard-line statements from the government and concentrate on the effort to bring about a negotiated outcome. From 9 April 1920 Basil Thomson of Scotland Yard opened up a relationship with a senior American correspondent, Carl Ackerman, who then acted as one of the back channels with Sinn Fein. In May 1920 C. J. Phillips told Ackerman: 'Within three years Ireland would be a republic in everything but name, and in less time than that all the British troops would be out of Ireland.'[42] On 16 June 1920 Cope reported to Lloyd George that he had already made contact with prominent Sinn Feiners, and, indeed, reasonably quickly Cope made contact with Collins himself.[43] Basil Thomson told Ackerman on 26 June that the government was very anxious to make peace in Ireland, but could find no one with authority to speak for Sinn Fein.[44] Ackerman passed the message rapidly on to the Sinn Fein leadership.

The new team in Dublin Castle was quite prepared to utilize tough measures. On 22 May 1920 General Sir Henry Tudor was appointed police

[38] M. Headlam, *Irish Reminiscences* (Dublin, 1949), 216; M. Hopkinson (ed.), *The Last Days of Dublin Castle: The Diaries of Mark Sturgis* (Dublin, 1999), 16–17; Alvin Jackson, *Home Rule: An Irish History* (London, 2003), 164.

[39] Leon O'Broin, *W. E. Wylie and the Irish Revolution* (Dublin, 1989), 44–5; see also John Wheeler-Bennet, *John Anderson: Viscount Waverley* (London, 1962), 61–3.

[40] 'The Life of a Civil Servant', NLI, Ms 31689, p32.

[41] For Kerr see G. K. Peatling, *British Opinion and Irish Self-Government 1865–1925: From Unionism to Liberal Commonwealth* (Dublin, 2003), 172.

[42] Carl Ackerman, 'Janus-Headed Ireland', *Atlantic Monthly* (June 1922), 812.

[43] O'Broin, *Wylie*, 68–9.

[44] Ackerman Diaries, Ackerman Ms, Library of Congress, Washington, DC, 28 June 1920, 16 July 1920.

adviser, a classic 'securocrat'. Internment without trial led to the detentions of thousands of young men. Martial law was imposed in several counties. The army was reinforced and re-equipped. To prop up the RIC, the 'Black and Tans' were supplemented by the Auxiliary Division of ex-soldiers who gained a reputation for being gun-happy.[45] Nevertheless, Anderson and his allies saw all these measures as being designed to bring about a compromise with the IRA. Inevitably, this was a messy business. British violence, temporarily at least, stiffened IRA resolve. Irish violence, temporarily at least, made it harder for a British government to compromise with 'terrorists': a particularly 'violent outrage' tended to make the government 'stiffen their backs for fear of seeming to give way to murder'.[46] Echoing the views of his aide, C. J. Phillips, Curzon told the Cabinet on 23 July 1920: 'You must negotiate with Sinn Fein. We shall be driven to dominion Home Rule sooner or later.'[47] Balfour, who felt that some in Dublin Castle, like Wylie, had 'lost their nerve',[48] replied: 'That won't solve the question. They will ask for a republic.' But who was right—Balfour or Curzon? This special meeting of the British Cabinet, with Irish government officials and James Craig representing northern Unionists, on 23 July was described by H. A. L. Fisher as 'the first wide-ranging review of Irish policy since the war'.[49] Wylie blasted the existing government strategy, pointing out that the British machinery of government no longer operated in large areas of the country. He claimed that Sinn Fein would agree to a county option for Ulster and a retention of British defence interests in Ireland. Wylie also appeared to believe that Sinn Fein would accept Dominion status. General Tudor, in stark opposition, argued for a policy of military repression. Crucially, Dr Leon O'Broin, Wylie's highly sympathetic, scholarly biographer and, in his youth, an active Sinn Fein supporter, has observed that 'one may question the accuracy of Wylie's opinion as to what "the goods" were in the eyes of Sinn Fein'.[50]

At the same Cabinet conference both Lloyd George and Churchill were attracted to the idea of re-forming the Ulster Volunteer Force (UVF)—an officially sponsored Unionist force of special constabulary—as a way of

---

[45] Arthur Mitchell, 'Alternative Government: Exit Britannia—the Formation of the Irish National State, 1918–21', in Joost Augusteijn (ed.), *The Irish Revolution 1913–23* (New York, 2002), 80; Charles Townshend, *Ireland: The Twentieth Century* (London, 1999), 100.

[46] Wilfrid Ewart, *A Journey in Ireland* (London and New York, 1921), 9, interview with senior official.

[47] Martin Gilbert, *Winston Churchill, 1874–1965*, companion vol. 4 *(1917–22)*, 1,149, H. A. L. Fisher Diary, 23 July 1920; O'Broin, *Wylie*.

[48] O'Broin, *Wylie*, 81.

[49] Hopkinson, *The Irish War of Independence*, 64; O'Broin, *Wylie*, 88.

[50] O'Broin, *Wylie*, 120.

relieving troops for duty not only in the south of Ireland but elsewhere in the Empire.[51] It was a highly controversial line of thinking. During the Home Rule crisis of 1912–14 the Ulster Unionist leadership had displayed at least some control over working-class Protestant violence, but now this control began to slip, as the challenge from the IRA became more intense and British irresolution was all too visible. The IRA murder of Lt.-Col. G. B. Smythe of Banbridge, Divisional Commander of the RIC in Munster, allegedly on account of his advocacy of an aggressive 'shoot to kill' police policy,[52] played directly into the justification given for sectarian anti-Catholic violence in Belfast. In the summer of 1920 shipyard-workers took matters into their own hands and expelled Catholic workers and 'rotten Protestants',[53] Labour or socialist types. Craig sent wary signals of support to the angry Protestant workers, but was fully aware of the dangers. These included the absolute destruction of the social fabric of his own city and the weakening of the moral case of Unionism in London. The all-Protestant Ulster Special Constabulary A, B, and C Specials security force emerged in this crisis—with British funding; a possible means of control for Craig, a bitter blow to working-class Catholics in Belfast. But if unionist militants were gaining a grip in Belfast, republicans were doing the same in the south and west. The Dail had decreed as early as August 1919 that a scheme of national courts be set up and a committee appointed to devise appropriate schemes. But progress at first was rather slow and very limited in geographical range.[54]

This was to change, however, in the early months of 1920, as the Dail court project intensified. The British were well aware that the Dail courts constituted a form of dual power in the countryside, which made it difficult to envisage the restoration of any form of Dublin Castle rule.

The Dail courts were an enormous success for Sinn Fein—winning plaudits from a vast array of commentators for their fairness and even social conservatism.[55] There was perhaps a downside: tough methods had to be employed by the IRA against the land-hungry, and some of the rural poor in the west seemed to have responded by a surprisingly

[51] Kevin Matthews, *Fatal Interference: The Impact of Ireland on British Politics* (Dublin, 2004), 23.

[52] J. A. Gaughan, *Memoirs of Constable Jeremiah Mee* (Naas, 1975), 294–301.

[53] Henry Patterson, *Class Conflict and Sectarianism* (Belfast, 1980), 136–42; Austen Morgan, *Labour and Partition: The Belfast Working Class* (London, 1991), 265–85.

[54] Mary Kotsonouris, *Retreat from Revolution: The Dail Courts 1920–24* (Dublin, 1994), 24.

[55] NLI Ms 17055, Sinn Fein document, 26 April 1920, 'Land and Property Claims'; M. Ó Suilleabhain, *Where Mountainy Men Have Shown* (Kerry, 1965), 177; *Blackwood's Magazine*, 21 Nov. 1921, p. 623.

unenthusiastic level of support for 'the war'.[56] Sinn Fein leaders like Erskine Childers might rail privately against the strong farmers he met in Limerick—'dull unimaginative lot of Redmondites not interested in anything but their own profit'—but in the end Sinn Fein bowed to such men rather than the landless.[57] Sir Hamar Greenwood told the House of Commons in November 1920: 'The Sinn Fein court has disappeared, except in backrooms, where it is held for the purposes of propaganda, especially in the American press.'[58] But the *Irish Bulletin* had no difficulty in showing the continued effective working of the courts.[59]

At the beginning of August 1920 Lloyd George dropped vague hints about Dominion Home Rule to an Irish delegation in Downing Street.[60] Making sure that he sat visibly by friends of the Ulster Unionists, in mid-August Lloyd George was more explicit in Parliament. He offered to engage Sinn Fein in talks if they accepted three conditions:

First of all, that the six counties which represent the north-east of Ulster must be accorded separate treatment. The second is that under no conditions will we assent to any proposal which will involve, directly or indirectly, the secession of Ireland or any part of Ireland, from the United Kingdom. The third is—though hardly in a different category, I put it separately in order to make it clear—we could not agree to anything that would involve any loss of the security of these islands and their safety in days of war.

To the dismay of Mark Sturgis, the Irish reaction was bitterly dismissive: he wondered if the Irish believed that 'the government must come hat in hands and fill their mouths and ask them to spit it out if it's not completely to their liking'.[61]

The evil effects of the McCurtain murder still had to play themselves out. Because of his alleged involvement, the IRA murdered District Inspector O. R. Swanzy outside his church in Lisburn on 22 August; this led to

---

[56] F. Gallagher, *Four Glorious Years*, 2nd edn. (Dublin, 2005), 72; *Sean Moylan In His Own Words: His Memoir of the Irish War of Independence* (Aubune, 2003), 22; Silvain Briolloy, *L'Irlande insurgée* (Paris, 1921), 55; David Fitzpatrick, *Politics and Irish Life*, 234–5; Terence Dooley, 'The Land for the People', in *The Land Question in Independent Ireland* (Dublin, 2004); Paul Bew, 'Sinn Fein and Agrarianism in the War of Independence', in D. G. Boyce (ed.), *The Revolution in Ireland, 1879–1923* (London, 1988), 217–34; Fergus Campbell, 'The Lost Land War: Kevin O'Sheil's Memoir of the Irish Revolution', *Archivium Hibernicum*, 57 (2003).
[57] Trinity College, Dublin (TCD) Ms 7812, Childers diary, 5 June 1920.
[58] *Hansard*, vol. 138, cols. 511–12.
[59] *Irish Bulletin*, 22 Dec. 1920. See also Mary Kotsonouris, *Retreat from Revolution: The Dail Courts* (Dublin, 1994), 24; Heather Laird, *Subversive Law in Ireland 1879–1920: From Unwritten Law to the Dail Courts* (Dublin, 2005), 123–7.
[60] *Freeman's Journal*, 5 Aug. 1920.
[61] Ibid., 17 Aug. 1920; Hopkinson (ed.), *The Last Days of Dublin Castle*, 23.

attacks on the property and person of many Lisburn Catholics. Over the next several days there were thirty violent deaths in Belfast. The British authorities insisted that, compared to deaths caused by sectarian conflict or the IRA campaign against police and soldiers, the number of deaths caused by British forces was small.

There was some truth in this defence up to midsummer of 1920, but matters soon changed. A more or less official policy of 'reprisals' was put in place: in part a function of the frustration generated by the experience of the spring mass release of IRA prisoners under threat of hunger strike and mass public pressure, and in part simply an expression of growing rage. It remains the case, however, that 'government escalation followed the IRA's lead, lagging by months in a kind of echo effect'.[62] The attitude of the Cabinet and senior military men is clear enough. By the end of August Sir Henry Wilson, the Chief of the Imperial General Staff, had learnt—to his dismay—from General Sir Nevil Macready that the Black and Tans were 'carrying out wild reprisals'. On 6 September Wilson noted in his diary: 'Macready says that Tudor's Black and Tan officers are all cut-throats ... they terrorise ... as much as Sinn Fein. These cut-throats are the invention of Winston and Tudor, but how any of these worthies hopes to solve the Irish question by counter-terrorism, I can not imagine.'[63] It is essential to keep in mind that the government did not hope to solve the problem by counter-terrorism alone: there was also a policy of dialogue with the leadership of 'the enemy'. In early September 1920 the British raided the home of a senior Sinn Fein figure, only to find a note on Dublin Castle paper: 'I am having the papers you require sent to you'—signed by Cope.[64] Churchill drew up a memorandum on reprisals for the Cabinet. General Radcliffe explained the logic to Sir Henry Wilson: 'If there is a definite scheme of reprisals ... made known beforehand, it should be very easy to get the troops to restrain their unofficial efforts.'[65] Lloyd George told H. A. L. Fisher: 'You can not, in the exciting state of Ireland, punish a policeman who shoots a man whom he has every reason to suspect has connived with the police murders. This kind of thing can only be met by reprisals.'[66] It seems clear that events like the Black and Tan sacking of Balbriggan on 20 September 1920 and the sacking of Cork (11–12 December) were not inconsistent with official policy at the highest level.[67]

---

[62] Peter Hart, *The IRA at War* (Oxford, 2003), 72.

[63] Gilbert, *Churchill*, iv. 1,214.

[64] William Sheehan, *British Voices: From the Irish War of Independence 1918–1921* (Cork, 2005), 86.

[65] General Radcliffe to Sir Henry Wilson, 23 Sept. 1920, Gilbert, *Churchill*, iv. 1,214.

[66] Ibid. 1,215, H. A. L. Fisher Diary, 24 Sept. 1920.

[67] Hopkinson, *The Irish War of Independence*, 80–1.

These views gained public credibility when General Sir Nevil Macready gave what the press called an 'astounding apology' for the behaviour of Crown forces. It is important to understand that Macready was no crude military reactionary. Two months before this interview, he had told the Chief Secretary that: 'Nothing but a bold dramatic political stroke will solve this matter. I do not, for one instant, think that the British public would stand martial law as I understand it for a week.'[68] Macready felt, as he later told Carl Ackerman, that the IRA operated outside the Geneva Convention: 'They neither wear uniforms nor fight fairly.'[69] It is this tone of bitterness and exasperation which pervades his words to the Associated Press.

In this interview, given at the end of September 1920, General Macready denied that reprisals 'for assassinations of police officers taken at Balbriggan by "Black and Tans" and elsewhere by the regular police or military were actuated by any set policy formulated by Government authorities'. But Macready also said that American army officers understood the realities of war: officers had to make their men love them. 'When in battle, soldiers go over the top, and their officer is killed in the charge, they go on with the determination to avenge his death on the enemy.'[70] Formerly in Ireland, if a police officer was murdered his colleagues simply sought to bring the perpetrator to justice.

But now the machinery of the law having been broken, they feel there is no certain means of redress and punishment, and it is only human that they should act on their own initiative. Punishment for such acts is a delicate matter, inasmuch as it might be interpreted as setting at naught the hoped-for effect of the training the officers have given their men.

In the Balbriggan case, for example, Inspector Burke, who had been killed there by the IRA, was very popular with the young police recruits he had trained. 'It was human nature that they should feel that they ought to avenge his death, knowing full well that the organisation responsible for the crime would shelter rather than give up on the culprits.'[71] The *Freeman* rightly commented that this interview was hardly a denial that reprisals had taken place, and Macready suggested that an official policy of reprisals might become necessary in the future. It seemed to hint that the 'horrors of Balbriggan might become Britain's official policy'. According to Macready, 'a policy of reprisals might become necessary'.[72]

In the light of these remarks, later government denials of a policy of reprisals are hardly convincing. In fact, one British secret service agent told

[68] Macready to Hamar Greenwood, 17 July 1920, National Archives (Kew), Colonial Office, CO 904/188/429.
[69] CO 904/188/715.   [70] *Weekly Freeman*, 2 Oct. 1920.
[71] Ibid., 5 Feb. 1921.   [72] Ibid., 20 Oct. 1920.

John A. Bethune that, while the early reprisals were acts of spontaneous revenge, retaliatory violence became official policy: 'A very definite scale of reprisals was laid down, and it fell largely to the lot of the secret service to carry them out.'[73] The *Freeman* asked sarcastically, again comparing British repression with German wartime crimes: 'There is no government policy of reprisals. Granard is sacked. Tralee shares the fate of Aerschot. From Killybegs to Killorglin, government forces establish a reign of terror. But there is no government policy of reprisals.'[74] There was a significant growth of opposition to government policy in England, led by *The Times* newspaper. Captain Wedgwood Benn MP insisted that, having condemned German methods in Belgium, the English were now using the same methods in Ireland. But it was very difficult to control the forces of the state, who were under intense onslaught. On 30 September District Inspector James Joseph Brady was killed by the IRA in Co. Sligo. Brady was the nephew of a former Redmondite MP, P. J. Brady, defeated by Sinn Fein for the St Stephens Green seat in 1918.[75] A 22-year-old ex-Irish Guards officer, Brady died as a result, his colleagues believed, of being hit by expanding 'dum-dum' bullets; infuriated, they went on a rampage against property in Tubercurry.[76] The Chief Secretary declared angrily: 'I have a right to complain of reprisals, because I am responsible for the discipline of the Irish constabulary—but those men who supported the murder of D. I. Brady ... have no right to complain of reprisals.'[77]

In October public attention focused on Terence MacSwiney, the Mayor of Cork and McCurtain's successor. He had been arrested in possession of sensitive police intelligence on 12 August and soon went on hunger strike. Fearing the polarizing effects of his death, Sir John Scott, the High Sheriff of Cork, and Serjeant Sullivan KC both urged the King to order MacSwiney's release. So did John Redmond's nephew L. G. Redmond Howard, who recalled the sacrifices of his uncles. George V took this seriously enough to send a reply, saying it was up to his ministers. Having intercepted messages from MacSwiney's family to Richard Mulcahy of Sinn Fein, seeking an end to the hunger strike, the government sent a back-channel message (via Ackerman) to Sinn Fein—if MacSwiney was released, would they compromise?[78] In Carl Ackerman's words: 'A game

---

[73] 'Secret Service in Ireland', *Northern Whig*, 21 July 1922.
[74] *Irish Times*, 12 Oct. 1920; *Weekly Freeman*, 13 Nov. 1920.
[75] *Weekly Freeman*, 5 Oct. 1920.
[76] Richard Abbot, *Police Casualties in Ireland 1919–1922* (Cork, 2000), 128–9; Proinnsíos Ó Duigeneáin, *Linda Kearns: A Revolutionary Irish Woman* (Nure, 2002), 26–8.
[77] C. J. C. Street, *The Administration of Ireland* (Belfast, 2001), 115.
[78] Ackerman, p. 441.

of political chess began. The British intercepted a letter from one of the Lord Mayor's nearest relatives, requesting that Mulcahy ask him to come off his hunger strike. They allowed this communication to go through and then made their offer, but Collins and Mulcahy refused to play.'[79] On 25 October, on the seventy-fifth day of his hunger strike, MacSwiney expired. Since Brady's death on 30 September the IRA had killed twenty-one policemen—the majority of them Irish Catholics; but their sacrifice was quickly forgotten. Terence MacSwiney's 'martyrdom' constituted a huge triumph for Sinn Fein, attracting widespread attention in the United States and Europe. Even sceptical British observers like Joyce Nankevell and Sydney Loch regarded the mass celebrated by Archbishop Walsh for MacSwiney in Dublin's Pro-Cathedral as a 'stupendous experience'[80] of profound emotional power. Another British intelligence officer admitted: 'It is a tribute to the sincerity of the grief of the people of Dublin that absolute order prevailed that day, and not a shot was fired in the whole city.'[81]

Every incident connected with MacSwiney's remains became a focus of intense controversy. The British military briefly separated family mourners from the coffin when it was set on the SS *Rathmore* bound for Cork—a 'revolting desecration'.[82]

For a while the gallant little band of Irishmen and Irishwomen watched her [the *Rathmore*] in silence. Then, dropping on their knees, they answered the Rosary, which was recited by the 'indomitable Capuchin' Father Dominic. It was a scene never to be forgotten by those who witnessed it, as the brilliant moonlight illuminated every detail of the fast speeding vehicle and threw a soft light over the kneeling crowd in which the most conspicuous figures were the sorrowing women in black and the bearded Capuchin in his brown habit.[83]

For all the power and unifying impact of the imagery of the MacSwiney martyrdom, though, even now not everyone was swept along. But those who did not answer the call were brutally treated. William Kennedy refused to close his chemist's shop as a mark of respect for MacSwiney: he was supported in this by his close friend T. J. O'Dempsey, who took an action for intimidation in the courts. Both men were immediately shot dead. Both had been loyal active Redmondites. O'Dempsey, an old Clongownian like Redmond himself, had been a co-founder, with Tom Kettle, of the Young Ireland branch of the United Irish League and later

[79] Ibid.   [80] *Ireland in Travail* (London, 1922), 86.
[81] *Northern Whig*, 21 July 1922.   [82] *Weekly Freeman*, 6 Nov. 1920.
[83] Ibid., 'Back to His Own: How the Dead Hero Came to the Land He Loved'; 5 Feb. 1921.

became the secretary of the Wexford branch of the Irish Party.[84] The mood created by MacSwiney's death seemed to legitimize attacks on those with constitutionalist connections. On 31 October the new District Inspector, Philip Kelleher, Military Cross holder and Irish rugby hero, was shot dead in the bar of the Greville Arms Hotel in Granard—the hotel owned by the family of Michael Collins's fiancée, Kitty Kiernan. Tim Healy, who knew the Kelleher family—Philip's father was the Macroom coroner—believed that the IRA could not have done such a thing; but, of course, they had.[85] The degree of Healy's distress over this case contrasts strongly with his considerably more detached view of a Protestant and Unionist IRA victim, Frank Brooke, a few weeks earlier.[86]

In November 1920 medical student Kevin Barry was executed in Mountjoy Jail for the murder of a soldier even younger than Barry himself. On the day of his execution, at Kevin Barry's alma mater, University College, Dublin, Sean MacBride—who was 'amazed' at how few students were in the IRA—found that 'nobody seemed to be paying very much attention'. MacBride arranged for a protest to be made by 'a few people'; but the more general attitude should not be surprising: the UCD medical school had produced numerous doctors for the British army in the First World War.[87] On 21 November came the horrific events of 'Bloody Sunday'. IRA death squads, including young activists like Sean Lemass, on the order of Michael Collins, systematically shot dead fourteen suspected secret service agents in their Dublin homes.[88] The list of those actually killed that night undoubtedly included some who were not intelligence officers[89]—for example, the Irish ex-soldier Captain Patrick MacCormack, a veterinary

---

[84] *Weekly Freeman*, 26 Mar. 1921; *Enniscorthy Guardian*, 26 Mar. 1921; R. B. McDowell, *Crisis and Decline* (Dublin, 1997), 96. In a private communication, Dr Conor Cruise O'Brien has told me that he thinks O'Dempsey may well have been the best man at his parents' wedding.

[85] Tim Healy, *Letters and Leaders of My Day* (London, 1928), ii. 629.

[86] Healy does speak of 'poor Brooke', but adds: 'He allied himself with French in the worst way, even to the extent of depriving Ireland of a grant of money which England wished to give for communications.' NLI Ms 23,266, Healy to Lord Beaverbrook, 31 July 1920. Frank Brooke was a privy councillor and a relative of Sir Basil Brooke, later an Ulster Unionist prime minister, 1943–63.

[87] Sean MacBride, *That Day's Struggle: A Memoir* (Dublin, 2005), 23. I am indebted to Prof. Greta Jones for the information that University College, Dublin, Medical School won some 47 military crosses.

[88] *Weekly Freeman*, 27 Nov. 1921.

[89] F. Costello, *Michael Collins: In His Words* (Dublin, 1997), 21; T. Ryle Dwyer, *The Squad and the Intelligence Operations of Michael Collins* (Cork, 2005), 176. British intelligence believed that the shooting of ex-soldiers and others who were known not to be spies was an integral and deliberate part of the IRA's campaign, in order that the population might be the more easily dominated. PRO CO 904/156.

surgeon from Co. Mayo, who had served in Egypt. Incidentally, the squads' victims included Major John Fitzgerald of Tipperary, and another old Clongownian, who had recently joined the RIC. The effect of the assassinations on the mood of the British army was striking. The twelve dead British army officers brought to the Castle—nine of them in their bloodied pyjamas—included five field intelligence officers and four Dublin Castle official handlers, but also popular, ordinary officers who had won the loyalty of their men.[90] 'The men were longing to shoot. They were mad with passion', wrote one sympathetic observer. In the afternoon the Black and Tans opened fire on a 15,000-strong crowd at a Gaelic football match in Croke Park, killing twelve. Many more were wounded and laid out on shop counters all the way from Croke Park to Upper O'Connell Street. Michael Hogan, a member of the Tipperary team, was killed on the pitch. Who fired first on that day? It is not impossible that an armed IRA man attending the match opened fire first; dozens of abandoned IRA firearms were discovered by Crown forces.[91] It is, however, more likely that—as some of the police evidence suggests—the forces of the state began the firing.[92] The *Weekly Freeman*'s special football reporter 'emphasised as a fact that it was from the uniformed men that the first and only shots came'. The *Freeman*, the constitutionalist organ, declared in its headline: 'Dublin's Amritsar: Horrible Scenes of Slaughter at a Football Match.' The same page carried a further headline: 'Fresh Horror/Three Prisoners Shot Dead in Dublin/Trying to Escape.' The story detailed the victims as IRA men Peter Clancy, Richard McKee, and T. C. Clune.[93] Clune was the nephew of the Catholic archbishop of Perth, Australia.

[90] 'Secret Service in Ireland: Sinn Fein Strikes at the British Secret Service, Leaving its Mark', *Northern Whig*, 21 Aug. 1922; 'Experiences of an Officer's Wife in Ireland', *Blackwood's Magazine*, 209: 1367 (May 1921), 586. Note the interesting observation: 'The American Consul had dined at our house, the night before the murders. They had played bridge till it was very late, and he had been pressed to stay the night. If he had, there probably would have been an American citizen less, as there is no doubt the men and boys who visited our house were mostly quite incapable from fright of distinguishing friend from foe. One of the wounded officers told me he was placed against a wall in the hall and eight men took, or tried to take, careful aim at him.' Prof. M. R. D. Foot, whose distinguished career, both in British wartime intelligence and as a academic historian, has given him access to documents not seen by others, has told me that Collins's efforts to hit intelligence officers was successful in a ratio of two to one amongst the dead.
[91] *Irish Times*, 22 Nov. 1921; and not contested in the *Irish Bulletin*, the IRA propaganda organ which contested much else of the government's version of this event.
[92] Tim Carey and Marcus de Búrca, 'Bloody Sunday 1920: New Evidence', *History Ireland*, 11: 2 (Summer 2003), 10–16; Brian P. Murphy, *The Origins and Organisation of British Propaganda in Ireland* (Cork, 2006), 56–8.
[93] *Weekly Freeman*, 27 Nov. 1920.

The southern unionist *Irish Times* coverage of Croke Park was of some interest.[94] It reported the implicitly reliable testimony of ex-soldiers that they had seen unprovoked firing by the state forces: indeed, the same point was made by some police evidence to the subsequent military inquiry. On 26 November Sinn Fein leaders Arthur Griffith, Eoin MacNeill, and Eamon Duggan were arrested. Griffith, in particular, did not find prison easy to endure: he shocked Ackerman, who visited him, by his dishevelled and distraught appearance. On 28 November the IRA hit back by carrying out its most successful ambush of the entire conflict on a group of cadets at Kilmichael. It had been a frenzied, if successful, attack. The Cork coroner, Dr Kelleher, who had to examine the bodies of the IRA victims, found that most of the cadets had been riddled with bullets. Three had been shot at point-blank range (probably by guns held to their heads), several had been shot after death, and another had had his head smashed open, probably with a club or an axe.[95] By late 1920 elements in the security forces mounted a sustained underground effort to terrorize the republican movement and its supporters into submission. 'Intelligence' encompassed political murders and death squads on both sides. But such politics were combined with the policy of back-channel contacts with Sinn Fein leaders, which, in effect, secured for those contacted a de facto immunity,[96] and gradually inclined those leaders towards a compromise. There was an official policy of 'embargo' on de Valera's arrest, while Anderson did not even bother to reply to security force requests that a reward be put on the head of Collins.[97] The 'peace process' and ruthless selective violence, not for the last time in Irish history, went hand in hand. British policy was summed up by one of its toughest practitioners, Ormond Winter, as being one of hitting the insurrection on the head by the methods of Tudor and Macready and offering its leader 'a bouquet' via the underground negotiations of Cope.[98]

Despite his anger over both Bloody Sunday and Kilmichael, Lloyd George was directly responsible for Archbishop Clune's undercover peace missions in December and the safe conduct which allowed him access to Sinn Fein and the IRA leaders. But in the end Lloyd George set too high a price. Whether driven by a sense of the IRA's underlying weakness—as some, like Stephen Gwynn, suspected[99]—or by a fear that he could not be seen

---

[94] *Irish Times*, 21 Nov. 1920; Carey and de Búrca, 'Bloody Sunday 1920', 10–16.
[95] Hart, *The IRA and its Enemies*, 24.   [96] Hart, *British Intelligence*, 15.
[97] Co 904/188/628, 10 Jan. 1921, C. Prescott Decie to Anderson; Co 904/188/710, 8 Apr. 1921, C. Prescott Decie to Anderson.
[98] Winter, *Winter's Tale* (London, 1955), 309.
[99] *A Student's History of Ireland* (Dublin and Cork, 1925), 529. At this very moment, Gwynn was drawing the attention of the British authorities to cases of misconduct by

to be negotiating under the impact of Bloody Sunday and Kilmichael, he insisted that the IRA decommission its weaponry as part of a deal. Although Lloyd George later claimed that his Irish officials all supported this, he was not telling the truth:[100] Bonar Law was the most likely advocate of this policy.[101] The negotiations of December 1920, which at one point looked rather hopeful, eventually collapsed. The deeper truth is that violence on a large scale creates an emotional context, because of the investment of those involved on both sides, which inclines in its early phases towards the defeat of peace processes. It is only when a moment has been reached when the combatants know for sure that further violence is unlikely to vindicate their project, and may even lead to dreadful defeat and demoralization, that the negotiators can gain the upper hand over the militarists.

Given his obsessive interest in the importance of intelligence operations, Collins was well aware by 1921 that the British had regained the initiative in this field: many new agents were in place and working effectively. One intelligence report sarcastically reported: 'If it is possible to extend sympathy to those who have been particularly devoid of it, then the seizure of a leader's entire office correspondence each successive month is possibly a worthy subject for it.'[102] Indeed, by March 1921 British intelligence penetration in Dublin, if not the country, was advanced, even to the extent of being counter-productive, as, for example, where the interception of de Valera's warlike communications (signed 'Godfather') with Irish-American militants temporarily inclined Lloyd George to the view that a compromise was impossible.[103] But then came an interesting signal from an experienced intermediary. On 20 March 1921 the British received the hopeful news (via the redoubtable Carl Ackerman) that de Valera was willing to see Sir James Craig to discuss 'the welfare of Ireland', though it was insisted that the real quarrel was between the English and Irish nations.[104] It was an

---

soldiers: Prescott Decie to Jonathan Anderson, 24 Jan. 1921, National Archives, CO 904/188/634.

[100] Hopkinson (ed.), *The Last Days of Dublin Castle*, 29.

[101] F. P. Crozier, *The Men I Killed* (Belfast, 2002), 99.

[102] PRO CO 904/156/53. This report is the work of 'O'—Brigadier Ormonde de l'Epée Winter. Dr Eunan O'Halpin observes: 'Winter may be dismissed as a Micawberish figure, but there is other evidence to suggest that, despite personal rivalries and continuing inefficiencies, what might be termed the continuing bureaucratisation of intelligence, slowly bore fruit after 1920.' See O'Halpin's 'Collins and Intelligence, 1919–1923', in Doherty and Keogh (eds.), *Michael Collins*, 73. O'Broin, *Wylie*, 132, describes Winter as 'smart, probably entirely amoral'.

[103] Ackerman, 'Janus-Headed Ireland', 811. For further recent evidence of British penetration, see Michael T. Foy, *Michael Collins' Intelligence War: The Struggle Between the British and the IRA 1919–1921* (Stroud, 2006), 230–2.

[104] Hopkinson (ed.), *Last Days of Dublin Castle*, 443.

encouraging moment. On 23 March 1921 Archbishop Gilmartin of Tuam made a powerful appeal for peace. The *Freeman* commented approvingly: 'Since the beginning of the year the conflict has resulted in 400 deaths. Who desires a continuance of this bloodshed?'[105] On 27 March the British had a further triumph in the security field. They successfully raided the offices of Sinn Fein's principal organ, the *Irish Bulletin*. The British report of the raid (26–7 March) mentioned that they had raided the headquarters of the Sinn Fein propaganda, but it did not mention this was also the offices of the *Bulletin*, to the surprise of many in Sinn Fein.[106] On 29 March the rapidly reconstituted *Bulletin* boldly claimed that Britain had once regarded the paper as the organ of a murder gang; was it now saying that it merely did the work of 'general publicity'? In fact, one member of the *Bulletin*'s staff, the editor Erskine Childers, was deeply disturbed. Childers called on Horace Plunkett's friend, R. A. Anderson, 'very much shaken, as he thought that evidence against him had almost certainly been discovered at the offices of the [*Irish*] *Bulletin* which was raided a day or two ago. He asked if he might sleep that night in Anderson's study, and he, of course, accepted.'[107] Yet, when the British finally caught up with Childers and arrested him in May, their discussions with him were of an amicable sort. Andy Cope in Dublin Castle was really only interested in developing his policy of dialogue and negotiation with Sinn Fein.

Lord Derby, meeting Ackerman after a trip to Ireland, recorded, at the end of April, his 'opinion that the first step in an Irish settlement is a meeting between Sir James Craig and de Valera'.[108] On 3 May Cope left Dublin for Belfast in an effort to persuade Craig to meet de Valera in Dublin. Hamar Greenwood's covering note to Craig of the same day declared: 'The bearer of this letter will explain his mission, and you must act as you deem best.' But it added: 'You know the desire of the government for peace based on goodwill, and subject to certain

---

105 *Weekly Freeman*, 26 Mar. 1921.

106 Gallagher, *Four Glorious Years 1918–21*, 95.

107 Mark Pottle (ed.), *Champion Redoubtable: The Diaries and Letters of Violet Bonham-Carter, 1914–1945* (London, 1998), 131, diary entry for 1 Apr. 1921. There is a gap in Childers's own diaries held in Trinity College, Dublin, for this period. Childers breaks off on 14 March 1921 and does not pick up again until the end of April. Childers's concern was, of course, well founded. The *Irish Bulletin* denied that anything of an incriminating nature was found in the raid—the records of Childers and Anderson suggest otherwise.

108 Carl Ackerman's Diary, Library of Congress, Washington, DC, 28 Apr. 1921. Ackerman records in his notes on 'Talk with Lord Derby' that Derby had said: 'British government would accept whatever Craig and de Valera ask for. Independence is impossible. A separate army and navy is impossible, but Ireland can have anything she wants within the Empire and can have a uniform police force instead of an army.'

strategical and other considerations.' Craig was told: 'We all admire [the way] you are conducting your cause ... You are gathering strength among your countrymen of both religions in the south as well as Ulster, by your straightforward and tolerant attitude.'[109] Craig—who now worked closely with the Anderson–Cope–Sturgis group—took the initiative by making a public pronouncement that he would gladly see de Valera. The meeting took place on 5 May 1921 in the suburbs of North Dublin. Sturgis recorded: 'Everyone agrees that Craig has done a really big thing. The Sinns ought to recognise this. Andy [Cope] said to O'F [Father O'Flanagan] "What do you think of that—I call that brave." O'F said: "Yes, Craig is a big man and an honest one." '[110] While there were real hopes that the two men might actually deal with substantive matters, these were to be disappointed. Craig and de Valera may well have talked past each other, but they did agree to another meeting, Craig playfully suggesting an Orange Hall as the next venue. But the really crucial development was Craig's willingness to put himself into the hands of the Dublin Castle 'liberal' peace faction, signalling that he had no objection to their strategy, provided it did not hurt Ulster's Unionist interests. Craig, indeed, went so far as to offer Andy Cope the headship of the Northern Ireland civil service.[111] Indeed, Craig was actively serving that strategy, because by exploiting the willingness of Sinn Fein to talk to other 'Irishmen', he had broken the taboo on talks with the British government. If 'Orange' Craig, a former British minister, could talk directly with de Valera, it became absurd to deny that eventually there could be talks with a British Liberal premier who merely had to face the fact that his 1920 Ireland Act would not in itself do the trick.[112] On the other hand, the British believed that by meeting Craig—who was instructed to make clear his opposition to the Republic—de Valera was tacitly conceding that the Republic was unattainable and was, more generally, receiving an education in the complexity of the issues. The meeting effected a mood-change which tipped the balance against the continuation of military conflict. On 5 May Craig and de Valera had talked about a meeting after the forthcoming elections: both expected that these elections would strengthen their respective hands.

[109] PRONI T3775/14/1.

[110] Hopkinson (ed.), *The Last Days of Dublin Castle*, 171.

[111] Ibid. 177, entry for 13 May 1921. 'Andy told me that Craig asked him to come to him as head of the Northern Ireland civil service. He does not want Ernest Clarke, who, as he says, is not liked by his Ministers. Andy has told me this—and only me—as he wants me to advise what he should do. It is difficult. I don't think he could be spared from here at present, yet he would be a tremendous link between North and South if he went. I doubt, too, whether, after the thing got fairly started, it would be a big enough job for him'.

[112] Ibid. 176.

The nomination day for the general election to the two parliaments established by the Government of Ireland Act was 13 May 1921. All candidate nominations for election to the Southern Ireland Parliament were returned unopposed (124 Sinn Feiners and four Independents). On 24 May the Northern Ireland general election was held—forty Unionists were returned as against six Nationalists and six Sinn Fein. Then came a last application of de Valera's quixotic approach to military strategy: an 'open' act of warfare. On 25 May the Custom House, Dublin, was destroyed and several lives lost in an attack by the IRA. The records of the Local Government Board and other bodies were included in the destruction. But it was something of a pyrrhic victory for the IRA: some 100 members of its Dublin Brigade were captured.

But the deeper problem for the Sinn Fein leadership was not the traditional hostility of the military element in Dublin Castle, but the growing irritation and impatience of the 'politicos' like Sturgis, Anderson, and Cope. They wanted Sinn Fein to work towards a Dominion status deal, and were irritated by attempts to patronize the northern Unionist leadership—a 'childish vanity'.[113] Cope, however, did not allow the Custom House fiasco to deter him. Tim Healy told his brother on 16 June: 'Cope continually meets the Sinn Fein leaders, including Michael Collins. The military desire trouble, for to crush is their job.'[114] But eventually it was decided to give the Sinn Fein leadership a tougher message. Collins reported to de Valera the message of another British intermediary ('Not Cope', he specified) on 18 June 1921: 'He is in a veritable panic and anxious to avert the awful times.' The message had been a simple one—if there was no response, the British were prepared to triple the number of soldiers in Ireland and back this up with a policy of martial law, heavy investment of troubled areas, and internment.[115] The Dublin Castle elite had made up its mind: the Ulster Unionists were prepared to offer all-Ireland institutions as part of a new dispensation of Dominion status—it was now up to Sinn Fein to respond positively. On 22 June George V opened the new Parliament in Belfast with a broadly conciliatory speech. On 9 July the British pressure finally paid off, and a truce was agreed by representatives of the British and the IRA. At the time of the truce the IRA, in some counties—Kerry and Cork, for example—was in confident and optimistic mood. But it should

---

[113] Hopkinson (ed.) 187–8, 202.

[114] Tim Healy to Maurice Healy, *Letters and Leaders of My Day*, ii. 638, 16 June 1921. For Collins's unconvincing demands for such a meeting and the subsequent controversy, see Brian P. Murphy, *Patrick Pearse and the Lost Republican Ideal* (Dublin, 1999), 114–20.

[115] CO 904/23/no 53/6094, epitome of a document seizure at de Valera's Blackrock home.

be noted that in other counties, such as Longford and Clare, there was an air of exhaustion rather than aggression.[116]

What were the purely military determinants? In mid-April 1921 'Ormonde Winter gave Sturgis the internment figures at that time: they composed 18 brigade commanders, 44 brigade staff officers, 71 battalion commanders, 166 battalion staff officers, 1,165 company officers and 1,479 other ranks.' Leon O'Broin comments: 'The list is enormous; but it is impossible to evaluate its significance.' But he adds: 'British intelligence, on the other hand, had undoubtedly become more effective'[117]—a view shared by Peter Hart.[118] One British intelligence agent, who paid full tribute to IRA effectiveness in the field, nonetheless told John A. Bethune: 'At the time of the armistice [June 1921], the British had an adequate secret service throughout the length and breadth of Ireland, a service so widespread and encircling that every move projected by the republicans was known in Dublin Castle before it could be carried out.'[119]

In March 1922 Collins said that Cathal Brugha, the Irish Minister of Defence, told him in July 1921 that the IRA could not hope to eject the British in this generation.[120] Collins later offered a sober assessment of the state of play in April 1922: 'In July last there were many parts of Ireland where the British forces could operate without the slightest interference. There were some parts where they could operate with difficulty. There were no parts where they could not operate even by a small concentration of numbers.'[121]

What other considerations may have had an impact upon the republican leadership? There is little doubt that the IRA was developing a distinctly sectarian tinge, and some, at least, of the republican leadership were disturbed by it. Hart has demonstrated the existence of an anti-Protestant colouring to the IRA's activity in Cork.[122] In Co. Cork, for example, the IRA deliberately shot over 200 civilians between 1920 and 1923, of

---

[116] Sinead Joy, *The IRA in Kerry 1916–1921* (Cork, 2005), 122–3
[117] O'Broin, *Wylie*, 128. [118] Hart (ed.), *British Intelligence in Ireland*, 12–15.
[119] 'Secret Service in Ireland', *Northern Whig*, 18 July 1922.
[120] *Munster Express*, 26 Aug. 1922.
[121] *Co. Cork Eagle*, 29 Apr. 1922. Stephen Gwynn agreed: 'In June 1921, the military strength of Great Britain in Ireland was increasing, and the IRA were running short of rifles and ammunition. Sinn Fein had strong military reasons for getting what it could while it could', *A Student's History of Ireland*, 305.
[122] Peter Hart, 'The Protestant Experience of Revolution in Southern Ireland', in R. English and G. Walker (eds.), *Unionism in Modern Ireland: New Perspectives on Politics and Culture* (Dublin, 1996), ch. 5, p. 89; see also the shocked testimony of a Protestant nationalist, Willie Kingston, 'From Victorian Boyhood to the Troubles: A Skibbereen Memoir', *Skibbereen and District Historical Society*, 1 (2005), 32–4; Peter Cottrell, *The Anglo-Irish War: The Troubles of 1913–22* (Oxford, 2006), 79, claims, of 'the 122 people executed in Cork between 1919 and 1923, only 38 were British spies'.

whom seventy (or 36 per cent) were Protestant, five times the percentage of Protestants in the civilian population; this is a higher rate of attrition than that suffered by the other beleaguered minority, the Catholics of Belfast, who, though only 28 per cent of the population, suffered 58 per cent of the city's violent deaths between 1920 and 1922.[123] Protestant farmers were also shot in Leitrim[124] and Tipperary.[125] In Cavan, the 80-year-old Protestant clergyman Dean John Finlay was murdered at Bawnboy on 12 June.[126] On 30 June 1921 a band of thirty armed men shot the two eldest sons of the Pearson household at Coolacreese, Cadamstown, Co. Offaly. Even as the murders were perpetrated, the IRA volunteers made assurances that this was not happening because the Pearsons were Protestants—but could not actually give a reason as to why it was happening.[127] The British tended to believe that this increase in attacks on loyalists—relatively soft targets—was the IRA's means of sustaining military pressure in a contest whose overall military logic was going against the IRA.[128] There were republican leaders who took a very hostile attitude towards such low-grade sectarianism. Stephen Gwynn wrote of Austin Stack: 'The Fenian tradition in its best form is represented by him. When Protestants in County Cork and elsewhere were largely attacked, the same thing was planned on a complete scale in Kerry, but Stack stopped it.'[129]

THE NEGOTIATION OF THE TREATY

On 20 July 1921 Lloyd George wrote to de Valera, outlining the proposals of the British government for an Irish settlement. The Prime Minister

[123] *Irish News*, 5 Nov. 2000, Eamon Phoenix, 'The Story of a Scarred City'.

[124] *Roscommon Herald*, 30 Apr. 1921.   [125] *Western News*, 18 June 1921.

[126] George Seaver, *John Allen Fitzgerald Gregg, Archbishop* (London, 1963), 113–14.

[127] Alan Stanley, *I Met Murder on the Way: The Story of the Pearsons at Coolacreese* (Naas, 2005), 12–13. For a critique which argues that the Pearsons were executed because of their involvement in an armed attack on the IRA, see Pat Muldonney, 'I Met Humbug on the Way', *Church and State*, 84 (Spring 2006), 17–24.

[128] William Sheehan (ed.), *British Voices: From the Irish War of Independence 1918–1921* (Cork, 2005), 130.

[129] *Observer*, 23 Apr. 1923. Then there was another, somewhat more eccentric but well-documented, facet of Collins's thinking. Collins, possibly something of a womanizer by the Irish Catholic standards of his day, rather mysteriously seems to have been much affected by a concern that the violence was having a destructive and negative effect on Irish womanhood. He told Ackerman that he was worried about an increase in the number of stillbirths, and he also told a disbelieving James Malone that he felt that the brutalizing conflict was stripping Irish women of their maternal and nurturing qualities. Patrick Twohig (ed.), *Blood on the Flag* (Cork, 1996), 155; Carl Ackerman, 'Inside the Irish Revolution', *New York Times*, 7 Aug. 1921; id., 'Dream of Ireland's Lincoln', *Hearst's International*, 23 Aug. 1922.

argued that Dominion status would grant Ireland complete autonomy on taxation and finance; that 'she shall maintain her own courts of law and judges'; that the country would also have its own army and police force, plus control of all aspects of public policy. The Prime Minister's letter did make reference to Britain's security and strategic interests: for example, the RAF 'will need facilities for all purposes that it serves'. The British forces should still be free to recruit in Ireland. Interestingly also, to avert the possibility of 'numerous trade wars', it was suggested that the 'British and Irish governments shall agree to impose no protective duties or other restrictions upon the flow of transport, trade and commerce'. As for the spectre of partition, the British government regarded that as a 'matter for Irishmen themselves'.[130] In August 1921, Eamon de Valera replied:

'Dominion status' for Ireland—everyone who understands the conditions, knows them to be illusory. The freedom which the British dominions enjoy, is not much the result of legal enactments or of treaties as of the immense distances which separate them from Britain and have made interference by her impracticable.[131]

The correspondence between the two dragged on. In a reversal of the classic role, the British, on 24 August 1921, urged the Irish to place matters in historical perspective. Daniel O'Connell and Thomas Davis had asked for self-government, not separation: 'The British Government have offered Ireland all that O'Connell and Thomas Davis asked, and more; and we are met only by an unqualified demand that we should recognise Ireland as a foreign power.'[132] De Valera's text had made one important concession on the northern question. He stated explicitly: 'We do not contemplate the use of force.'[133] The Prime Minister, in his reply, grasped this olive branch: 'We are profoundly glad to have your agreement that Northern Ireland can not be coerced.'

In this correspondence, Lloyd George failed to break de Valera's resolve on the issue of independence. But de Valera did accept the concept of a conference founded on the broad principle of government by the consent of the governed. At the time, de Valera was formulating the doctrine that later became known as external association. The idea here was that an independent Ireland could be associated with the British Commonwealth without allegiance to the king. On 7 September Andy Cope addressed a special meeting of the British Cabinet: he convinced that body that a formal prior insistence on Irish allegiance to the Crown would prevent any conference. The Cabinet resolved that the Prime Minister would repeat

---

[130] Tim Coates (ed.), *The Irish Uprising 1914–1921: Papers from the British Parliamentary Archive*, HMSO (London, 2000), 156–62.
[131] Ibid. 165.   [132] Ibid. 180.   [133] Ibid. 171.

that the consent principle was the core principle of British constitutional development, but that the British government did not necessarily accept any Irish nationalist interpretation of that principle. De Valera was asked if he was prepared to enter a conference on the position of Ireland with respect to the other nations in the British Empire.[134]

In the end, this sparring culminated with de Valera's agreement on 30 September 1921 to hold a conference in London, 'to ascertain how the association of Ireland with the community of nations known as the British Empire might best be reconciled with Irish national aspirations':[135] a formula which in itself ruled out the achievement of a separatist Irish republic. De Valera then made the interesting and controversial decision not to go to London for the negotiations, but to send Collins and Griffith. He told Joseph McGarrity in December 1921 that he remained at home to avoid compromising the republic, as a reserve against the tricks of Lloyd George, and so as to be in a position to influence extreme republicans to consent to external association with the British. Over sixty-one years de Valera constantly refined and expanded this fundamental explanation. Yet, at the time, few observers could have predicted the denouement.[136]

Collins, after all, seemed to be the greater militant. In April 1921 he had told Ackerman, for publication: 'When I saw you before, I said that the same effort which would get us dominion home rule, would get a republic.'[137] The Irish side was instructed to press for 'external association'—the idea that Ireland would be associated with, but not be a member of, the British Commonwealth—in exchange for a promise of 'essential unity': a phrase which captivated nationalist commentators. Horace Plunkett told James Bryce that there was no 'respectable' way out of the difficulty, but one would be found. Even so, he was surprised, as were so many others, by Sinn Fein's insouciance on the Ulster issue. The negotiations began well. Childers recorded: 'Conference at Colonial Office—Beatty, Churchill, Mick, me, Dalton. Interesting. They were not as stiff as we thought.'[138] But the mood soon deteriorated. 'Memo presented. Great flutter. Long argument.'[139] Collins regarded Childers's *idée fixe*—that the

---

[134] Cornelius O'Leary and Patrick Maume, *Controversial Issues in Anglo-Irish Relations 1910–21* (Dublin, 2004), 122–3.

[135] Coates (ed.), *The Irish Uprising*, 208.

[136] Murray, 'Obsessive Historian: Eamon de Valera and the Policing of his Reputation', 54, 15, 65. For subtle defence of de Valera's strategy, see John Regan, *The Irish Counter-Revolution 1921–36* (Dublin, 1999), 33.

[137] *Weekly Freeman*, 30 Apr. 1921. Ackerman interviewed Nevill Macready on 21 April 1921: when asked about Collins's remarks, Macready replied that, when selling a horse, 'an Irishman always asks twice what he expects to get'.

[138] TCD Ms 7812, Childers Papers, 13 Oct. 1921.   [139] Ibid., 18 Oct. 1921.

British had no strategic interests at stake—as so self-evidently absurd as to involve a degree of bad faith. On the other hand, Collins regarded his British interlocutors as straight-talking and logical.[140] By the beginning of November personal relations between Childers and Griffith were frayed.[141] Lloyd George, having brought Arthur Griffith to the point of accepting the offer of Dominion status with safeguards for British defence, began to bring pressure to bear on the government of Northern Ireland to exchange the sovereignty of Westminster for that of Dublin. Even at this moment, Sir James Craig, who clearly did not think the proposal was acceptable to his party, was determined to display a reasonable face. On 8 November one senior Conservative Unionist noted that 'James Craig has been consulted and is ready to do what he can, but doubts whether his people will accept any such terms. If there is an absolute deadlock, the Government will resign.'[142] Lloyd George called Lord Beaverbrook on 7 November to Downing Street. The Beaverbrook press then declared: 'Ulster is asked to get under a green umbrella. That there is a sentimental objection to this new departure, deeply rooted in the unhappy memories of the past, is clear. But is it worth the perpetuation of strife and disaster for every part of the United Kingdom, including Ulster?'[143] In similar tone, the *Daily Mail* appealed to Craig to set aside the 'age-long enmity between North and South'.

On 10 November 1921 Lloyd George formally told Craig of his new plan of settlement. The crucial clauses of this new document were C and D: according to Clause C, 'the Government of Northern Ireland would retain all the powers conferred upon her by the Government of Ireland Act', but according to Clause D, 'the unity of Ireland would be recognised by the establishment of an all-Ireland parliament, upon which would be devolved the further powers necessary to form the self-governing Irish state'. Lloyd George's letter explicitly discussed the possibility of the Irish government using economic pressures against the Northern Ireland government; it offered to discuss ways of resolving such fears. But the nub of the matter was admitted: 'Her Majesty's Government are fully aware of the objections which the people of Northern Ireland may feel to participation on any terms in an all-Ireland parliament.'[144]

---

[140] Hayden Talbot, *Michael Collins' Own Story* (London, 1922), 149–50.

[141] Childers Papers, 2 Nov. 1920.

[142] George Boyce, 'British Politics and the Irish Question 1912–1922', in Peter Collins (ed.), *Nationalism and Unionism: Conflict in Ireland 1888–1921* (Belfast, 1994), 103.

[143] *Weekly Freeman*, 12 Nov. 1921.

[144] O'Leary and Maume, *Controversial Issues in Anglo-Irish Relations*, App. 1, p. 147.

Craig's reply clearly exploited the Council of Ireland arrangements proposed in the Act of 1920 *against* Lloyd George's attempted manoeuvre. He replied on 11 November:

The possible unity of Ireland is provided for by the establishment of the Council of Ireland under the Act of 1920, together with the machinery for creating a Parliament for all Ireland, should Northern and Southern Ireland mutually agree to do so. The proposal now made to establish an all-Ireland parliament by other means, presupposes that such agreement is not necessary. An all-Ireland parliament can not, under existing circumstances, be accepted by Northern Ireland.[145]

The British, having failed to 'bounce' Craig, now placed pressure again on the Irish side. Childers angrily recorded in his diary: 'Cope urged me to support peace ... I thought of the fate of Ireland being settled hugger-mugger by ignorant Irish negotiators', adding for good measure that Griffith was 'muzzy with whiskey' and 'in genuine sympathy with many of the English claims'.[146] Sean MacBride, then employed as a courier for the talks team, also noted 'excessive drinking', which, he claimed, involved not only Griffith but also Collins.[147]

The negotiations concluded on 5 December, when Lloyd George, offering the threat of a resumption of war, balanced by the last-minute concession of fiscal autonomy for the new Irish state, demanded immediate agreement on a Dominion status settlement. On 6 December the delegates signed a treaty, creating the Irish Free State as a self-governing Dominion within the British Commonwealth. The Oath of Allegiance was the invention of an unlikely combination of the Colonial Secretary, Winston Churchill, and Harold Laski.[148] When the London Conference ended, and the Irish delegates were leaving the conference room in Downing Street, Collins walked over to a corner where there was an American rifle, the first manufactured in the United States for the world war, presented to Lloyd George by President Wilson. This he picked up, while the Cabinet watched in amazement. Walking over to Lloyd George's chair, he sat down and said to the minister: 'Now the Prime Minister can take a photograph of a gunman.'[149] Erskine Childers, despite, or perhaps because he was a distinguished British ex-serviceman, did not share the mood: 'When we left the room,' said Lloyd George, 'we met Erskine Childers outside, sullen with disappointment and

[145] O'Leary and Maume, *Controversial Issues in Anglo-Irish Relations*, App. 1, 149.
[146] TCD, Childers Papers, ms 7814, diary, 1 Dec.
[147] Sean MacBride, *That Day's Struggle* (Dublin, 2005), 45.
[148] Kenneth O. Morgan, *Consensus and Disunity: The Lloyd George Coalition Government 1918–1922* (Oxford, 1979), 264.
[149] Ackerman, 'Janus Headed Ireland', 812.

suppressed wrath at what he conceived to be the surrender of principles he had fought for.'[150]

What role did the threat of renewed British force play in the Irish decision to compromise in the treaty negotiations? There is no question that the threat of a massive British troop investment in Ireland played a role in the decision of the IRA leadership to call a ceasefire. There is also no doubt that in the later phases of the negotiations both Churchill and Lloyd George were seen to go out of the way to make sure that C. P. Scott, the editor of the *Manchester Guardian*, heard some blood-curdling threats; the British leader may well have calculated that, through J. L. Hammond of the *Guardian*, these threats would reach the Sinn Fein leadership.[151] But how credible were these threats, given the mood of British public and elite opinion? Scott himself acknowledged that parts of the British political establishment could never have countenanced a renewal of war.[152] Michael Collins insisted that Lloyd George never made a 'threat of immediate and terrible war'.[153] Perhaps more revealingly, the *Daily Chronicle*, Lloyd George's own organ, stated that if talks broke down with the Sinn Fein delegation they would be followed, not by renewed fighting, but by further negotiation. Dr Morgan concludes: 'Peace was logical and inevitable.'[154] This was a view shared by one intellectual anti-Treatyite, who had excellent experience in newspapers. Frank Gallagher, one of Sinn Fein's sharpest propagandists, noted that the proof of the vagueness of any Lloyd Georgian threat of war was easy to find: all Lloyd George's friends in the media had been briefed to argue, not for a return to war, but for an extension of the truce if no deal could be achieved in the short term.[155]

Frank Gallagher believed that a bad deal had been struck, a betrayal of the Irish cause. The hard right, like C. H. Bretherton, sneered that the Irish had fought a war to avert partition and break the link with the Crown: now they had ended up accepting both.[156] Terence MacSwiney's sister best expressed the incredulity of the republican faithful:

Of course, there were people who talked of Dominion home rule in Cork, but they were people who had never counted, and never would count, people who did nothing to gain the victory, but who will reap the gains of others. I remember mentioning to different volunteers the fact that the people [in Dublin] had mentioned Dominion

---

[150] Lawless and MacDonagh, *Ireland*, 471.

[151] Trevor Wilson (ed.), *The Political Diaries of C. P. Scott 1911–1928* (London, 1970), diary 28, 29 Oct. 1921, p. 403; 2, 5 Dec. 1921, p. 407.

[152] Ibid., 3 Dec. 1921, p. 409.   [153] Talbot, *Michael Collins' Own Story*, 172.

[154] Morgan, *Consensus and Disunity*, 264.

[155] Gallagher, *Four Glorious Years*, 335–6.

[156] *Atlantic Monthly*, (Nov. 1922), 695.

home rule, and they just laughed lightly and said: 'The decision rests with us—the army will see that the Republic is established'.[157]

From an old Sinn Fein point of view, the Treaty was a good deal. At the height of the Home Rule crisis Arthur Griffith's *Sinn Fein*[158] had argued that Redmondite Home Rule would leave to the Imperial Parliament the management of all Imperial affairs—the army, navy, foreign relations, customs, Imperial taxation, and matters pertaining to the Crown and colonies. The Treaty now conceded all this work to an Irish parliament: the old Arthur Griffith *Sinn Fein* agenda had triumphed over the Redmondite one. But it was not the republican agenda for which a minority had sacrificed so much—and inflicted so much.

Bretherton's remark—however brutal—contains the genesis of the civil war. The Dail began to deliberate on this issue in a debate which began on 14 December and ended on 7 January 1922. De Valera had often been associated with moderation between 1917 and 1921, but now he led the opposition to the Treaty and stood for 'the republic'. His own position was, however, more complex and nuanced. In a private session of Dail Eireann on 15 December, de Valera produced a new draft of the Treaty, which became known as Document No. 2. In this document he developed his idea of 'external association': de Valera argued that the Treaty was unacceptable. Document 2 accepted Ireland's 'association' with the states of the British Commonwealth. Whereas the Treaty included an oath of allegiance that embraced the king, de Valera's document (Article C) proposed for the purposes of the association: 'Ireland shall recognise his Britannic Majesty as head of the association.'[159] This ingenious attempt to resolve the sovereignty issues fudged in the Treaty was combined with a commitment to forswear the use of force in the North. For his opponents, de Valera's plan was a supreme illustration of the difference between 'Tweedledum and Tweedledee'.[160] On 7 January Dail Eireann approved the Anglo-Irish Treaty by sixty-four votes to fifty-seven. On Sunday, 8 January, de Valera declared that he would not accept 'self-determination at the cannon's mouth'. He added: 'I say today, and I repeat it, the heart of Ireland is absolutely for complete independence.'[161] On 9 January de Valera resigned as president of Dail Eireann and stood for re-election: Griffith was elected in his place. On 16 January the new members of the provisional

---

[157] Regan, *Irish Counter-Revolution*, 36.
[158] Arthur Griffith, *Sinn Fein*, 8 Apr. 1911.
[159] For de Valera's subsequent sensitivity on Document 2, see Murray, 'Obsessive Historian: Eamon de Valera and the Policing of his Reputation' 43.
[160] 'The Alternative Plan', *Co. Cork Eagle* and *Munster Advertiser*, 7 Jan. 1922.
[161] *Weekly Freeman*, 14 Jan. 1922.

government were received at Dublin Castle, and the formal transfer of power took place.

NORTH–SOUTH RELATIONS: THE IMPACT OF PARTITION

The 1922 meetings between Sir James Craig, staunch Ulster Unionist Prime Minister, and Michael Collins, IRA leader and head of the new provisional government in Dublin, surprised many contemporaries. After all, Irish Unionists suspected wrongly that Collins had murdered Frank Brooke, a cousin of prominent northern Unionist Sir Basil Brooke, 'with his own hand',[162] either because of his role in a Dublin Castle advisory committee or because of connection to the attempt to defeat the railway strike of 1920, which had strong nationalist overtones. Yet, the immediate context is clear. Craig's intelligence services had told him at the beginning of December that it was 'the intention of the Sinn Fein authorities to send 500 men to Ulster to carry on guerrilla warfare'.[163] On the other hand, the scant references to the North made during the Treaty debate encouraged Craig to hope that perhaps there was a way of avoiding violence.[164]

A contemporary journalist, Padraig de Brun, watching Collins speak on 9 December 1921 in the Dail debate on the Treaty, perceived a softening of tone on the Ulster question. 'For the first time also, Michael Collins struck another new note. He alluded to Ulster. His plea was the possibility of the North coming in with good will under the Treaty.'[165] Later, on 22 December 1922, when a republican opponent, Belfast man Sean MacEntee, challenged the Treaty for its betrayal of the North, there was an immediate response from the pro-Treaty side: 'Is the speaker prepared to coerce the

---

[162] See John Butler (ed.), 'Lord Oranmore's Journal', *Irish Historical Studies* (1995), 589, entry for 27 Aug. 1922. For a report of the murder, see *Weekly Freeman*, 7 Aug. 1920. See also Maj. C. J. C. Street, *The Administration of Ireland* (Belfast, 2001), 83; Charles Townshend, 'The Irish Railway Strike of 1920: Industrial Action and Civil Resistance in the Struggle for Independence', *Irish Historical Studies*, 21: 8 (Mar. 1979), 265–82. Frank Brooke's murderers were, in fact, Tom Keogh, Jim Slattery, and Vinny Byrne, see T. Ryle Dwyer, *The Squad and the Intelligence Operations of Michael Collins* (Cork, 2005), 123–4.

[163] PRONI SB 24/4710, Divisional Commissioner's report, signed E Gilligan and dated 2 Dec. 1921.

[164] For the most recent scholarly discussion of the role of Ulster in the Treaty debate, see Jason N. Knirck, *Imagining Ireland's Independence: The Debates over the Anglo-Irish Treaty of 1921* (New York, 2006), 152–3.

[165] Patrick Murray (ed.), Padraig de Burca and John F Boyle, *Free State or Republic: Pen Pictures of the Historic Dail Treaty Session of Dail Eireann 1922* (Dublin, 2002), 14.

six counties?'[166] Such conflicting signals obviously created a predisposition on Craig's part to deal with the new government in Dublin—perhaps its intentions, since the signing of the Anglo-Irish Treaty in late 1921, were now peaceable? Craig later explained that he wanted to get on to the 'ground floor' before some damaging proposition was advanced on either side or, indeed, before the London and Dublin governments approached him with some unsatisfactory initiatives of their own. 'I thought that I ought to get in before irretrievable harm was done, before some contract was made behind my back, or before some statement was issued by the Free State on which it might be impossible to go back.'[167] Collins also hoped to secure the release of some recently captured IRA prisoners in the North.

On 14 January Dan Hogan of the 5th Northern Division of the IRA was one of several men arrested by B-Specials on their way to a game in Derry City. The men, in fact, had intended to rescue three IRA men under death sentence. Symptomatically, Collins was unable to secure their release because he would not take Craig's advice that they apply for bail, thus recognizing the northern courts.[168] Both men wanted to sort out any possible changes in the territory of Northern Ireland as quickly as possible, though they had very different views as to how extensive these might be. Craig wanted small adjustments, whilst Collins was looking for something more radical. Collins wanted to see Catholic workers in Belfast receive better treatment; Craig wanted an end to the economic boycott of northern businesses by the South—though largely for reasons of 'political atmosphere', as perhaps only 10 per cent of northern businesses were affected in an economic sense. They were both willing to consider measures of practical co-operation on an 'all-Ireland' basis. The terms of the agreement between the two men were published in the press on 21 January 1922: the Boundary Commission, as outlined in the Treaty, was to be altered by mutual agreement. Collins was to call off the nationalist boycott of Belfast businesses, while Craig was pledged to aid the return of Catholic workers to the shipyards. The two Irish governments were to produce a better system than the Council of Ireland for dealing with the problems of all Ireland. That night Churchill and Collins dined together at Hazel Lavery's house in London—both jubilant that a deal had been done.[169]

In his press conference afterwards, Sir James Craig declared that he had had no idea in his mind of coming to a specific agreement on anything,

---

[166] Patrick Murray (ed.), 33.   [167] *Weekly Freeman*, 4 Feb. 1922.
[168] Fearghal McGarry, *Eoin O'Duffy: A Self-Made Hero* (Oxford, 2005), 99.
[169] John Julius Norwich (ed.), *The Duff Cooper Diaries* (London, 2005), 156.

but as time went on, he saw his opportunity, and Mr Collins saw his. Craig added:

For the credit of our land, we were able to put our joint names to a document which, on the one hand, is an admission by the Free State that Ulster is an entity of its own, with a head with whom they can at any rate confer ...

At any rate, I think our meeting has reassured the Loyalists throughout the south and west, that we, by recognising the government formally, will greatly aid the Unionists, Loyalists and level-headed men throughout the country to rally to that government—which at all events is endeavouring to restore order and stave off separation and 'the Republic', which is the party cry of the other side.[170]

To this end he was prepared to have a settlement which left the road open, at some future date, for 'Ulster' to decide whether it joined the 'Free State' or not. This explained why he had not vetoed Collins's proposal for a constitutional conference for Ireland as a whole. Addressing 500 key members of his own party on 27 January, Craig was unrepentant: 'My duty was, in effect, to lead.' He added:

What I was aiming at is Ulster's security, Ulster's close ties with Great Britain and the Empire, but as part of Ireland that it should be a free part of Ireland and not an Ireland at war. I have kept before my eyes all the time that in the long run it is better for the south and west and the Empire that we should be in the condition I have stated, because it seems to me we will be some little check on the hotheads in the south, if they know that by proclaiming the Republic, by trailing the Union Jack in the dust, by causing harm to the loyal people who belong to us—kith and kin of ours, that they only put the clock back for a century as far as any hope of getting Ulster in, whereas, as Lord Carson said in the House of Commons on a famous occasion: 'Ulster might be wooed by sympathetic understanding, she can never be coerced'.[171]

The more remarkable aspects of Craig's stand require some analysis. In the first place, it is clearly predicated on the assumption—to use modern Framework Document or Downing Street Declaration parlance—that Britain had no selfish strategic or economic interest in partition; in other words, it was for 'Ulster' and 'Ulster' alone—'Ulster' here meaning the six counties of Northern Ireland—to decide whether or not it chose to join up with the South. All that appeared to matter for Craig is that the principle of consent be respected; this could be achieved most effectively through Dublin's recognition of the northern parliament. There is also the willingness to take up the 'Council of Ireland' idea—purged of the unwieldy bureaucratic machinery proposed in the Government of Ireland

---

[170] *Co. Cork Eagle*, 4 Feb. 1922.
[171] *Irish Times*, 28 Jan. 1922. The reference is to the Carson speech of February 1914, discussed in P. Bew, *Ideology and the Irish Question* (Oxford, 1994), 103.

Act of 1920—as a means of providing a forum for North–South contact in matters with an 'all-Ireland' dimension. Craig was challenged by angry grassroots loyalists who argued that he had conceded too much, but he was able to carry the bulk of Ulster Unionist opinion—especially business opinion—with him. Behind the scenes, however, senior Ulster Unionists worried about the 'nebulous verbosity' and 'newly converted moderation' of the Craig stance.[172] As Craig himself said at the time, his duty was to lead, not to follow. It is, however, also worth noting that Craig laid great stress on the position of southern Protestants—in this he was, of course, strongly supported by Lord Carson, whose roots were in that community. He signalled that this community should rally to the support of the Free State government as the least-unpleasant available option—but he also argued that the North should signal a possible long-term willingness to come in with the South, in order to protect that community from republican onslaught. In later years, as the southern Protestant community went into rapid decline by the end of the 1920s, this consideration ceased to have a significant impact on Craig's approach.

However, despite the early joy of that dinner with Churchill at Hazel Lavery's, Collins also experienced some turbulence and unease. The *Freeman* and the Dail declared that co-operation was the key, 'if Ireland as a whole is not to rattle back into barbarism'.[173] Even so, Collins, just after his meeting with Craig, confessed his unease about the overall political situation in a letter of 27 January to his fiancée, Kitty Kiernan.[174] Collins, at a Cabinet meeting on 30 January, still considered himself to be carrying out a policy of non-recognition of the Craig regime; he was prepared to support schoolteachers and local bodies who refused to recognize the new state.[175] On 30 January Eoin Duffy, a senior protégé of Collins, proposed a dramatic escalation: the kidnapping of 100 prominent border Orangemen.[176] On 1 February Collins and Griffith met a delegation of northern nationalists and assured them they would insist on the transfer of large territories from the six counties—he reassuringly insisted that northern nationalists were pushing at an 'open door' on this point. Even more ominously, Collins assured this deputation: 'There were only two policies—peace or war. He and his colleagues were going to try the peace policy first.'[177]

Sir James Craig balefully noticed this delegation: he argued that the impact was a negative one. 'Yesterday,' he said, 'Mr Collins adopted a very

---

[172] PRONI D3480/59/43, R. C. Marshall to Sir Robert Lynn, 30 Jan. 1922.
[173] *Weekly Freeman*, 28 Jan. 1922.
[174] L. O'Broin (ed.), *In Great Haste*, revised extended edn. (Dublin, 1996).
[175] State Paper Office (Dublin), Provisional Government, Cabinet Conclusions, 30 Jan. 1922.
[176] McGarry, *O'Duffy*, 99.   [177] *Irish Times*, 2 Feb. 1922.

different attitude from that he showed at the first meeting ... It appeared that he had been driven by the extremists to reverse his earlier policy of conciliation.'[178]

Worse still, the Free State government appeared to switch immediately into warlike mode. The *Irish Times* reported grimly:

> We deplore the unofficial but authoritative reports which suggest that the provisional government is dallying with the fatal notion of war upon Ulster. It says that an attempt may be made to smash the machinery of the northern administration by reducing such services as the Post Office and the Land Commission to a state of chaos.[179]

On 7 February 1922 Collins wrote to Louis Walsh, a northern nationalist and former Sinn Fein candidate, expressing a certain frustration with northern nationalism. 'One thing that has struck me in the deputations from the North has been the lack of any real constructive programme. The lack even of any real fighting programme.' But he was confident that Sir James Craig was, in recent days, losing the battle for British public opinion. 'I am quite certain that his stand is now looked upon as being the unreasonable one and not ours,' Collins wrote. 'All the British statesmen are agreed that it was most disastrous on Craig's part to talk about agreeing nothing less than the six-county area.' Collins outlined tactics he intended to pursue with a view to destabilizing the northern parliament. In particular, he threatened to escalate the economic war from a semi-official boycott into one based on financial tariffs against Northern Ireland.[180]

On the night of 7–8 February Collins secretly approved a series of IRA raids across the border into Fermanagh and Tyrone, which led to the kidnapping of forty-two prominent loyalists, including the High Sheriff of Fermanagh: these were intended to be used as bargaining counters to secure the release of IRA prisoners. Three days later, five men died (four of them B-Specials) in a clash between B-Specials and IRA in Clones: the rest of the Specials were arrested. This, in turn, provoked violent loyalist reprisals in Belfast, including a bomb attack which killed six children. The decision of the B-Specials to travel from Newtownards to Enniskillen via Clones—where it was likely they would be spotted by the local IRA—is a strange one, especially because special constables had been involved, in January 1921, in looting a pub in Clones. At Westminster, Winston Churchill read out a letter from Eoin O'Duffy blaming the Specials for the deaths in Clones, and claiming that the provisional government was

---

[178] *Co. Cork Eagle*, 11 Feb. 1922.   [179] *Irish Times*, 3 Feb. 1922.
[180] 'Collins Letter Fetches £26,500', *Irish Times*, 22 Feb. 2003.

trying to secure the release of the captured loyalists.[181] Between 6 and 25 February forty-three people were killed in Belfast (twenty-seven Catholics and sixteen Protestants).[182] On 21 February the alarmed British government ordered the release of Dan Hogan in return for the hostages. London was particularly fearful that northern grievances could regenerate republican unity. In fact, in early February, a shadowy joint Ulster command, linking Collins, O'Duffy, and the anti-Treatyite Aiken, was established.[183]

On 5 March 1922 Collins defended the Treaty arrangement on partition. Regarding the arrangement dealing with north-east Ulster under the Treaty, he frankly confessed that it was not ideal. If the Free State was established, however, union, he said, was certain, as forces of persuasion and pressure were embodied in the Treaty which would bring the north-east into a united Ireland. 'With the British gone,' he said hopefully, the incentive to partition is gone.'[184] Blithely disregarding his own role in the deterioration of North–South relations, Collins sent an angry telegram to the British government on 6 Mar. 1922:

Belfast Parliament apparently powerless or unwilling to prevent bloodshed or to bring criminals to justice. Invariably your troops are called against our people and feeling running very high against this course of action. Suggest you send an independent investigator and my statements can be shown to be correct. Cannot over-emphasise the seriousness of the situation. Absolutely imperative that some action be taken.[185]

On 7 March 1922 Eamon de Valera met the deputies from Sinn Fein organizations in Ulster at a Belfast meeting: significantly, Joe McGrath, Minister for Labour in the new provisional government, was also present: de Valera condemned 'the present anarchy of north-east Ulster, and the campaign of murder and outrage of Nationalists because of their religious faith'.[186] Unionists objected to such obvious 'hobnobbing' between pro- and anti-Treaty forces and their willingness to accept a common stand on northern matters. Meanwhile Collins sanctioned an offensive which killed six policemen and Specials in the North, and the anarchy of north-east Ulster now took a turn for the worse. On 22 March armed men burst into the Antrim Road home of Owen MacMahon, a successful Catholic businessman, moderate home-ruler, and director of Glentoran FC, the soccer club then at the heart of Protestant East Belfast's sporting life.

[181] McGarry, *O'Duffy*, 100.
[182] Robert Lynch, 'The Clones Affray, 1922—Massacre or Invasion?', *History Ireland*, 12: 3 (Autumn 2004), 36.
[183] McGarry, *O'Duffy*, 101.   [184] *Leinster Leader*, 11 Mar. 1922.
[185] PRONI HA 31/1/28, telegram from Collins to Churchill, 6 Mar. 1922.
[186] *Weekly Northern Whig*, 11 Mar. 1922.

The father, three sons, and a barman were killed, while two other sons were wounded. Even by Belfast standards, the MacMahon murders were shocking in their cruelty, even in a month when thirty-five Catholics and eighteen Protestants had been killed in Northern Ireland. They shocked also because many suspected police involvement: the name of District Inspector Nixon, in particular, was frequently mentioned in this context. Dr Alan Parkinson, in the most recent scholarly study, has written: 'It is hard to refute the theory that either rogue policemen were directly involved in offensives such as that on the Antrim Road, or that Loyalist gangs executed them with the connivance of certain police officers.'[187]

Field Marshal Sir Henry Wilson now erupted and publicly denounced the whole pattern of the unfolding Anglo-Irish settlement. Churchill formally replied to Wilson in a speech at Northampton on 25 March; Wilson's description of southern Ireland as a 'welter of chaos and murder' was 'by no means a truthful representation of the facts'. In fact, in most cases there was complete normality. Churchill declared himself 'encouraged' by de Valera's avowed determination at Limerick to 'wade' through Irish blood to achieve the republic. 'This is the true spirit of the Bolshevik mania, that the world is so bad and hopeless that there is nothing for it but to wade through blood towards a distant doctrinaire ideal.'[188] This statement shows the massive extent of Churchill's investment in Collins: events in Dublin appeared to reinforce the wisdom of Churchill's strategy. Although a majority of the IRA leadership was in favour of the Treaty, this was not true of the rank-and-file. On 22 January 1922 Richard Mulcahy, the Dail Minister of Defence, reluctantly conceded to pressure, demanding an IRA convention within two months. Such a convention would surely have remained committed to the republican ideal. Mulcahy hurriedly turned to the task of establishing a national army, in order to counterbalance the threat of a coup. Mulcahy then tried to ban the convention in March, but it went ahead anyway: in an explicit challenge to the government, the delegates, on 26–7 March, elected a sixteen-man executive which looked rather like a republican military junta.

The logic of Churchill's support for both Craig and Collins was that they should be brought closer together, if only to counteract the argument that Ireland was collapsing into anarchy. Churchill decided to make a further

---

[187] Alan E. Parkinson, *Belfast to Unholy War: The Troubles of the 1920s* (Dublin, 2004), 237. The files at PRONI HA 32/1/28, HA/5/193, and HA/5/699 contain the official view that the McMahons themselves did not—the morning after the murders—allege that the police were responsible, though they did observe that four of the raiders wore waterproof coats and police caps. The leader of the murder gang did not fit Nixon's description.

[188] *Weekly Freeman*, 1 Apr. 1922.

effort to establish a renewed Craig–Collins understanding. At the end of the month the British government sponsored an attempt to renew the Craig–Collins pact. On the eve of this meeting Sir James Craig claimed that his government did not blame the provisional government for IRA outrages in the North—though he noted language explicitly supporting northern IRA violence had been used by senior figures closely associated with the regime, such as Sean MacEoin and Eoin O'Duffy. This rather tactful (if ambiguous) message clearly indicated that he was prepared to make a second serious effort to reach a settlement.[189] After rather difficult discussions, in which Collins apparently 'boasted'[190] of responsibility for outrages in the North, the terms of a new pact were dramatically announced by Churchill:

1 Peace is hereby declared.
2 From today, the two governments to co-operate in every way with a view to the restoration of peaceful conditions in the unsettled areas.

Its most important clause was the third one:

3 The police in Belfast to be organised in general accordance with the following conditions:
a The police in mixed districts to be composed of one half Catholics and of one half Protestants … All Specials not required for this force to be withdrawn to their homes and their arms handed in.
b An advisory committee, composed of Catholics, to be set up to assist in the selection of Catholic recruits for the Special Police.[191]

In addition, the British government was to make available at least £500,000 for relief works—at least one-third of which was to go to Catholic workers. The essence of the new pact is clear: a reformed, non-sectarian Northern Ireland so far as security and employment policy was concerned, in exchange for an end to IRA violence (Clause 6) and Dublin recognition. Many senior Unionists felt that Craig had conceded too much ground—but the Prime Minister himself seems to have been determined to work within the new arrangement. If there were perils for Craig, he was rescued by the ideological rigidity of his opponents. Eoin O'Duffy, for example, strongly supported the suggestion that Catholics should take up the places set aside for them in the Specials, arguing that the cream of the flying columns should enlist. However, the proposal failed because northern republicans refused to take the

189 *Irish Times*, 29 Mar. 1922.
190 Lady Spender's diary (6 Apr. 1922) records her husband Wilfrid Spender's view of these negotiations: 'Collins, who, he says, is like the hero of an American film drama, was very truculent … did not attempt to deny responsibility for outrages in Ulster … indeed, he boasted of them', PRONI D1633/2/24.
191 *Irish Times*, 31 Mar. 1922.

required declaration of allegiance to the northern state.[192] The *Weekly Northern Whig*, a staunch Unionist supporter of the regime, explained in an important editorial on the pact that 'friendly co-operation' between north and south should be the order of the day.[193] But the leader added: 'Ulster' would never accept 'forceful incorporation in the Free State'—indeed, 'every effort to bring it about is bound to result in further alienation of the people'.

Sir James Craig again faced significant internal criticism, but he was able to point to Winston Churchill's strong support. In the House of Commons, Churchill paid 'tribute … to the statesmanlike courage and earnest good will, which had been displayed at this most critical juncture in the fortunes of Ireland by Sir James Craig (cheers)—and his colleagues in the Ulster Cabinet'. Churchill expanded further on the potential significance of the new pact: 'But in addition, there is a hope in this agreement of co-operation between North and South (hear, hear)—a co-operation only forthcoming on the basis of the Treaty, a co-operation obviously fully and fatally destroyed were a republic to be set up (hear, hear).' Churchill added: 'The hope of the unity and co-operation undoubtedly opens out to Irishmen in all parts of Ireland, a prospect for the peaceful and progressive future of their country, which had never before been laid before them. In these two ways Ulster and the Ulster government have rendered supreme service not only to Ireland but to the whole Empire.' But for Churchill such a 'supreme service' imposed a strong reciprocal obligation on the British government to defend the 'soil' of Ulster.[194] Simultaneously, the repressive Special Powers Act was passed by the Northern Ireland Parliament.

But if Craig received a reward in London for striking a deal with Collins, Collins received no such reward in Dublin. Republicans were decidedly unimpressed by the new pact. On 2 April Eamon de Valera and Cathal Brugha addressed a republican meeting in Dundalk. They poured scorn on Collins and the latest fruits of his strategy. Brugha declared angrily: 'Mr Griffith was not helping Irish employment when he took off this boycott and allowed these Belfast wholesalers to send their shoddy English goods round the country.' Eamon de Valera asked if anyone of them would choose to be British subjects, to have King George as their king, or to disestablish the republic? (No!) He noted bitterly of Collins: 'Certain people who were running to London day after day reminded him of little boys going to be spanked.' De Valera's analysis of the second Craig–Collins pact was particularly scathing. He claimed that Sir Henry Wilson was massing an army in the North to carry out more murders, then asked of the new pact: 'What was it? It simply tells them in the north:—So murder our people and

---

[192] McGarry, *O'Duffy*, 102.   [193] *Weekly Northern Whig*, 1 Apr. 1922.
[194] Ibid., 8 Apr. 1922.

then, in order to prevent more murder, we will give up what we have been striving for.' Then de Valera went right to the heart of the matter: 'They were going to have the privilege of recognising the northern government if they wanted to. If they were going to recognise the northern government, they would have been far wiser to recognise it when the Partition Act came out.'[195]

This Dundalk statement of de Valera constitutes the essence of the republican critique of the compromise effected by Collins. The issue essentially was the political return on violence and suffering: if, at the end of this phase of struggle, there was to be no republic and no Irish unity, how was it rationally possible to justify the sacrifices accepted by some voluntarily, and imposed on others who were given no choice? But on the same day, in the west of Ireland, Michael Collins offered a defence of his course of action. Collins told a meeting in Castlebar on 2 April: 'We have won a position of freedom we have not had since the Norman invasion. What evil spell is upon us?' he asked. Collins added: 'If Mr de Valera and his friends will not join with us, if they will not co-operate in the work to be done, can they not adopt the policy of live and let live? There is now no enemy to fight in the greater part of Ireland.'

Collins then outlined a defence of his second pact with Craig: 'If we could speak with one voice to the north-east Ulster, how could we increase the hopes of near union?' He explained that he had been in consultation 'with the spokesmen of the north-east. We have arrived at an agreement which, we hope, will at last lead to peace in Belfast and put an end to the terrible doings which have shocked humanity.' Collins argued that such an understanding opened up the way for the gradual achievement of Irish unity based on dialogue and agreement.

That agreement and the co-operation it provides in preserving order, will bring, we trust, not only peace, but will lead to some degree of tolerance and mutual understanding in place of the present suspicion and distrust in that it opens up a new era of hope in the north-east and adds immensely to the prospect of union. The hopes of fulfilment of such a union would be made almost certain, and some understanding could be carried out among ourselves if something could be done to end the threats of civil war and the tendency towards disorder shown by our opponents' present tactics. It was for those who knew the value of Irish nationality to convert their countrymen in the north-east. That would take time, but they must show them that they could be practical upbuilders as well as idealists.[196]

This was impressive talk. Even so, the new pact was to fail as did its predecessor. Neither Craig nor Collins proved able to protect their respective minorities. 'Generous recognition for differing interests without regard to their numerical strength is the saving formula for Ireland', Stephen Gwynn had written. But it proved to be impossible to deliver such generous recognition. Two days after the pact was signed an RIC man from Brown Square barracks at the bottom of the Shankill Road in Belfast was shot dead. Within an hour uniformed police, apparently from Brown Square, brutally murdered four Catholics in the Arnon Street–Stanhope Street area. This time the evidence pointed clearly to the role played by District Inspector Nixon. Politically well connected in loyalist circles, Nixon was a thorn in Craig's side. The city's Unionist press described the Arnon Street murders as 'mob law at its worst'. In July 1922—to Nixon's fury—the Ministry of Home Affairs snubbed him by promoting a Catholic officer over his head,[197] but in 1923 Nixon had to be placated with an MBE,[198] before finally being dismissed in 1924.[199] Nixon and his allies did not have the strength on their own to push Craig away from his chosen strategy. But he did have the capacity to intensify the alienation of northern nationalism and thus contribute to further destabilization. Nixon was also able to have a career as a populist MP at Stormont. Similarly, Collins could not control events in his own state. On 31 March the Irish Free State (Agreement) Act 1922 provided for the transfer of powers to the provisional government, but on 14 April that same government was to be challenged by the anti-Treaty forces under Rory O'Connor, which seized the Four Courts in Dublin. Even more dramatically, fourteen Protestants were massacred in West Cork after an IRA man had been killed breaking into a house.[200] These events had precisely the same alienating effects on northern Unionists as the Arnon Street murders had on northern Catholics.[201]

At first, GHQ in Dublin reverted to a war policy against the North. O'Duffy made the decision on 5 May to launch a new mass offensive in Ulster on 19 May—with the knowledge of Michael Collins, but not the Cabinet.[202] One captured document (13 May) from the North-East Advisory Committee of Nationalists—Collins's northern representatives—spoke

---

[197] PRONI HA 31/1/254. Nixon's protest is dated 11 July 1922.

[198] Parkinson, *Belfast's Unholy War*, 346. For an early treatment of this file, see Paul Bew, 'The Political History of Northern Ireland Since Partition: The Prospects for North/South Co-Operation', *Proceedings of the British Academy*, 98 (1999), 401–18.

[199] C. Ryder, *The Fateful Split: Catholics and the Royal Ulster Constabulary* (London, 2004), 83. Ryder describes this as a 'grubby political episode' in which 'the Government set out to sack Nixon, backed down, decorated him and then acted only when his confrontational attitude left them no choice'.

[200] Hart, *The IRA and its Enemies*, 282–5.

[201] W. Ewart, *A Journey in Ireland* (New York and London, 1922), 153; Dennis Kennedy, *A Widening Gulf: Northern Attitudes Towards the Independent Irish State 1919–49* (Belfast, 1988), 117.

[202] McGarry, *O'Duffy*, 100.

of a 'definite plan of campaign to be adopted by the Nationalists of the north-east, whereby they can render impotent the so-called government of Northern Ireland'.[203] On 17 May the IRA initiated this new northern offensive, beginning with an attack on the Musgrave Street police station. On the weekend of 20–2 May fourteen people were killed in Belfast, including William John Twaddell, a Unionist member of the Northern Ireland Parliament.

The pattern seemed set. The dynamic of events implied a national-ist–unionist civil war, not a republican one. On 20 May a pact between Collins and de Valera provided for a panel of Sinn Fein candidates to be drawn from the pro- and anti-Treaty parties in proportion to their strength in the existing Dail. The anti-Treaty forces were offered a share in govern-ment proportionate to their electoral strength. Having relied so much on the good faith of Collins, Winston Churchill was genuinely shaken—to the alarm of his officials. In fact, Churchill need not have been quite so worried. For Collins, 'the function of the pact was to allow for a calm and peaceful election':[204] an election which he confidently expected to win. The great mass of the people supported the Treaty and the peace which it was expected to bring. The anti-Treaty IRA had the capacity to disrupt an election, and the pact was the only way to ensure that such an election took place. Sir James Craig's reaction to the pact was, hardly surprisingly, explosive. He was prepared, he said, to treat with the southern representatives of a Free State, who were within the ambit of the British Empire. 'I am not prepared to meet with a composite government, one half of which is Republican in sentiment, and the other half of which says it doesn't go back on its statement that the Treaty is a step towards a republic.'[205]

The northerners immediately feared that all southern guns would be turned on them. On 24 May 1922 Major General Arthur Solly-Flood, the Northern Irish government's military advisor, prepared a 'Guide for City and County Authorities in Connection with the Defence of Ulster'. Some of its proposals were draconian—in the event of 'war', disaffected areas were to be proclaimed; there was to be widespread use of censorship, and blacklists of suspect officials were to be drawn up.[206] This was immediately

---

203 PRONI HA 32/1/206.

204 Laffan, *The Resurrection of Ireland*, 390; see also 410; Tom Garvin, *1922: The Birth of Irish Democracy* (Dublin, 1996), 129.

205 *Weekly Freeman*, 27 May 1922.

206 PRONI HA 32/1/271. 'Disappearance of one of the military adviser's staff. Collins's spy, appointed by Solly-Flood on account of his good war record, later surfaced as a superintendent in the Irish police. See the graphic anecdote in Charles W. Magill (ed.), *From Dublin Castle to Stormont: The Memoirs of A. P. Magill* (Cork, 2003), 71.

removed by one of Collins's spies in Solly-Flood's office and taken to Dublin.

Towards the end of May Free State forces loyal to Michael Collins occupied Pettigo and an old fort at Belleek, Co. Fermanagh. Anti-Treaty forces were also active in the area, attacking and kidnapping local loyalists. By 30 May the local Northern Ireland forces—Specials under the command of Sir Basil Brooke—had felt it was wise to retreat, and Belleek was now patrolled by the IRA in an armoured car captured from the Specials.

On 4 June British forces, having come under fire and lost a driver, attacked Irish army positions in Pettigo, Co. Fermanagh, killing seven Irish soldiers and retaking the village. It was a very tense moment. The *Northern Whig* reported: 'It is understood that Mr Michael Collins took a very grave view of the occurrences in Pettigo, and that he has forwarded a request to the British government for an immediate inquiry into the whole affair.'[207] The former editor of the *Times of India*, Arthur Moore, stressed the decisive role of Winston Churchill: 'A man very different from the majority of his colleagues in the Cabinet, as events soon proved. He advanced regiments under a heavy fire, against the captured salient and saluted the invaders with six rounds from a field piece.'[208] Archbishop Gregg in Dublin intervened to urge moderation and restraint:

If I read the signs right, southern Ireland is running headlong towards a conflict with Northern Ireland. This seems to me at the moment even a greater danger than any questions of the immediate relations of the Provisional Government with Great Britain ... But if we are not already engaged in civil war in Ireland, civil war may be upon us this week or next.[209]

A civil war was clearly on the cards—but was it to be unionist versus nationalist, as Archbishop Gregg feared, or pro- versus anti-Treatyite? The principal objective of British policy was to ensure the survival of the pro-Treaty faction in government. This meant that, even after the ill-fated invasion of Fermanagh, Collins retained considerable potential leverage against Craig. Armed with the captured document from Solly-Flood's staff, Collins was able to insist that Craig's security forces were out of control. He was also able to insist that his own prestige depended on the willingness of the British government to bring Craig to heel.

On 16 June Craig travelled to London and succeeded in persuading Lloyd George that it would be wrong to attempt to placate Collins by setting up a public inquiry into the working of the Northern Irish security forces. Craig

---

[207] *The Weekly Northern Whig and Belfast Post*, 10 June 1922.
[208] 'Through an Ulsterman's Eye', *Atlantic Monthly*, 130 (Oct. 1922), 541.
[209] *Weekly Northern Whig*, 10 June 1922.

was helped by the fact that on the same day Collins gained his expected substantial victory over the anti-Treaty forces in the general election in the South. Craig did, however, agree to a secret inquiry by an eminent public official S. G. Tallents. It was hardly a controversial choice—Tallents was attached to Churchill's Irish Committee. Balfour was unhappy about this proposal as the meeting ended. 'A report from Tallents, if public, would have little effect in counteracting propaganda', he told Lloyd George. Lloyd George replied: 'Sir James had to carry his colleagues with him. A report from Mr Tallents, making it quite clear there was a ground for a public inquiry, would enable him to do this.'[210] On 19 June the IRA massacred six Presbyterians at Atnaveigh near Newry. Frank Aiken was the local IRA commanding officer and had ordered the action: like Nixon, he too had a long, respectable career in politics ahead of him. Just as Nixon may not actually have been present at the murder of the MacMahons, Aiken may have been absent at Altnaveigh. ' "Why are they doing this to us?" they asked at Altnaveigh. "You are all protestants, that's enough," the leader of the gang is said to have replied in a cultured southern accent.'[211] On 22 June Field Marshal Sir Henry Wilson, Solly-Flood's sponsor, was assassinated in London by two IRA men, probably loyal to Collins. When introduced to Collins by Lloyd George at No. 10, Wilson had turned his back and walked out of the room[212]—it may have been a fatal snub. The British government had immediately to issue a statement, denying that Wilson had been killed by IRA weapons.[213] Ironically, one of Wilson's first actions as Craig's military advisor had been to urge the removal of the hardliner Dawson Bates from the post of Minister of Home Affairs and his replacement by Lord Londonderry, more liberal and an ex-soldier.[214] Behind the scenes, Lloyd George faced excruciating pressure: Bonar Law confronted him on 24 June, and Lloyd George realized, it was claimed, that he was facing another 'potential' prime minister.[215] Lloyd George, in turn, pressed Collins—he must do something to prove his good faith.

Tallent's report, when it came at the end of June/early July, was unflattering towards the northern government and its officials. Only Craig received good marks: 'A great desire to do the right and important thing:

[210] PRO CO906126, minutes of Downing Street meeting.

[211] Robert Lynch, *The Northern IRA and the Early Years of Partition* (Dublin, 2006), 148; Dennis Kennedy, *The Widening Gulf: Northern Attitudes to the Independent Irish State 1919–49* (Belfast, 1988), 77.

[212] *Northern Whig*, 23 Mar. 1922.

[213] For this whole episode, see Hart, *The IRA at War*.

[214] PRONI T3775/17/1–2, Wilson to Craig, Mar. 1922.

[215] 'Centurion: Irish Treason and its Authors', *National Review*, 79 (1922), 843; R. O. Q. Adams, *Bonar Law* (London, 1949), 310–11 which also discusses Altnaveigh.

not a clever man', but one of good 'judgement' who could recognise a 'big issue'.[216] But despite his coolness towards the officials of the Ministry of Home Affairs, he accepted the thrust of their arguments. He placed the blame for the deteriorating situation on the IRA: 'I have no doubt that the failure to give effect to Clause 6 of the [Craig–Collins] Agreement, which provided for the cessation of IRA activity in the six counties, was the major cause of its failure.'[217] But by this stage the report had a largely academic status. Lloyd George had commissioned the report because he felt he was losing Michael Collins to de Valera—but on 28 June, at 4.10 in the morning, the provisional government attacked the IRA rebels occupying the Four Courts, thus marking the beginning of the Irish Civil War. It appears that two days earlier, on 26 June (under intense British pressure), the provisional government had decided to attack the Four Courts. On 27 June an army unit under Frank Thornton was ordered to intercept a republican raiding party at Ferguson's garage in the city. Given the continued unity of purpose in the North between pro- and anti-Treatyites it was a surprising move: Leo Henderson, the organizer of the raid, was, however, given tea.[218] For Griffith, it was an assertion of the legitimate authority of the new state: for Collins, it was a rather reluctant break with old comrades whom he had been desperately attempting to mollify. Sean MacBride has said in his memoir that arms were being delivered to republicans for use in the North right up to the moment of attack by the Free State.[219] One senior republican liaison officer was still expecting a 'call from Mick', who would fill posts in the Cabinet as agreed as part of the pact, when the fighting broke out.[220] Some 600 to 700 soldiers attacked: they used mainly rifles and machine-guns, but also some heavier weaponry. The noise of gunfire continued throughout the day. The *Freeman* noted grimly: 'The position was strikingly reminiscent of the tragic events of Easter week.'[221] A priest in soutane and biretta created an ugly scene in Capel Street by denouncing the Free State troops as Irish Black and Tans. The official statement issued by the government declared:

Statements that British troops are co-operating with the IRA are false and malicious. None but the Irish forces—with the co-operation of the citizens who are loyally

[216] PRO CO/24. For a broader, excellent, balanced discussion of these issues, see Kirsten Pedersen, 'Northern Ireland 1921–30: The Establishment of an Orange State', in Joost Augusteijn and Mary Ann Lyons (eds.), *Irish History: A Research Yearbook No 1* (Dublin, 2002).

[217] See the documents he found at PRONI HAS/139/6.

[218] Michael Hopkinson, *Green against Green: The Irish Civil War* (Dublin, 1988), 116–17.

[219] *That Day's Struggle* (Dublin, 2005), 58.   [220] *Irish Tribune*, 27 Aug. 1926.

[221] *Weekly Freeman*, 1 July 1922, 'Battle of the Four Courts'.

and enthusiastically supporting the government—are engaged in putting down the disorderly elements who attempt to tyrannise over the people and defy their will.

But one thing, at least, was clear—any probable attempt on the part of the Free State to attack Northern Ireland was immediately stymied by the outbreak of the civil war.[222]

Very rapidly the bitterness of the civil war reached a great intensity: all southern pressure on the Belfast government was relieved. In early August the captured diary of an irregular officer—reproduced in the *Irish Times* at the end of the month—records a belief that Collins had tried to open a dialogue with some opponents in Cork—but this mood did not last. As the attempts to murder him came closer and closer to success, Collins became increasingly bitter: on 18 August his car was attacked, but luckily for him, he was not in it. George Bernard Shaw met him a few days before the end. Collins was certainly not looking for a compromise.[223] In an *Irish Times* profile of the writer, Shaw stressed that Collins had been in aggressive, unforgiving mood towards his enemies: 'Ireland is obviously on the point of losing its temper.' Recalling the incident in 1946, Shaw added: 'His nerves were in rags: his hand kept slapping his revolver all the time he was talking pleasantly enough.'[224] On 22 August Collins was killed at Bealnablath, between Macroom and Bandon, Co. Cork. Even at his funeral a sniper fired some twenty shots during Richard Mulcahy's oration. 'In some of the back streets of Dublin the women were dancing jigs and reels.'[225]

The fundamental cause of the civil war was political. From 1916 to 1921 Sinn Fein had created, amongst its own supporters, a very high-level expectancy as to the likely outcome of the conflict. In the end, the disappointment of the final deal was too much for many to bear. William O'Malley aptly concluded: 'They doubted the Irish Party, it is true, but they have not got their republic, and they have had to put up with partition.'[226] It was this thought, nagging away in the soul of so many, which led them to reject the Treaty. What, after all, was the social dimension, if any, to the civil war? All scholars agree that within the nationalist political elite, which split over the Treaty, there is little correlation between class origin and support for the Treaty:[227] political calculations, ideological factors,

---

[222] Garvin, *1922*, 184.

[223] Bill Kissane, *The Politics of the Irish Civil War* (Oxford, 2005), 102.

[224] *Irish Times*, 21 Aug. 1922, 'GBS on Ireland'; Shaw to Alfred Douglas, 9 Nov. 1946, in Dan H. Laurence (ed.), *Bernard Shaw: Collected Letters 1926–50* (London, 1988), iv. 586. Shaw conveyed to the press something of the tone of his meeting with Collins when he advised the media not to worry 'about the difficulty of overcrowded prisons, because there will be no prisoners, the strain should be on the cemeteries'.

[225] *Galway Observer*, 2 Sept. 1922.   [226] Ibid., 28 Oct. 1922.

[227] Tom Garvin, *Nationalist Revolutionaries in Ireland* (Oxford, 1987), 142.

and personality disputes appear to have been far more important. The initiating cause appears to have been political, ideological, and personal, but this does not rule out a social dimension as events evolved. What, then, about the class dimension of the civil-war division within the broad nationalist community? It certainly existed in the rhetoric of the period, and opponents of the Treaty allowed some respect to those inspired by the Russian Revolution of 1917.[228]

J. J. Lee has argued that popular support for and against the Treaty 'did reflect socio-economic differences'.[229] Michael Hopkinson has further suggested that, while economic considerations did not account for the split in the Dail, they explained much in the country at large. Treaty support was more intense where there was most prosperity, where connections with the British economy were the most intimate, and where communications were the most developed. Opposition to the Treaty was strongest in the west of the country. In the west and in parts of the south, this opposition was linked to economic grievances, especially those arising out of the land question. Regions such as West Cork, Kerry, and Mayo became republican bastions during the civil war. Opinion in Leinster, however, was strongly supportive of the Treaty.[230]

The results of recent local studies are varied in the light they throw on this issue: Peter Hart's study of Co. Cork suggests that the IRA became more proletarian during the civil war,[231] but Michael Farry's equally interesting study of Sligo 'demonstrates clearly the absence of a social basis for the civil war in Co. Sligo'.[232] What is not in dispute, however, is that the pro-Treaty forces employed a language of relative social conservatism and tried to present the republican cause as contaminated by a dangerous social radicalism, if not communism. The headline themes of the pro-government press are particularly instructive in this context. The stress was always on the anarchy and chaos produced by republican activity: 'The Reign of Terror: Robberies, Shootings, Raid on Banks and Looting of Village';[233] 'Ruining Ireland: Campaign of Disturbance by Wreckers and Robbers goes on. Wholesale Plundering.'[234] The scale 'of almost unbearable inconvenience' imposed by the civil war was great enough—Cork city, for example, was completely cut off from North Kerry for a month in the autumn

---

[228] Emmet O'Connor, *Reds and the Greens: Ireland, Russia and the Communist International* (Dublin, 2004), 56.

[229] J. J. Lee, *Ireland 1912–85: Politics and Society* (Cambridge, 1989), 542.

[230] Michael Hopkinson, 'From Treaty to Civil War', in J. R. Hill (ed.), *A New History of Ireland*, VII, *Ireland 1921–1984* (Oxford, 2003), 5–6.

[231] *The IRA and its Enemies*, 160.

[232] *The Aftermath of Revolution* (Dublin, 2000), 204–5.

[233] *Weekly Freeman*, 23 Dec. 1922.   [234] Ibid., 13 Jan. 1923.

of 1922.[235] But the deepest horror of all was reserved for 'communist' experiments and land seizures, sometimes facilitated by the chaos of the civil war: 'The Toorahara Soviet—Bolshevist Ethics of Moscow Permeate into Co. Clare.'[236] The truth is that the weakness of the urban working class, combined with the virtual disappearance of the agricultural labourer—in a country that was dominated by farmer proprietors—meant that there was no real possibility of communism.[237] It is hard, therefore, not to sympathize with Frank Cunnane, a republican prisoner awaiting execution in Tuam: 'My Rosary beads I send home. Tell [Cissie] that in death I wear the Scapulars she gave me—we are not waging a war of Bolshevism of which the IRA is accused.'[238] The accusation of Bolshevism was made, however, and not without effect.

On 17 November began the first of a series of seventy-seven executions of Irregulars by shooting—the last taking place on 2 May 1923. Frank Cunnane, for example, was executed in Tuam barracks in April. Prestige and service to Ireland were no barrier to execution. Erskine Childers was tried by a military court for unlawful possession of a revolver and was shot on 24 November. On 8 December Rory O'Connor, Liam Mellows, and two other Irregulars were executed after their trial as a reprisal for the assassination of the pro-Treaty deputy Sean Hales. Stephen Gwynn was extraordinarily impressed by the toughness of the government—which he hailed in his *Observer* column. His house and library were burned down in retaliation. In early February the veteran nationalist Dr Sigerson resigned from the Senate as a result of republican threats. In 1868 Sigerson's book on Irish history had been regarded as crude pro-Fenian propaganda by Lord Kimberley, the Lord-Lieutenant. The veteran poet, scientist, and writer was a professor of history in the National University. He had also written a celebrated book on the treatment of political prisoners in the nineteenth century. But now even George Sigerson had had to bow to the republican whirlwind.[239] The Senate had become a gloomy place. Gwynn had already observed that the Senate's minute of silent prayer was a subject for a great writer. 'It would be a tempting subject for Mr James Joyce to write the thoughts, aspirations and emotions of these 60 seconds in those 60 consciousnesses.'[240] On 17 February 1923 the Cosgrave government publicly signalled that any suggestion that they were seeking a compromise with the rebels was false. On 18 February Free State forces killed Denny

[235] *Evening Echo*, 6 Sept. 1922.   [236] *Weekly Freeman*, 12 May 1923.

[237] David Fitzpatrick, 'The Disappearance of the Irish Agricultural Labourer, 1841–1912', *Irish Economic and Social History 1917–1980*, 7 (1980), 66–92.

[238] Nollaig Ó Gadhra, *Civil War in Connaught 1922–23* (Cork, 1999), 84.

[239] *Weekly Freeman*, 10 Feb. 1923.   [240] *Observer*, 28 Jan. 1923.

Lacey, the most prominent and formidable leader of the anti-Treaty forces in south Tipperary: 'The stubbornness of his views was only equalled by the remorseless energy of his actions.'[241] At this point, de Valera appeared to insist there could be no compromise on his part either.

The civil war, nonetheless, was gradually winding down. On 23 March a meeting of the republican army executive endorsed a proposal by de Valera that he would be empowered to enter into negotiations on the basis of three principles, namely: 'That the right of the Irish people to sovereign independence is inalienable; that the ultimate court of appeal on questions of national expediency is the people of Ireland; and that no person subscribing to these principles ought to be prevented from taking a full share in the nation's political life.'[242] In the next few weeks even Austin Stack, a great republican diehard, became increasingly disillusioned: he was joined in this by other stalwarts like Frank Barrett, Dan Breen, and Sean Gaynor. They designed a document authorizing the President of the Republic, to order 'an immediate cessation of hostilities'.[243] But there was still a significant element on the republican executive who opposed any acknowledgement of defeat. The *Weekly Freeman*, on 14 April, carried a captured document, addressed to Liam Lynch, which exuded disorganization and demoralization. Given Liam Lynch's absolutely pivotal role in the conduct of a war (in which activity de Valera had become increasingly marginal), this was an important moment.[244] Then, on 14 April, Stack, with three comrades, was arrested at Lismore.

By the spring of 1923 the Irregular campaign was nearing collapse: one of its last actions was the burning of two Protestant schools in Cork.[245] De Valera and Frank Aiken issued a statement on behalf of both the political and military wings of the republican movement. It announced 'a suspension of all offensive operations', but also inaugurated a new political philosophy: it accepted that the

ultimate court of appeal for deciding disputed questions of national expediency and policy is the people of Ireland, its judgement made by the majority vote of the adult citizenry; and the decision to be submitted to, and resistance by violence excluded, not because the decision is necessarily right ... but because acceptance of

[241] *Weekly Freeman*, 24 Feb. 1923.

[242] J. Anthony Gaughan, *Austin Stack: Portrait of a Separatist* (Naas, 1977), 231.

[243] From MT (Department of CS), GHQ Dublin, 22 Mar., to Chief of Staff, contains much gloom, of which this is typical: 'Army Order No 1 apparently met with a poor response. I wonder, will Army Orders No 2 and 3 work better?', *Weekly Freeman*, 14 Apr. 1923.

[244] For this complex relationship, see Bill Kissane, *The Politics of the Irish Civil War* (Oxford, 2005), 90–1.

[245] *Irish Independent*, 30 Apr. 1922.

this rule makes for peace, order and unity in national actions, and is the democratic alternative to arbitrariment by force.[246]

There were obvious ambiguities in these statements. Was a 'suspension of all offensive operations' a permanent end to the conflict? What was to be done about guns? Republicans announced they were dumping them. Cosgrave remarked that republicans still wanted access to their weapons 'any time they took it into their heads to interview a bank manager'.[247] But the pro-government *Irish Independent* editorial grasped the point that a new era was emerging: 'The constitutional way of resolving our political difficulties, upon which Mr de Valera laid stress in December 1921, should never have been departed from.' It added: 'We hope eventually, Mr de Valera would move the whole way to a constitutional position.'[248] Sir James Craig, the next day, held out an olive branch to the South:

The fact that certain Irishmen have taken a different view from what they held, would never prevent those in the North from expressing at all times the most earnest wish that prosperity, peace and happiness might belong to the others as well as to themselves. When they talked about prosperity in Northern Ireland, they could not help hoping that prosperity would extend to the whole of their beloved country.[249]

Craig was capable of generosity, in part because it looked as if radical republicans had suffered a decisive defeat. But it should be noted that the anti-Treaty IRA was still alive, if demoralized. An internal IRA document stated on 28 May 1923: 'The dumping of arms does not mean that the usefulness of the IRA is past, or release any member from its duty to his country. On the contrary, a disciplined volunteer force, ready for any emergency, will be a great strength to the nation in its march to Independence. It is clearly our duty to keep the Army Organisation intact.'[250] At the end of May 1923 the *Manchester Guardian* asked the question: 'How much electoral support remained for Republicans?'

In Leinster and Munster people believe that they will be snowed under by the votes of indignant materialists, farmers, shopkeepers and labourers, who will not easily forgive them for interrupting their business and burdening the country with debt. A Republican from a Republican stronghold in the county of Cork admitted to me that the Republicans today have no chance of half of the votes they would have got the week after the Treaty was signed.[251]

---

[246] *Irish Independent*, 30 Apr. 1922.   [247] Ibid., 10 May 1923.
[248] Ibid., 30 Apr. 1922.
[249] Ibid., 1 May 1923.   [250] Kissane, *The Politics of the Irish Civil War*, 123.
[251] *Weekly Freeman*, 2 June 1923.

Such a comment reveals both the scale of the defeat suffered by republicans, but also the possibility of a recovery when the most bitter memories of civil war anarchy had faded.

The civil war had dribbled to a close. The loss of Irish life was considerable. Perhaps 800 pro-Treaty soldiers were killed between the Treaty's signing and the war's end. There is no record of overall republican deaths—but it is probable that it was much higher. No figure exists for civilian deaths either. It is certain, however, that casualties were considerably in excess of the number of Irish Volunteers lost in the 1916–21 period.[252] In August 1923 the Free State election gave Cosgrave's Cumann na nGaedheal some sixty-three seats; the republicans gained forty-four, Labour fourteen, Farmers fifteen, independents and others some seventeen. The pro-Treaty faction's support base was some 39.1 per cent of the vote as against 27.4 per cent for the republicans.[253] Those who had decided to follow Michael Collins in acceptance of the Treaty compromise had a firm grip on the government of the new self-governing Ireland.

---

[252] Hopkinson, *Green against Green*, 273.   [253] *The Nation*, 25 June 1927.

10

'Melancholy Sanctity' in the South, 'Perfect Democracy in the North': Ireland 1923–1966

What really happened was that the exalting sense of Ireland's exceptional destiny, which had existed before 1922, simply faded into the sheer ordinariness of a paternal, pettifogging, fairly decent little republic. The dreams of the founders were unattainable. It was not going to be a Workers' Republic, as Connolly hoped, or a Gaelic-speaking one, as Pearse hoped, or a united one, as all the revolutionaries had hoped and assumed. The North was lost for good: left-wing extremism flickered and died in the Thirties; so did the right-wing extremism of the Blueshirts. A melancholy sanctity prevailed.

(Conor Cruise O'Brien, 'Two-Faced Cathleen', *New York Review of Books*, 29 June 1967)

As you get older, you get much more conservative, as I have done.

(Rockefeller Foundation Advice Center, Tarrytown, RF II, Project Ireland, 403, Box 1, folder 2, report from D. P. O'Brien and Dr Allen of a conversation with de Valera in the summer of 1942)

'The shadow of civil war and the poverty of the new state ensured there was little appetite for radical social and cultural change.'[1] The new Irish ministers were obsessed with issues of financial credibility, being understandably eager to demonstrate the seriousness of Irish national purpose by avoiding bankruptcy or extensive debt. They were determined to preserve the institutions of the state and to demonstrate that these institutions could themselves hollow out the last remnants of British rule. In short, they were determined to vindicate the celebrated claim of Michael Collins, that the Free State constituted the freedom to build freedom.

---

[1] Diarmaid Ferriter, *The Transformation of Ireland 1900–2000* (London, 2004), 296.

On 9 September 1922 the *Irish Times* profiled the new leader of Ireland, W. T. Cosgrave:

It is hard to imagine anybody who is less close to what we used to consider the Sinn Fein type than Mr Cosgrave. It is not only that he does not dress in the regulation way—trench-coat, leggings, slouch hat and the rest of it—but he has a thoroughly conservative face. He is neither a wild-eyed revolutionary nor a long-haired poet. He dresses generally in sombre hues, wears a bowler hat and looks rather like the general manager of a railway company.

The Irish people found themselves governed by intellectually severe and brusque martinets: men who believed not so much in the economy of truth as the necessary brutality of truth. One commentator in D. P. Moran's *The Leader*—which prided itself on its party-political neutrality—explained, at the moment of the government's fall, that 'whilst probably it is, or was, best for the people to be ruled with a strong, firm hand ... especially following on a period of war fevers, that kind of administration was bound to make the Government unpopular, as the Irish people have to be humoured'.[2] But the new leaders of the nation regarded humouring of the Irish people as an indulgence that could not be afforded. This was to be their eventual undoing, but not before they had established the firm basis for a viable parliamentary democracy. The paradox for Ireland's new rulers was a harsh one: they actually achieved the objectives which, they felt, were the really important ones for any serious Irish government, yet, nonetheless, progressively fell out of favour—over a period of a decade—with the Irish electorate. The growing disillusionment of the populace had one profound cause: Irish independence had long been freighted with a heavy weight of historical expectation as a development which would in itself reverse the harsh conditions of life for many of the plain people of Ireland, yet, while Irish independence provided much emotional satisfaction—Catholic nationalists were plainly in political control of the country—the material conditions of life for many ordinary people did not improve, and in some cases actually deteriorated.

Progress was, in the end, to be rather slow. From 1923 to 31 March 1932 the Land Commission acquired and distributed some 330,825 acres (on average of 36,758 per annum) amongst 15,687 allottees (an average of just under 20 acres each, regarded at the time as a standard holding). Thus, an average of 11,843 people per annum had benefited from acquisition and division: the practical reality, long obscured by the British and landlord presence, was now all too obvious. There was not enough land in Ireland

---

[2] *The Leader*, 27 Feb. 1932.

to satisfy all the uneconomic holders in the country.[3] Agrarian radicals obsessed about the remaining areas of landlord privilege: for example, the landed class was allowed to retain demesne or woodland or untenanted land in areas which were intermingled with woodland, 'as was commonly the case'. 'Romanus', in the *Catholic Bulletin*, declared that the legislation thus broke the 'moral law'.[4]

The land legislation of 1923 was the first clear indication of the government's style of work. Austere, prickly men attempted to do their duty with a fine disregard for sentimentality. The government did its business by drawing strong lines rather than offering fudges: the first key group to show discontent was the military.

On 18 February the government announced a reduction and reorganization of the national army: it infuriated some old political types in the force. By March the state faced what came to be known as the 'army mutiny', the collapse of which on 6 May 1924 may have been the last dangerous 'echo of civil war' and a decisive vindication of 'civilian control of the army'.[5] But it led to the resignation of Joe McGrath, the Minister of Industry, and other supporters of the government: the only real beneficiary was de Valera, looking in from the outside at the margins of politics.[6] The government, however, brought the same forceful and brutal realism to the next great issue on the agenda—pensions. On the eve of Irish independence, the British Exchequer had subsidized Irish pension arrangements to the tune of £4 million—three-quarters of that sum going to the twenty-six counties of the Irish Free State.[7] Without British subvention, the government realized that the cost of the British pension scheme was too high for Ireland to bear. Pension expenditure was, in fact, the great bulk of welfare spending. On 15 June 1924 Ernest Blythe, the Finance Minister, passed the Old Age Pensions Act, reducing old-age pensions from 10 shillings to 9 shillings a week—it was a significant moment, and, like the army mutiny, offered much solace to de Valera. There was more solace to come in 1925, with the Boundary Commission crisis. For, even on the subject of the 'unnatural' partition of Ireland, Free State ministers were inclined to give expression to tough-minded and unpopular assessments. Kevin O'Higgins was clear on the subject on 19 March 1925: he described partition 'as a problem of close

[3] Terence Dooley, *'The Land for the People': The Land Question in Independent Ireland* (Dublin, 2004), 94–5.
[4] 'The Truth about Irish Fascism', *Catholic Bulletin*, 23 (July–Dec. 1933), 40.
[5] Maryann Valialis, *Almost a Rebellion: The Irish Army Mutiny of 1924* (Cork, 1985), 120–1.
[6] Richard Mulcahy, *Mulcahy: A Family Memoir* (Dublin, 1999), 201–5.
[7] Cormac O'Grada, '"The Greatest Blessing of All": The Old-Age Pension in Ireland', *Past & Present*, 175 (May 2002), 122–3.

on a million people having different ideals and different traditions … that problem is not soluble at the present moment, and it is perhaps a problem that only time can solve'.[8] The Boundary Commission, established under Article 12 of the Anglo-Irish Treaty, had not started its work until 1924. It had been appointed by Ramsay MacDonald's minority Labour government, but it actually operated under Baldwin's Conservative one, which came to power in November 1924. The *Morning Post*, on 7 November 1925, carried a leak of the Boundary Commission report—a proposed rectified border, containing only minor rectifications.[9]

W. T. Cosgrave rushed to London to consult with Stanley Baldwin. He complained that the four-county concept, which had seriously been discussed at Buckingham Palace in 1914, appeared to have disappeared. But the British side pointed out that no such concept was to be found in the 1921 Treaty. The British told the Irish that they had, at all times, assumed that there would be a two-way transfer of territories. Cosgrave insisted that Lloyd George, the then Prime Minister, had given the 'impression' of more substantial concessions to the Irish side;[10] given that the British government was now led by Baldwin, who rather disliked Lloyd George, this cut very little ice. This was, after all, a British government composed either of men who had opposed the Treaty, or who, if they had taken responsibility for it, had 'long since learned the price they would pay for going against conservative opinion on this issue'.[11]

There was a possible way out for all concerned—the British, Irish, and Northern Irish governments. Article 5 of the Treaty had committed the Free State to a share of the United Kingdom public debt, subject to agreement between the two governments. A possibility existed, therefore, of a 'trade off'[12] between the abandonment of Article 12 and the securing of concessions under this article. This was the route taken by the Free State government. This tripartite agreement between the governments of the United Kingdom, the Irish Free State, and Northern Ireland revoked the powers of the Boundary Commission and maintained the existing boundary of Northern Ireland. The Irish Free State was released from liability for

---

[8] Sir James O'Connor, *History of Ireland 1798–1924* (London, 1926), ii. 203.

[9] Margaret O'Callaghan, ' "Old Parchment and Water": The Boundary Commission of 1925 and the Copper-Fastening of the Irish Border', *Bullan*, 4 (Winter–Spring 2000), 45; P. Murray, 'Partition and the Irish Boundary Commission: A Northern Nationalist Prospective', *Clogher Record*, 13: 2 (2004), 203, for important context.

[10] Enda Staunton, 'The Boundary Commission Debacle 1925: Aftermath and its Implications', *History Ireland*, 4: 2 (Summer 1996), 42.

[11] Kevin Matthews, 'Stanley Baldwin's Irish Question', *Historical Journal*, 43: 4 (2003), 1049.

[12] Staunton, 'The Boundary Commission Debacle of 1925', 44.

British public debt and accepted liability for notorious damage since 21 January 1919; the powers of the Council of Ireland in Northern Ireland were transferred to the Northern Ireland government. The new agreement, signed on 3 December by Craig, Cosgrave, and Baldwin, not only confirmed the territory of Northern Ireland, but also embodied Dublin's recognition of the status of Northern Ireland as part of the United Kingdom. In December 1925 the Dail debated the new Treaty. An exchange between Patrick Baxter, the Farmers' Party representative for Cavan, and Patrick McGilligan, himself a northern Catholic, captured the mood of the debate.

Baxter: No young Nationalist can go to a neighbour's house or a *cailidhe* without ... being liable to be stopped half a dozen times by a next-door neighbour with a revolver. Three or four Nationalists can not stand at a crossroads without 'B' Specials coming along to deny them their rights.

McGilligan: I have brothers who do all these things without any of this happening.[13]

James Craig was prepared at this point to talk in public, in a friendly and relaxed way, about relations with the government in the South. At this very moment, however, Eamon de Valera returned to the stage of Irish politics, bringing with him the possibility of a new cold war between North and South. He seized the opportunity created by the reality that those in power had so little to offer by way of populist appeal. Poverty, emigration, and high unemployment were widespread and affected most dramatically those who had taken the losing republican side of the civil war. In 1926 the Irish working class was small: only 13 per cent of the labour force worked in industry, about the same as the number of domestic servants, and far less than the 53 per cent who worked in agriculture. The government lacked any economic strategy other than reliance on the export of agricultural produce to the UK market, a policy that reinforced the support of large farmers and a consequent refusal to ameliorate the lot of the urban and rural poor.[14]

To the surprise, perhaps, of the government, de Valera proved to be flexible enough to respond to the opportunity posed. He broke, in April 1926, with the rump of Sinn Fein/IRA irreconcilables and founded a new party, Fianna Fail, with the intention of entering the Dail—though the issue of the oath of allegiance to the British Crown, obligatory for new Dail members, appeared to stand in the way. On 17 April 1926 the new party, Fianna Fail, issued its first press statement.

The text is a clear exposition of the world-view of Eamon de Valera, the Fianna Fail leader. The themes of political independence, language

[13] Staunton, 'The Boundary Commission Debacle of 1925', 44.
[14] Richard Dunphy, 'Fianna Fail and the Working Class, 1926–38', in Fintan Lane and Donal Ó Drisceol (eds.), *Politics and the Irish Working Class* (London, 2005), 249.

revival, land reform, and an end to partition are neatly intertwined: not all, of course, had equal weight. This language also recalled the themes of mainstream Irish nationalism from the Irish Republican Brotherhood of the 1860s through the Land League and Parnellite movements up to Sinn Fein. There is not a point to be found in the Fianna Fail press statement which could not have been comfortably located in an *Irish People* editorial of the 1860s. After a false start in the business of self-government, the Irish people were now being offered a chance to fulfil their destiny as defined by 'genuine' patriots.

This shift towards acceptance of the Free State institutions, fraught with ambiguity as it was, surprised some of de Valera's opponents; as D. P. Moran's the *Leader* sourly observed: 'The move was inconsistent with all he had said and done for the previous four years.'[15] Fianna Fail's break with the IRA had a decisive long-term significance. In the shorter term, this was less than obvious: the formation of the party in May 1926 did not see an immediate severing of ties with the IRA by its members. At the upper level many retained joint membership of the two organizations until 1927. Cases of rank-and-file dual membership survived until 1932. Outsiders assumed a broad identity of purpose and sympathy between the two groups.[16] De Valera, nonetheless, had decided that the moment required a fundamentally new type of politics. A good insight into his thinking is given in a letter to Joseph McGarrity, a leading émigré nationalist figure in the United States, in which de Valera fears the development of class politics unless he interfered.

Dr Richard Dunphy has argued that this is a classic example of that populist politics in which the leader, in this case de Valera, rejects the idea that groups in society have irreconcilable interests. Indeed, the task of leadership is to prevent the development of a consciousness of conflicting interests. This type of politics operates at the rougher edges of the playing-field of liberal democracy: this populism bases itself on an appeal against the established structures, in this case including, very superficially, the established structure of relationship with Britain.[17]

De Valera had decided that to allow such a government as Cosgrave's to continue in power when the main opponent was the Labour Party would have been precisely to risk the institutionalization of class divisions in the Free State: the Labour Party's relatively strong performance—12.6 per cent of the vote as against Fianna Fail's 26.1 per cent and the Cumann na nGaedheal's 27.4 per cent—in the first (June) election of

---

[15] *The Leader*, 29 Jan. 1927.
[16] Brian Hanley, *The IRA, 1926–36* (Dublin, 2002), 113.
[17] Dunphy, 'Fianna Fail and the Working Class', 247–9.

1927 demonstrated the danger. The June election was more marked by the decline in support for the government than for a substantial increase in 'republican sentiment': Labour held twenty-two seats, as against Fianna Fail with forty-four.

It is perhaps worth pointing out that the issue of partition had little, at a popular level, to do with Fianna Fail's emergence. As Eamon Donnelly, a northern nationalist active in Fianna Fail at this time, noted in *Honesty*: 'There is no use shirking the fact that one of the biggest crimes to their [the Cosgrave government's] credit isn't a live issue by any means. I refer to Ulster.'[18] However, the Boundary Commission report did, at least, mobilize oppositional political elites and create a sense of righteous indignation.

Everything was, however, changed by the murder of Kevin O'Higgins. O'Higgins was a particular *bête noire* for republicans. As Minister for Home Affairs (1922–7), he was identified with many harsh anti-republican measures: he was, for example, party to the decision that four republican prisoners, including Rory O'Connor, who had been best man at his wedding, should be shot as a reprisal for the assassination of Sean Hales TD on 7 December 1922. The desire to hit back was too much for some in the IRA. O'Higgins was murdered on 10 July 1927 near his home at Booterstown, Co. Dublin, while on his way to mass, by a group of republicans apparently acting without the authority of the IRA leadership.[19]   Responding to the assassination, the government passed emergency legislation, enforcing acceptance of the oath of allegiance as the sine qua non of participation in mainstream political life. In the end, though, de Valera gave way. Fianna Fail complied, whilst making it clear that they regarded the oath as an empty formula. On 11 August 1927, de Valera and Fianna Fail finally took their seats. The leading Republican propagandist Frank Gallagher could only tell his readers that the decision 'occasioned days and nights of anxiety'[20]—they can hardly have been surprised.[21]

The results of the election in September seemed to satisfy de Valera: the sitting government narrowly avoided being toppled. This time Labour had only thirteen seats to the fifty-seven gained by Fianna Fail. Fianna Fail's share of the vote rose from 26.1 to 35.2 per cent, whilst Labour's fell from 12.6 to 9.1 per cent. The broad trend was established; increasingly, Fianna Fail's language focused on economic and social themes: of particular importance here was the campaign against the payment of land annuities to Britain. In 1923 the government of the Irish Free State had undertaken

---

[18] *Mayo News*, 4 June 1927.　　[19] Hanley, *The IRA 1926–36*, 49.
[20] *The Nation*, 20 Aug. 1927.
[21] On these developments see Owen Dudley Edwards, *Eamon de Valera* (Cardiff, 1987), 110–12.

to collect and pay to the United Kingdom the moneys due from tenant-purchasers—that is, the annuities in respect of holdings purchased under the 1903 and 1909 British Land Acts. These annuities amounted to £3 million a year.[22]

The Fianna Fail manifesto of February 1932 contained specifically Republican political elements of largely symbolic importance: Fianna Fail in power would remove the oath of allegiance obligatory to members entering the Dail. It would seek to find a means of preventing the payment of pensions to former RIC members. But the key elements were the economic and social provisions. Fianna Fail committed itself to retaining the land annuities in the State Treasury. 'The British government is neither legally nor justly entitled to receive them.'[23] This, then, opened the way for a populist scheme of agricultural de-rating. 'With two of the three million pounds involved, the farmers can be relieved completely of the rates on their holdings.'[24] The manifesto also made clear that Fianna Fail had a new strategy for industrial growth. 'To organise systematically the establishment of the industries required to meet the needs of the community in manufactured goods. The aim would be to make ourselves as independent of foreign imports as possible and to provide for our people the employment that is at present denied them.' Suitable fiscal laws would be passed to give the protection necessary against unfair foreign competition.[25]

In 1932 Fianna Fail won the general election decisively with 44.5 per cent of the vote; it had gained seventy-two seats as against fifty-seven for Cumann na nGaedheal. In an atmosphere fraught with tension and wild rumours of 'coups' and 'counter-coups', de Valera took office as King George VI's 'last Irish Prime Minister'. John Wheeler Bennett was later to put this assessment to Eamon de Valera:

'I was what?' came the amazed reply. 'I do not recognise myself in that part'. 'I know you took the oath of allegiance in order to be able to abolish it,' I replied, 'but you did take it, and therefore you were his last Irish Prime Minister'. At first I thought the long saturnine face was to be convulsed with fury, and the fierce sightless eyes would blaze in anger, but what I took for anger, proved to be humour, and he laughed aloud.[26]

[22] Deirdre McMahon, *Republicans and Imperialists* (New Haven and London, 1984), 38–41.
[23] Alan O'Day and John Stevenson (eds.), *Irish Historical Documents Since 1800* (Dublin, 1992), 188.
[24] Ibid.   [25] Ibid. 189.
[26] John Wheeler-Bennett, *Friends, Enemies and Foreigners* (London, 1976), 151. I owe this reference to C. D. C. Armstrong. By 1933 de Valera had indeed successfully abolished the oath.

This did not exhaust the ambiguity of the moment. The losers in the civil war were now, ten years later, the winners of the political competition for the allegiance of the Irish electorate. As it had promised during the election campaign, Fianna Fail granted release to the twenty IRA men still held in the state's jails, in the likely knowledge that several, at least, would resume their subversive activity.[27] Perhaps even more profoundly, it was perceived that, after a decade-long right-wing dominance, mainstream Irish republicanism was returning to the true path—the agrarian radicalism of the old Fenian tradition, which would, at last, be put into effect. After a false start, Ireland was at last to receive the type of self-government for which the heroes of the independence movement had fought.

At last, the great themes of social Fenianism as derived from the radical wing of Young Ireland were to become government policy. Speaking in 1931 at Irishtown, where, in 1879, the Land League had been inaugurated, de Valera insisted: 'The land his party stood for was the Ireland of Fintan Lalor, a country which still was their own from sod to sky. With the country's resources fully developed, employment and a means of existence for a population of 20 million could easily supplied.'[28] Ireland was to break free from the pattern of structural underdevelopment which London had imposed, leading to mass emigration and depopulation. The principal methods—long rehearsed—were to be industrial protection and Irish control of Irish resources, combined with an agrarian policy unafraid of putting the interests of small producers first.

By the end of the 1920s Fianna Fail had secured the confidence of substantial sectors of Irish industry. The party was increasingly confident in its expression of support for a policy of industrial protection. In January 1932 de Valera told a meeting in Offaly that 'one couldn't expect an Irish manufacturer to show enterprise if he is driven out of the home market by a foreign combine selling goods here'.[29] De Valera assured the same audience that 'personally he believed that such protection would not be used for profiteering purposes'. In 1930 Fianna Fail's programme was in line with the National Agricultural and Industrial Development Association (an employers' organization): running full-page advertisements in newspapers, the NAIDA emphasized the number of jobs which could be created through the development of the home market.[30] This was the key message in Fianna Fail's concerted and successful drive to rally working-class and rural-labourer

[27] Seosama Ó Longaigh, *Emergency Law in Independent Ireland* (Dublin, 2006), 139.

[28] *Mayo News*, 10 Jan. 1931.

[29] Richard Dunphy, *The Making of Fianna Fail Power in Ireland 1923–48* (Oxford, 1995), 908.

[30] Ibid. 91.

support. The argument that unemployment was a function of the government's failure to protect Irish industry, and that Irish manufacturers, if given a fair chance by a policy of protection, could provide full employment was constantly stated.

Sometimes a more radical proviso was added: if the Irish industrial bourgeoisie failed in this task, then the state would intervene and instigate temporary and emergency employment, creating projects.

Hailing Fianna Fail's 'great victory' in de Valera's snap general election of January 1933—which saw his party rise from seventy-two to seventy-seven seats, while Cumann na nGaedheal fell from fifty-seven to forty-eight—the *Mayo News*, edited by P. J. Doris, who had a proud 'national' record as a friend of Michael Davitt and old Fenian, Land Leaguer, Sinn Feiner, and supporter of Fianna Fail, insisted: 'All agricultural workers must be provided with economic farms on the rich lands of Ireland now given over to the grazing principle in the eastern or middle counties of Ireland.'[31]

It is difficult to avoid the conclusion, however, that for all the hope vested in him by rural radicals, for de Valera the issue of land had, as its most profound significance, the fact that it allowed him to broach broader constitutional questions. De Valera exploited the issue of land annuities to pursue his dream of full sovereignty as distinct from the Dominion status which had emerged from the Treaty. As Dr Cronin has written: 'His behaviour in early negotiations with the British fits in with the general pattern of Treaty dismantlement which he pursued in office.'[32] In June 1932, at a meeting with the representatives of the British government in Dublin, Dominion Secretary J. H. Thomas and Secretary for War Lord Hailsham, to deal with the annuities issue, de Valera brought 'national, not economic, issues to the fore by haranguing the British once more with his document number two'.[33] At this meeting, de Valera told the British side that the next £3 million instalment of land annuities would not be paid. The British responded with the Special Duties Act on 14 July 1932 that put a 20 per-cent duty on most Irish agricultural imports. The Irish replied in turn on 22 July with the Emergency Duties Bill, which put a reciprocal 20 per-cent duty on British industrial exports such as coal, cement, and electrical machinery. Britain paid a price for this policy, but for Ireland the price was much higher. Some 96 per cent of all Irish exports went to Britain: the new policy was highly expensive, costing Ireland some £18 million per year for the duration of the war. In particular, this policy hit the stronger farmers, who were the mainstay of Irish cattle exports.

---

[31] *Mayo News*, 4 Feb. 1933.
[32] Mike Cronin, 'Economics and Informal Empire in the Irish Free State', in Mike Cronin and John M. Regan (eds.), *Ireland: The Politics of Independence, 1922–49* (London, 2000), 155.
[33] Ibid.

These angry rural conservatives allowed themselves to listen to the new leadership of Eoin O'Duffy, who admired continental fascism. The Blueshirt movement—relying in the main on strong farmers and their sons[34]—convulsed the Irish countryside in 1933–4: the government contained the threat. Fianna Fail policies may have been disruptive, but they were not quite so palpably disastrous as their opponents predicted.[35] The government also had sufficient pragmatism to back away from the wilder shores of agrarian radicalism.

As part of the price of defeating Blueshirtism, agrarian radicalism was destined to be disappointed. Pragmatism began to reassert itself in Anglo-Irish relations. The Irish government initiated a discussion with the British government. The British proved receptive, thanks in part to a fear that Irish farmers might be converted to German coal, which could deprive the depressed British coal industry of Irish markets. The Coal–Cattle pact of January 1935 increased the British quota on cattle imports from Ireland by one-third in return for a comparable increase in Irish coal imports from Britain; it would be renewed annually until superseded by the Anglo-Irish Trade Agreement of 1938 as 'a business transaction based on the mutual interests of the two countries'. Professor Lee notes: 'The pact marked a recognition by de Valera that historical illusion must sometimes succumb to historical reality.'[36]

Fianna Fail policies did enjoy some success. In fact, employment in manufacturing rose from 118,219 to 138,109 between 1926 and 1936, and the gains were heavily concentrated in the Dublin area and Leinster.[37] Fine Gael, the successor to Cumann na nGaedheal, began to change its approach in the beginning of 1936; by 1937 its manifesto gave full support to the industrial movement. Nonetheless, industrial development aside, as the 'economic war' with Britain was wound down, the government was clearly open to the charge that it was losing its radical nationalist tinge. By November 1937 the Department of Finance was increasingly assertive on

---

[34] For a recent discussion of this movement and its fascist leadership and mass base of rural conservatives, see Paul Bew, Ellen Hazelkorn, and Henry Patterson, *The Dynamics of Irish Politics* (London, 1989), 59–66; for two important studies in similar vein, see M. Cronin, *The Blueshirts and Irish Politics* (Dublin, 1979), 49–51 and F. McGarry, *Eoin O'Duffy: A Self-Made Hero* (Oxford, 2005), 242.

[35] This is the key point in the valuable anonymous essay, 'The Blueshirts and the IRA', *Quarterly Review*, 261: 518 (Oct. 1933), 303–4. The same writer, discussing the possibility of a fascist seizure of power, rejects it but adds: 'what is unimaginable is a majority vote of the electorate along the lines that bourgeois commonsense, or even philosophical liberalism, would dictate.'

[36] J. J. Lee, *Ireland 1912–85: Politics and Society* (Cambridge, 1989), 241.

[37] Mary Daly, *Industrial Development and Irish National Identity 1922–39* (Dublin, 1992), 109.

the subject of ending the economic war: an essential move, it was felt, in the battle to reduce the uncertainties which plagued the prospects for the Irish economy.[38] But there was to be at least a programme of compensating ideological work. The project of the 1937 constitution simultaneously allowed the government to maintain its new appeal to the centre with an attempt to massage sentiment in traditional heartlands. As Leon O'Broin puts it in his autobiography *Just Like Yesterday*, de Valera was 'trying to placate left-wing Republicans with national phrases and pious people with expressly Catholic bits'.[39]

The constitution, therefore, stresses the unifying elements of Irish political culture, which were patriarchal Catholicism, nationalism (the claim on the North), and, hardly surprisingly in a nation of peasant proprietors, property rights. Much of this ideology went back to the Cosgrave government. The Eucharistic Congress of 1932 had shown the intensity of popular Catholic piety. In February 1935 the sale or importation of contraceptives was forbidden—as late as 1974, a government bill to liberalize this legislation was defeated, with the Taoiseach voting against. As Angela Clifford remarks on the subject, there were very few discordant voices when the 'Constitution of a Catholic state' (Sean MacEntee) was being debated. She notes: 'The striking feature of the Dail discussion on divorce was that the legislators were indulging in the favourite Catholic practice of discussing the esoteric points of Church law, rather than examining the social results that would follow from the constitutional provisions.'[40] The constitution also reflected the very specific approach of Eamon de Valera.[41] Inevitably, the text reflected the Catholicity of the majority of the island's inhabitants. Article 44 declared that the state recognized the special position of the Holy Catholic Apostolic and Roman Church as the guardian of the Faith possessed by the great majority of its citizens. But Article 44 also afforded state recognition to the Protestant denominations, the Quakers, and the Jewish congregations. Article 41, however, gave a particular force to Catholic thinking: divorce was forbidden, as, indeed, it had been since 1925. The Irish language was formally declared to be the first official language. The 1937 constitution contained a crucial formulation on the partition question. Article 2 declared 'the national territory consists of the whole island of Ireland, its islands, the territorial seas'. Article 3 seemed to take the matter further. It spoke 'of the

---

[38] Thomas M. Feeney, 'Séan MacEntee and the Development of Public Policy in Independent Ireland', unpublished Ph.D thesis, University of Dublin (2005), 46.

[39] Leon O'Broin, *Just Like Yesterday* (Dublin, 1986), 184.

[40] Augela Clifford, *The Constitutional History of Eire-Ireland* (Belfast, 1987), 119.

[41] Sean Faughnan, 'The Jesuits and the Drafting of the 1937 Constitution', *Irish Historical Studies*, 26: 101 (May 1988); Dermot Keogh, *The Vatican, the Bishops and Irish Politics* (Cambridge, 1986), 209–13.

right of the [Dublin] Parliament and Government ... to exercise jurisdiction over the whole of that territory'. At the same time, this provision made a tactical retreat, in that, in effect, it stated 'that the laws enacted in Dublin have effect only in the Twenty-Six Counties'. The 1937 constitution intended itself to be a form of loyalty oath, a statement of national beliefs, ideals, and aspirations. At this level, it was a highly successful statement; unfortunately, it also excluded, even more forcefully, those people on the island of Ireland who felt themselves not to be a part of the Catholic nationalist bloc. Veteran republican Thomas Hales (Fianna Fail TD for Cork West) observed sardonically that those who were actually prepared to fight for Irish unity would find themselves imprisoned under Article 38, which set up the special courts. Eamon Donnelly, a Fianna Fail TD with strong northern roots, argued that Irish unity should precede the drafting of any constitution. Frank McDermott (Independent) was alone in stressing that the constitution could further alienate northern unionists. 'To achieve unity,' he declared, 'we have got to offer them an Ireland in which a place can be found for their traditions and aspirations, as well as ours. Until we are willing to do this, we are partitionists at heart, no matter how loudly we prate about unity.'[42]

Was this a fair charge? The Dail debate on the Anglo-Irish Treaty in 1938, in which de Valera won the return of the Treaty ports, is particularly revealing in this context. Mr Timothy Linehan (Fine Gael: North Cork) pointed out that de Valera had not attempted to persuade the British Prime Minister to improve the political conditions of the nationalist minority in the North.

He could have got some guarantees from Mr Chamberlain that would prevent this puppet parliament in the north from gerrymandering, that would prevent them from victimising and treating the Nationalist minority in the north as they have been treated for the last 16 or 17 years, and as they are still being treated today.

Mr Richard Anthony (Independent Labour: Cork City) interjected irreverently: 'Sure, we gerrymandered ourselves.' But Martin Corry, republican veteran and Fianna Fail TD for Cork East, acknowledged that the House had differing views as to how to achieve Irish unity. He had, however, his own final solution to the northern problem: 'I am personally in favour of storing up sufficient poison gas, so that when you get the wind in the right direction, you can start at the border, and let it travel, and follow it.'[43]

42 Clifford, *Constutional History*, 122.
43 *Dail Eireann Debates*, 29 Apr. 1938, cols. 315–18.

INTER-WAR NORTHERN IRELAND: 'ORANGE TERROR?'

In 1943 Eamon Donnelly was asked to read and comment upon a powerful new analysis of the partition problem. In Donnelly's view this work 'erred on the side of tolerance' and did not point vividly enough to the 'terrors, torture and persecutions' of the northern minority. What was this work? In August 1943 a writer using the pen-name 'Ultach' published *Orange Terror*,[44] the classic Catholic nationalist critique of the operation of the state in Northern Ireland. The author, J. J. Campbell (1910–79), was a clever young classicist and teacher at St Malachy's College. But, for all Ultach's emphasis on unjust and oppressive treatment of northern Catholics, he insisted 'that Catholics are persecuted ... is not due directly to the fact of partition itself, but is on the other hand an essential feature of the regime'.[45] It was not the 'result of some vicious streak in the character of the Orangemen ... it is a necessary feature of the administration'.[46] Employing Waldemar Gurian's theoretical analysis of the common features of the Nazi and Soviet systems, Ultach, in particular, claimed to find the Unionist regime had much in common with the totalitarian model. In particular, Ultach pointed out: 'Both governments [Nazi and Bolshevik] require a state of political high tension to keep the masses in movement.'[47] For Ultach, the Orange system worked in the same way, with the Catholics in Northern Ireland playing the same role as, for example, the Jew in Germany: the permanently insidious subversive threat. All of these regimes—Nazi, Soviet, and Unionist—presented measures of coercion as, in fact, measures of self-defence against dangerous enemies.

The Unionists, it is said, had permitted elections, but only those they were sure to win. Ultach argued, not without reason, that the abolition of proportional representation for the local parliament in 1929 had been designed to enforce a unanimity of opinion amongst Protestants. Ultach even claimed—less convincingly, perhaps—an analogy between the Unionist practice of allowing criticism of the government by extreme Orangemen with the Soviet practice of 'self-criticism'. In fact, though, Ultach's picture is clearly overdrawn. The Nazi regime was unwilling to tolerate any discrete subcultures, while the Unionists were prepared to tolerate the nationalist subculture, so long as it knew its limits.

---

[44] *Orange Terror*, Ard Righh Press edn. (Belfast, 1998), 50. This edition includes the responses of Donnelly, Blythe, and others.
[45] Ibid. 24.   [46] Ibid. 13.   [47] Ibid.

There is, however, no doubt that the Unionist political leadership, freed, after all, from the credible threat of violent subversion after 1922, displayed a significant hardening of opinion, reinforced by the dynamics of political competition within the Stormont system. Sir James Craig's views underwent a particularly significant evolution. Craig had entered politics when 'traditional Unionism' was challenged by serious social divisions in the 1902–6 epoch.[48] It left him with an indelible conviction that Protestant votes had to be earned and could not be taken for granted. However, during the great crisis which led to the establishment of the Northern Ireland Parliament, Craig had not been afraid to espouse 'broad views' and 'tolerant ideals', as he put it in 1921. He was also concerned to protect, so far as possible, the Protestant interest throughout the island. Provost Traill's original conception that partition would not be a 'carnival of reaction' in James Connelly's famous phrase, a feast of sectarian oppression, but rather would protect minority rights—if only because both states had vulnerable minorities, so that each felt concern for those on the other side of the border—appeared as if it might be borne out. But the Protestant community in the south and west dropped dramatically in numbers: by 1925 one-third of the pre-war population had gone. Craig ceased to think in broader terms: when, in 1934, Donegal Presbyterians petitioned en masse for transfer back to the North, they received little real attention.[49] Craig grew increasingly cynical about London politicians who had asked him to govern Northern Ireland in the most difficult and violent circumstances in 1921–2 and then tried, in his view, to undermine him. Increasingly, he saw Stormont as a bulwark against all enemies, internal and external.

But Stormont could be lost: in particular, Craig began to fear the emergence of extreme Protestant movements, with their vote-splitting capacities. The Scottish Protestant League, a populist political splinter-group in Glasgow, gave rise to the Ulster Protestant League, which he loathed. All the more reason to reassure the Protestant population that he had their concerns at heart. Of course, management of such a constituency was by no means an easy task. Lord Charlemont, his liberal Minister of Education, noted in February 1936 'the trend of present politics ... unless the Herodianism of the Protestant League can be out-Heroded, I, a supporter of the Government, will lose my seat to a Jackanapes.'[50] Charlemont's reference to the

---

[48] Alvin Jackson, 'Irish Unionism and the Russellite Threat, 1894–1906', *Irish Historical Studies*, 25: 100 (Nov. 1987), 376–404; T. P. Daly, 'James Craig and Orangeism', *Irish Historical Studies*, 24: 156 (Nov. 2005), 431–48.
[49] Dennis Kennedy, *The Widening Gulf* (Belfast, 1988), 225.
[50] Paul Bew, Kenneth Darwin, and Gordon Gillespie, *Passion and Prejudice: Nationalist/Unionist Conflict in Ulster in the 1930s and the Origins of the Irish Association*, (Belfast, 1993), 50.

Ulster Protestant League is instructive: the city council elections of May 1936 showed that prominent UPL candidates could defeat Ulster Unionists—for example, in Duncairn—and Craig typically was very nervous on the subject, noting that similar ultra-Protestant zealotry in Glasgow had helped Labour, but that in Northern Ireland, of course, the split in the centre-right vote would aid a far more dangerous enemy, nationalism.[51]

'I am convinced that to have accepted direct rule by Westminster in all matters, as an alternative to the Act of 1920, would in the long run have been against the interests of Ulster,' Craig declared in January 1934, adding: 'I believe Ulster and Belfast have been built on years and years of the most perfect democracy one could conceive.'[52] Sectarian language became more and more widely used in the 1930s. In March 1934 Sir Basil Brooke, then Minister of Agriculture, famously declared that Protestants should employ only 'Protestant lads and lasses',[53] and for all that he himself did not keep to this advice,[54] it had a strong and polarizing impact on political debate.[55] Craig had fallen increasingly into the acceptance of a new 'common sense'. In this mindset the solution to the Irish question was a simple one: Protestant majority rule in the north-east and Catholic majority rule in the south and west. Gone was his old acquaintance Stephen Gwynn's obsession and concerns about respect for the rights of minorities, even if a certain sentimental Irishry did not fully disappear: 'While we are Ulstermen, we are also Irishmen',[56] he insisted in May 1936.

On 15 January 1935 Lord Charlemont, the most liberal mind in the Cabinet, wrote to a close friend, Major-General Hugh Montgomery: 'Can a Roman Catholic be loyal to a Protestant government? Yes, I think so.' He added:

The thoughtful Roman Catholics in Ulster in these times will discount the exuberant utterances of politicians, even perhaps going so far as to allow for the circumstances in which they say them, for he knows that the ordinary Roman Catholic can go about his business without interference from anyone in the administration.

Charlemont added: 'It's far worse to live under oppressive laws than to have to read speeches in the *News Letter*.'[57] Of course, Charlemont here is setting the bar rather low and asking rather a lot of his Catholic fellow

[51] Graham Walker, ' "Protestantism before Party!": The Ulster Protestant League in the 1930s', *Historical Journal*, 28: 4 (1985), 965.
[52] *Irish Times*, 8 Jan. 1934.
[53] Brian Barton, *Brookeborough: The Making of a Prime Minister* (Belfast, 1989), 84–9.
[54] *Guardian*, 24 Aug. 1992.
[55] Jonathan Bardon, *A History of Ulster* (Belfast, 1982), 538–9.
[56] *Irish News*, 7 May 1936.
[57] Bew, Darwin, and Gillespie, *Passion and Prejudice*, 7.

citizens. 'Going about business' is here loosely defined, and running into 'B' Specials late at night could be a frustrating and unpleasant experience for ordinary Catholics. Nor was it always possible to go about one's business without interference. The month of July 1935 was to be dominated by large-scale sectarian violence. The death-toll stood at seven Protestants, three Catholics—but while only a handful of Protestants had to leave their houses, some 2,000 Catholics had to move from their dwellings.[58] The liberals in the Cabinet reproached themselves for not taking a stronger stand: Charlemont wrote to Montgomery on 14 August: 'I don't think the [liberals] have been sufficiently outspoken in their opinions; it is agreeable to be in a cabinet, the members of which are all friends, but it has its drawbacks from the point of view of public policy.'[59] But by the end of the month the tone of the discussion had deteriorated. A working-class Unionist figure, William Grant MP, wrote to the press insisting that 99 per cent of Catholics were disloyal and thus responsible for the suspicions of the majority. The main Catholic newspaper, the *Irish News*, responded with a weary dignity: 'Northern Nationalists had, for a long time past, recognised that the Northern Ireland Parliament has come to stay for a long time.' The *Irish News* concluded: 'The truth, however uncongenial, is that [the Catholics] are not rebels: they are loyal citizens and outside a few quarters of Belfast and a few fanatics in the country, they are recognised and respected as loyal citizens by their fellow Protestant countrymen.'[60] But this call for mutual respect was met in 1936 by the radical local-government gerrymander in the Unionist interest in the city of Derry:[61] at first designed to be only a temporary move, it lasted for more than three decades.

The key problem for the Unionist government was the nature of the response to moderate overtures from the nationalist community. Should it encourage a line of populist exclusiveness which served only to alienate further the minority? Or should it seek to encourage the acquiescence of the minority? It became clear, when the archives of the inter-war Unionist regime were opened, that there was considerable internal debate within and around the Cabinet about these matters. But, in most instances, it was resolved in favour of those who stressed the importance of maintaining Protestant unity against developing a more flexible approach towards the Catholic minority. The consequence was a growing Whitehall unease

[58] A. C. Hepburn, *A Past Apart: Studies of the History of Catholic Belfast* (Belfort, 1996), 183.

[59] Bew, Darwin, and Gillespie, *Passion and Prejudice*, 11.

[60] *Irish News*, 26 Aug. 1935.

[61] Tom Hennessy, *A History of Northern Ireland 1920–1996* (Dublin, 1997), 113; Patrick Buckland, *Factory of Grievances* (Dublin, 1997), 242–3.

about conditions in the North: an unease which had a particular political importance, because Northern Ireland's growing financial dependence in the harsh inter-war years weakened Belfast's industrial strength.[62] As Sir Richard Hopkins at the Treasury was to put it near the end of the decade:

When the Northern Irish government was set up, it was expected that their revenues would be sufficient both to meet their expenses and to provide a substantial contribution to Imperial services (defence, debt etc.). This expectation was realised at first fully and later in a diminishing degree. Since 1931 Northern Ireland has been, in effect, a depressed area. So, far from receiving any large Imperial contribution, we have invented a series of *dodges* and *devices* to give them *gifts* and *subventions* within the ambit of the Government of Ireland Act so as to save Northern Ireland from coming openly on the dole as Newfoundland did.[63]

Hopkins's note implies that the general position of Britain and Northern Ireland, within the world economy, was not subject to control by the Northern Irish government. Other documents make it clear that this was, in fact, his view, and explain his willingness to resort to what he later described as 'wangles' and 'fudges' to help the regime.[64] 'The fact is that they copy all our legislation and that, therefore, we set their general standard, for better or worse. In times like these, that standard means bankruptcy for a small community which is suffering terribly from unemployment.'[65]

But everyone wanted to ensure the continued flow of funds from Westminster. Even the highly conservative Sir Wilfred Spender admitted: 'I am sharply concerned that the Ulster working classes appreciate the benefits of the British connection, but if this were severed a large proportion of those resident in Northern Ireland would change to socialistic tendencies.'[66] Inevitably, however, some of these benefits trickled through to the Catholic population.

Crucial to an understanding of northern Catholic attitudes towards partition is the issue of material welfare. As far back as August 1927 Cahir Healy, the greatest leader of inter-war republicanism and nationalism, advised a Fermanagh curate that this problem, if not tackled, 'could act as a barrier to national unity'. In 1939 he and other northern nationalist

---

[62] See Paul Bew *et al.*, *The State in Northern Ireland* (Manchester, 1979), chs. 2–3.

[63] PRO T 160/1138/15586. Hopkins's document for Sir F. Philips, 8 February 1939. As early as 24 November 1930 Bewley wrote to Waley: 'Any honest statement of the position cannot help pointing out the fact that we now subsidise Northern Ireland to the tune of a million a year or more', PRO T 160/430/12302.

[64] PRO T 160/550/F6562/021/1, Hopkins to the Chancellor, 16 May 1933.

[65] Ibid., same to same, 10 May 1933.

[66] PRONI D715, Spender to Gen. Montgomery, 2 Nov. 1937.

leaders warned de Valera of the erosion of 'national spirit' by the 'English dole system and other social services'.[67]

Ernest Blythe was reflecting on this reality when he rejected 'Ultach's talk of the six-county 'state' and rejected the comparison with international totalitarianism. But there is a powerful sense in which Ultach tacitly admitted this himself. Ultach specifically refused to advocate a traditional nationalist campaign; it was precisely for this reason that Eamon Donnelly mocked his moderation. Ultach insisted, instead, that the focus should be on a campaign against religious discrimination.

The weakness of the Orange position is in the fact that its politics are based on the persecution of a group whose only overall distinguishing feature is its religion. Admittedly, the restoration to Catholics of their political rights would not mean the immediate end of partition: but it would mean that the north would settle down to a normal social and political life: that a body of political opinion could be formed in freedom and that the people could be persuaded of the futility of partition.

Ultach added: 'Again, the persecution of a religious minority is the one injustice which you can take before any tribunal. English people don't like it.'[68] A good propaganda campaign in England would completely discredit the Northern Irish government and bring about a new policy. Needless to say, no genuinely totalitarian regime could be challenged by such methods, and Ultach is here tacitly moving away from the comparison of Ulster Unionism with Soviet Communism or German Nazism. He was also putting his finger on the Belfast administration's ultimate vulnerability.

Dean W. S. Kerr, a Wicklow Protestant with good memories of Catholic toleration in that county, responded to Ultach's arguments. Kerr, an anti-Catholic polemicist in certain moods, had, in his writings during the First World War, shown a capacity for a certain type of relatively thoughtful Unionist argumentation. He now developed a stronger anti-nationalist line. In 1901 there were 84,992 Catholics in Belfast; in 1937 the number had risen to 104,372. In the independent part of Ireland the population had fallen between 1901 and 1936 by 104,351. These figures hardly implied that Northern Ireland was an especially unfriendly place for Catholics. Kerr cited several recent examples of Protestant willingness to elect Catholics to leading positions in the professional life of the province. He argued that the repression of the Irish state against republicans was harsher than that of Northern Ireland, but that a double standard operated in the evaluation of the activities of the state in Northern Ireland. With the outbreak of the

---

[67] Enda Staunton, review of Eamon Phoenix, 'Northern Nationalism: Nationalist Politics, Partition and the Catholic Minority in Northern Ireland 1890–1940', *Irish Political Studies*, 10 (1995), 238.

[68] *Orange Terror*, 61.

Second World War both states took stern action against the IRA, but the de Valera regime was, indeed, rather more harsh. But the really striking passage in Kerr's essay lay in his exploration of Ernest Blythe's comment on Ultach. Blythe stressed the

importance of the existence, both north and south, of an illegal underground military organisation. He tells how its activities have led to arrests, police searches and internment in the south. I see no reason to doubt that its existence and activities in the north are the main cause of the continuance into the present day of the police activities of which *Ultach* complains so bitterly ... Catholic opposition [is] to the very existence of the northern 'state' in general; and when a secret military organisation is operating against the said 'state', it is only natural that politicians should be ready to suspect almost any Catholic.[69]

But Ultach had, in his own way, sidetracked that argument: 'I am leaving out the physical force solution ... if taken as granted that there must be no wholesale coercion, then the alternative is agreement.'[70]

Orange Terror, for all its excessive polemical zeal, had exposed the weakness of the Unionist system. Ultach had posed the question—what would happen if the English paymaster of the Northern Irish system decided that the sectarian prejudices of the Unionist leadership were simply no longer acceptable? When that moment came, in 1969, 'Ultach', who had never told his children that he was the author of *Orange Terror*, was available as the distinguished academic, Professor J. J. Campbell of Queen's University, to be one of the three co-authors of the Cameron Report, which spelled the end of the most obviously blatant features of sectarianism in the Northern Ireland state.

WORLD WAR AND ITS AFTERMATH: IRISH NATIONALISM

The British decision to concede the Treaty ports to de Valera in 1938 took on a very different aspect in 1940: what had seemed in 1938 a civilized *rapprochement* with Ireland—setting a good example for all Europe—appeared foolhardy in 1940. To the fury of Sir Wilfrid Spender, who cared obsessively about this matter of imperial security, Sir James Craig himself had encouraged the deal—provided he received further financial concessions from the

---

[69] 'Slander on Ulster', one of a series of articles published in the *Bell*, Dublin (Feb. 1944), issued by the Ulster Unionist Council, Glengall Street Belfast, p. 2. See also Daithi Ó Corráin, ' "Ireland in his heart north and south": The Contribution of Ernest Blythe to the Partition Question', *Irish Historical Studies*, 35: 137 (May 2006), 61–81.
[70] 'Slander on Ulster', 61.

Treasury. Craig, like many others, had believed that Chamberlain's policy of appeasement would work. When this proved not to be true, Britain found itself strategically exposed on its Irish flank. In the lead-up to the Treaty negotiations, David Lloyd George had declared on 18 July 1921:

> There can be no doubt in the mind of any reasonable man that if Ireland were given complete independence, with its own army and control of its own ports and powers to enter into treaties with foreign nations, whether they were friendly or hostile to us, that would place Britain in a position of such peril that I should hesitate to think what would befall in the event of a repetition of either the great struggle with Napoleon or the great struggle with Germany.[71]

But, in effect, this was the position Britain now found itself in. Exposed, vulnerable, and worried, the British exerted pressure for a deal which would garner them Irish support in the war. The new United States ambassador to Dublin, David Gray, arrived in Dublin in April 1940. Gray, a cousin of the President, Franklin Delano Roosevelt, had attended a private family dinner at the White House shortly before leaving for Europe, and had gained an intimate grasp of the President's strategy. He was well aware of Roosevelt's desire to break the grip of isolationist forces in US politics and support Britain against Hitler. In such a situation, Gray felt it incumbent upon him to facilitate such an outcome. In the Irish context this meant pushing the British and Ulster Unionists towards Irish unity as part of a deal whereby Ireland would support Britain in the war, and part of US anti-war opinion (the Irish-American section) would be broken down.[72] For example, before leaving for a visit to Northern Ireland in June 1940, Gray was visited by the British representative in Dublin, Sir John Maffey. Maffey was, at this point, doing his utmost to bring London and Dublin closer together, at the expense, it should be noted, of the Belfast government: at the beginning of May 1940 he arranged, with de Valera's consent, for two of his ministers, Lemass and Ryan, to call at Buckingham Palace.[73] Maffey told Gray that Craig (now Lord Craigavon) had recently been called to London, where he had been given 'merry hell' and all but ordered to 'end partition on the best terms he could'.[74]

---

[71] Centurion, 'The Irish Treason and its Authors', *National Review*, 79 (1922), 697–8.

[72] For Gray's resolute activity in this respect, see T. Ryle Dwyer, *Irish Neutrality and the USA* (Dublin, 1977), ch. 3, 'David Gray, the USA and Partition'.

[73] DO130/84/275/29. Maffey recalls this moment in the minute of a conversation with Eamon de Valera, held on 16 October 1947. This document is also to be found at Prem 8/847/Secret Serial No 4, with a note from Philip Noel Baker, Colonial Secretary, recommending it to the Prime Minister. Maffey always believed that Lemass was pro-Allies and not a supporter of Irish neutrality. *Irish Times*, 2 Jan. 1995, 'British profile held Lemass was opposed to neutrality'.

[74] Dwyer, *Irish Neutrality and the USA*, 54.

Gray was delighted with this news. At this point he had significant emotional sympathy for Irish nationalism, and regarded the Ulster Unionist leadership as parochial 'Bourbons', who were the sole obstacle to Irish unity and, therefore, gaining Irish support for the anti-Nazi alliance. It was a view which he slowly came to change; in the end, Gray concluded that de Valera had no intention of supporting Britain, even if Irish unity was delivered, and that Lord Craigavon's suspicions were entirely justified.

My pro-Irish sympathies had made me a sitting duck for the Great Idealist [Gray later wrote]: He believed that Germany would win the war. He wanted Northern Ireland without strings. In payment, he had secretly offered an Irish neutrality which would tear the allies from the German ports, also Irish influence in America to prevent American intervention in the war.

Craigavon 'outmanoeuvred him', said Gray later and to good effect.

But in the summer of 1940 David Gray's views were rather different: the Ulster Unionists should ally quickly with de Valera. Irish unity was a small price to pay for the defeat of Hitler. But the cause of diplomacy was to be complicated by espionage and the triumph of German armies on the continent. On 5 May Dr Hermann Goertz, a German spy, parachuted safely into Co. Meath. He landed on the estate of Captain Harry Fowler, but lost his parachute: this was recovered by one of Fowler's cowherds, who reported the matter to the police.[75] The Irish authorities were thus aware of the parachute drop, but until 22 May they did not know who had been dropped or why.[76] Within a few days Ireland was shaken by further threatening news. On 10 May Germany invaded Holland, Belgium, and Luxembourg. At Galway, de Valera said in response:

I was at Geneva [i.e. the League of Nations] on many occasions ... The representative of Belgium and the Netherlands were people that I met frequently, because we co-operated not a little with the northern group of nations. Today, these two nations are fighting for their lives, and I think I would be unworthy of this small nation, if, on an occasion like this, I did not utter our protest against the wrong which has been done to them.[77]

But suddenly, the Irish state's line appeared to change. On 14 May Frank McDermott, the Irish correspondent of the London *Sunday Times*, submitted his copy, praising and quoting de Valera's Galway speech, with the idea that it would appear in the newspaper on 19 May. To his surprise,

---

[75] Gray Mss, 'Behind the Green Door', University of Wyoming Library, ch. 8, p. 7.
[76] Mark Hull, *Irish Secrets: German Espionage in Wartime Ireland* (Dublin, 2003), 87–93.
[77] Coogan, *De Valera*, 547.

the Irish censor excised the paragraphs praising the speech. The German ambassador in Dublin, Eduard Hempel, it appears, had protested against de Valera's language, and Irish Foreign Minister, Frank Aiken, had decided to uphold Hempel. David Gray argued it was 'de Valera's tragedy' that, on 12 May 1940, he recognized the 'decisive gulf' between Nazism and his own Christian values and then almost immediately decided 'secretly to apologise for it and suppress Irish discussion of the difference between the Nazis and the Christian way of life'.[78]

On 15 May 1940 Colonel Liam Archer of Irish Intelligence told Guy Liddell, MI5's Director of Counter-Intelligence, that if the Germans landed Irish resistance would not last more than a week. 'He was quite emphatic that Eire would be thinking about their independence and that many people would not mind Great Britain getting a licking. On the other hand, somebody who had expressed this view to him concluded by saying: "But what would happen to us if they did?" '[79]

At this point, the Irish government received yet more worrying news. Stephen Held, an Irish citizen of German extraction, dismissed his domestic servant, giving her an unusually large cash gift.[80] The girl reported the matter to the police, and on 22 May the police raided Held's house. The spy, Hermann Goertz, was able to make his escape and stay at large until 27 November 1941. But his German uniform was discovered, as well as his transmitter and the suit bought for him in Switzers by Mrs Francis Stuart and Maude Gonne MacBride. (Ironically, David Gray, a man with strong literary interests, had already called at the house of Francis Stuart, the novelist, only to discover he was in Berlin.)[81] Most disturbing of all was a cache of papers concerning the preparations for an airborne attack. The Germans, it seemed, were on the verge of an invasion in alliance with the IRA. Despite the anti-Fascist line of the movement in the early and mid-1930s, the IRA had drifted into an alliance with the Nazis. Dr Brian Hanley has argued that the marginalization and decline of the IRA—membership fell from 12,000 in 1933 to 2,000 by the late 1930s—contributed to the Nazi alliance.[82] But the fact remains: in January 1939 the IRA felt strong enough to begin its bombing campaign in Britain, which led to seven civilian

---

[78] Gray, 'Behind the Green Door', ch. 7, is devoted to this incident.

[79] Nigel West (ed.), *The Guy Liddell Diaries*, vol. 1: *1939–1942* (London, 2005), 15 May 1940, p. 79.

[80] Gray, 'Behind the Green Door', ch. 10, p. 1.

[81] A serious republican and novelist, Francis Stuart was a broadcaster for the Nazis in this period, see David O'Donoghue, *Hitler's Irish Voices* (London, 1998), esp. 99–105.

[82] Brian Hanley, 'Oh Here's to Adolf Hitler: The IRA and the Nazis', *History Ireland*, 13: 3 (May–June 2005), 31–5.

deaths and the execution of two IRA men. The IRA Magazine Fort raid of 23 December 1939 seized all the Irish army ammunition stocks, 1 million rounds, and provoked intense fears of subversion.[83] When he arrived in Dublin in April 1940, the American ambassador David Gray observed that the IRA could place significant bodies of reasonably impressive marching men on the streets, and was, to his surprise, still a factor in national and international politics.

These discoveries came as a bombshell. They indicated that the IRA had far more effective German links than had been suspected, and had developed a plan for joint action in Northern Ireland—the scenario which de Valera most feared.[84] The biggest threat of this kind was 'Plan Kathleen'. Goertz told his Irish captors, following his arrest in November 1941: 'The general idea of the plan was an invasion of Northern Ireland by German forces with the assistance of the IRA, who would come in from Ballyshannon and Dundalk.'[85] The plan envisaged a landing in the neighbourhood of Londonderry (in the manner of Narvik) and a successful conquest of Ulster with assistance from the IRA. The IRA intended to contribute a ground offensive beginning in Co. Leitrim, with a front on Lower and Upper Lough Erne, which would, somehow, lead to the destruction of all British forces in Northern Ireland.[86]

The original author of Plan Kathleen was an amateur military strategist, a Belfast man, Liam Gaynor.[87] Gaynor was a former Dail civil servant, who met Stephen Held in mid-July 1939. Their early conversations took a historical turn. Gaynor vigorously defended Wolfe Tone against the charge of being a 'Protestant adventurer'. He pointed out that 'Tone had cut adrift from his own Protestant associates and worked and suffered with his downtrodden Catholic brothers'.[88] Held was impressed by Gaynor's intellectual ability; by September 1939 the discussion had moved from the historical to more pressing political matters. Held asked him 'what he would consider necessary for the Germans to do if they thought of invading this country'.[89] Plan Kathleen was the result of Gaynor's musings on this topic.

[83] NLI Lr. Col. Niall C. Harrington Ms, 40,633/1–4, Harrington's 30-page analysis, 27 Jan. 1942, unflinchingly reveals the scale of official embarrassment.
[84] Eunan O'Halpin, *Defending Ireland: The Irish State and its Enemies Since 1922* (Oxford, 1999), 249.
[85] National Archives, 'The Plan Kathleen', KV2/1323, MIF/BIH, 28 Feb. 1942.
[86] Mark M. Hull, *Irish Secrets: German Espionage in Wartime Ireland* (Dublin, 2003), 90.
[87] Ibid. 91.
[88] National Archives, London, KV2/1323. Liam Gaynor—117 Homefarm Road, Drumcondra, Dublin—author of the 'Kathleen Plan'. This document is based on intelligence provided by Irish intelligence to London.
[89] Ibid.

Gaynor may have been an armchair general, but de Valera was shaken: it was the potential political appeal of the strategy which frightened him. On 6 June 1940 de Valera discussed affairs with Gray.

He went to the map of Donegal Bay, where Lough Esk extends north of the border, 50 miles to the north-east, the head of Lough Swilly. 'If I were the Germans,' he said, 'I would land at these points and proclaim myself a liberator. If they should do that, what I could do, I do not know'. [He might have added that, in 1804, another potential invader, Napoleon, also saw the strategic significance of Lough Swilly]. Then he added: 'Please don't mention that to anybody. It might get around'.[90]

Gray was impressed by de Valera's tone, and his view of the Taoiseach as a genuine anti-Nazi was reinforced. Gray reported to the President of the United States on 6 June 1940:

I think I have mentioned to you that de Valera always maintains such a dead pan—no meeting of the eye—that the idea comes back to me that I am taking a big personal responsibility in giving my English friends and you the picture of him as out and out anti-Nazi. Well, a little thing occurred at our last session, which really assured me. He was talking about a German (Jew), a Nobel Prize winner, who left Germany, engaged for the Institute for Advanced Studies, Professor Schroedinger. The man is now in abject terror in Ireland, fearing that the Gestapo is going to get him, and de Valera is more concerned over him than many much more important matters. In asking if I could help in getting him to America, he spoke of the Germans in a way that left no doubt of his feelings.

In fact, Schroedinger, though undoubtedly an enemy of the Nazis, was not Jewish; he was attending Protestant church services in Dublin, while having his daughter raised as a Catholic. However, for an entirely different and rather more profound reason, Gray, many years later, reviewed his own report to the President with some scepticism. 'The protection of Professor Schroedinger ... will always perplex those who deliver the final verdict on Eamon de Valera. At the present moment, I can only interpret them as another example of that "specious openness", which was his most effective technique of deception.'[91] Gray also felt that the discussion of the IRA–German war plan was also an example of 'specious openness': the technique being to display such apparent frankness of emotion as to deceive

---

[90] 'Behind the Green Door', ch. 8, p. 5. This is a key moment in the formulation of de Valera's tougher policy towards the IRA which led to the execution of George Plant in March 1942; five other IRA men were executed during the war, and another three allowed to die on hunger strike.

[91] Hilary Mantel, 'Schroedinger in Clontarf', *London Review of Books*, 27: 13 (7 July 2005), 13.

the listener into believing that de Valera's core values, at least, were the same as those of his companion in the room.

Later in June 1940 the moderate and conciliatory Irish politician Frank McDermott visited Northern Ireland: on 25 June a northern minister admitted frankly that the Cabinet was divided, but told him that, 'in view of the gravity of the situation and the acute need for the Eire ports, he himself would possibly resign if Craigavon refused to co-operate with Westminster'.[92] MacDermott's source was Basil Brooke, who added that the Cabinet would split on the issue. At the same time, Brooke told his son: 'if we were faced with the choice of losing our civilisation or accepting the unification of Ireland, he would find it a very difficult decision. He regarded western civilisation as of greater worth than anything else, being absolutely convinced of the menace of Nazi Germany'. His son concluded: 'It was my impression ... that in those circumstances, he would do his best to ensure Irish unity.'[93] Returning to Dublin with his hopeful story, MacDermott called upon Frank Aiken. The response was blunt and uninterested: 'MacDermott, get this clear: we are never going to abandon our neutrality.'[94] On 28 June 1940 Neville Chamberlain, the British Prime Minister, conveyed to Eamon de Valera the British offer of unity. The first item was apparently unambiguous: 'A declaration to be made by the United Kingdom government forthwith, accepting the principle of a united Ireland. This declaration would take the form of a solemn undertaking that the union is to become, at an early date, an accomplished fact, from which there shall be no turning back.'[95] The Northern Irish government was effectively ordered to work out the details of union with the government of Eire. Craigavon accused Chamberlain directly of treachery to 'loyal Ulster'. Chamberlain denied this, rather weakly, suggesting that the Northern Ireland government's role as part of the 'joint body' with the government of Eire, set up to work out the 'union of Ireland', would be protection enough. Craigavon replied by saying that, anyway, his 'confidential information' suggested that de Valera was 'under German dictation' and was 'past reasoning with'.[96] The price for Dublin was, of course, a high one: full military co-operation with Britain in the war against Hitler, at a moment

[92] This was Sir Basil Brooke, later Lord Brookeborough, Prime Minister of Northern Ireland; see Barton, *Brookeborough*, 162. There is evidence that MacDermott also had this view.
[93] Hennessy, *A History of Northern Ireland 1920–96*, 89.
[94] John Bowman, *De Valera and the Ulster Question* (Oxford, 1982), 237; Gray, 'Behind the Green Door', ch. 11, p. 4.
[95] O'Day and Stevenson (eds.), *Irish Historical Documents Since 1800*, 201.
[96] PRONI T3775/20/1–8, contains the Craigavon–Chamberlain telegrams, 27–8 June 1940.

when Hitler was very much in the ascendant. On 7 July 1940 Chamberlain wrote to his sister Ida:

The real basic fact is that it is not partition which stands in the way at this moment, but the fear of Dev and his friends that we shall be beaten. They don't want to be on the losing side, and, if that is unheroic, one can only say that it is the attitude of the world from the USA to Romania, and from Japan to Ireland.[97]

The next major subversive German effort was Operation Sealion: Sean Russell and Frank Ryan, two IRA leaders, were to be delivered to Ireland by submarine in August 1940. Russell, however, died suddenly on board before he could be landed. The operation was under the control of Admiral Canaris, who was later executed because of his alleged collusion with the Allies. This has raised the question—was the operation doomed from the start? Later, General Lahousen, when being debriefed by the Allies, told the British authorities: 'Canaris was accused, wrongly, by certain circles of the German Foreign Office of having liquidated Russell.'[98] Lahousen was more inclined to believe that the leftist Ryan murdered Russell, but this is even more unlikely. In August 1940 three northern nationalist politicians—Senator McLaughlin for Armagh (a close associate of Cardinal Macrory), and John Southwell and Peadar Murney for Newry—'decided' at a meeting in Dublin, attended by Hempel, 'to place the Catholic minority in the north under the protection of the Axis powers'.[99]

The British offer in the summer of 1940 of Irish political unity in return for belated entry into the war on the Allied side did not disturb de Valera's resolve to remain outside the conflict. De Valera, in fact, did not turn this offer down out of hand; negotiations continued for several weeks. What decisively determined him to reject Chamberlain's offer? One of de Valera's successors as Taoiseach, Garret FitzGerald, has stressed the role of Joe Walshe, the influential Secretary of the Department of External Affairs, who wrote to de Valera a few days after the negotiations to say that 'if we joined the losing allied side, we would "deservedly have lost our independence"'.[100] Walshe, a believer in the German New Order and the absolute impossibility of German defeat, was so close to the German ambassador Eduard Hempel, that Hempel's children knew him as 'Uncle

[97] *Irish News*, 29 June 1992; Brian Girvin, *The Emergency: Neutral Ireland 1939–45* (London, 2006), 134–5.

[98] NA KV2/1292.

[99] Brian Barton, *Northern Ireland in the Second World War* (Belfast, 1995), 123. This analysis is based on a report by the Irish police to the Department of Justice.

[100] Garret FitzGerald, 'Wartime Neutrality: Theoretical Rather than Real', *Irish Times*, 29 Jan. 2005.

Joe'.[101] Walshe appears to have believed that Germany would leave Ireland alone after it had defeated Britain, because it would not wish to alienate the United States. David Gray came to believe in an even more sinister interpretation: he linked de Valera's frequent public talk in the late 1930s about solving the partition problem by an exchange of populations—the 'Irish' in England for the Protestants of the north of Ireland—with his wartime strategy. Gray concluded:

> The accumulating evidence supports the view that, even before the fall of France in 1940, de Valera believed that Hitler would win the war and that in payment for keeping the allies out of the Eire ports, he would obtain Northern Ireland on his own terms. This would have enabled him to invoke his formula of exchange of populations, expel 800,000 Ulstermen and invite in an equal number of exiles.[102]

A second British offer of unity was to be made in far more propitious circumstances—for the British. On the early morning of 8 December 1941 Sir John Maffey, the British representative in Dublin, delivered a special message to de Valera from Churchill. The context was clear: in the immediate aftermath of the Japanese attack on Pearl Harbor, American involvement in the war against the Axis was certain. The note passed over included the celebrated: 'Now is your chance, now or never, a nation once again.'[103] Churchill's message can, of course, be read, perhaps rather pedantically, as meaning only that Ireland could redeem her national honour by joining the war. But it is worth noting that Churchill was aware that important elements in the Unionist Cabinet would accept Irish unity as a price for Irish support in the war against Hitler. This, therefore, gives the message rather more potential meaning. But did de Valera miss an opportunity to solve the partition issue? His son denies the point. 'Such a theory is without foundation, grossly misleading and patently false, for to take one important point, the Unionists had not been consulted.'

In defence of his father's policy, Terry de Valera has recently written that Britain rather than Germany was the more likely invader of Ireland, and that Britain's intentions towards Ireland were less benign than those of the Nazis. In particular, Terry de Valera stresses the significance of a British War Cabinet memorandum of 8 October 1940, in which it was decided that, in the event of a German invasion of Ireland, the RAF should be prepared to use poison mustard gas, a gas which could hardly have

[101] Gray, 'Behind the Green Door'.
[102] W. A. Carson, *Ulster and the Irish Republic* (Belfast, n.d.), p. v. For de Valera's proposal for an exchange of populations between Irish emigrants in Britain and the Protestants of Northern Ireland, see Bowman, *De Valera and the Ulster Question 1917–73*, 209.
[103] Terry de Valera, *A Memoir* (Dublin, 2004), 212.

discriminated between Irish and German.[104] Terry de Valera's observation also adds that his father's inclination was not to explore the offer: 'As he told me, his primary worry and concern at this point in time was not the solution to partition, but rather the grave danger of an imminent invasion by the British on some pretext for such.'[105]

But although de Valera turned down Churchill's offer, the American entry into the war did lead to a different type of Irish neutrality. Professor O'Halpin's valuable edition of the recently declassified British official history of MI5's Irish section gives, in effect, the founding text of what, in Ireland, is known as the 'pragmatic pro-neutrality argument'.[106] As Christopher Andrew makes clear in his introduction, the document is an anti-Churchill critique. It argues that Irish neutrality on balance helped Britain. Dr Garret FitzGerald has recently argued that it was hardly neutrality, properly understood, at all.[107] The thesis essentially is that de Valera could not have brought a partitioned Ireland into the war on the British side without creating massive internal Irish conflict. In that event, Ireland's contribution of 42,665 men and women to the British armed forces, and many more to her industrial labour force, could not have been made. Meanwhile, potential intelligence problems were sorted out by an unusually high degree of co-operation—a remarkable level, indeed, given traditional Anglo-Irish tensions. In the Goertz case, the real Irish co-operation in this was that they voluntarily agreed to allow his messages to Germany to run, and enabled the British to read them without knowing what they might reveal or that Irish nationals might be compromised; in fact, the messages did reveal that the GoC of the 2nd Division of the Eire Army (Hugo MacNeill), who was well known to be anti-British and pro-German, had been in touch with Goertz before his arrest.

It need hardly be said that no allusion was ever made to this by either side. There is no doubt that this co-ordination was largely due to Colonel Dan Bryan as an intelligence officer and to Dr Hayes' cryptographic zeal. It is very doubtful if his military superiors agreed to the passing of the ciphers to the British and certainly his political superiors would not have done so.[108]

But such an account suppresses two key questions. In a context in which a move to end neutrality was linked to a firm British statement of support

---

[104] Terry de Valera, *A Memoir* (Dublin, 2004), 176; cf also J. P. Duggan, *Ireland and the Third Reich* (Dublin, 1985). But see Ray Raymond, 'Irish Neutrality and Anglo-Irish Relations 1921–41', *International History Review*, 9: 3 (Aug. 1987), 459.

[105] Terry de Valera, *A Memoir*, 212.

[106] *MI5 and Ireland 1939–45: The Official History* (Dublin, 2003).

[107] Garret FitzGerald, *Ireland in the World: Further Reflections* (Dublin, 2005), 124.

[108] O'Halpin (ed.), *MI5 and Ireland 1939–45*, 76.

for Irish unity, it might not have been beyond de Valera's political capacity to persuade a majority of the electorate.[109] Secondly, this MI5 document does not face up to the full strategic thrust of Churchill's argument that the Irish 'Treaty ports' (given up by Britain in 1938, much to his anger) were vital to British security. Beerehaven, after all, was beyond the range of German dive-bombers and long-range fighter air cover; it would have offered sure anchorage for British ships waiting to counter German surface raiders trying to break out to attack the Atlantic convoys. With facilities in Ireland, the effective air reconnaissance essential to anti-submarine warfare would have been much easier. Denial of the Irish ports to the Royal Navy was reckoned by the Admiralty to have cost 368 ships and 5,070 lives during the war. James Dillon wrote: 'I could never forget that the west coast of Ireland was littered with the bodies of English seamen who had been bringing supplies to us.'[110] As the MI5 document does, at least, conclude:

There can be very little doubt that when de Valera decided to adopt the policy of neutrality, entailing as it did, the refusal to grant the British Navy the use of the Eire ports, he provided the British people with an overwhelming case for the maintenance of partition, which he himself would so much have liked to see ended.

It has to be acknowledged also that the self-referential culture of Irish nationalism was ill equipped to rise to the moral challenges of world war. There had been little instinctive sympathy with the plight of international Jewry. This was perhaps more particularly the case in the North, where the nationalist community took a brisk view of the suffering of others who, anyway, might well have deserved it. A leading figure of the West Belfast nationalist intelligentsia, Dr Brian Moore, father of the celebrated novelist of the same name, had declared in 1936: 'The hatred of the German people against the Jews was instructive, and he believed there must be some reason for it, because a whole nation would not look down upon the Jews without some justification.'[111] The point is not so much the existence in Ireland of a casual anti-Semitism (so widespread in Europe), as the strength of the related belief that the most oppressed people in Europe in the 1940s were to be found in Ireland. The *Irish Press*, with some insouciance, stated on 1 April 1943: 'There is no kind of oppression visited on any minority in Europe which the six-county Nationalists have not also endured.' This

---

[109] Henry Patterson, *Ireland Since 1939: The Persistence of Conflict* (Dublin, 2006), 57–61.
[110] Maurice Manning, *James Dillon: A Biography* (Dublin, 1999), 169.
[111] *Irish News*, 2 Mar. 1936; for the son's reaction against such a world-view, see Patricia Craig, *Brian Moore: A Biography* (London, 2002), 57–74.

was, as Professor J. J. Lee has observed, a 'revelation that would no doubt have helped the victims lining up for the Auschwitz gas chambers place their plight in consoling comparative perspective if only circumstances had permitted them to gratefully clutch their copies of the "Truth in the News"'.[112] As news of the holocaust of European Jewry began to reach the public in Ireland after the war ended and much horrifying information was released, the response of the Irish government was both parochial and defensive. The research of Patrick Maume has shown that the *Sunday Independent* in Dublin published a report (with photos) from an anonymous correspondent, revealing the horror of the Bergen–Belsen concentration camp. Eamon de Valera denounced the report as 'anti-national propaganda': for de Valera, it was important to see the participants in the war as being morally equivalent. De Valera, of course, knew that the reports were true, but he objected to them being publicly discussed. He felt that debate on the issue was divisive and retrospective; criticism would lead to doubts about his government's policy which he increasingly equated with the national interest. In effect, this amounted to saying that crimes which had taken place outside Ireland's borders were irrelevant. The *Sunday Independent* then published a second report from Belsen, written by an Irish doctor serving in the British armed forces, who had been tending concentration camp survivors.[113] De Valera's celebrated message of condolence to Hempel on the death of Hitler is no more remarkable than his dispute with the *Independent*.

The inevitable isolation of Ireland, imposed by neutrality, had suited de Valera. He ruled supreme as the philosopher king of Irish pastoralism and frugal comfort. In the summer of 1942 he met three times with Dr D. P. O'Brien of the Rockefeller Foundation in New York. After a period of illness, de Valera's eyesight had improved, and he was believed to be reading widely again. O'Brien was impressed: 'In fact, he was better informed physically, and certainly on the state of the health of the nation, than were his ministers in various fields.' O'Brien felt that de Valera's ministers were relatively insignificant figures. He noted 'that it is clear that he is attempting to bring about, before he passes out of the picture, a balanced Ireland, a national Ireland, an Ireland that can maintain itself as an integral body of the union of nations on earth'.[114] But revealingly, de Valera confessed

---

[112] Lee, *Ireland 1912–1985*, 266–7.

[113] 'De Valera denounced Reports of Holocaust as "Propaganda"', *Observer*, 8 May 2005.

[114] Rockefeller Foundation Archive Center, Tarrytown, RF 1 1, Project Ireland 403, Box 1, Folder 2, D. P. O'Brien, *Report on Conditions in Ireland 1942*, ch. 4, 'Personalities: Mr Eamon de Valera called Taoiseach'. For the important role played by the Rockefeller Foundation in funding Irish medical projects, see Greta Jones,

to his interlocutor from the Rockefeller Foundation that he had grown increasingly 'conservative' with age. Less favourably, but realistically, the report noted:

A great deal of the political life of Ireland has been nourished on shibboleths and vague generalities, frequently based on an emotional background. No plans for Ireland's future can afford to overlook the tremendous role played by the religious belief of the people, which is dominated by the Catholic clergy of the country.[115]

For the Rockefeller analysts there was 'little doubt' that in Ireland there were 'thousands of citizens' so anti-British that they might almost be classified as pro-German.[116] Certainly, in 1942 there was no public crisis over the values of Fianna Fail. The economic strategy of self-sufficiency—which had come under increasing strain in the late 1930s—now seemed to be fully vindicated. The whole range of Fianna Fail slogans, from protection to increased tillage, seemed to be justified; though from 1943 onwards, opposition, both in the country and the Dail, became more vocal.

More privately, there was an intense policy debate going on within the Fianna Fail Cabinet: in the 1930s some in the party managed a wry commentary on the performance of the Irish industrial elite. Erskine Childers, son of the executed republican, admitted to 'cynical moods'.[117] But Sean Lemass's Ministry for Industry now questioned government policy more profoundly. He began to hint of the need for foreign investment: he argued that Irish farmers were deeply inefficient. He stressed that British social democracy—operative in the North—would prove to be a seductive model for many Irish people. Intellectually vigorous though the debate was,

---

'The Rockefeller Foundation and Medical Education in Ireland in the 1920s', *Irish Historical Studies*, 30: 120 (Nov. 1997); see also the same author's '*Captain of all these Men of Death': The History of Tuberculosis in Nineteenth- and Twentieth-Century Ireland* (New York and Amsterdam, 2001), 193–4. For the more general difficulties of Irish public health in this epoch, see James Deeny's classic *To Cure and to Care* (Dublin, 1989), 77, which spells out a general crisis. One example also suffices: the British had a particular concern about louse-bourn typhus in Ireland: 'Therefore it was imperative that people who had louse infestation (as so many had during the war) and who were possibly carrying the rickettsia, should not travel across the water. Accordingly, a Health Embarkation Scheme was set up to de-louse all those who were going to Britain to join the armed forces or to take up employment. It was a fairly hush-hush affair, and people did not talk about it lest national feelings should be hurt.'

[115] *Report*, 12.
[116] *Report*, ch. 5, App. 2, p. 4. See also R. M. Douglas, 'The Pro-Nazi Underground in Ireland', *Historical Journal*, 49 (2006), 1180–1.
[117] 'The Spread of Industry', *Ireland Today*, 2: 4 (Apr. 1937).

action was slight. Other members of the Cabinet adopted more traditionalist positions closer to conservative Catholic social theory.[118]

In 1948 an ill-assorted coalition of radical republicans, Fine Gael, and Labour, defeated Fianna Fail in the general election. When the new government first entered the Dail, Dr Thomas O'Higgins of Fine Gael accompanied Sean MacBride of the republican Clann na Poblachta. Fianna Fail TDs cried out: 'Fine company you are keeping, Dr O'Higgins'; a reference to MacBride's alleged role in the murder of Kevin O'Higgins, his brother. O'Higgins then privately asked the Ministry of Justice if it was possible to prosecute another minister for murder.[119] A former chief of staff of the IRA, MacBride did, however, evolve a new policy to end partition. In March 1949 he made it clear to George Garrett, the American envoy in Dublin, that Ireland would accept the Atlantic pact and join NATO if partition was ended.[120] The inter-party government eventually collapsed, following a major internal row in the so-called 'Mother and Child Affair', an attempt by Dr Noel Browne to bring in a very limited measure of social medicine—free health-care for the mother six weeks after birth. The significant role of the Catholic hierarchy in this crisis further strengthened the Ulster Unionist case.[121]

Fianna Fail returned to power in 1951, but Lemass did not really gain a grip on the agenda until the late 1950s. The crisis of a stagnant economy and society intensified as the policy prescriptions of the inter-war period appeared to be inadequate in the post-war world. The *Irish Times* declared in a famous editorial on the fortieth anniversary of the Easter Rising: 'If the present trend disclosed continues unchecked … Ireland will die—not in the remote unpredictable future, but quite soon.'[122] The Belfast Unionist press noted with some satisfaction the scale of demoralization within Irish nationalism.[123]

---

[118] Paul Bew and Henry Patterson, *Sean Lemass and the Making of Modern Ireland* (Dublin, 1982), 16–59.

[119] O'Broin, *Just Like Yesterday*, 88.

[120] George Garrett to Secretary of State, 18 Mar. 1949, R to G 84, US Legations Records (Dublin), File 1949 (Atlantic Pact), Box 703, Washington National Records Centre. I owe this reference to Dr Ray Raymond.

[121] Kevin Rafter, *The Clann: The Story of Clann na Poblachta* (Dublin, 1996), 140–8; Noel Browne, *Against the Tide* (Dublin, 1986), 141–56. Noel Browne was later to tell the author that when his party leader, former IRA leader Sean MacBride, forced his resignation, he protested to Noel Hartnett, an equally disillusioned colleague, that MacBride's arrogance, dismissing him from the room as he tipped ash from his cigarette, was intolerable. Hartnett replied that the last time he had seen MacBride make that gesture, the offending party was shot in the head.

[122] Bew and Patterson, *Sean Lemass*, ch. 3.

[123] Mary Daly, *The Slow Failure: Population Decline and Independent Ireland 1920–73* (Madison, Wisc., 2006), 193.

By summer 1957 even the tightly controlled *Sunday Press* editorial and letter pages carried items in favour of foreign capital. Lemass also came out more and more strongly for an expansion of state expenditure—even in areas which were not, in the narrow technical sense, productive. In the general election of 1957 Fianna Fail was armed with a modernizing programme based on vulgar Keynesianism, and capitalized on disenchantment with the coalition's economic performance. It was perhaps Fianna Fail's last chance, but it was a chance that was taken.

Lemass carefully deconstructed the legislative apparatus of economic nationalism, which he himself had created in the 1930s. The highly intelligent government chief economic advisor, T. K. Whitaker, dismantled the last vestiges of the Irish agrarian radical tradition in his report *Economic Development* of 1958, which accepted the dominance of grassland production: precisely 100 years on from the founding of the Fenian movement, which had, in effect, created that tradition.

In a memorandum of 1929 Sean Lemass had asserted that the 'goal of our efforts should be to keep the Irish people in Ireland and provide prosperity for here. Everything else, even cheap living or accepted notions about efficiency, must be sacrificed to that end.'[124] The 'everything else' which had to be 'sacrificed' for that end now turned out to include Lemass's earlier policies of economic nationalism, but it cannot be disputed that the sacrifice was a success. The commentator and writer Desmond Fennell, a nationalist and traditionalist, detected a subversive element in the legacy of Lemass. He argued that while Lemass achieved the 'relegitimation' of a state which the economic crisis of the 1950s had threatened, unfortunately he did this in material terms above all. But herein lay the problem: 'For a state legitimised by its economy can not inspire its citizens to anything and makes them a profoundly apathetic and dissatisfied crowd of people.'[125] The Lemass era was the 'point of departure from the high point of de Valera's Ireland and the beginning of a journey that led to the EU and the so-called Celtic tiger'.[126] For better or worse, Ireland now became a modernized country like the others—less inspired by Catholicism or the campaign to save the language—but because a country like the others, still open to the appeals of nationalism.

---

[124] Enda Delaney, 'Emigration, Political Cultures and the Evolution of Post-War Irish Society', in Brian Girvan and Gary Murphy (eds.), *The Lemass Era: Politics and Society in the Ireland of Sean Lemass* (Dublin, 2005). Whitaker later recalled: 'I was spurred by a cartoon in *Irish Opinion* showing Ireland a still beautiful but somewhat bedraggled lady asking a fortune-teller "Have I a future?".' *Irish Times*, 13 Dec. 2006.

[125] 'The Two Faces of Fianna Fail', *Sunday Press*, 4 Jan. 1981.

[126] Brian Girvin and Gary Murphy, 'Whose Ireland? The Lemass Era', in *The Lemass Era*, 4.

ULSTER UNIONISM: THE IMPACT OF WAR AND WELFARISM

The Second World War was a major watershed in British social and political history, and, try as its rulers might, Northern Ireland could not remain untouched by the effects of the conflict. The war led to a substantial increase in state planning and economic management.[127] A young British civil servant, Norman Dugdale, appointed to the Ministry of Commerce by a panel including G. C. Duggan, recalled of this moment: 'Especially for the poor and afflicted, life was going to be better, and everybody, whether protestant or catholic, would benefit from the new dispensation.'[128] There is little doubt that—added to the welfare state, which, at a stroke, resolved many of the key problems of inter-war Unionist government—Irish neutrality was a tremendous boon to Ulster Unionism. In the late 1930s there was a rising tide of criticism in Whitehall of the Stormont system. One key theme is worthy of note: Eamon de Valera had separated himself from the IRA in a way that Lord Craigavon had failed to match in separating himself from the Orange Lodges.[129] The Unionist leadership was perceived still—eighteen years after S. G. Tallents first made the criticism—as being too close to their followers. Worse still, this intimacy required special funding by the Treasury. However, the Irish decision to stay neutral led to a reappraisal. Northern Ireland's importance was strategic and economic rather than as a source of recruits.

Irish nationalism, rather than Ulster Unionism, suffered the most discredit in British eyes in the years between 1940 and 1945. The fact that a significant part of the northern nationalist leadership had placed their community under the protection of the Third Reich remained a secret, tucked away in the Irish police files until the 1990s. But a voluble rhetorical anti-Britishness was no such secret.[130] The Belfast IRA's support for the Hitler project was also no secret: wartime IRA internees in Belfast plotted the advance of Hitler's armies, first with delight and then despair. Eamon de Valera's visit of condolence to the German legation on the death of Hitler—having made no such visit to the US embassy on the death of Roosevelt—is a classic illustration of a somewhat closed mentality. Churchill's famous thrust against de Valera, 'frolicking with Hitler',

---

[127] E. J. Hobsbawm, *Industry and Empire* (London, 1972), 245.

[128] PRONI, 'Waiting for the Barbarians', Ms, p. 52. For Norman Dugdale, see 'Stormont's Secret Poet Revealed', *Belfast Telegraph*, 9 Apr. 1997.

[129] Paul Bew et al., *Northern Ireland 1921–2001*, 66.

[130] Hennessy, *A History of Northern Ireland*, 85.

included by contrast an exaltation of Northern Ireland's vital role in the war: the 'light of freedom' had been kept alive by brave little Ulster, making its ships and bombers, and providing a home for British shipping and Allied servicemen. In Ireland, de Valera's response was enthusiastically received: proof of the gap in perception between the two states.

David Gray's emotional passage on this subject deserves recall, if only because it has so little resonance in American life today:

Such Ulster names as James Craig, Basil Brooke, the Abercorns, J. M. Andrews, will pass into our history with the Ulstermen who, two centuries before, stood by George Washington in his darkest days. They, like the comradeship forged during the dangerous years, have become part of our American heritage.[131]

By contrast, Nicholas Mansergh, who worked in the Ministry of Information in London, drawing up lists of brave and decorated Irish officers in the Allied forces, warned his Irish allies that publicity on such a matter had to be carried on in a private and low-key way.[132] The need to respect the formal position of the Irish state implied a certain restraint in any publicity effort.

Even with the election of a Labour government, little changed in British eyes. The diplomatic briefing prepared for the trips of Irish ministers to London on economic issues in the 1940s are more than mildly contemptuous. In the winter of 1947 de Valera attempted to engage Philip Noel Baker, Secretary of State for the Colonies, on the northern issue. Noel Baker ignored de Valera's new advocacy of Irish unity: de Valera offered considerable autonomy to the North within an Irish parliament. The British minister was unimpressed. De Valera was even batted away on the subject of Stormont's policy on 'Eireann infiltration' (southerners moving north to take up jobs), a subject on which London had once differed with Belfast. Noel Baker explained bluntly: 'The use of Northern Ireland air and naval forces had literally saved us from destruction, when Hitler's main attack had been on our Atlantic convoys, and the country would never forget it.'[133] Ireland's declaration on Easter Sunday 1949 by the inter-party government of a republic produced a strong pro-Unionist response in the Government of Ireland Act of 1949. Far from undermining Northern Ireland's position within the United Kingdom, Eire's gesture seemed only to have strengthened it. The tone of the official memorandum, prepared by Norman Brook

---

[131] 'Behind the Green Door', ch. 1, p. 6.
[132] PRONI D2661/C/1/N/3/76, Mansergh to Gen. Hugh Montgomery, 3 Jan. 1944: 'I am afraid it is considered essential that the document with awards made to men from Eire in HM forces be considered unofficial, and, therefore, that no reference be made to the fact that it is compiled in this ministry.'
[133] National Archives, DO/130/84, 'Notes of conversation, 4 November 1947'.

for Prime Minister Clement Attlee's use in the House of Commons debate on the Ireland bid in 1949, is striking: it endorsed every key theme of Ulster Unionist thinking. Father O'Flanagan's celebrated insistence that a geographical entity was not necessarily a political entity was noted. The real enemy to Irish unity was an Irish nationalism which had broken away from the United Kingdom. Both Northern Irish business interests and the social condition of the working men depended on staying within the United Kingdom. The notion pioneered by the Irish Foreign Minister, Sean MacBride, that a united Ireland would be an asset to NATO, was derided.

It is ludicrous to suggest that if the anti-Partitionists had their way, and Northern Ireland were made part of the Irish Republic, there could be a united Ireland which could shoulder the Atlantic Treaty obligations more effectively. There would be no real unity with a large minority which would feel that it had been coerced and betrayed.[134]

In his speech on the Bill on 11 March 1949, Herbert Morrison (grandfather of Peter Mandelson, a later Northern Ireland Secretary), paid obeisance to the idea that 'discussions' among Irishmen might one day change the shape of the question: nonetheless, the British government would not take the initiative in any scheme to diminish the size of the United Kingdom. Given that the Labour Party had a significant 'Friends of Ireland' grouping and many voters of Irish descent, the strength of official British endorsement of partition is all the more impressive. The process of Northern Ireland's implementation of British welfarism remained a complex and at times inconsistent one. Brooke's diary of 21 August 1951 describes a meeting with the Ulster Unionist Council: 'I told them that the Convention on Human Rights compelled us to be fair, and I insisted that I was not going to be responsible for discrimination.' In early 1956 Brooke, however, was initially only prepared to support a Family Allowances Bill which abolished payments for the fourth and subsequent children—a clearly anti-Catholic provision.[135] The Unionist MPs at Westminster forced him to drop this idea. Brooke's return to more uncompromising sectarian attitudes may, in part, have been related to the stirrings of republican militancy, which led to a reopening of the IRA campaign on 12 December 1956; the fact remains that this campaign fizzled out, and was formally ended on 26 February 1962.[136]

Much now would depend on the quality of Brooke's successor as premier, Terence O'Neill. O'Neill's political background is interesting. A product of

---

[134] O'Day and Stevenson (eds.), *Irish Historical Documents*, 207.
[135] Henry Patterson, *Ireland Since 1939* (Oxford, 2002), 122.   [136] Ibid. 128.

one of Ireland's greatest landed families, his father had been the first British MP to die at the front in the First World War. O'Neill was the child of the most scandalous (in a political sense) marriage of the day: his father a strong Ulster Unionist, his mother the daughter of one of the great Liberal, pro-Home Rule political families, as the daughter of the Marquess of Crewe. This made O'Neill the great-grandson of Lord Houghton, friend of William Smith O'Brien, the Young Ireland leader. He was, as a consequence of his father's death, raised under the influence of his mother's family and connections, which were aristocratic and metropolitan Liberal. Before the war he drifted aimlessly in the City of London. A 'good war' gave him direction and reinforced his distrust for those who sat it out in provincial self-regard. In October 1946 Terence O'Neill was returned unopposed as the Unionist member for Bannside in the Stormont parliament, like Parnell returning to cash a local family name and tradition for the purpose of personal ambition. In 1956 he was sworn of the Privy Council (Northern Ireland) and became Minister of Home Affairs and then of Finance, forming a politically important relationship with a reform-minded private secretary, Kenneth (later Sir Kenneth) Bloomfield. Another important member of O'Neill's circle was the *Belfast Telegraph* editor Jack Sayers. When, in 1963, O'Neill became Prime Minister of Northern Ireland, unlike his three Unionist predecessors there was little trace of anti-Catholic bitterness on his record. His Orangeism was notably cool and formal. Yet, he was to disappoint some, at least, of his liberal friends.

The subsequent intensity of the sectarian conflict has obscured the fact that, in his early years in office. O'Neill was primarily concerned to win back Protestant support which the Unionist Party had lost to the Northern Ireland Labour Party in the period since 1958. 'Stealing Labour's thunder'—to use O'Neill's own term—rather than allaying Catholic resentments, was his main preoccupation. It should be noted, however, that O'Neill did not gratuitously misrecognize the political context: nationalism was at such a discount (the poor economic record of Dublin undermined dramatically the appeal of the IRA campaign relaunched in the north in 1956), and Labour appeared to be the greatest local threat. O'Neill, nonetheless, had a generous, even impulsive, streak and was capable of the occasional conciliatory grand gesture towards the minority, such as his famous visit to a Catholic school. In the main, however, he espoused a rhetoric of planning and modernization by which nationalist grievances would be dissolved by shared participation in the benefits of economic growth. He saw little role for structural reform. His speeches in this early period resonate with a pious little-Ulsterism, in which devolution emerges not just as an inevitable and reasonable historical compromise but as a responsive communal form of government superior to that of the class-based party system in the rest of the United Kingdom. That UK system was, however, economically sustaining the Stormont regime: a fact of which O'Neill was more aware than the Unionist electorate.

O'Neill's early lack of responsiveness to Catholic grievances was sharply criticized by liberal Unionist groupings, such as the leadership of the Northern Ireland Labour Party and the *Belfast Telegraph*, but in the short term O'Neillism was quite effective politically. Despite electoral success, O'Neill was widely perceived to be a poor party manager. Normally secretive and aloof, at times he was capable of indiscreet and hurtful sarcasm at the expense of prickly senior colleagues. And, ironically, his 1965 triumph played a key role in marginalizing a party (Labour) which gave radicals from the Catholic community an outlet. Instead, O'Neill gave priority to improving relations with the South: yet, since 1932, North and South had drifted further and further apart.

The broad cultural differences were profound. In the period from 1930 to 1939 the Irish state banned 70 per cent of the books reviewed in the *Times Literary Supplement*;[137] and there is no evidence of any post-war liberalization in the 1950s.[138] Divorce and contraception were forbidden in the South—with dramatic and negative implications for the quality of life of many Irish women.[139] But important though other issues were, they were, given the social conservatism of Irish Protestants, perhaps less important than the role played by the language issue, a role which effectively bore out the fears expressed both by unionists and leading constitutional nationalists in the Home Rule crisis. Eamon de Valera had insisted in 1921: 'It is my opinion that Ireland, with its language and without its freedom, is preferable to Ireland with freedom and without the language.'[140] On 19 June 1947, however, he told Lord Rugby: 'It is undoubted that, with the achievement of their liberty, the people of the 26 counties had lost interest in the Gaelic revival.'[141] Remarkable though this admission was, it omitted to mention the one important effect of the compulsory language policy. For, as John Dillon had foreseen, the most profound source of Protestant alienation in independent Ireland was the compulsory language issue. John Dillon's son, Myles Dillon, became one of the foremost Gaelic scholars of the twentieth century in Ireland, Director of the School of Celtic

---

[137] Peter Martin, *Censorship in Two Irelands* (Dublin, 2006), 194.

[138] James Kelly, 'The Operations of the Censorship of Publications Board: The Notebooks of C. J. O'Reilly 1951–5', *Analecta Hibernica*, 38 (2004), 223–69.

[139] Greta Jones, 'Marie Stopes in Ireland—The Mother's Clinic in Belfast 1936–47', *Social History of Medicine*, 5: 2 (1992).

[140] *Roscommon Herald*, 6 Aug. 1921.

[141] National Archives, Prem/8/824/4487.

Studies in the Dublin Institute of Advanced Studies.[142] But in 1958 Dillon wrote sadly:

The language is rapidly ceasing to have any symbolic value at all, because it has been turned into an instrument of discipline. The policy was launched in 1925, and it was inspired, I have long suspected, by the purpose in the minds of a few people who pressed for it, of using the language as a means of transferring power—or rather authority. At that time ... all the cultural institutions of the country were in the hands of Protestants: the Royal Irish Academy, the National Library, the National Gallery, the Royal Irish Academy of Music, the Royal Dublin Society, the Museum, the College of Science, the Botanical Gardens, even the Society of Antiquaries. All that must now be changed: a new administrative class was to be established, and the language was one of the means used. Lyster, Eglinton, Praeger, Best, Armstrong, Westropp, Sir Frederick Moore, none of these men could have passed the test. None of them could stand a chance of civil service appointment now. I shall not dwell upon that painful subject: but I believe that far from helping the language movement, this turning of the screws has destroyed its value as a form of allegiance.[143]

There were also important economic and social differences between North and South to be taken into account. Four years after the publication of his *Northern Ireland: Success or Failure?*, G. C. Duggan published, in 1954, *A United Ireland*, a pamphlet which first appeared as nine articles in the *Irish Times* in December of that year. The pamphlet is dominated by a massive personal contradiction; despite his strong sympathy for the Unionist cause during the Home Rule crisis and the three decades of services to the Stormont regime, concluding as Comptroller and Auditor-General, Duggan was, in principle, a believer in a united Ireland. In *Northern Ireland: Success or Failure?*, he revealed Lord Craigavon's comment in a private interview in 1937: 'Duggan, you know that in this island we can not live always separated from one another. We are too small to be apart for the border to be there for all time. The change will not be in my time, but it will come.'[144] Duggan added: 'I felt that the words were not lightly spoken and had in them something prophetic.' But Duggan was also a realist. *A United Ireland* recorded faithfully the massive economic and financial obstacles in the way of unification. Duggan opens his pamphlet by flagging up the difficulty: 'The financial and administrative integration of the two parts of Ireland has become increasingly difficult as the 33 years that have already elapsed since Ireland was one lengthen their span.' The discussion of the working of social services was particularly striking.

[142] Joachim Fischer and John Dillon (eds.), *The Correspondence of Myles Dillon 1922–1928: Irish–German Relations and Celtic Studies* (Dublin, 1999), 9.

[143] Ernest Blythe, 'The Significance of the Irish Language for the Future of the Nation', Myles Dillon, 'Comment', *University Review*, 2: 2 (1958), 24.

[144] G. C. Duggan, *Northern Ireland: Success or Failure* (Dublin, 1950), 21–2.

The assistance bill in the six counties is £4, 500, 000. In Eire, where external public assistance is drawn on much more austere lines, it is under £2, 000, 000. If the Northern Ireland model were followed in the South, the latter figure would have to be multiplied by above five. In a welfare state, the taxpayer's purse is bottomless, especially if a wealthier neighbour is prepared to guarantee and help to finance parity of treatment.

Put bluntly, if one was poor and vulnerable, it was better to be born on the northern side of the Irish border. Duggan insisted that *all* the citizens of Northern Ireland benefited significantly from Northern Ireland's financial integration with Great Britain. A united independent Ireland would very quickly face an unpalatable question: are the Northern Ireland 'local' services to be brought down to the Eire level, or are the latter to be raised to the higher standards, and if so, how is the money to be found? Is it clear beyond all doubt—Duggan wanted to know—that those in the six counties who wish to see Ireland reunited, are prepared to see their land rated again, their agricultural produce left to fend for itself in an unsubsidized market, their unemployment benefit and children's allowance reduced, their medical attendance and hospital treatment charged for?[145]

It is precisely because of the Republic's disadvantages that O'Neill felt safe enough to enter into a new relationship with Dublin. Psychologically attracted to new talks of 'summits' between the two premiers, much less psychologically attracted the complex political work of reform within Northern Ireland, O'Neill looked to the Irish Republic. This was the Irish Republic of Sean Lemass, which Terence O'Neill wanted to bring closer to the North: a country which still had a privileged position for the Catholic Church, which censored much mainstream literary work, and whose compulsory Irish-language policies had had a negative effect on intellectual life. A country with a poor economic record. Thus, in 1966, on the fiftieth anniversary of the Easter Rising, the population of the Republic, at 2.88 million, was less than it had been in 1926 (2.97 million), whilst that of the part of Ireland still 'unfree' was larger (1.25 million in 1926 and 1.48 million in 1966). These figures were perhaps, above all, a tribute to the presence of the British welfare state in one part of Ireland and its absence in the other. Yet, the paradox remains that, thanks more to Lemass than to any other politician, all these 'realities' were in the process of rapid change, creating the basis for a potentially more positive relationship between the two parts of Ireland. The era of melancholy sanctity was closing; signalled, above all, by the sharp decline in priestly vocations in the late 1960s. In a 1959 conversation with the

145 Deeny, *To Cure and to Care*, 73.

British ambassador to Ireland, Sir Alexander Clutterbuck, Lemass said 'that he fully realised on looking back that a great number of mistakes had been made by the government here in relation to the North; these he would work to rectify'.[146] With what success, we will see in the next chapter.

[146] Michael Kennedy, 'Northern Ireland and Cross-Border Co-Operation', in *The Lemass Era*, 99.

11

'Unbearably Oldfashioned and Pointless': The Era of the Troubles, 1968–2005

> That's my dream for Northern Ireland. I would like to see those Orange bastards just wiped out.
>
> (North Belfast Republican cadre, in Fionnuala O'Connor, *In Search of a State: Catholics in Northern Ireland* (1993))

> No genuine negotiation can take place if a tiny minority of the Irish people is allowed to become involved on the basis that, if the parties representing the other 95 per cent of the people of the island do not accept its terms, it will relaunch a murder campaign against a large section of its fellow Irishmen and women.
>
> (Garret FitzGerald, *Irish Times*, 20 Aug. 1994)

> The conclusion to all this came on 28 July 2005, when the IRA announced the formal end to its armed campaign.
>
> (Gerry Adams, *The New Ireland: A Vision for the Future* (2005), 120)

Ireland made its original application to join the European Community in 1961: Professor Brian Girvan has argued that this was a most significant moment, revealing that 'the specific dynamic that had driven Irish Nationalism from the Act of Union to the consolidation of a republican regime had become exhausted'.[1] It was the positive proof that Lemass and Whitaker had destroyed the world of insularity and protectionism. In fact, Irish officialdom was nagged by a constant fear throughout the 1960s that the EEC would overlook Ireland's application in the difficult period following the sudden suspension of British–EEC negotiations in February 1963: in July 1963 the German Foreign Minister omitted to mention Ireland in

---

[1] Brian Girvan, *From Union to Union: Nationalism, Democracy and Religion in Ireland: Act of Union to European Union* (Dublin, 2002), 201.

the list of countries Germany would like to see in the Common Market. Ambassador Gallagher was subsequently assured by a senior German Foreign Office official that the omission was entirely accidental and that 'Britain had to come in as a full member because she was too important and powerful, and Ireland and Britain naturally went together; it is all the British Isles anyway'.[2] In 1967, as in 1963, the French veto on British entry had automatically brought with it a failure of the Irish application.

There were other signs of a more pragmatic, less ideological, approach on the part of the Irish state. The immediate prelude to the 'Troubles' was, in fact, a period of apparent rapprochement in North–South relations. As with the economy, however, Lemass's path on the North was complex and tortuous: in the lead-up to his own path-breaking meeting with Terence O'Neill, he made life difficult for the northern premier by emphasizing traditional anti-partitionist themes. An important moment of clarification, however, came when the first Irish Catholic President of the United States, John F. Kennedy, told the Irish ambassador in March 1963 that he could not support the idea that Britain should be cajoled into making a declaration in favour of Irish unity. The ambassador outlined Kennedy's response: 'There is a long built-in history involved, which includes religious differences, and it has to be seen like that from the British point of view; he is convinced that no British minister could feel able to make a public statement of the kind suggested.'[3] At a Fianna Fail dinner in Tralee in July 1963, Lemass recognized that 'the Government and the Parliament there exist with the support of a majority in the six-county area,'[4] and insisted that the solution to the problem of partition was one to be found in Ireland by Irishmen. In October 1963 Charles Haughey, son-in-law of Lemass and Minister of Justice, sent his top official, Peter Berry, north to work with Stormont: the Gardai helpfully employed intelligence gathered by the RUC to close down IRA training camps in the South.[5]

Much now would depend on the response of the Northern Irish premier, Terence O'Neill, who saw himself, at least, as a liberal modernizer. But what was his immediate political context? Northern Irish Catholics clearly suffered discrimination: though core political and socio-economic rights (as delivered by the UK state, much superior to those on the rest of the

[2] Joe Humphreys, 'Constant Fear on Ireland's Standing within Europe', *Irish Times*, 1 and 2 Jan. 1999.

[3] Henry Patterson, 'Sean Lemass and the Irish Question 1959–65', *Journal of Contemporary History*, 34: 1 (1999), 155.

[4] Ibid. 154.

[5] Peter Berry, 'Berry–Craig Second Meeting', *Magill* (June 1980). I am grateful also to Professor Bob Stout for allowing me to see the memorandum by his father, W. F. Stout, which confirms Peter Berry's account.

island) and religious freedoms were not denied.[6] Catholics actually had a disproportionately large share of local-authority houses, but this reality coexisted with another: in, for example, the town of Dungannon the council was gerrymandered, and not one new Catholic family had been offered a permanent house for twenty-four years.[7] The texture of political life was set by the dominance of an ethnically determined Protestant unionism: only the development of a more civic, liberal unionism could have conceivably reduced the Catholic sense of alienation. On the other hand, the consequences of intercommunal polarization were potentially disastrous. In 1975 Edwin Aunger, the Canadian political scientist, argued on the basis of his analysis of the 1971 census that Catholics were significantly disadvantaged. They were more likely than Protestants to be low on the economic scale. Within each class, there was a tendency for Catholics to cluster in the lower reaches. Catholics were much more likely to be in industries with lower status and more unemployment, such as construction, while Protestants dominated in industry and engineering that ranked higher in pay and prestige. In the Protestant community the unskilled section of the working class was diminishing as a proportion of the workforce; in the catholic community it was actually increasing. No less than a quarter of the non-agricultural workforce was confined to unskilled labour, excluded not only from political life but from the rising standard of living enjoyed by other classes. In a context of inflamed sectarian passions, this sector constituted an immense reservoir of opposition to unionism and indifference to moderation.[8] To aggravate matters, there was a substantial minority of Protestants who were as badly off as their Catholic neighbours, and thus provided an equally militant grouping ready to engage on the streets.

Perhaps because these local realities were so intractable, modernizing elements within unionism tended to lay greater stress on island-wide, North–South possibilities for change. Even the *Belfast News Letter*, the loyal organ of the Ulster Unionist Party, called for a North–South meeting to discuss matters such as tourism, transport, and trade. Terence O'Neill now had sufficient reason to believe that the mood within unionism allowed him to move ahead. Whilst symptomatically keeping most of his Cabinet colleagues in the dark, he held a summit with Lemass on 14 January 1964 at Stormont. But apparent progress on an inter-state level was to prove an illusion. The fiftieth commemoration of the Easter Rising was

---

[6] Thomas Hennessy, *Northern Ireland: The Origins of the Troubles* (Dublin, 2005), 383.

[7] Henry Patterson, *Ireland Since 1939* (Oxford, 2002), 195.

[8] E. A. Aunger, 'Religion and Occupational Class in Northern Ireland', *Economic and Social Review*, 7 (1975); for a discussion of Aunger's work, see Paul Bew, Peter Gibbon, and Henry Patterson, *Northern Ireland 1921–2001* (London, 2002), 141–3, 146.

to be associated with a rise in tension in both states: on 29 June loyalist extremists murdered Catholics in Belfast—in a ghastly anticipation of the later Troubles—and the senior leadership of the RUC became seriously concerned with the subversive potentiality of this extremism, which it rated as more dangerous than the IRA.[9] A southern source documented perhaps a thousand members.

Sean Lemass thought he could control all the meanings and emotions generated by the 1966 celebrations. He declared: 'There is no question that James Connolly would be with us now in what we're doing in the Fianna Fail government.'[10] Not many were convinced that this was an accurate reading of the great socialist republican. In fact, Lemass was in profound error. The 'passionate' celebrations of the Easter Rising helped the IRA, still demoralized after the failure of the '56 campaign, to grow to a membership of over 1,000;[11] it assisted a 'backlash' of ultra-Protestant feeling, led by the Revd Ian Paisley, who began to establish a significant base of support in this period.[12]

It was, however, the civil-rights demonstration on 5 October 1968 in Derry which opened up the modern Ulster crisis. The television coverage—especially the work of the RTE cameraman Gay O'Brien—changed the course of Irish history. The media gave widespread coverage to the unrestrained batoning by the RUC of civil-rights demonstrators, including MPs, without 'justification or excuse' (according to the later Cameron Commission). Cocooned in their devolutionist shell, the Unionists found it particularly difficult to defend the peculiarities of their system to outsiders. They found it particularly difficult to explain themselves to the London political elite. For the first time in their careers, the Ulster Unionist leadership, used in recent decades to easy victories and stability, found themselves having to deal with a real crisis—complicated, it has to be said, by the confused cross-currents of student radicalism.[13]

Irish neutrality during the Second World War had weakened nationalism's credibility in London. The arrival of the welfare state in the North contrasted with mass emigration to the United Kingdom from the Republic in the 1950s; these developments provided the circumstances that bred

---

[9] Margaret O'Callaghan and Catherine O'Donnell, 'The Northern Ireland Government, the Paisleyite Movement and Ulster Unionism in the 1960s', *Irish Political Studies*, 2: 2 (June 2006), 203–32; Tom Hennessy, *The Origins of the Troubles* (Dublin, 2005), 95–8.

[10] Paul Bew, '1950's', in Luke Dodd (ed.), *Nationalisms, Visions and Revisions* (Dublin, 1999), 36.

[11] Paul Dixon, *Northern Ireland: The Politics of War and Peace* (London, 2001), 75.

[12] Clifford Smyth, *Ian Paisley: Voice of Protestant Ulster* (Edinburgh, 1987), 14–15.

[13] On this topic, see Simon Prince, 'The Global Revolt of 1968 and Northern Ireland', *Historical Journal*, 49: 3 (Sept. 2006), 851–75.

a generation of complacent Unionist politicians that believed, wrongly, that they held all the political and economic cards. In particular, it was a political generation used to relatively untroubled relations with London. Furthermore, in 1966, after fifty years of independence, the population of the Republic (at 2.88 million) was less than it had been in 1926 (2.97 million), while that of the part of Ireland still 'unfree' was larger (1.25 million in 1926, 1.48 million in 1966). The nationalist leadership in Northern Ireland itself was provincial, unsophisticated, and almost permanently on the defensive. Slow to see the positive implications for Irish nationalism of the Lemass revolution in economic strategy, the Unionist leaders felt that economic trends remorselessly strengthened unionism, while at the same time undermining the logic of nationalism.

The response of Brian Faulkner (Minister of Commerce) to the events in Derry reflected these assumptions. While William Craig, the Minister of Home Affairs, had claimed simply that the Northern Ireland Civil Rights Association had been infiltrated by the IRA, and that 'majority opinion in the IRA Council was Communist', Faulkner stressed the economic advantages of the status quo: 'All the lurid accusations and every bit of sensational political mud-slinging rebounded not only on Orange and Unionist Ulstermen, but endangered the pay packets of every Nationalist citizen of Northern Ireland as well.'[14] As Faulkner acknowledged in the same speech, 'unfortunately for Northern Ireland, the attempt to equate Nationalism with civil rights... was an effective one in the eyes of the world'. Terence O'Neill immediately grasped the fact that the Northern Ireland government had no alternative save to pursue reforms. He told his Cabinet within days of the Derry confrontation: 'Northern Ireland's standing and reputation has been most seriously damaged... He must remind his colleagues of Northern Ireland's utter financial dependence: in these circumstances a directive from Downing Street could have grave repercussions.'[15] The Prime Minister told the media: 'We might get back to a situation of 1912, when a Liberal government tried to interfere in Irish affairs.' There was still, at this point, support for O'Neill in London. But even a sympathetic Whitehall observer noted that London 'does not universally support the methods and objectives of all organs of the Northern Ireland government'.[16] Harold Wilson, in particular, was perfectly willing to resort to the threat of financial pressure. Pressure was not

---

[14] Paul Bew and Gordon Gillespie, *A Chronology of the Troubles 1968–1999* (Dublin, 1999), 5.

[15] G. K. Peatling, *The Failure of the Northern Ireland Peace Process* (Dublin, 2004), 39.

[16] Rachel Donnelly, 'London pins Hopes on "Liberal" O'Neill', *Irish Times*, 1 and 2 Jan. 1999.

long in coming. Prime Minister Wilson told Northern Ireland Ministers on 4 November that if further reforms were not forthcoming the British government would feel compelled to propose a 'radical' course involving the complete 'liquidation' of all financial agreements with Northern Ireland.[17]

On the same day, the Unionist Cabinet received an interesting letter from a former Unionist attorney-general, Edmund Warnock. Warnock argued that the electoral gerrymander of Derry, which had effectively deprived a local nationalist of control of the city council in 1936, had been intended to be only temporary. 'If ever a community had a right to demonstrate against a denial of civil rights, Derry is the finest example.'[18] On 22 November the RUC Inspector-General reported to the Cabinet that many unionists, were sympathetic to the civil-rights protest, adding that the civil-rights movement was not on IRA front and, absent electoral reforms, was unlikely to weaken.[19] O'Neill's answer was a five-point plan on 22 November. It dealt with the most obvious grievances signalled by the civil-rights movement. The business vote in local government elections was abolished, and the local government system was to be reformed within three years. Fair allocation of local authority housing was promised. There was to be an ombudsman to investigate grievances arising out of central government administration. The Special Powers Act was to be reviewed and clauses conflicting with the United Kingdom's international obligations to be removed. The Derry City Council was to be superseded by the Development Commission. A prominent critic of the regime in the mid-1960s Charles (later Sir Charles) Brett, had once insisted that the 'Unionists will assert that they can not in any circumstances afford the blow to their prestige of losing Derry.'[20] But now the Unionists had to accept precisely such a blow to their prestige. It did not, however, offer an immediate resolution of the 'one man, one vote' issue in local government. It thus allowed the civil-rights movement to retain its most effective mobilizing slogan.

However, O'Neill's position as Prime Minister and leader of the Unionist Party was not strengthening. The party's council had endorsed the government's reform package on 6 December 1968, but only after O'Neill had given a commitment not to introduce any further reforms, especially of the local government franchise, without prior consent. The following day O'Neill unburdened himself to Sir Andrew Gilchrist, the British ambassador

[17] Hennessy, *Origins*, 151–5.   [18] PRONI Cab 4/140/14, 14 Nov. 1968.

[19] *Irish Times*, 1 and 2 Jan. 2007, 'Tensions on how to handle civil rights campaign'.

[20] Aaron Edwards, 'Labour Politics and Sectarianism: Interpreting the Political Fortunes of the Northern Ireland Labour Party' unpub. Ph. D thesis, Queen's University, Belfast (2006), 11–12.

in Dublin. O'Neill was in an extremely pessimistic and depressed mood. Although he could understand the reaction of ordinary Protestant people to reform, O'Neill was exasperated by their failure to grasp the implications of financial dependence upon London. This sense of Northern Ireland's financial dependence was the one issue which firmly linked Harold Wilson and Terence O'Neill in agreement.

Nevertheless, O'Neill was still strong enough to set the agenda. On 9 December he appealed over the heads of his Cabinet critics to the general public for support in a celebrated TV broadcast: 'Ulster stands at the crossroads.' He concluded his peroration:

Unionism armed with justice will be a stronger cause than unionism armed merely with strength ... What kind of Ulster do you want? A happy and respected province in good standing with the rest of the United Kingdom? Or a place continually torn apart by riots and demonstrations and regarded by the rest of Britain as a Political outcast?

He implied support for 'one man, one vote' in local government, pointing out that it would not substantively reduce Unionist power. On 10 December the *Belfast Telegraph* printed a coupon on its front page that declared: 'I approve of Captain O'Neill's broadcast and support his effort to heal the divisions in our community.' On 11 December, buoyed up by significant signs of public support within both communities, O'Neill sacked his hardline Cabinet opponent William Craig. On 12 December a meeting of Unionist MPs at Stormont gave overwhelming support to O'Neill. The 'I back O'Neill' campaign received over 150,000 letters and telegrams of support. Terence O'Neill was voted 'man of the year' by the readers of the *Sunday Independent* newspaper in Dublin.

O'Neill, therefore, ended the year on an ambiguous kind of high. There was, however, one significant danger looming on the horizon. On 20 December the People's Democracy, a student-based radical faction of the civil-rights movement, rejected the mainstream leadership's advice and called for a protest march from Belfast to Londonderry. It claimed that the march would be modelled on the famous march from Selma to Montgomery in the United States, led by Martin Luther King. In one respect, at least, this claim was true: such a march, passing as it did through many Protestant areas on a seventy-mile trek, had the capacity for provoking violence: like 'honest' Jack Lawless in 1828, the genuine non-sectarian radicalism of the young marchers had the capacity to provoke a major destabilization.

The march left Belfast City Hall on 1 January 1969. The failure of the Unionist government to deal with the problems posed by the march was one of the gravest errors of the 'Troubles'. There was little support for the march at the outset—only a few dozen left Belfast. Activists like Gerry Adams, on his own account a founder member of the civil-rights movement,[21] did not participate. Banning the march might have brought little reaction. Having allowed the march to go ahead, the government should have given more thought to its policing. The consequences of the loyalist attack on the (to them) extremely provocative march transformed the situation and strengthened the hostility of many Catholics to the state. It could be argued that the march marks the pivotal point at which the Troubles changed from being primarily about civil rights to being about the more traditional disputes concerning national and religious identities. The attitude of People's Democracy was, perhaps, naive. Though the march was modelled on the Selma–Montgomery march in Alabama, there was one crucial difference: the issue of statehood, at least, was not an issue in the US civil-rights struggle. The marchers believed that they were participating in a protest for civil rights and socialism; in reality, they had helped unearth layers of ethno-nationalist animosity and hatred that had remained at least partly buried over the previous decades. As Eamon McCann, one of the leftist leaders of the PD march, came to admit only a few weeks later:

It is perfectly obvious that people do still see themselves as Catholics and Protestants, and the cry 'Get the Protestants' is still very much on the lips of the Catholic working class. Everyone applauds when one says in a speech that we are not sectarian, we are fighting for the rights of all Irish workers, but really that's because they see this as the new way of getting at the Protestants.[22]

The PD march determined the fall of O'Neill. The Prime Minister managed to retain considerable moderate Protestant support, but after the attack on the marchers at Burntollet he lost his appeal to middle-class Catholics. They felt that he had allowed Orange rednecks to pummel the flower of their educated youth. His project was fatally wounded by the general polarization in the public mood. O'Neill decided, in one last desperate throw of the dice, to call an election in February, a course of action he had specifically rejected in his 'Crossroads' broadcast. For the first time in its history, the Unionist Party entered an election campaign in a divided state. Support for O'Neill was strongest in the suburban constituencies of the greater Belfast area, while anti-O'Neillism was strongest in the border counties and in working-class Belfast constituencies.[23] The result was less than a resounding triumph. In his Bannside constituency O'Neill was himself run close by Ian Paisley, who polled 6,331 votes against

---

[21] *Irish Times*, 8 Nov. 2005, see also Adams's memoir, *Before the Dawn* (London, 1996).
[22] *New Left Review*, 55 (May–June 1969), 11.
[23] Bew, Gibbon, and Patterson, *Northern Ireland*, 179.

O'Neill's 7,745. O'Neill was later to lament that his failure to win Catholic votes, while he shed hardline Protestant votes to Paisley, had been a significant blow.

There was an added significance: the emergence of a young Catholic, John Hume, who won a seat in Foyle standing on an independent ticket—Hume asked for a mandate to work for 'the foundation of a new political movement based on social democratic principles'.[24] Hume was to place himself at the centre of constitutionalist nationalist politics over the next generation: at first he was identified with a conciliatory approach towards Unionism, but over time his perspectives were to become more nationalist. O'Neill staggered on, but, behind the scenes, everyone asked—would his eventual fall mean the introduction of direct rule from London? John Chilcot, a young Home Office official, had been set to work on this project in January. In February 1969 Home Secretary James Callaghan told a committee of ministers that direct rule was a serious option.[25] Unionists in Belfast were soon aware that contingency plans of this sort existed. On 3 March Lord Cameron's commission was appointed to investigate the cause of violence in Northern Ireland: J. J. Campbell ('Ultach' of the 1940s) was to be the Catholic representative. On 17 April Bernadette Devlin, a 21-year-old civil-rights marcher, who had been attacked at Burntollet, was returned to the House of Commons for mid-Ulster on a 92 per-cent turnout. In her maiden speech on 22 April she advocated direct rule as an admittedly radical but effective solution for the Northern Ireland problem.[26] But when so 'unrelenting' a radical declared for direct rule, how could a respectable government go so far, so fast? With the mood in the province becoming ever more edgy, however, O'Neill made one final effort to achieve stability. On 23 April 1969 he announced that his government accepted the principle of 'one man, one vote' (the principal demand of the civil-rights movement) to be applied at the next local government election. This was his last major act: on 28 April he resigned, saying: 'Look about you at the present state of our country and try to answer the question "Is this really the kind of Ulster that you want?" I asked you that question once before; and now, as then, it is only you who can answer.'[27] Despite much conjecture—and the discussion behind the scenes of direct rule—London allowed James Chichester-Clark to take over from O'Neill. Contrary to the widespread rumour, Chichester-Clark had not succeeded via a private understanding

[24] Hennessy, *The Origins of the Troubles*, 195.

[25] Peter Rose, *How the Troubles Came to Northern Ireland* (Basingstoke, 1997), 150–5; Geoffrey Warner, 'Putting Pressure on O'Neill: The Wilson Government and Northern Ireland 1964–69', *Irish Studies Review*, 13: 1 (2005), 34.

[26] W. D. Flackes, *Northern Ireland: A Political Directory* (Dublin, 1980), 180.

[27] Terence O'Neill, *Ulster at the Crossroads* (London, 1969), 201.

with O'Neill, a kinsman.[28] Nevertheless, he brought the same range of qualities and deficiencies as O'Neill to the post: a soldier's bravery, a sense of decency, and a profound absence of any skills of political presentation. To complicate matters further, his police advice told him that Ian Paisley's policy of 'countermarching' simply intensified and ignited protest.

In the middle of August 1969 the sequence of events which prompted the British army's *longue durée* in Northern Ireland began. On 12 August the annual parade of the Protestant Apprentice Boys in Derry was stoned by Catholic youths: this led to violent clashes between Bogside Catholics and the police, who were followed by a Protestant crowd. The Bogside was now in an apparent state of siege, its determination symbolized by the public militancy of Bernadette Devlin MP. But how would events be perceived in the South? Matters were complicated by the fact that the Taoiseach Jack Lynch had collapsed in mid-1969 at a function in Ballinasloe.[29] Exaggerated fears about his health promoted a leadership push by both C. J. Haughey and Neil Blaney; each claimed to be the more patriotic. Haughey was particularly anxious to bury his reputation of being a self-interested 'capitalist roader' without patriotic credentials. On 13 August a troubled Jack Lynch broadcast that the Irish government 'can no longer stand by and see innocent people injured and perhaps worse', and was asking the British government to request the immediate dispatch of a UN peacemaking force to Northern Ireland, and that field hospitals were being prepared in Co. Donegal and other border areas. The effects within Northern Ireland of this broadcast were profoundly destabilizing, as many working-class Protestants genuinely feared an Irish army invasion. On 14 August the rioting in Derry continued and spread to Belfast, where there was rioting involving now Catholic and Protestant crowds. On 15 August the rioting continued in Belfast, and many homes were burned in Bombay Street, in the Catholic Clonard area; Catholic refugees in Belfast fled to the Republic. In the afternoon British troops took up their positions and established a peace-line between Catholic and Protestant areas in Belfast. There were no state-sponsored attacks on Catholics; there was no IRA conspiracy to overthrow the state: but there had been a sectarian conflict of the most bitter sort on the streets of Belfast. On 16 August the Irish Cabinet gaves Charles J. Haughey full discretion to provide aid for Catholics in the North.[30]

---

[28] See C. D. C. Armstrong's important essay on Clark in the *Oxford DNB* (2006); http://www.oxforddnb.com/view/printable/76880.

[29] Michael Mills, *Hurler on the Ditch* (Dublin, 2005), 50.

[30] Hennessy, *Origins of the Troubles*, 390. Ronan Fanning, 'Living in Troubled Times', *Sunday Independent*, 2 Jan. 2000.

Many shrewd observers were later to conclude that the Stormont government's (incorrect) assumption that a request for British troops would lead to the immediate abolition of Stormont had created a context in which an overstretched police force was given responsibility for massive public-order problems, which the earlier utilization of British troops would have averted.[31] It is, however, arguable that the eventual decision to send in the troops, while leaving the Stormont regime intact, was the greatest mistake of British policy during the Troubles. The effect was to allow the Provisional IRA to present the British army as the tool of the 'Orange' Stormont ascendancy regime. The Provisionals also had the great advantage that they had a realistically achievable transitional objective: the abolition of Stormont. Austin Currie, one of the leaders of the new modernizing nationalist grouping, the Social Democratic and Labour Party (SDLP), founded in August 1970, was later to argue powerfully that the British government 'should have taken that extra step and suspended Stormont. Had that happened in 1969, then I believe that a lot of the trouble, and a lot of the deaths that occurred after that, could have been avoided.'[32] Was 1969 the appropriate moment for direct rule? It should be noted that the balance of Home Secretary James Callaghan's very serious discussions of the issue behind the scenes still inclined him to caution, even if British troops were deployed on the streets of Belfast and Derry.[33] Stormont was allowed to stay in existence.[34] It is clear that this decision was not taken casually or lightly, yet the fact remains that the government's strategy allowed it to garner the worst of both worlds: the apparent threat to implement direct rule in 1969 if British troops were called in led to a dreadful deterioration in the streets of Belfast; but the failure to implement direct rule once these troops had arrived assisted the generation of a radicalizing momentum in Catholic politics.

On 19 August the Northern Irish ministers met British ministers in London. It was confirmed that the British GOC in Northern Ireland would have overall responsibility for security. The two governments committed themselves to maintaining the 'momentum of reform', and to ensure 'equality of treatment for all citizens of Northern Ireland' as prevailed 'in the rest of the UK'. Oliver Wright, a senior British Foreign Office official,

---

[31] See the important remarks of Arthur Green, the Secretary to the Scarman Commission, which was set up to analyse the crisis of this violence, 'Lessons Scarman may have for Saville', *Belfast Telegraph*, 26 Feb. 2002.

[32] Paul Bew and Gordon Gillespie, *Northern Ireland: A Chronology of the Troubles 1968–90*, 2nd edn. (Dublin, 1999), 20.

[33] Hennessy, *The Origins of the Troubles*, 233–6.

[34] I am indebted to the late Lord Callaghan for discussions of this point at the Witness seminar for the Centre of Contemporary British History.

was appointed as the British government's representative in Northern Ireland. The Hunt Committee was established to examine the recruitment and organization of the RUC and the Ulster Special Constabulary. The Scarman Tribunal was appointed to inquire into the recent disturbances, while on 12 September the Cameron Commission reported on the origins of the civil-rights crisis. The Cameron Report's (para. 142) verdict was decisive:

> The conclusions at which we arrived after the evidence was heard and finished, [are] that certain at least of the grievances fastened upon by the Northern Ireland Civil Rights Association and its supporters, in particular those which were concerned with the allocation of houses, discrimination in local authority appointments, limitations on local electoral franchise and deliberate manipulation of ward boundaries and electoral areas, were justified, a fact which is confirmed by decisions already taken by the Northern Ireland government since these disturbances began.

Cameron was not based on 'a comprehensive survey of practices in Northern Ireland's local authorities; rather, it was a snapshot of the contentious'.[35] While insisting on this point, Chichester-Clark did, however, acknowledge that some authorities had behaved improperly, and that it would have been better if the problem had 'been well—and I say this frankly—if we had grasped this nettle some time ago. Perhaps they underestimated the effect which even isolated cases of injustices could have in a divided community.'[36]

At first, British troops were well received in nationalist areas. Nevertheless, as early as 11 September the Home Secretary, James Callaghan, was confiding to Richard Crossman: 'Life was very bleak ... there was no prospect of a solution. He had anticipated [that] the honeymoon wouldn't last very long and it hadn't. The British troops were tired and were no longer popular, and the terrible thing was that the only solutions would take ten years, if they would ever work at all.'[37] The full intractability of the conflict was becoming tragically clear to British policy-makers; the outline of the modern Ulster crisis was already in place. On 10 October the Hunt Committee reported and recommended the replacement of the Ulster Special Constabulary by the Ulster Defence Regiment, to be fully under British army control. The loyalist Shankill Road exploded, and the first policeman to die in the Troubles (Constable Victor Arbuckle) was shot dead. A member of the loyalist paramilitary body, the Ulster Volunteer Force (UVF), was found to have blown himself up at the foot of a pylon in Ballyshannon, Co. Donegal. Ulster loyalism appeared to be on the defensive and lashing out rather wildly.

[35] Hennessy, *The Origins of the Troubles*, 303.   [36] Ibid. 303.
[37] Richard Crossman, *Diaries of a Cabinet Minister*, vol. 3 (London, 1977), 636.

But it should not be assumed that the Irish state contemplated the implementation of the territorial claim on Northern Ireland as stated in the 1937 constitution. In fact, officials were keen to insist on an acceptance of the validity of the 1925 Agreement, which had accepted Northern Ireland's status as part of the United Kingdom. A document prepared for the Irish Cabinet on 16 August 1969 insisted:

> With regard to the International Court of Justice, the main difficulty resides in the probability that the British would take their principal standing on the 1925 Agreement, and we could not afford in any circumstances to have the validity of this Agreement made the determining factor in the UN approach to the question.[38]

It is true that in 1969 a detailed contingency plan for invasion of the North was drawn up in late September.[39] But others were in a less militant frame of mind. A second 'secret' Irish memorandum, dated 26 October 1969, considered the claim that the 1925 Agreement did not survive the 1932 change of government and the 1937 constitution, only to conclude: 'The basic principle of respect for Treaties (*pacta sunt servanda*) means they may not be unilaterally terminated. International relations would be very haphazard and unstable if changes of government or unilateral acts by governments were to mean a termination of their international commitments.' The same text also quoted from a ruling of the permanent Court of International Justice in 1932 that a state 'could not cite its own constitution as evidence, but had to rely on international laws and obligations'. The memorandum concluded that Ireland's dispute with Britain 'was a political dispute', and they had 'little basis on which to make it a legal one'.[40] This implicitly cautious tone was not accepted by all in the Department of Foreign Affairs.[41] But the Taoiseach, Jack Lynch, fully accepted the need to be circumspect and paid much attention to the realistic advice of T. K. Whitaker.

The Irish premier's caution had no counterpart in the attitudes of Belfast republicans. Behind the scenes, the leadership of a new IRA was preparing for war. Brendan Hughes has described the fatal decision taken by the Provisional IRA, as it became known, to go on the offensive: 'I recall Billy McKee saying that this is our opportunity now with the Brits on the

---

[38] Angela Clifford, *August 1969: Ireland's Only Appeal to the United Nations* (Belfast, 2006), 30.

[39] *Irish News*, 10 Aug. 2004.

[40] Enda Staunton, 'The Boundary Commission Debacle of 1925: Aftermath and Implications', *History Ireland*, 4: 2 (Summer 1996) 45.

[41] See Ronan Fanning, 'Playing it Cool: The Response of the British and Irish Governments to the Crisis in Northern Ireland 1968', *Irish Studies in International Affairs*, 12 (2001), 57–85.

streets, this is what we wanted, open confrontation with the army.'[42] It was this decision to attack the British army which transformed the relations between the army and the Catholic community. Early in January 1970 the Provisional Army Council formally confirmed an all-out offensive against the 'British occupation system'.

Simultaneously, Jack Lynch told the Fianna Fail ard fheis that 'like it or not, we have to acknowledge that two thirds of the one and a half million people who make up the population of the six counties wish to be associated with the United Kingdom'. The 'plain truth' was that: 'Would we want to adopt the role of an occupying conqueror over the million or so six-county citizens who, at present, support partition?'[43] But not everyone listened to Lynch's message or bothered to answer his question. On 11 January, failing to obtain a two-thirds vote in favour of parliamentary abstention, some eighty delegates (supporters of a new Provisional Army Council) out of 257 at a Sinn Fein ard fheis in Dublin walked out. The split between the left-wing 'politicized' officials and the Provisionals, then seen as more right-wing and militaristic, was formalized. Perhaps even more disturbing was the evidence that 'the Troubles' of the North were destabilizing the Irish elite at the highest level. Northern delegations incessantly pestered Dublin for guns, and some sought support for a new struggle for Irish unification. The Irish government, as a government, on 6 February asked a reluctant military command to prepare for a 'Doomsday' scenario: remarkably, the Irish state theoretically contemplated engaging with a subversive organization with a view to the seizure of the territory of a friendly power.[44] But it is important to note that Jack Lynch was still more than aware of the dangers in any adventurous drive for unity.

In February 1970 an important delegation representing senior northern nationalists and Republicans met the Taoiseach in Dublin. He explained categorically that Ireland could not afford the financial burden of unity.[45] Not everyone was as clear-headed on the matter as Lynch at this moment. Early in 1970 the ailing Minister for Justice told two other ministers in the Lynch Cabinet that some of their colleagues were 'doing something' they should not be doing. In March the provisional IRA began its bombing campaign in Belfast.

On 2 April 1970 500 rifles mysteriously arrived in lorries at the Dundalk barracks of the Irish army from, it was claimed, Irish army sources. The rifles did not have the normal escort, nor were they accompanied by the usual

[42] Hennessy, *Origins of the Troubles*, 367.
[43] Patterson, *Ireland since 1939*, 180.
[44] Hennessy, *Origins of the Troubles*, 366–7, 393.
[45] Paddy Doherty, *Paddy Bogside* (Cork, 2001), 22.

documentation. When Jack Lynch was informed, he ordered the lorries to stay in Dundalk and then return to Dublin the following morning. Later that evening a group of men arrived at the barracks gate demanding the rifles: the police dispersed the crowd, and the next day the weapons were returned to Dublin.[46] But given such incidents, it was hardly a complete surprise when, on 6 May 1970, Jack Lynch dismissed two ministers, Charles Haughey, Minister for Finance, and Neil Blaney, Minister for Agriculture. Lynch stated as his rationale that 'I am satisfied that they do not subscribe fully to government policy in relation to the present situation in the Six Counties as stated by me at the Fianna Fail ard fheis in January last'.[47] Blaney and Haughey were arrested on charges of conspiring to import arms and ammunition. On 6 October the trial of Haughey, Captain James Kelly, an Irish army officer, Albert Luykx, and John Kelly began in Dublin: they were all to be acquitted on 23 October.[48]

Haughey's behaviour during the arms trial itself was highly significant. It was alleged that Haughey gave Captain Kelly, an Irish army officer, £10,000 on 19 February 1970 to buy the following: 200 sub-machine guns, 84 light machine-guns, 50 general purpose machine-guns, 50 rifles, 200 grenades, 70 flak-jackets, 200 pistols, and 250,000 rounds of ammunition. (Self-evidently, this sort of weaponry implied an aggressive IRA campaign rather than simply a defence of beleaguered Belfast Catholics.) The first attempt to land arms, via Dublin port, failed because—significantly—there was no government paperwork. The second attempt was checked by the arrival of the Gardai, sent by Peter Berry, a senior official of the Department of Justice. But when it came to the trial, Haughey betrayed his co-defendants. Luykx, Captain Kelly, and John Kelly all argued that there was a government plan to buy arms. Haughey denied this and then offered a defence designed to protect himself but expose his colleagues. (This strategic retreat by Haughey was bitterly criticized in the 1970s and 1980s by Kevin Boland, a minister of ultra-republican views who had not been privy to the arms plot but believed Lynch had been wrong to disown it, resigned from the Cabinet—and subsequently from the Dail and Fianna Fail—in protest, and spent the remainder of his life denouncing what he perceived as a crucial betrayal of the party's republican principles.)

Haughey preferred to perjure himself rather than risk his political career. It was an important moment; if Haughey had had the courage of his

[46] Padraig Faulkner, *As I Saw It: Reviewing over Thirty Years of Fianna Fail in Irish Politics* (Dublin, 2005), p94.
[47] Ibid. 99.
[48] Justin O'Brien, *Modern Prince: Charles J. Haughey and the Quest for Power* (Dublin, 2002), 25–55; see also Mills, *The Hurler in the Ditch*.

apparent convictions, he might well have unleashed 'a tidal wave of naked nationalism' by proclaiming that he had acted in the best interests of Ireland. His discretion was a key moment in the unfolding hypocrisy and realism of the Irish political class on the North.[49] Lynch, nonetheless, retained a widespread popularity in Irish public-opinion polls and the control, also, of the Fianna Fail party. Irish opinion on this point may well have included a significant sneaking admiration for those prepared to take risks for northern nationalists, but the predominant sentiment saw the stability of the Irish state as a greater value. To this extent, Jack Lynch's speech in January had set the tone for the turbulent year. Fear of contagion with the violence of the North became widespread in the South. The events of the arms trial remain highly controversial. The Irish army intelligence officer on trial, Captain James Kelly, always insisted up to his death that he was merely following orders from the Cabinet, and that his trial was unjust: surviving supporters of Jack Lynch, such as the then Minister for Education, Padraig Faulkner, a member of the Cabinet subcommittee on the North, insist equally strongly that the evidence strongly suggests that there was no Cabinet decision to import weapons.[50]

The Provisionals themselves were primarily the creation of the sectarian explosion in Belfast itself—but it is not in doubt that the early rapid strengthening of the movement owed much to support from leading figures in the Fianna Fail government, some of them concerned to head off the socialist radicalism of the 'official' IRA, the Provisionals' challengers for support in West Belfast. It seems likely, for example, that the Dundalk weapons were intended for Ballymurphy, where the IRA was engaging the British army in three nights of serious rioting. On 18 June 1970 Harold Wilson lost the UK general election and the Conservative leader Edward Heath inherited the Ulster problem.[51] On 27 June, following Orange parades, republicans 'defending' the small Catholic enclave of Short Strand in East Belfast killed two Protestants, while republicans killed three more on the Crumlin Road: the sectarian head-count on the night—five Protestants dead and one Catholic—established the ghetto credibility of the 'Provos' against the more cautious left-wing 'officials'. Whitehall took the view that 'if the protestants were the main aggressors in August 1969, on this

---

[49] John-Paul McCarthy, 'Let the Mourning be Brief for "Father of the Peace Process" ';
Eoghan Harris, 'Death of Chieftain: The Enigma was Empty', *Sunday Independent*, 13 June 2006.

[50] Faulkner, *As I Saw It*, 93–104.

[51] For the ambiguous history of the Tory–Ulster Unionist relationship, which had diminished throughout the century, see Jeremy Smith, 'Ever Reliable Friends? The Conservative Party and Ulster Unionism in the Twentieth Century', *English Historical Review*, 121 (Feb. 2006), 71.

occasion, there is convincing evidence that the catholic side is to blame'.[52] The British army's subsequent resolve to 'do something', combined with the intense rivalry between the Official and Provisional IRA, led to the dramatic Falls Road curfew of July 1970. In August 1970 the Provisionals killed their first unarmed Royal Ulster Constabulary member, though they did not manage to kill a British soldier until February 1971. The campaign, which was to see the loss of 3,700 lives, but not the attainment of its stated purpose, Irish unity, had begun.

Following a particularly shocking Provisional IRA murder of three soldiers in Belfast on 10 March 1971, the sense of crisis deepened. On 12 March 1971 4,000 shipyard workers, claiming to represent all shades of political and religious opinion, marched on Unionist Party headquarters, Glengall Street, Belfast, to demand the internment of IRA leaders. An experienced soldier, James Chichester-Clark had his doubts about the effectiveness of such a policy. Chichester-Clark placed his faith in a different set of measures: in particular, he wanted to see permanent military bases in nationalist areas to prevent the growth of 'no-go areas', and the return of the RUC to its 'rightful role' on security policy. The army refused and Chichester-Clark resigned. On 20 March 1971 Brian Faulkner, whom the London government had long considered to be the most talented of the Unionist politicians, became the leader of the Unionist Party and Prime Minister of Northern Ireland. Faulkner was Ulster Unionism's last hope in his generation, and the policy of internment was its last card. For his election did nothing to stem the tide of violence or the political deterioration. Even before the introduction of internment, the SDLP, now the dominant force in Northern Irish political nationalism and much influenced by John Hume, announced its withdrawal from the Northern Ireland Parliament after a refusal of an inquiry into the shooting of two men by the army on 18 July. Driven by a fear that society could not stand such constant terror, including regular bomb explosions, from the Provos, Faulkner attempted to persuade the army and the British government to try internment.

On 5 August 1971 Faulkner met with Heath, who told him that the army GoC was not, at present, advocating internment. Nevertheless, the British government was prepared to give Faulkner support, but 'if they did not succeed ... the only further option would be direct rule'. Faulkner replied that direct rule would be a calamity, and 'if they could get a grip on the security situation, there was a genuine hope, not merely of restoring the pre-'68 situation, where people had, for the most part, been living harmoniously, but of moving forward to something better'. Faulkner's

---

[52] Geoffrey Warner, 'The Falls Road Curfew Revisited', *Irish Studies Review*, 4: 3 (Aug. 2006), 329.

account of these discussions in his memoir recalls that Sir Alec Douglas Home expressed extreme hostility to direct rule on 18 August. Faulkner was wrong to take comfort from the Foreign Secretary's attitude. The Prime Minister's words of 5 August were the best guide to future policy.[53] Internment was a desperate gamble. It had worked in the past when simultaneously applied in the South: in 1922–4, for example, it had led to a dramatic reduction in violence.[54] But this time it failed, and failed dramatically. In 1971, prior to internment, there were thirty-four deaths from political violence in the North: between internment and the end of the year there were 139.[55] On 9 August, the day it was introduced, Father Hugh Mullan was murdered while administering the last rites during rioting in Belfast. Private Winston Donnell, shot at a roadblock near Strabane, was the first UDR soldier to be killed. As Northern Ireland hung on the brink of outright civil war, Protestants were forced out of the Ardoyne area of Belfast, setting fire to 200 houses as they left rather than have them occupied by Catholics. Two thousand Protestants were left homeless, while 2,500 Catholics left Belfast for refugee camps set up in the Republic. In the following days barricades were erected in Catholic working-class areas, and even the Official IRA engaged in a gun battle with the army in Belfast.

By 12 August twenty-two people had been killed and up to 7,000 people (the majority Catholics) left homeless, as houses were burned to the ground. While internment in itself provided decidedly limited security benefits, the social and political reaction it created far outweighed these. As a result, violence increased for the rest of the year, and the SDLP refused to become involved in political talks while internment continued. It is clear, however, that the main winners from the introduction of internment were the Provisional IRA: the popularity of that movement within the Catholic community was decidedly enhanced.[56]

The intensity of the reaction also made it difficult for the British government to openly consider direct rule at that time, as this was the goal the IRA proclaimed as an intermediate step towards a united Ireland. Despite this, as Faulkner's gamble visibly failed and the British army found itself the target of vastly increased Catholic animosity, the introduction of direct rule was widely expected. On 27 September a two-day meeting began at Chequers, involving the British, Irish, and Northern Irish prime

---

[53] Brian Faulkner, *Memoirs of a Statesman* (London, 1978), 127–8.
[54] Laura K. Donahue, 'Regulating Northern Ireland: The Special Powers Acts, 1922–72', *Historical Journal* 41 (1998), 1089–120; Seosamh O'Longaigh, *Emergency Law in Independent Ireland 1922–48* (Dublins 2006), 21 and 277.
[55] M. Farrell, *The Orange State* (London, 1975), 287.
[56] Patrick Bishop and Eamonn Mallie, *The Provisional IRA* (London, 1987), 189.

ministers, to discuss matters of common concern. At the beginning of October 1971 Edward Heath still felt it right to assert:

Taking full account of the political dangers of further alienating the minority population in Northern Ireland, and of the risks of strain on our relations with Dublin, we believed that the first priority should be the defeat of the gunmen using military means, and that in achieving this, we should have to accept whatever political penalties were inevitable.[57]

But within days officials were provoking a rethink. It is worth looking at Cabinet Secretary Sir Burke Trend's minute of 6 October 1971. Secretary to the Cabinet since 1962, the Prime Minister respected his 'formidable intellect, which he used to penetrate to the heart of any problem':[58] Trend had none of the spontaneous unionism of his predecessor, Sir Norman Brook, who had believed that the possession of Northern Ireland gave strategic advantages to the United Kingdom. Trend was already thinking that Northern Ireland required a power-sharing government, going beyond the limits of Brian Faulkner's cautious 'green paper' proposals, which gestured in this direction. Trend became increasingly interested in the idea of holding a border poll. The concept was to build up unionist self-confidence and thus permit unionists to make a generous power-sharing deal. Trend asked: 'Can the proposals in the Green Paper be supplemented by a broadening of the government at Stormont? Would the recruitment of non-militant Republican Catholics be made more palatable if it were agreed there would be no change in the border without a referendum?'[59] In principle, the border poll might have been a consciously pro-unionist one, a device to allow greater reform and accommodation with a view to maintaining the union on a more stable basis ad infinitum—but that is not how Trend saw it. On the contrary, the border poll was seen as a device which kept open the future possibility of a united Ireland. The minutes, taken by Trend himself with his usual precise accuracy, of the Downing Street discussion of this meeting of 2 October 1971 are of particular importance here:

In general discussion, the meeting recognised it was essential to define the main object of the government's Northern Ireland policy. If this were to maintain the *status quo* constitutionally, it was probable that the terrorist problem should be overcome as a first priority. On the other hand, if the object were to preserve the

---

[57] 'Visit of the Prime Minister of Northern Ireland', Cabinet Office, 2 Oct. 1971. The meeting considered the brief for the Prime Minister's meeting with Mr Faulkner on 7 October 1971.

[58] Edward Heath, 'Baron Trend 1914–1987', in C. S. Nichols (ed.), *The Dictionary of National Biography 1986–1990* (Oxford, 1996), 456.

[59] Burke Trend document, 'Northern Ireland', 6 Oct. 1971.

option of creating a united Ireland at some time in the future, it might be better to seek first for a political solution in which the minority were persuaded to participate in the government of Northern Ireland. If Mr Faulkner can be persuaded to broaden his government to include non-militant Republicans, the support for the terrorist campaign would be undermined ... Despite the difficulty of reaching a political or military solution, the meeting recognised that the continuation of the present trends might lead to a situation in which direct rule would prove to be inevitable.[60]

Burke Trend's highly unsentimental analysis—from a traditional unionist point of view—was in keeping with the broader tone of thinking in the government's policy-making apparatus. The Central Policy Review staff at this very moment declared:

The fact that Northern Ireland is part of the United Kingdom is no more or less relevant than the fact that Algeria was part of metropolitan France ... if the Six Counties ceased to be British, the net saving to public expenditure would be considerable ... Some form of deal with the Irish Republic seems the best option available.

Trend submitted the document to the Cabinet.[61] Inevitably, these discussions do not appear to have taken place in a hermetically sealed atmosphere; Dublin journalists and opinion-formers picked up on the discourse,[62] and it fed into a mood of nationalist expectancy. The *Economist* declared at the beginning of 1972: 'Ministers have made little secret of their belief that the most satisfactory solution in the end would be if a political solution were created over the years in which the protestant majority in the north would come to recognise a future for itself in a united Ireland.' Encouraged by such sentiments, the Provisional IRA declared that 1972 would be the year of victory.

Jack Lynch, the Irish premier, was beginning, slowly, to establish a working relationship with Edward Heath. The first draft of his private exchange with Heath on 6 December 1971 records his admission that it was 'understandable' for British troops to fire shots across the border. Later, when Heath suggested that the state might extradite suspects from the South, Lynch replied that 'he would have no inhibition about extradition', adding, however, evasively that it would be a matter for the Irish courts.[63]

---

[60] 'Visit of the Prime Minister of Northern Ireland', Cabinet Office, 2 Oct. 1971, pp. 25–6.

[61] *Sunday Tribune*, 29 Dec. 2002.

[62] On this glib and deeply unserious application of the so-called Algerian analogy, see the powerful and impressive work of one of the great modern Anglophone scholars of Algeria, Hugh Roberts, *Northern Ireland and the Algerian Analogy* (Belfast, 1986); *The Battlefield—Algeria 1988–2002: Studies in a Broken Polity* (London, 2003).

[63] 'State Papers: History Revealed—Papers Show Lynch Weak on North', *Sunday Business Post*, 6 Jan. 2002.

Five weeks later the British Cabinet reviewed the situation in the north on 11 January 1972: the IRA, on the retreat in Belfast, was still very strong in Derry. A major military operation might be required—but it should only take place *after* a substantial political initiative designed to win over the Catholic population.[64]

At this point, the Ministry of Defence appears to have registered that much of the discussion within the policy-making elite presumed that Britain had no strategy or security interests in Northern Ireland. But was this true? In mid-January 'a short note on the defence implications of a united Ireland'[65] was prepared: this agnostic document argued that while there were some significant strategic advantages in the status quo, everything really depended on the unknowable context in which a united Ireland would come about.

In mid-January also, Peter Jenkins, then the doyen of the *Guardian*'s political columnists, recorded that the most senior British military were tired of dealing with local Stormont politicians and officials and wanted direct rule.[66] On 23 January 1972 Heath met with Lynch in Brussels. The Taoiseach spoke of the need for a political initiative—though Heath found his thinking a little obsessive. Heath's aide, Sir Robert Armstrong, formed the impression that Mr Lynch was saying 'that we were reaching the point where a political initiative might have some hope of success, because the IRA campaign of violence had received a severe setback (at any rate in Belfast), but the Protestants might still be sufficiently alarmed to be prepared to contemplate change'. There appears, at this moment, to have been a growing consensus amongst the most senior officials at the Home Office and the Foreign Office that a period of direct rule was inevitable and that some new form of power-sharing was the way forward for Northern Ireland.[67]

Then a dramatic and horrific event in Derry took centre stage. On 30 January 1972 thirteen men, all unarmed, were shot dead and seventeen were wounded by the Parachute Regiment in Londonderry. Another man died later. The shooting began at the end of a civil-rights rally, attended by nearly 10,000 people, when part of the crowd tried to climb over a street barrier and was forced back by the army with rubber bullets and spray from a water cannon. On numerous occasions over the previous months troops had battled huge crowds in the Creggan against a backdrop of gunfire

---

[64] For more context see Paul Bew, 'The Role of the Historical Adviser and the Bloody Sunday Tribunal', *Historical Research*, 78: 199 (Feb. 2005), 120.

[65] PRO DE FFE 2/25/295/1068. 'A short note on the defence implications of a united Ireland', 13 Jan. 1972. I owe this reference to Dr Tom Hennessy.

[66] *The Guardian*, 17 Jan. 1972.

[67] Bloody Sunday Tribunal website, OS4.182 KW3.75, 78, 79.

and bombs, and had only occasionally killed people. On Bloody Sunday the crowd was actually less violent than it had been during the earlier confrontations. Dr Niall Ó Dochartaigh has acutely observed: 'Thus, to many in Derry, the army appeared to have carried out a calculated massacre of unarmed rioters, deliberately escalating the conflict.'[68]

Given the tone of its discussion of Derry on 11 January, 'Bloody Sunday' definitely was not a product of a 'conspiracy' at the level of the British Cabinet, whose priorities lay elsewhere, or of the Northern Irish Cabinet, which was too powerless to achieve such an outcome. Brian Faulkner, though, immediately grasped the significance of the fact that it was not clear that any of the dead were IRA men. Faulkner declared: 'When were a dozen gunmen ever killed in a crowd situation, with no civilian casualties?' He also reflected ruefully on the political implications of the tragedy: 'This is London's disaster, but they will use it against us.'[69]

At the highest level of military thinking there was, however, an element of dangerous confusion. In the autumn of 1971 the army had attempted a conciliatory policy in Derry, but found that rioting and violence had intensified. Some senior officers grew increasingly exasperated and were inclined towards a harsher policy—one employing greater lethal force; others were less convinced. British army orders for the day reflect both this ambiguity and the fraught nature of the objective situation.[70] The concept of projected army activity was laid out as 'lowest possible key', but soldiers were also warned to expect sniper fire in the event of rioting. In its defence, the British army later denied that it opened the firing and blamed the IRA; it is a denial which has never been accepted in nationalist Ireland.

The least that might be said was said by the Widgery Tribunal in 1973, that some soldiers lost their discipline and fired recklessly, taking innocent life.[71] John Hume soon reported that Bogsiders 'feel now that it's a united Ireland or nothing'. In a debate in the House of Commons, Bernadette Devlin, speaking of the Home Secretary, Reginald Maudling, said: 'The minister has stood up and lied to the House. Nobody shot at the paratroops,

---

[68] *From Civil Rights to Armalites: Derry and the Birth of the Irish Troubles* (Cork, 1997), 283; see also the same author's 'Bloody Sunday and the Divisions in British Security Policy', paper presented at the Political Studies Association of Ireland Conference, Belfast (Oct. 2005).

[69] Bloody Sunday Inquiry: Statement made at the request of the Inquiry's solicitors, by Dr Robert Ramsay CMG (Lately Director General European Parliament: NICS and NIO 1965–83), p. 9, Brussels, 5 Jan. 2002. I am indebted to Dr Ramsay for a discussion of the issues.

[70] Bew, 'Bloody Sunday', 113–27

[71] *Report of the Tribunal appointed to enquire into the Events on 30th January 1972, which led to loss of Life in Connection with the Procession in Londonderry on that Day by the Rt Hon Lord Widgery, OBE, TD* (London, 1972), paras. 89–104.

but somebody will shortly ... I have a right, as the only representative in this House who was an eyewitness, to ask a question of that murdering hypocrite.' She then ran across the Chamber, pulled Maudling's hair, and slapped his face. Later she said: 'I didn't shoot him in the back, which is what they did to our people.'[72] Reaction in the Irish Republic was equally hostile. The main pro-government journal, the *Irish Press*, declared: 'If there was an able-bodied man with Republican sympathies within the Derry area who was not in the IRA before yesterday's butchery, there will be none tonight.' The Irish ambassador to Britain was recalled in protest at the events of the previous day, and on 1 February the Minister for Foreign Affairs, Dr Patrick Hillery, arriving in New York on his way to speak to the United Nations, declared that his objective was to get Britain out of Ireland. The repercussions of the Derry killings continued on 2 February, when, after a series of anti-British demonstrations throughout the day, the British embassy in Dublin was burned down after it was attacked by a crowd of more than 20,000.

Amid the torrent of international criticisms of Britain as a result of the killings, Edward Heath announced the setting up of a tribunal of inquiry into the shootings in Londonderry, to be headed by Lord Chief Justice Widgery. Perhaps most importantly, Bloody Sunday was also the final straw for the British government as far as Stormont was concerned, and in the wake of the incident it decided that London had to assume control of the security forces, a decision that would bring about the end of the Stormont regime. Faulkner's sharp observation to Ramsey was to be borne out by the subsequent developments.

Indeed, the fact that the Provisionals were so obviously aiming for direct rule was the main factor in delaying its implementation. However, by the end of March, Heath moved to strip away security powers and then to prorogue Stormont. The Parliament of Northern Ireland met for one last time on 28 March 1972. There is no doubt that when the end came for Stormont, it was due to a British perception that the United Kingdom could not continue to suffer the damaging international perception that it was linked to militarism in Northern Ireland. In retrospect, the introduction of internment was the turning-point; had that move proved effective, then direct rule could have been averted.

For the Provisionals, direct rule was a victory. They declared that it 'places us in a somewhat similar position to that prior to the setting up of partition and the two statelets. It puts the "Irish question" in its true perspective—an alien power seeking to lay claim to a country for which it has no legal

---

[72] *Hansard*, 5th ser., vol. 830, cols. 37–43.

right.'⁷³ In fact, the more profound local significance of direct rule lay elsewhere: its introduction represented the definitive end of the 'Orange state'; it allowed the British government the space to introduce a strategy of reform 'from above'. Loss of control of the local state also helped generate a long period of disarray and confusion in Unionist politics; indeed, for almost a decade it was marked by the rise of Ian Paisley and the Democratic Unionist Party (DUP) and the weakening of the Ulster Unionist Party. It was to take almost two decades for the Unionist Party to re-establish itself as the dominant force in Protestant politics, before losing that position again in 2003. The introduction of direct rule was the most decisive moment of the crisis; it is the sine qua non for all later developments, including the Anglo-Irish Agreement of 1985, which was, in effect, merely a rather significant 'green' appendage to the direct-rule machine.

POLITICS WITHOUT STORMONT, 1972–1974

The other sine qua non for all later developments was the public opinion in the Irish Republic: strongly nationalist in emotional sympathy but reluctant to pay any real price for reunification.⁷⁴ The internal political life of the Republic was dominated by the issue of Europe. The French veto on British (and therefore Irish) entry was lifted in May 1971; in May 1972 an Irish referendum showed a majority for entry of 83 per cent. Accession to the community took place on 1 January 1973: the implication was profound—'the two parts of Ireland and Britain were all moving forward into a new relationship'. But it is worth noting that the absence of peace reduced greatly the chances of a positive effect. For Ireland, the European connection brought major economic benefits, including the structural funds which were to play an important role in the modernization of the economy. Ireland significantly had been able to enter 'Europe' without either joining NATO or giving up its constitutional claim on Northern Ireland. It had been willing to do either or both if required, but it was not required. Not that there was a strong desire in the Irish political leadership to give any reality to the claim on the North. Sir John Peck, British ambassador in Dublin, reported a significant conversation with the Irish Prime Minister on 31 July 1972:

I asked [Lynch] how serious an issue reunification had been in the by-election, and how much it mattered to the Irish people as a whole. His answer amounted to

⁷³ Bew and Gillespie, *Chronology*, 50.
⁷⁴ Peter Mair, 'Breaking the Nationalist Mould: The Irish Republic and the Anglo-Irish Agreement', in Paul Teague, *Beyond the Rhetorics: Politics the Economy and Social Policy in Northern Ireland* (London, 1987), 91.

saying that they could not care less. As far as he was concerned, he wanted peace and justice in the north and close friendship and co-operation with us.[75]

It should never be forgotten that Northern Ireland was convulsed by frenetic levels of violence in 1972 and 1973. There was also the beginning of a serious intelligence war: on 2 October 1972 the IRA smashed a British intelligence-gathering exercise in West Belfast, using the cover of a laundry business. Gerry Adams described this as a 'devastating blow', akin to the strike against the British secret service by Collins in Dublin in November 1920. But he added significantly that the IRA took their 'eye off the ball' while British intelligence regrouped: in this respect, history was to repeat itself.[76] These were years in which the collapse of the Stormont regime—for so long apparently impregnable—gave rise to the most millenarian of expectations on the republican side and the most paranoid of fears on the unionist side. This orgy of murder was never to be repeated; these two years account for over a quarter of all deaths from political violence between 1969 and 1990. These years saw an intense republican onslaught, but the largest single group of casualties was amongst Catholic civilians, who suffered 254 deaths out of a total of 759, which included also 125 Protestant civilians, 167 British army soldiers, twenty-six members of the UDR, and twenty-four policemen.[77] These are figures which describe a grim civil war, complicated only by the British state's efforts to act as a peacemaker. The broad outlines of policy continued along the lines set out by Burke Trend in the autumn of 1971. It is a simple matter to detect the further outworking of Trend's thinking.

On 8 March 1973 the border poll he had recommended took place. The poll offered the alternatives: 'Do you want Northern Ireland to remain part of the United Kingdom?' and 'Do you want Northern Ireland to be joined with the Republic of Ireland outside the United Kingdom?' The result was a vote of 591,820 (57.5 per cent of the electorate) in favour of retaining the union, while 6,463 voted for unity with the South. Most nationalists had boycotted the poll. The prospect of a certain strong victory probably also reduced the unionist turnout—even so, it is striking that the unionist vote exceeded significantly the total support for the Unionist parties. But having, as it were, settled the union question, the government then, on 20 March, advanced its *Northern Ireland Constitutional Proposal* White Paper. The White Paper insisted that any settlement must be based on

[75] Irish voters could not care less about unification. 'Jack Lynch: New Documents reveal Taoiseach's amazing Candour to British Ambassador about Northern Ireland', *Sunday Tribune*, 25 May 2003.

[76] *Before the Dawn*, 212.

[77] David McKittrick, *Lost Lives* (Edinburgh and London, 1999), 1473.

some form of executive power-sharing and would have an 'Irish dimension': 'New institutional arrangements for consultation and co-operation on an all-Ireland basis.' Brian Faulkner won the battle to prevent the Ulster Unionist Party rejecting the White Paper outright (27 March). In the Assembly election of June 1973 Faulkner Unionists won 191,729 votes; the non-sectarian Alliance Party won 66,541 and the Northern Ireland Labour Party some 18,675 votes. This might be described as the moderate unionist vote. But various factions of anti-White Paper unionists achieved some 255,406 votes.[78]

Behind the scenes, the British government hoped that its support for a power-sharing plus Irish dimension would lead to greater security co-operation with Dublin. Hopes may have risen on this score, with the election of a Fine Gael–Labour coalition in February 1973; for Britain this represented a 'less green' option than a Fianna Fail government. On 14 April 1973 the Taoiseach was handed a dossier on IRA border activities, which was a combined British army/RUC assessment. It marks the beginning of serious British attempts to engage the Republic in the work of security co-operation: 'We are looking for a marked improvement on the part of the South.' The British were aware that the response might be disappointing, and 'that we will have to tax them ... if improvement is not forthcoming'. Nevertheless, F. A. Rowley's memorandum was touched by an exaggerated optimism. 'It may be that [the Irish authorities] will wait for some blatant attack before making an arrest; it may be that they will move immediately; it may be that the Active Service Units will merely get the message that the good old days are over and themselves quietly decide to disperse.'[79] It is difficult not to see this document as the first sign of an understandable but somewhat unrealistic British obsession with the possibilities of Dublin government security co-operation, which was to have a significant political effect in later years.

The British entered a bidding war, which they always lost: ever greater concessions to the Republic in exchange for that illusory act of decisive cross-border co-operation. But at this point the signs for such a policy were promising. Following Fianna Fail's general election defeat, the newly elected Cosgrave government had sent out conciliatory signals on Ulster—only to be castigated by John Hume of the SDLP, a reversal of Hume's earlier relationship with Dublin.[80] As a result, Brian Faulkner, who had been confronted with a British demand that he accept power-sharing in 1971–2, found in 1973 that Britain intensified the pressure on his leadership. They

[78] See Richard Rose, *Northern Ireland: A Time of Choice* (London, 1976), 30.
[79] NAFCO 87/243, Border Co-Operation, F. A. Rowley, 17 Apr. 1973.
[80] Patterson, *Ireland Since 1939*, 238.

now urged him to accept also a Council of Ireland, which would allow greater co-operation on an all-Ireland basis. Faulkner was told that there would be an inbuilt unionist veto on its progress. In fact, all-Ireland co-operation was not, in principle, an impossibility: it had an honourable unionist tradition going back to Sir James Craig—Faulkner would have been well aware of the work which went on in this area while he was a member of the Northern Ireland Cabinet in the 1960s. But there was a key element of symbolism here. Were the all-Ireland institutions to be presented as an embryonic form of Irish unity? Some members of the SDLP had an exalted opinion of what the Council of Ireland would mean.

The general approach of the SDLP to the talks was to get all-Ireland institutions established, which, with adequate safeguards, would produce the dynamic that could lead ultimately to an agreed single state for Ireland. That meant, of course, that SDLP representatives would concentrate their entire efforts on building up a set of tangible executive powers for the Council, which, in the fullness of time, would create and sustain an evolutionary process.[81]

The British government was also partly responsible for creating this situation. By failing to define clearly those areas that the Council of Ireland would control and those that it would not, it succeeded in inflating nationalist aspirations, while at the same time raising loyalist fears of the Council as a means of forcing them into a united Ireland. But, of course, such a failure had its roots in the underlying pro-Irish unity rationale of Trend's original documentation.

In retrospect, it is clear that the Faulknerite Unionists were the principal losers at the Sunningdale constitutional conference, though they were under pressure from almost all the other parties involved in the talks to give ground. When Faulkner came out strongly against the southern government having any say on the police, Edward Heath joined the SDLP and the Irish government to pressure him into accepting that the Council of Ireland would be consulted with regard to the composition of the new police authority. In return, Heath gave a largely meaningless pledge in the Sunningdale communiqué to discuss the devolution of responsibility for policing 'as soon as the security problems were resolved and the new institutions were seen to be working effectively'. One liberal Unionist at Sunningdale has recorded his despair on account of 'the Irish government's inability to offer us terrorist extradition to balance the concession of a Council of Ireland. It was at this point that the Unionists could see the futility of it all.'[82]

---

[81] Paddy Devlin, *The Fall of the Northern Ireland Executive* (Belfast, 1975), 32.
[82] Basil McIvor, *Hope Deferred: Experiences of an Irish Unionist* (Belfast, 1998), 102. But see also, for a different assessment of, at least, Brian Faulkner's mood, Austin Currie, *All Hell Will Break Loose* (Dublin, 2004), 241.

On 16 January 1974 Mr Justice Murnaghan's ruling in the Dublin High Court in response to an action taken by Kevin Boland, the former Fianna Fail minister now transformed into keeper of the republican faith, was announced. Boland's challenge to Sunningdale was thrown out, but at a high price. The Irish government's defence amounted to a declaration that its territorial claim to Northern Ireland was still in force. Faulkner protested bitterly: 'It had to be said that the publication of the defence by Dublin had robbed him of all credibility on the question of status.'[83] Almost two decades later Garret FitzGerald, who had been Irish Foreign Minister in 1975, conceded to Roy Bradford, a Unionist minister in the power-sharing executive: 'Our legal defence involved demolishing the entire political position which we had built up with you.'[84] Then, if possible, matters took a further turn for the worse. On 17 January Hugh Logue of the SDLP spoke at Trinity College, Dublin. Logue was reported as saying that the Council of Ireland could 'trundle' unionists as to a united Ireland. He denied it—but his actual words were hardly less infuriating for unionists. 'Britain,' said Logue in mid-January 1974, 'is in the process of disengaging herself from this country.' Logue quoted with approval the words of Desmond Boal QC, a leading advisor to the Revd Ian Paisley. Mr Boal had stated: 'We have just got to understand that the connection at this moment is in the process of being broken, no matter how many strangulated screams at this suggestion come from people who have been blind to the significance of recent history.' In Logue's analysis, the fearful unionist barrister had got it just right.[85] At the same time, it should be noted, a promise by Heath to the SDLP that he would phase out internment and begin releasing detainees as soon as possible also failed to materialize.[86]

A general election, called in February, in the United Kingdom facilitated a concentrated expression of Unionist discontent:[87] Unionists opposed to Sunningdale received only just over 50 per cent of the votes cast, but won eleven of the twelve (then) Northern Ireland seats in the House of Commons. The general election also replaced Heath's government in London with a Labour government under Harold Wilson.

When the new Prime Minister was appraised of the election results in Northern Ireland, he decided that the power-sharing experiment was

[83] Eamon Phoenix, 'Faulkner says Cosgrave's Declaration of North's Status was Devalued', *Irish Times*, 17 Jan. 2004.

[84] Centre for Contemporary British History, Witness Seminar, 11 Feb. 1993.

[85] 'Sunningdale gives Unity Declaration sought by De Valera', *Irish Times*, 17 Jan. 1974.

[86] Paddy Devlin, *The Fall of the Northern Ireland Executive* (Belfast, 1975), 39.

[87] G. K. Peatling, *The Failure of the Northern Ireland Peace Process* (Dublin, 2004), 47.

doomed. Harold Wilson, according to Bernard Donoughue, head of the policy unit at 10 Downing Street, was 'very committed' to a solution of the Northern Irish question, whilst being rather 'laid back' on the great questions of the day, Britain's relationship with Europe and income policy. The Prime Minister immediately became obsessed with a radical 'nuclear option' for Northern Ireland. He wished to achieve a British withdrawal by a complex, indirect route: 'What people in the Labour party don't understand is that the troops are the last to come out.' Wilson immediately established a secret committee to discuss such a policy: all this went on in blissful ignorance of Dublin's views. But Donoughue then received a call from the Irish Assistant Cabinet Secretary, Dermot Nally, who said: 'I get the impression you are planning something a bit radical on the North.'[88] Donoughue, who was slightly shaken, because the Downing Street discussions were supposed to be secret, asked: 'What do you think, Dermot?' Nally's reply was direct: 'I don't think it would be very welcome here.' Donoughue, who had great personal admiration for Nally, regarding him as a first-rate operator in a second-rate system, gently chided him with the charge of 'humbug'[89] and hypocrisy. Was Britain not proposing to do what Ireland had long rhetorically demanded? But Nally remained unmoved: the new British thinking was at best 'premature'. It was at this point, according to Donoughue, that the Ulster workers' strike intervened and physically brought down the power-sharing executive.

Throughout March and April an effort of sorts was made to save the executive. On 13 March Liam Cosgrave told the Dail: 'The factual position of Northern Ireland within the United Kingdom can not be changed, except by a decision of a majority of the people of Northern Ireland.'[90] But the damage done by the Boland case could not be undone by such a queasy formulation, for all that it actually represented the real position of the Irish government. Wilson visited Northern Ireland on 18 April for talks with police and army commanders, members of the executive, trade-unionist, and church leaders. He insisted that there was no alternative to the Sunningdale Agreement: privately, his view was the exact opposite.

In any case, the Sunningdale Agreement was doomed. On 15 May the loyalist Ulster Workers Council called for general work stoppages. The strike began with power-cuts and factory closures. On 17 May twenty-two people were murdered, and over 100 were injured, when three car bombs exploded during the rush hour in Dublin. Five others were murdered and

---

[88] Centre for Contemporary British History, Witness Seminar, 11 Feb. 1993.
[89] Lord Donoughue interview, 17 Aug. 2005.   [90] *Dail Debates*, vol. 271, col. 8.

twenty injured by a car bomb in Monaghan. The eventual death toll of thirty-three was the greatest number of people killed on any one day of the 'Troubles'. On 20 May the beleaguered executive met and agreed: 'Support for the strike was based on a false understanding of Sunningdale. Once this had been removed by a clear agreed statement from the Executive, support for the strikers would diminish.'[91] In a desperate last effort to save the executive, the SDLP agreed to 'phase' in the Council of Ireland. But the strike remained strong, and the performance of the state and the army in resisting it was hardly impressive. Wilson remarked privately: 'They've capitulated before they are supposed to know.'[92] But this flip remark—while revealing much about his own predilections—begs the question: if Downing Street believed the executive was doomed, why would army officers on the ground risk all for an already failed project? It also ignores the factor of surprise, which worked for the strikers. Informed opinion at the outset did not expect a successful, effective strike[93]—quite the contrary, there had been a recent history of rather feeble loyalist minor strikes. There was an assumption that the May strike would be of the same order—but over the first two days the strikers acquired a vice-like grip on the life of the province. It became very difficult to think of any military strategy which could have broken it without serious loss of life, with incalculable consequences.[94] It is also worth noting that the Prime Minister's own actions merely strengthened loyalist intransigence.

On 25 May 1974 the Prime Minister made a television and radio broadcast: it became known as the 'sponger's speech'. The strike, he said, was run by thugs dependent on the generosity of the British taxpayer for their livelihoods. Very unusually for Wilson, the speech was his own work—his principal advisors were excluded. The effect on the unionist community was the generation of a deep, cold anger, which further aided the strikers. On 28 May Faulkner and the five other Unionist members of the executive resigned, leading to the collapse of power-sharing.

It can easily be seen that Harold Wilson's decision not to support the executive with the army did not reveal any wish on his part to accommodate loyalist demands: quite the contrary, in fact. On 20 May 1974, five days before the 'spongers' broadcast, the Prime Minister decided to establish

[91] Minutes of Executive meeting, cited in Bew and Patterson, *The British State and the Ulster Crisis*, 65.
[92] Donoughue, Witness seminar, 11 Feb. 1993.
[93] Gordon Gillespie, *The Origins of the Ulster Workers' Strike*. *Études Irlandaises* (2004), 141; see e.g. David McKittrick's *Irish Times* article (14 Mar. 1974).
[94] Senior British army testimony to the Witness seminar, Centre for Contemporary British History, 11 Feb. 1993.

a small contingencies committee in Northern Ireland, to consider the 'unmentionable': British withdrawal from Northern Ireland.[95] A Cabinet subcommittee, which he chaired, held meetings from the end of the strike well into 1975. A number of options, including withdrawal and partition, were considered. The Prime Minister's own leaning was certainly in favour of withdrawal.

The fall of the executive was a bitter blow for the SDLP—it seemed to confirm that militant unionists had the strength to veto power-sharing in the North. John Hume increasingly insisted that the way forward lay through the path of a British–Irish imposed solution. But this was to be a long-term development, taking some ten years. In the short term, Hume had to face an Irish state which was reluctant to help. In an important 1975 discussion, he acknowledged to a senior British official that the IRA bombing campaign was designed to strengthen political reaction within the unionist community: he called for the British to 'destroy' the Provisionals.[96] Hume was even prepared to praise the 'courage and agility' of Faulkner, but the 'triumph of the demagogues and paramilitaries on the extremes of unionism'[97] left him deeply embittered. By 1979 he spoke of the unionist community in more aggressive tones: 'They are one of the most right-wing forces in Europe; nobody else would stand for them anywhere.'[98] Their failure to show 'any generosity either in the present or in the past' was the reason why Hume's policy after 1974 had, as its focus, the winning of British support for an imposed initiative. Hume's approach was to be resisted unsuccessfully within the SDLP by both Gerry Fitt and Paddy Devlin, who feared its polarizing effect; but both were marginalized, in consequence, within their own community.

HAROLD WILSON AND THE IRISH QUESTION: THE BRITISH PROJECT OF WITHDRAWAL?

What about the impact on the British government of the failure of power-sharing? At the end of May 1974 Harold Wilson remarked in the aftermath of the UWC strike: 'It is clear that we are in the position of "responsibility without power"'. The traditional prerogative of something

---

[95] Bernard Donoughue, *Downing Street Diary: With Harold Wilson in No. 10* (London, 2005), 20 May 1974, p. 124.

[96] *Irish Times*, 31 Dec. 2005.

[97] 'The Irish Question: A British Problem', *Foreign Affairs*, 58 (1979–80), 305.

[98] Interview with Seamus Deane and B. Fitzpatrick, *The Crane Bag*, 4: 2 (1980), 40.

very unpleasant through the ages—I think a eunuch [*sic*].'⁹⁹ The Prime Minister argued that, in this worsening situation, drastic measures might soon become inevitable. It was necessary, therefore, to evolve a 'Doomsday scenario'—a scenario which, Wilson acknowledged, was open to important objections. Wilson's plan was to give Northern Ireland a type of Dominion status, which effectively severed it from Britain. Under the plan, which was circulated only to his closest advisors, all British funding would have been cut off within five years, although a small army garrison would have been retained. The scheme would have effectively returned Northern Ireland to Protestant majority rule, would provoke international outcry, and could have led to massive bloodshed. Wilson acknowledged: 'It is open to nearly all the objections' which he then listed: 'Outbreak of violence and bloodshed, possible unacceptability to moderate Catholics, ditto to the Republic, the United Nations and the possible spread of trouble across the water, to name but a few.'¹⁰⁰ This was the 'malign scenario' which began to dominate the mind of Conor Cruise O'Brien, a minister in the Irish Cabinet in this epoch.

The Irish government was dismayed by the drift of the British Prime Minister's thinking. Although there is no evidence that this was Wilson's actual intention—his subjective support for British withdrawal appears to be genuine—he forced a process of tough-minded realism within the higher echelons of the Irish state. In June and July 1974 the Irish IDU (Inter-Departmental Unit) began to study the problem intensively. Ireland designed a plan to invade the North; but this plan acknowledged that a large army would be required to put down Protestant resistance. On 2 July 1974 the IDU, led by Dermot Nally, concluded:

An army of the order of 60,000 would be required to control Northern Ireland with the majority population in revolt against southern authority and to deal with possible counter attacks in this part of the country. This would be on the basis of total war. The willingness of any government in modern society to contemplate such action is open to doubt.

Tellingly, no plans were put in place to increase the size of the Irish army; the strength of the Irish defence forces in 1974 was 11,333 men, but it was decided that any plans to increase substantially those numbers would merely have destabilized the situation, or worse still, encouraged the British in their aspiration to withdraw. 'Any excessive actions on our part could make certain the holocaust mentioned by the British Prime Minister, that is likely

⁹⁹ 'Doomsday Plan made in Secret by No 10', *Belfast Telegraph*, 1 Jan. 2005; 'British had Doomsday Withdrawal Plan in '74', *Irish News*, 3 Jan. 2005.
¹⁰⁰ 'British had Doomsday Withdrawal Plan', *Irish News*, 3 Jan. 2005.

to involve the whole island. There is no rational basis for trying to assess the outcome of a situation which was developed in this way.'[101] All efforts were devoted to pushing the British away from the path of reunification. The Irish Foreign Minister, Garret FitzGerald, was so concerned about the possibility of British withdrawal that he mentioned it to Henry Kissinger in Washington. FitzGerald reminded Kissinger of Libyan involvement with the IRA and Cuba's long-distance role in Angola.[102]

But inside the British government more cautious attitudes began to prevail. Possibly as a result of Irish government pressure in Washington, the UK ambassador in Washington reported that the US government was opposed to withdrawal 'with or without a period of notice'. This development had a definite impact. 'Above all, we must avoid a drift to civil war, defeat and withdrawal', runs a memo to the Prime Minister in October 1974.[103] The British, but not the Prime Minister or Roy Jenkins, Home Secretary, were increasingly reconciled to direct rule: direct rule 'with a difference' was an aspiration expressed on 3 December. On 4 December 1974 Bernard Donoughue noted: 'Ahead stretches an endless period of direct political rule—which is why HW wants to get some movement towards pulling out.'[104] Roy Jenkins tended to support Wilson's view: 'Everything he heard made him more convinced that Northern Ireland was nothing to do with the rest of the UK.'[105] By mid-December a 'top secret' policy document had no illusions about a quick fix: 'We have a further considerable period of direct rule ahead of us.'[106] On 10 December, however, a group of Protestant clergymen met with the Provo leadership, military and political, in Feakle, Co. Clare: a rather bizarre encounter was disrupted, but not ended, by the appearance of the Irish Special Branch.[107] The British state felt it had to respond to any possible opportunity for 'peace' implied by the Feakle meeting.

The Provisional IRA announced on 20 December 1974 a temporary ceasefire, due to last from 22 December to 2 January, and eventually extended to 17 January. During all this time government officials engaged in dialogue with the leadership of Provisional Sinn Fein. Over the Christmas

---

[101] Ronan Fanning, 'Holocaust Fear if British left the North', *Sunday Independent*, 2 Jan. 2005; Stephen Collins, 'Doomsday Plan gave Part of North to Republic', *Sunday Tribune*, 2 Jan. 2005.

[102] Garret FitzGerald, *All in a Life* (Dublin, 1993), 259.

[103] Richard Bourke, 'Britain Clearly Wanted to Disengage from the North', *Irish Times*, 1 and 3 Jan. 2005.

[104] Donoughue, *Downing Street Diaries*, 253.   [105] Ibid. 254.

[106] Richard Bourke, 'Digging in for the Long Haul of Direct Rule', *Irish Times*, 4 Jan. 2005.

[107] Denis Cooke, *Peacemaker: The Life and Work of Eric Gallagher* (Peterborough, 2005), 212–24.

period the republicans were in receipt of a message from the British that 'HMG wished to devise structures of disengagement from Ireland'.[108] On 9 February the Provisional IRA announced an indefinite ceasefire to begin the following day. 'Incident centres', manned by Provisional Sinn Fein, were set up to monitor the ceasefire in liaison with the British government: the President of Provisional Sinn Fein called them the 'very legs on which the truce stands', while Maire Drumm, another key Sinn Fein leader, said that they constituted a power-base for Sinn Fein.[109] At a minimum, the Provisional IRA was being offered hegemony in nationalist areas: a hegemony it exploited to move against its local rivals, either republican or constitutionalist. The ceasefire was, however, more often observed in the breach: for example, on 13 August the Provisionals killed five Protestants in a Shankill bar, and on 1 September four more were killed at an Orange Hall in Newtownhamilton.

The game carried on, therefore, in Belfast. The *Irish Times* northern correspondent at the time was subsequently to recall a dinner party given for local newspaper editors by Merlyn Rees, Secretary of State for Northern Ireland, and Frank Cooper, a senior mandarin, at which Cooper had said that withdrawal would come in about five years. He added that in the first two months of 1975, 'officials at Stormont began to lace their dinner conversations and political *tête-à-têtes* with predictions of a pull-out. It now seems that this was aimed at creating an atmosphere which convinced the Provos that their main aim, a declaration of intent, was soon to become a reality.'[110]

British policy enunciated a form of tough love for the province: a kind of 'hands off' approach, sanctioned by the Prime Minister, which signalled psychological withdrawal. John Whale commented in the *Sunday Times*: 'The central fact about British policy ... is that the government has made the clear-eyed decision to have no policy, because it has no power to enforce one.' Whale concluded: 'The nub of the Provisionals' dream is an Ireland without British influence. Now they have it ... It has not happened in quite the way they expected it, and it will not have the consequences they once looked for: but these things never do.'[111] In similar vein, Louis Branney, in the FCO Research Department, speculated that the Provisional IRA might be induced to accept an independent Ulster, because 'in the tradition of Wolfe Tone, the republicans have always regarded the north as in some way different and separate, but no less Irish'.[112] This memo was

---

[108] *Irish Times*, 30 Apr. 1992
[109] Paul Bew and Henry Patterson, *The British State and the Ulster Crisis: From Wilson to Thatcher* (London, 1985) 66.
[110] *Irish Times*, 9 June 1978.   [111] *Sunday Times*, 23 June 1975.
[112] National Archives (London), FCO Research Department, 28 Aug. 1975.

attached to the relevant recent press cuttings: and in this way media and mandarin speculation mutually reinforced each other. The British driver seemed determined to send out a message: 'look, no hands.' It was not so much a question of not having a selfish strategic interest in Ulster policy; rather a matter of not caring less. Emotional disengagement was the order of the day. In July 1975 the *Guardian's* Belfast correspondent, Derek Browne, aptly summed up the situation:

> Constitutionally, politically and militarily, the solution in Northern Ireland has never been so fluid or open to speculation. So-called solutions like independence, restored majority rule and British withdrawal are openly canvassed and debated in the best informed circles, and with every day that passes, the wilder predictions are growing more credible.[113]

Perhaps in response to these uncertainties, in September 1975 there was a brief flicker of movement in unionist politics. The former hardliner William Craig, backed by, amongst others, David Trimble, a young academic lawyer, urged a unionist voluntary coalition, including the SDLP, for Northern Ireland.[114] Paisley vacillated and then crushed the proposal, thus winning the first round in a struggle which Trimble was to reopen two decades later.

The leader of the republican movement, Ruairí Ó Bradaigh, was later to give two principal reasons for the failure of his strategy of his negotiation with the British. He was to stress the great increase in loyalist anti-Catholic violence during the period of the truce: fear of a sectarian bloodbath in the event of British withdrawal undoubtedly had an impact on the British state machinery as a whole. But Ó Bradaigh also acknowledged another potent factor: 'The Dublin government indicated to the British that a withdrawal must not be contemplated.'[115] Dublin was becoming increasingly 'twitchy at the continuation of the truce and talks', the British representative said. Dublin hunted down and arrested David O'Connell, a key republican leader, in September 1975.

In this sense, Ó Bradaigh's defence of his handling of the dialogue with British officials has a certain limited credibility. There was an impulse towards 'withdrawal' within the British system, and it had the support of the

---

[113] Derek Browne, 'The Treacherous Truce', *Guardian*, 15 July 1975.

[114] See J. A. McKibben, 'Ulster Vanguard: A Sociological Profile', unpublished Master's thesis, Queen's University Belfast (1990), 172–208; Henry Patterson and Eric Kaufman, *Unionism and Orangeism in Northern Ireland since 1945* (Manchester, 2007), 180–5.

[115] *Irish Times*, 22 Dec. 1992. For a fuller statement of Ó Bradaigh's case, see Robert W. White, *Ruairí Ó Bradaigh: The Life and Politics of a Revolutionary* (Bloomington and Indianapolis, 2006), 219–47. Interestingly, Michael Oatley, one of the British interlocutors in the early phase of the dialogue, has insisted it was 'minutely monitored at the highest level', *Prospect* (Sept. 2006), 5.

Prime Minister. British intentions were unclear, and they reflected differing views within the Cabinet and the civil service. There is, however, evidence to sustain the argument that the Prime Minister's views never gained hegemony within either the political class or higher civil service, which, especially given Dublin's hostility to withdrawal and the pressure Dublin exercised via America, was always in a more cautious, less anti-unionist, place than the Prime Minister. According to a secret British document, written in early January 1975, the British, in entering into an understanding with the Provos, had two aims: first, to 'string [the IRA] along to the point where their military capacity went soggy' and where Catholic community support disappeared,[116] and secondly, 'to give the doves the excuse to call it all off without [the British] making substantial concessions'. In February the British ambassador in Dublin reassured the Irish Minister for Foreign Affairs, Garret FitzGerald, that the ongoing contact between the British and the IRA was 'to explain British policy and not to negotiate'. The Northern Ireland Office officials had found the Sinn Fein representatives were 'still politically naïve and did not seem to have the remotest understanding of British policy'.[117]

This was a reassurance greatly welcomed in Dublin. On 7 July 1975 Dermot Nally told the Taoiseach that the relative advantages of a continued British presence in the North were 'so great that we should do everything possible to bring it about'.[118] Nally insisted that northern nationalist ambitions should not be allowed to threaten the stability of the southern state. Despite all this British sensitivity, in September 1975 the Irish Department of Foreign Affairs was still fearful that the British had 'plans ... for shuffling off the Northern coil'.[119] The British embassy in Dublin had a definite responsiveness to the nervousness of the Irish state: in mid-October 1975 it warned that British withdrawal would generate 'more or less permanent instability on the whole island': the creation of a 'Portugal on our doorstep ... leaving aside any moral considerations about our obligations to the democratic majority in Northern Ireland and the bloodshed which would follow a withdrawal, it is in our own best interest, selfishly defined to stay in the province'.[120]

---

[116] Rory Rapple, 'Sifting through Sunningdale', *Sunday Business Post*, 1 Jan. 2006.

[117] John Bowman, 'Files Highlight Warnings of British Plans for North', *Irish Times*, 29 Dec. 2005.

[118] Ronan Fanning, 'How Dublin prepared for the Threat of NI Doomsday', *Sunday Independent*, 1 Jan. 2006.

[119] John Bowman, 'Files Highlight Warnings of British Plans for North', *Irish Times*, 29 Dec. 2005.

[120] National Archives (London), FCO (17 Oct. 1975), report prepared for the Republic of Ireland desk. In 1976 Nally warned lest Irish criticisms might intensify British irritations and lead to withdrawal, *Irish Times*, 29 Dec. 2006. For further evidence of Nally's caution see Eamon Delany, 'Operation Doomsday', *Magill* (Nov. 2006).

But even responsiveness to Irish fears did not place the British and Irish governments in exactly the same place. The British had an unwelcome problem on their plate, placed there by the Provisional IRA, which drew its legitimacy from the wider Irish nationalist story as articulated by Irish governments. The fact that the Irish government did not actually want a united Ireland—painfully evident to the British—did not necessarily make the British job of managing the North easier in the absence of a decisive Irish government political, ideological, and military assault on the republican movement. The British, therefore, felt that they had a perfect right to explore any possible way out of their problems: there was no question of accepting any Irish veto on a dialogue with republicans. While the British might sometimes be tempted to regard extreme republicans in the North as potential politicians, struggling to change the nature of terrorist organizations, Michael Daly of the British embassy in Dublin acknowledged: 'In the eyes of the Dublin government, the IRA are an armed conspiracy, bent on subverting the very fabric of the state.' On the other hand, for the British there was a fundamental consideration, which has to be respected, regardless of Irish concerns: 'If the extremists are to be induced to give up their violent role', the corollary of this was 'that they might be allowed to seek a political one to replace it'.[121] In the end, the Provisional leadership *was* deceived as to British intentions, but it was deceived so effectively, in part because of the genuine degree of division on the British side, and because the Provos should have given more thought to the implications of Dublin's attitude.

Sir Frank Cooper later said the truce had been the means of getting rid of internment—a 'noose round the neck of the government'—and of perhaps separating the political element from the 'militarists'. The dialogue with the Provos had been one of 'mutual obfuscation',[122] but this does not mean that Ó Bradaigh was necessarily simply the victim of a cunning plan—as the new leadership of Gerry Adams was to allege—but rather, that the balance of forces within both British and Irish politics foreclosed against the republican project and the British Prime Minister's inclination to foster it, because that project was essentially unrealistic. But a legacy of mistrust remained: one of the first actions of the British representative upon renewing negotiations with the republican leadership in 1990 was to explicitly reassure the IRA that this time Britain was 'sincere' and not out to 'con' them. There was much irony here: because this time, the British faced a northern leadership of the IRA (Adams, McGuinness), which had exploited

---

[121] National Archives, FCO 87/471, Michael F. Daly, British Embassy, Dublin, 24 Nov. 1975.
[122] Bew and Patterson, *British State and the Ulster Crisis*, 108.

the 'naivety' of the old southern leadership (Ó Bradaigh and his allies) to push them on to the sidelines.[123] Labour Party politicians, including both Merlyn Rees and Roy Mason, and NIO officials later claimed that the sole purpose of the truce was to divide the Provisional leadership and to create the conditions for ending internment and for criminalizing the Provisionals: but had policy been quite so defined and so cynical for the Prime Minister?

Certainly, when the truce formally broke down on 22 September, Harold Wilson—supported in this by Roy Jenkins—continued to dream of withdrawal. 'But the politicians were not interested,' Donoughue recorded in his diary in mid-November 1975, 'Rees, Healy and Callaghan all said "Do nothing" ... HW and Jenkins were the only two looking for something different in the longer term—separation from Britain.'[124] On 10 January Wilson produced a self-confessed apocalyptic note on the theme of an independent Northern Ireland. As late as early March 1976 the Prime Minister was still thinking of ways of punishing the (Northern) Irish for financial subsidies, now running at £600 million a year;[125] but even here he met with stubborn resistance from other ministers. The Irish government hoped that Wilson was reconverted to direct rule after a 5 March meeting—but he was not.[126]

The period of great indeterminacy in British policy finally idled to a close with Wilson's surprise resignation in mid-March 1976. With Callaghan's premiership came the appointment, in September 1976, of Roy Mason as Secretary of State for Northern Ireland. Mason, more than any other secretary of state before or since, defended direct rule as a form of government which both communities could tolerate.

A STABILIZATION OF POLICY? THE ROAD TO THE HUNGER STRIKE

In June 1976 Merlyn Rees, the then Secretary of State, revealed that soon after the end of the truce and the release of the last detainees, the Bourne Committee had been set up by the NIO to investigate the problem of recovering 'greater effectiveness of the police in enforcing the rule of the

---

[123] Sinn Fein, *Setting the Record Straight: A Record of Communications between Sinn Fein and the British Government October 1990–November 1993* (Belfast, 1993), p. 28, 23 Mar. 1993, report of meeting with British government representative.
[124] Donoughue, *Downing Street Diaries*, 11 Nov. 1975, p. 562.
[125] National Archives, CJ4/1250/1358; Donoughue, *Downing Street Diaries*, 5 Mar. 1976, p. 685.
[126] Ibid., 26 Feb. 1976, p. 678. *Irish Times*, 29 Dec. 2006.

law'. The moral ambiguities of the ceasefire and the incident centres now forgotten, Rees now defined the 'security problem' as one of the 'small groups of criminals'.[127] In the months before his appointment, Roy Mason as Secretary of State for Defence had supported a tougher military response in Northern Ireland: 'He asked to dispatch the "Spearhead" battalion straightaway—the instruction was sent from the Cabinet Room. He also suggested sending in the SAS; using computerised intelligence information, closing the border and designating Armagh a special security area under martial law.'[128] At his first press conference as Northern Ireland Secretary, Mason surprised the assembled media representatives by claiming that his concern over the poor state of Northern Ireland's economy exceeded any worries he had about the political situation or security: 'Unemployment, little new investment, too many businesses closing down, these are the questions which must receive priority.'[129] Mason later added for good measure: 'The majority of people in Northern Ireland want to stay inside the United Kingdom. People feel they get as good a deal out of direct rule as they do out of any other form of rule.'[130]

The Provisionals, slowly weaned off the opiate of secret negotiation with government, elaborated the long-war strategy. A new, younger northern leadership emerged under Gerry Adams and Martin McGuinness: it explicitly defined itself by saying that it would never again negotiate with a British government until the British set a date for withdrawal. In the end, the long war was to fail in this objective, and the new leadership found themselves compelled to go down the same road—parlaying with the British—for which they had condemned the old, with what was left of the old loudly condemning them.[131]

The Mason epoch was a discouraging one for the Provisionals—a fact reflected in contemporary comment—provoking them into a major reorganization and creation of a cellular structure which, it is now clear, only partially reduced their vulnerability to informers for a while. It was also relatively stabilizing for unionism: in a desperate attempt to radicalize his base, Paisley threatened to leave politics if a second strike in 1977[132]—against the direct rule machine—failed. But this time the unionist community was much less moved. There was close co-ordination between the Secretary of State, the army GoC, and the Chief Constable, while the NIO also successfully played a delaying game with the electricity workers, whose

127 *Hansard*, vol. 913, 14 June 1976, col. 50.
128 Donoughue, *Downing Street Diary*, 6 Jan. 1976, p. 621.
129 *The Times*, 28 Sept. 1976.   130 Ibid., 27 Nov. 1976.
131 Ed Molony, *A Secret History of the IRA* (London, 2002).
132 For a recent discussion of this strike see *Sunday Tribune*, 10 Dec. 2006.

support was crucial to the success or failure of the stoppage. The strike failed, but Paisley did not keep his promise to leave politics, and enjoyed a compensating triumph in the 1977 local elections and the European elections of 1979.

In June 1977, in a 'pork-barrel election',[133] Jack Lynch unexpectedly led Fianna Fail back into government with a twenty-seat majority—the biggest in the history of the state. With sharp insight, he noted on the night of his victory that the majority was too large and could create problems. Lynch called for a new initiative on the North and criticized the new British emphasis on direct rule. But his private objectives on the North were rather limited: after a September meeting with the Prime Minister, James Callaghan, in London, he claimed that he had been reassured that there would be no drift towards greater integration of Northern Ireland within the United Kingdom.[134] But a weak Callaghan government, with a slender parliamentary majority, was in no position to turn against the Ulster Unionist MPs in the House of Commons, who were leaning towards an integrationist and non-devolutionist stance, and who had won a convert in Airey Neave, the Tory opposition spokesman, who was assassinated by Irish republicans of the Irish National Liberation Army (INLA) in the Palace of Westminster on 30 March 1979,[135] two days after the fall of the Callaghan government on a confidence vote by 311 to 310.

But would Neave's integrationism survive his murder? At first, it seemed that it would. The Conservative manifesto for the general election stated: 'In the absence of devolved government, we seek to establish one or more regional councils with a wide range of powers over local services.' There was no mention of power-sharing.[136] Margaret Thatcher swept to power in May 1979, but she was soon to be tested by the IRA's most effective military intervention for years.

In fact, the Irish policy of the Thatcher government was to be characterized by a vacillation not to be found in other aspects of policy. The Queen's cousin, Earl Mountbatten, and other members of his party, including two teenagers, were killed in a bomb attack on his boat outside the harbour of Mullaghmore in Co. Sligo on 27 August 1979. On the same day, nineteen soldiers were blown up at Warrenpoint. In the aftermath of these events the new British Prime Minister insisted on greater security co-operation with Dublin. Jack Lynch conceded permission for British helicopters to cross

---

[133] Dermot Keogh, *Twentieth Century Ireland: Nation and State* (Dublin, 1994), 327.
[134] *Irish Times*, 29 Sept. 1977.
[135] Jack Holland and Henry McDonald, *INLA: The Story of One of Ireland's Most Ruthless Terrorist Organisations* (Dublin, 1997), 212–18.
[136] Bew and Patterson, *The British State and the Ulster Crisis*, 111.

the border for a limited distance in cases of 'hot pursuit': after all, Ireland allowed British helicopters to assist in air–sea rescues. But Lynch had failed to grasp the neuralgic symbolism of the issue: when the Taoiseach, jetlagged and reeling from two by-election losses in his Cork base, admitted his change of policy at the National Press Club in Washington DC, a Fianna Fail backbencher, Dr Bill Loughnane, called him a 'liar' and demanded his resignation. Sile de Valera TD supported Loughnane on this issue, and Lynch's effort to fire Loughnane from the Parliamentary Party failed. Lynch decided it was time to resign on 5 December 1979: mistakenly, he believed that his deputy, George Colley, was likely to succeed him. In the event, Charles James Haughey, the veteran of the arms-trial crisis, won by forty-four votes to thirty-eight.

Haughey was a vehement critic of what he saw as the place-hunting, venality, and corruption of the Redmondite political party.[137] But he did not regard such anti-corruption flapdoodle as having any relevance to his own activities. While Colley, as part of his self-image as representative of old-style Fianna Fail decency, imitated the self-consciously modest lifestyle of de Valera, Haughey revelled in a lifestyle far beyond his apparent financial means. In fact, a rationalization for his inexplicably wealthy existence was ready at hand. Patrick Gallagher of the Gallagher Construction Group, in 1979, helped to write off Haughey's £1 million debt with Allied Irish Banks. 'Haughey was financed in order to create the environment which the Anglo-Irish enjoyed and we as a people could never aspire to', he explained in a 1998 interview. Gallagher added: 'Everything was planned. Someone had to live in the big house.'[138] The big house in question, in Kinsealy, was the Palladian mansion originally built by the Ascendancy politician John Beresford in the late eighteenth century. In fact, the new Fianna Fail leader mimicked his eighteenth-century Anglo-Irish precursor not just in styles of conspicuous consumption and a taste for profane and vulgar language, but in a crude indifference to those groups which stood outside this new Dublin establishment, 'Hail fellow, well met', but cold at heart; once again the Palladian mansion echoed to the 'volley of execrations'—in a famous interview with *Hot Press*, Haughey gave a view of some Irish political commentators: 'I could instance a lot of fuckers whose throats I'd cut and push off the nearest cliff.'[139] More significant was his contemptuous attitude towards northern unionists. One of the leading journalists of the

[137] Martin Mansergh (ed.), C. J. Haughey, *The Spirit of the Nation: The Speeches and Statements of Charles Haughey* (Cork, 1986), 310; James McConnell, ' "Jobbing with Tory and Liberal": Irish Nationalists and the Politics of Patronage', *Past & Present*, 188 (Aug. 2005), 105–31, analyses the Redmondite record.

[138] Peter Murtagh, 'Power, Corruption and Lies', *Irish Times*, 17 June 2006.

[139] *Sunday Times*, 18 June 2006, 'A New Reformation for the Language of Diplomacy'.

early Troubles period was to write: 'I vividly recall the burden of Haughey's conversation: that Ulster protestants were secondary to the future of Ireland and that—his own words—"they've never achieved anything".'[140] This sectarianism was combined with a powerful parochialism, as befitted one of the most energetic and ruthless of the first generation of children born in Ireland in the 1920s.

The son of a Free State army officer from the North, Haughey first achieved some public notice on VE Day in May 1945: in celebration of the end of the war in Europe, some Trinity College students flew the Union Jack from the flagpole facing College Green: Haughey, in retaliation, burned another Union Jack, and there was a minor riot.[141] Haughey was also uncomprehending of Samuel Beckett's decision to stay in wartime France and win a Croix de Guerre for his services to the resistance rather than come back to peacetime Ireland.[142] In office, Haughey stopped the Irish army attending the British Legion Remembrance Sunday services in St Patrick's Cathedral, thus creating a context whereby the Irish army was present at the Glen of Imaal to honour the Nazi dead of the Second World War, but was not present to honour the Irish dead of that conflict.[143] On domestic policy, Haughey promised to reverse Lynch's policy of expenditure based on unsustainable borrowing. In the end, in his first two years as Taoiseach he did nothing to contain spending or Exchequer borrowing, which averaged just under 16 per cent of Gross National Product during his first term. National debt rose from 85 per cent of GNP to 102 per cent in that period, while inflation was just short of 20 per cent. In frustration, Haughey turned to the 'North' as an issue, and there was plenty to engage him.[144] Dublin now had a rhetorically 'green' premier, but his early efforts to put pressure on a British government, led by Margaret Thatcher since 1979, were woefully unsophisticated and easily rebuffed.[145] Thatcher insisted: 'No democratic country can voluntarily abandon its responsibilities in a part of its territory against the will of a majority of the population there.'[146]

[140] Henry Kelly: 'Haughey polluted the air of Irish politics. His rules were his own, his vanity was breathtaking', *Sunday Telegraph*, 18 June 2006.

[141] Bruce Arnold, *Haughey* (London, 1993), 14.

[142] *Ireland on Sunday*, 18 June 2006; Terry Eagleton, 'Political Beckett?', *New Left Review*, 2nd ser., 40 (July–Aug. 2006), 67–77.

[143] Kevin Myers, 'On his watch corruption became part of Irish life', *Irish Independent*, 14 June 2006.

[144] Marc Coleman, 'Celtic tiger's father left a haunting legacy', *Irish Times*, 20 June 2006.

[145] Frank Dunlop, *Yes, Taoiseach* (Dublin, 2004), 217. See also C. J. Haughey, 'Northern Ireland: A New Approach', *Études Irlandaises*, NS 5 (Dec. 1980), 153–63.

[146] 'In Memory of Airey Neave', *Études Irlandaises* (Dec. 1980), 145.

The end of internment had led to a new British policy of 'criminalization', as republicans called it: above all, the denial of political status to prisoners. The hunger-strike weapon lay to hand. The historic role of the hunger strike in the history of the IRA was well known—it was inevitable that, from 1977 onwards, the Provos should begin to consider a new hunger strike.[147] As the level of violence fell significantly from 1977 to 1979, there was a strong sense of a campaign petering out. The hunger strikes transformed the political character of the Northern Ireland problem. Now republican prisoners appeared in the role of men prepared to accept suffering for their cause rather than simply inflicting suffering on others. The first wave of hunger strikes disintegrated before Christmas 1980. A second, more determined wave, led by Bobby Sands, the Provisionals' 'commanding officer' in the Long Kesh jail, began in March 1981. The hunger-strikers and their supporters articulated, as Terence MacSwiney in 1920 had done before them, 'a tribal voice of martyrdom, deeply embedded in the Gaelic, Catholic, Nationalist tradition'. The main Catholic daily paper, the *Irish News*, was filled with obituary notices on the lines of 'God's curse on you, England, you cold-hearted monster', and invocations of 'Mary, Queen of Ireland'. The remarkable murals that began to cover gable walls in many Catholic areas of Belfast displayed religious feeling in many ways, the hunger-striker as Christ with rosary beads being frequently displayed. Young activists on public demonstrations switched seamlessly from political chant to deal out a decade at the rosary. 'A moment before, they had been shouting "One, two, three, four, open up the H-block door". Now, on the steps of Enniskillen Town Hall, the Rosary was said, rhythmic, flowing, automatic, and passing Catholic housewives joined in. Prayer and protest are easy companions in Fermanagh.'[148] New political possibilities were opened up—first indicated by Bobby Sands himself, when he won a by-election for the Westminster constituency of Fermanagh and South Tyrone on 9 April 1981.

The impact of the hunger-strikers can not be measured simply at this popular electoral level. The most distinguished Irish writers, men like Sean O'Faolain and Seamus Heaney, who had refused to accept many nationalist pieties,[149] were moved to sympathy and even a kind of moral support. Sean O'Faolain saw in the hunger-strikers a revival of the pre-Christian habit described in the ancient Irish laws of 'fasting against a person of exalted state

[147] See Ed Moloney's report in *Hibernia* (Oct. 1979); and the discussion in Bew and Patterson, *The British State and the Ulster Crisis*, 118.

[148] *Irish Times*, 4 May 1981.

[149] See Heaney's acceptance of Unionist political rights in his fascinating interview 'The Art of Poetry', in *Paris Review*, 144 (Fall 1997), 114. Sean O'Faolain had issued a celebrated rebuke on the subject of the IRA's sacrifice of Irish Catholic policemen in 1919–21.

in order to enforce a claim against him'.[150] Seamus Heaney has described the impact of a hunger-striker's death, that of Francis Hughes, the second to die after Bobby Sands: 'I had walked to Mass with his sisters and had worked in the summertime in the Bogside with his father.' Heaney has described the return of the body, under police escort, to the hunger-striker's home village of Toomebridge.

By what right did the steel ring of the defence forces close round the remains of one who was son, brother, comrade, neighbour, companion? The nationalist collective felt that the police presence was an assault on what the Irish language would call their *duchas*, their entire sense of community: hence the fury of the local crowd.[151]

But set against Heaney's commentary was the observation of the senior policeman Alan McQuillan, whose principal memory was the horrible violence done to children who were among Hughes's dozen or so victims:[152] 'He was an extremely good terrorist. He killed a lot of people. A terrible and ruthless opponent—and in some way brave. But I saw a lot of people he murdered, including a child, which gives a different perspective.' One community saw a hero, the other a brutal child-murderer. The hunger-strike movement greatly assisted the political rise of Sinn Fein: but it also deepened the profound incomprehension and mutual hostility of the two communities. Unionists reacted to attempts to capture sympathy for hunger-strikers with cold contempt. In the May 1981 local government elections, they gave the DUP a majority over the UUP for the first time, despite the UUP's 'integrationist' success of the late 1970s.

Haughey dissolved the Dail on 21 May 1981, claiming that he was calling the election because of the grave and tragic situation in Northern Ireland. Terry Keane, his self-proclaimed mistress, recalled:

He was sure he'd win it on the northern ticket, but I said, 'don't be ridiculous, nobody gives a fiddlers about the North, the Irish electorate only cares about money'. He was a bit needled and said: 'Oh, you Wimbledon women, what would you know?' This was because I had grown up in England, but I was proven right.[153]

In the general election campaign of 1981 Haughey insisted: 'I believe there is always in the general, in the mind, the Irish public mind, a wish for a

---

[150] 'Living and Dying in Ireland', in Karl Miller, introduction, *London Review of Books, Anthology 1* (London, 1981), 62.

[151] 'Translating a Classic', *Proceedings of the American Philosophical Society*, 48: 4 (Dec. 1994), 412.

[152] *Sunday Tribune*, 23 Oct. 2005.

[153] Terry Keane, 'An electrifying first meeting was quickly followed by a secret encounter in a London hotel', *Ireland on Sunday*, 18 June 2006.

solution to this problem, a wish for ultimate Irish unity. I believe that's as present today as ever it was.'[154] The bulk of the electorate, however, 'continued to focus doggedly on the domestic issues of taxation, inflation and unemployment'.[155] Haughey clung to power by striking highly expensive deals with independents and smaller parties, but eventually fell on a vote of no confidence in November 1982: a Fine Gael–Labour coalition took office in December.

Two other hunger-strikers were elected in the Republic's general election in June, and in the aftermath of Sands's death his election agent, Owen Carron, was elected for his constituency on 20 August. The story of martyrdom for the cause was also a story of cold political calculation. In a powerful recent account—which has drawn support from other independent sources—Richard O'Rawe, a Provisional at the centre of the hunger-strike crisis in the Maze Prison, argues that after the death of the first four hunger-strikers the British made an improved offer: 'I thought the offer was sufficient for us to settle the dispute honourably.'[156] O'Rawe describes a crisis of personal faith: 'I tried time and again, I search for a counterbalancing argument to the charge that the Republican leadership let hunger strikers die to get Carron elected.'[157] The tenth and last hunger-striker to die did so on 20 August, the day of Carron's election. By June 1983 Sinn Fein had obtained some 13.4 per cent of the vote in the North, which compared well with the SDLP's 17.9 per cent. The British government faced the real possibility that the political wing of the Provisional IRA would take over from the SDLP as the principal representative of northern Catholics.

The new Irish government, led by Garret FitzGerald, was gripped by a fear that revolutionary nationalism would displace constitutional nationalism in the North. It became the task of Irish diplomacy to persuade the British state to take on board this fear and take action—anti-unionist action, if necessary—to prevent this dire outcome. In May 1984 Dublin issued the Forum Report in an effort to change British policy and turn it towards a more amenable direction.

In fact, since late 1983 negotiations of a very tentative sort had stated between the British and Irish governments, 'the initiative [coming] from the Irish side'. The negotiations were carried on in great secrecy and confined to a small group of officials working under the two prime ministers. One of the two key British officials (alongside Sir Robert Armstrong), Sir David

---

[154] O'Brien, *The Modern Prince*, 191.   [155] Patterson, *Ireland Since 1939*, 277.
[156] Richard O'Rawe, *Blanketmen: An Untold Story of the Hunger Strike* (Dublin, 2005), 180, 254. For the new support for O'Rawe's argument, see the remarks of Denis Bradley, who acted as an intermediary between the IRA and the British, 'IRA was offered deal, says Bradley', *Sunday Times*, 30 Apr. 2006.
[157] *Blanketmen*, 254.

Goodall, has given us his view of the negotiating position of the Irish Prime Minister:

Dr FitzGerald was prepared drastically to lower Nationalist sights on Irish unification in the interests of promoting stability in Northern Ireland and halting the political advance of Sinn Fein. This meant trying to reconcile Nationalists to the union rather than breaking it; but ... this could only be done if the Republic were associated in some institutionalised way in the government of Northern Ireland.[158]

The fear of Sinn Fein superseding the SDLP, carefully cultivated and even exaggerated by the Irish government, was the decisive impulse behind the process that led to the signing of the Anglo-Irish Agreement.

ANGLO-IRISH AGREEMENT? THE HILLSBOROUGH ACCORD OF 1985

The hunger strikes, not in themselves but through later political developments, had therefore been one of the turning-points of the Troubles, a turning-point that eventually had deep implications for the local Protestant community—ironically in many respects, because they had not been directly involved in the original dispute between the British government and the hunger-strikers. As slightly mystified onlookers, few leading unionists grasped the drift of events, and they found themselves effectively excluded from negotiations. Even unionist leader Jim Molyneaux's sympathetic biographer, Ann Purdy, concluded: 'His peculiar characteristic of being able to have a "long view" and of recognising the eventual outcome of a policy even before it has left the drawing board, failed on this occasion.'[159] This time Molyneaux had been cut out of 'the loop', and, in part at least, the responsibility was his own and that of Enoch Powell, now a key figure in the Unionist parliamentary party. Powell had been delegated the task of 'managing' Thatcher, but Powell's austere personality rendered him useless for the purpose,[160] , despite his huge intellectual influence on Thatcherite Conservatism. In October 1984 the IRA exploded a murderous bomb at the Conservative Party Conference in Brighton, almost killing the Prime Minister, but failing to derail the Anglo-Irish negotiations.

The Anglo-Irish Agreement of November 1985 sent a shudder of horror through the unionist community. There was a huge demonstration of

---

[158] David Goodall, 'The Irish Question', Headmaster's lecture given at Ampleforth 1992, *Ampleforth Journal*, 98 (Spring 1992), 471.
[159] Ann Purdy, *Molyneaux: The Long View* (Greystone, 1989), 9.
[160] Simon Heffer, *Like the Roman: The Life of Enoch Powell* (London, 1998), 897.

protest. It accentuated fears of British betrayal, and Margaret Thatcher, who only shortly before had appeared as a reassuring figure, became the focus of much rage. Thatcher herself, rather like Gladstone in 1881, underestimated the radicalism of her own actions; unlike Gladstone, she came to regret these. Ian Paisley told his congregation at the Martyrs' Memorial Church: 'We pray this night that thou wouldst deal with the Prime Minister of our country. O God, in wrath take vengeance upon this wicked, treacherous, lying woman: take vengeance upon her, O Lord, and grant that we shall see a demonstration of thy power.' Much anger was also focused locally on the NIO, though in fact the Foreign Office and, more particularly, the Cabinet Office had taken the decisive role in committing Britain to the Agreement, while the NIO had been profoundly sceptical.[161] In the midst of much heated rhetoric—especially about the failure to consult unionists—it was difficult to detect the real significance of the Agreement.

Above all, the Anglo-Irish Agreement ushered in an era of direct rule with a green tinge, symbolized by the permanent presence of Irish government officials at Maryfield, Co. Down. The Agreement was novel in its explicit acceptance of a role for the Irish government in the affairs of the North, as a defender of the interests of the nationalist community. This role was much less than the joint authority proposed by the New Ireland Forum—shared responsibility for all aspects of the administration of government—but it was more than purely consultative. Much of the confusion in unionist politics arose from the difficulties involved in coping with this fact. The Agreement also acknowledged that the British government would support a united Ireland if majority consent existed for it in the North. Here it was less novel: the same point had been enunciated in 1973 at the time of the Sunningdale Agreement.

The text of the Anglo-Irish Agreement explicitly attempted to encourage devolution on a cross-community basis, but, despite a later inaccurate claim by Thatcher to this effect, it was not possible to 'knock out' its institutions by agreeing to power-sharing. It is important to note the view of the Northern Ireland Office that mere 'lip service' was being paid to power-sharing devolution, and the Agreement was, in fact, an alternative.[162]

---

[161] Mark Stuart, *Douglas Hurd: The Public Servant* (Edinburgh and London, 1988), 147. Hurd's diary entry for 9 May 1985 notes a 'very important meeting in the Northern Ireland Office to chart the way forward. Officials are negative … Officials like direct rule without Dublin or devolution'.

[162] Bew, Gibbon, and Patterson, *Northern Ireland 1921–2001*, 205–9. I am indebted to senior sources within the Northern Ireland Office for this information. I am indebted also to Sir David Goodall for allowing me to consult his papers at Churchill College, Cambridge, including his important 78-page account of the Anglo-Irish Agreement.

In the absence of any agreement on devolution, the Anglo-Irish Agreement gave a paradoxical shape to the governmental institutions of the North. In substance, the system was, administratively and economically, increasingly integrated with the United Kingdom. This integration was intensified by the growing reliance of the entire community on the British subvention. Nevertheless, the new role of the Irish government in Northern Ireland affairs appeared to be irreversible, and for many this implied the eventual evolution of a formalized system of joint authority.

Thatcher's eventual decision to support the Agreement owed much to American pressure: Ronald Reagan pressed the Prime Minister in this direction, in part, at least, because the President wished to have a means of softening Speaker Tip O'Neill's critique of his Nicaragua policy.[163] The impact of this Anglo-American *realpolitik* was suppressed at the time. Senior Tories deceived themselves as to the balance of the negotiation, claiming, for example, an illusory victory on the principle of consent. 'The Unionists had a negative grievance against the secrecy of the negotiations, but when the agreement was reached, they failed to see that they had gained a huge success in the recognition of consent.'[164] In fact, there was no particular victory on consent: the Irish government's rhetorical constitutional claim remained in force—an ideological provocation to unionists, even if it meant nothing in international law. But the real problem lay elsewhere: it lay with the poisonous impact of the Agreement of 1985 on community relations, an impact which mocked the Agreement's stated objective of reconciliation.

In 1983, in his Oak Room speech, Garret FitzGerald had insisted that the Irish people were 'too wise' to seek to impose a deal with the British over the heads of the unionists. In 1985 FitzGerald explicitly reversed his position, in a way which echoed Redmond's reversal in 1910 of his earlier views of the 1890s. For a second time in the twentieth century, a moderate nationalist leader, who had promised a conciliatory approach to unionism—ruling out the manipulation of the power of the British state against it—had reneged on that promise. Garret FitzGerald has explained that this was a reluctant change of mind, forced upon him by the electoral rise of Sinn Fein, which, in his view, made the status quo in the North unsustainable. But in the European elections of 1984 and the local elections of 1985, the dramatic electoral progress of Sinn Fein which existed in the 1981–3

---

[163] John A. Farrell, *Tip O'Neill and the Democratic Century* (Boston, 2001), 624. 'We hoped to use this [Irish policy] as a lever against Tip, in order to get contra aid money', wrote one National Security Council official in a memo. To this extent, Powell's obsession with US influence was justified, Heffer, *Like the Roman*, 822.

[164] Douglas Hurd, *Memoirs* (London, 2003), 308.

period had stalled. The damage to trust was, therefore, incalculable, and the possibility of stabilizing Northern Ireland on the basis of some democratic compromise was to recede for more than a decade.[165] FitzGerald's original reformist project was also changed in other ways—in particular by the brutal instrumentality of Charles J. Haughey. In an RTE interview on 27 September 1981, Garret FitzGerald had laid out the principles of what became known as his 'constitutional crusade'. He said: 'What I want to do is to lead a crusade, a republican crusade, to make this a genuine republic on the principles of Tone and Davis.' He added:

If I were a northern protestant today, I can't see how I would be attracted to getting involved with a state that is itself sectarian—not in the acutely sectarian way in which Northern Ireland was, in which catholics were repressed [but] the fact is, our laws and our constitution, our practices, our attitudes reflect those of a majority ethos and are not acceptable to protestants in Northern Ireland.[166]

Yet, at first, FitzGerald's brave statement of principle had little effect. Indeed, if anything, the Irish constitution appeared to be moving in an even more Catholic direction. Abortion was illegal in Ireland, but some Catholic activists, fearing the growth of secularization, sought a change to the constitution as a further bulwark against any future attempt to alter the law. Haughey inspired the wording of a new constitutional prohibition on abortion, passed in 1983, which passed with 66.5 per-cent support. In 1985, on a different issue, Haughey was less successful: he opposed the FitzGerald government's decision to legalize contraception and thereby lost a senior Fianna Fail politician, Dessie O'Malley, who then founded the Progressive Democrats, who, though sometimes in coalition with Fianna Fail, were to be a thorn in the party's side over the next decades. In 1986, however, the FitzGerald government lost a referendum which would have allowed the introduction of divorce in Ireland. When this divorce referendum was called, Haughey returned from a weekend in Paris with his mistress Terry Keane to broadcast what he called a purely personal statement of his unshakeable belief in the importance of the family.[167] The coalition failed in this first effort to change the constitution and introduce divorce.

In the aftermath of the Agreement, John Hume predicted that Unionists would negotiate with him to bring about a power-sharing agreement by

---

[165] Paul Bew and Henry Patterson, 'The New Stalemate: Unionism and the Anglo-Irish Agreement,' in Paul Teague (ed.), *Beyond the Rhetoric: Politics, Economy and Social Policy in Northern Ireland* (London, 1987), 41–57.

[166] Bew and Gillespie, *A Chronology*, 157.

[167] Fintan O'Toole, 'A Life and a Legacy', *Irish Times*, 14 June 2006.

the end of 1986. British government ministers predicted that Sinn Fein electoral support would collapse. Both Hume and the British were destined to be disappointed. The Unionists, infuriated by the SDLP's role in bringing about the humiliation of 1985, refused to negotiate within the terms of an Agreement which they loathed. Meanwhile, the general election of May 1987 revealed that Sinn Fein's share of the vote had fallen only slightly in the wake of the Agreement: from 11.8 per cent to 11.4 per cent.[168] In 1987, political violence was also on the rise with almost 100 deaths as against sixty-two in 1986 and fifty-four in 1985. As early as March of that year, Prime Minister Thatcher had decided that the much-vaunted security returns of the Agreement were inadequate.[169]

The Agreement, therefore, had an important impact on the Northern Irish body politic—but it was not the impact which was anticipated, or by which it had originally been justified. The security rewards were likely to be chimerical anyway, given that the Agreement coincided with massive IRA arms shipments from Libya. The first clear proof of unintended consequences was John Hume's seven-month long dialogue with Sinn Fein in 1988. As early as 1986–7, a series of complex contacts behind the scenes between Sinn Fein and the British government defined, in principle, a definition of British withdrawal. This effectively defined withdrawal as a promise not to interfere politically in all-party talks about the future of Northern Ireland. On this basis, the long, ambiguous march of Sinn Fein into constitutional politics began.[170]

The themes of Hume's seven-month-long dialogue had a similar significance. Hume argued that the Agreement of 1985 had, in effect, rendered Britain 'neutral' on the question of partition. Sinn Fein insisted that Britain still had a strategic interest in fostering Irish division. The Sinn Fein–SDLP meetings were abruptly terminated by Hume after the accidental killing by the IRA of two of his Catholic constituents. Then the two parties made public a series of lengthy and rather instructive documents. The SDLP attempted to place itself on the classic ground of constitutional nationalism. The decisive moment in their document is the endorsement of Parnell's speech, given in Belfast in May 1891: 'Until ... the prejudices of the [Protestant] minority, whether reasonable or unreasonable, are conciliated ... Ireland can never enjoy perfect freedom, Ireland can never be united.'[171]

The Fine Gael–Labour government of 1982–7 had done little to tackle the problems of the Irish economy: taxation was raised in order to sustain

---

[168] For the general election figures, see Paul Bew, 'How Northern Ireland Really Voted', *Irish Political Studies*, 3 (1988).

[169] Margaret Thatcher, *The Downing Street Years* (London, 1983), 402–15.

[170] Moloney, *A Secret History of the IRA*, 394.   [171] *Northern Whig*, 23 May 1891.

government spending. In 1987 unemployment rose to 232,000 and national debt rose to 125 per cent of GNP. With unemployment heading for a quarter of a million and 40,000 people leaving the country annually, a new context was created for C. J. Haughey. Elected again as Taoiseach in 1987, he faced a repeat of the Lemass–Whitaker moment of the 1950s. The crisis had reached such a point that a decisive change of policy became unavoidable: at this moment he was helped by Alan Dukes, the new leader of Fine Gael, who committed his party to supporting Haughey's minority administration from opposition. Between 1987 and 1992 Haughey's new strategies enjoyed significant success. He facilitated a new social partnership between employers and unions, which led to wage moderation and stability in the labour movement. He established the International Finance Centre, which attracted financial institutions to Ireland with special tax treatment. He also abandoned Fianna Fail's opposition to the Single European Act in order to enhance Ireland's access to structural funds. In 1989 Haughey went prematurely to the country in order to achieve an overall majority. He lost Fianna Fail seats and found himself in government with his bitter opponents, the Progressive Democrats, who had split from Fianna Fail over both the northern policy and his early financial recklessness. But 'blending social partnership with his coalition partners' fondness for tax cuts', Haughey made 'a virtue out of necessity'.[172] He had also opened the door in 1987 to a secret peace process. At the centre of this project, whether reaching out to the British or Irish state, was the intermediary Father Alec Reid, a redemptorist priest from Tipperary, who was based in West Belfast. It was a remarkable achievement, because there was nothing in the public language in the republican movement that indicated any private softening of line.

The leading Sinn Fein propagandist Danny Morrison declared that if Thatcher had been killed at Brighton, British withdrawal would have come more quickly. In 1985 Morrison published a fascinating pamphlet, *The Good Old IRA*. Issued by the Sinn Fein publicity department, this was designed to destroy the comfortable pieties of mainstream Irish constitutional nationalism. The leaders of modern Ireland—Danny Morrison thought—had forgotten just how murky the origins of the Irish state were. His pamphlet dismisses the idea that the old IRA of 1919–21 had a democratic mandate. 'Nobody was asked to vote for war in 1918', he states. Sinn Fein had subsequently used its muscle to reshape the electoral system in its own interest. Morrison insists that the 'old IRA' launched an aggressive war against 'fellow Irishmen'—before the Black and Tans arrived. He draws attention to the extensive list of civilian casualties and

172 *Irish Times*, 20 Apr. 1995.

the many refined acts of cruelty perpetrated by the old IRA. Politicians who inherited the state thus created had no right to condemn the new northern IRA. The Irish Foreign Minister had described Northern Ireland as a 'nationalist nightmare': surely such language justified war? The opening words of the pamphlet proclaim the message: 'The IRA, 16 years into this phase of the struggle, states confidently that it *will* successfully conclude the national struggle.'

In line with the confidence and militancy displayed by Danny Morrison, Gerry Adams told the *Andersonstown News* in March 1986 that 'armed struggle is a necessary form of resistance ... armed struggle becomes unnecessary only when the British presence has been removed ... if at any time Sinn Fein decide to disown the armed struggle, they won't have me as a member'. At the 1986 Sinn Fein ard fheis Martin McGuinness emphatically stated: 'Our position is clear, and it will never, never change. The war against British rule must continue until freedom is achieved.'[173] But, as events were to prove, this rhetoric was hollow, and a 'peace process' was opening up behind the scenes.

THE PEACE PROCESS

In 1986 Father Reid had opened up the line of communication between the Northern Ireland Office and the Sinn Fein leader.[174] Reid did not allow horrific events like the 'Poppy Day' massacre in Enniskillen to deter his activities. Martin Mansergh has also noted Reid's role in involving the Irish government:

The origins of the peace process will be a matter for ongoing debate ... I personally regard the Enniskillen bomb as the psychological turning point, because it was in November 1987 that Father Alec Reid ... put a written proposal for dialogue between the SDLP and Sinn Fein, and it was then that Haughey judged it worthwhile to explore the readiness of republicans to make peace.[175]

In an interview given to a press agency in November 1989, the Northern Ireland Secretary Peter Brooke conceded that the British and the IRA were in a military stalemate.[176] But if 'a debate broke out in the terrorist community' which led to a cessation of violence, the government would have to be imaginative. Brooke's interview was 'not authorised' or cleared

[173] Anthony MacIntyre, 'Modern Irish Republicanism: The Product of British State Strategies', *Irish Political Studies*, 10 (1995), 101.
[174] Molony, *A Secret History of the IRA*, 246–8.
[175] Martin Mansergh, 'Secrecy on the Path to Peace', *Sunday Tribune*, 8 May 1996.
[176] Molony, *A Secret History of the IRA*, 242.

first with Mrs Thatcher in Downing Street; but he was gratified by the support he received from that quarter—in particular from Charles Powell, the Prime Minister's senior aide.[177]

As in 1974–5, such secret contacts between the British and republicans were to exasperate the Irish government, which believed that the republican movement might easily become the victim of its own romanticization of the ways of the secret world. What, in the end, was the use, reasoned the Irish government, of a tantalizing hint of Irish unity from British intelligence operatives, if a British government would not stand over it in the House of Commons?[178] But this time the Irish government 'played the game', in a way it had refused to do in 1974–5.

From late 1990 through to 1992, first Peter Brooke, then his successor Sir Patrick Mayhew sponsored round-table talks between the main constitutional parties on the way forward for the province. But the participants in these talks always feared that the real initiative lay elsewhere: indeed, the Unionists feared that John Hume, the leader of the SDLP, placed more emphasis on a 'peace' deal with Sinn Fein. They were right to have such a concern.

In the autumn of 1991 Charles Haughey discussed with John Hume a document which might alter the stalemate,[179] but on 6 February 1992 Albert Reynolds became Taoiseach in place of Haughey, who was plagued with allegations that he had ordered the phone-tapping of journalists. (Five years later Haughey was to fall victim to financial scandal.[180]) In February 1992 Sinn Fein, in similar fashion, sent a draft to Dublin of a declaration which, it suggested, should be made jointly by the British and Irish governments. The key sentence was the demand for a British commitment to Irish unity: 'The British government, consequently, commits itself to such unity (within a period to be agreed) and to use all its influence and energy to win consent for this policy.'[181] But the British were not in that place. In December 1992 Sir Patrick Mayhew had insisted at Coleraine:

[177] Peter Brooke interview, Edinburgh, 29 Nov. 2005. Charles Powell's younger brother Jonathan was at the heart of Mr Blair's efforts to open and sustain a dialogue with the IRA from 1997 to 2006.

[178] Martin Mansergh, 'Secrecy on the Path to Peace', *Tribune Magazine*, 5 May 1996.

[179] *Irish Times*, 9 July 2005.

[180] In December 2006 the Moriarty Tribunal concluded that the scale of secretive payments from members of the business elite devalued the quality of a modern democracy. In 2006 terms the sum amounted to at least 40 million euros. *Irish Times*, 20 Dec. 2006.

[181] Draft of a declaration which Sinn Fein suggests should be made jointly by the British and Dublin governments, p. 374. Eamonn Mallie and David McKittrick, *The Fight for Peace: The Secret Story Behind the Irish Peace Process* (London, 1996), 374.

The reality is that if Northern Ireland's position as part of the UK is ever going to change, it will only be by the will of a majority of its people ... We are not indifferent, we are not neutral in our resolve to protect and deliver the people of Northern Ireland from terrorist violence. We are not neutral in defending the right of the Northern Ireland people to democratic self-determination.

The British, however, had now deepened their dialogue with the republican movement. The IRA's Warrington bomb killed a small child and a 12-year-old boy on 20 March 1993. But on 23 March the British government representative, undeterred, told his republican contact:

Mayhew had shed marginalisation, defeating the IRA, etc. That's gone ... Mayhew is now determined. He wants Sinn Fein to play a part, not because he likes Sinn Fein, but because it cannot work without them. Any settlement not involving all of the people north and south won't work. A north/south settlement that won't frighten Unionists. The final solution is union. It is going to happen anyway. The historical train—Europe—determines that. We are committed to Europe. Unionists will have to change. This island will be as one.

Just in case the historical train needed encouragement, the IRA exploded a devastating car bomb in the City of London, causing damage estimated at over £1 billion.

The more normal processes of political dialogue at the Brooke–Mayhew talks had revealed a growing liberalization of the position of the Ulster Unionists—in effect, conceding in principle both power-sharing and an Irish dimension. But this movement in the early 1990s by the Unionists did not lead to a deal with the SDLP. The SDLP remained wedded, throughout the process, to a 'European model', which suggested one EEC, one Dublin, and one London nominee on a six-member Northern Ireland executive commission. Moreover, the proposed parliamentary assembly was to be modelled on the European Parliament: that is to say, it was to be a largely advisory body, without a legislative role, and with no effective control over the executive. Those proposals, predictably, found no favour with the UUP and DUP; less predictably, they found no favour with the Alliance Party or the British government. Few observers in Brussels believed that the EC was keen to play such a role. The talks were also deadlocked on the issue of Articles 2 and 3 of the constitution of Ireland.

As the talks collapsed on 10 November 1992, press briefings by the NIO referred to the possibility of a change in the SDLP's attitude when the party's ordinary membership realized how much was on offer. Such a development was, however, rather unlikely. The Anglo-Irish Agreement had created a context in which it became logical—almost compellingly so—for constitutional nationalists and the British Labour Party to argue for a form of joint authority, perhaps with a European dimension. It has to be understood, too, that the *manner* of the collapse of the 1974 experiment made it very difficult for the SDLP to trust Unionists. There remained, too, the reality of the Provisional IRA's campaign. At the end of twenty-five years of the Troubles, it can be seen that there was a new subtlety in political discourse. Mainstream unionists now conceded ground on power-sharing and the Irish dimension, while constitutional nationalists aimed for joint authority rather than a united Ireland. Nevertheless, a widely acceptable solution was not yet in sight: indeed, the 'power-sharing plus Irish dimension' plan that had magnetized so many people of good will was, temporarily at least, losing its political relevance. In a *Sunday Tribune* article at the beginning of July 1993, Gerry Adams significantly declared that republicans might be prepared to accept joint authority as a part of the process towards the end of partition.[182] To explain this shift in emphasis, it is helpful to turn to the words of Martin Mansergh, then the principal adviser to Albert Reynolds:

In June 1993, not without much soul-searching on the Republican side, the draft [of a 'formula for peace'] was handed over to the British Government by the Taoiseach. To say they handled it with kid gloves would be something of an understatement. They were prepared to discuss, but not negotiate it, and on several occasions in the autumn of 1993 many of them would have preferred to set it aside. But an initiative that might bring peace was always going to be more important than attempts to restart inter-party talks, or even early discussions of the Framework Document.[183]

Mansergh has a serious point here: Sir Patrick Mayhew's speech at the British–Irish Association in Cambridge in September 1993 was an indication of his reluctance—the emphasis was entirely on the 'constitutional' parties. Mansergh is, however, also right to say that the British remained 'engaged' with the Provos.

There is a little doubt that the British state was aware, thanks to its extensive intelligence penetration of the republican political class,[184] that the Provisional leadership had an overly positive view of the likely advance of the Catholic demographic in Northern Ireland, but did nothing to discourage such exaggerated opinion. As Adams wryly noted, British intelligence had 'regrouped'—indeed, just as it had done after Collins's blows in November 1920. As with Collins, the British offered the 'bouquet'

182 *Sunday Tribune*, 4 July 1993.
183 'The Background to the Peace Process', *Irish Studies in International Affairs* (1995), 154.
184 Jack Holland and Susan Phoenix, *Policing the Shadows: The Secret War Against Terrorism in Northern Ireland* (London, 1936), 207–8.

of negotiation or the alternative of more violence—a violence which, in the early 1990s, was clearly having its effect on republican morale. The dynamisms of a 'dirty war' were now longer and more drawn out in the case of Adams than they were against Collins, but they were essentially similar. This is the clue to the British refusal to abort the secret dealing with the Provos, even after the Shankill bomb which killed ten civilians on 23 October.

The Irish government clearly had a similar agenda, based on the belief that the Adams leadership was sincerely interested in peace. On 2 November 1993 Dublin leaked a plan for the future of Northern Ireland, which was drawn up by Department of Foreign Affairs officials. The plan called on the British to 'acknowledge the full legitimacy and value of the goal of Irish unity by agreement'. In short, the British were urged to take on the role of becoming persuaders for Irish unity: privately, senior British officials dismissed the *Irish Press* document as fantasy. On 28 November 1993 the *Observer* newspaper in London broke the story that, despite all denials, the British government had had a secret channel of communication with Sinn Fein and the IRA for three years.[185] The House of Commons was surprisingly sympathetic to the Northern Ireland Secretary, who was judged to have been taking risks for peace; but on 2 December Sinn Fein published a set of documents, *Setting the Record Straight: A Record of Communications between Sinn Fein and the British Government October 1990–November 1993*. The effect of these events on public opinion in Northern Ireland was dramatic. The British government defended itself by claiming that it had received a message that the Provisionals recognized that the war was over and that they stood by the consent principle in their discussions. While the government genuinely believed it had, in substance, received such a message, the Provisionals denied it; it was always likely, as was later confirmed, that intermediaries had gilded the lily.

It became necessary for the British government, however, to act decisively to place the Northern Ireland problem in a safer context. This helps to explain the sudden move towards the strategy embodied in the Downing Street Declaration of 15 December 1993. All the 'leaks' about secret negotiations had created a dangerously unstable public mood; there was a need for a highly public clarification of policy, one which might also set out the parameters of future policy. Remarkably, the British managed to keep 'Molyneaux unionism' on board. The lessons of 1985 had, in this sense, been grasped. Molyneaux was given a prior insight into the secret talks before the *Observer* exclusive. In the next few days the British went further, by allowing Molyneaux and other Unionists a contribution to the

[185] *Observer*, 28 Nov. 1993.

negotiations, leading up to what became the Downing Street Declaration of December 1993; for example, Archbishop Robin Eames played a hand in drafting paragraphs 6–8 of the Declaration.

The Downing Street Declaration proved to be a document of considerable originality and sophistication. In the same document, the Irish government was to note that Irish unity would 'be best achieved with the agreement and the consent of the people of Northern Ireland'. But the agreement of a majority in the North was now an absolute prerequisite for Irish unity. This changed the Irish position in the draft sent from Dublin in June 1993, which saw unionist consent as only desirable.[186] For unionism it formalized a distasteful message—albeit one already sent by Peter Brooke in 1990: 'The Prime Minister ... reiterates on behalf of the British Government that they have no selfish strategic or economic interest in Northern Ireland.' In truth, though, a selfish strategic interest did not ever imply that Britain could not have an unselfish strategic interest—for example, a concern for the stability of the island of Ireland.

The real novelty of the Downing Street Declaration lay elsewhere. It is necessary at this point to consider the complex language of the Declaration's fourth paragraph. After the Declaration, the phraseology of the Hume–Adams agreement continued to dominate the political scene, but its content was dramatically altered. One of the most effective slogans of Irish nationalism had been given a new, decidedly softer, conceptual content; and this had been done by a Fianna Fail government. The self-determination of the Irish people was conceded by Britain, but solely on the basis that the Irish government only wished to operate that principle in favour of Irish unity with the support of a majority in the North.

Superficially, the rhetoric of the Hume–Adams process had been conceded, but, in essence, the process had been stripped of its content in a quite dramatic way. The British, it is true, were now 'facilitators'—not for Irish unity, but for an agreed Ireland; and an 'agreed' Ireland, by definition, could not be a united Ireland until there was majority consent in Northern Ireland. As paragraph 4 of the Downing Street Declaration stated: 'The role of the British Government will be to encourage, facilitate and enable the achievement of such agreement over a period through a process of dialogue and co-operation based on full respect for the rights and identities of both traditions in Ireland.' As Martin Mansergh explained later: 'The British Government wish to promote enough political agreement to prevent the two communities from fighting each other and harming British

---

[186] Eamon O'Kane, 'Anglo-Irish Relations and the Northern Ireland Peace Process: From Exclusion to Inclusion', *Contemporary British History*, 18: 1 (Spring 2004), 95.

interests ... They had made it clear that they will not be persuaders for a united Ireland, nor do they wish to see it come about.'[187]

The Irish government insisted also, on the day of the Downing Street Declaration, that the IRA prove its good faith by handing over its weapons. Why did the Irish government accept such a limited and disappointing outcome from a republican point of view? The answer lies, in part, in the economic realities of the Irish question. In 1989 Professor Joseph Lee published his brilliant statement of frustrated patriotism, denouncing Irish 'economic performance ... the least impressive in western Europe'.[188] Very quickly, these words ceased to be appropriate: the 1990s saw a dramatic improvement in economic performance, perhaps the result of the delayed introduction of mass education and the subsequent victory over the forces of conservatism in Irish society, the Church and small farmers. But despite the dramatic improvements of the 1990s and early twenty-first century, significant economic constraints remained in place.[189] As recently as 2003—ten years after the Downing Street Declaration—Garret FitzGerald has warned:

The achievement of the EU level of GNP does *not* mean, however, that average Irish living standards in the broadest sense have now attained the EU level. Because Ireland's infrastructure—roads, public transport, hospitals, schools etc.—still largely reflect inadequacies untouched from the pre-1990 period, when Ireland was 40 per cent poorer than all its neighbours, a huge programme of public investment is required in order to expand and modernise these inadequate facilities—and will continue to be required for perhaps 10–15 years.[190]

Despite Irish economic advances, Dublin still could not pay for Irish unity. The doctrine of parity assumed an equality of citizenship throughout the United Kingdom, and alongside this an assumption that Northern Ireland was entitled to its proper share of the entire services of the UK public sector. Harold Begbie's *The Lady Next Door* (1914) gave an early glimpse of that 'welfare unionism'[191] which remained so formidable an element in the modern Irish question. Encountering a Belfast socialist and radical, Begbie assumed that the man, as a singularly enlightened member of the working class, would be a home-ruler. 'I should think not! No, I am a Unionist, out and out. England is absolutely essential to us. An Irish parliament would be entirely Tory ... But we can screw out of England all we want, bit by

---

[187] *Irish Times*, 3 July 1995.
[188] J. J. Lee, *Ireland 1912–1985: Politics and Society* (Cambridge, 1989), 521.
[189] Tom Garvin, *Preventing the Future* (Dublin, 2004), 186–7.
[190] Garret FitzGerald, *Reflections on the Irish State* (Dublin, 2003), 33–4.
[191] Iain McLean and Alistair McMullan, *The State of the Union: Unionism and the Alternatives in the United Kingdom Since 1707* (Oxford, 2006), 157.

bit, and she can help us to pay the bill.'[192] By 2006 the cost of paying the bill was £5 billion per annum for the London Exchequer,[193] thus allowing Northern Ireland a prosperity which the Republic's Exchequer could not sustain: this is a significant clue to the ultimate moderation of the Irish government's negotiating stance.[194]

Despite their sharp initial criticism of the Downing Street Declaration as inadequate, the IRA delivered a 'complete cessation of military operations' on 31 August 1994. The cajoling, even bullying, of the Provisional leadership by the Irish government appears to have been the decisive factor, Albert Reynolds bluntly remarking: 'I told them if they don't do this right, they can shag off.'[195] Nor could the Sinn Fein leadership assume that the SDLP's good offices would always remain available. On 18 May 1994 Eddie McGrady, the MP for South Down, met with Chris McCabe, a senior NIO official. The official note of this meeting declared: 'Mr Eddie McGrady is not a happy man. He disagrees fundamentally with the way John Hume is acting, which he thinks is elevating Sinn Fein/PIRA to a position of respectability they do not deserve (more than once he described them as the "scum of the earth").'[196]

On the other hand, if there was an understanding between the Provisionals and the British government, it was inevitably an imperfect one. The British, in their private communications, had refused all talk of withdrawal. Instead, they had offered vague murmurings about the European Union, the logic of history being unity, and so on. They had also made it clear in public that the IRA would have to decommission its arms before the admittance of Sinn Fein to all-party talks—as Gerry Adams fully admitted in his interview with Tom Collins in the *Irish News* on 8 January 1994. Few on the Irish side paid any attention to this admission. It became an article of faith in Irish political culture to insist that the Adams leadership had known nothing of the British concern for decommissioning before it called the ceasefire. Few on the British side reflected on their own rather obvious historical 'lesson': Lloyd George's preoccupation with the IRA handing over arms may have delayed the deal in 1921. It is doubtful, too, if the British had shared with Adams their commitment to a Northern Ireland referendum to underpin any negotiated settlement, as was announced by

[192] Harold Begbie, *The Lady Next Door* (London, 1914), 11.

[193] For the evolution of the doctrine of 'parity', see the important paper by the senior NICS official Arthur Green, 'Parity: The Political Premises' (Nov. 1977), 7.

[194] Viewed at least from the perspective of traditional nationalism. See e.g. Anthony Coughlan, *Fooled Again* (Cork and Dublin, 1986).

[195] S. Duignan, *One More Spin on the Merry Go Round* (Dublin, 1995), 147, diary entry for 12 Aug. 1994.

[196] *Irish News*, 12 Apr. 2003.

the Prime Minister John Major in September. All in all, the caginess which characterized British reaction to the ceasefire probably reflected genuine emotion.

In a way, the ceasefire was a footnote to the Anglo-Irish Agreement, which was now working in a way no one had intended. It had given the Irish government a prestigious role in the North, and this allowed it to act as a broker for a ceasefire in a way that would have been inconceivable a decade earlier. But still the question remained: what did the republican movement expect to get out of the peace process? Throughout the whole Hume–Adams process and the secret contacts with the government, it had sought a commitment from the British government that it would act as a 'persuader' for Irish unity. Yet, at no point does the British government appear to have given such a commitment; still less had it accepted the concept of joint authority.

The next major step in the process was the British and Irish governments' decision to issue the Joint Framework Document. This would outline the intergovernmental assessment of the best political future for Northern Ireland. The internal arrangements (strand one) were the work of the British government itself: in fact, the Irish did not see the strand one material until the day of publication. But the controversial area concerned the North–South arrangements: it was necessary here to encourage republicans to believe that a settlement which was transitional to Irish unity was close at hand, while encouraging unionists that the process would guarantee their place in the United Kingdom. It was a tough, almost impossible task, and the Framework Document, almost inevitably, failed it.

In January 1995 *The Times* published a leaked version of an early text of the Document. The Document's generalized 'green' tone terrified unionists, who reacted with great dismay. Molyneaux, who had handled the Downing Street Declaration with a measure of competence, now looked—as he had done with the Anglo-Irish Agreement of 1985—marginalized and out of touch. In the aftermath of *The Times* leak, John Major told a group of thirty or forty Tory MPs, crowded into his room at the House of Commons: 'It's like the first chapter of an Agatha Christie, it doesn't tell the whole story.'[197] He was right, but few in Northern Ireland believed him. Molyneaux's leadership now entered its final descent, and he was replaced in September 1995 by David Trimble, as the party leadership skipped a generation.

The Framework Document was duly published on 22 February. By this stage it reflected the imprint of much eleventh-hour negotiation. Following *The Times* leak, the British government accepted the need to move away

---

[197] Gyles Brandreth, *Breaking the Code: Westminster Diaries May 1990–May 1997* (London, 1999).

from the generalities about cross-borderism in that leak—profoundly unsettling to unionists—towards the more concrete and specific. Major drew up a list of forty-three amendments, and at the eleventh hour the new Dublin government of Fine Gael leader John Bruton accepted most of these.[198] It was a decisive proof of Bruton's sophisticated and conciliatory approach to the Northern Ireland question. Bruton had benefited fortuitously from the collapse of the Reynolds government—brought about by the ramifications of the state's handling of the case of a paedophile priest, Father Brendan Smyth. Bruton was determined to seize the chance to weaken the atavistic strain in Irish politics; in 1996 the divorce referendum, for example, was at last carried. Thanks to Bruton's subtlety, *The Times* leak, so often described as profoundly destabilizing, effectively performed a benign service for what was coming to be known as the 'peace process'. In the final version—as opposed to the text leaked to *The Times*—the banality and low-key nature of much of the proposed cross-borderism was made explicit in Paragraph 33,[199] as was the so-called 'triple lock', making clear that the agreement of the local parties was required. The final text did not, however, deal comprehensively with the Irish territorial claim to Northern Ireland; the language employed still retained a significant element of ambiguity. Unionists, however, were only slightly reassured: in general, their overreaction played into republican hands, creating a mood of republican contentment, which was to last for some months.[200]

But all this superficial success contained the seeds of disappointment for Irish republicans. Privately, some leading republicans said they had received a signal that the British would withdraw within ten years and that a deal had been struck to this end between the then Taoiseach, Albert Reynolds, and John Major. Given these assumptions, the first eighteen months of the 1994 ceasefire had seemed like one long process of obstruction. In essence, the British government refused to pressure the Unionists into all-party talks while an atmosphere of threat and undiminished republican armament remained. Eventually, the contentment induced in republicanism by the publication of the Framework Document evaporated. Much of 1995 was dominated by bitter arguments concerning the failure to make any progress

[198] Anthony Seldon, *Major: A Political Life* (London, 1997), 530.

[199] Para. 33 lists 'by way of example' the proposals at a harmonizing level: 'The category of agriculture and fisheries might include agricultural and fisheries research, training and advisory services, and animal welfare, health might include comparative ventures in medical, paramedical and nursing training, cross-border provision of hospital services and major emergency/accident planning; and education might include mutual recognition of teacher qualifications, co-operative ventures in higher education, in teacher training, in education for mutual understanding and education for special needs.'

[200] Brandreth, *Breaking the Code.*

towards the objective of all-party talks. Apart from the usual mistrust and ethnic antagonism of Ulster politics, the problem was complicated by the arms issue. The Downing Street Declaration had declared that only a 'permanent' renunciation of violence entitled Sinn Fein to a place at the 'talks table'; but how was that permanence to be demonstrated? Both the Irish and British governments had declared that it required the handing over of weapons.

THE MAKING OF THE GOOD FRIDAY AGREEMENT, 1996–1998

Eventually, the governments delegated the problem to another interested party: the United States. In January 1996 Senator George Mitchell's report on the arms issue suggested the waiving of this precondition. It proposed, instead, a surrender of arms during talks. The British government accepted the Mitchell report, but seizing on one of his more casual suggestions, announced an electoral process in Northern Ireland as a form of compensation for unionists. This was widely seen by republicans in Northern Ireland as 'binning the Mitchell report', and while technically untrue, this phrase did, in fact, reflect the truth that the Major government was less than impressed by the senator's handiwork. But on 9 February 1996 matters changed radically: the IRA ended its ceasefire with a large, murderous bomb at Canary Wharf, London. Sinn Fein now settled in to await the election of a Labour government under Tony Blair; a government which, it rightly calculated, would have little instinctive sympathy for Ulster Unionism. Following Tony Blair's landslide win in May 1997, the Provisionals moved rapidly to restore their ceasefire. In return, they were offered a place at the talks table, having effectively destroyed the Downing Street Declaration precondition that they make a permanent renunciation of violence. Having taken so radical a step, Blair attempted, in this phase, to protect the Ulster Unionist leader David Trimble, by imposing a moderate agenda on the talks process.

In the Irish Republic the June general election also saw a change in government. Bertie Ahern was elected Taoiseach at the head of a Fianna Fail–PD Coalition. Since 1969 the Irish electorate had thrown out all governing parties or governing coalitions which presented themselves for re-election. Ahern[201] was to break that pattern when re-elected for a second

---

[201] Karen Gilland Lutz argues that in the 2002 general election Irish political debate was characterized by the absence of serious policy differences: the Northern Ireland

term in 2002. The Republic's dominant politician for a decade, Ahern's political character requires analysis. A self-proclaimed 'socialist', he has presided over Ireland's competitive capitalist transformation.[202] Although he emerged as a Haughey lieutenant, he denounced the financial scandals of the Haughey era. When asked about his father's famous description of Ahern as the 'most devious' and the 'most cunning', Sean Haughey TD commented: 'I suppose that's a matter for the two gentlemen concerned in their complex political relationship.'[203] Ahern was a very public Catholic, who publicly shared his life with a partner (not his wife) for many years. Above all, he pointedly rebuked John Bruton's decision to have a portrait of Redmond in the Taoiseach's office by replacing it with one of Padraig Pearse—but he nevertheless pursued Redmond's northern policy rather than that of Pearse. He opened up a serious private engagement with David Trimble and approached the Northern Ireland question with a studied moderation.[204] Perhaps for this reason, or perhaps—and it is just as likely—for reasons of personal pique and jealousy, Charles Haughey in retirement not only castigated Ahern's government as the 'worst in the history of the state', but denounced Ahern's greatest achievement, the Good Friday Agreement, as 'inherently unstable, an unstable settlement in which the Provisional IRA demonstrates its willingness only to protect the nationalists within a failed state'.[205]

Though there had been many suggestions for a political agreement during the course of the Troubles, after the publication of the 'Heads of Agreement' document in January 1998 it was clear that the only settlement on offer was one consisting of balanced constitutional change by the British and

issue was actually the main area of cleavage, even though it, too, was surrounded by much consensus. Slight though these differences, they were deeply felt: in such a context—weak opinion, strongly held—personality is of particular importance, 'Irish Party Competition: Change or *Plus ça Change*', *Irish Political Studies*, 18 (2003), 40–59.

[202] Nicola Jo-Anne Smith, *Showcasing Globalisation? The Political Economy of the Irish Republic* (Manchester, 2005), 135. A recent study by Philip Lane and Francis Ruane points out that American companies counted for 77% of the Republic's exports. The authors argue that US companies are exporting profits to Ireland, transferring by a simple process of bookkeeping the cost of added value in the sale of a computer, reckoning that Ireland's 12.5% corporation tax rate makes it a more rewarding profit centre than the US or most European countries, including Britain., 'Ireland's Dispossessed are Real Threat to Celtic Tiger', *The Times*, 19 Apr. 2006.

[203] As Eoghan Harris pointed out in his shrewd article, *Sunday Independent*, 19 Feb. 2006.

[204] See e.g. his interview, 'For Compromise not Victory', with the present author, published in *Parliamentary Brief*, 5: 4 (Mar. 1998), 8–11; Stephen Collins, *The Power Game: Fianna Fail Since Lemass* (Dublin, 2000), 317.

[205] O'Brien, *The Modern Prince*, 9. Haughey is the senior source here interviewed, 24 July 2002. My thanks to Justin O'Brien for this information.

Irish, a Northern Ireland Assembly, a replaced Anglo-Irish agreement, and a British–Irish Council linking the Assembly to other United Kingdom bodies and North–South structures.

Given the conflicting agendas and mutual suspicions of those involved in the talks, it was hardly surprising that the final agreement was characterized by safeguards, vetoes, and some areas of ambiguity. The core of the agreement, however, was unambiguous: the union of Great Britain and Northern Ireland would continue as long as it was supported by a majority of the people of Northern Ireland. In return for this acceptance by the British and, crucially, also by the Irish government and other nationalists, unionists were required to accept power-sharing and cross-border co-operation. Perhaps the most difficult area for unionists, however, was that, in return for the ending of the IRA campaign of violence and a formal Dublin acceptance of the legitimacy of the North's position within the United Kingdom, they had to allow Sinn Fein a 'soft landing'. In practice, this soft landing was likely to focus on the contentious issues of the release of prisoners, policing, and the decommissioning of weapons.

Sinn Fein had accepted that the talks would not create a united Ireland. Writing in *Ireland on Sunday* on 8 March 1998, Gerry Adams defined Sinn Fein's bottom line as including powerful cross-border bodies, operating independently of a Northern Ireland assembly; policing and the courts coming within the remit of new all-Ireland institutions; the disbanding of the RUC, withdrawing the army, and releasing all paramilitary prisoners; and the retention of the territorial claim in the Irish constitution. It is striking how, in constitutional political matters, the Sinn Fein agenda was comprehensively defeated. Articles 2 and 3 of the Irish constitution were transformed, for example, and cross-border bodies were tied to the Assembly. The Good Friday Agreement, insofar as it represented the thinking of the local parties, was a triumph for the SDLP and the Ulster Unionists. Their negotiating approach had driven the process. Adams did not 'sign' the Agreement, and was agnostic and noncommittal on Good Friday itself.[206] Sinn Fein contributed but little to the political details — 'in the dunces' corner', as one Irish official put it.

But, with great tactical brilliance, Adams moved rapidly to embrace the Agreement and claim ownership of it against those who had actually made it. At the 'Talking to One's Opponents' conference (Armagh 2001) Adams recalled the moment: 'we went to a special Ardfheis of our party, and then we went to another special Ardfheis of our party and we turned policy

---

[206] G. Adams, 'When we have democratically come to a conclusion, we will let you know', *Irish Times*, 11 Apr. 1998; Austen Morgan, *The Belfast Agreement: A Practical Legal Analysis* (London, 2000), 9.

on its head.' It should also be noted that on policing and prisoners and other military matters—more narrowly, the 'politics of the gun'—Sinn Fein was much more successful. The RUC was not disbanded, but it was remodelled by the Patten Commission in a way which left many of its members feeling humiliated. Prisoners were rapidly released, and by 2005 the British government had agreed to disband the home service battalions of the Royal Irish Regiment. In 2006 the British government established a willingness to finance restorative justice schemes run by loyalist and republican paramilitaries. In short, a pattern was soon established: the formal political properties of the union were preserved. The Ulster Unionist leadership was able, quite correctly, to claim a triumph for the principle of consent and assert the democratic legitimacy of partition. The whole *raison d'être* of the IRA's war had been to smash that legitimacy. Nevertheless, in reserved areas of policy—security, policing, and legality—the British government was exceptionally keen to placate republicans in such a way as to greatly intensify fears of a mafia state. Most remarkable of all, IRA decommissioning of its weaponry—promised in the Agreement for 2000—was delayed until 2005.

In a province desperate for peace and prosperity, it proved possible, in 1998, to win a 71 per-cent majority for the Agreement—a slight majority of Unionists supplemented by a large majority of Nationalists. In the ensuing Assembly election, the pro-Agreement Ulster Unionist Party was the largest party in the Assembly, but the support of the UUP voters for the Trimble project was fragile. If the Agreement failed to deliver political stability on a creditable basis, many were capable of bolting to Ian Paisley's DUP. While David Trimble finally compelled the IRA to start decommissioning in the autumn of 2001, it was too late to preserve the UUP's majority position within unionism. The election result also emphasized the narrowing of the gap in electoral support between Sinn Fein and the SDLP that had taken place in the 1990s. In 1992 the SDLP won approximately 70 per cent of the nationalist vote, compared with Sinn Fein's 30 per cent; in 1993 it was 64 per cent to 36 per cent; in the general election of May 1997 it was 60 per cent to 40 per cent; and in the district council elections three weeks later it was 55 per cent to 45 per cent. In the 1998 Assembly election the SDLP received 55.2 per cent of the nationalist vote compared to Sinn Fein's 44.2 per cent. The election also confirmed the growth in the combined SDLP and Sinn Fein votes as a proportion of the total vote. In the May 1997 general election the total nationalist vote reached a new high point at 40.2 per cent, though the figure fell slightly to 39.7 per cent in the Assembly election. By the general election of 2001 Sinn Fein had overwhelmed the SDLP, and this, with continued republican illegal behaviour, greatly weakened the Agreement's prospects of retaining sufficient unionist support.

Yet, successful as the republican movement was at the polls, progress towards Irish unity was unimpressive. In a meeting on the transitional programme for the new Assembly, a senior British mandarin of the Wilson era, surveying the mundane tasks facing that body, asked the question: 'If Gerry Adams was a fly on the wall, what would he think of this?' Some, after all, had worked in Downing Street in the Wilson era when withdrawal was seriously contemplated. In short, how could a revolutionary movement settle for such a prosaic, even dull outcome, which fell so drastically short of its stated objectives? Perhaps this helps to explain the IRA's consistent compensating adventurism in this period: some in the IRA had to be reassured that there was still a revolutionary agenda of sorts, hence the decision, for example, to set up a spy ring at Stormont, or to rob the Northern Bank in the massive heist in 2004.

The 'Stormontgate' spying scandal of 2002 led to suspension of the institutions of the Good Friday Agreement, which had seen a power-sharing executive operate for nineteen months.[207] The Irish government was critical of the police raid at Stormont, which had signalled publicly the discovery of the alleged spy ring. Partly as a means of conveying to Dublin the seriousness of the situation, the Prime Minister visited Belfast to make a major speech at the office of the Harbour Commissioners. This speech insisted that the IRA must make radical 'acts of completion' in order to reassure unionists that Sinn Fein was now committed to democracy.[208] First the British government and then David Trimble—in what the unionist leader has subsequently acknowledged as an act of 'hubris'[209]—attempted to engage the republican leadership on an agenda which would have revived the institutions. The best that could be achieved was an IRA commitment to accept the peaceful and democratic methods of the Agreement: the IRA, which had stood outside the Agreement when it was signed, now, in some sense, came within its ambit. There was also a third act of decommissioning, but once again the details were vague and unimpressive in their impact on public opinion.

[207] The outstanding treatment of this period is Dean Godson, *Himself Alone: David Trimble and the Ordeal of Ulster Unionism* (London, 2004). But see also, on its final crisis, Martina Purdy, *Room 21: Stormont—Behind Closed Doors* (Belfast, 2005), 330–41; Christopher Farrington, *Ulster Unionism and the Peace Process in Northern Ireland* (London, 2006), 162–80.

[208] See Paul Bew, 'Where now in Belfast?', *Parliamentary Brief*, 10: 3 (Feb. 2006), 17–18.

[209] Frank Millar, *David Trimble: The Price of Peace* (London, 2004), 172; Joan Boucher, 'Mapping Unionism: A Comparative Study of the Evolution of Ulster Unionism Since the 1960s', unpublished Ph.D thesis, University of Ulster (2005), 144.

THE BREAKING OF THE GOOD FRIDAY
AGREEMENT

At this point the capacity of the Blair–Trimble relationship to sustain the Good Friday Agreement as the template for Northern Ireland was destroyed. Although Trimble had been visible short-changed by republicans, in Autumn 2003 Blair called a new election for the Assembly, which, above all, both Sinn Fein and the DUP, feeding on the mutual polarization of the population, desperately wanted. The decision to rush an election to a suspended Assembly which was not able to sit for years to come requires some explanation. In the Irish government, and also in the US State Department, there was a constituency which believed that the logic of the process required a further embrace of the 'extremes': that a DUP–Sinn Fein deal was not only possible but desirable. Both the Irish and the State Department in Washington were very excited by DUP contacts in Washington from the summer of 2002, which encouraged them to believe that that party harboured a new pragmatism and willingness to share power with Sinn Fein. Tony Blair was a very late convert to this position, indeed, only really adopting it in late 2003, when he bowed to Irish and American pressure to hold an election, while still hoping that Trimble's leadership of unionism would be retained. Blair had, in the summer of 2003, resisted such pressure and postponed the election, but in the autumn his resolve cracked, with consequences, in the medium term at least, which were entirely as negative as he had feared. In the end, Trimble, still at this point topping the poll in his own constituency, went down to a relatively narrow but strategically crucial defeat. The reason is clear: most unionists interpreted the decision to go ahead with an 'election to nothing' as a sign that the republican movement dominated the process and that Trimble's capacity to influence Blair was at an end. Even after the horror of the Omagh bomb in 1998—even after 9/11 in New York in 2001—the British government had continued to behave as if it believed that the IRA had a realistic option of a return to war and that this fear determined their priorities.

Throughout 2004 every effort was made to achieve a deal between the DUP and Sinn Fein. These negotiations appeared to proceed surprisingly well, and in late November–early December the media—encouraged by the governments and a section of the DUP leadership—speculated freely that the 'mother of all deals' was close. The British, Irish, and American governments tried to tempt the DUP into a new deal by supporting the concept of 'visible' decommissioning, backed up by photographic evidence.

The modernizing wing of the DUP appears to have been optimistic that the photographs would be delivered by the IRA; those closest to the Paisley leadership were clear in their minds that the photographs were not coming. On this more correct basis, they were consistently pessimistic about the possibility of an agreement.[210] This pessimism was apparently vindicated when it became clear that the IRA was still committed to running a criminal empire, and before the end of the month the movement underlined the point by pulling off the greatest bank robbery in the history of the United Kingdom at the headquarters of the Northern Bank in Belfast. It also became clear that the British government had at no point during the negotiations laid any firm emphasis on the criminality question. When the IRA refused to make commitments in this area, the British tried to persuade the Irish government to ignore it.[211]

The repercussions were serious. This time the Irish state, which, in the aftermath of Stormontgate, had been critical of British security assessments and action, agreed with the British view that the IRA was responsible. The DUP moved its position to the point where one of its leading modernizers declared it would require a generation to pass before any power-sharing deal with Sinn Fein–IRA was possible. Such rhetoric has to be taken with a pinch of salt, but it had a certain significance. Sinn Fein leaders insisted that the IRA would be kept in existence until there was a united Ireland. Both governments appeared to accept this as a 'reality'. Polling confirmed that even after the IRA disbanded and disarmed totally and in public, most unionists now did not want to share power with Sinn Fein.

Sinn Fein leadership responded to this crisis with a predictably effective move. Following an extensive negotiation involving British officials Jonathan Powell and Dr Jonathan Phillips, the IRA once again promised to be peaceful in a statement on 28 July 2005, and both governments declared their hope that all criminality and paramilitary activity was at an end. Peaceful and democratic means were to be respected. There were to be no other activities whatsoever—though the IRA refused to disband. In fact, the statement of 2005 mirrored, in rather precise ideological and linguistic terms, the statement of 1923: above all, the IRA was still to remain in existence with its mission intact. Of course, such ideological 'corrections' may not actually describe the exact political situation. It became clear quickly that Sinn Fein had succeeded in reactivating its agenda on policing and demilitarization without paying the price of photographic evidence of decommissioning, while only a few months before, in late 2004, the governments had deemed this to be necessary. In September the IRA, at

---

[210] Brian Rowan, *Paisley and the Provos* (Belfast, 2005), 92–102.
[211] Stephen Collins, 'Ourselves and Blair Alone', *Sunday Tribune*, 11 Mar. 2005.

last, decommissioned, but *sans* the 'Kodak moment'. This was a defeat for the DUP, which provoked much Sinn Fein gloating.

Two prime ministers and the Sinn Fein leadership remain committed to the revival of the Good Friday Agreement, and it was possible that the DUP leadership, which was currently estranged from the project, may well feel compelled to return to it. Even DUP militants, opposed to modernizers, seemed in 2006 to offer little more than to delay a deal with Sinn Fein by, say, two years. But whatever happened, as long as he lived Ian Paisley now controlled the timing of any final decision. Perhaps Trimble was not completely surprised. In 1975 'Calvin McNee' had written in *Fortnight* that no deal was possible without Paisley's endorsement: 'Even if it got 70/30 backing at the polls in a referendum.'[212] Calvin McNee was the nom de plume employed by a young Belfast law lecturer, David Trimble.

The broad outline history of violent death in the Troubles is not in dispute. Republicans were the largest single agent of death—58 per cent of all the victims fell at their hands. Significantly, the Provos managed to kill at least five people for every death they suffered, causing over 1,000 deaths and suffering 200. It is a statistic which reveals much about the way in which modern liberal democracy copes with terror. Republicans killed 713 innocent civilians. The largest number of republican paramilitaries killed in the conflict were murdered not by the RUC or British army, but by their own comrades: The INLA and the IRA have been responsible for the deaths of 164 of their own members. The army, RUC, and loyalist paramilitaries killed 161. These are squalid details of a squalid conflict, to which we must add one other—innocent Catholic civilians killed by loyalists (whose war on republican terrorists was only sporadic in intensity) were the largest single group to die in 'the Troubles'.

Three thousand six hundred and thirty human beings had been slaughtered in a largely sectarian conflict in the First World—between two peoples, the Protestant Irish and the Catholic Irish, who, between them, had produced many of the intellectual avatars of that world—in science, the arts, and the economy. Ironically, it was the hostility of the government of the Irish Republic rather than that of the United Kingdom which destroyed, for the twentieth century at least, the possibility of a united Ireland. It adds but little to this humiliation to discover that the brutal and erratic Ugandan dictator Idi Amin offered himself as a good-faith mediator 'between the opposing sides in the crisis that is tearing Northern Ireland apart'.[213] The brutality of the IRA campaign bred another brutality by intensifying a loyalist predilection for violence already visible in 1966.

212 *Fortnight*, 31 Oct. 1975.
213 'Dictator Amin offered to broker Ulster deal', *Belfast Telegraph*, 1 Jan. 2005.

Yet all this horror was underpinned by the safety-net provided for by the British state—this was, after all, the first war in history in which a single government paid and housed both sides.[214] Prime Minister Tony Blair concluded on 6 April 2006, in his speech at the Navan Centre, Armagh: 'The way this struggle was being conducted was indeed brutal and bloody, but most of all unbearably oldfashioned, out of date and pointless. No one was ever going to win.' By the time these words were spoken, terrorism had indeed gone out of vogue. But the fact remains that for a quarter of a century, for many in Ireland and indeed in supportive constituencies, both in America and England, it did not seem like that: brutal, essentially sectarian violence had indeed been quite the fashion. Even the young undergraduate Tony Blair, it emerged in the summer of 2006, had asked the junior common room of his Oxford College, St Johns, to subscribe to *An Phoblacht/Republican News* in the early years of 'the Troubles'.[215]

---

[214] Kevin Myers, *Watching the Door: A Memoir, 1971–78* (Dublin, 2006), 155.

[215] It would be unfair to single out Mr Blair. In the 1970s it seemed that all shades of opinion—from American neo-con hero Senator 'Scoop' Jackson to the leading avant-garde Marxist Louis Althusser—could find something 'progressive' in the Northern Ireland conflict.

12

Conclusion

Irish is a word of most composite signification.

(Henry Giles, *Lectures and Essays on Irish and other Subjects*
(1869), 42)

It is impossible to conclude a history of the union without going into
the consequences, and therefore dealing with present politics, which
is not in general desirable in what aspires to be a general history. I can
not, therefore, help it; and must have the charge of writing a party
pamphlet on account of two or three concluding pages.

(W. E. H. Lecky, February 1890, in Elisabeth Lecky, *A Memoir of
the Rt Hon William Edward Hartpole Lecky* (1909), 219)

The situation in Ireland at this moment demands the most serious attention and
ought to engage them to leaving nothing undone to prevent the calamity that would
arise to Great Britain from a civil war in that kingdom. The value and importance
of Ireland can not be adequately be estimated or sufficiently prized, its loss or
separation would be the most mortal blow that this kingdom could receive. This
is well known to everyone who is acquainted with the relative weight of the two
kingdoms.[1]

This paper, signed by the Prince of Wales, calling the Cabinet's attention
to the state of Ireland in mid-February 1797, is proof of the importance
of Ireland to the security of Britain. The 'Protestant wind' in Bantry Bay
might have averted a French invasion of Ireland in December 1796, but
the French had demonstrated that the Royal Navy could be evaded and
could not itself guarantee Ireland's security. It was a psychological blow of
immense importance, as the Prince of Wales acknowledged. In 1798 the
French actually did invade to assist the rising of the United Irishmen; a
rising which was put down with telling brutality.

There can be no question, therefore, that strategic considerations in the
1790s played a dominant role in the British decision to implement a union

---

[1] PRONI T3319/42, 14 Feb. 1797.

with Ireland. Even so, these strategic considerations coexisted ultimately with, and were reinforced by, political and economic calculations: all of which seemed to suggest that the union was the most benign way of ensuring the most tranquil and progressive development of Irish society. The 1790s saw the emergence of a militant republicanism and an equally militant loyalism on Irish soil. Professor Thomas Bartlett has described the 1790s as the 'crucible of modern Ireland when separatism, Republicanism, Unionism and Orangeism captured the Irish political agenda'.[2] But there is even more to be said. In the 1790s the relationship between the British state and the Catholic masses of Ireland began to change. London's decision to concede the right to vote in 1793 was of major significance: a 'turning point'[3] in the history of Protestant ascendancy. The unsuccessful attempt during the Fitzwilliam viceroyalty of 1794–5 to push on to full Catholic political emancipation was also of great significance. One scholar has suggested: 'If emancipation had arrived ... in the Relief Bill of 1795, and Parliament had remained in Dublin, the two nations would surely have become one.'[4] In 1843 Daniel Madden wistfully wrote: 'It is certainly a great pity that the two nations in Ireland are not joined into one. Their union would produce a far finer people than either of the Irish nations is at present.'

Inspired by Edmund Burke, leading politicians in Britain began to accept the argument that the security of Britain required some kind of rapprochement with Catholic Ireland. Burke died in 1797, but the accuracy of his analysis was validated by the rising of 1798: the 'half-citizens', as Burke had described the people of Catholic Ireland, had become the full 'Jacobin'—precisely as he had predicted. In his *Reflections on the Revolution in France*, Burke was, as Professor Derek Beales has put it, 'virtually coming out' as a sympathizer with Catholicism, sensing that the revolution offered an opportunity to represent it to British and Irish protestants in a more favourable light'.[5] But Duigenan and Fitzgibbon, Irish Protestants of Catholic descent, refused the offer of such a reassessment. Whether reformist or reactionary in their attitude, local Irish forces knew, post-Burke, that the agenda had changed, and the struggle for full Catholic emancipation would be resolved, above all, in London, not Dublin or Belfast.

Burke's influence over the British premier's advocacy of the union in 1799 was significant. Pitt presented the union in the most exalted terms. He borrowed Burke's language: a man could not speak as a true Englishman

[2] Thomas Bartlett, *Theobald Wolfe Tone* (Dublin, 1997), 5.
[3] J. C. Beckett, *The Making of Modern Ireland 1603–1923* (London, 1966), 52.
[4] Adrian Hastings, *The Construction of Nationhood: Ethnicity, Religion and Nationalism* (Cambridge, 1997), 94.
[5] 'Edmund Burke and the Monasteries of France', *Historical Journal*, 48: 2 (2005), 434.

unless he spoke as a true Irishman, and a man could not speak as a true Irishman unless he spoke as a true Englishman. Unionists invoked the spread of 'liberal' sentiment flowing from the more sophisticated body politic of the wider United Kingdom. This, combined with the influx of English capital, would raise the condition of Irish society. The evil tendencies of the 1790s in Ireland—extremist French Jacobin influence, combined with the bitterest Catholic–Protestant sectarianism—would gradually fade from memory. There is no denying the dominance of the strategic calculation, but the union reflected more than a narrow conception of British strategic interest. There is no reason to doubt the sincerity of these benign aspirations: it is difficult to sustain the view—later vigorously expressed—that the union was deliberately designed, as Daniel O'Connell put it, 'that Ireland might be robbed with greater facility'.[6]

The union presented itself as a double reconciliation. In the first place, it was designed, according to its supporters, to reconcile Catholic and Protestant interests in Ireland itself. William Cusack Smith explained in 1800: 'By making them (the Catholics) one to four, instead of being three to one', the union alone had the capacity to diminish sectarian antagonism. In a striking phrase, Cusack Smith reminded his readers that, 'by being Catholic, they have not ceased to be Irishmen'.[7] The phrase is so striking because it represents an assumption that Irish Protestants had the first claim on the title 'Irish': an assumption destined to disappear rapidly. The union writers also argued that the union would bring reconciliation, not only within the island of Ireland, but also between the islands of Ireland and Britain. The union pamphleteers insisted that the union would create a new imagined community, 'one people', in the United Kingdom. The Prime Minister, William Pitt, was a particularly enthusiastic advocate of the 'one people' theme. A double source of instability was to be removed: the Protestant fear of the Catholic majority in Ireland and the Catholic resentment of their 'exclusion from certain rights and privileges'.[8]

Pitt, following Burke, had presented the union in the most exalted terms. Against this, anti-union pamphleteers insisted that the pro-union prospectus was false. The English capital would never come. Why would it come to Ireland, when it already dominated local markets, asked one

[6] See Liam Kennedy, *Colonialism, Religion and Nationalism in Ireland* (Belfast, 1996), 47; see also Liam Kennedy and D. S. Johnson, 'Nationalist Historiography and the Decline of the Irish Economy', *Ireland's Histories: Aspects of State, Society and Ideology* (London, 1991).

[7] *Letter to Henry Grattan*, 3rd edn. (Dublin, 1800), 35.

[8] *Speech of the Rt. Hon. William Pitt in the House of Commons, Thursday 31 January 1799* (Dublin, 1799), 38.

anguished writer.[9] Ireland would be turned into a powerless, impoverished province, the divisions between Catholic and Protestant would intensify. Henry Grattan famously argued that the union project was not about the creation of one people or the identification of two nations. Rather, he said, it was the merger of the parliament of one nation with that of another. Thomas Moore's *Captain Rock* (1824) welcomed the union as opening up the space for a clear 'field of combat' between the Ascendancy and the people.[10]

The promise of a new union was to be blighted by the failure to accompany the measure with Catholic emancipation. This had been Pitt's intention, but in frustration he was forced to resign in 1801. The Irish Protestant elite (with mainstream British backing) successfully mobilized the King against Catholic emancipation and made such a move impossible for a generation. Nothing is more remarkable than the way in which Protestant ascendancy opponents of Pitt's project, like Sir John Parnell or Sir John Foster, speedily reconciled themselves to it, whilst self-conscious Burkeans and Catholic emancipationists, like Sir William Smith or J. W. Croker, who had supported the union, were rapidly disillusioned. Paradoxically, the continuing hostility of the poor decreased Britain's security—and thus undermined the other plank of the union. In 1807 Arthur Wellesley felt compelled to draw up new plans for the defence of Ireland and passed them into the Home Office; in 1831 he discussed similar plans with Maurice Fitzgerald, the Knight of Kerry.[11] These plans assumed little popular support for the union. But if the Irish did not love the British Parliament, did the British Parliament take Ireland seriously?

Ireland became the object of serious British investigation. Between 1810 and 1833 there were 114 Royal Commissions and some sixty Select Committees on Irish matters.[12] Even so, in 1819, for example, Robert Peel lamented the 'inattention' and 'listlessness' with which the House of Commons treated important Irish issues.[13] Above all, Catholic emancipation was long delayed. When emancipation was eventually conceded in 1829,

---

[9] *An Address to the People of Ireland against an Union: In which a Pamphlet Entitled Arguments for and against that Measure is considered with Considerable Alterations and Additions*, by a Friend to Ireland (Dublin, 1799), 19.

[10] Thomas Moore, *Memories of Captain Rock: The Celebrated Irish Chieftain with some Account of his Ancestors Written by Himself*, 4th edn. (London, 1824), 364.

[11] NLI Ms 2007, Knight of Kerry, diary entry 31 Jan. 1831.

[12] Alan O'Day, 'Ireland and the United Kingdom', in George Boyce and Roger Swift (eds.), *Problems and Perspectives in Irish History Since 1800* (Dublin, 2003), 20–1.

[13] Quoted in Michael Staunton, 'Reason for a Repeal of the Legislative Union between England and Ireland', in *Repeal Prize Essays: Essays on the Repeal of the Union* (Dublin, 1845), 117; *Freeman's Journal*, 21 Dec. 1834: 'Sir Robert Peel at one time pathetically lamented the apathy with which anything related to Ireland was sure to be treated by the

it came about not as a result of a free and generous British concession of the justice of the case, but as a result of the massive pressure generated by Daniel O'Connell. Catholic emancipation was accomplished without a 'grace towards the Roman catholics'. As J. W. Croker commented in his 1848 *Quarterly Review* article, with some precision:

The priests alone—the really influential body—got nothing by the emancipation, and they, whom, above all, it was of the most vital importance to conciliate, were rejected and, of course, additionally mortified and exasperated. This explains the otherwise inexplicable fact that every concession to the Romanists has been followed by increased discontent—that is, every new concession to the laity left the clergy still further behind.[14]

As early as 1833 J. O'Driscoll was writing in terms radically different from those of William Cusack Smith: he identified an 'emphatic people', possessed by an 'absurd emphatic Irishism'; a militant Catholic democracy, which denied Irishness—'cast out in public opinion'—to all the other groups on the island.[15]

It was now the Protestant gentry and not the Catholic masses who had a fight on their hands to be considered Irish.[16] The *Spectator*, in 1836, opined: 'We have often said that the union so called was not a real union of the two nations. It was the union of the governing class of Ireland with the governing class of England.'[17] The writer might have added that it had been the union of the Protestant governing class of Ireland with the Protestant governing class of England. But surely, with emancipation settled, the union might have, as the *Spectator* wanted, a second chance? There was some legitimate basis for the *Spectator*'s hope. In 1834 O'Connell argued in his motion: 'From our first connexion with England, we have been treated as an inferior caste and a war of atrocities, such as might well put barbarism to the blush, had for centuries been carried on against [us].' But in the same speech, O'Connell insisted that he 'valued highly the British connexion with Ireland'.[18] Following the failure of the repeal campaign in parliament and the compact with the Whigs at Lichfield House, O'Connell spoke of his readiness to consent to the union if steps were taken to produce 'an identity of laws, an identity of institutions and an identity of liberties'. What he

Imperial Commons, and observed that the bare allusion to any topic purely Irish was a sign for members to retire from the House.'

14 'Outlines of the History of Ireland', 600.
15 *A View of Ireland, Political and Religious*, 2 vols. (London, 1833), 238.
16 Ibid.   17 *Spectator*, 30 Jan. 1836.
18 Peter Jupp, 'Government, Parliament and Politics in Ireland 1801–1841', in Julian Hoppit, *Parliaments, Nations and Identities in Britain and Ireland 1660–1850* (Manchester, 2003), 151.

looked for, he said, was a new state in which there was an identification between 'Yorkshire' and 'Carlow'. O'Connell declared in 1839: what is 'union without identification?'[19]

It is worth noting that, as late as the Gladstone ministry (1868–74), it seemed possible that Liberalism might become 'the political vehicle of Irish Catholic and Presbyterian identities against the old regime':[20] but it became clear by the mid-1880s that the future of Irish politics lay with the nationalist mobilization of Catholics on the one hand, and the unionist mobilization of Protestants on the other: clear proof of the failure to create 'one people'. Notwithstanding the significant minorities of Catholics or Protestants who refused the general trend, the brute fact remains: in 1885–6 every constituency with a Catholic majority in Ireland returned a nationalist.[21] From this point onwards, the concession of self-government to a Dublin parliament was, if not an absolute inevitability, a very likely probability. There is, at any rate, no doubt that the Prime Minister of the day presented the measure of Home Rule as a product of the flawed nature of the original union concept. There is also no doubt of the dominant sectarian strain on Irish political life. By 1886 John Bright, who had, in 1852, criticized Belfast liberalism in Belfast for lacking a sense of a broader Irish identity, now had a different target: 'I think that some of these fellows [the Irish members] are too fond of talking of Ireland as a catholic nation. They do harm.'[22]

Why then did that unionist conception fail, at least to this extent? There are three distinct reasons. First, Britain failed to achieve a moral hegemony to match its political, military, economic, and even linguistic dominance. Second, the pattern of Irish economic and social development tended to undermine the union—except in the north east—and even in the north-east economic success came at a high price. Third, a continuing strategic interest bedeviled British efforts to govern Ireland for much of the nineteenth century.

CHURCH–STATE RELATIONS

Britain's failure to achieve moral hegemony in Ireland was, however, not a matter of mere oversight. It was not a failure to see the need for the creation

[19] *Freeman's Journal*, 26 Apr. 1834.
[20] Patrick Maume, *The Long Gestation* (Dublin, 1999), 3.
[21] Brian Walker, 'The 1885 and 1886 General Election in Ireland', *History Ireland*, (Nov.–Dec. 2005), 38.
[22] R. Barry O'Brien, *Charles Stewart Parnell*, vol. 2 (London, 1899), 146.

of a stratum which could mediate between the rulers and 'the people', and thus bridge a growing chasm. From the moment of the Lichfield House compact of 1835, British governments made serious attempts to incorporate the Catholic middle classes in the magistracy and civil service. The system of national education initiated in 1831 effectively achieved a widespread achievement of English literacy in Ireland.[23] But all these efforts and achievements were greatly diminished on account of one failure: the failure to win over the Catholic priesthood. The state, for all that it might be said to be suffering a certain crisis of legitimacy throughout much of the period, still managed to deliver a high level of literacy and educational achievement more generally, a centralized police force, and a working, though at times highly controversial, legal system. There was a centralized civil service and a rather bureaucratic system of poor relief. There were other, rather striking indications of successful delivery. In his 1873 pamphlet *The Intellectual Resources of Ireland*, R. B. Lyons, Vice-President of the College of Physicians in Ireland, claimed that there was one graduate to every 3,095 people in Ireland as compared with one to every 6,486 in England.[24] Yet, Britain could never generate a pro-British organic intelligentsia in Ireland because of its failure to establish a real connection with the Catholic priesthood; the sons of the tenant-farming elite.[25]

The Catholic priest was the central and most respected figure of Irish life throughout the nineteenth century—indeed, until vocations began to fall off in 1968–70 and the Church became subsequently mired in sexual scandal. William Carleton's celebrated story *The Poor Scholar* tells of the sacrifices required to 'make' a priest. No one could become a priest without years of study: it became a matter of pride throughout small local impoverished communities to play a part in helping. But Stephen Gwynn also noted the feeling (perhaps subconscious) that every member of the beaten-down people who attained an education raised the people with him.[26] Many of the most intelligent British commentators of the nineteenth century—men who otherwise differed comprehensively, like Lord John Russell, J. W. Croker, W. Cooke Taylor, and Lord Houghton—saw the full significance of this reality. In 1845 the former Cambridge 'apostle' and friend of William Smith O'Brien, Richard Monckton Milnes, now

---

[23] Tony Crowley, 'The Struggle between the Languages: The Politics of English in Ireland', *Bullán: An Irish Studies Journal*, 5: 2 (Winter–Spring 2001), 15.

[24] Greta Jones, 'Catholicism, Nationalism and Science', *Irish Review*, 20 (Winter–Spring 1997), 48.

[25] Emmet Larkin, *The Pastoral Role of the Roman Catholic Church in Pre-Famine Ireland, 1750–1850* (Dublin, 2006), 260.

[26] Stephen Gwynn, *Irish Literature and Drama in the English Language* (London, 1936), 64.

Lord Houghton, published a pamphlet, *The Real Union between Britain and Ireland,* supporting the concept of state provision for the Catholic priesthood, as the clue to transforming the relationship between Ireland and England.[27] Another sophisticated liberal thinker, influential Dublin Castle adviser William Cooke Taylor, discussed the case for state support of the Catholic clergy in 1849: 'Had Pitt taken such a step in 1799, *before* the union was carried, it is all but certain that George the Third must have concurred in all his assignments.' Cooke Taylor added ominously:

We see what might have been done then—we do not see what can be done now. The state of imperfection in which the union was left, has generated elements that must long seriously impede, if not prevent, its completion. Principles of cohesion have been crushed by storm or wasted by time from the unfinished edifice; and the temporary expedients employed to fill up these gaps, have seriously impaired the stability of the entire structure.[28]

Cooke Taylor's tone was that of a man who felt he has been writing fifty years too late.

W. E. H. Lecky was a strong supporter of Cooke Taylor's argument—but he also shared his pessimism. There 'was a moment', Lecky declared, when it would have been quite possible to create an arrangement for

the special education of the priests with Dublin University and thus to secure for the teachers of the Irish people a high level of secular education and a close and friendly connection with their Protestant counterparts. If this course had been adopted, and if it had been combined with a state payment of the priests, the whole complexion of later Irish history might have been changed.[29]

Lecky and Cooke Taylor were intellectual liberals; J. W. Croker was most decidedly not an intellectual liberal. Croker, rather a high Tory, spoke of the 'hereditary indolence and squalor' in Ireland, but he believed it would have dissolved if other conditions had been right.[30] The failure to follow the policy of Burke and Pitt on Catholic emancipation—'the injustice and impolicy of such a distribution of political power were flagrant'[31]—was the principal source of the social evils of Ireland. 'The priests hold in their hands the peace of Ireland, and until you disarm, or divide, or conciliate them, there can be no tranquility, no security for life or property.'[32] As late as 1848 Croker argued the case for a state provision for the priesthood: 'Let us

[27] *The Real Union Between Britain and Ireland* (London, 1845); T. Wemyss Reid, *The Life, Letters and Friendships of Richard Monckton Milnes, First Lord Houghton* (London, 1891), i. 353.
[28] *Athenaeum* (1849), 110–11.
[29] W. E. H. Lecky, *Democracy and Liberty* (London, 1896), ii. 3.
[30] 'Outlines of the History of Ireland', *Quarterly Review*, 83: 606 (Sept. 1848), 598.
[31] Ibid. 599. [32] Ibid. 603.

look at the matter more practically, we recognise and protect Mahometan worship in the East, and downright Roman Catholic establishments in Malta or Canada.'[33] Croker asked: 'Is it now too late? We trust not.'[34] But it was, though not everyone realized it. Sir James Graham, the senior Peelite, wrote to Cornewall Lewis in 1852: 'If the time really has gone by when it was possible to deal with the religious divisions in that country and to ally the Roman catholic priesthood to the state, I would fear that the case was desperate, and the root of the evil can not be touched.' But he did not feel that moment had quite been reached.[35] As late as 1867, Lord John Russell—Croker's great ideological enemy in all matters, especially Irish matters[36]—visited Belfast, actively supporting a scheme of state provision for the Catholic clergy. Thomas MacKnight's comment has a certain resonance:

When I left him in the Royal Hotel, I was surprised and, indeed, somewhat mortified, that a statesman who had been twice Prime Minister, and a Liberal leader in the House of Commons for many years, did not see that the Catholic bishops would, in those days, not allow their priests to become mere stipendiaries of the state. The words attributed to the Swedish Chancellor Oxenstierna occurred to me: 'Knowest thou not, my son, with how little wisdom the world is governed?'[37]

ECONOMIC AND SOCIAL DEVELOPMENT

The union had been presented as the key to achieving a higher level of Irish economic success: expectations were deliberately raised in order to offer compensation for possible political frustrations. By this standard, though not necessarily by other, more empirical, less exalted indicators,[38] the union disappointed. The broad pattern of Irish development under the union is not in dispute.[39] Ireland had a unique demographic history: rapid population growth until the 1840s, followed by the appalling famine crisis (1846–50), and then a steady decline up to 1911. Only the north-eastern corner of the island achieved significant industrialization: de-industrialization was

---

[33] 'Outlines of the History of Ireland', *Quarterly Review*, 83: 606 (Sept. 1848), 605.
[34] Ibid. 603.
[35] Charles Stewart Parker, *Life and Letters of Sir James Graham* (London, 1907), ii. 76.
[36] *Correspondence between the Rt. Hon. John Wilson Croker and the Rt. Hon. Lord John Russell in some Passages of Mr Moore's Diary. With a Postscript by Mr Croker Explanatory of Mr Moore's Acquaintance and Correspondence with him* (London, 1854).
[37] *Ulster As It Is* (London, 1896), i. 124.
[38] See e.g. Frank Geary, 'Examining Ireland's Post-Famine Economic Growth Performance', *Economic Journal*, 112 (2002), 919–35.
[39] This section owes much to Gearóid Ó Tuathaigh, 'Ireland under the Union: Historiographical Reflections', *Australian Journal of Irish Studies*, 2 (2002), 1–22.

the norm for most of the country. In a typical travellers' comment, John Gamble wrote in 1818 that Belfast was a great commercial town: 'You might imagine yourself in Liverpool or Glasgow, only that the accent is a little too English for one and a great deal too Scottish for the other.'[40] A wry reference covered the moment when Belfast was known for its political radicalism as much as its economic success: the modern Belfast, it was made clear, had a primary focus on material advancement.[41] Even the one area of the union's undoubted economic success, the north-east, did not unambiguously enhance the broader project, although it undoubtedly enhanced support in Protestant Ulster.

Emerson Tennent's classic reply to O'Connell's speech in favour of the repeal of the union stated bluntly: 'The north of Ireland had, every five years, found its trade doubled since the union.'[42] Henry Cooke made the increasing prosperity of Belfast a major part of his defence of the union.[43] But it is important to note that Cooke's economic argument for the union linked Belfast's prosperity to the 'genii of Protestantism and liberty'. The question was asked: if Belfast could prosper under the union, why not the rest of the country? Cooke had no doubt as to the answer—the absence of 'protestantism' and 'liberty' in the south and west. The unionist–nationalist divide within the working-class communities of Belfast was evident as early as the 1840s, when Protestant and Catholic workers were mobilized in the pro- and anti-repeal cause. This fundamental antagonism was exacerbated by evangelical ministers and repeal leaders: the new division was 'grafted on to the existing sectarian divide imported from the Ulster countryside in the early nineteenth century in the form of the Ribbon and Orange societies'.[44]

In short, Belfast was the great industrial success of nineteenth-century Ireland, but that success generated its own destabilizing tensions. Belfast grew even more rapidly after O'Connell's visit, as the introduction of shipbuilding and engineering added to the established textile industry. Thousands of workers, many of them Catholic, were attracted from the countryside. In 1800 an estimated 10 per cent of Belfast's 20,000 population was Catholic, but by the census of 1861 34 per cent of Belfast's 121,000

---

[40] John Gamble, *View of Society and Manners in the North of Ireland written in the Year 1818* (London, 1819), 366.

[41] 'About 40 years ago the presbyterians of Ulster who, humanly speaking, had so few real evils to complain of, heated their fancies with, I could almost say, imaginary ones', ibid. 295.

[42] *Freeman's Journal*, 28 Apr. 1834.

[43] Patrick Maume (ed.), *William McComb: The Repealer Repulsed* (Dublin, 2003), p. xvi.

[44] Catherine Hirst, 'Politics, Sectarianism and the Working Class in Nineteenth-Century Belfast', in Fintan Lane and Donal Ó Drisceoil, *Politics and the Irish Working Class 1880–1945* (London, 2005), 78.

population was Catholic. This influx had been associated with long-running sectarian rioting following the Twelfth of July Orange celebrations in 1857, 1864, and 1872.

But the great famine of 1846–50 most definitely mocked the union's claims to generate prosperity and well-being. Following the disastrous failure of the potato crop, a million Irish died within a supposedly United Kingdom. English public opinion, generous and sympathetic at first, soon became markedly less so, as compassion fatigue set in over the years of the famine. Reports which stressed Ireland's culture of agitation rather than self-help; the selfish grabbing of relief intended for the poorest by better-off farmers; the local rather than the 'national' nature of Irish distress—all served to confirm in the English mind an assumption that the English poor were more deserving recipients of support in hard times. The decision made in the summer of 1847 to meet the famine primarily through reliance on the Poor Law was, in effect, a sentence of death for tens of thousands. It was well known that the Irish Poor Law system was not designed to meet such a challenge.[45] The role of a punishing providentialism—a conviction that God was punishing the Irish for the sin of laziness—in the direct formulation of British policy was slight. But a harsher strain of British public opinion did exist, which was prepared to make the argument that the British state should not exert itself lest it interfere with the operation of God's just chastisement of a feckless people. Inevitably, such sentiment poisoned the Anglo-Irish relationship and deepened Irish resentment. Without a stronger British aid, Irish society simply lacked the resources to help itself. This was not just a matter of money, but of a broader social disarticulation. The *Dublin Evening Mail* expressed the point eloquently:

There is still no social community, no public opinion, in this country; there are a few possessors of real property; a small mercantile and professional class; a large class of semi-barbarous money-hoarders, a larger mob and a priesthood; but among these several classes, there is neither reciprocity of feeling nor harmony of action.[46]

Inevitably, a sense of bitter Irish resentment was the pervasive legacy: a sense that Ireland's voice had not been heard. The *Cork Examiner* asked: 'What would happen if Queen Victoria closed the doors of the House of Commons on the 105 representatives of this country? But would it be worse than what has actually happened?'[47]

Even during the famine and its aftermath, there were serious efforts made to rebuild the Anglo-Irish relationship. In 1847 Sir Robert Peel

[45] Herman Merivale, *Five Lectures on the Principles of a Legislative Provision for the Poor of Ireland Delivered in 1837* (London, 1838), 34.
[46] *Dublin Evening Mail*, 5 May 1847.   [47] *Cork Examiner*, 13 Jan. 1852.

subjected the electors of Tamworth to large selections from Edmund Burke's letter to Richard Burke: arguably the most eloquent assault on the concept of Protestant ascendancy ever written.[48] Burke's letter, he informed a perhaps slightly bemused English electorate, would be the basis of his future policy on Ireland. Peel also advanced schemes of economic regeneration which would lead to high levels of investment in Ireland. This idea was enthusiastically welcomed by W. Neilson Hancock:

The employment of capital will necessarily lead to the employment of labour; thus all classes in the community will be benefited together, and the mutual co-operation naturally resulting from the free intercourse of enterprising capitalists, and industrious because well paid labourers will lead to the peace and good feeling between different classes, to which, in the artificial state Ireland has been placed, they have long been strangers.[49]

Professor Hancock's fine hopes were to be disappointed. The post-famine reconstruction of Irish society failed to bring about the era of 'peace and good feeling'. The *Freeman's Journal*, at the beginning of 1863, felt justified in stating: 'Ireland has been united to the Empire, and one of the most frequent arguments used to win her compliance was the assurance of sharing in the prosperity of England. That hope, if entertained by any, has not been realised, nor has the promise yet been fulfilled.'[50] Fenianism launched itself on its doomed trajectory as an insurrectionary movement in the 1860s.

In 1868, in the aftermath of the defeat of the Fenian rising of 1867, Lord Stanley, the Foreign Secretary, declared that Ireland and England were inseparable 'now and forever'. He also denounced as evil 'the wild suggestion, broached in more than one quarter, that the present tenants of the soil should be converted into proprietors, subject only to the payment of existing rents to their landlords'.[51] But not every senior politician in England struck the same note: Gladstone publicly stated that he would govern Ireland by conforming as much as possible to Irish ideas.[52]

In 1877, in Dublin, Gladstone signalled a willingness to contemplate a specifically Irish path of development in agrarian matters, and so, indeed, it

[48] David Bromwich (ed.), *On Empire, Liberty and Reform: Speeches and Letters of Edmund Burke* (New Haven and London, 2000), 415–40.

[49] W. Neilson Hancock, *Statistics Respecting Sales of Encumbered Estates in Ireland: A Paper Read Before the Statistical Section of the British Association at Edinburgh 6 August 1850* (Dublin, 1850), p10.

[50] *Freeman's Journal*, 23 Jan. 1863.

[51] Ibid., 14 Jan. 1868. Stanley discussed in his diary (8 Feb. 1868) the case for a new 'Devon Commission to enquire into the Irish land system case … to dispel a multitude of existing delusions'. J. R. Vincent (ed.), *Disraeli, Derby and the Conservative Party: Journals and Memoirs of Edward Henry, Lord Stanley, 1849–1869* (Hassocks, 1978), 328.

[52] *Freeman's Journal*, 30 Jan. 1868.

transpired. The land question in Ireland was resolved by means of agrarian revolution: prolonged to be sure—the Land Acts stitched together from 1870 to 1909 first weakening and then eliminating 'landlordism' in the countryside. A large class of peasant proprietors was created: they were 3 per cent as opposed to 97 per cent of tenants in the 1870s, but they swelled to become 97.4 per cent in 1929 as opposed to 2.6 per cent of tenants.[53] But at the heart of this great revolution lay a profound ambiguity. The great agrarian mobilization of the land war of 1879–82 depended on the exploitation of the grievances of the poor and most vulnerable sections of the Irish farming community. Yet, when Parliament dealt with the issue in 1881, it had ballooned into 'the Irish land question' as a whole, and strong and middling farmers were the main beneficiaries of concession. The land struggle moved away from the small farmers of Co. Mayo, who had given birth to it. In Mayo, in 1881 and 1882, there was little sign of popular agitation, and the numbers of those emigrating rose dramatically from 1881 to 1883.[54] Parnell, on the other hand, became the 'hero' of the bourgeoisie; more importantly, the strong farmer class gained a grip on the island's material resources which, while it was briefly challenged in 1933–4, had a hegemonic influence on Irish economic and social mores until the era of the Celtic Tiger.

SELFISH STRATEGIC INTERESTS?

The attitude of Lord Melbourne, Prime Minister of the United Kingdom in 1834–5 and 1836–41, towards Ireland is particularly instructive. The Lichfield House Compact of 1835 held out the hope of a new relationship between Catholics and the state. Melbourne believed that 'the majority of the [Irish] population were bigoted Roman catholics'. The Protestants and the Orange lodges were equally bad, sunk in the 'absurdity and impracticality of their own objects'. Since Melbourne held fast to the idea that the political union of the two islands was not open to question, he had to accept the importance of loyal Irish Protestantism. As a consequence, the loyalists were to be treated 'with firmness and justice, but at the same time with caution and consideration, not only for their feelings, but even their prejudices'.[55]

---

[53] Philip Bull, *Land, Politics and Nationalism: A Study of the Irish Land Question* (Dublin, 1996), 195–200.

[54] Don Jordan, *Land and Popular Politics in Ireland: County Mayo from the Plantation to the Land War* (Cambridge, 1994), 312.

[55] L. G. Mitchell, *Lord Melbourne 1779–1848* (Oxford, 1997), 179.

In 1845, in the face of the 'repeal' threat, the Duke of Wellington was prepared to argue that Protestants should be armed and trained as a yeomanry or volunteer force, holding commissions under the Crown, a proposition which other senior members of Peel's government felt could only lead to a religious war in Ireland,[56] despite a concern that a 'Protestant massacre on a large scale' was on the cards in the autumn of 1843.[57] Faced with the Young Ireland revolt in 1848, the government, caught up in exaggerated fears, winked at the arming of Orangemen. The mood soon passed, and in October 1849 *The Times*, especially close to Lord Clarendon in Dublin Castle, announced:

The great lessons that Ireland requires and that we have undertaken to teach her, are unity of affection, equality of rights and the absolute supremacy of law. The Imperial government has proclaimed war to the knife with all that sets class against class, and leads one class of men to imagine themselves to be favoured and the others to be opposed. It has dismissed and proscribed every form of political sectarianism.[58]

But much as the British establishment tried to free itself from any taint of Orangeism, John Mitchel was always there to remind nationalists of the embarrassing truth.[59] In fact, freeing oneself from the legacy of the past could not be achieved quite so quickly or painlessly. As late as 20 October 1881, Earl Spencer, with much Irish experience in Cabinet, wrote to Lord Cowper in Dublin: 'the active support of Orangemen and Protestants is the ultimate resource of English rule in Ireland but ought to be kept until every other card has been played.'[60] This 'last resort' became more and more implausible as time passed. In March 1883 the *Irish Nation* reported that Gladstone had told a French political leader a 'short time ago that he was trying to wake the humblest Irishman[,] that he had a governing agency, and that the government [was] carried on by him and for him'.[61] Gradually the impact of Gladstone's conversion to Home Rule in 1886 (which Spencer endorsed) found an echo on the Conservative and Unionist side, an echo which implied that a moral unionism had to abandon a divide-and-rule policy. Twenty-two years later a Conservative and unionist Chief Secretary would claim:

I had convinced my colleagues, a majority of our supporters in the House … that it was right to foster union among Irishmen and to obliterate the vestiges of ancient

[56] Kevin B. Nowlan, *The Politics of Repeal* (London, 1965), 52.

[57] S. R. Gibbons, *Captain Rock, Knight Errant: The Threatening Letters of Pre-Famine Ireland* (Dublin, 2004), 36.

[58] *The Times*, 11 Oct. 1849.

[59] *An Apology for the British Government in Ireland* (Dublin, 1882), 31.

[60] Countess Cowper, *Earl Cowper KG: A Memoir by his Wife*, privately printed (London, 1915), 533–5.

[61] *Irish Nation*, 17 Mar. 1883.

feuds without troubling ourselves about the ultimate effect of social regeneration on Ireland's attitude towards the home rule versus union controversy.[62]

But, by this point, and indeed at least two decades previously, Catholic Ireland had concluded that British policy in Ireland had been tainted by a 'divide and rule' agenda, which placed Catholic Ireland at a disadvantage, because the Orangemen, however often condemned by British statesmen, were, despite all the rhetoric, the privileged allies of the state. The Home Rule crisis of 1912–14 seemed to this audience to provide an objective proof of such a view.

Nevertheless, a decisive shift in British mentality had taken place: underpinned, it should be said, by a sense of the economic irrelevance of Ireland.[63] Britain ceased to regard Irish self-government as involving a strategic risk: British naval and military power combined with the obvious Redmondite pro-imperial enthusiasm to produce such an effect. Colonel Wilfrid (later Sir Wilfrid) Spender was unique in giving the issue such weight as to make it central to his career.[64]

In mainstream British political life, Home Rule as such did not provoke any serious concerns about strategic issues. Liberal home-rulers assumed that British garrisons would remain in Ireland. The Redmondite Irish Press Agency in London embossed its notepaper with the Foreign Secretary Sir Edward Grey's speech on the colonial question, which hailed the 'healing' effect of granting self-government. Given such profuse promises of reconciliation, it would seem to have been almost paranoid to be obsessed with questions of security. It is here that the Redmondite conception that, once Home Rule paid the debt owed to history by the establishment of an Irish parliament, the two democracies would find common cause, worked its magic. The Easter Rising, of course, changed the terms of this whole debate, and in the 1921 Treaty negotiations there was clear evidence of British concern about possible strategic vulnerabilities.[65] It remained, though, almost impossible for Britain to desert the Protestant community in Ireland, more particularly that community in the six north-eastern counties

---

[62] J. W. Mackail and Guy Wyndham, *Life and Letters of George Wyndham* (London, 1925), i. 472–3.

[63] As early as 1886 Sir Robert Giffen, the distinguished economist, had noted: 'We grow a whole new people, equal to the whole disaffected parts of Ireland at the present time every ten years. In a few generations, at this rate, Ireland must become, relatively to Great Britain, very little more than a somewhat larger Isle of Man, or Channel Islands. To let Ireland split partnership would differ in no kind, and comparatively little in degree, as far as business is concerned, from letting the Isle of Man remain a separate state.' 'The Economic Value of Ireland to Great Britain', *Nineteenth Century*, 19 (Mar. 1886).

[64] Geoffrey Lewis, *Carson: The Man Who Divided Ireland* (London, 2005), 149.

[65] Peter Hart, *Mick: The Real Michael Collins* (London, 2005), 149.

where it formed a majority. It was always difficult for British statesman to formulate a language which justified the expulsion of a settled community of a million citizens from the United Kingdom polity, or even unilaterally radically altered the terms of membership of that polity, as in 1985.[66]

Even Gladstone, who, by the mid-1880s was in thrall to an essentially nationalist view of Irish history, still implied in 1893 that he would concede partition if Irish unionists would settle for it.[67] By coming so late in the day to this conclusion Gladstone squandered his moral authority to do what he clearly believed, as the first Prime Minister to concede the Irish case for self-government, he had the capacity to do: win Irish Party support for a partition settlement. Lloyd George summed up what had become London's pro-consent Irish position in 1919, as the War of Independence (as nationalists saw it—unionists termed it a civil war) got under way:

Mr de Valera says that Ireland is a nation [cries of No! and Two Nations!]. The mere fact it is an island is not proof it is a nation. Britain is an island, but it has three nations. In religion, in temperament, in tradition and outlook, in everything that constitutes a nation, unfortunately they [the Irish] differ ... they [Irish nationalists] are not satisfied with getting self-determination for themselves without depriving others of the right of self-determination.[68]

In 1922 the south and west of Ireland having just seceded from the union, Harold Cox, editor of the *Edinburgh Review*, hailed the 'new United Kingdom'. Let the South go, he argued, rely instead on 'Saxon stock' in the North. Cox invoked an important shared moment linking Belfast and London, according to a Belfast report of one of his speeches: 'His home was in Kent, and when the wind was from the south, they, at night, could hear the noise of the guns booming on the Somme. Ulstermen on the Somme were fighting for the defence of Kent.'[69] But such (mainland) emotional warmth was the exception rather than the rule. Harold Cox's reaction was untypical. W. D. Allen's brilliantly evocative 1925 essay on the Tyrone 'Black' men more correctly locates the uneasy Ulster Protestant (or more accurately, Ulster loyalist) place in the wider British culture:

Under the streamers in the long and wet and narrow cobbled streets, in the early afternoon they are forming columns. They are marching in ragged line—that great nuisance of today—the Protestants of Ulster. Where are they marching along the muddy road, solemnly and ponderously, and fixedly ... ? You may laugh, you overeducated, you supercilious, you townbred froth of things. The sign post says

[66] Paul Bew, *Ideology and the Irish Question* (Oxford, 1994), 51–2; Arthur Aughey, *Nationalism, Devolution and the Challenge to the United Kingdom State* (London, 2001), 31.
[67] *Northern Whig*, 5 May 1893.   [68] *Times Literary Supplement*, 17 Mar. 2001.
[69] *Northern Whig*, 31 Mar. 1922.

'to the asylum'—their muddy hobnailed boots go splashing into a wet and peaty meadow bordered with rich, green, swaying trees, cut by a savage wind, needled with driving rain, grey cloud looming over. Cheerfully, quickly, methodically, they roll the banners, for they are expensive banners ... bought with the weekly threepences and sixpences of working men. Four men ... noticeable for their gaunt and bitter aspect, maimed and bemedalled, roll out a banner, ordered in black crêpe, Thiepval 1916 it reads. So comfortably remote, remoter ever than the 'relief of Derry', they are celebrating. Silently, humorously, doggedly, they mass around a dripping platform, a remarkable feudal patriarchal, tribal, historical anachronism in these days of moderation, toleration—whine, don't fight—enlightenment.[70]

W. D. Allen, one of the more intellectual of Ulster Unionist MPs, had grasped more accurately than Harold Cox that Ulster had an uncertain and unloved place in the United Kingdom firmament. More typical of mainstream British attitudes was a frequently unenthusiastic acceptance of the fact that it was impossible to coerce Ulster: an attitude which inevitably rubbed up against the desire for an 'equal citizenship', characteristic of any democratic society, even Northern Ireland.

The transfer of the Treaty ports to Irish sovereignty in 1938 is a further case in point. The British belatedly gave the ports back to de Valera: the decisive calculation was a political one—a desire to show the value of 'jaw jaw':[71] though it was also underpinned by a sense of historical guilt for some about Britain's treatment of Ireland. Britain hoped to demonstrate to Hitler that negotiations with old enemies would achieve mutual benefit without recourse to war. Little thought was given to the long-term strategic issues. When the Second World War broke out, it turned out that the Irish ports had a strategic importance. Berehaven was beyond the range of German dive-bombers and long-range fighter air cover. It was, therefore, much less vulnerable than Milford Haven or Portsmouth. Possession of Berehaven and Foynes would have greatly assisted British air reconnaissance, so essential to anti-submarine warfare. It would also have allowed for easier interception of German long-range reconnaissance aircraft. Above all, retaining the Irish Treaty ports would have permitted faster turnaround time for Atlantic convoys. Nevertheless, while Winston Churchill bitterly resented the military costs of the neutrality, British intelligence came to the conclusion that the neutrality had been compatible with British interests. In fact, this was due to the remarkable co-operation offered to the allies by Colonel Dan Bryan, head of Irish military intelligence; ironically, Bryan

[70] W. D. Allen, *Beld-es-isba* (London, 1925).
[71] David Gray, 'Behind the Green Door', University of Wyoming Library, 2, speaks of Chamberlain being 'illuminated by the dream of European peace and appeasement. The Prime Minister apparently was not interested in punishing them for their violation of Treaty obligations, but using their predicament to test the appeasement formula.'

may be seen as following the logic of Joseph Pollock in 1796. Pollock had dropped his nationalism and radicalism because he feared the consequences of a Franco-British conflict on Irish soil. In substance, Dan Bryan, like Joseph Pollock, believed that Irishmen had every reason to make sure that Britain had no incentive at all to fight a continental enemy on Irish soil.[72] Churchill's brutal criticism of Irish neutrality did, however, generate a certain legacy. The notion of a British strategic interest, long dormant, now revived. In 1955 the British Cabinet was informed:

It must be recognised that the possession of Northern Ireland is of capital importance in the defence of Great Britain. The gravity of the loss of the naval base at Queenstown in the Irish Republic was acutely apparent during the last war. If this had been accompanied by the loss of Northern Irish harbours, aerodromes and shipbuilding capacity, the result may well have been disastrous.[73]

This memorandum stressed the consequent need to treat the 'irritating' demands of Ulster Unionists with some sensitivity: twenty years later Downing Street was occupied by men considerably less sensitive (if not actually hostile) to these irritating demands, but even so, it was axiomatic that any political settlement of the 'Troubles' should protect Britain's defence interests.[74]

As late as May 1982 Nicholas Scott, a minister at the Northern Ireland Office, told an Irish-American interviewer, Padraig Ó Malley, that an IRA victory in Ireland would lead to an 'offshore island—centre for subversion that would not be very dissimilar from what the United States and the central and northern parts of Latin America have endured from Cuba in the last 20 years'.[75] There is no doubt, however, that the British public discussion of strategic issues moved to a new place in the 1990s. In that decade, following upon the collapse of the Soviet Union and the end of the Cold War, Britain reached a new position: a confident public insistence that it had no selfish and strategic interests at stake in Ireland.[76] On 9 November 1990, in a speech in his own constituency, Peter Brooke, the Secretary of State for Northern Ireland, declared that Britain had no 'strategic or economic interest' in Northern Ireland and would 'accept the

---

[72] I am grateful to Patrick Maume for discussions on this point.

[73] Marc Mulholland, *Northern Ireland at the Crossroads: Ulster Unionism in the O'Neill Years, 1960–69* (London, 2000), 16.

[74] Bernard Donoughue, *Downing Street Diary: With Harold Wilson in No. 10* (London, 2005), 31 Oct. 1975, p. 550.

[75] Padraig Ó Malley, *The Uncivil Wars: Ireland Today* (Boston, 1983), 236–7.

[76] Michael Cox, 'Northern Ireland After the Cold War', in Michael Cox, Adrian Guelke, and Fiona Stephen, *A Farewell to Arms? From Long War to Long Peace in Northern Ireland* (Manchester, 2000), 249–62.

unification of Ireland if consent existed for it'.[77] The effect of Peter Brooke's pronouncement, later formalized in the Downing Street Declaration of 1993, was to make Irish unity—in John Hume's famous phrase—a matter for those who believed in it persuading those who did not. In fact, it was remarkable how little nationalist effort went into the task of gentle persuasion and how much ethnic grinding, albeit—and this is vitally important—without bombs and bullets, remained the order of the day in Northern Irish politics. It is also remarkable how often the ethnic grinders were effectively underwritten by powerful outside forces in Dublin, London, and even, at times, in Washington. The failure of Irish nationalists to seize the opportunity for a new agenda for the advocacy of Irish unity as being in the interests of Protestant, Catholic, and Dissenter alike is very striking.

AMBIGUITIES OF THE PEACE PROCESS

But if nationalism has devoted little energy to conjuring up a vision of a new Irish nation at ease with itself, there has been no wider vision of the purpose of the union, with one remarkable exception: a speech given by Sir Patrick Mayhew, then Northern Ireland Secretary, to the Irish Association in Dublin in May 1994. Sir Patrick argued that unionism was an authentic Irish political tradition: sometimes it was sectarian and embattled, but it should not be characterized as a purely negative movement. At the heart of Irish unionism lay a positive vision, a:

belief that all the people of these islands—English, Welsh, Scots and Irish too—share far more than divides them; a belief that there is as much value in their confirmed and various diversity as there is in their actual conformity; a belief that in a democratically established union there is more strength to be found than in the sum of its constituent parts; a belief, therefore, that it will gain from being freely associated together with a union that is a union.

Shortly after his general election victory of May 1997, Tony Blair made a major speech at Balmoral in Belfast. He said: 'The union binds the four parts of the United Kingdom together. I believe in the United Kingdom. I value the union.' The speech—designed to create the space for David Trimble to achieve a successful negotiation of what was to become known as the Good Friday Agreement—was effective in its way, but it provoked a great row behind the scenes with the Irish government.

---

[77] Paul Bew and Gordon Gillespie, *Northern Ireland: A Chronology of the Troubles*, 2nd edn. (Dublin, 1999), 242.

Blair has been reluctant to return to the theme. This is in itself revealing, because though the Prime Minister told us that he values the union, he did not (unlike Sir Patrick Mayhew) tell us why: indeed, one of Blair's later appointments as Secretary of State for Northern Ireland, John Reid, was visibly reluctant to assert that the British government valued the union, apparently believing that such a statement would compromise his 'neutrality'. This leaves modern Irish politics in a strange condition, in which the dominant ideologies (nationalism and unionism) are strong in terms of numerical support, but less strong morally and intellectually. Unionism lacks that warm recognition in London it would love to have: nationalism generates more warmth in Dublin, but also, less visibly, a degree of unease.

For if the union, both in theory and practice, has proven to be a highly flawed conception, it has its counterpart in the failure of Irish nationalism to rise above a narrow ethnic or religious base. For all the valiant efforts to insist that the spirit of Tone or Davis infuses modern Irish nationalism,[78] the painful historical truth belies this claim. Tone's pleasure that the pope was being burnt in effigy has been shared by Orangemen but not mainstream nationalists. Davis had a distinctive non-sectarian, liberal vision, a vision which O'Connell defeated, with profound implications for Irish attitudes to broader educational questions. The vicissitudes of the civic nationalist project of Young Ireland is worth noting here. In 1845 John Mitchel passionately identified with the political ecumenism of his close friend Thomas Davis—'a deep enough root those planters have struck into the soil of Ulster, and it would now be ill striving to unplant them'.[79] But the emotional radicalism generated in Mitchel's soul by the famine, which led him to embrace not only the theory of British genocide, but anti-Semitism and slavery too, also changed Mitchel's tone on this topic. By 1858 Mitchel had dismissed Davis' optimism about winning over the forces of Orange Tory conservatism. He 'was too sanguine as we can now all see'. In a devastating sentence, Mitchel wrote: 'In the sanctuary of the Orange heart, no angel dwells—of the better sort.'[80] The Orange refusal to respond to the many blandishments of the Young Irelanders in 1848 left a bitter legacy. Mitchel also injected into the bloodstream of nationalism a conviction that evil Britain had, by definition, no reformist intent on the land question and that representation in Parliament at Westminster was of little avail. These concepts permeate the strategy of radical Land Leaguers and the later generation of Sinn Fein.

---

[78] The classic text is Martin Mansergh, *The Legacy of the Past* (Cork, 2003).
[79] John Mitchel, *Life of Hugh O'Neill* (Dublin, 1845), p. viii.
[80] Patrick Maume (ed.), *The Last Conquest of Ireland (Perhaps)* (Dublin, 2005), 86.

In their different but not entirely dissimilar ways, Butt and Parnell attempted to protect the Davis project against the more militant and aggressive strains of nationalism. Parnell's celebrated speech of May 1891, which insisted that 'conciliation' was the only possible nationalist response to the 'reasonable or unreasonable' sentiments of the unionist community in the north-east, may have come rather late in the day. It seemed to exploit rather opportunistically Parnell's own damaged relationship with the Catholic Church in order to make a desperate bid for 'Orange' support.

It is beyond doubt that Parnell's message would have been much more effective if stated in the days of his pomp in the mid-1880s. But the fact remains that Parnell had never accepted the premises of his neo-Fenian Land League allies, and hoped to lead Irish nationalism along conservative and non-sectarian lines. After Parnell's death in 1891, both Redmond and William O'Brien—even as they disagreed with each other over tactics and timing—sought to defend the concept of a nationalism which amounted to being more than the voice of the resurgent Catholic democracy. By the early twentieth century accommodation or confrontation was the 'stark choice'[81] facing those politicians who had exploited the land question as the engine of popular mobilization for Home Rule during the previous twenty years. William O'Brien and (more privately but with equal intensity) John Redmond believed, after the Wyndham Land Act of 1903, that the old politics of agrarian agitation was now much less relevant, and the opportunity existed to reconcile all creeds and classes (including landlords and other elements of the Protestant ascendancy) and move towards consensus politics and the creation of a new Ireland unburdened by the sectarian and class tensions of the past. Dr Philip Bull has described the failure of this conciliatory strategy as due, ultimately, to the 'inability of the political culture to free itself of the habits of mind and action created by the land issue'.[82] 'These habits were confrontational, class-riven and resonating in sectarian recrimination and accusation.'[83] The conciliatory strand of nationalist politics in the Redmond era lacked a grassroots validation.[84] Even so, Redmond's project—Home Rule within the Empire—came

[81] Gearóid Ó Tuathaigh, 'Political History', in Laurence M. Geary and Margaret Kelleher, *Nineteenth-Century Ireland: A Guide to Recent Research* (Dublin, 2005), 18.

[82] Philip Bull, *Land, Politics and Nationalism* (Dublin, 1996), 76; Sally Warwick Haller, 'Seeking Conciliation: William O'Brien and the Ulster Crisis, 1911–1914', in D. G. Boyce and Alan O'Day (eds.), *The Ulster Crisis 1885–1921* (London, 2005), 146–64.

[83] Ó Tuathaigh, 'Political History', 19.

[84] Michael Wheatley, *Nationalism and the Irish Party: Provincial Ireland 1910–1916* (Cambridge, 2005).

close to success, and had he delivered self-government he might have had enhanced power to shape grassroots sentiment.

Home Rule was an ambiguous concept: it could be interpreted as anything from a modest form of devolution to a stepping-stone to separation. But there is little question as to Redmond's interpretation: Redmond saw Home Rule as a debt owed to history, which, once paid, opened up new reconciling possibilities. Combined with the process of land reform, it removed Ireland's traditional grievance; once implemented, there was no need for a disciplined nationalist political machine to stay in place; rather, the opportunity would be created for new forces to emerge. 'After home rule is granted, the home rule party as we have known it, will disappear', he regularly opined. The educated intelligentsia and business classes of Ireland would then move onto the stage. In Redmond's vision, a Home Rule parliament would have continued Westminster links; Irish Party MPs would stay at Westminster and could even, in principle, serve in British Cabinets. Redmond's great vulnerability, of course, was the inability to deal with Ulster Unionist opposition to his project. The insurrectionaries who seized the initiative at Easter 1916 and destroyed Redmond's leadership, claimed to have an answer to that question—they certainly exploited Redmond's apparent weakness on the issue. Stephen Gwynn has, however, argued that the republican resort to violence in the 1916–23 period merely exacerbated the damage caused by the failure of the constitutional nationalists to grasp the need for compromise over Ulster. The violence that republicans have used against Irishmen of the unionist tradition has, indeed, historically been self-defeating, as it has made it less likely that 'the Unionist people will ever trust a Catholic majority enough to throw their lot in with them'.[85]

As a former Redmondite MP, Stephen Gwynn feared precisely this outcome: the continuation of partition and sectarian bitterness. This is why he sought to defend a broad definition of Irishness. In 1923 he defended the poet W. B. Yeats:

Mr Yeats and those with whom he associates are nonetheless Irish, because they belong to the Anglo-Irish stock. Irish nationality is a real thing, nonetheless real, because it defied definition. The real is that which is present in sensation; a man is Irish if he feels Irish and can make others feel the same of him: you destroy the reality if you seek to attach it to shibboleth.[86]

In 1926 though, Gwynn appeared to concede defeat. The first sentence of his autobiography has a kind of tragic resignation: 'I was brought

---

[85] Charles Lysaght, 'Squaring the Rhetoric and Reality of the 1798 Rising', *Sunday Independent*, 4 Apr. 2004.

[86] *Observer*, 18 Nov. 1923. R. F. Foster has pointed out that Gwynn returned to this theme 16 years later, *W. B. Yeats: A Life*, vol. 2, *The Arch Poet* (Oxford, 2003), 659.

up to think myself Irish, without question or qualification, but the new generation prefers to describe me and the like of me as Anglo-Irish.'[87] This was not the gloomiest of Stephen Gwynn's assessments. In his essay on 'Hatred', published in his 1938 volume *Fond Opinions*, he declared in a striking passage: 'We know in Ireland, and probably they know in Poland, in Slovakia and in Russia, and a score of other countries where revolution has succeeded, what is the cost of victorious hate.'[88] Ten years later, writing in the *Bell*, he reiterated the same point he had made in 1924: Ireland was still not a nation, and much of the blame lay with an all-too-vigorous project of 'Gaelicisation'.[89] In 1887 William O'Brien hailed the generosity of Irish nationalism: 'A single Smith O'Brien redeems a whole pedigree'; but this was not how Stephen Gwynn, Smith O'Brien's grandson, experienced it.[90] At times it seems as if for modern Irish republicanism the movement is everything and the goal of unity and reconciliation (always in the middle distance) is nothing. Nonetheless, such determined futility invites consideration of a neglected topic: the basis for communal hatred in modern Ireland.

In 1914 Lord Bryce, an Ulsterman who was a serious judge of these matters, with considerable local and international experience, was inclined to downplay the issue:

Protestants and catholics in Ireland have, especially in northern Ireland ... a spirit of collective antagonism, not personal hatred to one another. There is no danger of religious persecution. There are little weaknesses in human nature, which we must be prepared for in all countries, but they do not amount to oppression or persecution.[91]

To understand these matters, it is necessary to go beyond Bryce to Burke. Edmund Burke's 'Letter to Sir Hercules Langrishe' is the *foundational* text: Burke brilliantly showed how impossible it is for a community to accept an ascendancy with a large and often mediocre base. Trapped in this relationship since the seventeenth century, very many northern Catholics have unreservedly embraced a rhetoric of victimhood. They have placed their own suffering on a par with that of the victims of Nazism and apartheid. When two leading figures, President Mary McAleese and Father Alec Reid, advanced this thesis, the letter pages of the Belfast nationalist press displayed but little embarrassment.[92] There is no escaping here the

---

[87] *Experiences of a Literary Man* (London, 1926), 11.
[88] Stephen Gwynn, *Fond Opinions* (London, 1938), 37.
[89] Stephen Gwynn, *The Bell*, 15: 6 (Mar. 1948), 85.
[90] 'Lost Opportunities of the Irish Gentry', *Irish Essays* (London, 1893), 26.
[91] *Hansard*, vol. 64, 1 July 1914, col. 551.
[92] See e.g. the *Irish News*, 13–14 Oct. 2005.

role of discrimination and often the envenoming power of anecdote,[93] even if the distinction between second-class citizenship and the loss of all citizenship rights, and then the right to life itself, has to be preserved. In a most interesting recent discussion of the discrimination issue, Marc Mulholland asks the key question: 'Why did Unionists discriminate?' In a well-documented essay, he locates a number of key components in the discriminatory Ulster Unionist world. They were triumphalism, anti-Catholicism, social prejudice, and populism—to which Mulholland adds the influence of cabals, particularly the Londonderry 'cabals', and most plausibly of all, concerns about security.[94] Stephen Gwynn's *Observer* articles in the early 1920s give powerful evidence of a former nationalist MP arguing that Sinn Fein–IRA penetration of the British state machinery in Ireland made inevitable the elaborate precautions taken by unionism. The memoir of Eamon Collins, *Killing Rage*, provides striking evidence of a similar republican modus operandi, and it is perfectly clear that the dismantling of the traditional unionist defences in these areas made the British state in Northern Ireland exceptionally vulnerable to spying scandals like 'Stormontgate', exposed in 2002. Mulholland's unflinching conclusion is of particular importance. 'This [was done] not with a desire to crush catholics but rather to keep them in their place.' But, as Mulholland observes, the growing acceptance of the principle of consent by the Irish government has created a context where these practices have lost some of their supposed rationale. In Mulholland's view, had nationalist Ireland acknowledged this principle earlier, 'orchestrated discrimination to maintain a one-party state would have been much less virulent'.[95]

But where does this leave the Irish nationalist project? In principle, it opens up benign possibilities, but there are difficulties. Sinn Fein already dominates northern nationalism; it has made substantial electoral inroads into the Irish Republic. It is true that this progress depends on the continuation of the IRA ceasefire in Northern Ireland; but it is also true that Sinn Fein is not the subject of sustained mainstream reproach in the Irish Republic for its role in the violence of Northern Ireland. Many spectacular acts of cruelty have been forgotten or, perhaps more remarkably, excused in the public mind by reference to the obstinacy and unreasonableness of the (largely Ulster Protestant) victims. On the other

---

[93] For an unpleasant example in the 1960s, in a particular locale, of local government exclusion, see Grainne McCoy, 'The Role of Local Government Conflict Management: Portadown, the Case Study', University of Ulster Ph. D thesis (2006), 99.

[94] Marc Mulholland, 'Why Did Unionists Discriminate?', in Sabine Wichert (ed.), *From the United Irishmen to Twentieth-Century Unionism: A Festschrift for A. T. Q. Stewart* (Dublin, 2004), 187–206.

[95] Ibid. 206.

hand, in the North the recollection of violent acts heavily determines the Protestant community's attitude towards the republican elite. The leader of Sinn Fein, Gerry Adams, stands in the polls as the third most respected Irish politician, while his party was at 10 per cent.[96] Sinn Fein is attempting to effect a change in the terms of the traditional relationship between northern and southern nationalism. The 'melt had been broken in these people',[97] de Valera dared lecture Armagh nationalists, when they failed to support Sinn Fein. The election of Mary McAleese as President of Ireland in 1997 has, at least, proved, in certain contexts, the domestic acceptability of the northern nationalist accent. Now it is northern republicans who lecture Dublin: where is the green paper on Irish unity the Irish government is so reluctant to produce? Significantly, though, the lecturing has yet to produce an effect.

In recent years Northern Irish republicans have sought to saunter onto the political stage of the Irish Republic almost in the fashion of returning war-heroes. The collapse of left-wing alternatives such as the Democratic Left has helped the rise of Sinn Fein. So also has the prevalence of widespread evidence of financial corruption which has tarnished both the major parties—Fianna Fail and Mr Haughey particularly—and other key institutions of Irish respectability, such as the banking system.

There is an irony, of course. All this has taken place while the republican movement claimed to be the legitimate government and actively recruited and trained a private army which was heavily involved in massively lucrative criminal fund-raising activities. But the northern leadership presents a certain asceticism, nonetheless. 'We have suffered', it seems to say, 'for Ireland.' 'The hunger strikes of our dead comrades, the years in prison, the risks undertaken—all this for a certain vision of Ireland.'

Mainstream society in the Irish Republic looks on nervously. Influential 'non-revisionist' columnists worry about the Provo claim to be the 'sole franchise holder' on Irish self-determination or, quite simply, that the Provisionals lie in a way which is qualitatively different from the (relatively harmless) evasions and self-deceptions of southern society. For the policy-making apparatus of the state, there is a harsh but unavoidable choice: one senior Irish diplomat once declared: 'Irish nationalism is like a shark. It must keep moving or it dies.'[98] But is such an attitude compatible with the Irish state's principal objective: stability on the island of Ireland? This is

---

[96] Kevin Rafter, *Sinn Fein 1905–2005: In the Shadow of Gunmen* (Dublin, 2005), 240–1.

[97] *Roscommon Herald*, 6 Feb. 1918.

[98] Eamon Delaney, *Accidental Diplomat: My Years in the Irish Foreign Service* (Dublin, 2001), 305.

the question which dominates all others in modern Ireland and much will depend on the answer. The Irish Foreign Minister, Dermot Ahern, has recently opined that 'we can no longer have two histories, separate and in conflict'.[99] But the official tone of the 2006 celebrations of the 1916 Rising did little to change the reality that in Ireland there are, indeed, 'two histories, separate and in conflict'. The Redmondite perspective was written out of the story, whilst the impact of the Rising on deepening the partition in men's minds was not discussed: nor was the broad failure of Sinn Fein economic, social, and cultural policies. The paradox of 1916 remains: a Catholic revolt against a Catholic political establishment which could only justify itself by claiming a more intense, 'pure' emotion on the religious, national, and linguistic issues of the day. Meanwhile, in the North, a kind of domesticated Paisleyism ruled the roost. The absence of any real connection between these two worlds was symbolized, above all, in the Dublin riots which greeted the 'Love Ulster' march, organized by unionist activists, to commemorate the northern victims of IRA violence in 2006. Yet, the Taoiseach was right to say that without a 'shared past' we cannot have a shared future. The beginning of genuine civility on the island of Ireland requires no less: in this sense, the first large-scale commemoration in the Republic of the Irishmen who died at the Battle of the Somme was an important and positive moment.[100]

Even more remarkably, Frank Millar, the most realistic and shrewd analyst of Northern Irish politics, argued that a Paisley–Sinn Fein coalition administration in Northern Ireland is a question of when, not if.[101] This is the true significance of the St Andrews Agreement of Autumn 2006: it signalled, at last, Paisley's willingness in principle to do a deal with Sinn Fein; it also signalled Sinn Fein's willingness in principle to embrace the police in Northern Ireland. As ethnic rage gives way to ethnic vanity, is it really possible that the enmities of Irish history are losing their power to hurt and destroy?[102]

---

[99] *Irish Political Review*, 21: 2 (Feb. 2006), 23.   [100] *Irish Times*, 3 July 2006.
[101] *Irish Times*, 18 Jan. 2007.
[102] For a discussion of this moment, see Paul Bew *The Making and Remaking of the Good Friday Agreement* (Dublin, 2007). This text takes the discussion up to the eve of Ahern's third general election triumph and Sinn Fein's unexpectedly poor performance.

Index

Abbot, Charles 67
Abercorn, Duke of 33, 260, 262
Abercorn, Lord 479
Aberdeen, fourth Earl of 239
Ackerman, Carl 400, 405, 406, 410,
    411, 412, 418
Act of Union 61–2, 62–3, 212, 363,
    486, 557–8, 563
  and bribery 60–1
  and Castlereagh 2, 46, 53
  and Cornwallis 51
  presentation of viii
  see also parliamentary union
Acton, Lord 32 n 132
  and Gladstone 294
Adams, Gerry 493, 510, 522, 524, 537,
    540, 541, 542, 544, 545, 551, 580
  and the Good Friday Agreement
    (1998) 549–50
Addington, Henry (Viscount
    Sidmouth), 64, 67
agrarian depression 249
agrarian disturbances 97, 108, 137
agrarian violence 135, 139–40, 147–8,
    218, 270, 296, 321, 323, 332
  see also Rockite movement
agriculture 299–300
  graziers 214–15
  and rural economy 297–8
  transition to pasture 250
  see also potato crop
Ahern, Bertie 547–8
Ahern, Dermot 581
Aiken, Frank 428, 436, 441, 466, 469
Algeria 505
Allen, W.D. 571–2
Allen, William (Fenian) 264, 265
Alliance Party 511, 539
Allied Irish Banks 526
Althusser, Louis 555 n 215
American Civil War 255, 257
Amin, Idi 554
Amnesty Association 271

see also Fenianism; Fenians
Ancient Orders of Hibernians 366
Anderson, Sir John 400, 401, 410,
    413, 414
Anderson, R.A. 412
Anderson, Sir Robert 266
Andersonstown News, The 537
Andrew, Christopher 472
Andrew, Sir Robert 532 n 162
Andrews, J.M. 479
Anglesey 131, 133, 134, 136, 137,
  British rule in Ireland 134–5
  dreadful vista 116–17
  and O'Connell 135, 138
Anglo-French war 24
Anglo-Irish Agreement (1985) 509,
    531–3, 535, 539–40, 545
Anglo-Irish Treaty (1921) 396, 570
  negotiated 416–20
  debated in the Dail 422
Anglo-Irish Treaty (1938) 454, 456,
    572
Angola 518
An Phoblacht/Republican News 555
Anster, John 166
Anthony, Richard 456
anti-Irish racism 202–5
anti-tithes campaign 132–3, 136–8
  Midleton, co. Cork 138
Arbuckle, Victor 497
Archer, Colonel Liam 466
Argyll, Duke of 276, 318 n 72, 349
Armagh, 524, 555, 580
  disturbances 120
  Orange assault on Maghery 127
  sectarian clashes 32–4
Arms Bill 184, 186
Armstrong, E.C.R. 483
Armstrong, Sir Robert 506, 531
'Army mutiny' (1924) 446
Arnold-Forster, May Florence 333
Arnold, Matthew
  'The Incompatibles' 340

Ascendancy 10, 27, 29, 83,
  Burke's critique 16–18, 93
  and Jacobinism 36
Ashbourne, Lord 343
Ashe, Thomas 384
Asplen, G.W. 243
Asquith, Henry Herbert 370, 381
Atkinson, Edward 299–300
Atkinson, Wolsey 42
Attlee, Clement 480
Auckland, Lord 58
Aud
  arms shipment (1916) 375
Aunger, Edwin 488
Austen, Jane 223
Auxiliary Division 401

B-Specials, *see* Ulster Special
  Constabulary
Baker, Philip Noel 464 n 73, 479
Balbriggan 404, 405
Baldwin, Stanley 447
Balfour, Arthur 354–5, 401
  law and order 354
  tour of west 358
Ball, F. Erlington 22–3
Ball, John 227
Ballot Act (1872) 286
Ball, Robert 11
Ballybay events 119
Ballymena Observer 243
Banim, John 91–2
Bantry Bay *see* French fleet
Barnes, George 1, 82
Barrett, Eaton Stannard 78
Barrett, Frank 441
Barrett, Michael 265
Barrington, Sir Matthew 167
Barry, Kevin 408
Bartlett, Thomas, 557
Barton, Sergeant John D. 397
Bates, Richard Dawson 436
Battle of the Diamond 33
Battle of the Somme
  commemoration of 581
  nationalist fatalities 383
  Ulster Division at 382, 571
Baxter, Patrick 448
Beales, Derek, 557
Beaverbrook, Lord 419
Beckett, Samuel 527
Bedford, Duke of 78, 145
Begbie, Harold 543–4

Belfast 460, 492, 494, 496, 499, 500,
  506, 519, 551, 564, 571
  expansion 263
  expulsion of shipyard workers
    in, 402
  Fenian threat 263–4
  industrialisation 368–9, 565
  sectarian violence in 351, 404,
    427–9, 434, 460, 489, 495,
    501, 503, 566
Belfast News Letter 44, 63, 73, 459, 488
  and Act of Union 61–2
  and McKnight 232
Belfast Telegraph 481, 482, 492
Bell, The 578
Bell, Alan 399
Bellew, Robert 38
Bellew, Sir Edmund 101
Belmore, Earl of 286
Benn, Captain Wedgwood 406
Bennett, William
  and famine 194–5
Bentinck, Lord George 118, 193–4
Beresford, John 27, 31, 58, 67–8, 526
Berry, Peter 487, 500
Berwick, Walter 230
Bessborough (formerly
  Duncannon) 184, 283–4
Best, R.I. 483
Bethel, Isaac Burke 53
Bethune, John A. 406, 415
Bianconi, Charles 105 n 91
Biggar, Joseph Gillis 279, 307, 318
Birch, Thomas Ledlie 46
Birrell, Augustine 365, 366, 368, 374
'Black and Tans', the 397, 401, 404,
  409, 536
Blacker, William 42
Blackwood, Lord Basil 372
Blair, Tony 547, 551, 552, 555, 574–5
Blake, J.A.
  and Atkinson (Ed.) 300
Blakeney, Sir Edward 220
Blaney, Neil 495, 500
Blennerhasset, R.P. 280
'Bloody Sunday'
  1921, 408–10
  1972, 506–8
Bloomfield, Sir Kenneth 481
Blueshirts 454
Blythe, Ernest 395, 446, 462–3
Boal, Desmond 513
Boland, Harry 377 n 73, 394

Boland, Kevin 500, 513, 514
Botanical Gardens, the 483
Botha, Louis 381
Boundary Commission 424, 446–8,
    450, 498
Bourke, Canon Ulick J. 253
Bourke, Colonel Walter 315, 338, 355
Bourke, Mrs 315
Bourne Committee 523–4
Bousfield, Bernard 13
Boyce, Father 246
Boyton, Michael 333, 339
Bradford, Roy 513
Brady, District Inspector James Joseph
    Brady 406
Brady, Joe 335–6
Brady, Maziere 184
Brady, Michael 391
Brady, P.J. 406
Branney, Louis 519
Breen, Dan 394, 441
Brennan, Thomas 329, 339, 355
Bretherton, C.H. 421, 422
Brett, Sergeant 264
Brett, Sir Charles 491
Bridge, Patten Smith 298
Bright, John 213, 256, 276, 277, 348,
    561
Brighton bomb (1984) 531
British policy in independent Ireland
    and Northern Ireland (1921–)
  abolition of Stormont 508–9
  the Army in Northern
    Ireland 495–6, 497, 506–7,
    550
  civil rights marches 490–1
  contact with Provisional
    republicanism 518–19, 535,
    537, 539, 540–1
  contact with Sinn Fein (1920–1)
    404, 410, 414
  the Craig-Collins pact 430
  criminalization of Provisional
    republicanism 524, 528, 553
  the declaration of an Irish Republic
    (1949) 479–80
  decommissioning 544, 547
  direct rule 494, 496, 502–3, 504,
    506, 508–9, 518, 523, 524, 532
  the Downing Street Declaration
    (1993) 541–4
  the economic war with the Irish Free
    State 453–4

  end of Cold War 573
  the European Union 486–7
  Good Friday Agreement
    (1998) 549–50
  the Irish Civil War 437
  the Irish dimension and Northern
    Ireland 510–11, 512
  Joint Framework Document 545–6
  land question 325–9
  power-sharing in Northern
    Ireland 504–5, 506, 510–11,
    512–14, 515, 525, 532–3
  the Second World War 464,
    469–72, 479, 572–3
  sponsoring a DUP-Sinn
    agreement 552–4
  subsidising Northern Ireland 461,
    482, 492
  the truce (1921) 414
  US pressure on 533, 552
  withdrawal from Northern
    Ireland 513–14, 516–18,
    519–22, 523
Brook, Sir Norman 480, 504
Brooke, Sir Basil (Lord
    Brookeborough) 423, 435, 459,
    469, 479, 480
Brooke, Frank 408, 423
Brooke, Peter 537–8, 539, 542, 573–4
Brooks, Sydney 364
Brougham, Lord 144
Browne, Denis
  and Threshers 84
Browne, Derek 520
Browne, Noel 476
Bruce, William
  Belfast Politics 11
Brugha, Cathal 395, 415, 431
Bruton, John 546, 548
Bryan, Colonel Dan 472, 572
Bryce, James (Lord Bryce) 334, 340,
    365, 366, 418
  on Parnell 305–6, 306, 336
  on sectarianism 578
Buckingham Palace talks 370
Buckland, Dr William 175
  and potato crop 176
Buckle, Thomas
  History of Civilisation 203–4
Buckley, Nathaniel 298–9
Budeley, Revd John 232
Bull, Philip 576
Burdet, Sir Francis

Burdet, Sir Francis (*cont.*)
  Catholic Emancipation Bill
    (1825) 110
Burgoyne, Sir John 190, 197–200
  famine appeal with
    Trevelyan 198–200
Burke, Edmund 1, 4, 21 n 87, 25, 51,
    57, 93, 558
  on Ascendancy 16–18, 36, 567
  on Britain and Ireland 18–19
  and Catholic emancipation 28, 29,
    30
  Catholic sympathies 14–17, 21–2,
    25–6
  contacts 22–3
  and Duigenan 30–1, 37–9, 57,
    82–3
  family background 14
  and Hamilton 14–15
  and Home Rule debate 349–50
  'Letters on a Regicide Peace' 35
  'Letter to Hercules Langrishe' 23,
    93, 578
  Miles's attack 34–5
  political testament 35–7
  Reflections on the Revolution in
    France 7, 16, 557
  and Paine 7–8, 9
  refutations of 13
  and Tone 12–13, 34
  Townsend's defence of 35
Burke, Inspector 405
Burke, Julianne (EB's sister) 14
Burke, Richard (EB's father) 14,
Burke, Richard (EB's son) 18, 23, 24,
    26, 567
  and Catholic Committee 19–20, 21
Burke, Richard O'Sullivan 265
Burke, Thomas
  assassination 336
Burkean legacy 58
  rhetoric 53–4 n 26
Burns, Elizabeth 160
Burntollet march (1969) 493, 494
Bushe, Charles Kendal 55
Butt, Isaac 157–8, 270–1, 298, 305,
    307, 330, 576
  assessment of 308
  and education 292–3
  and federalism 283–4, 310
  and Fenianism 271, 272
  and Home Rule 278–9, 281–6, 291
  and Home Rule Conference 284–5

Irish Federalism 284
  and land reform 273–4, 297
  O'Brien's lawyer 222
  O' Connell repeal debate 158–9
  and Parnell 307, 308, 310
  Ulster Times 158
Byrne, Edward 357
Byrne, Patrick 19

Caird, James 208
Cairnes, J.E.
  and land reform 274–5, 276
  and university reform 289
Cairns, Earl
  and peasant proprietorship 331
Callaghan, James 494, 496, 497, 523,
    525
Cambrai, Philip 368
Cambridge and Oxford Review 188–9
Cambridge, Duke of 271
Camden, first Earl of 8, 29, 30, 44–5
Cameron Report 463, 489, 494, 497
Campbell, J.J. 457, 462–3, 494
Campbell, Revd Theophilius 224
Campbell, Sir George
  and land reform 275–4
Canaris, Admiral 470
Canary Wharf bomb (1996) 547
Canning, George 79, 102, 114
Carleton, William 96, 304
  'The Poor Scholar' 98, 562
  Wildgoose Lodge 95–6
Carlisle, Earl of (formerly Lord
    Morpeth) 251, 255
  'flocks and herds' doctrine 241–2
Carlyle, Thomas
  political outlook 155
  and Tipperary 162–3
  and Young Ireland 163 n 207
Carnarvon, Lord 352
  and Parnell 343
Carnot, Lazare 34, 36
Carrickshock deaths 137
Carroll, Dr William 309
Carron, Owen 530
Carson, Edward 354, 368, 370, 372,
    381, 391
Casement, Sir Roger 374
  and Easter Rising 375
  hanged 379–80
Casey, John Sarsfield 298
Castlereagh, Viscount, Second
    Marquess of Londonderry 1–2,

6–7, 39, 40 n 178, 45, 46, 52, 59,
  60, 64 n 77, 87, 102 n 77, 371
accusations of betrayal 46–7
and Catholic emancipation 88, 100,
  102, 104
and Emmet rebellion 74–5
and French Revolution 8–9, 12
and Louis XVIII 53
and parliamentary union 46, 59–60
and Presbyterianism 62
see also Stewart family
Catholic Association 107–8, 118,
  120–1
  banned 109
  and O'Connell motion 115
  relaunched 114
  suppressed 122
Catholic Board 90
Catholic Bulletin 379, 446
Catholic Church 360, 562, 563–4,
  576
  and education 171–2, 173–4, 287
  and famine 208–9
  and Fenians 255–6
  ne temere decree 368
  position of in independent
    Ireland 455, 475, 476, 484,
    534
Catholic clergy 562
  militant language 226
Catholic Committee 23–4 n99, 34, 88
  resignations 101
Catholic conventions 26
Catholic Defence Association
  and Tenant League 237
Catholic emancipation 23, 27–9, 30,
  58, 75, 77, 89, 102, 110, 113,
  115, 116, 131–2, 557
  conceded 121–2, 559–60
  and Dawson 117–18
  and Lawless 118–20
  Northern Whig 131–2
  and O'Connell 109–10, 112,
    114–15, 122–3, 131
  and parliamentary union 63, 559
  and Pitt 76–7, 87
  and rebellion (1798) 49
'Catholic exclusion' 52
Catholic Ireland, 561
  and French Jacobinism 32
Catholicism 10–11, 12, 48, 62, 63,
  170
  Gladstone on 293

Catholic minority in Northern
  Ireland 424, 430, 432–3, 457,
  459–60, 461–2, 473, 487–8,
  493, 540
  and British Army 497, 499, 502,
    503
  deaths in 'the Troubles' 554
  and the hunger strikes (1981) 528
Catholic Relief Act (1793) 25
Catholic Relief Bill (1793) 24
Catholic Relief Bill (1795) 28
Catholic university 286
Cavan 416
Cavanaugh, Father 314, 315
Cavendish, Lord Frederick
  assassination 336
Ceannt, Eamonn 371, 373
  and Easter Rising 379
Celtic Tiger 477, 568
Chamberlain, Ida 470
Chamberlain, Joseph 323, 331
Chamberlain, Neville 456, 464,
  469–70, 572 n 71
Charlemont, Earl of 19
Charlemont, Lord James 458, 459,
  460
Chichester-Clark, James 494–5, 497,
  502
Chilcot, John 494
Childers, Robert Erskine (1870–1922)
  403, 412, 418–19, 420, 440
Childers, Erskine Hamilton (1905–74)
  475
Christie, Agatha 545
Churchill, Lord Randolph 344
Churchill, Winston Spencer 370,
  401–2, 404, 420, 421, 424, 426,
  427, 429, 435, 478, 572–3
  on the second Craig-Collins
    pact 430–1
  alarm at Collins-de Valera pact 434
  offer of united Ireland to de Valera
    (1941) 471–2, 473
Church of Ireland
  disestablishment 268–70
Church Temporalities Act (1833) 139
Cicero 23
Civil Rights 490, 492–3, 506
  media coverage of 489
  Unionist support for 491
Civil War 437–43
Clancy, Peter 409
Clancy, Seán 389

Clann na Poblachta 476
Clare 415, 518
Clarendon, Lord 224, 226, 227, 230,
  569
  dismissal of Roden 230
  and Orangemen 225
  and Protestants 224–5
  and Russell 236
  Clarke, Ernest 413 n 111
Clarke, James Chichester 176
Clarke, Thomas James 339, 371, 373,
  374
  and Easter Rising 375, 379
Clerkenwell explosion 265–7
  see also Fenians
Clery, Arthur 387
Clifford, Angela 455
Cloncurry, Lord 124, 133
Clune, Archbishop 410
Clune, T.C. 409
Clutterbuck, Sir Alexander 485
Cobbett, William 111, 113
coercion 332, 344
  debates (House of
    Commons) 323–4
Coercion Bill (1833) 139
'Coercion Bill' (1881)
  and Habeas Corpus Act 323
coercive legislation 339–40
Colclough, John 42–3
Cole, Henry Robert 69
Colley, George 526
Collins, Eamon
  Killing Rage 579
Collins, General Patrick 340–1
Collins, Michael 386, 394, 397, 400,
    407, 410, 414, 435–6, 443, 444,
    510, 540–1
  Anglo-Irish Treaty
    negotiations 418–420
  Civil War 437
  Craig-Collins pact 423–8, 430–3
  death of 438
  election pact with Eamon de
    Valera 434
  intelligence 411
  orders 'Bloody Sunday' (1921) 408
  on the weakness of the IRA 415
Collins, Tom 544
Comerford, R.V. 172
Compensation for Disturbance Bill
  (1880) 318
Confessions of a Whitefoot 167

Congested District Board 358
Congress of Vienna 53, 102
Connellan, Corry 184
Conner, William 168, 214, 218–19
  and Repeal Association 162
Connolly, James 365, 370, 373, 458,
  489
  and Easter Rising 376, 377, 379
  and IRB 374
  Workers' Republic 373
Connolly, Lily 379
conscription
  nationalist opposition 389
consent *see* principle of consent
Conservative Party, 525, 531
Convention Act (1793) 26, 88
Cooke, Edward 40, 60, 67–8
Cooke, Revd Henry 5, 90–1, 128–9,
  152, 270, 565
Cooper, Austin
  murder of 147, 149
Cooper, Sir Frank 519, 522
Cope, Andy 400, 404, 410, 412, 413,
  414, 417, 420
Cork 404, 410, 414–16, 438, 439,
  441, 526
Cork Examiner ix, 57, 179, 219, 220,
  234, 235, 239, 251, 263, 566
  and Act of Union 212
  and famine 187, 196, 200, 201
Cornwallis, General 45, 49, 52, 60, 64,
  77
  and Act of Union 51
Corry, Martin 456
Cosgrave, Liam 511, 514
Cosgrave, W.T. 440, 442, 443, 445,
  449, 455
  and the Boundary
    Commission 447–8
  and Easter Rising 378–9
  'German Plot' arrest 388
Council of Ireland
  in the 1920s 395–6, 420, 425, 448
  in the 1970s 511–12, 513, 515
Country Gentleman's Magazine
  Irish tenant mentality 274
Cowper, Lord 569
Cox, Harold 571, 572
Cox, Watty
  Irish Magazine 80, 81, 82, 90
Craig, Sir James (Lord Craigavon) 381,
    395, 400, 401, 411, 412, 435–6,
    478, 483, 512

agrees to meet Eamon de Valera
(1921) 413
Anglo-Irish Treaty
negotiations 419–20
Boundary Commission 448
Civil War 442
Collins-de Valera pact 434
Craig-Collins pact 423–8, 430–3
governing philosophy 458–9
Second World War 463–5, 469,
479
shipyard-worker expulsions 402, 424
Craig, William 490, 492, 520
Craigavon, Lord *see* Craig, Sir James
Crawford, Sharman 92, 128, 205, 237,
239
Down election 237–8
land reform Bill 218
Creagh, Father John
denunciation of Jews 364 *see also*
Limerick
Creevey, Thomas 75, 123
Crewe, Marquess of 481
Crimean War 240
Crimes Act (1887) 354
Croke, Archbishop of Cashel 320, 341
and No Rent Manifesto 329
Croker, John Wilson 64, 69, 79, 83,
85, 94, 110, 113–14, 118, 130–1,
147, 179, 559, 562
Quarterly Review article 281, 560,
563–4
Crolly, William, RC Bishop of Down
and Connor 129
Cromwell, Oliver 313
Cronin, Mike 453
Crossman, Richard 497
Crowley, Peter O'Neill 263
Crozier, J.A. 130
Cuba 398, 518, 573
Cullen, Dr Paul 256, 261, 270
RC Archbishop of Armagh 236
and Crimean War 240
on Fenians 253
and MacManus funeral 254
O'Connell correspondence 154
and O'Keefe case 287–8
political outlook 256–7
and population decline 257
and university reform 289
Cumann na nGaedheal 443, 449, 451,
453, 454
Cunnane, Frank 440

Curragh Camp
'pre-emptive mutiny' 370
Curran, John Philpot 27, 31, 70
Curran, Sarah 70
Currie, Austin 496
Curzon, Lord George 400, 401
Cusack, Miss 37
Cusack Smith, Thomas Berry 165
Cusack Smith, William (Baron) 22–3,
34, 41, 60, 72, 85, 86, 106, 169,
558, 560
and Catholic emancipation 27–9,
30
House of Commons motion 140–2
court ruling 114–15
and parliamentary union 54–5, 55,
58–9, 83
The Patriot 23
report on party feeling (1813) 93
The Rights of Citizens 22, 23
A Sketch of the State of Ireland 83

Dail Eireann, first (1919–21) 393
Anglo-Irish Treaty debates 422
courts 402–3
Dail Eireann, second (1921–2) 426
Daily Chronicle 421
Daily Mail 419
Daly, Michael, 522
Dargan, William 240
Daunt, W. J. O'Neill 66, 83, 256
Davis, Thomas 154, 155–6, 168, 173,
417, 534, 575
clash with O'Connell 171
death 175
and education 171, 174
federalism 166
influence of 175–6
on Tone's career 2
and Young Ireland 176
Davitt, Michael 146, 259, 312, 324,
341, 344, 346, 354, 355, 363, 453
and famine 207
and Limerick Jews 364
Dawson, Colonel George 110, 153
and Catholic emancipation 117–18
Deasy, Timothy 264
de Beaumont, Gustave 148
de Brun, Padraig 423
Decrès, Vice-Admiral 75
Defenders 31–2, 33–4, 39, 40, 73
De Grey, Lady 156
de Lamartine, Alphonse 222

Delane, J.T. 259
Democratic Left 580
Democratic Unionist Party
    (DUP) 509, 539, 553, 554
    and elections 529, 550, 552
Dempsey, Anthony
    eviction 316
de Nie, Michael 191, 202, 348
Derby, Lord 278, 282, 283 n 254, 307,
    308, 313, 318–19, 322
    n 86, 328, 330, 334, 340, 412
    government 239
Derry 467, 495, 496, 506
    civil rights marches in 489, 490, 492
    gerrymandering of 460, 491
de Toqueville, Alexis 119–20
de Valera, Eamon 384, 385, 386–7,
    390, 392, 394, 397–8, 410, 412,
    414, 416, 429, 437, 446, 454,
    462, 463, 477, 482, 571, 572,
    580
    1937 constitution 455–6
    Anglo-Irish Treaty
        negotiations 416–18
    assumes power 451
    Civil War 441–2
    conscription 391
    and the Easter Rising 378
    election pact with Michael
        Collins 434
    and the 'Emergency' 464–74,
        478–9
    executions of IRA men 468 n 90
    founds Fianna Fail 448–9
    'German Plot' arrest 388
    Irish Volunteer convention
        (1917) 385
    and land annuities 453
    meeting with Sir James Craig 1921,
        411, 413
    and Northern Ireland 428, 479
    opposition to the Anglo-Irish Treaty
        and resignation 422
    rejects Craig-Collins pact 431–2
    takes Dail seat 450
de Valera, Sile 526
de Valera, Terry 471–2
de Vere, Aubrey 199
Devine, Thomas 384
Devlin, Bernadette 494, 495, 507–8
Devlin, Joe 366, 372
Devlin, Paddy 516
devolution 363, 365

Devon Commission report 167–8
Devoy, John 228, 291, 309, 330
    and *Catalpa* rescue 309
    and Fenians 248
    and Land League 331
    and land reform 312
    and New Departure 309–10
    and Parnell 309–11
Dewee, Francis P.
    The Molly Maguires 339
Dickson, Rev. Steel 5
Dickson, T.A. 329
Dillon, James 473
Dillon, John 292, 346, 363, 366, 368,
    482
    and Sinn Féin 385–6, 392
Dillon, John Blake 154, 256, 324, 329
Dillon, Luke 225, 356
Dillon, Myles 482–3
Disraeli, Benjamin viii, 165, 193–4,
    262, 268, 269, 291
    and Home Rule 290–1
    and O'Connell 126
Dissenters 10, 11, 23
    and French Revolution 11–12
Dobbs, Francis 73
Doheny, Michael 225, 246
Dolan, C.J. 366
Dolly's Brae
    sectarian clash 229–30
Donahue's Magazine
    and land question 300
Donegal 495, 497
Donegall, Marquess of 11
Donnell, Winston 503
Donnelly, Eamon 450, 456, 457, 462
Donnelly, James S.
    famine in Irish culture 208–9
Donoughue, Bernard 514, 518, 523
Doris, P.J. 453
Dorrian, Hugh 214
Dougherty, Sir James Browne 372
Douglas, Sylvester (Lord
    Glenbervie) 26–7
Down 532
Downing Street Declaration
    (1993) 541–4, 545
Downpatrick Recorder 238
Downshire, Marquess of 237–8
Doyle, Bishop of Kildare and
    Leighlin 108, 135, 140
Doyle, Seán
    Spark 373

Drennan, William 1, 9, 14, 23, 24, 25–6, 27, 47, 74, 78
Drumgoole, Dr 102
and Catholic principles 89–91
Drumm, Maire 519
Drummond, Thomas 83, 144, 192
and law enforcement 147–8
support for 149
Dublin 414, 433, 500, 508, 514
Dublin Castle administration 50, 67, 70, 88, 225, 374, 569
and Catholic emancipation 89
and land question 154, 323
and Lalor (J.F.) 218
Lord-Lieutenant's powers 65
'Ministry of All the Talents' 77–9
Dublin Evening Herald 225
Dublin Evening Mail 91, 153, 193, 194, 226, 566
and English rule in Ireland 228–9
Dublin Journal 46, 69–70, 73, 81
and Burke's influence 93
Dublin Review 83
Dublin University Magazine 14, 193
and O'Connell 113, 215
see also Butt, Isaac
Dufferin, Marquess of 273, 325–6
Duffy, Charles Gavan 119, 154, 166, 194 n 93217, 219, 234, 244, 270
and Crimean War 240
and McKnight 231–3
and *Vindicator* 232
Duffy, Ned 247, 297
Dugdale, Norman 478
Duggan, Eamon 410
Duggan, G.C. 400, 478, 483
Duigenan, Patrick 30–1, 49–50, 51, 63 n 72, 60, 68, 80, 90, 557
critique of Burke 37–9, 57–8, 82–3
Duke of Wellington *see* Wellesley, Sir Arthur
Dukes, Alan 536
Dumouriez, General 84
Dundas, Henry, Viscount Melville 19, 20, 25, 63
Dungannon 488
Dungannon Convention 24, 26, 88
Dunlop, Andrew 295 n 312
Dunphy Richard 449
Dunraven, Lord 362, 363
DUP *see* Democratic Unionist Party
Durham, Bishop of 236
Dwyer, Michael 69

Eames, Archbishop Robin 542
Easter Rising (1916) 570, 577
British response 378
and Casement 375, 379–80
and Ceannt 379
and Clarke 375, 379
and Connolly 376, 377, 379
and Cosgrave 378–9
and de Valera 378
effect of executions 380–1
Fannin on 376
fatalities 376–7
fiftieth anniversary of 484, 488–9
and Irish Volunteers 375
leaders executed 379–80
and McNeill 375
and Markiewicz 377
ninetieth anniversary of 581
and Pearse 375–6, 377, 379
plans 374–5
proclamation 375, 377–8
and Sheehy-Skeffington 376
Stephens on 376
Eastwood, Sir John 191
Ecclesiastical Titles Bill (1851) 236
economic prosperity, 564
accounts of 242–3
Economist, The 505
Edgeworth, Maria 144, 205–6
The Absentee 5–6, 205
Castle Rackrent 205
Edinburgh Review 571
education
and Catholic Church 171, 173–4, 287, 290
Catholic University 253
national school system 135–6, 562
third-level 169–72, 289–90, 292–3
Egan, Patrick 279, 320, 321–2, 328, 335, 339, 356
'Eglinton, John' (W. K. Magee) 483
Eire (1937–1949)
1937 constitution of 455–6
and censorship 482
and the 'Emergency' 463–74, 478–9, 572–3
position of Roman Catholic Church in 455, 475
Eldon, Lord 75
Elizabeth II 525
Elliot, Walter 60
Elliott, Marianne 70
Elliott, William 78, 79

Emergency, the *see* World War II
Emergency Duties Bill (Irish Free State)
  (1932) 453
emigration 296
Emmet, Robert 68–71, 72,
  221
  rebellion 68–70, 74–5
  speech from the dock 70
Emmet, Thomas Addis 68
Encumbered Estates Act (1849) 208,
  242
Engels, Frederick
  and Irish landlords 328
  and O'Connell 160–1, 162–63
Enniskillen bomb (1987) 537
Ensor, George 32
Established Church in Ireland 10, 132,
  154–5, 268–70
  reform 139
  see also Protestant Church; tithes
Eucharistic Congress (1932) 455
European Union (EU) 477, 486–7,
  509, 539, 543, 544
evictions 273, 277–8, 316–17
  famine 210
  Gerrard estate 182
Ewart, Wilfred 395–6

famine 188, 189, 194–5, 200, 201,
  202, 229
  British government response 205,
    211–12
  clearances 214–15
  in Cork 187–8, 193
  English press 195–6
  English public opinion 182, 210,
    229, 566
  evictions 210
  Indian corn shipment 177
  in Irish culture 208–9
  Irish landlords 195–6
  and Irish language 207
  Mitchel's genocide thesis 209–10,
    211
  and *The Nation* 177–8
  observations on 243
  and O'Connell Tribute 178–80
  population decline 206, 207
  relief measures 181–2, 186–7
  and Shaftesbury 184 n 43
  soup kitchens 189, 190, 194
Fannin, Albert
  Easter Rising 376

farmers
  and Sinn Féin 386, 389
Farmers Clubs 311
Farrell, M. 395
Farry, Michael 439
Faulkner, Brian 490, 502–3, 504, 505,
  508, 516
  and 'Bloody Sunday' 507
  resigns from the power-sharing
    executive 515
  and the Sunningdale
    Agreement, 511–12 513
Faulkner, Padraig 501
federalism 166
Fenian Brotherhood 246
  see also Fenians
Fenianism 245, 267, 567
  in America 245–6
  in Australia 272
  and Belfast 263–4
  and Butt 271
  and evictions 316
  in Ireland 247
  and *Irish People* 247
  and loyalism 264
  military defeat 261
  objectives 249–50
  and Parnell 309, 576
  political strength 262–3
  and sectarianism 263
Fenians 277
  attempted arms seizure at
    Chester 259, 308
  and Catholic Church 255–6
  Clerkenwell explosion 265–7
  and constitutionalists 268
  and Cullen 253
  Engels on 266
  and Irish Parliamentary Party 339
  at Iveragh peninsula 259
  and land reform 312
  Manchester hangings 264–5
  Manchester rescue 264
  Marx on 248, 265–6
  military activities in North
    America 258–9
  and Parnell 306–7
  and priests 252, 253–4
  prisoners 271–2, 273
  1867 rebellion 259–61, 567
  social philosophy 252
  and Spencer 271–2
  submarine tests 339

and Tenants' Defence
Associations 297
Fennell, Desmond 477
Fennell, Thomas 394
Ferguson, Samuel 176
Fermanagh 427, 435, 528
Ferriter, Diarmaid 195
Fianna Fail 487, 489, 499, 511, 526,
580
and the arms trial 500–1
assumes power (1932) 451–2
and economic policy 453–5
elections (1927) 449–50; (1933)
453; (1948) 476; (1957) 477;
(1977) 525; (1989) 536; (1997)
547; (2002) 547–8
and the Emergency (1939–45) 475
enters Dail 450
founded in 1926 448–9
and the principle of consent 542
Financial Times 368
Fine Gael 454, 476, 511, 530, 535,
536, 546
Fingall, Lord 75, 76, 100, 104, 110
Pitt meeting 76–7
Finlay, Dean John 416
Finlay, F.D. 149–50
Fisher, H.A.L. 341, 401, 404
Fisher, Warren 399
Fitt, Gerry 516
FitzGerald, Desmond 391
Fitzgerald, Lord Edward 41, 42
FitzGerald, Garrett 470, 472, 513,
518, 521, 530, 534, 543
and the Anglo-Irish Agreement
(1985) 533
Fitzgerald, Major John 409
Fitzgerald, Maurice, Knight of
Kerry 46, 60, 63, 559
Fitzgerald, Vesey 115, 116
Fitzgibbon, John (Earl of Clare) 21–2,
25, 27, 37, 50–1, 60, 68, 557
Fitzwilliam, Lord 27, 28, 29, 30, 31,
557
fixity of land tenure 153–4
Flanagan, Father John 379
Flanedy, John 164–5
Fleming, John 338
Fogarty, Bishop of Killaloe 384–5
Foot, M.R.D. 409 n 90
Forster, May Florence Arnold- 333
Forster, W.E. 323, 330, 332, 333,
334–5, 335

and repression 331
Fortescue, Chichester 255, 259, 272,
276, 340
forty shilling freehold
abolished 122
40 shilling freeholders 110, 111, 112,
117, 130, 148
Foster, Sir John 27, 64, 559
Foster, T. Campbell 200
Fowler, Captain Harry 465
Fox, Charles James 77–8, 78–9
Fox, Lieutenant-General Henry 69
France 2, 471, 487, 505, 509, 527
Franchise Bill (1884) 341
Frazer's Magazine 205
Freeman's Journal 91, 112, 163,
165–6, 173, 199, 206, 238–9,
249, 394, 398–9, 405, 406, 567
effect of 1916 executions 381
and Gladstone 293
and intellectual materialism 292,
293
French fleet
at Bantry Bay 40, 556
French, Laurence 35
French, Lord John 394, 399
French, Lord Thomas, 89
French revolution (1789) 2
attitudes to 8–9
Froude, James Anthony viii, 3, 250
and Home Rule 280–1

Gaelic League 361
compulsory Irish 366
Gallagher Construction Group 526
Gallagher, Ambassador 487
Gallagher, Frank 421, 450
Gallagher, Patrick 526
Gallipoli
nationalist fatalities 383
Galway Independent 124
Gamble, John, 565
Gardai Siochana 487, 500
Garrett, George 476
Gaynor, Liam 467
Gaynor, Sean 441
general elections (Westminster)
(1832) 138; (1841) 153; (1847)
216; (1874) 290; (1881) 317–18;
(1885) 344; (1906) 365; (1910)
367; (1918) 390–1
Geoghegan, Dr Patrick 57
George III 63, 79, 563

George IV 104, 124
George V 406, 414, 431
George VI 451
George, Lloyd 381
Germany 464–5, 468, 471, 472,
    486–7
'German Plot'
    arrests 388–9
Giffard, John 90
Giffen, Sir Robert
    Ireland's economy 570 n 63
Gilchrist, Sir Andrew 491
Gilmartin, Archbishop 412
Ginnell, Laurence 365–6, 367
Girvan, Brian 486
Gladstone, Herbert 332, 345
Gladstone, William Ewart 139, 170–1,
    240, 266, 267, 271, 272, 273,
    287, 288, 317, 323, 333, 341,
    343, 532, 561, 569
    Anglicanism 269
    and Catholicism 293–4
    Church of Ireland
        disestablishment 268–70
    and Compensation for Disturbance
        Bill (1880) 318
    Hancock's influence 295
    and Home Rule 279–80, 330, 340,
        345, 346–7, 357
    and Home Rule Bill (1886) 348,
        349, 352
    and Ireland 295–6, 350, 567
    and Irish nationalism 345
    land reform 276, 326–7, 346, 347
    and Molly Maguires 339
    and O'Connell 303
    and Parnell 303, 336, 337, 347,
        357, 358–9, 360
    and partition 362, 571
    university reform 289–90, 292–3
Glengall, Lord 148
Goertz, Hermann 465, 466, 467, 472
Gonne, Iseult *see* Stuart, Mrs Francis
Goodall, Sir David 43 n 198, 533
    n 132, 531
Good Friday Agreement (1998) 548,
    549–51, 552, 574
Goodhall, William 50
Gordon, Delia 314–15
Gordon, James 82
Gordon, Mrs P.J. 314–15
Gordon, P.J. 315, 323, 338
Goschen, G.J. 334, 348

Gosford, Lord 33
Gosselin, Major 356 n 236, 357, 376
Gough , General Sir Hubert 370 n 48
    'pre-emptive mutiny' 370
Goulburn, Henry 96–7, 105,
    Unlawful Oaths Bill (1823) 107
Government of Ireland Bill (1886) *see*
    Home Rule Bill
Government of Ireland Act
    (1920) 381, 395, 461
Government of Ireland Act
    (1949), 479
Graham, Sir James 169, 564
Grant, James 228
Grant, William 460
Granville, Lord 347–8, 349
Grattan, Henry 20, 22, 27, 28, 35, 41,
    60, 84, 91, 100 n 70, 179, 203,
    291
    and Catholic emancipation 77, 80,
        81, 101–2
    death 103
    and parliamentary union 65, 559
    and 1798 rebellion 51
    Relief Bill (1813) 89
Grattan, Henry (junior) 245
Gray, David 464–5, 466, 467, 468,
    471, 479
Gray, Edward Dwyer 298
Gray, Sir John 256
Gray, Sam 119, 120, 145, 298
graziers 214–15
Green, Arthur 496 n 31
Greenwood, Sir Hamar 399, 403, 405,
    406
Gregg, Archbishop 435
Gregory, William 89
Grenville, Lord 3, 63, 77–8, 87
Greville, Charles 223
Grey, Charles (Second Earl
    Grey) 46–7, 138
Grey, Sir Edward 381, 570
Griffith, Arthur 228, 363–4, 371, 373,
    410, 418, 419, 420, 422, 426,
    431, 437
    'German Plot' arrest 388
    and Limerick Jews 364
    Nationality 373
    The Resurrection of Hungary 364
Griffith, Sir Richard
    valuation of Irish land 320
Grimshaw, Robert 132, 152
Gurian, Waldemar 457

Gwynn, Stephen 4, 176, 324, 360, 378, 381, 410, 416, 433, 440, 459, 562, 579
and Irishness 577–8

Habeas Corpus Act 264, 323
Hackett, Francis 253, 368
Hailsham, Lord 453
Hales, Sean 440, 450
Hales, Thomas 456
Haliday, Dr 20
Hall, Charles 55
Hamilton, Revd Dr 99
Hamilton, Edward 337, 345
Hamilton, Sir Robert 342
Hamilton, William 14–15
Hammond, J.L. 398, 421
Hancock, Dr W. Neilson 249, 272, 295, 567
Hanley, Brian 466
Hanningan, D.F.
'Parnell and Cromwell' 303
Harcourt, W.V. 349
Harding, Sir Henry
duel challenge to O'Connell 127
Hardwicke, third Baron and third Earl of 26, 67, 64, 69
Hardy, Alfred E. Gathorne 307
Harrington, Timothy 342
Harris, Matthew 297, 298, 320–1
Hart, Charles 220
Hart, Peter 415, 439
Hartington, Marquess of 296 n 314, 349
Hartnett, Noel 476 n 121
Hatherley, Lord 321
Haughey, Charles J. 487, 495, 526, 529, 534, 548, 580
and the arms trial 500–1
and Northern Ireland 529–30, 536, 537, 538
parochialism of 527
Haughey, Sean 548
Hay, Edward 50
Hayden, J.P. 252 n 110
Roscommon Messenger 383
Hayes, Dr 472
Healy, Cahir 461
Healy, Denis 523
Healy, Maurice 414
Healy, Tim 340–1, 342, 346, 408, 414
attack on Parnell 360
Heaney, Seamus 528–9

Heath, Edward 501, 502, 504, 512, 513
and 'Bloody Sunday' (1972) 508
and Jack Lynch 505, 506
Held, Stephen 466, 467
Hempel, Eduard 466, 470, 474
Henderson, Leo 437
Heron, Denis Caulfield 272–3
elected MP 273
Hertford, Lady 88
Hertford, Marquess of 129–30
and Strachan, 131
Higgins, Francis 40, 66
Hill, Lord Edwin 238, 243
Hillery, Patrick 508
Hippisley, Sir John 38
Hitler, Adolf 464, 465, 469–70, 471, 474, 478, 479, 572
Hobart, Lady Emily 2
Hobart, Major 20, 21, 57
Hobsbawm, Eric ix
Hoche, General 34, 36, 40
Hoche (French ship) 45
Hoey, J. Cashel 290
and Gladstone 294
Hogan, Dan 424, 428
Hogan, Michael 409
Holland, Denis 115, 118, 208
Holmes, Finlay 129
Holocaust, the 474
Home, Sir Alec Douglas 503
Home Rule 343, 363, 380, 561, 576
Ambiguities of 577
Belfast riots 351
and Butt 278–9, 281–6
Confederation of Great Britain 308, 309
Conference 284–5
electoral endorsement 344
federalism 283–4
and Froude 280–1
and Gladstone 279–80, 330, 340, 345, 346–7, 348, 349, 352
League 305
and Parnell 355
post-1916 381–2
and Redmond 577
and Ulster 370
Unionist resistance 352–3, 570
Home Rule Bill (1886) 348
debate 348–52
Home Rule Bill (1893)
House of Lords defeat 361

Home Rule Bill (1912) 367–8, 371
Honesty 450
Hopkins, Sir Richard 461
Hopkinson, Michael 439
Horner, Francis 84
Hot Press 526
Houghton, Lord *see* Milnes, Richard Monckton
Howth gun-running 371
Hughes, Brendan 498
Hughes, Francis 529
Humbert, General Jean 45
Hume, John 494, 502, 507, 511, 574
 dialogue with Sinn Fein 535, 538, 542, 544, 545
 on Unionism 516, 534
Hunger-strike
 in 1920 399
 Terence MacSwiney's death from 1920, 407, 528
 in 1980–1 528–9, 530, 531
Hunt Committee, the 497
Hussey, Thomas 18, 32, 35
Huxley, T.H. 303

Independent Ireland*see* Irish Free State (1922–37); Eire (1937–49); Republic of Ireland (1949–)
Inglis, Lieutenant 187
Ingram, John Kells 47
Insurrection Act (1807) 84
Inter-Departmental Unit (IDU) 517
Invincibles
 Phoenix Park murders 336
International Finance Centre 536
Internment without trial
 in 1920 401
 in 1922–4 503
 in 1971 502–3, 508, 513, 522, 528
IRA *see* Irish Republican Army; Official Irish Republican Army; Provisional Irish Republican Army
IRB *see* Irish Republican Brotherhood
Ireland on Sunday 549
Ireland Under Lord Mulgrave 150
Irish Arms Bill 161
Irish Bulletin 399, 403, 412
Irish capitalism
 north-south gap 368–9
Irish Catholic 379
Irish character
 assessments of 203–5
 see also anti-Irish racism

Irish Charitable Donations and Bequests Bill (1844) 169
Irish Colleges Bill (1845) 170–1, 211
Irish Confederation 185, 221, 222
 clubs 223
Irish Felon 223
Irish Free State (1922–37) 444
 establishment of 422–3
 relations with Northern Ireland 423–38, 447–8
 social and economic policies 445–6, 452–4, 482
Irish Free State (Agreement) Act (1922) 433
Irish history
 writing of ix
Irish House of Commons 6
Irish Independent 396, 442
Irish Land Act (1881) 327–8, 328
Irish Land Committee 319
Irish Land Purchase Bill (1885) (Ashbourne Act) 343
Irish language 455, 477, 482–3
Irish language movement 366–7
Irish Loyal and Patriotic Union 354
 The Law and the League 353
Irish loyalists 341–2
Irish Magazine 15
Irishman 208
Irish Nation 569
 on Marx 248–9
Irish National Liberation Army (INLA) 525, 554
Irish National Volunteers 370
 military exercises 374
Irish National Land League *see* Land League
Irish National League 340, 354, 358
Irish neutrality
 Second World War viii, 463–74, 478–9, 572–3
Irish News 460, 528, 544
Irish Opinion 387
Irish Parliament 6, 10, 16, 60
Irish Parliamentary Party 318, 323, 363, 364, 366, 367, 381, 385, 386, 388, 389, 526
 economic policy 368
 electoral performances (1914–16) 372–3
 and Fenians 339
 1918 election 390
 and Sinn Féin 386–8

split 359–60
Irish People 247, 249, 250, 449
  and MacManus funeral 254
  police raid 258
Irish Poor Law Commission 150–1
Irish Press 473, 508, 541
Irish Press Agency 570
Irish republic *also see* Irish Free State
  (1922–37); Eire (1937–49);
  Republic of Ireland (1949–)
  proclamation of (1916) 375, 377–8
Irish Republican Army
  (IRA, 1919–69) 397, 401, 463,
  487, 495, 544, 579
  1926 split 448–9
  1966 commemoration of the Easter
  Rising 489
  assassinations 398, 399, 402, 403,
  405, 406, 407–9, 436, 450
  bombing campaign in Britain 466–7
  border campaign (1956–62) 480,
  481
  civil rights campaign 490, 491
  Civil War 437–43
  at Kilmichael 410
  at Knocklong 395
  Nazi links 466–7, 468, 470, 478
  Northern Division of 424, 427, 434,
  436
  Provisional republican perception
  of 536–7
  release of prisoners 404, 452
  sectarianism of 415–16
  Treaty splits 429, 434
  the truce 1921, 414
Irish Republican Army (IRA 1969–),
  see Provisional Irish Republican
  Army
Irish Republican Brotherhood
  (IRB) 246, 307, 371, 449
  military council 373
  organisational structure 246–7
  supreme council 373
  see also Fenians; republicanism
Irish Revolutionary Brotherhood *see*
  Irish Republican Brotherhood
Irish Times 410, 427, 438, 445, 476,
  483, 519
  and Parnell 322
  and Sinn Féin 392
Irish University Bill (1873) 289–90
Irish Volunteers, 394
  at GPO 375

Jackson, Revd William 27
Jackson, Senator 'Scoop' 555 n 215
Jacobinism 22, 30, 32, 36, 41, 47, 51,
  64
Jalland, Patricia 367
Jenkins, Peter 506
Jenkins, Roy 518, 523
Johnstone, Charles 363
Johnston, William 264, 349
Joint Framework Document
  (1995) 540, 545
Jones, W. Bence 319
Joyce, James 360, 367 n 32, 440
Joyce, Myles 342
Jupp, Peter 122

Kavanaugh, Ann C. 50
Kay, Joseph 210
Keane, Terry 529, 534
Kearney, Hugh 211–12
Keegan, Lames 92
Kelleher, Dr 410
Kelleher, District Inspector Philip 408
Kelly, Edward 263
Kelly, Captain James 500, 501
Kelly, John 500
Kelly, Colonel Thomas 259, 264, 265
Kennedy, John F. 487
Kennedy, William 407
Kenyon, Father 225, 227
Keogh, Dr Daire 70
Keogh, John 17, 79
Keogh, William 237, 239
Ker, David Stewart 238
Kerr, Donal 226
Kerr, Philip (Lord Lothian) 400
Kerr, Dean W. S. 462–3
Kerry 414, 416
Kettle, Andrew 304, 325, 329, 343–4
Kettle, Tom 407
  death at Somme 383
Kickham, Charles 247, 273
  Knocknagow 251–2
  tenant-right politics 252
Kiernan, Kitty 408, 426
Kilkenny Whitefeet 139
Killeen, Lord 110
Kilmainham Treaty 334, 354, 355
Kilmartin, James 310
Kilmichael 410
Kilwarden. Lord 68, 69, 70
Kilwarlin, Lord 5
Kimberley, Lord ix, 350, 440

King, David Bennett 302
King, Martin Luther 492
King-Harman, Colonel 279
Kirk, William 238
Kirwan, Thomas 88, 107–8
Kissinger, Henry 518
Knock apparitions 314–16
　and cures 315
　and Land League 315–16
　newspaper reports 316 n 61
Knocklong 395

Labouchere, Henry 184
Labour Party (British) 479, 480, 513,
　514, 523, 540, 547
Labour Party (Irish) 443, 449–50,
　476, 511, 530, 535
Lacey, Denny 440–1
Laffan, Michael, 381, 395
Lahousen, General 470
Lake, General 41
Lalor, James Fintan 185, 452
　Holy Cross meeting 218–19
　and land question 217–19, 223–4
　and Meagher 226–7
Lalor, Patrick 185
Lalor, Richard
　passive resistance 137
Land Act (1923) 446
Land Commission (Irish Free
　State) 445
Land Conference (1902) 362, 363
Landlord and Tenant (Ireland) Act
　(1870) 276, 277–8, 296, 296–7,
　319
　and evictions 277–8
　and landlords 278
　and Lecky 276–7
　Shaw Lefevre Committee 298
Land League 277, 312, 314, 365, 449,
　452, 568, 575, 576
　Convention (1879) 313
　and evictions 316–17
　and Knock apparitions 315–16
　mobilisation 319–21
　and No Rent Manifesto 329
　and *United Ireland* 328–9
landlords 250, 251, 278, 301, 316,
　328, 568
　Irish Land Committee 319
　and Parnell 347
land reform 273–8, 568
　and Butt 273–4

and Cairnes 274–5, 276
and Campbell 275–4
and Gladstone 276, 277–8
and Mill 274–5
and Murphy 274
and Parnell 310–11
Langrishe, Sir Hercules 16, 21,
Lansdowne, Lord 115
Larcom, Thomas 262
Larkin, Philip (Fenian) 264, 265
Larne gun-running 370, 371 see also
　UVF
Laski, Harold 420
Lattin, Patrick 56–7
Lavelle, Father Patrick 253, 257
　and MacManus funeral 254
Lavery, Lady Hazel 424, 426
Law, Andrew Bonar 411, 436
Lawless, Jack, 492
　and Catholic Emancipation 118–20
　and O'Connell 109, 111, 112
Lawless, J.V. 391
Leader, The vii–viii, 445, 449
Leahy, Archbishop of Cashel 261
le Caron, Henri 258, 339, 356–7
Lecky, W.E.H. ix, 16, 27, 47, 63, 76,
　100, 276–7, 297, 368, 563
　and Butt 286
　and Irish Land Act (1881) 327–8
　and land reform 326–7
Lee, J.J. 313, 439, 454, 474, 543
Lefevre, G.S. Shaw 134, 144, 337
Lefroy, Baron 223
Leitrim 416, 467
Lemass, Sean 408, 464, 536
　and the 1966 commemoration of the
　　Easter Rising 489
　dismantles protectionism 475, 477,
　　484, 486
　meets Terence O'Neill 488
　and Northern Ireland 484–5, 487,
　　490
Lewis, Sir George Cornwall, 564
　and Irish character 204
Libya 518, 535
Liddell, Guy 466
Liberals
　landslide victory (1906) 365
Lichfield House compact
　(1835) 143–4, 151, 282, 334,
　568
Limerick
　boycott of Jews 364

Limerick Leader 399
Linehan, Timothy 456
Lismore, Lord 257–8
Liverpool, Lord 88, 102
    cabinet 87
Lloyd George, David 400, 401–2, 403,
    435–6, 437, 571
    and Anglo-Irish Treaty
        negotiations 416–22, 447,
        464, 544
    and contacts with
        republicans 410–11, 413
    and reprisals 404
Loch, Sydney 407
Locke, John 225
    Limerick repeal rally 159
Logue, Hugh 513
Lomasney, William 338–9
Londonderry, Lord Charles Stewart
    (seventh Marquess of
    Londonderry) 436
Londonderry, Lord Robert Stewart (first
    Marquess of Londonderry) 2, 5
Long, Walter 367, 395–6
Long Kesh (the Maze) 528, 530
Longfield, Colonel 89 n 9
Longford 415
Lothian, Lord *see* Kerr, Philip
Loughnane, Bill 526
Louis XVI 9
'Love Ulster' march (2006) viii, 581
Louis-Philippe
    abdication 220
Loyalist ideologues 49
Loyal National Repeal Association 152,
    154, 162, 180, 232, 283
Luby, Thomas Clarke 247, 254m 262
Lucas, Frederick
    The Tablet 239
Luykx, Albert 500
Lyell, Sir Charles 204
Lynch, Edward
    burning of family 95–6;
    see also Carleton
Lynch, Jack 495, 498, 500, 501, 525,
    527
    and the British Government 505,
        506, 526
    and Irish unity 499, 509–10
Lynch, Liam 441
Lyons, R.B.
    *The Intellectual Resources of
    Ireland* 286–7, 562

Lyster, Thomas 483

McAleese, Mary 578, 580
MacBride, John 371
MacBride, Maud Gonne 466
MacBride, Sean 408, 420, 437, 476,
    480
McCabe, Chris 544
McCalman, Ian 22
McCann, Eamon 493
McCarthy, Justin 359
    on Fenians 248
    journalistic career 213
    and Mitchel 213
McCartney, J.W.E. 286 n 268
Macauley, James
    and O'Keefe case 288
McClintock, Pastor Kenny 524 n 132
MacColl, Malcolm 350–1
MacCormack, Captain Patrick 408
McCracken, Henry Joy 31
    Belfast Politics 11
MacCrone, Eliza 62
MacCullagh, Torrens 176, 184
McCurtain, Tomas 398–9, 403
McDermott, Frank 456, 465, 469
MacDermott, Seán 371, 373
Mac Diarmada, Seán *see* MacDermott
MacDonagh, Michael 373, 375
MacDonagh, Oliver 62–3, 172
MacDonagh, Thomas 371
    and blood sacrifice 375
MacDonald, Ramsey 447
McDonald, Dr Walter 173
McDonnell, Eneas 160
McDonnell, Thomas 16
MacEntee, Sean 423, 455
MacEoin, Sean 430
McGarrity, Joseph 418, 449
McGee, Thomas D'Arcy 225, 226, 228,
    228 n 268
McGilligan, Patrick 448
McGrady, Eddie 544
McGrath, Joe 428, 446
McGrath, Terence
    on Irish landlords 301
McGregor, Pat 186
McGuinness, Joseph P. 384
McGuinness, Martin 522, 524, 537
McHale, John, Archbishop of
    Tuam 171
McIvor, Basil 512
McKee, Billy 498

McKnight, Dr James 218, 276–277
  Banner of Ulster 233
  and Duffy 231, 232–4
  and tenant right agitation 233–5
McKnight, Thomas 24, 269, 272,
  564
McLaughlin, Senator 470
MacLoghlin, Cornelius 178
McLoughlin, Mary 314
MacMahon murders 429, 436
MacMahon, Owen 428–9
MacMahon, Patrick MP 202, 209
MacManus, Thomas Bellew
  at Ballingarry 227
  funeral 254–5
MacNally, Leonard 7–8
'McNee, Calvin' see Trimble,
  David, 554
MacNeill, J.G. Swift 350 n 208
MacNeill, Eoin 370, 371, 410
  and Easter Rising 375
MacNeill, Hugo 472
McParlan, James 339
MacPherson, Ian 399
McQuillan, Alan 529
McSkimmin, Samuel 40–1
MacSwiney, Mary 421–2
MacSwiney, Terence 406, 408, 528
  death of 407
  *Robert Emmet: Irish
    Fundamentalist* 371
Maamtrasna murders 342
Macready, Sir Nevil 399, 404, 405,
  410
Macrory, Cardinal 470
Madden, Daniel O. 142, 176, 557
Maffey, Sir John 464, 471
Maguire, John Francis 256, 280
Maguire, T. 126
Maguire, Dr Thomas 357
Maguire, Father Thomas
  court case 114–15
  and Young Ireland 219
Maher, Revd James 257
Mahoney, R.J. 327, 328
Major, John, 545 546, 547
Malcolm, John 238
Malone, James 386
  effect of 1916 executions 381
Manchester Guardian 398, 421, 442,
  506, 520
Mandelson, Peter 480
Manners, Lord John 89, 116, 183

Mansergh, Martin 43 n 198, 537, 540,
  542–3
Mansergh, Nicholas 479
Markiewicz, Constance
  and Easter Rising 377
Marsden, Alexander 37, 69
Marsh, Robert 398
Martineau, Harriet 203
Martin, John 227, 278–9, 280, 284,
  306
  and *United Irishman* 219–20
Marx, Karl 144, 155
  Capital 250
  on Fenians 248, 265–6
  Irish Nation assessment 248–9
  and Palmerston 241
Mason, Roy 523, 524
Mason, W. Shaw 95, 168
Mathew, Father 187
Maudling, Reginald 507–8
Maume, Patrick 394, 474
Maw, Father 239
Mayhew, Sir Patrick 538, 539, 540,
  574, 575
Maynooth College Bill 170
Mayo 568
Mayo News 453
Meagher, Thomas Francis 154, 185,
  222, 225
  and James Fintan Lalor 226–7
  physical force 221
Meath 465
Meehan, P.F. 366, 390
Melbourne, Lord 135, 137, 143–4,
  150–1, 568
Mellows, Liam 440
Methodists 89–90
MI5 472, 473
Miles, William Augustus 34
Military Service bill (1918) 389
Mill, John Stuart 122, 124, 213, 289
  Morning Chronicle 191
  England and Ireland 274–5
Millar, Frank 581
Milnes, Richard Monckton (Lord
  Houghton) 216, 228, 240, 481,
  562
  *The Real Union between Britain and
    Ireland* 562–3
'Ministry of All the Talents' 77–9
Mitchel, John 154–5, 182–3, 185,
  200, 212–14, 219, 221, 240,
  291–2, 569

death in Ireland 291
famine genocide thesis 209–10,
    211, 575
and land question 217–18, 234
and *The Nation* 176, 199,
and O'Connell 215, 222
trial and conviction 222–3
and *United Irishman* 219–20
Mitchell, George 547
Mitchelstown, Co. Cork
killings 354
Molly Maguires 339
Molyneaux, Jim 531, 541, 545
Monaghan 515
Monahan, J.H. 184
Montgomery, Revd Henry 128–9
and O'Connell 129, 131–3
Whig article 130
Montgomery, Major-General
    Hugh 459, 460
Monypenny, W.F. 365
Moore, Arthur 435
Moore, Brian 473
Moore, Sir Frederick 483
Moody, Dr John 5
Moore, George Henry 237
Parnell and his Island 328
Moore, Richard 184
Moore, Thomas 80–1, 86, 130, 134,
    140
'Lalla Rookh' 353–4
Captain Rock (1824), 559
Moran, D.P. 445, 449
Morgan, Kenneth O. 421
Moriarty, Bishop of Kerry 257, 269
Morley, John 277, 306, 345, 353
Morning Chronicle 191, 199
Morning Post 447
Mornington, Earl of 45
Morpeth, Lord 144, 192
Morris, Gillian 398
Morris, Michael 258, 305, 346
Morris, William O'Connor x, 76, 149
on Carlisle 241–2
Morrison, Danny 536–7
Morrison, Herbert 480
Moser, Joseph 35
'mosquito' press 373
'Mother and Child Affair' 476
Mountbatten, Earl 525
Mountjoy Prison, Dublin 399, 408
Mountnorres, Lord 321
Mulcahy, Richard, 406–7 429, 438

Mulgrave, Lord [Francis Henry]
    administration 144–5, 147–8
Mulholland, Marc 579
Mullan, Father Hugh 503
Mullin, James 305
Munroe, 44
Murnaghan, Mr Justice 513
Murney, Peadar 470
Murray, RC Archbishop 171
Murphy, Father 116
Murphy, James H. 146
Murphy, J.J.
and land reform 273–4
Murtagh, Constable 398
Musgrave, Sir Richard 38, 49–50, 51

Naas, Lord, Earl of Mayo 258, 262
Nagle, David 14, 98
see also Rock
Nally, Dermot 514, 517, 521
Nankevell, Joyce 407
Napoleon I 68, 75, 94, 101, 159, 464,
    468
Nation, The 154, 155, 164, 176, 182
and famine 177–8, 194, 199
and O'Connell 180–1
and O'Connell Tribute 178–9
and Parnell 310–11
and Phoenix Society 244
and Russell 184, 185
see also Young Ireland
National Agricultural and Industrial
    Development Association
    (NAIDA) 452
National Association (1864)
    Great Aggregate Meeting 256
National Association of Ireland
    see Loyal National Repeal
        Association
National Gallery of Ireland 483
National Library of Ireland 483
National Press Club, Washington
    DC 526
NATO *see* North Atlantic Treaty
    Organisation
Nazis, the 457, 462, 465, 466, 471,
    478, 527
Neave, Airey 525
Neave, Sir Digby 229
Neilson, Samuel 39
Newell, Edward 41
Newenham, Edward 34
Newenham, Thomas 67, 81–2

Newenham, Thomas (*cont.*)
opinion of Irish 85–6
New Ireland Forum 530, 532
Newman, John Henry 286–7
Catholic University 253
Newport, Sir John 78, 79
Newry Magazine 95
New York Globe 397
Nicholls, George
workhouse system 150–1
Nixon, District Inspector John
W. 429, 433, 436
Nolan, John 'Amnesty' 271, 279, 307
'No Popery' election (1807) 79
No Rent Manifesto 329
North Atlantic Treaty Organisation
(NATO) 476, 480, 509
Northern Bank 551, 553
Northern Ireland 419, 458, 464, 469,
483, 521, 538–9
abolition of Stormont 508–9
Anglo-Irish Agreement
(1985) 531–3, 535
border poll in (1973) 510
Catholic minority in 414, 424, 430,
432–3, 457, 459–60, 461–2,
470, 473, 487–8, 490, 493, 540
civil rights marches in 489, 490,
491, 492–3, 494
declaration of an Irish
Republic 479–80
direct rule in 494, 496, 502–3, 504,
506, 508–9, 518, 523, 524
discrimination in 579
Downing Street Declaration
(1993) 541–3, 574
DUP-Sinn Fein deal 552–4, 581
economy of 461, 484, 490, 492,
524, 544
end of Cold War, 573–4
establishment of 395–6
Good Friday Agreement
(1998) 549–51, 552
human cost of 'the Troubles' 554
hunger-strikes (1981) 528–30
independence 519, 523
introduction of internment in
(1971) 502–3
Joint Framework Document
(1995) 545–6
O'Neillism 481–2
PIRA ceasefires 518–19, 544–6,
547

Protestantism 458–60, 488
relations with the South 423–38,
447–8, 484, 487, 543
Second World War 464, 467, 469,
471, 478–9
Sunningdale Agreement
(1973) 512–15
totalitarianism 457, 462, 578
Northern Ireland Civil Rights
Association 490, 497
Northern Ireland Labour Party 481,
482, 511
northern nationalists
and Home Rule 382
in Northern Ireland 414, 424, 430,
432–3, 457, 459–60, 461–2,
470, 473, 487–8, 490, 493, 540
Northern Star 41
Northern Whig ix, 116, 119–20,
121–2, 129–30, 131, 153, 179,
196, 225, 243, 435
and education 172
and evictions 182
and Gladstone 293–4
and O'Connell 132, 152
Northern Whig Club 6, 7
Norton, Desmond 191–2
Nugent, General 44
Nugent, General Sir Oliver
Battle of the Somme 382

O'Beirne, Lewis, Bishop of Meath 59
Ó Bradaigh, Ruairi 520, 522–3
O'Brien, Barry 306
O'Brien, Conor Cruise 20, 172, 517
O'Brien, D.P. 474
O'Brien, Sir Edward 116
O'Brien, Edward Smith 297
O'Brien, Gay 489
O'Brien, Gerard 232
O'Brien, Michael (Fenian) 264, 265
O'Brien, Sophie Raffalovich 366 n 27
O'Brien, William 272, 273, 290, 291,
298–9, 311, 328, 341, 342, 346,
351, 361, 576, 578
No Rent Manifesto 329
and Parnell 353
Plan of Campaign 353
United Irish League 362, 366
O'Brien, William (Labour Party) 371
O'Brien, William Smith 161, 164,
168, 180, 181, 185, 222, 225,
244, 270, 313, 481, 562, 578

background 216–17
at Ballingarry 227
physical force 221
transportation 227
O'Broin, Leon 401, 415, 455
Observer, The 541, 579
obstruction (parliamentary tactic) 307, 310, 324
O'Callaghan, Jeremiah 197
O'Callaghan, Seán 391
O'Connell, Daniel x, 77, 88, 91–2, 98, 100, 105, 107, 116, 118, 149–50, 176, 179–80, 283, 302–3, 330, 417, 558, 565, 575
and agrarian crime 99–100
and agrarian terrorism 139–40
and Anglesey 117, 135
arrest 163
in ascendant 109–12
assessments of 215–16
Belfast repeal speech 152–3, 232
and British parliament 369
and Butt 158–9
Carlyle's criticism 162–3
Catholic emancipation 109–10, 112, 114–15, 122–3, 131, 391, 560
Catholic nationalism 369
Clare by-election 115–16
Clontarf meeting banned 163
Coercion Bill (1833) 139
consistency 113
'council of 300' 162
critique of parliamentary union 66
Cullen correspondence 154
and Cusack Smith 140–2
and Dawson 153
death 215
and Devon Commission 168
and Disraeli 126
Drumgoole speech 90
and education 171–2
electoral strategy 113–14
fatal duel with D'Esterre 91
federalism 166
financial support 108, 118
General Association 131
general election (1832) 138
and George IV 104
Harding duel challenge 127
inner bar 136
international humanitarian 126
Irish question in Britain 166
jail sentence 165
as landlord 179 n 14
leadership role 108–9
'Letter to the People of Ireland' 127
liberal credentials 172–3
liberal readings of 172, 172–3
Lichfield House compact 143–4, 334
Lords' Select Committee address 111–12, 128, 171
Loyal National Repeal Association 152
monster meetings 159–60
and Montgomery 129, 131–3
and Mulgrave administration 144–5, 147–8
and Napoleon 159–60
and *Northern Whig* 132, 179
Observations on Corn Laws 157
and Orangemen 131
patent 'of precedency' 110–11,
and Peel 160, 170, 170–1
poor law debate 150–1
post-emancipation challenges 125–6, 560–1
prosecution 164, 165
Reform Bill (1831) 133–4, 135
release from jail 166
relations with Protestants 109, 128, 129–33
and repeal 126–7, 142–3, 151–2, 157–8, 172, 180–1
and Repeal Association 185
reversal of positions 122–3
royalist enthusiasm 146–7
and Russell (PM) 183, 184, 186
sectarianism 172, 173
and slavery 172 n 250
and Stanley 135
and tithes 127, 143, 150
Tribute collection 178–80, 210
and veto 100–1, 112, 172
violent language 92, 106
and Young Ireland 156, 164, 180–1, 184–5, 211
O'Connell, David 520
O'Connellism
radical dimension 100
and Catholic ascendancy 132
O'Connell, John 203
and Young Ireland 185
O'Connor, Arthur 9n, 22, 41–2
O'Connor, Feargus 138, 172, 203

O'Connor, Rory 433, 440, 450
O'Conor, Revd Charles 80–1
O'Conor, Norreys Jephson
 Changing Ireland viii
O'Dempsey, T.J. 407
Ó Dochartaigh, Niall 507
O'Donnell, Frank Hugh 304, 307
O'Driscoll, J. 560
O'Duffy, Eoin 427, 430, 433, 454
O'Faolain, Sean 528
O'Farrell, Fergus 128
Offaly 416
Official Irish Republican Army
 (OIRA) 501–2, 503
O'Flanagan, Father Michael 383–4,
 413, 480
 two nations in Ireland 387
 'Orange and Green' lecture 387–8
Ogle, George 59
O'Gorman, Richard 177, 178, 221,
 222, 225, 226
Ó Gráda, Cormac 186
O'Grady, Standish 71–2
O'Hagan, Thomas Lord 126 n 3, 145,
 173, 244, 271, 283
 and O'Keefe case 288
O'Halloran, Dr Clare 50–1
O'Halpin, Eunan 472
O'Higgins, Kevin 390, 446, 450,
 476
O'Higgins, Thomas 476
O'Keefe, C.M. 264
O'Keefe, Father Robert
 suspension and sacking 287–8
O'Kelly, James J. 279, 309
O'Kelly, Seán T. 371, 391
Old Age Pensions Act (1924) 446
O'Leary, Cornelius 394
O'Leary, John 247–8
O'Loghlen, Michael 145
Omagh bomb (1998) 552
O'Mahony, John 245, 255, 258
O'Malley, Dessie 534
O'Malley, Ernie 395
Ó Malley, Padraig, 573
O'Malley, William 438
O'Malley, Father Thaddeus 151
O'Neill, Colonel John 258
O'Neill, Captain Terence 480
 and civil rights 490, 491
 fall of 493–5
 and reforming Northern
  Ireland 481–2, 492

relations with Republic of
 Ireland 484, 487
 and Sean Lemass 488
O'Neill, Tip 533
Orange Boys 33
Orangeism 80, 270, 330
Orange Order 42, 44, 93, 119, 222,
 224–5, 233, 236, 382–3, 565,
 566, 569, 575, 576
 banning of 109
 'bludgeon men' 238
 celebrations repressed 106–7
 clashes with Catholics 95, 127
 Dolly's Brae violence 229–30
 foundation of 33
 Grand Lodges dissolved 146
 and O'Connell 131
 and parliamentary union 59
 and royal plot 145–6
 reconstitution 107
 reported arming of 225
O'Rawe, Richard 530
O'Reilly, Archbishop, 75
O'Reilly, John Boyle 317
O'Reilly, Myles 229
O'Reilly, Major Myles 253, 255
O'Shea, Captain William Henry 321
 divorce proceedings 357, 358
 and Parnell 331, 332–3, 345–6
O'Shea, Father
 The Tenants Protection Society 234
O'Shea, Mrs Katharine
 family connections 321
 and Gladstone 336–7, 347
 Healy attack 360
 and Parnell 321, 329, 331, 346
Ó Súilleabháin, Amlaoibh, 206
O'Sullivan, Jeremiah 265
O'Sullivan, Father John 244
O'Sullivan, Michael Malachy 297,
 312, 339
O'Sullivan, 'Morty' 151
Oswald, Eleazar 26
Ó Tuathaigh, Gearóid 137–8

Paget, General Sir Arthur 370
Paine, Thomas 7–8, 9, 23
Paisley, Revd Ian 489, 493–4, 495,
 509, 513, 520, 524–5, 532, 550,
 553, 554, 581
Pall Mall Gazette 354
Palmerston, Lord 161, 240–1, 268,
 307

and Irish Catholics 170
and Irish character 204
final Irish policy statement 256
Marx on 241
Sligo estates 191–2
Papal Irish Brigade of St Patrick
    in Italy 253
'Papist Boys of Ireland' 82
Parkinson, Alan 429
parliamentary union 53, 54–5, 87,
    194, 281, 283, 342, 556–7, 563
    assessments of 83
    critiques of 65–6
    opposition to 55
    support for 55–6
    see also Act of Union
Parker, Dame Dehra 176
Parnell, Anna 322
    The Tale of the Land League 321
Parnell, Charles Stewart 302–9, 324,
    328, 330, 334, 347–8, 350–1,
    481, 535, 568
    arrest 329
    and Butt 307, 308, 310
    and Carnarvon 343
    character 305–6
    and Claude Sophie (child) 331
    conciliation 576
    conspiracy trial 323
    death 360
    electoral triumph (1885) 355
    and Fenians 306–7
    funds raised 341
    and Gladstone 336, 337, 347, 357,
        358–9, 360
    government surveillance 355–6
    and Home Rule 355, 357, 359
    and Irish Parliamentary Party 318,
        323, 324–5
    Irish Times 322
    and land agitation 312
    and Land League 314
    and landlords 347
    and land reform 310–11, 357
    leadership under attack 358–60
    No Rent Manifesto 329
    and O'Brien (W.) 353
    and 'obstruction' in parliament 307,
        310
    and O'Shea (Captain) 331, 332,
        345–6
    and O'Shea divorce 358
    and O'Shea (Mrs) 321, 331, 346

and Rhodes 356
and Sheridan (P.J.) 335
Special Commission evidence 356
and Plan of Campaign 353–4
political objectives 322
and protectionism 343–4
religious convictions 304–5
Times forged letter 355
To The People of Ireland 359
in the United States 316–17
and violence 335–6, 336, 337, 355,
    356–7
Parnell, Fanny 329
Parnell, Henry 304
Parnell, Sir Henry Brooke 75, 78, 98,
    102 n 77, 120
Parnellism, 361, 362
Parnell, John Henry (CSP's father) 304
Parnell, Sir John 20, 559
Parnell, Thomas
    and Carleton, 304
Parnell, William 78, 88
Parnell, William Henry (CSP's
    grandfather) 303–4
Parsons, Sir Laurence 50–1
partition viii–ix, 362, 381, 382, 388,
    395, 396, 419, 450, 457, 458,
    462, 464, 476, 479, 516, 535,
    540, 550, 571
    North-South relations 423–38,
        455–6, 479–80, 483–4, 487,
        499
    and the Second World War 469–73
Party Procession Act (1850) 230, 264
Patten, Colonel John Wilson *see*
    Winmarleagh, Lord
Patten Commission 550
Paul, Jeffrey 43
Payon, Professor
    potato crop warning 175
PD *see* People's Democracy
PDs *see* Progressive Democrats
Peace Preservation Act (1814) 96
Peace Preservation (Ireland) Act
    (1881) 332
Pearce, R.R. 107
Pearse, Patrick 371, 374, 375, 548
    and blood sacrifice 375
    and Easter Rising 375–6, 377, 379
peasant proprietorship 331
peasantry
    social structure 99
Peck, Sir John 509

'Peelers' 96–7
Peel, Robert 88–9, 96, 97, 103, 107,
    116, 141, 153, 156, 165, 176–7,
    203, 255, 281, 282, 559
  assessment of Ireland 92–3, 94
  awareness of sectarianism 95
  Burke's influence 168–9, 566–7
  and Catholic emancipation 118,
    120–1, 123, 124
  and Corn Law crisis 180, 181
  Indian corn shipment 177
  Irish attitudes 183
  Irish policy 161
  Irish Poor Law debate 207–8
  Maynooth College grant 169–70
  and O'Connell 170, 170–1
  Protestant principles 102–3
  resignation 180
Peel, Robert (father of PM) 55
Peep Of Day Boys 33
Pelham 29–30
People's Democracy (PD) 492–3
Perceval, Spencer 74
Percy, William
  Irish Salvation 60
Perrin, Louis 136
Persse, Stratford 105
Peterson, Marianne 107
Petty, Lord Henry 75
Phillips, C. J. 400, 401
Phillips, Jonathon 553
Phoenix Park murders 336, 337, 355,
    356
Phoenix Society see Fenianism;
    Fenians
Pigot, D.R. 184
Pigott, Richard
  Parnell letters forgery 357
Pim, Herbert
  What Emmet Means 371
Pim, Jonathan 201, 211
Pitt, William 3, 12, 15, 22, 26–7, 27,
    34, 35, 42, 47, 61, 76, 122–3, 563
  and Anglo-Irish relationship 52–3
  and Catholic emancipation 29, 64.
    76–7, 87
  death 77
  and parliamentary union 53–4,
    55–6, 65, 557, 558, 559
  and 1798 rebellion 51
  resignation 63–4
Pius VI 52
Pius VII 52

Pius IX 235–6
Plan Kathleen 467
Plan of Campaign 353–4
  Mitchelstown killings 354
Plunket, William Conyngham 74, 107,
    110, 111
  and Catholic emancipation 103–4
Plunkett, George Noble Count 384
Plunkett, Sir Horace 412, 418
Plunkett, Joseph Mary 371, 373
  and blood sacrifice 375
Pollock, Allan
  estate clearance 242
Pollock, Hugh 395–6
Pollock, John 84–5
political Protestantism 75
  anti-Catholicism 93
  and Russell 235–6
Pollock, Joseph 24, 39–40, 573
Ponsonby, George 78
Poor Law Amendement Act
    (1847) 190
poor law debate 150–1 see also
    Nicholls
Poor Law Inspectorate (1869) 276
poor law system 190–1
poor, the
  fear of 206–7
population decline 250, 564
  Cullen's pastoral 257
Porter, Grey 176
Porter, J.L. 337 n 155
Portland, Duke of 27, 32
Portugal 521
potato crop 176–7, 188
  dependence on 211
  failure (1817) 97; (1822) 105
  warning 175
  see also famine
Pouchet, Professor
  potato crop warning 175
Powell, Charles 538
Powell, Enoch 531
Powell, Jonathan 538 n 177, 553
Power, John 178
Power, John O'Connor 259, 279,
    307–8, 312
Praeger, R.L. 483
Pratt, Charles, first Earl of Camden 8
Prendergast, T.P.
  *The Cromwellian Settlement of
    Ireland* 250
Presbyterianism 90

and Catholic emancipation 91
divisions 128–9
principle of consent viii, 369, 381,
383, 425, 514, 532, 533, 539,
542, 549, 573–4, 579
Progressive Democrats (PDs) 534, 536,
547
Property Defence Association 321
protectionism 343–4
Protestant ascendancy 27, 29
Protestant Church 59, 65, 89
clergy meet PIRA leaders 518
and Church of Ireland
disestablishment 268–70
Protestant conversion work 101
Protestantism 172
nature of Northern Ireland 458–60,
488
Protestant loyalists 39
Protestants 48, 224–5, 561
and the Anglo-Irish Agreement
(1985) 532
and Britain 369, 568
and the hunger-strikes (1981) 529,
531
and Rockite movement 99
in the South of Ireland 426, 432–3,
441
and the War of
Independence 415–6
Provisional Irish Republican Army
(PIRA 1969–) 496, 498, 499,
500, 505, 506, 507, 511, 521,
535, 540, 543, 548, 551, 554,
573, 580, 581
and assassinations 502–3, 519, 525
and bombings 502, 516, 525, 531,
537, 539, 541, 547
and ceasefires 518–19, 544–6, 547,
579
and decommissioning 550, 551,
552–4
and direct rule 508
early support from senior Fianna Fail
figures for 501
and the hunger strikes 528–30
and intelligence 510, 540
and internment 503
propaganda of 536–7
Public Works (Ireland) Bill 181–2
public-works policy
and famine 186
Purdy, Ann 531

Quakers 190
Quarterly Review 144, 179, 196,
267–8, 281
Quigley, Father 41, 46

Radcliffe, General 404
Radio-Telefis Eireann (RTE) 489, 534
Ramsey, Robert 508
Ray, T.M. 153, 185
Reagan, Ronald 533
Rebellion Act (1799) 68
reclamation tenantry 250–1
Galtee Hills 298–9
Redesdale, Lord 69, 74, 75, 76, 87,
104, 268–9, 274
Redington, Thomas 183–4
Redmond, John 361, 362, 365, 373,
383, 407, 526, 533, 548, 570,
576, 581
balance of power at Westminster 367
and British war effort 371
and conciliation 576–7
invitation to join British
Cabinet 372
and Irish National Volunteers 370
vision of Home Rule Ireland 577
Redmond-Howard, L.G. 379, 406
Rees, Merlyn 519, 523–4
Reform Bill (1831) 133–4
Reform Act (1832) 281–2
Reid, Father Alec 536, 537, 578
Reid, John 575
Reilly, Thomas Devin 220, 221, 226
and *United Irishman* 219–20
Renan, Ernest ix
repeal 133, 138, 151–3,
House of Commons motion
defeat 142–3
Limerick rally 159
monster meetings 159–60
new basis of campaign 153–4
and O'Brien (W.S.) 217
and O'Connell 126–7, 142–3,
151–2, 157–8, 172, 180–1
O'Connell-Butt debate 158–9
Sectarian divisions, 565
and Young Ireland 156
repealers 138, 153, 216
'council of 300' 162
Republic of Ireland (1949–)
the Anglo-Irish Agreement
(1985) 532–3, 545
Catholic social teachings 476, 534

Republic of Ireland (1949–) (*cont.*)
  censorship 482
  declaration of a Republic 479
  dismantling of protectionism 477,
    484, 486
  and the Downing Street Declaration
    (1993) 542–4
  economy of 477, 484, 486, 535–6,
    543
  emigration 489
  the European Union 477, 486–7,
    509
  and the Good Friday Agreement
    (1998) 549, 554
  and the Joint Framework Document
    (1995) 545–6
  and Northern Ireland 484, 487,
    495, 498, 499–500, 509,
    529–30, 538, 541, 545, 551,
    552, 554, 575, 579
  opposes British withdrawal from
    Northern Ireland 514,
    517–18, 520–2
  reaction to 'Bloody Sunday'
    (1972) 508
  and the Sunningdale Agreement
    (1973) 512–13
Reynolds, Albert 538, 540, 544, 546
Rhodes, Cecil 356
Ribbonism 94, 108
Ribbonmen 94, 96, 100, 108, 146,
  229–30, 238, 247, 565
Richardson, Dr William 33
Richmond, Duke of 3, 79
Rights of Man 7–8 *see also* Paine
Robinson, Seamus 394
Rockefeller Foundation, New
  York 474–5
Rock, General John 97–8
  spirit of 130
  and tithes 132–3
  see Nagle
Rockite movement 97–9
  and Protestants 99
Roden, Lord
  dismissed by Clarendon 230
Roman Catholic Relief Act (1829) 121
Roosevelt, Franklin 464, 478
Ross, Revd Alexander 95
Ross, David 176
Rossa, Jeremiah O'Donovan 244
  dynamite explosions in
    England 338–9

  elected MP 272–3
Rowan, Archibald Hamilton 27
Rowley, F.A. 511
Royal Dublin Society 483
Royal Irish Academy 483
Royal Irish Academy of Music 483
Royal Irish Constabulary (RIC) 397,
  401, 451
Royal Irish Regiment (RIR) 550
Royal Ulster Constabulary (RUC) 487,
  489, 497, 502, 511, 549, 550, 554
  and civil rights marches 489, 491
Rudd, Pemberton 53
Rugby, Lord 482
rural economy 297
Russell, Charles 351–2, 357
Russell, Lord John 143–4, 161, 165,
  180, 183–4, 189–90, 191, 193,
  205, 206, 243, 281–2, 562, 564
  Durham letter 236, 282
  and Irish character 204
  and *The Nation* 184, 185
  and O'Connell 183, 184, 186
  and O'Keefe case 288
  and Orangemen 225
  and political Protestantism 235–6
Russell, Sean 470
Russell, Thomas 3, 13, 31, 39, 72
  execution 71
  political outlook 73–4
Rutherford, John 245
Ryan, Frank 470
Ryan, Dr James 464

Sadleir, John 237, 239
St Andrews Agreement (2006) 581
St George, Mansergh 157
St John's College, Oxford 555
St Patrick's College, Maynooth 32
  grant 169–70
Salisbury, Lord 331, 344, 362
Sampson, William 3, 13, 40, 47
Sands, Bobby 528–9, 530
Saunders Newsletter 242
Saunderson, Colonel Edward vii
  *Two Irelands: Loyalty versus
    Treason* 351
Saunderson, Somerset 399
Saurin, William 80, 89, 105
  rejection of peerage 106
Sayers, Jack 481
Scarman Tribunal 497
Schroedinger, Professor 468

Scott, C.P. 421
Scott, Sir John 406
Scott, Nicholas, 573
Scottish Protestant League 458
Scrope, George Poulett 214–15
Scullabogue 43, 48
Scully, Denys 52
SDLP *see* Social Democratic and
  Labour Party
sectarianism 32–4, 42, 55, 57, 74, 93,
  120, 172, 173, 229–30, 561
  in 1798 rebellion 49, 50
  of the IRA (1919–21) 415–16
  in north of Ireland 95, 243, 263,
    351, 404, 427–9, 434, 460,
    489, 495, 501, 503, 566
  O'Connell-Cullen
    correspondence 154
Seely, Colonel 370
Senior, Nassau 201–2
Sexton, Thomas 315, 329
Shaftesbury, Earl of
  and famine 184 n 43
Shankill bomb (1993) 541
Shawe-Taylor, Captain 398
Shawe-Taylor, John 338, 362
Shaw, Frederick 141
Shaw, George Bernard 367 n 32, 438
Shaw, William 324, 342–3
Sheehy, Father 14
Sheehy-Skeffington, Francis
  execution 376
Sheridan, P.J. 333, 334, 339, 357
  and Parnell 335, 355
Sheridan, Dr Edward 88
Sheridan, Mrs P.J. 315
Sheridan, Richard Brinsley 56
Shiel, Richard Lalor 91–2, 100, 101,
  110, 111, 142
Shrewsbury, Earl
Shrewsbury, John Talbot, sixteenth earl
  of 121, 157
  Pitt meeting 76–7
Sidmouth, Viscount *see* Addington,
  Henry
Sigerson, George 440
Sinclair, Thomas 174
Single European Act 536
Sinn Fein (1905–1970) 364, 366, 383,
  385, 397, 400, 403, 413, 575,
  579
  and 1926 split 448–9
  and 1970 split 499

and the Anglo-Irish Treaty
  negotiations 416–22
and the Anglo-Irish Treaty split 422
and the Dail courts 402–3
Dillon on 385–6
elections (1914–16) 372; (1917)
  383–384; (1918) 390–1, 392;
  (1921) 414; (1923) 443
and the establishment of the first
  Dail 393
and farmers 386, 390
'German Plot' arrests 388–9
and the Irish Party 386–8
and physical force 390–2
Sinn Fein (Provisional, 1970–) 536,
  547, 551, 553, 579–80, 581
  dialogue with the British
    Government 518–19, 520,
    521, 522–3, 524, 535, 540–1
  dialogue with the SDLP 535, 537,
    538, 542, 544
  and elections 530–1, 533–4, 535,
    550, 552
  and the Good Friday Agreement
    (1998) 549–50, 554
  and the hunger-strikes
    (1981) 529–30
  propaganda of 536–7
Sinn Fein (weekly) 367, 422
Sirr, Major Henry 42, 225
Sligo 406, 439, 525
Sligo Journal 45
Sloan, James 33
Smith, Elizabeth 199, 223 n 235
Smith, George Lewis 76
Smith, Sir William 559
Smyth, Father Brendan 546
Smythe, Lt.-Col. G. B. 402
Social Democratic and Labour Party
  (SDLP) 496, 502, 503, 513, 516,
    520, 530, 540, 550
  and dialogue with Sinn Fein, 535,
    537, 538, 542, 544
  and the 'European model', 539
  and the Good Friday Agreement
    (1998), 549
  and the Irish dimension, 512, 515
Society of Antiquaries 483
Solly-Flood, Major General
  Arthur 434, 435, 436
Soloheadbeg, Co. Tipperary 394
Somerville, Alexander 167
Somme *see* Battle of the Somme

soup kitchens 189, 190, 194
Soup Kitchens Act (1847) 190
Southwell, John 470
Soviet communism 457, 462
Soviet Union, 573
Soyer, Alexis 194
Spankie, Robert
  and Cusack Smith 141
Special Air Service (SAS) 524
Special Duties Act (London)
  (1932) 453
Special Powers Act (Northern Ireland)
  (1922) 431, 491
Spectator 123, 187–8, 194–5, 196,
  200, 200–1, 203, 208, 560
  and Fenians 263
  and O'Connell 215, 216
Spencer, Lord [Earl] 290, 338, 347–8,
  357
  and Fenians 271–2
  and Home Rule 350, 352
  and Irish peasantry 300
  law-and-order policy 342
Spender, Sir Wilfrid, 461, 463, 570
  Battle of the Somme 382
Spenser, Earl 63, 87, 569
Spring-Rice, Cecil 352 n 220
Stack, Austin 416, 441
Stanley, Lord 92, 134,135, 140–1,
  267, 567
  national school system 135–6
Stawel, William 97
Steele, Tom 139–40, 185
Stephens, James 244–5, 248, 257–8,
  379
  American tour 255
  at Ballingarry 227
  deposed 258–9
  The Insurrection of Dublin 376
  and Irish Republican Brotherhood
    (IRB) 246–7
  and MacManus funeral 254
Stewart, Alexander R. 238
Stewart family 4–5
  and Downshire interests 5
Stewart, Robert 2, 3, 4, 5, 24–5, 30,
  39 correct
  election, 6–7
Stewart, Robert (senior) 5
'Stormontgate' 551, 553, 579
Stout, W.F. 487 n 5
Strachan, Lady 131
Stuart, Francis 466

Stuart, Mrs Francis (Iseult Gonne) 466
Sturgis, Mark 400, 403, 413, 414, 415
Sullivan, A.M. Donal 188, 189, 223,
  244
Sullivan, Daniel
  and Fenianism 272
Sullivan, Serjeant A.M. 341, 406
Sullivan, T.D. 244
  on Fenian rebellion 261
  'God Save Ireland' 265
  The Nation 328–9
Sunday Independent 474, 492
Sunday Press 477
Sunday Times 465, 519
Sunday Tribune 540
Sunningdale Agreement
  (1973) 512–15
Swanzy, O.R. 403
Swift, John vii

Tallents, S.G. 436–7, 478
Talleyrand, Charles Maurice 68
Taylor, Sir John 399
Taylor, William Cooke x, 52, 71, 76,
  134, 142, 156, 173, 176, 562, 563
  Whiteboy ballads 149
Teeling, Charles 39
Teeling, Luke 39
Temple, Sir Richard 304
Tenant League 234–5, 236, 239
  and Catholic Defence
    Association 237
  three Fs 234
tenant right 130, 251–2, 312
  agitation 233–5
  Peel's criticism 256
  Ulster custom 167–8
  Ulster Tenant Right Association 218
tenants
  classes of 319 n 74
Tenants' Defence Associations 297,
  311
Tennent, Revd John 62, 152–3
Tennent, Emerson 152–3, 565
  Belfast economic success 142–3
Tennent, William 62
Tests and Corporations Act (1791) 103
Thatcher, Margaret 525, 527–8, 533,
  536, 538
  and the Anglo-Irish Agreement
    (1985) 531–2, 535
Thomas, J.H. 453

Thomson, Sir Basil 400
Thomson, James 44
Thornton, Frank 437
Thornton, General 119
Thornton, W.T. 201
Threshers, the 83–4
Tierney, Dom Mark 329
Times, The 182, 188, 194, 195, 203,
    230, 242, 397, 406, 545, 546, 569
    forged Parnell letter 355
Times Literary Supplement, The 482
Tipperary, 416
    Carlyle's comments 162–3
    disturbances 120
    landlords 148–9
    violence 147–8
tithes 127, 132–3, 153–4
    settlement of issue 150 *see also*
        anti-tithes campaign
Toibín, Colm 195
Tone, Theobald Wolfe 1–4, 7, 9, 22,
    27, 40, 49, 467, 519, 534, 575
    *An Argument on Behalf of the
        Catholics of Ireland* 3–4
    and Burke 12–13, 34
    capture 45
    and Catholic Committee 20
    Cave Hill oath 31
    colonial scheme 3, 12
    death 46
    on Dissenters' change of
        attitude 11–12
    in France 34
    on Irish society 10–11
    political thought 4
    trial 45–6
Tonna, Charlotte Elizabeth
    Recollections 98–9
Torrens, McCullagh 302–3
Towers, J. 13
Townsend, Thomas
    defence of Burke 35
Treason Felony Act (1848) 222
Trench, W.S. Chevenix 188, 195
Trevelyan, Sir Charles 156, 197–200,
    202, 205, 210, 275
    famine appeal with
        Burgoyne 198–200
    famine relief 186
    letters to Father Mathew 197
    and state's role 211
Trevelyan, George O. 337, 338
Traill, Anthony 458

Treacy, Sean 394, 395
Trend, Sir Burke 504, 510, 512
Trimble, David 520, 545, 547, 548,
    550, 551, 552, 554, 574
Trimleston, Lord 101
Trinity College, Dublin 513, 527
Trollope, Anthony 290
Trotter, J.B. 78
Troy, Archbishop 52, 75, 104
Tuam News 314, 315
Tudor, General Sir Henry 400, 401,
    404, 410
Twaddell, William John 434
Tyndall, John 176, [292], 367
Tyrone 427, 571

UIL *see* United Irish League
Ulster Defence Regiment (UDR) 497,
    503, 510
Ulster Division
    Battle of the Somme 382
Ulster Magazine 243
Ulster Protestant League, 458–9
Ulster Special Constabulary 402, 435,
    497
    B-Specials, 424, 427, 460
Ulster Tenant Right Association 218
Ulster Unionist Council (UUC) 480,
    491
Ulster Unionists 363, 369, 381, 396,
    426, 457, 459, 476, 488, 491,
    502, 525, 538, 573,
    577
    affect of abolition of Stormont
        on 509
    and the Anglo-Irish Agreement
        (1985) 531, 535
    commitment to power-sharing and
        an Irish dimension 539, 540
    contributes to the Downing Street
        Declaration (1993) 541–2
    discrimination in Northern
        Ireland 579
    divisions within 493
    elections (1918) 390; (1921) 414;
        (1973) 511
    and the Good Friday Agreement
        (1998) 549–50
    and the hunger-strikes (1981) 529
    and the Joint Framework
        Document 545–6
    and nationalism 368
    and Second World War 464–5

Ulster Unionists (*cont.*)
  Solemn League and Covenant
    pledge 368
  and the Sunningdale Agreement
    (1973) 512, 515
  threat of force 392
Ulster Volunteer Convention 9
Ulster Volunteer Force (UVF)
  1900–20, 368, 369, 401–2
  1960s–2000s, 497
Ulster Workers Council
  (UWC) 514–15, 516
'Ultach', see Campbell, J.J.
Union Flag 65
United Irish League (UIL) 362, 365,
  407
  national convention (1909) 366
United Irishman 219–20, 221, 353,
  364
United Irishmen 7, 10, 12, 13, 19, 24,
  31, 40–1, 42, 43, 47, 73
  Burke 36
  and Defenders 34, 39
  Dublin 24, 27, 42
  rebellion (1798) 42–5
United Irish rebellion (1798) 42–5
  Lecky's view 47
  in north 43–5
  reaction to 49–51
  in west 45
  in Wexford 42–3
United Nations (UN) 495, 498, 508,
  517
United States (US) 464, 465, 471, 472,
  479, 487, 492, 493, 518, 521,
  526, 533, 547, 552, 555, 573, 574
University College, Dublin 408
UVF *see* Ulster Volunteer Force

Verner, Colonel 127
veto on Catholic bishops 51–2, 80, 90,
  98, 100–1, 112, 113, 172
Victoria, Queen 146–7
Vindicator 232
Vinegar Hill 49
Viridicus 50 *see also* Musgrave

Wales, Prince of (Prince Regent 88)
  88, 556
Walsh, Louis 427
Walsh, Archbishop William, 407
  Irish Party and partition 388

Walshe, Joe 470–1
Walter, Revd 390
Walters, John 202–3
Warnock, Edmund 491
War of Independence (1919–21)
  393–414, 571
Warrenpoint bomb (1979) 525
Washington, George 479
Waterloo 94
Wayland, Francis
  murder of 147
Weekly Freeman's Journal 372, 409,
  412, 426, 437, 441
Weekly Northern Whig 430
Welfare State 478
Wellesley, Sir Arthur (Duke of
  Wellington) 25, 79, 94
  and Catholic emancipation 115,
    116, 118, 123
  Dublin Castle military plan 220,
    559
  military defence of Ireland 79–80,
    569
Wellesley family 78, 79, 104–5
Wellesley-Pole, William 45
Wellesley, Richard, Marquess 104, 105
  marriage 107
  protest against 106
Western Argus 124
Westmeath Journal 31
Westminster
  Irish representation in Union
    Parliament 65
Westminster Review 195–6
Westropp, Thomas 483
Whale, John 519
Whately, Archbishop of Dublin 135,
  150, 270
Wheeler-Bennett, John 451
Whelan, Dr Irene 101
Whitaker T.K. 477, 486, 498, 536
White, Henry 112
White, Luke 70
Whiteboyism 14
Whiteboys 11, 106
Wickham, William 1, 69, 71, 72,
  and Emmet 74
Widgery, Lord Chief Justice 508
Widgery Tribunal 507, 508
William III 33
William IV 136, 146
Wilson, Harold 490–1, 492, 501, 551
  and British withdrawal from

Northern Ireland 513–14,
516–18, 523
and the Ulster Workers Council
strike (1974) 515
Wilson, Field Marshal Sir Henry 404,
429, 431, 436
Wilson, Woodrow 396
Windham, William 63
Winmarleigh, Lord (John Wilson
Patten) 262, 318–19
Winter, Ormonde 410, 415
Wiseman, Cardinal Nicholas,
Archbishop of Westminster, 235
and famine 243
Wodehouse, Lord (later Earl of
Kimberly) 255, 350
Wood, Henry Evelyn 321
Workers' Republic 365
World War I (1914–18) 371
World War II (1939–45) 463–75,
478–9, 527, 572–3
Wright, Oliver 496

Wylie, W.E. 378, 400, 401
Wyndham, George 363, 569–70
Wyndham Land Act (1903) 362, 576
Wyse, Thomas 114, 161, 171

Yeats, W.B. 247, 360, 577
Young, Revd Augustus 376
Young Ireland 248, 452, 481, 575
anticlericalism 219
attack at Ballingarry (1848) 227, 569
and Carlyle 155, 163 n 207
dispersal 227–8
and famine 177, 210
influence 228
Irish Confederation 185, 221, 222
and land question 217–18
mobilization 225, 226
and O'Connell 156, 164, 180–1,
184–5, 211, 215, 216
and repeal 156